Microsoft® Office

PowerPoint® 2007

Comprehensive Concepts and Techniques

Gary B. Shelly

Thomas J. Cashman

Susan L. Sebok

COURSE TECHNOLOGY
CENGAGE Learning

Australia • Brazil • Japan • Korea • Mexico • Singapore • Spain • United Kingdom • United States

COURSE TECHNOLOGY
CENGAGE Learning

Microsoft® Office PowerPoint® 2007:
Comprehensive Concepts and Techniques
Gary B. Shelly
Thomas J. Cashman
Susan L. Sebok

Executive Editor: Alexandra Arnold

Product Manager: Heather Hawkins

Associate Product Manager: Klenda Martinez

Editorial Assistant: Jon Farnham

Senior Marketing Manager: Joy Stark-Vancs

Marketing Coordinator: Julie Schuster

Print Buyer: Denise Powers

Director of Production: Patty Stephan

Production Editor: Matthew Hutchinson

Developmental Editor: Laurie Brown

Proofreader: John Bosco

Indexer: Rich Carlson

QA Manuscript Reviewers: John Freitas,
    Serge Palladino, Chris Scriver, Danielle Shaw,
    Marianne Snow, Teresa Storch

Art Director: Bruce Bond

Cover and Text Design: Joel Sadagursky

Cover Photo: Jon Chomitz

Compositor: GEX Publishing Services

For product information and technology assistance, contact us at
Cengage Learning Customer & Sales Support, 1-800-354-9706
For permission to use material from this text or product, submit all requests online at **cengage.com/permissions**
Further permissions questions can be emailed to
permissionrequest@cengage.com

ISBN-13: 978-1-4188-4347-2

ISBN-10: 1-4188-4347-4

Course Technology
25 Thomson Place
Boston, Massachusetts 02210
USA

Cengage Learning is a leading provider of customized learning solutions with office locations around the globe, including Singapore, the United Kingdom, Australia, Mexico, Brazil and Japan. Locate your local office at:
international.cengage.com/region

Cengage Learning products are represented in Canada by Nelson Education, Ltd.

For your lifelong learning solutions, visit **course.cengage.com**

Purchase any of our products at your local college store or at our preferred online store
www.ichapters.com

Printed in the United States of America
5 6 7 8 9 10 09

Microsoft® Office

PowerPoint® 2007
Comprehensive Concepts and Techniques

Contents

Microsoft Office PowerPoint 2007

Contents

Appendices

Preface

The Shelly Cashman Series® offers the finest textbooks in computer education. We are proud of the fact that our series of Microsoft Office 4.3, Microsoft Office 95, Microsoft Office 97, Microsoft Office 2000, Microsoft Office XP, and Microsoft Office 2003 textbooks have been the most widely used books in education. With each new edition of our Office books, we have made significant improvements based on the software and comments made by instructors and students.

Microsoft Office 2007 contains more changes in the user interface and feature set than all other previous versions combined. Recognizing that the new features and functionality of Microsoft Office 2007 would impact the way that students are taught skills, the Shelly Cashman Series development team carefully reviewed our pedagogy and analyzed its effectiveness in teaching today's Office student. An extensive customer survey produced results confirming what the series is best known for: its step-by-step, screen-by-screen instructions, its project-oriented approach, and the quality of its content.

We learned, though, that students entering computer courses today are different than students taking these classes just a few years ago. Students today read less, but need to retain more. They need not only to be able to perform skills, but to retain those skills and know how to apply them to different settings. Today's students need to be continually engaged and challenged to retain what they're learning.

As a result, we've renewed our commitment to focusing on the user and how they learn best. This commitment is reflected in every change we've made to our Office 2007 books.

Objectives of This Textbook

Microsoft Office PowerPoint 2007: Comprehensive Concepts and Techniques is intended for a eight- to ten-week period in a course that teaches PowerPoint 2007 as the primary component. No experience with a computer is assumed, and no mathematics beyond the high school freshman level is required. The objectives of this book are:

- To offer a comprehensive presentation of Microsoft Office PowerPoint 2007
- To expose students to practical examples of the computer as a useful tool
- To acquaint students with the proper procedures to create presentations suitable for coursework, professional purposes, and personal use
- To help students discover the underlying functionality of PowerPoint 2007 so they can become more productive
- To develop an exercise-oriented approach that allows learning by doing

The Shelly Cashman Approach

Features of the Shelly Cashman Series Microsoft Office PowerPoint 2007 books include:

- **Project Orientation** Each chapter in the book presents a project with a practical problem and complete solution in an easy-to-understand approach.
- **Plan Ahead Boxes** The project orientation is enhanced by the inclusion of Plan Ahead boxes. These new features prepare students to create successful projects by encouraging them to think strategically about what they are trying to accomplish before they begin working.
- **Step-by-Step, Screen-by-Screen Instructions** Each of the tasks required to complete a project is clearly identified throughout the chapter. Now, the step-by-step instructions provide a context beyond point-and-click. Each step explains why students are performing a task, or the result of performing a certain action. Found on the screens accompanying each step, call-outs give students the information they need to know when they need to know it. Now, we've used color to distinguish the content in the call-outs. The Explanatory call-outs (in black) summarize

Q&A

What is a maximized window?

A maximized window fills the entire screen. When you maximize a window, the Maximize button changes to a Restore Down button.

Other Ways

1. Click Italic button on Mini toolbar

2. Right-click selected text, click Font on shortcut menu, click Font tab, click Italic in Font style list, click OK button

3. Click Font Dialog Box Launcher, click Font tab, click Italic in Font style list, click OK button

4. Press CTRL+I

BTW

Minimizing the Ribbon

If you want to minimize the Ribbon, right-click the Ribbon and then click Minimize the Ribbon on the shortcut menu, double-click the active tab, or press CTRL+F1. To restore a minimized Ribbon, right-click the Ribbon and then click Minimize the Ribbon on the shortcut menu, double-click any top-level tab, or press CTRL+F1. To use commands on a minimized Ribbon, click the top-level tab.

what is happening on the screen and the Navigational call-outs (in red) show students where to click.

- **Q&A** Found within many of the step-by-step sequences, Q&As raise the kinds of questions students may ask when working through a step sequence and provide answers about what they are doing, why they are doing it, and how that task might be approached differently.

- **Experimental Steps** These new steps, within our step-by-step instructions, encourage students to explore, experiment, and take advantage of the features of the Office 2007 new user interface. These steps are not necessary to complete the projects, but are designed to increase the confidence with the software and build problem-solving skills.

- **Thoroughly Tested Projects** Unparalleled quality is ensured because every screen in the book is produced by the author only after performing a step, and then each project must pass Course Technology's Quality Assurance program.

- **Other Ways Boxes and Quick Reference Summary** The Other Ways boxes displayed at the end of most of the step-by-step sequences specify the other ways to do the task completed in the steps. Thus, the steps and the Other Ways box make a comprehensive reference unit. A Quick Reference Summary at the end of the book contains all of the tasks presented in the chapters, and all ways identified of accomplishing the tasks.

- **BTW** These marginal annotations provide background information, tips, and answers to common questions that complement the topics covered, adding depth and perspective to the learning process.

- **Integration of the World Wide Web** The World Wide Web is integrated into the PowerPoint 2007 learning experience by (1) BTW annotations that send students to Web sites for up-to-date information and alternative approaches to tasks; (2) a Microsoft Business Certification Program Web page so students can prepare for the certification examinations; (3) a Quick Reference Summary Web page that summarizes the ways to complete tasks (mouse, Ribbon, shortcut menu, and keyboard); and (4) the Learn It Online section at the end of each chapter, which has chapter reinforcement exercises, learning games, and other types of student activities.

- **End-of-Chapter Student Activities** Extensive student activities at the end of each chapter provide the student with plenty of opportunities to reinforce the materials learned in the chapter through hands-on assignments. Several new types of activities have been added that challenge the student in new ways to expand their knowledge, and to apply their new skills to a project with personal relevance.

Organization of This Textbook

Microsoft Office PowerPoint 2007: Comprehensive Concepts and Techniques consists of six chapters on Microsoft Office PowerPoint 2007, three special features, seven appendices, and a Quick Reference Summary.

End-of-Chapter Student Activities

A notable strength of the Shelly Cashman Series Microsoft Office PowerPoint 2007 books is the extensive student activities at the end of each chapter. Well-structured student activities can make the difference between students merely participating in a class and students retaining the information they learn. The activities in the Shelly Cashman Series Office books include the following.

CHAPTER SUMMARY A concluding paragraph, followed by a listing of the tasks completed within a chapter together with the pages on which the step-by-step, screen-by-screen explanations appear.

LEARN IT ONLINE Every chapter features a Learn It Online section that is comprised of six exercises. These exercises include True/False, Multiple Choice, Short Answer, Flash Cards, Practice Test, and Learning Games.

APPLY YOUR KNOWLEDGE This exercise usually requires students to open and manipulate a file from the Data Files that parallels the activities learned in the chapter. To obtain a copy of the Data Files for Students, follow the instructions on the inside back cover of this text.

EXTEND YOUR KNOWLEDGE This exercise allows students to extend and expand on the skills learned within the chapter.

MAKE IT RIGHT This exercise requires students to analyze a document, identify errors and issues, and correct those errors and issues using skills learned in the chapter.

IN THE LAB Three all new in-depth assignments per chapter require students to utilize the chapter concepts and techniques to solve problems on a computer.

CASES AND PLACES Five unique real-world case-study situations, including Make It Personal, an open-ended project that relates to student's personal lives, and one small-group activity.

Instructor Resources CD-ROM

The Shelly Cashman Series is dedicated to providing you with all of the tools you need to make your class a success. Information about all supplementary materials is available through your Course Technology representative or by calling one of the following telephone numbers: Colleges, Universities, and Continuing Ed departments, 1-800-648-7450; High Schools, 1-800-824-5179; and Career Colleges, Business, Government, Library and Resellers, 1-800-477-3692.

The Instructor Resources CD-ROM for this textbook include both teaching and testing aids. The contents of each item on the Instructor Resources CD-ROM (ISBN 1-4239-1226-8) are described on the following pages.

INSTRUCTOR'S MANUAL The Instructor's Manual consists of Microsoft Word files, which include chapter objectives, lecture notes, teaching tips, classroom activities, lab activities, quick quizzes, figures and boxed elements summarized in the chapters, and a glossary page. The new format of the Instructor's Manual will allow you to map through every chapter easily.

LECTURE SUCCESS SYSTEM The Lecture Success System consists of intermediate files that correspond to certain figures in the book, allowing you to step through the creation of a project in a chapter during a lecture without entering large amounts of data.

SYLLABUS Sample syllabi, which can be customized easily to a course, are included. The syllabi cover policies, class and lab assignments and exams, and procedural information.

FIGURE FILES Illustrations for every figure in the textbook are available in electronic form. Use this ancillary to present a slide show in lecture or to print transparencies for use in lecture with an overhead projector. If you have a personal computer and LCD device, this ancillary can be an effective tool for presenting lectures.

POWERPOINT PRESENTATIONS PowerPoint Presentations is a multimedia lecture presentation system that provides slides for each chapter. Presentations are based on chapter objectives. Use this presentation system to present well-organized lectures that are both interesting and knowledge based. PowerPoint Presentations provides consistent coverage at schools that use multiple lecturers.

SOLUTIONS TO EXERCISES Solutions are included for the end-of-chapter exercises, as well as the Chapter Reinforcement exercises. Rubrics and annotated solution files, as described below, are also included.

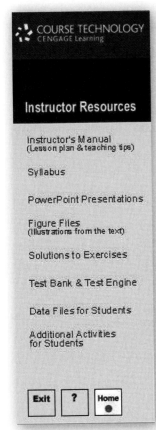

RUBRICS AND ANNOTATED SOLUTION FILES The grading rubrics provide a customizable framework for assigning point values to the laboratory exercises. Annotated solution files that correspond to the grading rubrics make it easy for you to compare students' results with the correct solutions whether you receive their homework as hard copy or via e-mail.

TEST BANK & TEST ENGINE In the ExamView test bank, you will find our standard question types (40 multiple-choice, 25 true/false, 20 completion) and new objective-based question types (5 modified multiple-choice, 5 modified true/false and 10 matching). Critical Thinking questions are also included (3 essays and 2 cases with 2 questions each) totaling the test bank to 112 questions for every chapter with page number references, and when appropriate, figure references. A version of the test bank you can print also is included. The test bank comes with a copy of the test engine, ExamView, the ultimate tool for your objective-based testing needs. ExamView is a state-of-the-art test builder that is easy to use. ExamView enables you to create paper-, LAN-, or Web-based tests from test banks designed specifically for your Course Technology textbook. Utilize the ultra-efficient QuickTest Wizard to create tests in less than five minutes by taking advantage of Course Technology's question banks, or customize your own exams from scratch.

LAB TESTS/TEST OUT The Lab Tests/Test Out exercises parallel the In the Lab assignments and are supplied for the purpose of testing students in the laboratory on the material covered in the chapter or testing students out of the course.

DATA FILES FOR STUDENTS All the files that are required by students to complete the exercises are included. You can distribute the files on the Instructor Resources CD-ROM to your students over a network, or you can have them follow the instructions on the inside back cover of this book to obtain a copy of the Data Files for Students.

ADDITIONAL ACTIVITIES FOR STUDENTS These additional activities consist of Chapter Reinforcement Exercises, which are true/false, multiple-choice, and short answer questions that help students gain confidence in the material learned.

Assessment & Training Solutions
SAM 2007

SAM 2007 helps bridge the gap between the classroom and the real world by allowing students to train and test on important computer skills in an active, hands-on environment.

SAM 2007's easy-to-use system includes powerful interactive exams, training or projects on critical applications such as Word, Excel, Access, PowerPoint, Outlook, Windows, the Internet, and much more. SAM simulates the application environment, allowing students to demonstrate their knowledge and think through the skills by performing real-world tasks.

Designed to be used with the Shelly Cashman series, SAM 2007 includes built-in page references so students can print helpful study guides that match the Shelly Cashman series textbooks used in class. Powerful administrative options allow instructors to schedule exams and assignments, secure tests, and run reports with almost limitless flexibility.

Student Edition Labs

Our Web-based interactive labs help students master hundreds of computer concepts, including input and output devices, file management and desktop applications, computer ethics, virus protection, and much more. Featuring up-to-the-minute content, eye-popping graphics, and rich animation, the highly interactive Student Edition Labs offer students an alternative way to learn through dynamic observation, step-by-step practice, and challenging review questions.

Online Content

Blackboard is the leading distance learning solution provider and class-management platform today. Course Technology has partnered with Blackboard to bring you premium online content. Instructors: Content for use with *Microsoft Office PowerPoint 2007: Comprehensive Concepts and Techniques* is available in a Blackboard Course Cartridge and may include topic reviews, case projects, review questions, test banks, practice tests, custom syllabi, and more.

Course Technology also has solutions for several other learning management systems. Please visit course.com today to see what's available for this title.

CourseCasts Learning on the Go. Always Available…Always Relevant.

Want to keep up with the latest technology trends relevant to you? Visit our site to find a library of podcasts, CourseCasts, featuring a "CourseCast of the Week," and download them to your portable media player at http://coursecasts.course.com.

Our fast-paced world is driven by technology. You know because you are an active participant — always on the go, always keeping up with technological trends, and always learning new ways to embrace technology to power your life.

Ken Baldauf, a faculty member of the Florida State University (FSU) Computer Science Department, is responsible for teaching technology classes to thousands of FSU students each year. He knows what you know; he knows what you want to learn. He is also an expert in the latest technology and will sort through and aggregate the most pertinent news and information so you can spend your time enjoying technology, rather than trying to figure it out.

Visit us at http://coursecasts.course.com to learn on the go!

CourseNotes

Course Technology's CourseNotes are six-paneled quick reference cards that reinforce the most important and widely used features of a software application in a visual and user-friendly format. CourseNotes will serve as a great reference tool during and after the student completes the course. CourseNotes for Microsoft Office 2007, Word 2007, Excel 2007, Access 2007, PowerPoint 2007, Windows Vista, and more are available now!

About Our New Cover Look

Learning styles of students have changed, but the Shelly Cashman Series' dedication to their success has remained steadfast for over 30 years. We are committed to continually updating our approach and content to reflect the way today's students learn and experi- 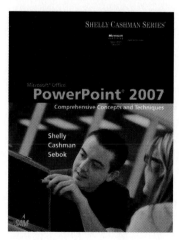 ence new technology. This focus on the user is reflected in our bold new cover design, which features photographs of real students using the Shelly Cashman Series in their courses. Each book features a different user, reflecting the many ages, experiences, and backgrounds of all of the students learning with our books. When you use the Shelly Cashman Series, you can be assured that you are learning computer skills using the most effective course-ware available. We would like to thank the administration and faculty at the participating schools for their help in making our vision a reality. Most of all, we'd like to thank the wonderful students from all over the world who learn from our texts and now appear on our covers.

To the Student . . . Getting the Most Out of Your Book

Welcome to *Microsoft Office PowerPoint 2007: Comprehensive Concepts and Techniques*. You can save yourself a lot of time and gain a better understanding of the Office PowerPoint 2007 program if you spend a few minutes reviewing the figures and callouts in this section.

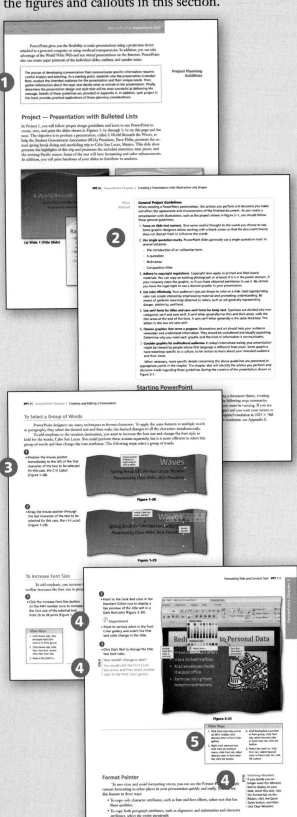

1 PROJECT ORIENTATION

Each chapter's project presents a practical problem and shows the solution in the first figure of the chapter. The project orientation lets you see firsthand how problems are solved from start to finish using application software and computers.

2 PROJECT PLANNING GUIDELINES AND PLAN AHEAD BOXES

Overall planning guidelines at the beginning of a chapter and Plan Ahead boxes throughout encourage you to think critically about how to accomplish the next goal before you actually begin working.

3 CONSISTENT STEP-BY-STEP, SCREEN-BY-SCREEN PRESENTATION

Chapter solutions are built using a step-by-step, screen-by-screen approach. This pedagogy allows you to build the solution on a computer as you read through the chapter. Generally, each step includes an explanation that indicates the result of the step.

4 MORE THAN JUST STEP-BY-STEP

BTW annotations in the margins of the book, Q&As in the steps, and substantive text in the paragraphs provide background information, tips, and answers to common questions that complement the topics covered, adding depth and perspective. When you finish with this book, you will be ready to use the Office programs to solve problems on your own. Experimental steps provide you with opportunities to step out on your own to try features of the programs, and pick up right where you left off in the chapter.

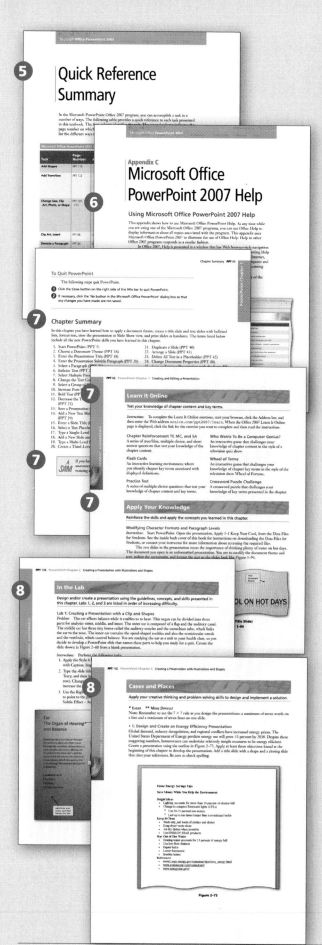

5 OTHER WAYS BOXES AND QUICK REFERENCE SUMMARY
Other Ways boxes that follow many of the step sequences and
a Quick Reference Summary at the back of the book explain the
other ways to complete the task presented, such as using the
mouse, Ribbon, shortcut menu, and keyboard.

6 EMPHASIS ON GETTING HELP WHEN YOU NEED IT
The first project of each application and Appendix C show you
how to use all the elements of Office Help. Being able to answer
your own questions will increase your productivity and reduce
your frustrations by minimizing the time it takes to learn how to
complete a task.

7 REVIEW, REINFORCEMENT, AND EXTENSION
After you successfully step through a project in a chapter, a
section titled Chapter Summary identifies the tasks with which you
should be familiar. Terms you should know for test purposes are
bold in the text. The SAM Training feature provides the opportunity for addional reinforcement on important skills covered in
each chapter. The Learn It Online section at the end of each chapter offers reinforcement in the form of review questions, learning
games, and practice tests. Also included are exercises that require
you to extend your learning beyond the book.

8 LABORATORY EXERCISES
If you really want to learn how to use the programs, then you
must design and implement solutions to problems on your own.
Every chapter concludes with several carefully developed
laboratory assignments that increase in complexity.

1 | Creating and Editing a Presentation

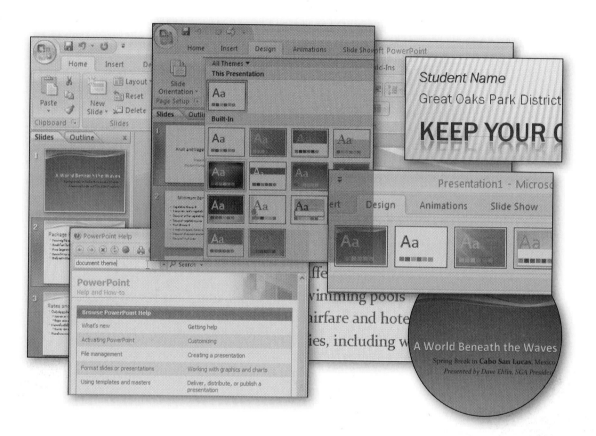

Objectives

You will have mastered the material in this chapter when you can:

- Start and quit PowerPoint
- Describe the PowerPoint window
- Select a document theme
- Create a title slide and text slides with single- and multi-level bulleted lists
- Save a presentation
- Copy elements from one slide to another

- View a presentation in Slide Show view
- Open a presentation
- Display and print a presentation in grayscale
- Check spelling
- Use PowerPoint Help

1 | Creating and Editing a Presentation

What Is Microsoft Office PowerPoint 2007?

Microsoft Office PowerPoint 2007 is a complete presentation graphics program that allows you to produce professional-looking presentations (Figure 1–1). A PowerPoint **presentation** also is called a **slide show**.

PowerPoint contains several features to simplify creating a slide show. For example, the results-oriented user interface can boost productivity by making tasks and options readily accessible. Professionally designed standard layouts help you save time by formatting and creating content. You then can modify these layouts to create custom slides to fit your specific needs. To make your presentation more impressive, you can add diagrams, tables, pictures, video, sound, and animation effects. Additional PowerPoint features include the following:

- **Word processing** — Create bulleted lists, combine words and images, find and replace text, and use multiple fonts and type sizes.
- **Outlining** — Develop your presentation using an outline format. You also can import outlines from Microsoft Word or other word processing programs.
- **Charting** — Create and insert charts into your presentations and then add effects and chart elements.
- **Drawing** — Form and modify diagrams using shapes such as arcs, arrows, cubes, rectangles, stars, and triangles. Then apply Quick Styles to customize and add effects. Arrange these objects by sizing, scaling, and rotating.
- **Inserting multimedia** — Insert artwork and multimedia effects into your slide show. The Microsoft Clip Organizer contains hundreds of media files, including pictures, photos, sounds, and movies.
- **Saving to the Web** — Save presentations or parts of a presentation in HTML format so they can be viewed and manipulated using a browser. You can publish your slide show to the Internet or to an intranet.
- **E-mailing** — Send your entire slide show as an attachment to an e-mail message.
- **Collaborating** — Share your presentation with friends and coworkers. Ask them to review the slides and then insert comments that offer suggestions to enhance the presentation.
- **Preparing delivery** — Rehearse integrating PowerPoint slides into your speech by setting timings, using presentation tools, showing only selected slides in a presentation, and packaging the presentation for a CD.

This latest version of PowerPoint has many new features to increase your productivity. Graphics and other shape effects allow you to add glow, shadowing, 3-D effects, and other appealing visuals. Typography effects enhance the design's impact. PowerPoint themes apply a consistent look to each graphic, font, and table color in an entire presentation. Digital signatures enable you to verify that no one has altered your presentation since you created it, and the Document Inspector removes private data, such as comments and hidden text.

PowerPoint gives you the flexibility to make presentations using a projection device attached to a personal computer or using overhead transparencies. In addition, you can take advantage of the World Wide Web and run virtual presentations on the Internet. PowerPoint also can create paper printouts of the individual slides, outlines, and speaker notes.

Project Planning Guidlines

The process of developing a presentation that communicates specific information requires careful analysis and planning. As a starting point, establish why the presentation is needed. Next, analyze the intended audience for the presentation and their unique needs. Then, gather information about the topic and decide what to include in the presentation. Finally, determine the presentation design and style that will be most successful at delivering the message. Details of these guidelines are provided in Appendix A. In addition, each project in this book provides practical applications of these planning considerations.

Project — Presentation with Bulleted Lists

In Project 1, you will follow proper design guidelines and learn to use PowerPoint to create, save, and print the slides shown in Figures 1–1a through 1–1e on this page and the next. The objective is to produce a presentation, called A World Beneath the Waves, to help the Student Government Association (SGA) President, Dave Ehlin, promote the annual spring break diving and snorkeling trip to Cabo San Lucas, Mexico. This slide show presents the highlights of this trip and promotes the included amenities, tour prices, and the inviting Pacific waters. Some of the text will have formatting and color enhancements. In addition, you will print handouts of your slides to distribute to students.

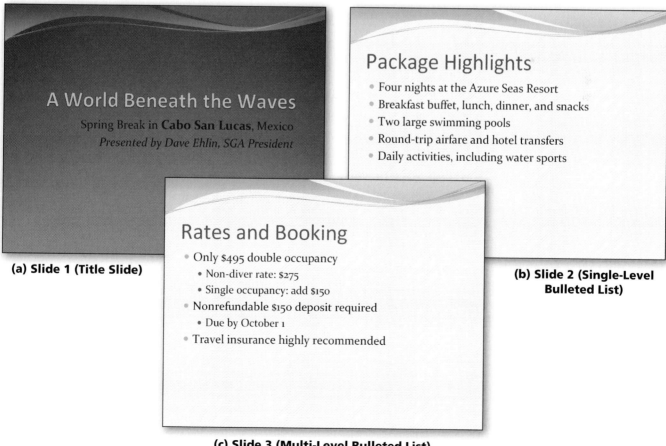

(a) Slide 1 (Title Slide)

(b) Slide 2 (Single-Level Bulleted List)

(c) Slide 3 (Multi-Level Bulleted List)

Figure 1–1

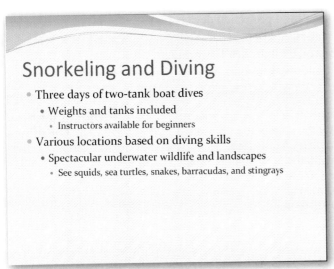

(d) Slide 4 (Multi-Level Bulleted List)

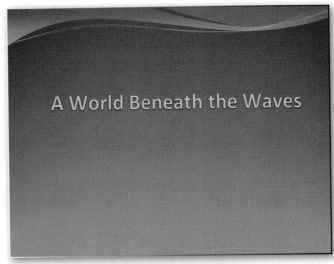

(e) Slide 5 (Closing Slide)

Figure 1–1 (continued)

PowerPoint allows you to produce slides to use in an academic, business, or other environment. One of the more common uses of these slides is to enhance an oral presentation. A speaker may desire to convey information, such as urging students to participate in a food drive, explaining first aid, or describing the changes in an employee benefit package. The PowerPoint slides should reinforce the speaker's message and help the audience members retain the information presented. An accompanying handout gives audience members reference notes and review material after the presentation's conclusion.

Overview

As you read this chapter, you will learn how to create the presentation shown in Figure 1–1 by performing these general tasks:

- Select an appropriate document theme.
- Enter titles and text on slides.
- Change the size, color, and style of text.
- View the presentation on your computer.
- Save the presentation so you can modify and view it at a later time.
- Print handouts of your slides.

Plan Ahead

General Project Guidelines

When creating a PowerPoint document, the actions you perform and decisions you make will affect the appearance and characteristics of the finished document. As you create a presentation such as the project shown in Figure 1–1, you should follow these general guidelines:

1. **Find the appropriate theme.** The overall appearance of a presentation significantly affects its capability to communicate information clearly. The slides' graphical appearance should support the presentation's overall message. Colors, fonts, and layouts affect how audience members perceive and react to the slide content.

2. **Choose words for each slide.** Use the less is more principle. The less text, the more likely the slides will enhance your speech. Use the fewest words possible to make a point.

(continued)

(continued)

**Plan
Ahead**

3. **Format specific elements of the text.** Examples of how you can modify the appearance, or **format**, of text include changing its shape, size, color, and position on the slide.

4. **Determine where to save the presentation.** You can store a document permanently, or **save** it, on a variety of storage media including a hard disk, USB flash drive, or CD. You also can indicate a specific location on the storage media for saving the document.

When necessary, more specific details concerning the above guidelines are presented at appropriate points in the chapter. The chapter also will identify the actions performed and decisions made regarding these guidelines during the creation of the slides shown in Figure 1–1.

Starting PowerPoint

If you are using a computer to step through the project in this chapter and you want your screen to match the figures in this book, you should change your screen's resolution to 1024 × 768. For information about how to change a computer's resolution, read Appendix E.

Note: If you are using Windows XP, see Appendix F for alternate steps.

BTW

Decreasing Resolution
You may need to decrease your computer's resolution if you know you are going to run your presentation on another computer that uses a lower resolution, such as 800 × 600 or 640 × 480. This lower resolution, however, may affect the appearance of your slides.

To Start PowerPoint

The following steps, which assume Windows Vista is running, start PowerPoint based on a typical installation. You may need to ask your instructor how to start PowerPoint for your computer.

1

• Click the Start button on the Windows Vista taskbar to display the Start menu.

• Click All Programs at the bottom of the left pane on the Start menu to display the All Programs list.

• Click Microsoft Office in the All Programs list to display the Microsoft Office (Figure 1–2).

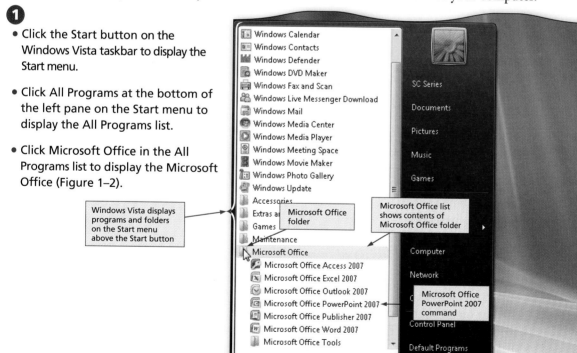

Figure 1–2

2

- Click Microsoft Office PowerPoint 2007 to start PowerPoint and display a new blank document in the PowerPoint window (Figure 1–3).

- If the PowerPoint window is not maximized, click the Maximize button next to the Close button on its title bar to maximize the window.

Q&A

What is a maximized window?

A maximized window fills the entire screen. When you maximize a window, the Maximize button changes to a Restore Down button. When you restore a maximized window, the Restore Down button changes to a Maximize button.

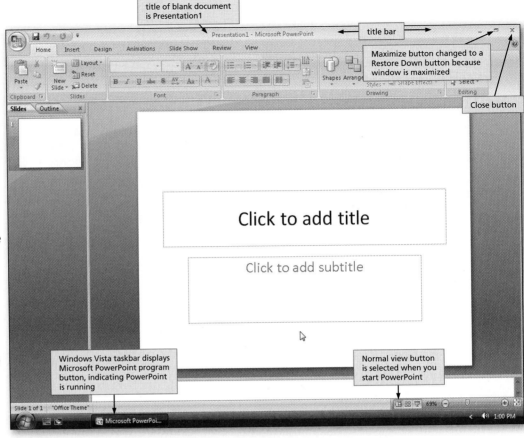

Figure 1–3

Other Ways

1. Double-click PowerPoint icon on desktop, if one is present
2. Click Microsoft Office PowerPoint 2007 on Start menu

BTW

Portrait Page Orientation

If your slide content is dominantly vertical, such as a skyscraper or a person, consider changing the slide layout to a portrait page orientation. To change the orientation, click the Slide Orientation button in the Page Setup group in the Design tab and then click the desired orientation. You can use both slide and portrait orientation in the same slide show.

The PowerPoint Window

The PowerPoint window consists of a variety of components to make your work more efficient and documents more professional. These include the document window, Ribbon, Mini toolbar and shortcut menus, Quick Access Toolbar, and Office Button. Some of these components are common to other Microsoft Office 2007 programs; others are unique to PowerPoint.

PowerPoint Window

The basic unit of a PowerPoint presentation is a **slide**. A slide may contain text and objects, such as graphics, tables, charts, and drawings. **Layouts** are used to position this content on the slide. When you open a new presentation, the default **Title Slide** layout appears (Figure 1–4). The purpose of this layout is to introduce the presentation to the audience. PowerPoint includes eight other built-in standard layouts.

The default (preset) slide layouts are set up in **landscape orientation**, where the slide width is greater than its height. In landscape orientation, the slide size is preset to 10 inches wide and 7.5 inches high when printed on a standard sheet of paper measuring 11 inches wide and 8.5 inches high.

The PowerPoint window in Figure 1–4 contains placeholders, a mouse pointer, and a status bar. Other elements that may appear in the window are discussed later in this and subsequent chapters.

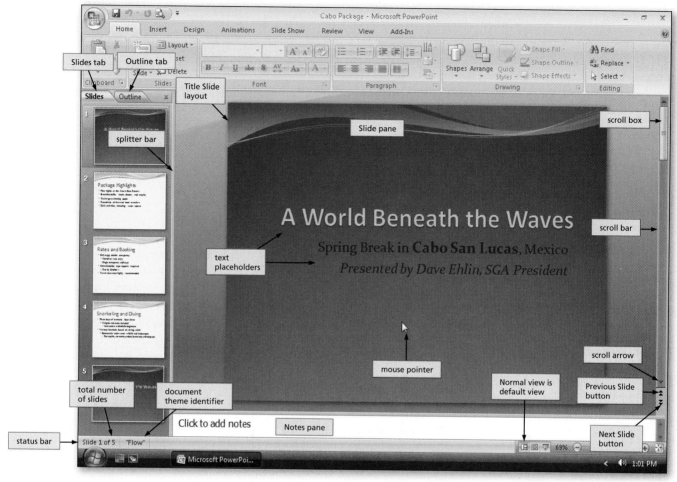

Figure 1–4

PLACEHOLDERS   **Placeholders** are boxes with dotted or hatch-marked borders that are displayed when you create a new slide. All layouts except the Blank slide layout contain placeholders. Depending on the particular slide layout selected, title and subtitle placeholders are displayed for the slide title and subtitle; a content text placeholder is displayed for text, art, or a table, chart, picture, graphic, or movie. The title slide in Figure 1–4 has two text placeholders where you will type the main heading, or title, of a new slide and the subtitle.

MOUSE POINTER   The **mouse pointer** becomes different shapes depending on the task you are performing in PowerPoint and the pointer's location on the screen. The mouse pointer in Figure 1–4 is the shape of a block arrow.

SCROLL BAR   You use the **vertical scroll bar** to display different slides in the document window. When you add a second slide to a presentation, this vertical scroll bar appears on the right side of the Slide pane. On the scroll bar, the position of the **scroll box** reflects the location of the slide in the presentation that is displayed in the document window. A **scroll arrow** is located at each end of a scroll bar. To scroll through, or display different portions of the document in the document window, you can click a scroll arrow or drag the scroll box to move forward or backward through the presentation.

The Previous Slide button and the Next Slide button appear at the bottom of the vertical scroll bar. Click one of these buttons to advance through the slides backwards or forwards.

The **horizontal scroll bar** also may appear. It is located on the bottom of the Slide pane and allows you to display a portion of the slide when the entire slide does not fit on the screen.

STATUS BAR The **status bar**, located at the bottom of the document window above the Windows Vista taskbar, presents information about the document, the progress of current tasks, and the status of certain commands and keys; it also provides controls for viewing the document. As you type text or perform certain commands, various indicators may appear on the status bar.

The left edge of the status bar in Figure 1–4 shows the current slide number followed by the total number of slides in the document and a document theme identifier. A **document theme** provides consistency in design and color throughout the entire presentation by setting the color scheme, font and font size, and layout of a presentation. Toward the right edge are buttons and controls you can use to change the view of a slide and adjust the size of the displayed document.

PowerPoint Views

The PowerPoint window display varies depending on the view. A **view** is the mode in which the presentation appears on the screen. PowerPoint has three main views: Normal, Slide Sorter, and Slide Show, and also Notes Page. The default view is **Normal view**, which is composed of three working areas that allow you to work on various aspects of a presentation simultaneously. The left side of the screen has a Tabs pane that consists of a **Slides tab** and an **Outline tab** that alternate between views of the presentation in a thumbnail, or miniature, view of the slides and an outline of the slide text. You can type the text of the presentation on the Outline tab and easily rearrange bulleted lists, paragraphs, and individual slides. As you type, you can view this text in the **Slide pane**, which shows a large view of the current slide on the right side of the window. You also can enter text, graphics, animations, and hyperlinks directly in the Slide pane. The **Notes pane** at the bottom of the window is an area where you can type notes and additional information. This text can consist of notes to yourself or remarks to share with your audience. If you want to work with your notes in full page format, you can display them in **Notes Page view**.

In Normal view, you can adjust the width of the Slide pane by dragging the **splitter bar** and the height of the Notes pane by dragging the pane borders. After you have created at least two slides, **scroll bars**, **scroll arrows**, and **scroll boxes** will appear on the right edge of the window.

Ribbon

The **Ribbon**, located near the top of the PowerPoint window, is the control center in PowerPoint (Figure 1–5a). The Ribbon provides easy, central access to the tasks you perform while creating a slide show. The Ribbon consists of tabs, groups, and commands. Each **tab** surrounds a collection of groups, and each group contains related commands.

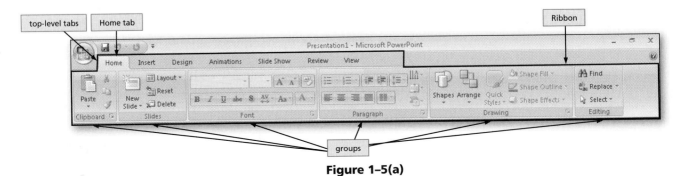

Figure 1–5(a)

When you start PowerPoint, the Ribbon displays seven top-level tabs: Home, Insert, Design, Animations, Slide Show, Review, and View. The **Home tab**, called the primary tab, contains the more frequently used commands. To display a different tab on the Ribbon, click the top-level tab. That is, to display the Insert tab, click Insert on the Ribbon. To return to the Home tab, click Home on the Ribbon. The tab currently displayed is called the **active tab**.

To display more of the document in the document window, some users prefer to minimize the Ribbon, which hides the groups on the Ribbon and displays only the top-level tabs (Figure 1–5b). To use commands on a minimized Ribbon, click the top-level tab.

Each time you start PowerPoint, the Ribbon appears the same way it did the last time you used PowerPoint. The chapters in this book, however, begin with the Ribbon appearing as it did at the initial installation of the software. If you are stepping through this chapter on a computer and you want your Ribbon to match the figures in this book, read Appendix E.

Figure 1–5(b)

In addition to the top-level tabs, PowerPoint displays other tabs, called **contextual tabs**, when you perform certain tasks or work with objects such as pictures or tables. If you insert a picture in a slide, for example, the Picture Tools tab and its related subordinate Format tab appear (Figure 1–6). When you are finished working with the picture, the Picture Tools and Format tabs disappear from the Ribbon. PowerPoint determines when contextual tabs should appear and disappear based on tasks you perform. Some contextual tabs, such as the Chart Tools tab, have more than one related subordinate tab.

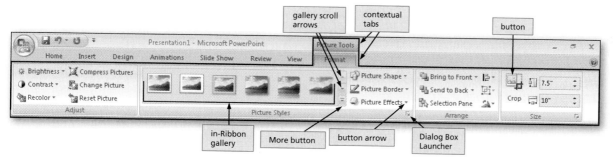

Figure 1–6

Commands on the Ribbon include buttons, boxes (text boxes, check boxes, etc.), and galleries (Figure 1–6). A **gallery** is a set of choices, often graphical, arranged in a grid or in a list. You can scroll through choices on an in-Ribbon gallery by clicking the gallery's scroll arrows. Or, you can click a gallery's More button to view more gallery options on the screen at a time. Some buttons and boxes have arrows that, when clicked, also display a gallery; others always cause a gallery to be displayed when clicked. Most galleries support **live preview**, which is a feature that allows you to point to a gallery choice and see its effect in the document - without actually selecting the choice (Figure 1–7).

BTW

Minimizing the Ribbon
If you want to minimize the Ribbon, right-click the Ribbon and then click Minimize the Ribbon on the shortcut menu, double-click the active tab, or press CTRL+F1. To restore a minimized Ribbon, right-click the Ribbon and then click Minimize the Ribbon on the shortcut menu, double-click any top-level tab, or press CTRL+F1. To use commands on a minimized Ribbon, click the top-level tab.

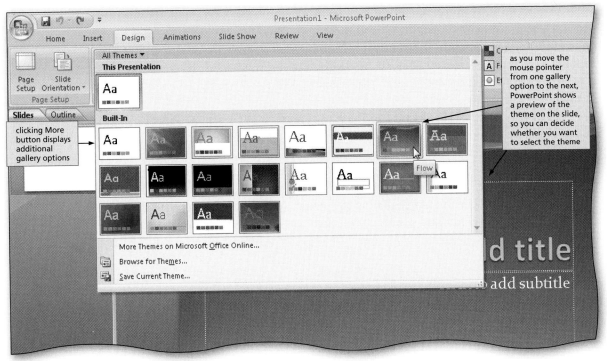

Figure 1–7

Some commands on the Ribbon display an image to help you remember their function. When you point to a command on the Ribbon, all or part of the command glows in shades of yellow and orange, and an Enhanced ScreenTip appears on the screen. An **Enhanced ScreenTip** is an on-screen note that provides the name of the command, available keyboard shortcut(s), a description of the command, and sometimes instructions for how to obtain help about the command (Figure 1–8). Enhanced ScreenTips are more detailed than a typical ScreenTip, which usually only displays the name of the command.

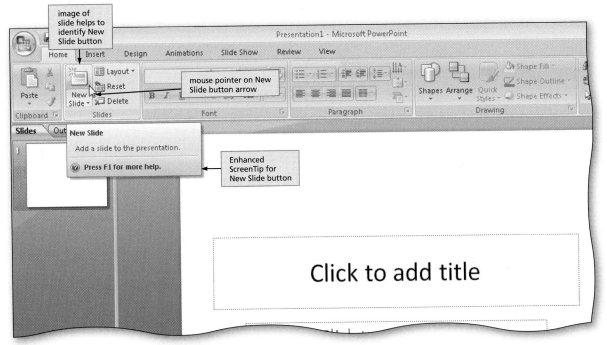

Figure 1–8

The lower-right corner of some groups on the Ribbon has a small arrow, called a **Dialog Box Launcher**, that when clicked displays a dialog box or a task pane with additional options for the group (Figure 1–9). When presented with a dialog box, you make selections and must close the dialog box before returning to the document. A **task pane**, by contrast, is a window that can remain open and visible while you work in the document.

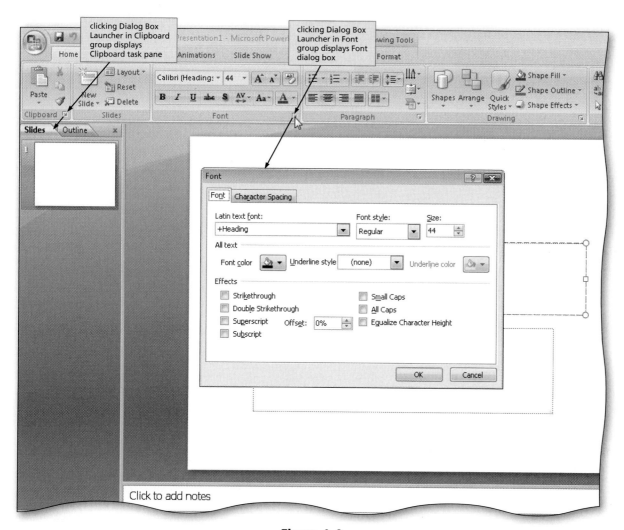

Figure 1–9

Mini Toolbar and Shortcut Menus

The **Mini toolbar**, which appears automatically based on tasks you perform, contains commands related to changing the appearance of text in a slide. All commands on the Mini toolbar also exist on the Ribbon. The purpose of the Mini toolbar is to minimize mouse movement. For example, if you want to use a command that currently is not displayed on the active tab, you can use the command on the Mini toolbar - instead of switching to a different tab to use the command.

When the Mini toolbar appears, it initially is transparent (Figure 1–10a on the next page). If you do not use the transparent Mini toolbar, it disappears from the screen. To use the Mini toolbar, move the mouse pointer into the toolbar, which causes the Mini toolbar to change from a transparent to bright appearance (Figure 1–10b on the next page).

BTW

Turning Off the Mini Toolbar
If you do not want the Mini toolbar to display, click the Office Button, click the PowerPoint Options button on the Office Button menu, and then clear the 'Show Mini Toolbar on selection' check box in the Popular panel.

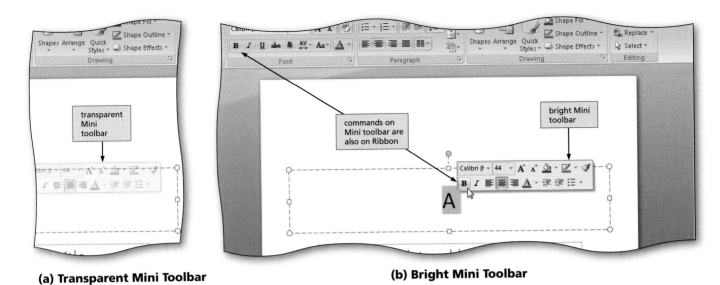

(a) Transparent Mini Toolbar

(b) Bright Mini Toolbar

Figure 1–10

A **shortcut menu**, which appears when you right-click an object, is a list of frequently used commands that relate to the right-clicked object. When you right-click a scroll bar, for example, a shortcut menu appears with commands related to the scroll bar. If you right-click an item in the document window, PowerPoint displays both the Mini toolbar and a shortcut menu (Figure 1–11).

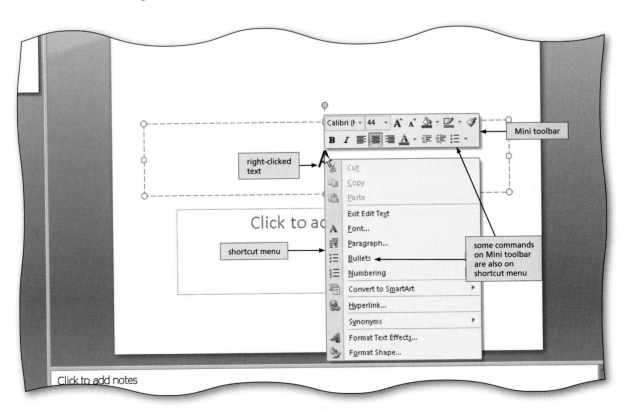

Figure 1–11

Quick Access Toolbar

The **Quick Access Toolbar**, located by default above the Ribbon, provides easy access to frequently used commands (Figure 1–12a). The commands on the Quick Access Toolbar always are available, regardless of the task you are performing. Initially, the Quick Access Toolbar contains the Save, Undo, and Redo commands. If you click the Customize Quick Access Toolbar button, PowerPoint provides a list of commands you quickly can add to and remove from the Quick Access Toolbar (Figure 1–12b).

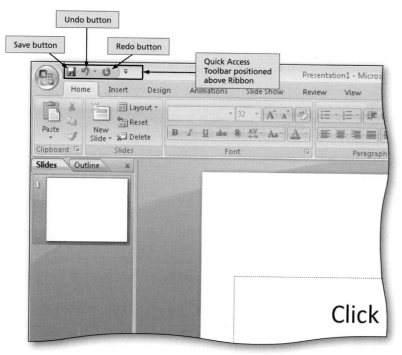

Figure 1–12(a) Quick Access Toolbar above Ribbon

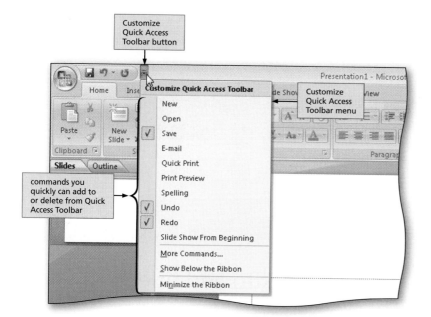

Figure 1–12(b) Customize Quick Access Toolbar

You also can add other commands to or delete commands from the Quick Access Toolbar so that it contains the commands you use most often. As you add commands to the Quick Access Toolbar, its commands may interfere with the document title on the title bar. For this reason, PowerPoint provides an option of displaying the Quick Access Toolbar below the Ribbon (Figure 1–12c).

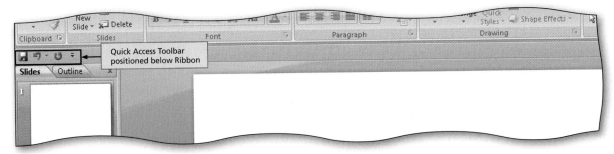

Figure 1–12(c) Quick Access Toolbar below Ribbon

Each time you start PowerPoint, the Quick Access Toolbar appears the same way it did the last time you used PowerPoint. The chapters in this book, however, begin with the Quick Access Toolbar appearing as it did at the initial installation of the software. If you are stepping through this chapter on a computer and you want your Quick Access Toolbar to match the figures in this book, you should reset your Quick Access Toolbar. For more information about how to reset the Quick Access Toolbar, read Appendix E.

Office Button

While the Ribbon is a control center for creating documents, the **Office Button** is a central location for managing and sharing documents. When you click the Office Button, located in the upper-left corner of the window, PowerPoint displays the Office Button menu (Figure 1–13). A **menu** contains a list of commands.

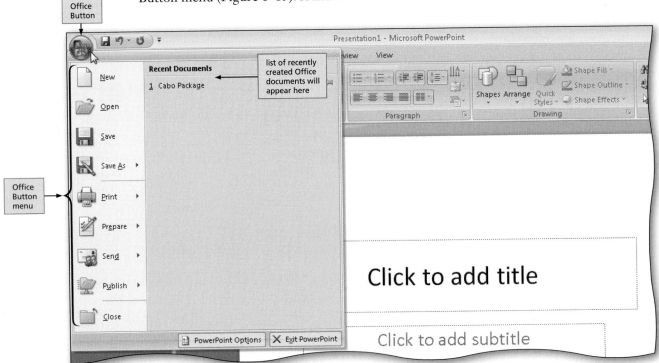

Figure 1–13

When you click the New, Open, Save As, and Print commands on the Office Button menu, PowerPoint displays a dialog box with additional options. The Save As, Print, Prepare, Send, and Publish commands have an arrow to their right. If you point to this arrow, PowerPoint displays a **submenu**, which is a list of additional commands associated with the selected command (Figure 1–14). For the Prepare, Send, and Publish commands that do not display a dialog box when clicked, you can point either to the command or the arrow to display the submenu.

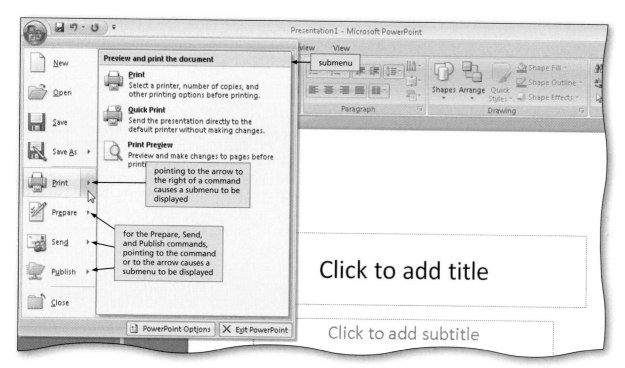

Figure 1–14

Key Tips

If you prefer using the keyboard instead of the mouse, you can press the ALT key on the keyboard to display a **Key Tip badge**, or keyboard code icon, for certain commands (Figure 1–15). To select a command using the keyboard, press its displayed code letter, or **Key Tip**. When you press a Key Tip, additional Key Tips related to the selected command may appear. For example, to select the New command on the Office Button menu, press the ALT key, then press the F key, then press the N key.

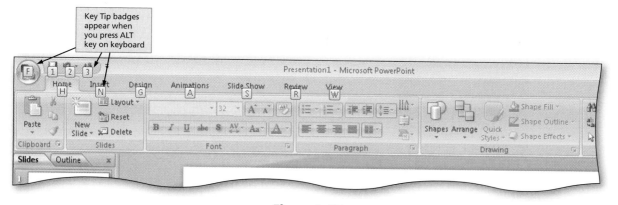

Figure 1–15

To remove the Key Tip badges from the screen, press the ALT key or the ESC key until all Key Tip badges disappear, or click the mouse anywhere in the PowerPoint window.

Choosing a Document Theme

You easily can give a presentation a professional and consistent appearance by using a document theme. This collection of formatting choices includes a set of colors (the color theme), a set of heading and content text fonts (the font theme), and a set of lines and fill effects (the effects theme). These themes allow you to choose and change the appearance of all the slides or individual slides in your presentation.

Plan Ahead	**Find the appropriate theme.**
	In the initial steps of this project, you will select a document theme by locating a particular built-in theme in the Themes group. You could, however, apply a theme at any time while creating the presentation. Some PowerPoint slide show designers create presentations using the default Office Theme. This blank design allows them to concentrate on the words being used to convey the message and does not distract them with colors and various text attributes. Once the text is entered, the designers then select an appropriate document theme.

To Choose a Document Theme

The document theme identifier shows the theme currently used in the slide show. PowerPoint initially uses the **Office Theme** until you select a different theme. The following steps change the theme for this presentation from the Office Theme to the Flow document theme.

• Click Design on the Ribbon to display the Design tab (Figure 1–16).

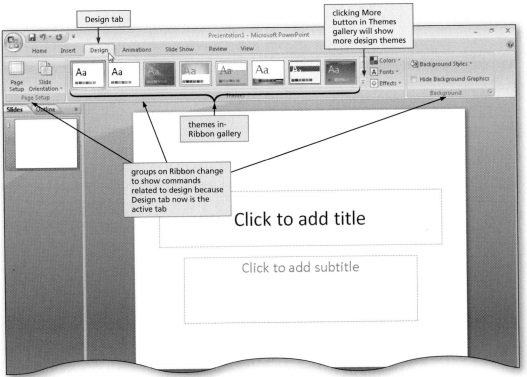

Figure 1–16

2

• Click the More button in the Themes gallery to expand the gallery, which shows more Built-In theme gallery options (Figure 1–17).

 Experiment

• Point to various document themes in the Themes gallery and watch the colors and fonts change on the title slide.

Q&A Are the themes displayed in a specific order?

Yes. They are arranged in alphabetical order running from left to right. If you point to a theme, a ScreenTip with the design's name appears on the screen.

Q&A What if I change my mind and do not want to select a new theme?

Click anywhere outside the All Themes gallery to close the gallery.

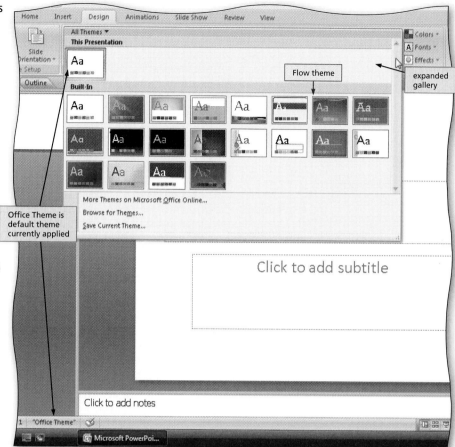

Figure 1–17

3

• Click the Flow theme to apply this theme to Slide 1 (Figure 1–18).

Q&A If I decide at some future time that this design does not fit the theme of my presentation, can I apply a different design?

Yes. You can repeat these steps at any time while creating your presentation.

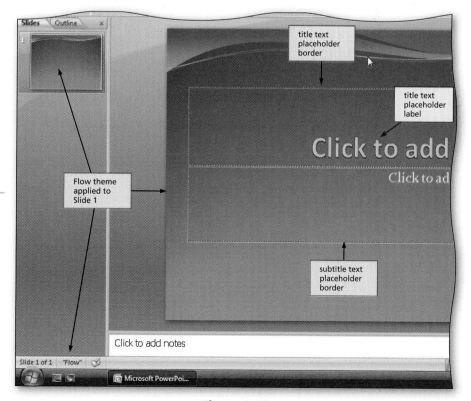

Figure 1–18

Creating a Title Slide

With the exception of a blank slide and a slide with a picture and caption, PowerPoint assumes every new slide has a title. Many of PowerPoint's layouts have both a title text placeholder and at least one content placeholder. To make creating a presentation easier, any text you type after a new slide appears becomes title text in the title text placeholder. The following steps create the title slide for this presentation.

Plan Ahead

Choose the words for the slide.

No doubt you have heard the phrase, "You get only one chance to make a first impression." The same philosophy holds true for a PowerPoint presentation. The title slide gives your audience an initial sense of what they are about to see and hear. It is, therefore, extremely important to choose the text for this slide carefully. Avoid stating the obvious in the title. Instead, create interest and curiosity using key ideas from the presentation.

Some PowerPoint users create the title slide as their last step in the design process so that it reflects the tone of the presentation. They begin by planning the final slide in the presentation so that they know where and how they want to end the slide show. All the slides in the presentation should work toward meeting this final slide.

To Enter the Presentation Title

As you begin typing text in the title text placeholder, the title text also is displayed in the Slide 1 thumbnail in the Slides tab. PowerPoint **line wraps** text that exceeds the width of the placeholder. The presentation title for Project 1 is A World Beneath the Waves. This title creates interest by introducing the concept of exploring the life under water. The following step creates the slide show's title.

- Click the label, Click to add title, located inside the title text placeholder to select the placeholder (Figure 1–19).

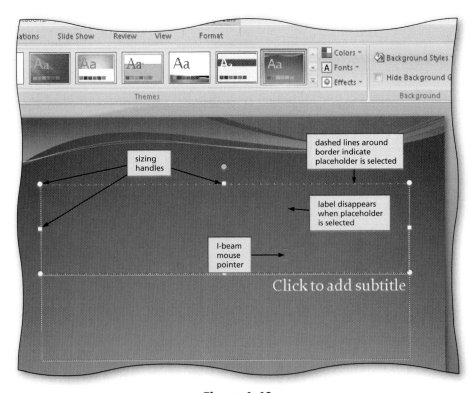

Figure 1–19

2

- **Type** A World Beneath the Waves in the title text placeholder. Do not press the ENTER key (Figure 1–20).

Q&A

What if a button with two lines and two arrows appears on the left side of the title text placeholder?

The **AutoFit** button displays because PowerPoint attempts to reduce the size of the letters when the title text does not fit on a single line. If you are creating a slide and need to squeeze an extra line in the text placeholder, you can click this button to resize the existing text in the placeholder so the spillover text will fit on the slide.

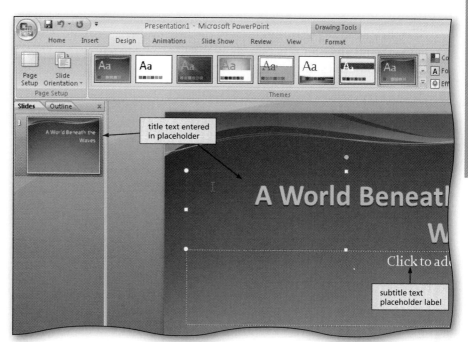

Figure 1–20

Correcting a Mistake When Typing

If you type the wrong letter, press the BACKSPACE key to erase all the characters back to and including the one that is incorrect. If you mistakenly press the ENTER key after typing the title and the insertion point is on the new line, simply press the BACKSPACE key to return the insertion point to the right of the letter s in the word Waves.

When you install PowerPoint, the default setting allows you to reverse up to the last 20 changes by clicking the Undo button on the Quick Access Toolbar. The ScreenTip that appears when you point to the Undo button changes to indicate the type of change just made. For example, if you type text in the title text placeholder and then point to the Undo button, the ScreenTip that appears is Undo Typing. For clarity, when referencing the Undo button in this project, the name displaying in the ScreenTip is referenced. You can reapply a change that you reversed with the Undo button by clicking the Redo button on the Quick Access Toolbar. Clicking the Redo button reverses the last undo action. The ScreenTip name reflects the type of reversal last performed.

Paragraphs

Subtitle text in the subtitle text placeholder supports the title text. It can appear on one or more lines in the placeholder. To create more than one subtitle line, you press the ENTER key after typing some words. PowerPoint creates a new line, which is the second paragraph in the placeholder. A **paragraph** is a segment of text with the same format that begins when you press the ENTER key and ends when you press the ENTER key again. This new paragraph is the same level as the previous paragraph. A **level** is a position within a structure, such as an outline, that indicates the magnitude of importance. PowerPoint allows for five paragraph levels.

To Enter the Presentation Subtitle Paragraph

The first subtitle paragraph links to the title by giving specific details about the vacation location, and the second paragraph gives information about the person who will be speaking to the audience. The following steps enter the presentation subtitle.

- Click the label, Click to add subtitle, located inside the subtitle text placeholder to select the placeholder (Figure 1–21).

Figure 1–21

- Type Spring Break in Cabo San Lucas, Mexico and then press the ENTER key.

- Type Presented by Dave Ehlin, SGA President but do not press the ENTER key (Figure 1–22).

Q&A Why do red wavy lines appear below the words, Cabo and Ehlin?

The lines indicate possible spelling errors.

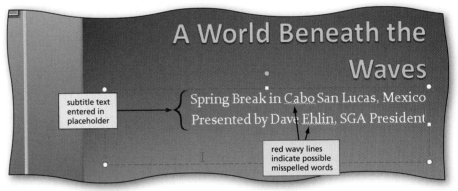

Figure 1–22

Plan Ahead

Identify how to format specific elements of the text.

Most of the time, you use the document theme's text attributes, color scheme, and layout. Occasionally, you may want to change the way a presentation looks, however, and still keep a particular document theme. PowerPoint gives you that flexibility.

Graphic designers use several rules when formatting text.

- Avoid all capital letters, if possible. Audiences have difficulty comprehending sentences typed in all capital letters, especially when the lines exceed seven words. All capital letters leaves no room for emphasis or inflection, so readers get confused about what material deserves particular attention. Some document themes, however, have a default title text style of all capital letters.

- Avoid text with a font size less than 24 point. Audience members generally will sit a maximum of 50 feet from a screen, and at this distance 24-point type is the smallest size text they can read comfortably without straining.

- Make careful color choices. Color evokes emotions, and a careless color choice may elicit the incorrect psychological response. PowerPoint provides a color palette with hundreds of colors. The built-in document themes use complementary colors that work well together. If you stray from these themes and add your own color choices, without a good reason to make the changes, your presentation is apt to become ineffective.

Formatting Characters in a Presentation

Recall that each document theme determines the color scheme, font and font size, and layout of a presentation. You can use a specific document theme and then change the characters' formats any time before, during, or after you type the text.

Fonts and Font Styles

BTW

Formatting Words
To format one word, position the insertion point anywhere in the word. Then make the formatting changes you desire. The entire word does not need to be selected for the change to occur.

Characters that appear on the screen are a specific shape and size. Examples of how you can modify the appearance, or **format**, of these typed characters on the screen and in print include changing the font, style, size, and color. The **font**, or typeface, defines the appearance and shape of the letters, numbers, punctuation marks, and symbols. **Style** indicates how the characters are formatted. PowerPoint's text font styles include regular, italic, bold, and bold italic. **Size** specifies the height of the characters and is gauged by a measurement system that uses points. A **point** is 1/72 of an inch in height. Thus, a character with a point size of 36 is 36/72 (or 1/2) of an inch in height. **Color** defines the hue of the characters.

This presentation uses the Flow document theme, which uses particular font styles and font sizes. The Flow document theme default title text font is named Calibri. It has a bold style with no special effects, and its size is 56 point. The Flow document theme default subtitle text font is Constantia with a font size of 26 point.

To Select a Paragraph

You can use many techniques to format characters. When you want to apply the same formats to multiple words or paragraphs, it is efficient to select the desired text and then make the desired changes to all the characters simultaneously. The first formatting change you will make will apply to the second paragraph of the title slide subtitle. The following step selects this paragraph.

1

• Triple-click the paragraph, Presented by Dave Ehlin, SGA President, in the subtitle text placeholder to select the paragraph (Figure 1–23).

Q&A

Can I select the paragraph using a technique other than triple-clicking?

Yes. You can move your mouse pointer to the left of the first paragraph and then drag it to the end of the line.

Figure 1–23

To Italicize Text

Different font styles often are used on slides to make them more appealing to the reader and to emphasize particular text. Italic type, used sparingly, draws the readers' eyes to these characters. The following step adds emphasis to the second line of the subtitle text by changing regular text to italic text.

- With the subtitle text still selected, click the Italic button on the Mini tool-bar to italicize that text on the slide and on the slide thumbnail (Figure 1–24).

Q&A

If I change my mind and decide not to italicize the text, how can I remove this style?

Select the italicized text and then click the Italic button. As a result, the Italic button will not be selected, and the text will not have the italic font style.

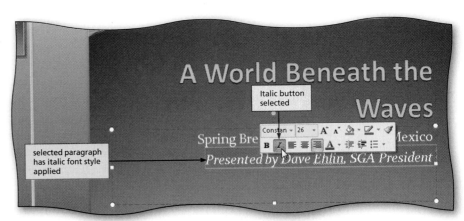

Figure 1–24

Other Ways
1. Right-click selected text, click Font on shortcut menu, click Italic in Font style list   2. Click Home tab, click Italic in Font group   3. Press CTRL+I

To Select Multiple Paragraphs

Each of the subtitle lines is a separate paragraph. As previously discussed, PowerPoint creates a new paragraph each time you press the ENTER key. To change the character formatting in both paragraphs, it is efficient to select the desired text and then make the desired changes to all the characters simultaneously.

The next formatting change you will make will apply to both title slide subtitle paragraphs. The following step selects the first paragraph so that you can format both paragraphs concurrently.

- With the second subtitle text paragraph selected, press the CTRL key and then triple-click the first subtitle text paragraph, Spring Break in Cabo San Lucas, Mexico, to select both paragraphs (Figure 1–25).

Q&A

Can I use a different technique to select both subtitle text paragraphs?

Yes. Click the placeholder border so that it appears as a solid line. When the placeholder is selected in this manner, formatting changes will apply to all text in the placeholder.

Figure 1–25

Identify how to format specific elements of the text.
When selecting text colors, try to limit using red. At least 15 percent of men have difficulty distinguishing varying shades of green or red. They also often see the color purple as blue and the color brown as green. This problem is more pronounced when the colors appear in small areas, such as slide paragraphs or line chart bars.

Plan Ahead

To Change the Text Color

PowerPoint allows you to use one or more text colors in a presentation. To add more emphasis to the title slide subtitle text, you decide to change the color. The following steps add emphasis to both subtitle text paragraphs by changing the font color from white to dark blue.

1

- With both paragraphs selected, click the Font Color arrow on the Mini toolbar to display the palette of Theme Colors and Standard Colors (Figure 1–26).

Q&A

If the Mini toolbar disappears from the screen, how can I display it once again?

Right-click the text, and the Mini toolbar should appear.

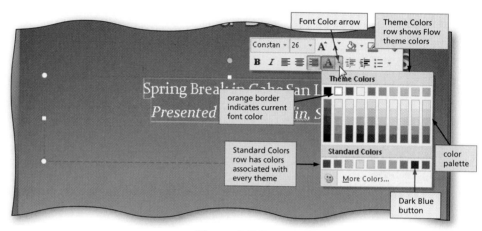

Figure 1–26

2

- Click the Dark Blue button in the Standard Colors row on the Mini toolbar (row 1, column 9) to change the font color to dark blue (Figure 1–27).

Q&A

Why did I select the color, dark blue?

Dark blue is one of the 10 standard colors associated with every document theme, and it works well with the shades of blue already on the slide. An additional consideration is that dark colors print well.

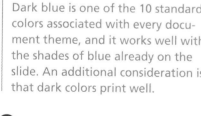

Figure 1–27

3

- Click outside the selected area to deselect the two paragraphs.

Other Ways

1. Right-click selected text, click Font on shortcut menu, click Font color button, click Dark Blue in Standard Colors row

2. Click Home tab, click Font Color arrow in Font group, click Dark Blue in Standard Colors row

To Select a Group of Words

PowerPoint designers use many techniques to format characters. To apply the same formats to multiple words or paragraphs, they select the desired text and then make the desired changes to all the characters simultaneously.

To add emphasis to the vacation destination, you want to increase the font size and change the font style to bold for the words, Cabo San Lucas. You could perform these actions separately, but it is more efficient to select this group of words and then change the font attributes. The following steps select a group of words.

- Position the mouse pointer immediately to the left of the first character of the text to be selected (in this case, the C in Cabo) (Figure 1–28).

Figure 1–28

- Drag the mouse pointer through the last character of the text to be selected (in this case, the s in Lucas) (Figure 1–29).

Figure 1–29

To Increase Font Size

To add emphasis, you increase the font size for Cabo San Lucas. The Increase Font Size button on the Mini toolbar increases the font size in preset increments. The following step uses this button to increase the font size.

- Click the Increase Font Size button on the Mini toolbar once to increase the font size of the selected text from 26 to 28 point (Figure 1–30).

Other Ways

1. Click Home tab, click Increase Font Size button in Font group
2. Click Home tab, click Font Size box arrow, click new font size
3. Press CTRL+SHIFT+>

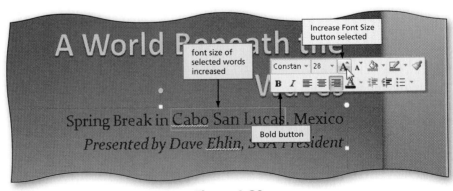

Figure 1–30

To Bold Text

Bold characters display somewhat thicker and darker than those that display in a regular font style. Clicking the Bold button on the Mini toolbar is an efficient method of bolding text. To add more emphasis to the vacation destination, you want to bold the words, Cabo San Lucas. The following step bolds this text.

- Click the Bold button on the Mini toolbar to bold the three selected words (Figure 1–31).

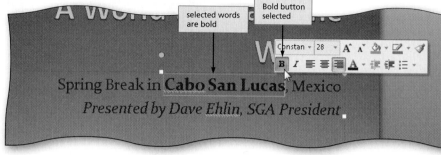

Figure 1–31

Other Ways
1. Click Home tab, click Bold button in Font group
2. Press CTRL+B

Identify how to format specific elements of the text.
Avoid line wraps. Your audience's eyes want to stop at the end of a line. Thus, you must plan your words carefully or adjust the font size so that each point displays on only one line.

Plan Ahead

To Decrease the Title Slide Title Text Font Size

The last word of the title text, Waves, appears on a line by itself. For aesthetic reasons, it is advantageous to have this word appear with the rest of the title on a single line. One way to fit text on one line is to decrease the font size. The process is similar to increasing the font size. Clicking the Decrease Font Size button on the Mini toolbar decreases the size in preset increments. The following steps decrease the font size from 56 to 48 point.

- Select the title slide title text, A World Beneath the Waves (Figure 1–32).

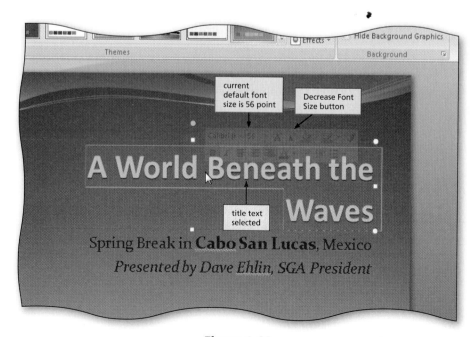

Figure 1–32

2

- Click the Decrease Font Size button on the Mini toolbar twice to decrease the font size from 56 to 48 point (Figure 1–33).

Figure 1–33

Saving the Project

While you are building a presentation, the computer stores it in memory. When you save a presentation, the computer places it on a storage medium such as a USB flash drive, CD, or hard disk. A saved presentation is referred to as a **file**. A **file name** is the name assigned to a file when it is saved.

It is important to save the presentation frequently for the following reasons:

- The presentation in memory will be lost if the computer is turned off or you lose electrical power while PowerPoint is open.

- If you run out of time before completing your project, you may finish your presentation at a future time without starting over.

Plan Ahead

BTW

Saving in a Previous PowerPoint Format
To ensure that your presentation will open in an earlier version of PowerPoint, you must save your file in PowerPoint 97–2003 format. Files saved in this format have the .ppt extension.

Determine where to save the document.
When saving a document, you must decide which storage medium to use.

- If you always work on the same computer and have no need to transport your projects to a different location, then your computer's hard drive will suffice as a storage location. It is a good idea, however, to save a backup copy of your projects on a separate medium in case the file becomes corrupted or the computer's hard drive fails.

- If you plan to work on your projects in various locations or on multiple computers, then you should save your projects on a portable medium, such as a USB flash drive or CD. The projects in this book use a USB flash drive, which saves files quickly and reliably and can be reused. CDs are easily portable and serve as good backups for the final versions of projects because they generally can save files only one time.

To Save a Presentation

You have performed many tasks and do not want to lose the work completed thus far. Thus, you should save the presentation. The following steps save a presentation on a USB flash drive using the file name, Cabo Package.

Note: If you are using Windows XP, see Appendix F for alternate steps.

1

- With a USB flash drive connected to one of the computer's USB ports, click the Save button on the Quick Access Toolbar to display the Save As dialog box. (Figure 1–34).

- If the Navigation pane is not displayed in the Save As dialog box, click the Browse Folders button to expand the dialog box.

- If a Folders list is displayed below the Folders button, click the Folders button to remove the Folders list.

Q&A
Do I have to save to a USB flash drive?

No. You can save to any device or folder. A **folder** is a specific location on a storage medium. You can save to the default folder or a different folder. You also can create your own folders, which is explained later in this book.

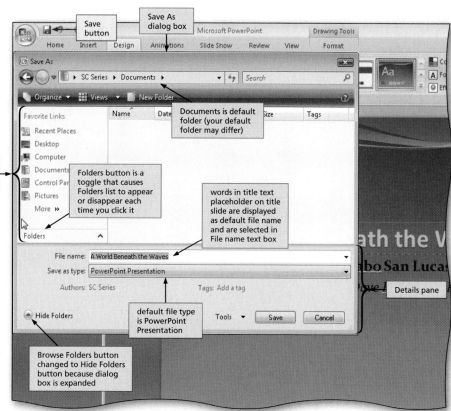

Figure 1–34

2

- Type Cabo Package in the File name box to change the file name. Do not press the ENTER key after typing the file name (Figure 1–35).

Q&A
What characters can I use in a file name?

A file name can have a maximum of 260 characters, including spaces. The only invalid characters are the backslash (\), slash (/), colon (:), asterisk (*), question mark (?), quotation mark ("), less than symbol (<), greater than symbol (>), and vertical bar (|).

Q&A
What are file properties and tags?

File properties contain information about a file such as the file name, author name, date the file was modified, and tags. A tag is a file property that contains a word or phrase about a file. You can organize and locate files based on their file properties.

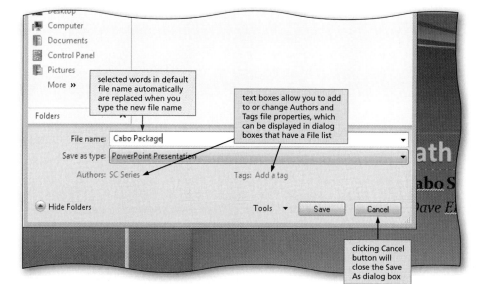

Figure 1–35

- If Computer is not displayed in the Favorite Links section, drag the top or bottom edge of the Save As dialog box until Computer is displayed.

- Click Computer in the Favorite Links section to display a list of available drives (Figure 1–36).

- If necessary, scroll until UDISK 2.0 (E:) appears in the list of available drives.

Q&A Why is my list of drives arranged and named differently?

The size of the Save As dialog box and your computer's configuration determine how the list is displayed and how the drives are named.

Q&A How do I save the file if I am not using a USB flash drive?

Use the same process, but select your desired save location in the Favorite Links section.

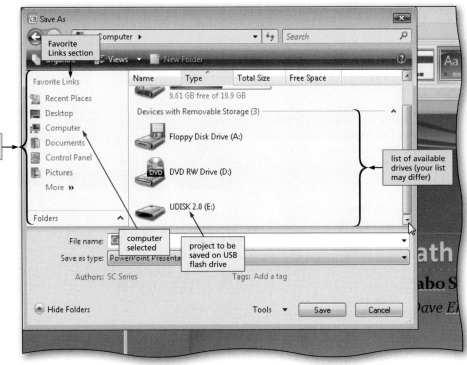

Figure 1–36

- Double-click UDISK 2.0 (E:) in the Computer list to select the USB flash drive, Drive E in this case, as the new save location (Figure 1–37).

Q&A What if my USB flash drive has a different name or letter?

It is very likely that your USB flash drive will have a different name and drive letter and be connected to a different port. Verify the device in your Computer list is correct.

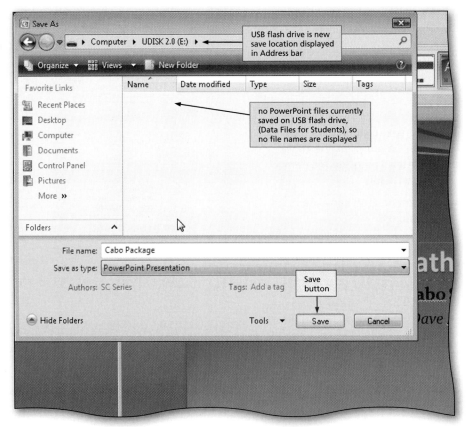

Figure 1–37

5

- Click the Save button in the Save As dialog box to save the presentation on the USB flash drive with the file name, Cabo Package (Figure 1–38).

Q&A How do I know that the project is saved?

While PowerPoint is saving your file, it briefly displays a message on the status bar indicating the amount of the file saved. In addition, your USB drive may have a light that flashes during the save process.

Q&A Why is .pptx displayed immediately to the right of the file name?

Depending on your Windows Vista settings, .pptx may be displayed after you save the file. The file type .pptx is a PowerPoint 2007 document. Previous versions of PowerPoint had a file type of .ppt.

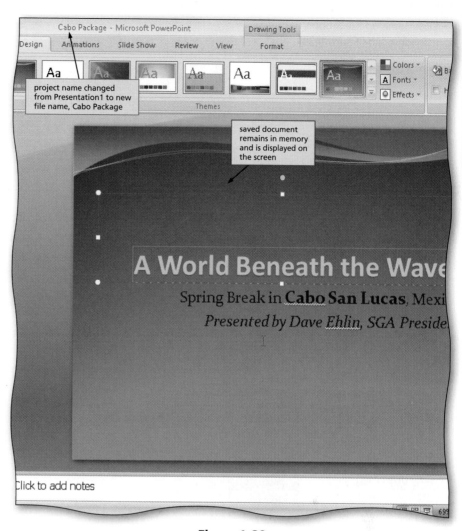

Figure 1–38

Other Ways

1. Click Office Button, click Save, type file name, click Computer, select drive or folder, click Save button

2. Press CTRL+S or press SHIFT+F12, type file name, click Computer, select drive or folder, click Save button

Adding a New Slide to a Presentation

With the title slide for the presentation created, the next step is to add the first text slide immediately after the title slide. Usually, when you create a presentation, you add slides with text, graphics, or charts. Some placeholders allow you to double-click the placeholder and then access other objects, such as media clips, charts, diagrams, and organization charts. You can change the layout for a slide at any time during the creation of a presentation.

To Add a New Text Slide with a Bulleted List

When you add a new slide, PowerPoint uses the Title and Content slide layout. This layout provides a title placeholder and a content area for text, art, charts, and other graphics. A vertical scroll bar appears in the Slide pane when you add the second slide so that you can move from slide to slide easily. A thumbnail of this slide also appears in the Slides tab. The following steps add a new slide with the Title and Content slide layout.

1

- Click Home on the Ribbon to display the Home tab (Figure 1–39).

Figure 1–39

2

- Click the New Slide button in the Slides group to insert a new slide with the Title and Content layout (Figure 1–40).

Q&A Why does the bullet character display a blue dot?

The Flow document theme determines the bullet characters. Each paragraph level has an associated bullet character.

Q&A I clicked the New Slide arrow instead of the New Slide button. What should I do?

Click the Title and Content slide thumbnail in the layout gallery.

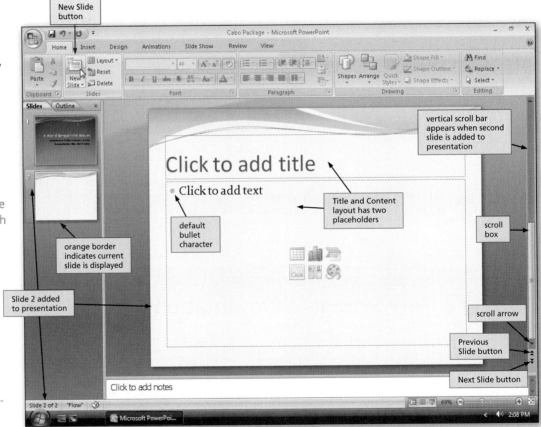

Figure 1–40

Other Ways

1. Press CTRL+M

Choose the words for the slide.
All presentations should follow the 7 × 7 rule which states that each slide should have a maximum of seven lines, and each line should have a maximum of seven words. PowerPoint designers must choose their words carefully and, in turn, help viewers read the slides easily.

Plan
Ahead

Creating a Text Slide with a Single-Level Bulleted List

The information in the Slide 2 text placeholder is presented in a bulleted list. All the bullets appear at the same paragraph level, called the first level.

To Enter a Slide Title

PowerPoint assumes every new slide has a title. The title for Slide 2 is Package Highlights. The following step enters this title.

- Click the label, Click to add title, to select it and then type Package Highlights in the placeholder. Do not press the ENTER key (Figure 1–41).

Q&A

What are those six icons grouped in the middle of the slide?

You can click one of the icons to insert a specific type of content: table, chart, SmartArt graphic, picture, clip art, or media clip.

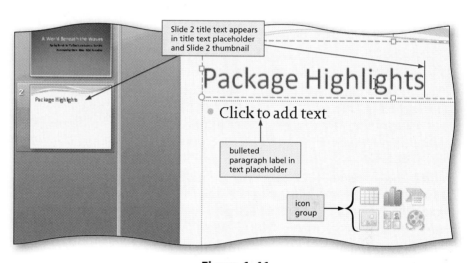

Figure 1–41

To Select a Text Placeholder

Before you can type text into the text placeholder, you first must select it. The following step selects the text placeholder on Slide 2.

- Click the label, Click to add text, to select the text placeholder (Figure 1–42).

Q&A

Why does my mouse pointer have a different shape?

If you move the mouse pointer away from the bullet, it will change shape.

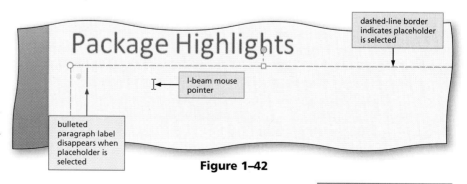

Figure 1–42

Other Ways
1. Press CTRL+ENTER

To Type a Single-Level Bulleted List

The content placeholder provides an area for the text characters. When you click inside a placeholder, you then can type or paste text. If your text exceeds the size of the placeholder, PowerPoint will attempt to make the text fit by reducing the text size and line spacing. **Line spacing** is the amount of vertical space between the lines of text.

As discussed previously, a bulleted list is a list of paragraphs, each of which is preceded by a bullet. A paragraph is a segment of text ended by pressing the ENTER key. The next step is to type the single-level bulleted list, which consists of five paragraphs (Figure 1–1b on page PPT 3). The following steps create a single-level bulleted list.

1

- Type Four nights at the Azure Seas Resort and then press the ENTER key to begin a new bulleted first-level paragraph (Figure 1–43).

Q&A Can I delete bullets on a slide?

Yes. If you do not want bullets to display on a particular paragraph, click the Bullets button in the Paragraph group on the Home tab or right-click the paragraph and then click the Bullets button on the Mini toolbar.

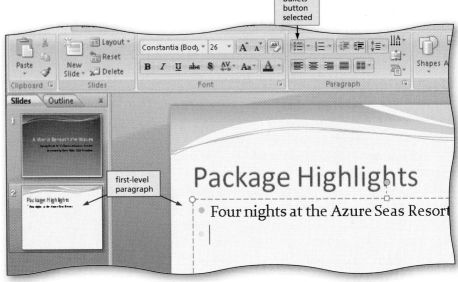

Figure 1–43

2

- Type Breakfast buffet, lunch, dinner, and snacks and then press the ENTER key.

- Type Two large swimming pools and then press the ENTER key.

- Type Round-trip airfare and hotel transfers and then press the ENTER key.

- Type Daily activities, including water sports but do not press the ENTER key (Figure 1–44).

Q&A I pressed the ENTER key in error, and now a new bullet appears after the last entry on this slide. How can I remove this extra bullet?

Press the BACKSPACE key.

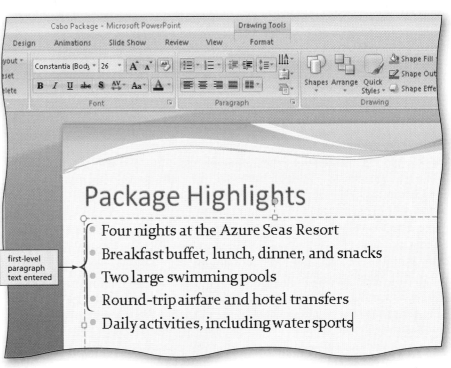

Figure 1–44

Creating a Text Slide with a Multi-Level Bulleted List

Slides 3 and 4 in Figure 1–1 on pages PPT 3–4 contain more than one level of bulleted text. A slide that consists of more than one level of bulleted text is called a **multi-level bulleted list slide**. Beginning with the second level, each paragraph indents to the right of the preceding level and is pushed down to a lower level. For example, if you increase the indent of a first-level paragraph, it becomes a second-level paragraph.

Creating a text slide with a multi-level bulleted list requires several steps. Initially, you enter a slide title in the title text placeholder. Next, you select the content text placeholder. Then, you type the text for the multi-level bulleted list, increasing and decreasing the indents as needed. The next several sections add a slide with a multi-level bulleted list.

To Add a New Slide and Enter a Slide Title

When you add a new slide to a presentation, PowerPoint keeps the same layout used on the previous slide. PowerPoint assumes every new slide has a title. The title for Slide 3 is Rates and Booking. The following steps add a new slide (Slide 3) and enter a title.

1
• Click the New Slide button in the Slides group on the Home tab to insert a new slide with the Title and Content layout (Figure 1–45).

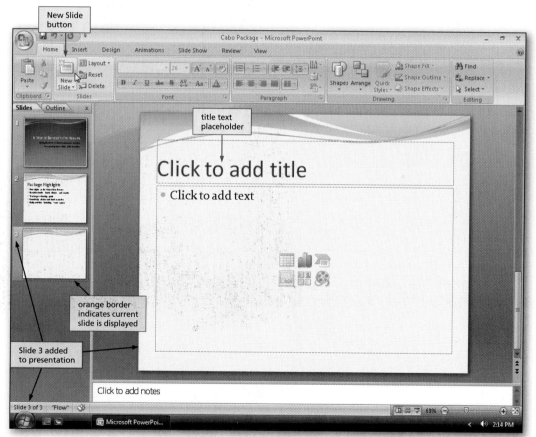

Figure 1–45

- Click the title text placeholder and then type `Rates and Booking` in this placeholder. Do not press the ENTER key (Figure 1–46).

Figure 1–46

Other Ways

1. Press SHIFT+CTRL+M

To Type a Multi-Level Bulleted List

In a multi-level bulleted list, a lower-level paragraph is a subset of a higher-level paragraph. It usually contains information that supports the topic in the paragraph immediately above it.

The next step is to select the content text placeholder and then type the multi-level bulleted list, which consists of six entries (Figure 1–1c on page PPT 3). Creating a lower-level paragraph is called **demoting** text; creating a higher-level paragraph is called **promoting** text. The following steps create a list consisting of three levels.

- Click the bulleted paragraph text placeholder.

- Type `Only $495 double occupancy` and then press the ENTER key (Figure 1–47).

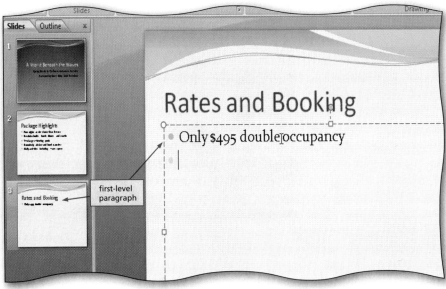

Figure 1–47

2

- Click the Increase List Level button in the Paragraph group to indent the second paragraph below the first and create a second-level paragraph (Figure 1–48).

Why does the bullet for this paragraph have a different size and color?

A different bullet is assigned to each paragraph level.

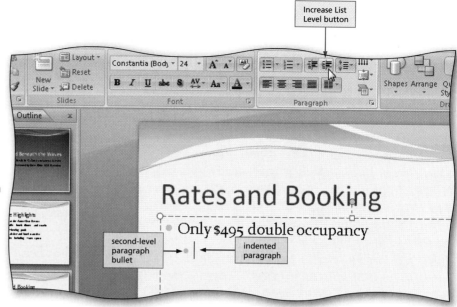

Figure 1–48

3

- Type Non-diver rate: $275 and then press the ENTER key to add a new paragraph at the same level as the previous paragraph.

- Type Single occupancy: add $150 and then press the ENTER key (Figure 1–49).

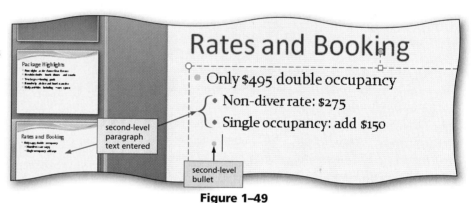

Figure 1–49

4

- Click the Decrease List Level button in the Paragraph group so that the second-level paragraph becomes a first-level paragraph (Figure 1–50).

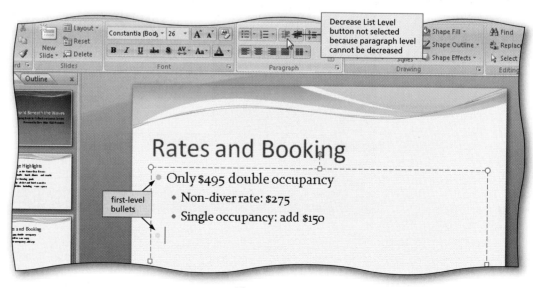

Figure 1–50

Other Ways

1. Press TAB to promote paragraph; press SHIFT+TAB to demote paragraph

To Type the Remaining Text for Slide 3

The following steps complete the text for Slide 3.

1 Type `Nonrefundable $150 deposit required` and then press the ENTER key.

2 Click the Increase List Level button in the Paragraph group to demote the paragraph.

3 Type `Due by October 1` and then press the ENTER key.

4 Click the Decrease List Level button in the Paragraph group to promote the paragraph.

5 Type `Travel insurance highly recommended` but do not press the ENTER key (Figure 1–51).

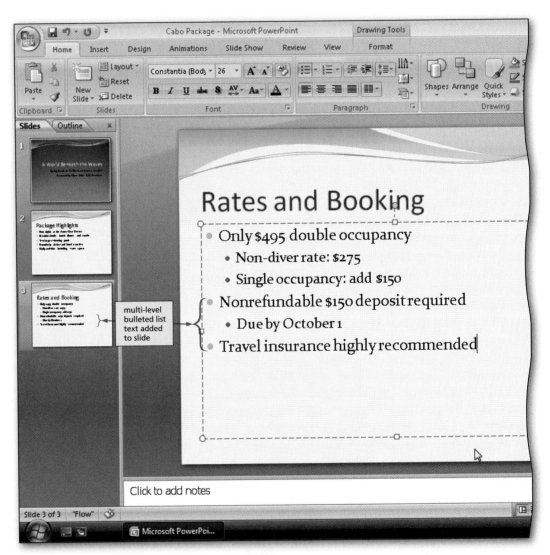

Figure 1–51

To Create Slide 4

Slide 4 is the final multi-level bulleted text slide in this presentation. It has three levels. The following steps create Slide 4.

1 Click the New Slide button in the Slides group.

2 Type Snorkeling and Diving in the title text placeholder.

3 Press CTRL+ENTER to move the insertion point to the text placeholder.

4 Type Three days of two-tank boat dives and then press the ENTER key.

5 Click the Increase List Level button. Type Weights and tanks included and then press the ENTER key (Figure 1–52).

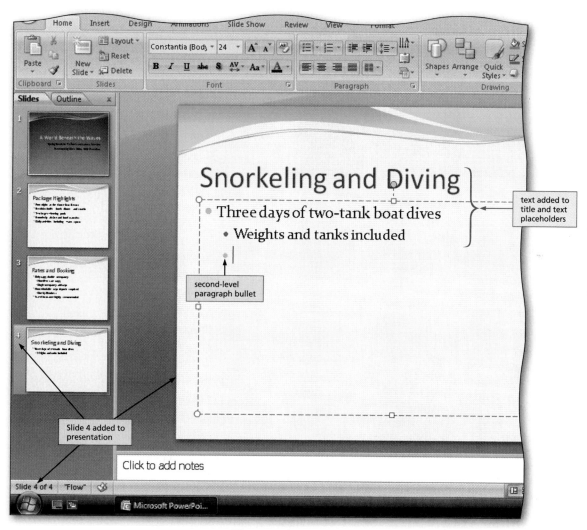

Figure 1–52

To Create a Third-Level Paragraph

Slide 4 contains detailed information about the particular dives. Each additional paragraph becomes more specific and supports the information in the paragraph above it.

The next line in Slide 4 is indented an additional level, to the third level. The following steps demote the text to a third-level paragraph.

1

- Click the Increase List Level button so that the second-level paragraph becomes a third-level paragraph (Figure 1–53).

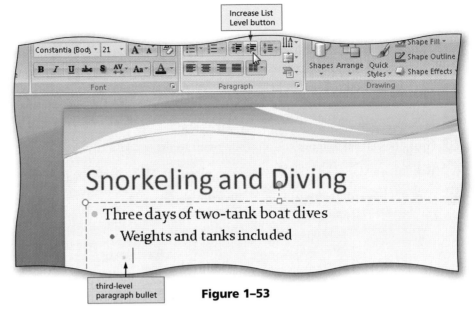

Figure 1–53

2

- Type Instructors available for beginners and then press the ENTER key to create a second third-level paragraph (Figure 1–54).

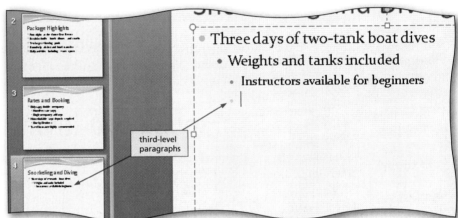

Figure 1–54

3

- Click the Decrease List Level button two times so that the insertion point appears at the first level (Figure 1–55).

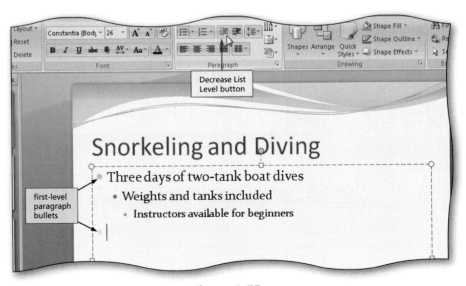

Figure 1–55

To Type the Remaining Text for Slide 4

The next three paragraphs concern what divers and snorkelers will view. The following steps type the remaining text for Slide 4.

1 Type `Various locations based on diving skills` and then press the ENTER key.

2 Press the TAB key to increase the indent to the second level.

3 Type `Spectacular underwater wildlife and landscapes` and then press the ENTER key.

4 Press the TAB key to increase the indent to the third level.

5 Type `See squids, sea turtles, snakes, barracudas, and stingrays` but do not press the ENTER key (Figure 1–56).

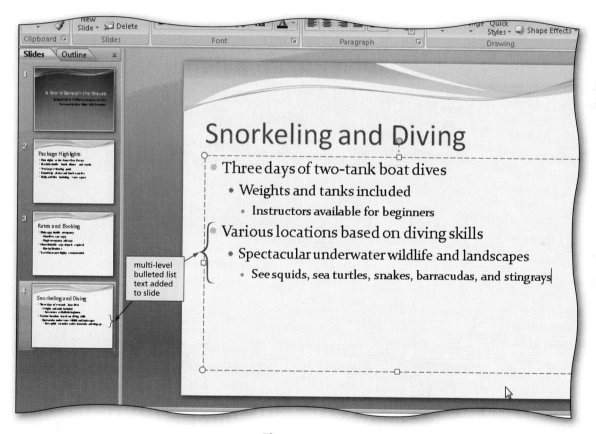

Figure 1–56

Choose the words for the slide.
After the last bulleted list slide in the slide show appears during a slide show, the default PowerPoint setting is to end the presentation with a **black slide**. This black slide appears only when the slide show is running and concludes the slide show, so your audience never sees the PowerPoint window. It is a good idea, however, to end the presentation with a final, closing slide to display at the end of the presentation. This slide ends the presentation gracefully and should be an exact copy, or a very similar copy, of your title slide. The audience will recognize that the presentation is drawing to a close when this slide appears. It can remain on the screen when the audience asks questions, approaches the speaker for further information, or exits the room.

Plan
Ahead

Ending a Slide Show with a Closing Slide

All the text slides are created for the Cabo Package slide show. This presentation thus far consists of a title slide, one text slide with a single-level bulleted list, and two text slides with a multi-level bulleted list. A closing slide that resembles the title slide is the final slide to create.

To Duplicate a Slide

When two slides contain similar information and have the same format, duplicating one slide and then making minor modifications to the new slide saves time and increases consistency.

Slide 5 will have the same layout and design as Slide 1. The most expedient method of creating this slide is to copy Slide 1 and then make minor modifications to the new slide. The following steps duplicate the title slide.

1
- Click the Slide 1 thumbnail in the Slides tab to display Slide 1 (Figure 1–57).

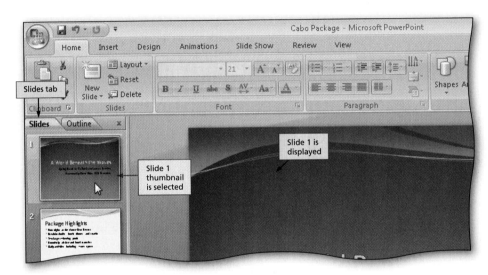

Figure 1–57

2
- Click the New Slide arrow in the Slides group on the Home tab to display the Flow layout gallery (Figure 1–58).

Figure 1–58

- Click Duplicate Selected Slides in the Flow layout gallery to create a new Slide 2, which is a duplicate of Slide 1 (Figure 1–59).

Figure 1–59

To Arrange a Slide

The new Slide 2 was inserted directly below Slide 1 because Slide 1 was the selected slide. This duplicate slide needs to display at the end of the presentation directly after the final title and content slide.

Changing slide order is an easy process and is best performed in the Tabs pane. When you click the slide thumbnail and begin to drag it to a new location, a line indicates the new location of the selected slide. When you release the mouse button, the slide drops into the desired location. Hence, this process of dragging and then dropping the thumbnail in a new location is called **drag and drop**. You can use the drag-and-drop method to move any selected item, including text and graphics. The following step moves the new Slide 2 to the end of the presentation so that it becomes a closing slide.

● With Slide 2 selected, drag the Slide 2 slide thumbnail in the Slides pane below the last slide thumbnail (Figure 1–60).

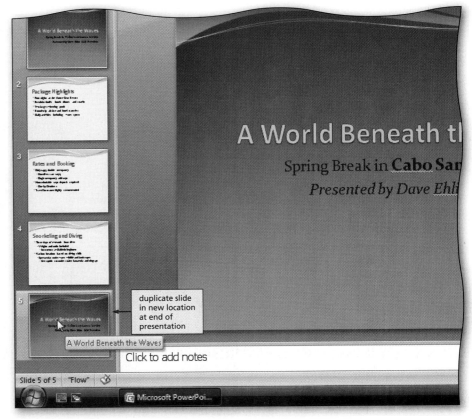

Figure 1–60

Other Ways

1. Click slide icon on Outline tab, drag icon to new location
2. In Slide Sorter view click slide thumbnail, drag thumbnail to new location

To Delete All Text in a Placeholder

To keep the ending slide clean and simple, you want only the slide show title, A World Beneath the Waves, to display on Slide 5. The following steps delete both paragraphs in the subtitle placeholder.

● With Slide 5 selected, click the subtitle text placeholder to select it (Figure 1–61).

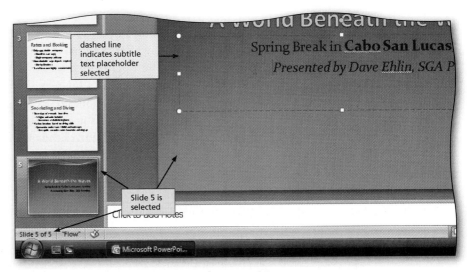

Figure 1–61

2
- Click the subtitle text placeholder border to change the border from a dashed line to a solid line (Figure 1–62).

clicking placeholder border changes border to solid line

Figure 1–62

3
- Click the Cut button in the Clipboard group on the Home tab to delete all the text in the subtitle text placeholder (Figure 1–63).

Cut button

subtitle paragraphs are deleted from placeholder

Figure 1–63

Changing Document Properties and Saving Again

PowerPoint helps you organize and identify your files by using document properties, which are the details about a file. **Document properties**, also known as **metadata**, can include such information as the project author, title, or subject. **Keywords** are words or phrases that further describe the document. For example, a class name or document topic can describe the file's purpose or content.

Document properties are valuable for a variety of reasons:

- Users can save time locating a particular file because they can view a document's properties without opening the document.
- By creating consistent properties for files having similar content, users can better organize their documents.
- Some organizations require PowerPoint users to add document properties so that other employees can view details about these files.

Five different types of document properties exist, but the more common ones used in this book are standard and automatically updated properties. **Standard properties**

BTW

Converters for Earlier PowerPoint Versions
The Microsoft Web site has updates and converters if you are using earlier versions of PowerPoint. The Microsoft Office Compatibility Pack for Word, Excel and PowerPoint 2007 File Format will allow you to open, edit, and save Office 2007 documents that you receive without saving them in the earlier version's file format.

are associated with all Microsoft Office documents and include author, title, and subject. **Automatically updated properties** include file system properties, such as the date you create or change a file, and statistics, such as the file size.

To Change Document Properties

The **Document Information Panel** contains areas where you can view and enter document properties. You can view and change information in this panel at any time while you are creating a document. Before saving the presentation again, you want to add your name and class name as document properties. The following steps use the Document Information Panel to change document properties.

1

- Click the Office Button to display the Office Button menu.

- Point to Prepare on the Office Button menu to display the Prepare submenu (Figure 1–64).

Q&A What other types of actions besides changing properties can you take to set up a document for distribution?

The Prepare submenu provides commands related to sharing a document with others, such as allowing or restricting people to view and modify your document, checking to see if your presentation will run in earlier versions of PowerPoint, and searching for hidden personal information.

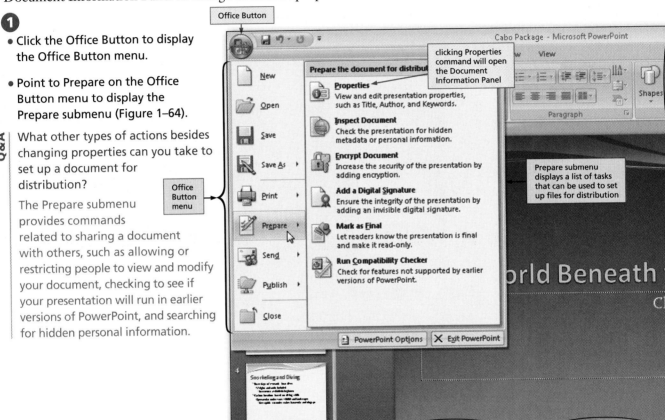

Figure 1–64

2

- Click Properties on the Prepare submenu to display the Document Information Panel (Figure 1–65).

Q&A Why are some of the document properties in my Document Information Panel already filled in?

The person who installed Microsoft Office 2007 on your computer or network may have set or customized the properties.

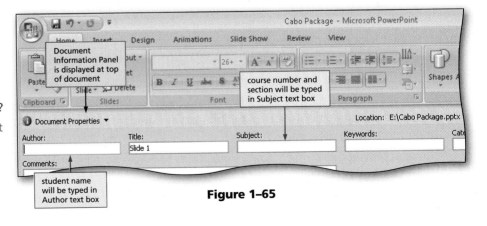

Figure 1–65

3

- Click the Author text box, if necessary, and then type your name as the Author property. If a name already is displayed in the Author text box, delete it before typing your name.

- Click the Subject text box, if necessary delete any existing text, and then type your course number and section as the Subject property (Figure 1–66).

Q&A

What types of document properties does PowerPoint collect automatically?

PowerPoint records such details as how long you worked at creating your project, how many times you revised the document, and what fonts and themes are used.

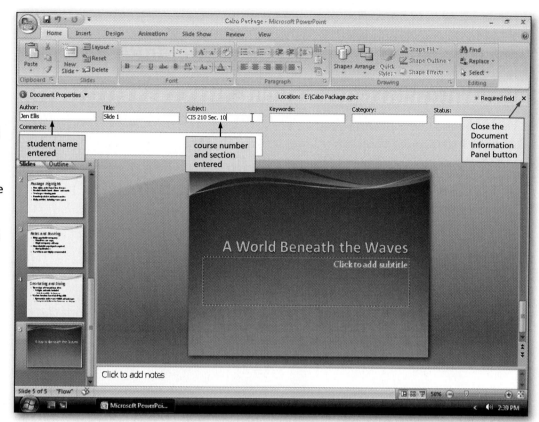

Figure 1–66

4

- Click the Close the Document Information Panel button so that the Document Information Panel no longer is displayed.

To Save an Existing Presentation with the Same File Name

Saving frequently cannot be overemphasized. You have made several modifications to the presentation since you saved it earlier in the chapter. When you first saved the document, you clicked the Save button on the Quick Access Toolbar, the Save As dialog box appeared, and you entered the file name, Cabo Package. If you want to use the same file name to save the changes made to the document, you again click the Save button on the Quick Access Toolbar. The following step saves the presentation again.

1

• Click the Save button on the Quick Access Toolbar to overwrite the previous Cabo Package file on the USB flash drive (Figure 1–67).

Q&A

Why did the Save As dialog box not appear?

PowerPoint overwrites the document using the settings specified the first time you saved the document. To save the file with a different file name or on different media, display the Save As dialog box by clicking the Office Button and then clicking Save As on the Office Button menu. Then, fill in the Save As dialog box as described in Steps 2 through 5 on pages PPT 27 through PPT 29.

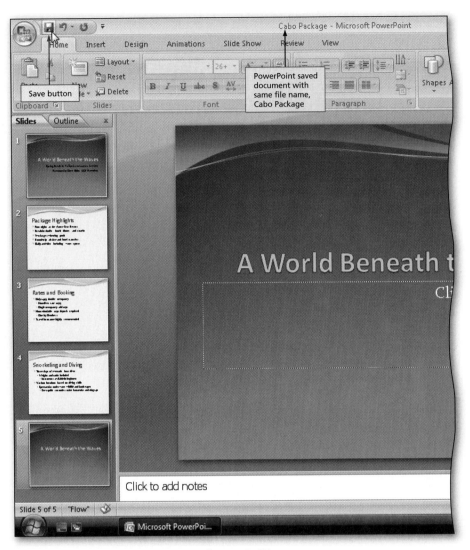

Figure 1–67

Other Ways

1. Press CTRL+S or press SHIFT+F12, press ENTER

Moving to Another Slide in Normal View

When creating or editing a presentation in Normal view, you often want to display a slide other than the current one. You can move to another slide using several methods.

• Drag the scroll box on the vertical scroll bar up or down to move through the slides in the presentation.

• Click the Next Slide or Previous Slide button on the vertical scroll bar. Clicking the Next Slide button advances to the next slide in the presentation. Clicking the Previous Slide button backs up to the slide preceding the current slide.

• On the Slides tab, click a particular slide to display that slide in the Slide pane.

To Use the Scroll Box on the Slide Pane to Move to Another Slide

Before continuing with developing this project, you want to display the title slide by dragging the scroll box on the vertical scroll bar. When you drag the scroll box, the **slide indicator** shows the number and title of the slide you are about to display. Releasing the mouse button shows the slide. The following steps move from Slide 5 to Slide 1 using the scroll box on the Slide pane.

- Position the mouse pointer on the scroll box.

- Press and hold down the mouse button so that Slide: 5 of 5 A World Beneath the Waves appears in the slide indicator (Figure 1–68).

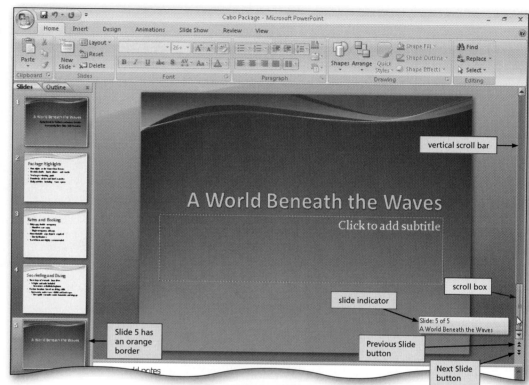

Figure 1–68

- Drag the scroll box up the vertical scroll bar until Slide: 1 of 5 A World Beneath the Waves appears in the slide indicator (Figure 1–69).

Figure 1–69

• Release the mouse button so that Slide 1 appears in the Slide pane and the Slide 1 thumbnail has an orange border in the Slides tab (Figure 1–70).

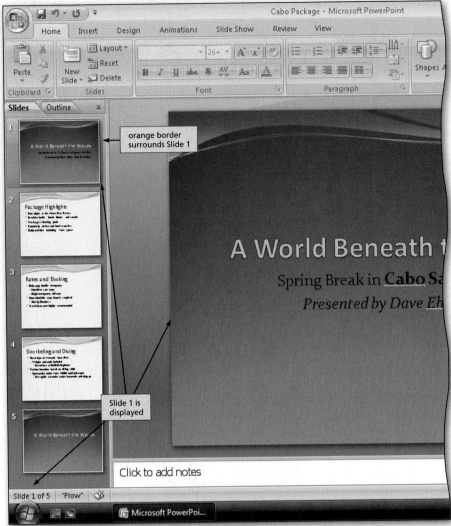

Figure 1–70

Viewing the Presentation in Slide Show View

The Slide Show button, located in the lower-right corner of the PowerPoint window above the status bar, allows you to show a presentation using a computer. The computer acts like a slide projector, displaying each slide on a full screen. The full-screen slide hides the toolbars, menus, and other PowerPoint window elements.

To Start Slide Show View

When making a presentation, you use **Slide Show view**. You can start Slide Show view from Normal view or Slide Sorter view. Slide Show view begins when you click the Slide Show button in the lower-right corner of the PowerPoint window on the status bar. PowerPoint then shows the current slide on the full screen without any of the PowerPoint window objects, such as the menu bar or toolbars. The following steps start Slide Show view.

 1

- Point to the Slide Show button in the lower-right corner of the PowerPoint window on the status bar (Figure 1–71).

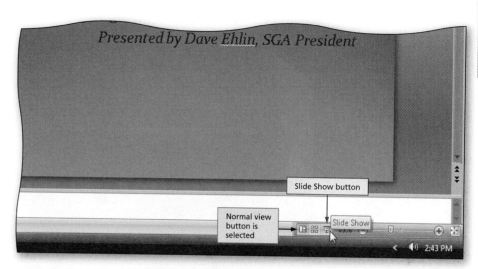

Figure 1–71

2

- Click the Slide Show button to display the title slide (Figure 1–72).

Q&A Where is the PowerPoint window?

When you run a slide show, the PowerPoint window is hidden. It will reappear once you end your slide show.

Figure 1–72

Other Ways

1. Click Slide Show tab, click From Beginning button in Start Slide Show group
2. Press F5

To Move Manually through Slides in a Slide Show

After you begin Slide Show view, you can move forward or backward through the slides. PowerPoint allows you to advance through the slides manually or automatically. During a slide show, each slide in the presentation shows on the screen, one slide at a time. Each time you click the mouse button, the next slide appears. The following steps move manually through the slides.

1

- Click each slide until Slide 5 (A World Beneath the Waves) is displayed (Figure 1–73).

Q&A I see a small toolbar in the lower-left corner of my slide. What is this toolbar?

The Slide Show toolbar appears when you begin running a slide show and then move the mouse pointer. The buttons on this toolbar allow you to navigate to the next slide, the previous slide, to mark up the current slide, or to change the current display.

Figure 1–73

2

- Click Slide 5 so that the black slide appears with a message announcing the end of the slide show (Figure 1–74).

Q&A How can I end the presentation at this point?

Click the black slide to return to Normal view in the PowerPoint window or press the ESC key.

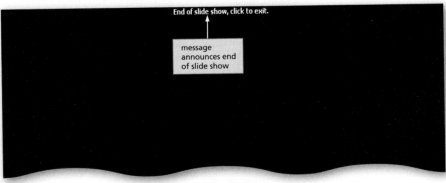

Figure 1–74

Other Ways

1. Press PAGE DOWN to advance one slide at a time, or press PAGE UP to go back one slide at a time

2. Press RIGHT ARROW or DOWN ARROW to advance one slide at a time, or press LEFT ARROW or UP ARROW to go back one slide at a time

3. If Slide Show toolbar is displayed, click Next Slide or Previous Slide button on toolbar

To Display the Pop-Up Menu and Go to a Specific Slide

Slide Show view has a shortcut menu, called a **pop-up menu**, that appears when you right-click a slide in Slide Show view. This menu contains commands to assist you during a slide show.

When the pop-up menu appears, clicking the Next command moves to the next slide. Clicking the Previous command moves to the previous slide. Pointing to the Go to Slide command and then clicking the desired slide allows you to move to any slide in the presentation. The Go to Slide submenu contains a list of the slides in the presentation. You can go to the requested slide by clicking the name of that slide. Additional pop-up menu commands allow you to change the mouse pointer to a ballpoint or felt tip pen or highlighter that draws in various colors, make the screen black or white, create speaker notes, and end the slide show. The following steps go to the title slide (Slide 1) in the Cabo Package presentation.

● With the black slide displaying in Slide Show view, right-click the slide to display the pop-up menu.

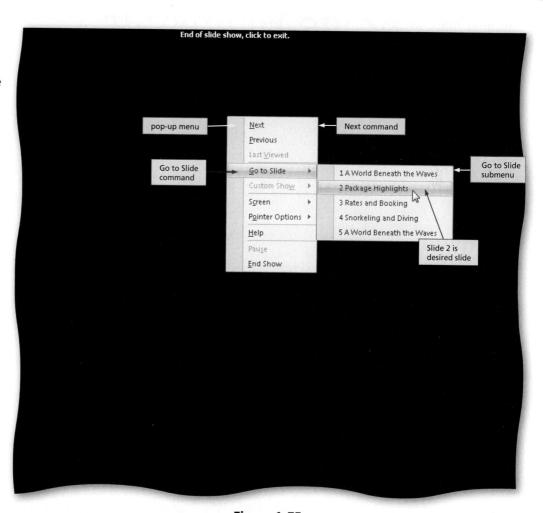

● Point to Go to Slide on the pop-up menu, and then point to 2 Package Highlights in the Go to Slide submenu (Figure 1–75).

Q&A Why does my pop-up menu appear in a different location on my screen?

The pop-up menu appears near the location of the mouse pointer at the time you right-click.

● Click 2 Package Highlights to display Slide 2.

Figure 1–75

To Use the Pop-Up Menu to End a Slide Show

The End Show command on the pop-up menu ends Slide Show view and returns to the same view as when you clicked the Slide Show button. The following steps end Slide Show view and return to Normal view.

- Right-click Slide 2 and then point to End Show on the pop-up menu (Figure 1–76).

- Click End Show to return to Slide 2 in the Slide pane in Normal view.

- If the Microsoft Office PowerPoint dialog box appears, click the Yes button.

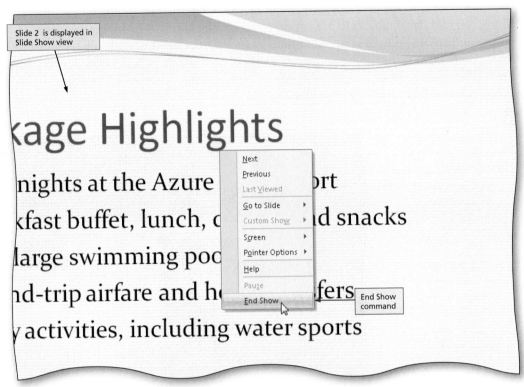

Figure 1–76

Quitting PowerPoint

When you quit PowerPoint, if you have made changes to a presentation since the last time the file was saved, PowerPoint displays a dialog box asking if you want to save the changes you made to the file before it closes that window. The dialog box contains three buttons with these resulting actions:

- Yes button — Saves the changes and then quits PowerPoint
- No button — Quits PowerPoint without saving changes
- Cancel button — Closes the dialog box and redisplays the presentation without saving the changes

If no changes have been made to an open presentation since the last time the file was saved, PowerPoint will close the window without displaying a dialog box.

To Quit PowerPoint with One Document Open

You saved the presentation prior to running the slide show and did not make any changes to the project. The presentation now is complete, and you are ready to quit PowerPoint. When you have one document open, the following steps quit PowerPoint.

1
Point to the Close button on the right side of the PowerPoint title bar (Figure 1–77).

2
- Click the Close button to quit PowerPoint.

Q&A
What if I have more than one PowerPoint document open?

You would click the Close button for each open document. When you click the last open document's Close button, PowerPoint also quits. As an alternative, you could click the Office Button and then click the Exit PowerPoint button on the Office Button menu, which closes all open PowerPoint documents and then quits PowerPoint.

Figure 1–77

Other Ways

1. With one document open, double-click Office Button
2. Click Office Button, click Exit PowerPoint on Office Button menu
3. With one document open, right-click Microsoft
   PowerPoint button on Windows Vista taskbar, click Close on shortcut menu
4. With one document open, press ALT+F4

Starting PowerPoint and Opening a Presentation

Once you have created and saved a presentation, you may need to retrieve it from your storage medium. For example, you might want to revise the document or print it. Opening a presentation requires that PowerPoint is running on your computer.

To Start PowerPoint

The following steps, which assume Windows Vista is running, start PowerPoint.

Note: If you are using Windows XP, see Appendix F for alternate steps.

1 Click the Start button on the Windows Vista taskbar to display the Start menu.

2 Click All Programs at the bottom of the left pane on the Start menu to display the All Programs list and then click Microsoft Office in the All Programs list to display the Microsoft Office list.

3 Click Microsoft Office PowerPoint 2007 on the Microsoft Office list to start PowerPoint and display a new blank presentation in the PowerPoint window.

4 If the PowerPoint window is not maximized, click the Maximize button on its title bar to maximize the window.

To Open a Presentation from PowerPoint

Earlier in this chapter you saved your project on a USB flash drive using the file name, Cabo Package. The following steps open the Cabo Package file from the USB flash drive.

1

• With your USB flash drive connected to one of the computer's USB ports, click the Office Button to display the Office Button menu (Figure 1–78).

Q&A

What files are shown in the Recent Documents list?

PowerPoint displays the most recently opened document file names in this list. If the name of the file you want to open appears in the Recent Documents list, you could click it to open the file.

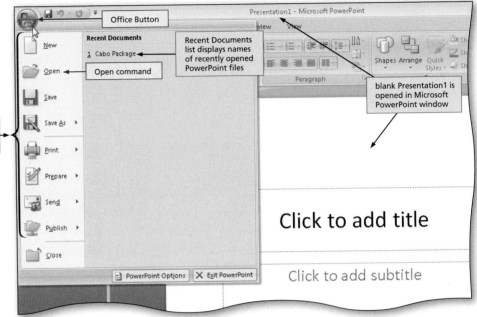

Figure 1–78

2

• Click Open on the Office Button menu to display the Open dialog box.

• If the Folders list is displayed below the Folders button, click the Folders button to remove the Folders list.

• If necessary, click Computer in the Favorite Links section and then scroll until UDISK 2.0 (E:) appears in the list of available drives.

• Double-click UDISK 2.0 (E:) to select the USB flash drive, Drive E in this case, as the new open location.

• Click Cabo Package to select the file name (Figure 1–79).

Q&A

How do I open the file if I am not using a USB flash drive?

Use the same process, but be certain to select your device in the Computer list.

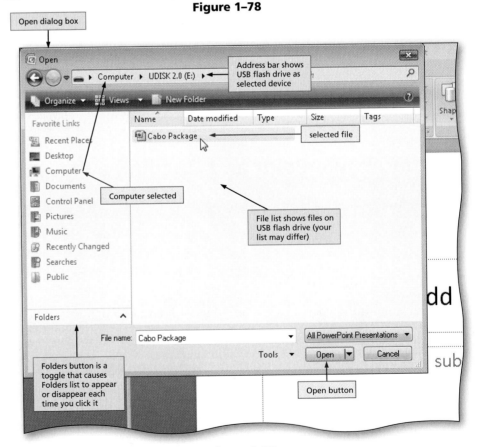

Figure 1–79

3

- Click the Open button to open the selected file and display Slide 1 in the PowerPoint window (Figure 1–80).

Q&A

Why are the PowerPoint icon and name on the Windows Vista taskbar?

When you open a PowerPoint file, a PowerPoint program button is displayed on the taskbar. The button contains an ellipsis because some of its contents do not fit in the allotted button space. If you point to a program button, its entire contents appear in a ScreenTip, which in this case would be the program name followed by the file name.

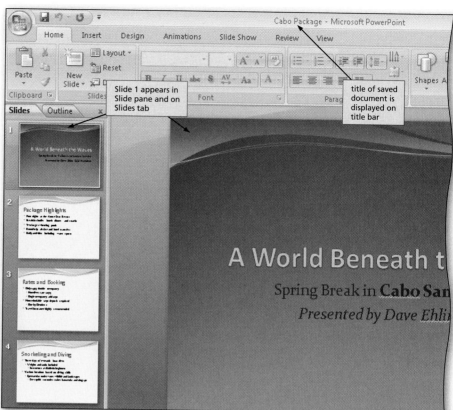

Figure 1–80

Other Ways

1. Click Office Button, double-click file name in Recent Documents list
2. Press CTRL+O, select file name, press ENTER

Checking a Presentation for Spelling Errors

After you create a presentation, you should check it visually for spelling errors and style consistency. In addition, you use PowerPoint's Spelling tool to identify possible misspellings. Do not rely on the spelling checker to catch all your mistakes. While PowerPoint's spelling checker is a valuable tool, it is not infallible. You should proofread your presentation carefully by pointing to each word and saying it aloud as you point to it. Be mindful of commonly misused words such as its and it's, through and though, and to and too.

PowerPoint checks the entire presentation for spelling mistakes using a standard dictionary contained in the Microsoft Office group. This dictionary is shared with the other Microsoft Office applications such as Word and Excel. A **custom dictionary** is available if you want to add special words such as proper names, cities, and acronyms. When checking a presentation for spelling errors, PowerPoint opens the standard dictionary and the custom dictionary file, if one exists. When a word appears in the Spelling dialog box, you can perform one of several actions.

Table 1–1 Spelling Dialog Box Buttons and Actions

Button Name	When To Use	Action
Ignore	Word is spelled correctly but not found in dictionaries	Continues checking rest of the presentation but will flag that word again if it appears later in document
Ignore All	Word is spelled correctly but not found in dictionaries	Ignores all occurrences of the word and continues checking rest of presentation
Change	Word is misspelled	Click proper spelling of the word in Suggestions list. PowerPoint corrects word, continues checking rest of presentation, but will flag that word again if it appears later in document.
Change All	Word is misspelled	Click proper spelling of word in Suggestions list. PowerPoint changes all occurrences of misspelled word and continues checking rest of presentation.
Add	Add word to custom dictionary	PowerPoint opens custom dictionary, adds word, and continues checking rest of presentation.
Suggest	Correct spelling is uncertain	Lists alternative spellings. Click the correct word from the Suggestions box or type the proper spelling. Corrects the word and continues checking the rest of the presentation.
AutoCorrect	Add spelling error to AutoCorrect list	PowerPoint adds spelling error and its correction to AutoCorrect list. Any future misspelling of word is corrected automatically as you type.
Close	Stop spelling checker	PowerPoint closes spelling checker and returns to PowerPoint window.

To Check Spelling

The standard dictionary contains commonly used English words. It does not, however, contain many proper names, abbreviations, technical terms, poetic contractions, or antiquated terms. PowerPoint treats words not found in the dictionaries as misspellings. The following steps check the spelling on all slides in the Cabo Package presentation.

- Click Review on the Ribbon to display the Review tab (Figure 1–81).

Figure 1–81

2

- Click the Spelling button in the Proofing group to start the spelling checker and display the Spelling dialog box (Figure 1–82).

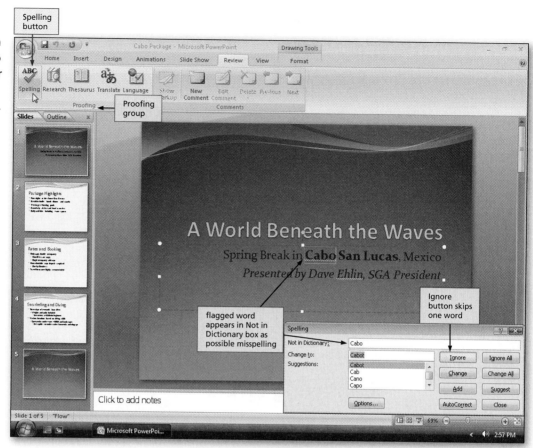

Figure 1–82

3

- Click the Ignore button to skip the word, Cabo (Figure 1–83).

Cabo is not flagged as a possible misspelled word. Why not?

Your custom dictionary contains the word, so it is recognized as a correct word.

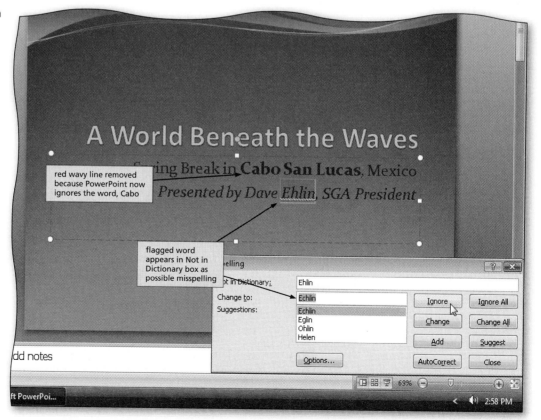

Figure 1–83

4
- Click the Ignore button to skip the word, Ehlin.

- When the Microsoft Office PowerPoint dialog box appears, click the OK button to close the spelling checker and return to the current slide, Slide 1, or to the slide where a possible misspelled word appeared.

- Click the slide to remove the box from the word, Ehlin (Figure 1–84).

Figure 1–84

Other Ways

1. Press F7

Correcting Errors

After creating a presentation and running the spelling checker, you may find that you must make changes. Changes may be required because a slide contains an error, the scope of the presentation shifts, or the style is inconsistent. This section explains the types of errors that commonly occur when creating a presentation.

Types of Corrections Made to Presentations

You generally make three types of corrections to text in a presentation: additions, deletions, and replacements.

- Additions are necessary when you omit text from a slide and need to add it later. You may need to insert text in the form of a sentence, word, or single character. For example, you may want to add the presenter's middle name on the title slide.

- Deletions are required when text on a slide is incorrect or no longer is relevant to the presentation. For example, a slide may look cluttered. Therefore, you may want to remove one of the bulleted paragraphs to add more space.

- Replacements are needed when you want to revise the text in a presentation. For example, you may want to substitute the word, their, for the word, there.

Editing text in PowerPoint basically is the same as editing text in a word processing program. The following sections illustrate the most common changes made to text in a presentation.

BTW

Certification
The Microsoft Certified Application Specialist (MCAS) program provides an opportunity for you to obtain a valuable industry credential – proof that you have the PowerPoint 2007 skills required by employers. For more information see Appendix G or visit the PowerPoint 2007 Certification Web page (scsite.com/ppt2007/cert).

Deleting Text

You can delete text using one of three methods. One is to use the BACKSPACE key to remove text just typed. The second is to position the insertion point to the left of the text you wish to delete and then press the DELETE key. The third method is to drag through the text you wish to delete and then press the DELETE key. Use the third method when deleting large sections of text.

Replacing Text in an Existing Slide

When you need to correct a word or phrase, you can replace the text by selecting the text to be replaced and then typing the new text. As soon as you press any key on the keyboard, the selected text is deleted and the new text is displayed.

PowerPoint inserts text to the left of the insertion point. The text to the right of the insertion point moves to the right (and shifts downward if necessary) to accommodate the added text.

Displaying a Presentation in Grayscale

Printing handouts of a presentation allows you to use them to make overhead transparencies. The Color/Grayscale button on the Color/Grayscale group on the View tab shows the presentation in black and white before you print. Pure Black and White alters the slides' appearance so that black lines display on a white background. Shadows and other graphical effects are hidden. Grayscale shows varying degrees of gray.

To Display a Presentation in Grayscale

The Color/Grayscale button on the Color/Grayscale group on the View tab changes from color bars to shades of black, called grayscale, and white. After you view the text objects in the presentation in grayscale, you can make any changes that will enhance printouts produced from a black and white printer or photocopier. The following steps display the presentation in grayscale.

- Click View on the Ribbon to display the View tab (Figure 1–85).

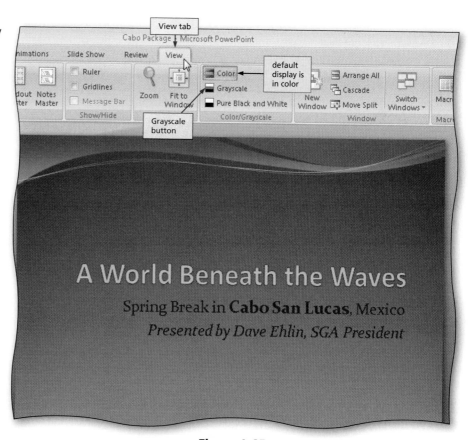

Figure 1–85

2

- Click Grayscale in the Color/Grayscale group to display Slide 1 in grayscale in the Slide pane (Figure 1–86).

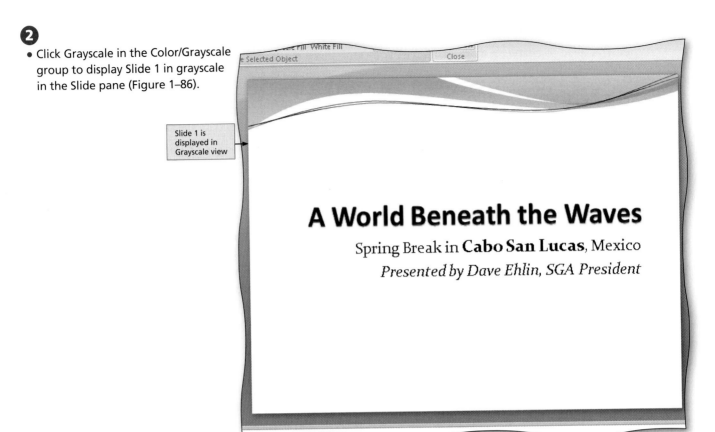

Figure 1–86

3

- Click the Next Slide button four times to view all slides in the presentation in grayscale (Figure 1–87).

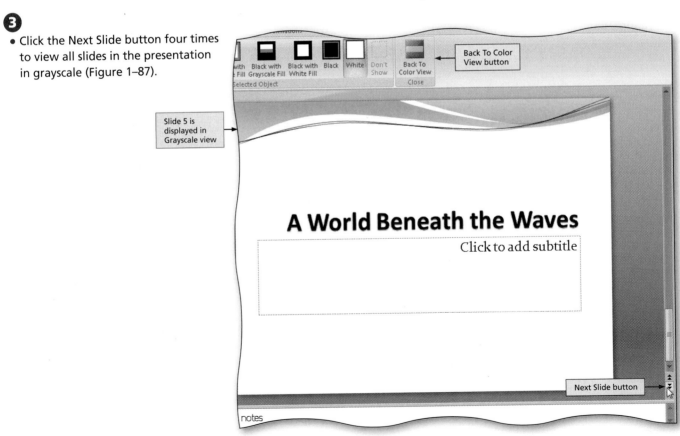

Figure 1–87

4

- Click the Back To Color View button in the Close group to return to the previous tab and display Slide 5 with the default Flow color scheme (Figure 1–88).

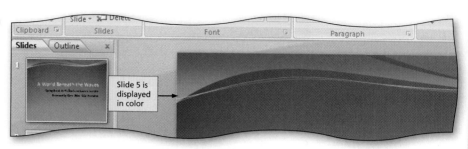

Figure 1–88

Printing a Presentation

After you create a presentation, you often want to print it. A printed version of the presentation is called a **hard copy** or **printout**.

Printed copies of your presentation can be useful for the following reasons:

- Many people prefer proofreading a hard copy of the presentation rather than viewing the slides on the screen to check for errors and readability.

- Someone without computer access or who could not attend your live presentation can view the slides' content.

- Copies can be distributed as handouts to people viewing your presentation.

- Hard copies can serve as reference material if your storage medium is lost or becomes corrupted and you need to re-create the presentation.

It is a good practice to save a presentation before printing it, in the event you experience difficulties with the printer.

To Print a Presentation

With the completed presentation saved, you may want to print it. The following steps print all five completed presentation slides in the saved Cabo Package project.

1

- Click the Office Button to display the Office Button menu.

- Point to Print on the Office Button menu to display the Print submenu (Figure 1–89).

 Can I print my presentation in black and white to conserve ink or toner?

Yes. Click the Office Button, point to the arrow next to Print on the Office Button menu, and then click Print Preview on the Print submenu. Click the Options button on the Print Preview tab, point to Color/Grayscale on the Options button menu, and then click Pure Black and White on the Color/Grayscale submenu. Click the Print button on the Print submenu.

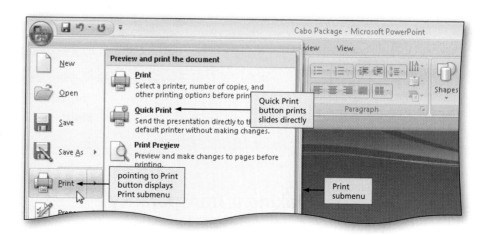

Figure 1–89

2

- Click Quick Print on the Print submenu to print the slides.

- When the printer stops, retrieve the hard copy of the five Cabo Package slides (Figures 1–90a through 1–90e).

Q&A

How can I print multiple copies of my document other than clicking the Print button twice?

Click the Office Button, point to Print on the Office Button menu, click Print on the Print submenu, increase the number in the Number of copies box, and then click the OK button.

Q&A

Do I have to wait until my presentation is complete to print it?

No, you can follow these steps to print your slides at any time while you are creating your presentation.

(a) Slide 1

(b) Slide 2

(c) Slide 3

(d) Slide 4

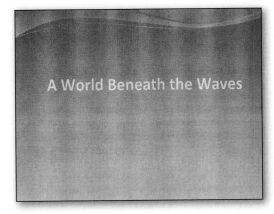

(e) Slide 5

Figure 1–90

Other Ways

1. Press CTRL+P

BTW

Quick Reference
For a table that lists how to complete the tasks covered in this book using the mouse, Ribbon, shortcut menu, and keyboard, see the Quick Reference Summary at the back of this book, or visit the PowerPoint 2007 Quick Reference Web page (scsite.com/ppt2007/qr).

Making a Transparency

With the handouts printed, you now can make overhead transparencies using one of several devices. One device is a printer attached to your computer, such as an inkjet printer or a laser printer. Transparencies produced on a printer may be in black and white or color, depending on the printer. Another device is a photocopier. Because each of these devices requires a special transparency film, check the user's manual for the film requirement of your specific device, or ask your instructor.

PowerPoint Help

At any time while using PowerPoint, you can find answers to questions and display information about various topics through **PowerPoint Help**. Used properly, this form of assistance can increase your productivity and reduce your frustrations by minimizing the time you spend learning how to use PowerPoint.

This section introduces you to PowerPoint Help. Additional information about using PowerPoint Help is available in Appendix C.

BTW

PowerPoint Help
The best way to become familiar with PowerPoint Help is to use it. Appendix C includes detailed information about PowerPoint Help and exercises that will help you gain confidence in using it.

To Search for PowerPoint Help

Using PowerPoint Help, you can search for information based on phrases such as save a presentation or format a chart, or key terms such as copy, save, or format. PowerPoint Help responds with a list of search results displayed as links to a variety of resources. The following steps, which use PowerPoint Help to search for information about using document themes, assume you are connected to the Internet.

1

• Click the Microsoft Office PowerPoint Help button near the upper-right corner of the PowerPoint window to open the PowerPoint Help window.

• Type document theme in the Type words to search for text box at the top of the PowerPoint Help window (Figure 1–91).

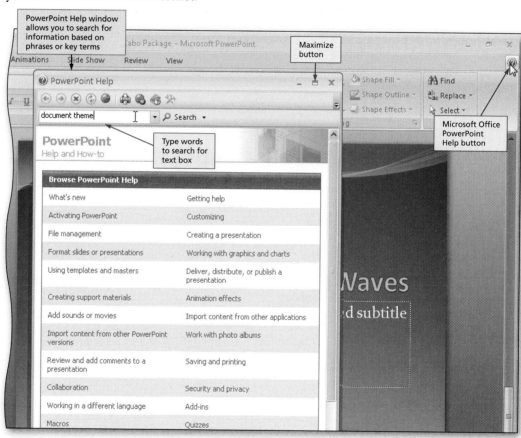

Figure 1–91

②

- Press the ENTER key to display the search results.

- Click the Maximize button on the PowerPoint Help window title bar to maximize the Help window (Figure 1–92).

Q&A

Where is the PowerPoint window with Slide 1?

PowerPoint is open in the background, but the PowerPoint Help window is overlaid on top of the Microsoft PowerPoint window. When the PowerPoint Help window is closed, the slide will reappear.

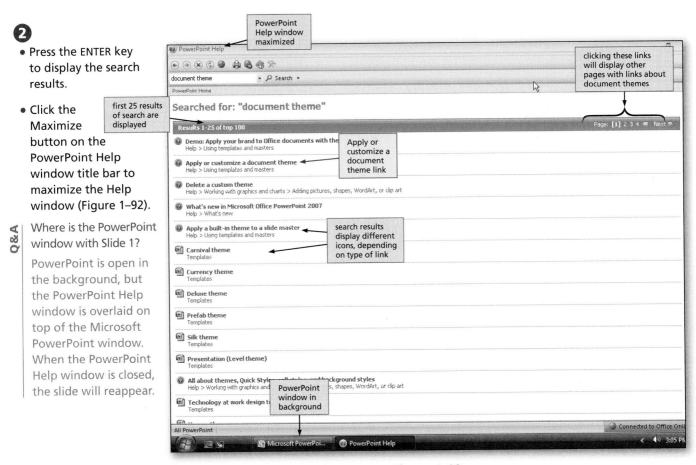

Figure 1–92

③

- Click the 'Apply or customize a document theme' link to display information regarding applying or customizing themes (Figure 1–93).

Q&A

What is the purpose of the buttons at the top of the PowerPoint Help window?

Use the buttons in the upper-left corner of the PowerPoint Help window to navigate through the Help system, change the display, show the PowerPoint Help table of contents, and print the contents of the window.

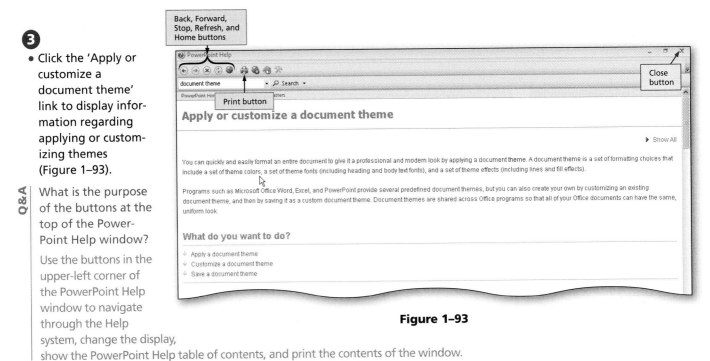

Figure 1–93

④

- Click the Close button on the PowerPoint Help window title bar to close the PowerPoint Help window and display Slide 5.

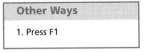

Other Ways
1. Press F1

To Quit PowerPoint

The following steps quit PowerPoint.

1 Click the Close button on the right side of the title bar to quit PowerPoint; or, if you have multiple PowerPoint documents open, click the Office Button and then click the Exit PowerPoint button on the Office Button menu to close all open documents and quit PowerPoint.

2 If necessary, click the No button in the Microsoft Office PowerPoint dialog box so that any changes you have made are not saved.

Chapter Summary

In this chapter you have learned how to apply a document theme, create a title slide and text slides with bulleted lists, format text, view the presentation in Slide Show view, and print slides as handouts. The items listed below include all the new PowerPoint skills you have learned in this chapter.

1. Start PowerPoint (PPT 5)
2. Choose a Document Theme (PPT 16)
3. Enter the Presentation Title (PPT 18)
4. Enter the Presentation Subtitle Paragraph (PPT 20)
5. Select a Paragraph (PPT 21)
6. Italicize Text (PPT 22)
7. Select Multiple Paragraphs (PPT 22)
8. Change the Text Color (PPT 23)
9. Select a Group of Words (PPT 24)
10. Increase Font Size (PPT 24)
11. Bold Text (PPT 25)
12. Decrease the Title Slide Title Text Font Size (PPT 25)
13. Save a Presentation (PPT 27)
14. Add a New Text Slide with a Bulleted List (PPT 29)
15. Enter a Slide Title (PPT 31)
16. Select a Text Placeholder (PPT 31)
17. Type a Single-Level Bulleted List (PPT 32)
18. Add a New Slide and Enter a Slide Title (PPT 33)
19. Type a Multi-Level Bulleted List (PPT 34)
20. Create a Third-Level Paragraph (PPT 37)
21. Duplicate a Slide (PPT 40)
22. Arrange a Slide (PPT 41)
23. Delete All Text in a Placeholder (PPT 42)
24. Change Document Properties (PPT 44)
25. Save an Existing Presentation with the Same File Name (PPT 45)
26. Use the Scroll Box on the Slide Pane to Move to Another Slide (PPT 47)
27. Start Slide Show View (PPT 49)
28. Move Manually through Slides in a Slide Show (PPT 50)
29. Display the Pop-Up Menu and Go to a Specific Slide (PPT 51)
30. Use the Pop-Up Menu to End a Slide Show (PPT 52)
31. Quit PowerPoint with One Document Open (PPT 53)
32. Open a Presentation from PowerPoint (PPT 54)
33. Check Spelling (PPT 55)
34. Display a Presentation in Grayscale (PPT 59)
35. Print a Presentation (PPT 61)
36. Search for PowerPoint Help (PPT 63)

 If you have a SAM user profile, you may have access to hands-on instruction, practice, and assessment. Log in to your SAM account (http://sam2007.course.com) to launch any assigned training activities or exams that relate to the skills covered in this chapter.

Learn It Online

Test your knowledge of chapter content and key terms.

Instructions: To complete the Learn It Online exercises, start your browser, click the Address bar, and then enter the Web address scsite.com/ppt2007/learn. When the Office 2007 Learn It Online page is displayed, click the link for the exercise you want to complete and then read the instructions.

Chapter Reinforcement TF, MC, and SA
A series of true/false, multiple choice, and short answer questions that test your knowledge of the chapter content.

Flash Cards
An interactive learning environment where you identify chapter key terms associated with displayed definitions.

Practice Test
A series of multiple choice questions that test your knowledge of chapter content and key terms.

Who Wants To Be a Computer Genius?
An interactive game that challenges your knowledge of chapter content in the style of a television quiz show.

Wheel of Terms
An interactive game that challenges your knowledge of chapter key terms in the style of the television show *Wheel of Fortune*.

Crossword Puzzle Challenge
A crossword puzzle that challenges your knowledge of key terms presented in the chapter.

Apply Your Knowledge

Reinforce the skills and apply the concepts you learned in this chapter.

Modifying Character Formats and Paragraph Levels
Instructions: Start PowerPoint. Open the presentation, Apply 1-1 Keep Your Cool, from the Data Files for Students. See the inside back cover of this book for instructions on downloading the Data Files for Students, or contact your instructor for more information about accessing the required files.

The two slides in the presentation stress the importance of drinking plenty of water on hot days. The document you open is an unformatted presentation. You are to modify the document theme and text, indent the paragraphs, and format the text so the slides look like Figure 1–94.

Perform the following tasks:
1. Change the document theme to Trek. Note that the Trek theme uses all capital letters for the title text. On the title slide, use your name in place of Student Name and bold and italicize your name. Increase the title text font size to 44 point.

(a) Slide 1 (Title Slide)
Figure 1–94

(b) Slide 2 (Multi-Level Bulleted List)

Figure 1–94 (continued)

2. On Slide 2, increase the indent of the second, fifth, and sixth paragraphs (Drink throughout the day; Do not substitute caffeinated beverages; Cool water is best for keeping hydrated) to second-level paragraphs. Then change paragraphs three and four (Start and end your day with water; Do not wait until you are thirsty) to third-level paragraphs.

3. Check the spelling, and then display the revised presentation in grayscale.

4. Change the document properties, as specified by your instructor. Save the presentation using the file name, Apply 1-1 Drink Water. Submit the revised document in the format specified by your instructor.

Extend Your Knowledge

Extend the skills you learned in this chapter and experiment with new skills. You may need to use Help to complete the assignment.

Changing Slide Theme and Text

Instructions: Start PowerPoint. Open the presentation, Extend 1-1 Nutrition, from the Data Files for Students. See the inside back cover of this book for instructions on downloading the Data Files for Students, or contact your instructor for more information about accessing the required files.

You will choose a theme (Figure 1–95), format slides, and create a closing slide.

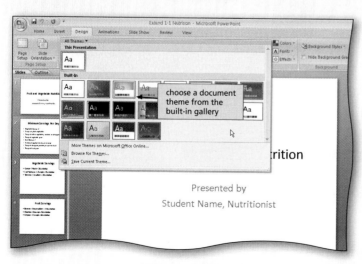

Figure 1–95

Perform the following tasks:

1. Apply an appropriate document theme.

2. On Slide 1, use your name in place of Student Name. Format the text using techniques you learned in this chapter, such as changing the font size and color and also bolding and italicizing words.

Continued >

Extend Your Knowledge *continued*

3. On Slide 2, adjust the paragraph levels so that the lines of text are arranged under vegetable and fruit categories. Edit the text so that the slide meets the 7 × 7 rule, which states that each line should have a maximum of seven words, and each slide should have a maximum of seven lines.

4. On Slides 3 and 4, create paragraphs and adjust the paragraph levels.

5. Create an appropriate closing slide using the title slide as a guide.

6. Change the document properties, as specified by your instructor. Save the presentation using the file name, Extend 1-1 Fruit and Vegetables.

7. Add the Print button to the Quick Access Toolbar and then click this button to print the slides.

8. Delete the Print button from the Quick Access Toolbar.

9. Submit the revised document in the format specified by your instructor.

Make It Right

Analyze a presentation and correct all errors and/or improve the design.

Correcting Formatting and List Levels

Instructions: Start PowerPoint. Open the presentation, Make It Right 1-1 Indulge, from the Data Files for Students. See the inside back cover of this book for instructions on downloading the Data Files for Students, or contact your instructor for more information about accessing the required files.

Correct the formatting problems and errors in the presentation while keeping in mind the guidelines presented in this chapter.

Perform the following tasks:

1. Change the document theme from Metro, shown in Figure 1–96, to Opulent.

2. On Slide 1, replace the words, Fall Semester, with your name. Format your name so that it displays prominently on the slide.

3. Move Slide 2 to the end of the presentation so that it becomes the new Slide 4.

4. Use the spell checker to correct the misspellings. Analyze the slides for other word usage errors that the spell checker did not find.

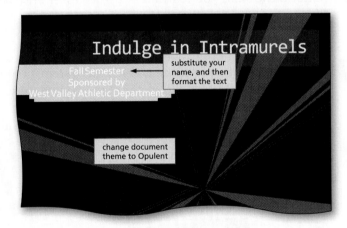

Figure 1–96

5. On Slide 2, increase the Slide 2 title (Athletic Events) font size to 40. Make the indent levels for paragraphs 2, 4, and 6 the same level.

6. On Slide 3, change the title text (Awards Ceremony) font size to 40. Make the indent levels for paragraphs 3 and 5 the same level.

7. Change the document properties, as specified by your instructor. Save the presentation using the file name, Make It Right 1-1 Intramurals.

8. Submit the revised document in the format specified by your instructor.

In the Lab

Design and/or create a presentation using the guidelines, concepts, and skills presented in this chapter. Labs 1, 2, and 3 are listed in order of increasing difficulty.

Lab 1: Creating a Presentation with Bulleted Lists

Problem: Many of the important steps you will take in your life are influenced by your credit report. Buying a car, renting an apartment, and even applying for a job often require a credit check. Your credit score can make or break your ability to obtain the goods you truly want and need. One of your assignments in your economics class is to give a speech about establishing credit. You develop the outline shown in Figure 1–97 and then prepare the PowerPoint presentation shown in Figures 1–98a through 1–98d.

Instructions: Perform the following tasks.

1. Create a new presentation using the Aspect document theme.

2. Using the typed notes illustrated in Figure 1–97, create the title slide shown in Figure 1–98a using your name in place of Marc Kantlon. Italicize your name. Decrease the font size of the title paragraph, Give Yourself Some Credit, to 40. Increase the font size of the first paragraph of the subtitle text, Understanding Your Credit Report, to 28.

3. Using the typed notes in Figure 1–97, create the three text slides with bulleted lists shown in Figures 1–98b through 1–98d.

Give Yourself Some Credit
 Understanding Your Credit Report
 Marc Kantlon
 Economics 101

Credit Report Fundamentals
 Generated by three companies
  Experian, Equifax, TransUnion
 Factors
  How much you owe to each company
  Payment history for each company
   Includes utilities, medical expenses, rent

How FICO Is Calculated
 Range - 760 (excellent) to 620 (poor)
  35% - Payment history
  30% - Amounts owed
  15% - Credit history length
  10% - New credit
  10% - Credit types

Improve Your FICO Score
 Pay bills on time
 Avoid opening many new accounts
  Open only if you intend to use
 Keep balances low
  Less than 25% of credit limit
 Review credit report yearly

Figure 1–97

Continued >

In the Lab *continued*

4. On Slide 3, change the font color of the number, 760, to green and the number, 620, to red.

5. Check the spelling and correct any errors.

6. Drag the scroll box to display Slide 1. Click the Slide Show button to start Slide Show view. Then click to display each slide.

7. Change the document properties, as specified by your instructor. Save the presentation using the file name, Lab 1-1 Credit.

8. Submit the document in the format specified by your instructor.

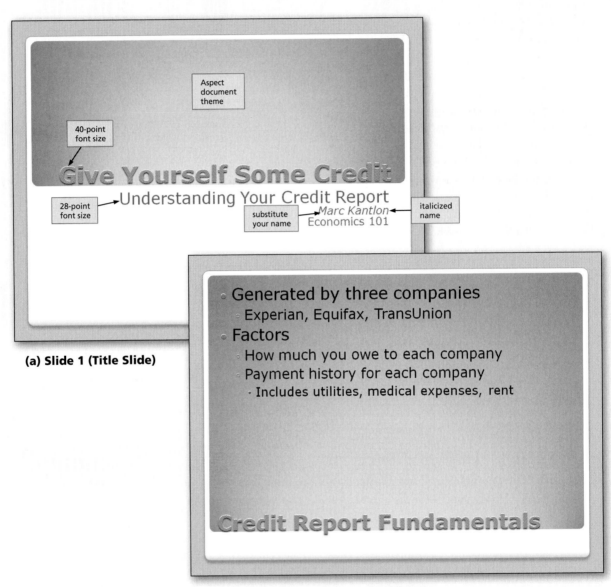

(a) Slide 1 (Title Slide)

(b) Slide 2

Figure 1–98

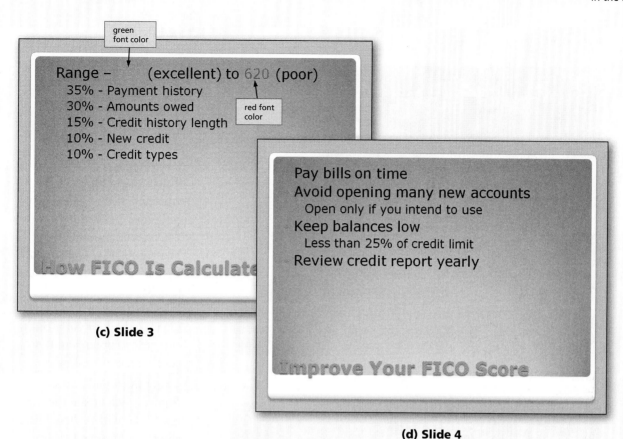

(c) Slide 3

(d) Slide 4

Figure 1–98 (continued)

In the Lab

Lab 2: Creating a Presentation with Bulleted Lists and a Closing Slide

Problem: Hybrid vehicles have received much attention in recent years. Everyone from environmentalists to movie stars are driving them, and potential buyers wait for months until the vehicles arrive in dealers' showrooms. You work part-time at Midwest State Bank, and the loan department manager, Jen Westbrook, has asked you to develop a PowerPoint presentation to accompany her upcoming speech. She hands you the outline shown in Figure 1–99 and asks you to create the presentation shown in Figures 1–100a through 1–100e.

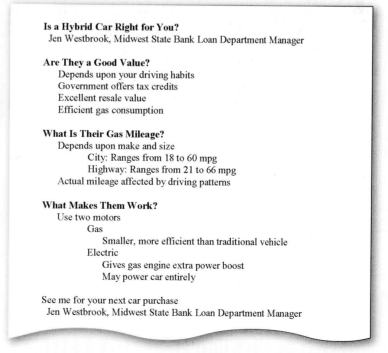

Figure 1–99

Continued >

In the Lab *continued*

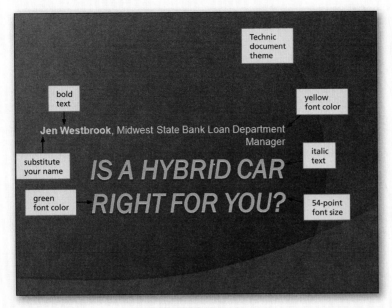

(a) Slide 1 (Title Slide)

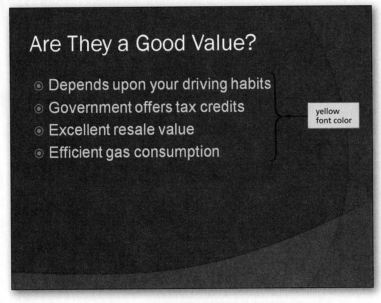

(b) Slide 2

Figure 1–100

Instructions: Perform the following tasks.

1. Create a new presentation using the Technic document theme.

2. Using the typed notes illustrated in Figure 1–99, create the title slide shown in Figure 1–100a using your name in place of Jan Westbrook. Bold your name. Italicize the title, Is a Hybrid Car Right for You?, and increase the font size to 54. Change the font color of the title text to green and the subtitle text to yellow.

3. Using the typed notes in Figure 1–99, create the three text slides with bulleted lists shown in Figures 1–100b through 1–100d. Change the color of all the bulleted list paragraph text to yellow.

4. Duplicate the title slide and then move the new closing slide to the end of the presentation. Change the Slide 5 title text, increase the font size to 66, and remove the italics.

5. Check the spelling and correct any errors.

6. Drag the scroll box to display Slide 1. Click the Slide Show button to start Slide Show view. Then click to display each slide.

7. Change the document properties, as specified by your instructor. Save the presentation using the file name, Lab 1-2 Hybrids.

8. Submit the revised document in the format specified by your instructor.

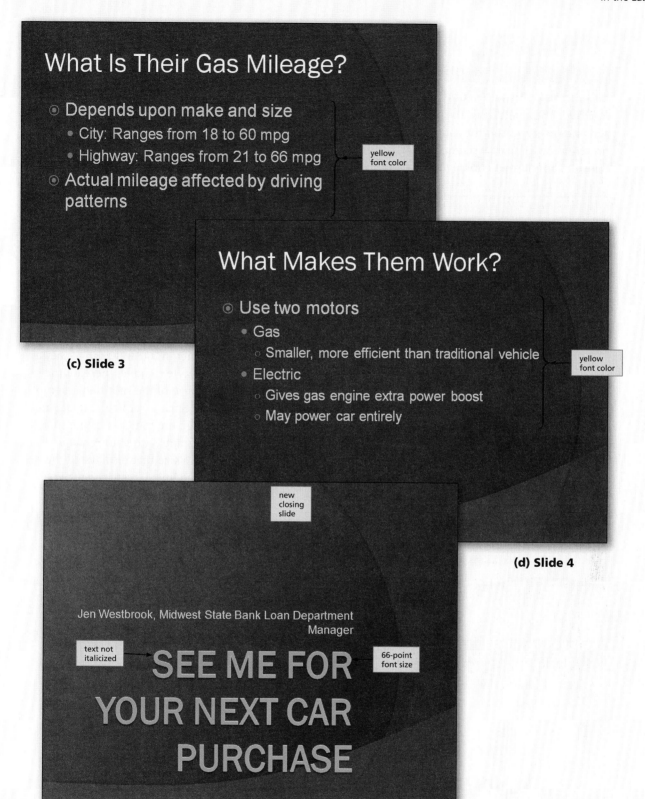

(c) Slide 3

(d) Slide 4

(e) Slide 5 (Closing Slide)

Figure 1–100 (continued)

In the Lab

Lab 3: Creating and Updating Presentations

Problem: Bobbie Willis, the public relations director for the South Haven Park District, plans activities every season for community residents and promotes the offerings using a PowerPoint presentation. The new seminars for senior citizens this spring are quilting and t'ai chi. Adults can register for gourmet cooking lessons and kickball. Teens can enroll in sailing and fencing lessons.

South Haven Park District
New Spring Seminars
Bobbie Willis, Director

Seniors' Seminars
    Quilting
        Quilts made from donated fabrics
        Sewing machines provided
    T'ai Chi
        Gentle warm-ups
        12 slow, continuous movements
        Easy cool-down exercises

Adults' Seminars
    Almost Gourmet
        Learn techniques from a professional chef
            Everyone prepares and enjoys the dinners
                Come hungry!
    Kickball
        Learn techniques and rules

Teens' Seminars
    Sailing
        Sail a 30-foot sailboat at your first class
    Fencing
        Three levels
            Level 1 – Beginning Foil
           Level 2 – Foil, Epee, and Saber
           Level 3 – Open Strip Fencing

Figure 1–101

Instructions Part 1: Using the outline in Figure 1–101, create the presentation shown in Figure 1–102. Use the Oriel document theme. On the title slide shown in Figure 1–102a, type your name in place of Bobbie Willis, increase the font size of the title paragraph, South Haven Park District, to 60 and change the text font style to italic. Increase the font size of the subtitle paragraph, New Spring Seminars, to 32, and change the font size of the subtitle paragraph with your name to 37 or to a size that displays all the text on one line. Create the three text slides with multi-level bulleted lists shown in Figures 1–102b through 1–102d.

Correct any spelling mistakes. Change the document properties, as specified by your instructor. Save the presentation using the file name, Lab 1-3 Part One Spring Seminars. Display the presentation in grayscale.

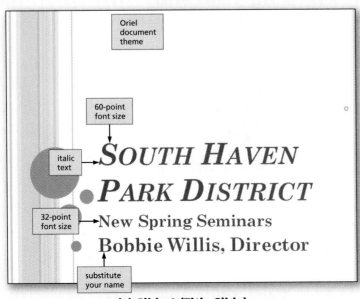

(a) Slide 1 (Title Slide)
Figure 1–102

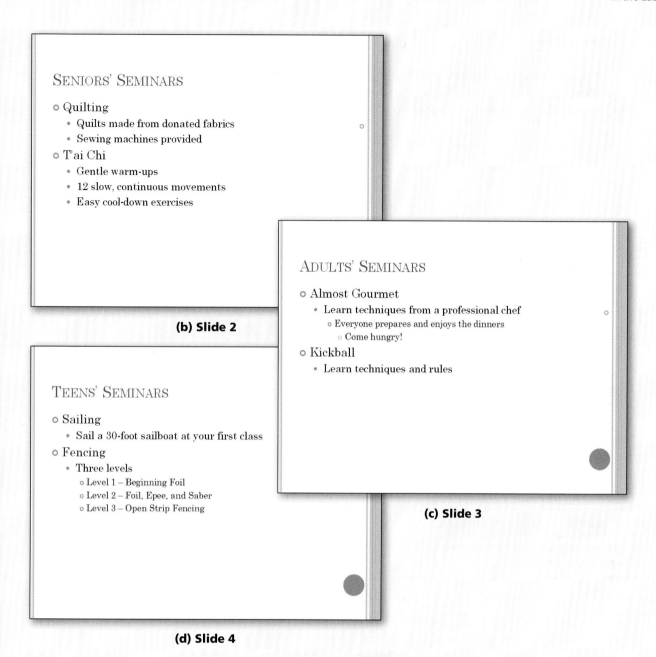

(b) Slide 2

(c) Slide 3

(d) Slide 4

Figure 1–102 (continued)

Instructions Part 2: The South Haven Park District staff members want to update this presentation to promote the new Fall seminars. Modify the presentation created in Part 1 to create the presentation shown in Figure 1–103. To begin, save the current presentation with the new file name, Lab 1-3 Part Two Fall Seminars. Change the document theme to Civic. On the title slide, remove the italics from the title paragraph, South Haven Park District, decrease the font size to 44, and bold the text. Change the first subtitle paragraph to New Fall Seminars. Then change your title in the second subtitle paragraph to Executive Director and change the font size of the entire paragraph to 28.

On Slide 2, change the first first-level paragraph, Quilting, to Quilting for the Holidays. Change the first second-level paragraph, Quilts made from donated fabrics, to Quilts will be raffled at Annual Bazaar. Change the title of the second seminar to Intermediate T'ai Chi.

On Slide 3, change the first second-level paragraph under Almost Gourmet to Holiday feasts and parties. Then change the second-level paragraph under Kickball to Seminar concludes with single elimination tournament.

On Slide 4, change the first class from Sailing to Climbing and then change the course description second-level paragraph to Covers verbal signals, rope, knots, harnesses, belaying.

Continued >

In the Lab *continued*

Correct any spelling mistakes, and then view the slide show. Change the document properties, as specified by your instructor. Display the presentation in grayscale. Submit both Part One and Part Two documents in the format specified by your instructor.

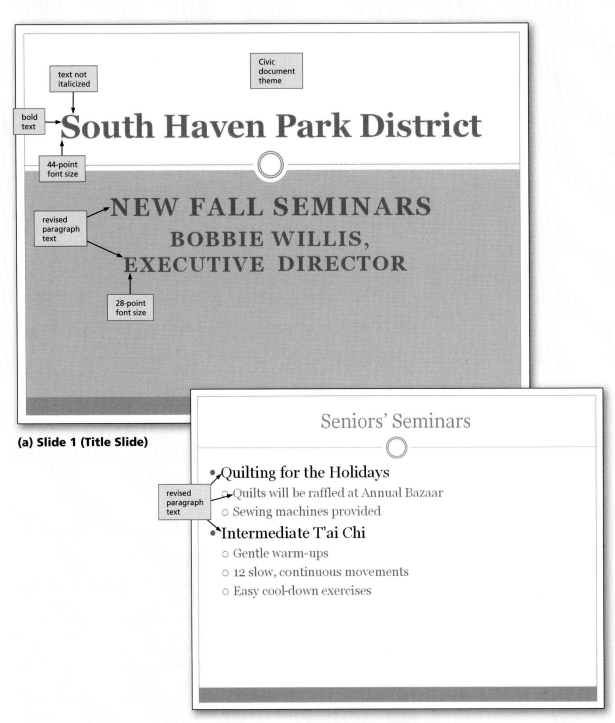

(a) Slide 1 (Title Slide)

(b) Slide 2

Figure 1–103

(c) Slide 3

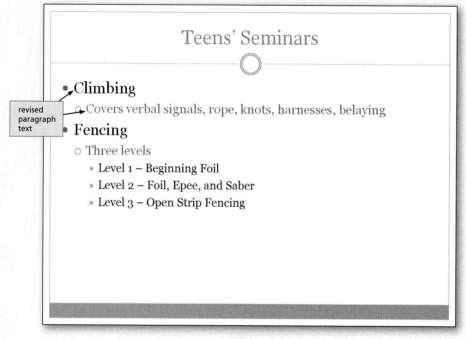

(d) Slide 4

Figure 1–103 (continued)

Cases and Places

Apply your creative thinking and problem solving skills to design and implement a solution.

• EASIER   •• MORE DIFFICULT

Note: Remember to use the 7 × 7 rule as you design the presentations: a maximum of seven words on a line and a maximum of seven lines on one slide.

• 1: Design and Create an Ocean and Seas Presentation

Salt water covers more than two-thirds of the Earth's surface. This water flows freely between the Earth's five oceans and seas, which all are connected. In preparation for your next snorkeling and diving adventure, you have been reading about the oceans and seas. You decide to prepare a PowerPoint presentation to accompany a speech that is required in your Earth Science class. You create the outline shown in Figure 1–104 about these waters. Use this outline along with the concepts and techniques presented in this chapter to develop and format a slide show with a title slide and three text slides with bulleted lists. Be sure to check spelling.

Water, Water, Everywhere
The Earth's Oceans and Seas
Jamel Thomas
Earth Science 203

Major Bodies of Water
Four oceans: Pacific, Atlantic, Indian, and Arctic
Pacific is largest and deepest
64,186,300 square miles
12,925 feet average depth
Fifth ocean delimited in 2000
Southern Ocean north of Antarctica

Coral Reefs
Form in shallow, warm seas
Made of coral polyps' skeletons
Grow on top of old skeletons
Spend adult lives fixed to same spot
Coral diseases increasing dramatically past 10 years
Responding to onset of bacteria, fungi, viruses

Ocean Zones
Sunlit (down to 650 feet)
Sea plants and many animals
Twilight (down to 3,300 feet)
Many different fish
Sunless (down to 13,100 feet)
Animals feed on dead food from above

Figure 1–104

• 2: Design and Create an Industrial Revolution Presentation

The Industrial Revolution changed the way people worked and lived in many parts of the world. With its roots in Britain in the 18th century, the Industrial Revolution introduced new machines, steam power, and trains. As part of your World History homework assignments, you develop the outline shown in Figure 1–105 about the Industrial Revolution and then create an accompanying PowerPoint presentation. Use the concepts and techniques presented in this chapter to develop and format this slide show with a title slide, three text slides with bulleted lists, and a closing slide. Be sure to check spelling.

The Industrial Revolution
1700 - 1850
Sonia Banks
World History 108

British Inventors
    First machines spun and wove cloth quickly
        Wealthy businessmen built factories
           Spinning Jenny machine spun 16 threads simultaneously
    Angered people who made cloth at home
        Luddites protested by smashing machines
           Led by Ned Ludd

Steam Power
    James Watt invented first steam engine in 1782
        Hundreds of his engines used throughout Britain
    George Stephenson designed steam train, The Rocket
        Peak speed: 30 mph
        Used to transport goods in 1829

Coal Mining
    Coal needed to boil water to create steam
    Mining towns boomed
        Deep mines dug
        Men, women, and children worked long hours
           Many people killed and injured

Figure 1–105

Continued >

Cases and Places *continued*

•• 3: Design and Create a Recycling Presentation

Many communities require recycling of household waste. Residents are required to separate paper, plastics, and glass and put each material in special bins or bags. Electronic equipment also can be recycled. Your community has developed a special program for broken or obsolete computers and peripherals, office equipment and products, small home appliances, and entertainment equipment. These items include personal computers, printers, cellular telephones, toasters, televisions, DVD players, and video game consoles. Community officials will be collecting these items during the next two Fridays at your local police station and a nearby shopping center. They will not accept air conditioners, humidifiers, and hazardous wastes. Using the concepts and techniques presented in this chapter, develop a short PowerPoint presentation to show at various businesses and offices in your community. Emphasize that recycling is important because electronic products have very short useful lives. They produce waste and may contain hazardous materials, but many components can be salvaged. Include one slide with acceptable products and another with unacceptable products.

•• 4 Design and Create Your Favorite or Dream Car Presentation

Make It Personal

Ever since Henry Ford rolled the first Model T off his assembly line in 1908, people have been obsessed with cars. From the sporty Corvette to the environmentally friendly Prius, everyone has a favorite car or dream car. Use the concepts and techniques presented in this chapter to create a slide show promoting a particular vehicle. Include a title slide, at least three text slides with bulleted lists, and a closing slide. Format the text using colors, bolding, and italics where needed for emphasis. Be sure to check spelling.

•• 5: Design and Create a Financial Institutions Presentation

Working Together

Financial institutions such as banks, savings and loans, and credit unions offer a variety of products. Have each member of your team visit, telephone, or view Web sites of three local financial institutions. Gather data about:

1) Savings accounts

2) Checking accounts

3) Mortgages

4) Certificates of deposit

After coordinating the data, create a presentation with at least one slide showcasing each financial institution. As a group, critique each slide. Submit your assignment in the format specified by your instructor.

2 | Creating a Presentation with Illustrations and Shapes

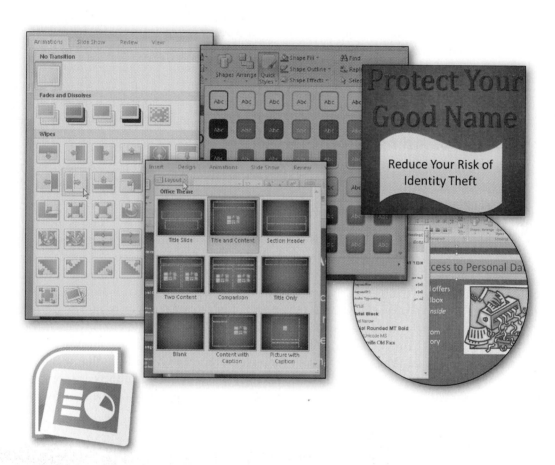

Objectives

You will have mastered the material in this chapter when you can:

- Create slides from a blank presentation
- Change views to review a presentation
- Change slide layouts
- Add a background style
- Insert, move, and size clip art
- Insert a photograph from a file
- Delete a placeholder

- Change font color
- Format text using the Format Painter
- Add and size a shape
- Apply Quick Styles to placeholders and shapes
- Select slide transitions
- Preview and print an outline and handout

2 | Creating a Presentation with Illustrations and Shapes

Introduction

In our visual culture, audience members enjoy viewing effective graphics. Whether reading a document or viewing a PowerPoint presentation, people increasingly want to see photographs, artwork, graphics, and a variety of type. Researchers have known for decades that documents with visual elements are more effective than those that consist of only text because the illustrations motivate audiences to study the material. People remember at least one-third more information when the document they are seeing or reading contains visual elements. These graphics help clarify and emphasize details, so they appeal to audience members with differing backgrounds, reading levels, attention spans, and motivations.

BTW

Delivery Skills
While illustrations and shapes help audience members retain important points in a slide show, keep in mind that a speaker's presentation skills are the most effective part of a presentation. The presenter's posture, eye contact, volume, gestures, and rate establish the tone and tempo of the presentation. A good presentation rarely overcomes poor delivery skills.

Project — Presentation with Illustrations and a Shape

The project in this chapter follows graphical guidelines and uses PowerPoint to create the presentation shown in Figure 2–1. This slide show, which discusses identity theft, has a variety of illustrations and visual elements inserted on a gray background. Clip art and photographs add interest. Transitions help one slide flow gracefully into the next during a slide show. Slide titles have a style that blends well with the background and illustrations. The slide handouts include an outline of the slides and print all four slides on one page.

This presentation uses Quick Styles, which are collections of formatting options for objects and documents. The Quick Styles, like the document themes introduced in Chapter 1, are created by Microsoft's visual designers and give your presentation a professional look. When you rest your mouse pointer on a Quick Style thumbnail in the Quick Style gallery, you will see how the various colors, fonts, and effects are combined, and you can select the image that best fits the impression you want to present in your slide show.

Overview

As you read through this chapter, you will learn how to create the presentation shown in Figure 2–1 by performing these general tasks:

- Create a new presentation from a blank presentation.
- Review presentation in a variety of views.
- Insert and format shapes.
- Insert photographs and clips.
- Print an outline and a handout.

(a)

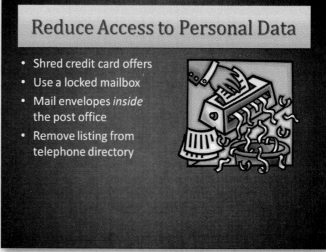

(b)

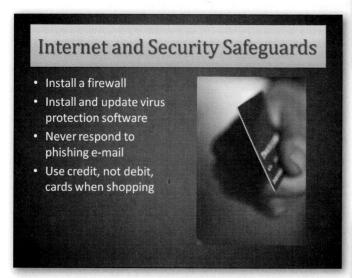

(c)

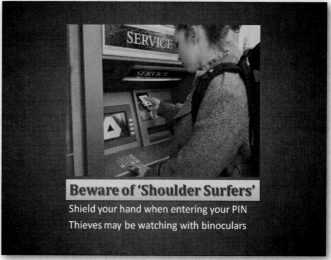

(d)

Figure 2–1

Plan
Ahead

General Project Guidelines

When creating a PowerPoint presentation, the actions you perform and decisions you make will affect the appearance and characteristics of the finished document. As you create a presentation with illustrations, such as the project shown in Figure 2–1, you should follow these general guidelines:

1. **Focus on slide text content.** Give some careful thought to the words you choose to use. Some graphic designers advise starting with a blank screen so that the document theme does not distract from or influence the words.

2. **Use single quotation marks.** PowerPoint slides generally use a single quotation mark in several instances.

   - The introduction of an unfamiliar term

   - A quotation

   - Nicknames

   - Composition titles

3. **Adhere to copyright regulations.** Copyright laws apply to printed and Web-based materials. You can copy an existing photograph or artwork if it is in the public domain, if your company owns the graphic, or if you have obtained permission to use it. Be certain you have the legal right to use a desired graphic in your presentation.

4. **Use color effectively.** Your audience's eyes are drawn to color on a slide. Used appropriately, color can create interest by emphasizing material and promoting understanding. Be aware of symbolic meanings attached to colors, such as red generally representing danger, electricity, and heat.

5. **Use serif fonts for titles and sans serif fonts for body text.** Typefaces are divided into two categories: serif and sans serif. A serif letter generally has thin and thick areas, with the thin areas at the end of the lines. A sans serif letter generally is the same thickness. The letters in this box are sans serif.

6. **Choose graphics that serve a purpose.** Illustrations and art should help your audience remember and understand information. They should be uncluttered and visually appealing. Determine why you need each graphic and the kind of information it communicates.

7. **Consider graphics for multicultural audiences.** In today's intercultural society, your presentation might be viewed by people whose first language is different from yours. Some graphics have meanings specific to a culture, so be certain to learn about your intended audience and their views.

When necessary, more specific details concerning the above guidelines are presented at appropriate points in the chapter. The chapter also will identify the actions you perform and decisions made regarding these guidelines during the creation of the presentation shown in Figure 2–1.

Starting PowerPoint

Chapter 1 introduced you to starting PowerPoint, selecting a document theme, creating slides with bulleted lists, and printing a presentation. The following steps summarize starting a new presentation. To start PowerPoint, Windows Vista must be running. If you are using a computer to step through the project in this chapter and you want your screen to match the figures in this book, you should change your computer's resolution to 1024 × 768. For more information about how to change a computer's resolution, see Appendix E.

To Start PowerPoint

Note: If you are using Windows XP, see Appendix F for alternate steps.

1 Click the Start button on the Windows Vista taskbar to display the Start menu.

2 Click All Programs at the bottom of the left pane on the Start menu to display the All Programs list and then click Microsoft Office in the All Programs list.

3 Click Microsoft Office PowerPoint 2007 to start PowerPoint and display a new blank presentation in the PowerPoint window.

4 If the PowerPoint window is not maximized, click the Maximize button next to the Close button on its title bar to maximize the window.

Plan Ahead

Focus on slide text content.
Once you have researched your presentation topic, many methods exist to begin developing slide content.

- Select a document theme and then enter text, illustration, and tables.
- Open an existing presentation and modify the slides and theme.
- Import an outline created in Microsoft Word.
- Start with a blank presentation that uses the default Office Theme. Consider this practice similar to an artist who begins creating a painting with a blank, white canvas.

  Experiment using different methods of developing the initial content for slides. Experienced PowerPoint users sometimes find one technique works better than another to stimulate creativity or help them organize their ideas in a particular circumstance.

Creating Slides from a Blank Presentation

In Chapter 1, you selected a document theme and then typed the content for the title and text slides using single- and multi-level bulleted lists. In this chapter, you will type the slide content for the title and text slides, select a background, and then format the text.

To Create a Title Slide

Recall from Chapter 1 that the title slide introduces the presentation to the audience. In addition to introducing the presentation, this project uses the title slide to capture the audience's attention by using title text and a shape, which is a movable, resizable graphical element. You will add this shape after you have typed the text for all four slides. The following step creates the slide show's title.

1 Type Protect Your Good Name in the title text placeholder (Figure 2–2 on the next page).

BTW

Introducing the Presentation
Before your audience enters the room, start the presentation and display Slide 1. This slide should be visually appealing and provide general interest in the presentation. An effective title slide gives a good first impression.

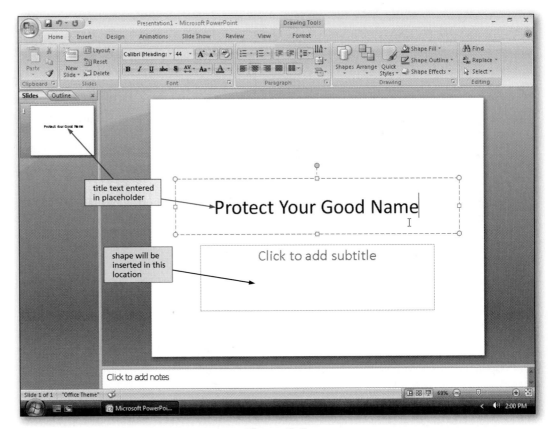

Figure 2–2

Plan Ahead

Use sans serif fonts for content text.

When a new slide is displayed during your presentation, your audience members focus on the title and then read the words in the content placeholder. Generally more words appear in the content placeholder, so designers use sans serif typefaces to decrease reading time.

To Create the First Text Slide with a Single-Level Bulleted List

The first text slide you create in Chapter 2 describes tips for helping prevent thieves from accessing personal information. The four suggestions are displayed as second-level paragraphs. The following steps add a new slide (Slide 2) and then create a text slide with a single-level bulleted list.

1 Click the New Slide button in the Slides group.

2 Type `Reduce Access to Personal Data` in the title text placeholder.

3 Press CTRL+ENTER, type `Shred credit card offers` in the content text placeholder, and then press the ENTER key.

4 Type `Use a locked mailbox` and then press the ENTER key.

5 Type `Mail envelopes inside the post office` and then press the ENTER key.

6 Type `Remove listing from telephone directory` but do not press the ENTER key.

7 Italicize the word, inside, in the third bulleted paragraph (Figure 2–3).

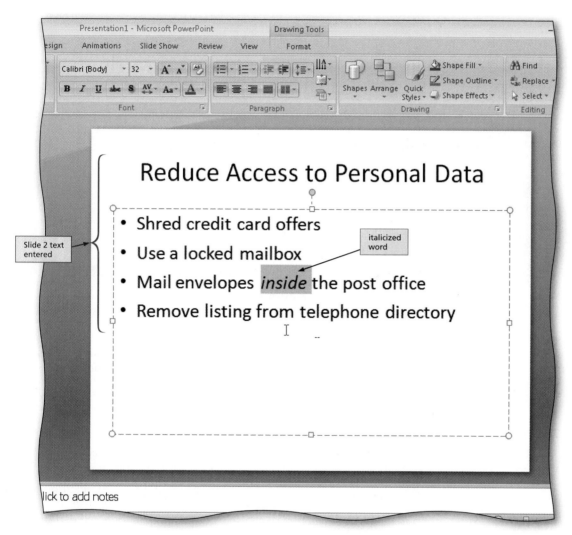

Figure 2–3

To Create the Second Text Slide with a Single-Level Bulleted List

The second text slide contains suggestions to help computer users protect their sensitive electronic files from cyber-intruders. The following steps add a new slide (Slide 3) and then create a text slide with a single-level bulleted list.

1 Click the New Slide button in the Slides group.

2 Type `Internet and Security Safeguards` in the title text placeholder.

3 Press CTRL+ENTER, type `Install a firewall` in the content text placeholder, and then press the ENTER key.

4 Type `Install and update virus protection software` and then press the ENTER key.

5 Type Never respond to phishing e-mail and then press the ENTER key.

6 Type Use credit, not debit, cards when shopping but do not press the ENTER key (Figure 2–4).

Figure 2–4

To Create the Third Text Slide with a Single-Level Bulleted List

The final text slide in your presentation provides information to protect people using an automatic teller machine (ATM). "Shoulder surfers" position themselves near an ATM and often use binoculars and cameras to capture a user's personal identification number (PIN). The following steps add a new slide (Slide 4) and then create a text slide with two second-level bulleted paragraphs.

1 Click the New Slide button in the Slides group.

2 Type Beware of 'Shoulder Surfers' in the title text placeholder.

3 Press CTRL+ENTER, type Shield your hand when entering your PIN in the content text placeholder, and then press the ENTER key.

4 Type Thieves may be watching with binoculars but do not press the ENTER key (Figure 2–5).

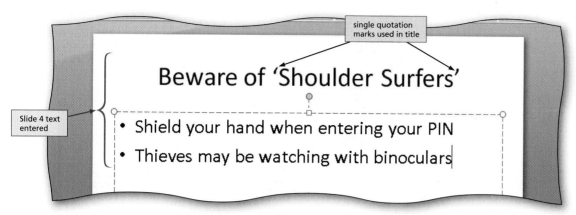

Figure 2–5

To Choose a Background Style

Now that the basic text paragraphs for the title and three text slides have been entered, you need to make design decisions. In creating Project 1, you chose a theme that determined the colors, fonts, and effects. You also can select these elements individually without choosing a theme. In Project 2, you will choose a background that fits the tone of your presentation and then choose fonts and effects. PowerPoint provides 12 white, ivory, blue, and black **background styles**. Background styles have designs that may include color, shading, patterns, and textures. **Fill effects** add pattern and texture to a background, which add depth to a slide. The following steps add a background style to all slides in the presentation.

1

- Click Design on the Ribbon to display the Design tab.

- Click the Background Styles button in the Background group to display the Background Styles gallery (Figure 2–6).

🔍 **Experiment**

- Point to various styles themes in the Background Styles gallery and watch the backgrounds changes on the slide.

Q&A Are the backgrounds displayed in a specific order?

Yes. They are arranged in order from white to black running from left to right. The first row has solid backgrounds; the middle row has darker fills at the bottom; the bottom row has darker fills on the sides. If you point to a background, a ScreenTip with the background's name appears on the screen.

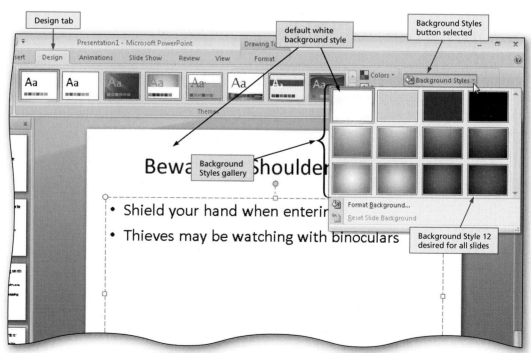

Figure 2–6

2

- Click Background Style 12 to apply this background to all the slides (Figure 2–7).

Q&A

If I decide later that this background style does not fit the theme of my presentation, can I apply a different background?

Yes. You can repeat these steps at any time while creating your presentation.

Q&A

What if I want to apply this background style to only one slide?

When the gallery is displaying, right-click the desired style and then click Apply to Selected Slides.

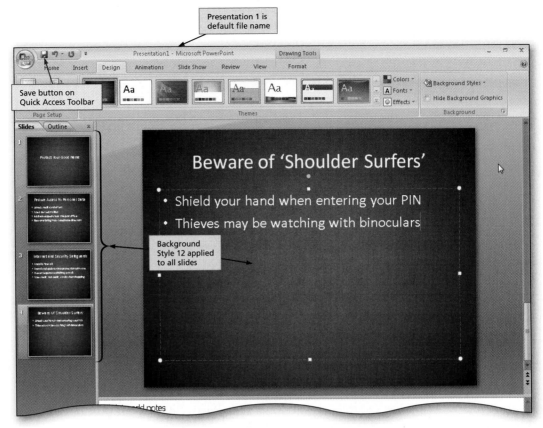

Figure 2–7

Note: If you are using Windows XP, see Appendix F for alternate steps.

To Save a Presentation

You have performed many tasks to create the slide show and do not want to risk losing the work completed thus far. Accordingly, you should save the presentation. For a detailed example of the procedure summarized below, refer to pages PPT 27 through PPT 29 in Chapter 1.

1 With a USB flash drive connected to one of the computer's USB ports, click the Save button on the Quick Access Toolbar to display the Save As dialog box.

2 Type Identity Theft in the File name text box to change the file name. Do not press the ENTER key after typing the file name. If Computer is not displayed in the Favorite Links section, drag the top or bottom edge of the Save As dialog box until Computer is displayed. Click Computer in the Favorite Links section.

3 Double-click your USB flash drive in the list of available drives.

4 Click the Save button in the Save As dialog box to save the presentation on the USB flash drive with the file name, Identity Theft.

BTW

Experimenting with Normal View
As you become more comfortable using PowerPoint, experiment with using the Outline tab and with closing the Tabs pane to maximize the slide area. To close the Tabs pane, click the X to the right of the Outline tab. To redisplay the Tabs pane, click the View tab on the Ribbon and then click Normal in the Presentation Views group.

Changing Views to Review a Presentation

In Chapter 1, you displayed slides in Slide Show view to evaluate the presentation. Slide Show view, however, restricts your evaluation to one slide at a time. Recall from Chapter 1 that Slide Sorter view allows you to look at several slides at one time, which is why it is the best view to use to evaluate a presentation for content, organization, and overall appearance. After reviewing the slides, you can change the view to Normal view to continue working on the presentation.

To Change the View to Slide Sorter View

You can review the four slides in this presentation all in one window. The following step changes the view from Normal view to Slide Sorter view.

- Click the Slide Sorter button at the lower right of the PowerPoint window to display the presentation in Slide Sorter view (Figure 2–8).

Q&A

Why is Slide 4 selected?

It is the current slide in the slide pane.

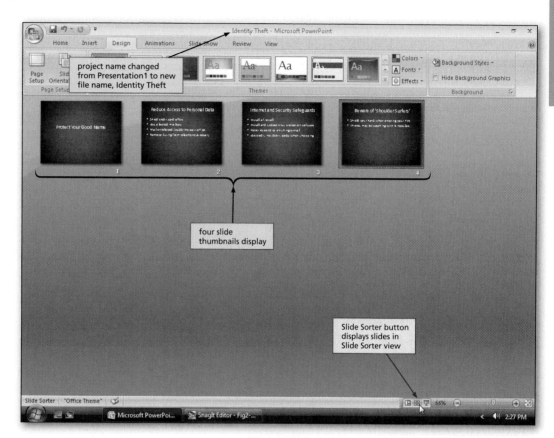

Figure 2–8

To Change the View to Normal View

You can make changes to text in Normal view and on the Outline tab. It is best, however, to change the view to Normal view when altering the slide layouts and formats so you can see the results of your changes. Switching between Slide Sorter view and Normal view helps you review your presentation, assess whether the slides have an attractive design and adequate content, and are organized for the most impact. The following steps change the view from Slide Sorter view to Normal view.

- Click the Normal button at the lower right of the PowerPoint window to display the presentation in Normal view (Figure 2–9).

Figure 2–9

BTW

Using the Find Command
Rather than viewing all the slides in your presentation to look for a particular word or phrase you typed, use the Find command to locate this text. Click the Home tab, click the Find button in the Editing group, type the text in the Find what text box, and then click the Find Next button.

Changing Layouts

When you developed this presentation, PowerPoint applied the Title Slide layout for Slide 1 and the Title and Content layout for the other three slides in the presentation. These layouts are the default styles. A **layout** specifies the arrangement of placeholders on a slide. These placeholders are arranged in various configurations and can contain text, such as the slide title or a bulleted list, or they can contain content, such as SmartArt graphics, pictures, charts, tables, shapes, and clip art. The placement of the text, in relationship to content, depends on the slide layout. You can specify a particular slide layout when you add a new slide to a presentation or after you have created the slide.

Using the **Layout gallery**, you can choose a slide layout. The nine layouts in this gallery have a variety of placeholders to define text and content positioning and formatting. Three layouts are for text: Title Slide, Section Header, and Title Only. Five are for text and content: Title and Content, Two Content, Comparison, Content with Caption, and Picture with Caption. The Blank layout has no placeholders. If none of these standard layouts meets your design needs, you can create a **custom layout**. A custom layout specifies the number, size, and location of placeholders, background content, and optional slide and placeholder-level properties.

When you change the layout of a slide, PowerPoint retains the text and objects and repositions them into the appropriate placeholders. Using slide layouts eliminates the need to resize objects and the font size because PowerPoint automatically sizes the objects and text to fit the placeholders.

To Change the Slide Layout to Two Content

Notice the slides have a significant amount of space and look plain. These observations indicate a need to add visual interest to the slides. The next several sections improve the presentation by changing layouts and adding clip art and photos. Before you add these graphical elements, you must change the slide layouts.

Adding clip art and a photograph to Slides 2, 3, and 4 requires two steps. First, change the slide layouts and then insert the clip or photo into the content placeholders. The following steps change the slide layout on Slide 2 from Title and Content to Two Content.

1
- Click the Previous Slide button on the vertical scroll bar twice to display Slide 2.

- Click Home on the Ribbon to display the Home tab.

- Click the Layout button in the Slides group on the Home tab to display the Layout gallery (Figure 2–10).

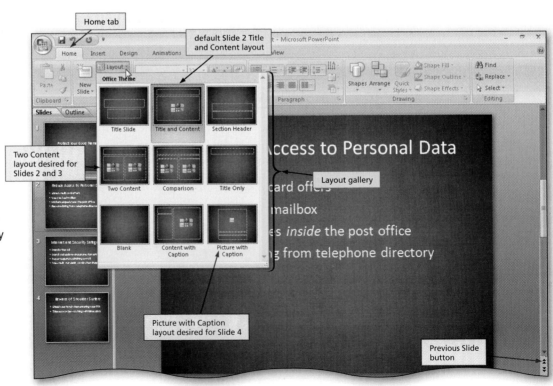

Figure 2–10

2

- Click Two Content to apply that layout to Slide 2 (Figure 2–11).

Q&A

Why did the bulleted list move to the left placeholder?

PowerPoint assumes you want your bulleted list to display on the left side of your slide. If you want the list to display on the right side, you will need to move the placeholders on the slide.

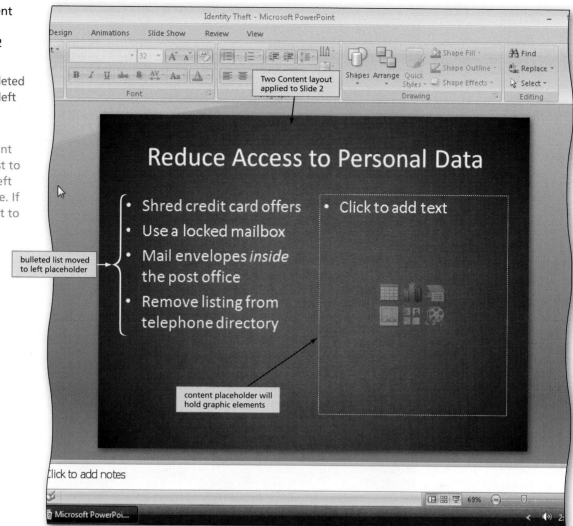

Figure 2–11

To Change the Slide Layout to Two Content

Slide 3 also will have a bulleted list and a graphic element, so the layout needs to change to accommodate this slide content. The following steps change the Slide 3 layout to Two Content.

1 Click the Next Slide button.

2 Click the Layout button in the Slides group on the Home tab to display the Layout gallery.

3 Click Two Content to apply the layout to Slide 3 (Figure 2–12).

Figure 2-12

To Change the Slide Layout to Picture with Caption

The Slide 4 text discusses exercising caution while using an automatic teller machine (ATM). You have a photograph of a person using an ATM, and you want to display this graphic prominently on the slide. The Picture with Caption layout serves this purpose well, so the layout needs to change to accommodate this slide content. The following steps change the Slide 4 layout to Picture with Caption.

1 Click the Next Slide button.

2 Click the Layout button in the Slides group.

3 Click Picture with Caption to apply the layout to Slide 4 (Figure 2–13).

Q&A Why did the font size of the title and bulleted list text decrease?

PowerPoint reduced the font size to make room for the large upper content placeholder. You can increase the font size of this text if you desire.

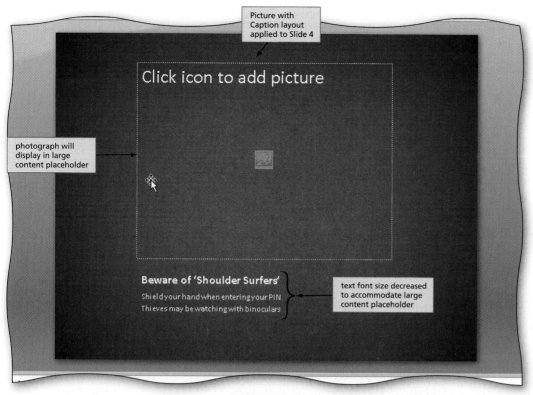

Figure 2–13

Inserting Clip Art and Photographs into Slides

A **clip** is a single media file, including art, sound, animation, and movies. Adding a clip can help increase the visual appeal of many slides and can offer a quick way to add professional-looking graphic images and sounds to a presentation without creating these files yourself. This art is contained in the **Microsoft Clip Organizer**, a collection of drawings, photographs, sounds, videos, and other media files shared with Microsoft Office applications. The **Office Collections** contains all these media files included with Microsoft Office.

You also can add your own clips to slides. You can insert these files directly from a storage medium, such as a USB flash drive. In addition, you can add them to the other files in the Clip Organizer so that you can search for and reuse these images, sounds, animations, and movies. When you create these media files, they are stored on your hard disk in **My Collections**. The Clip Organizer will find these files and create a new collection with these files. Two other locations for clips are Shared Collections and Web Collections. Files in the **Shared Collections** typically reside on a shared network file server and are accessed by multiple users. The **Web Collections** clips reside on the Microsoft Clip Art and Media Home page on the Microsoft Office Online Web site. They are available only if you have an active Internet connection.

BTW

Importing Clips
Previous versions of PowerPoint imported clips automatically the first time a user desired to insert clips. PowerPoint 2007 requires the user to import the clips on first use by clicking the Organize clips link in the Clip Art task pane, clicking the File menu in the Favorites – Microsoft Clip Organizer dialog box, pointing to Add Clips to Organizer in the File menu, and then clicking Automatically.

The Clip Art Task Pane

You can add clips to your presentation in two ways. One way is by selecting one of the slide layouts that includes a content placeholder with a Clip Art button. A second method is by clicking the Clip Art button in the Illustrations area on the Insert tab. Clicking the Clip Art button opens the Clip Art task pane. The **Clip Art task pane** allows you to search for clips by using descriptive keywords, file names, media file formats, and clip collections. Specific file formats could be for clip art, photographs, movies, and sounds. Clips are organized in hierarchical **clip collections**, which combine topic-related clips into categories, such as Academic, Business, and Technology.

Clips have one or more keywords associated with various entities, activities, labels, and emotions. In most instances, the keywords give the name of the clip and related categories. For example, an image of a cow in the Animals category has the keywords animals, cattle, cows, dairies, farms, and Holsteins. You can enter these keywords in the Search for text box to find clips when you know one of the words associated with the image. Otherwise, you may find it necessary to scroll through several categories to find an appropriate clip.

To Insert a Clip from the Clip Organizer into a Content Placeholder

Depending on the installation of the Microsoft Clip Organizer on your computer, you may not have the clip art used in this chapter. Contact your instructor if you are missing clips used in the following steps. If you have an open connection to the Internet, clips from the Microsoft Office Online Web site will display automatically as the result of your search results.

With the Two Content layout applied to Slide 2, you insert clip art into the right content placeholder. The following steps insert clip art of a shredder into the content placeholder on Slide 2.

- Click the Previous Slide button twice to display Slide 2.

- Click the Clip Art button in the content placeholder to display the Clip Art task pane.

- Click the Search for text box in the Clip Art task pane, delete any letters that are present, and then type shredder in the Search for text box (Figure 2–14).

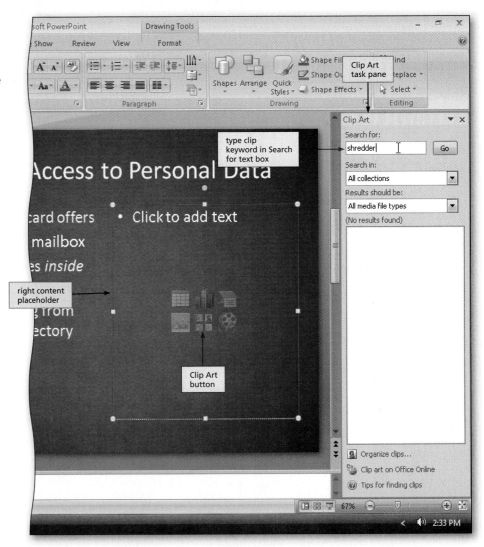

Figure 2–14

2

- Click the Go button so that the Microsoft Clip Organizer will search for and display all pictures having the keyword, shredder.

- If necessary, click the Yes button if a Microsoft Clip Organizer dialog box appears asking if you want to include additional clip art images from Microsoft Office Online.

- If necessary, scroll down the list to display the shredder clip shown in Figure 2–15

- Click the clip to insert it into the right content placeholder (Figure 2–15).

Q&A What if the shredder image displayed in Figure 2–15 is not shown in my Clip Art task pane?

Select a similar clip. Your clips may be different depending on the clips installed on your computer and if you have an open connection to the Internet.

Q&A What is the blue globe image that displays in the lower-left corner of the clips in the Clip Art task pane?

The globe indicates that the image was obtained from the Microsoft Office Online Web site.

Figure 2–15

Plan Ahead

Adhere to copyright regulations.
You have permission to use the clips from the Microsoft Clip Organizer. If you want to use a clip from another source, be certain you have the legal right to insert this file in your presentation. Read the copyright notices that accompany the clip and are posted on the Web site. The owners of these images and files often ask you to give them credit for using their work, which may be satisfied by stating where you obtained the images.

Photographs and the Clip Organizer

In addition to clip art, you can insert pictures into a presentation. These may include scanned photographs, line art, and artwork from compact discs. To insert a picture into a presentation, the picture must be saved in a format that PowerPoint can recognize. Table 2–1 identifies some of the formats PowerPoint recognizes.

You can import files saved with the .emf, .gif, .jpg, .png, .bmp, .rle, .dib, and .wmf formats directly into PowerPoint presentations. All other file formats require separate filters that are shipped with the PowerPoint installation software and must be installed. You can download additional filters from the Microsoft Office Online Web site.

Table 2–1 Primary File Formats PowerPoint Recognizes	
Format	**File Extension**
Computer Graphics Metafile	.cgm
CorelDRAW	.cdr, .cdt, .cmx, and .pat
Encapsulated PostScript	.eps
Enhanced Metafile	.emf
FlashPix	.fpx
Graphics Interchange Format	.gif
Hanako	.jsh, .jah, and .jbh
Joint Photographic Experts Group (JPEG)	.jpg
Kodak PhotoCD	.pcd
Macintosh PICT	.pct
PC Paintbrush	.pcx
Portable Network Graphics	.png
Tagged Image File Format	.tif
Windows Bitmap	.bmp, .rle, .dib
Microsoft Windows Metafile	.wmf
WordPerfect Graphics	.wpg

To Insert a Photograph from the Clip Organizer into a Slide

Next you will add a photograph to Slide 3. You will not insert this picture into a content placeholder, so it will display in the center of the slide. Later in this chapter you will resize this picture and then delete the right placeholder because it is not being used. To start the process locating this photograph, you do not need to click the Clip Art button icon in the content placeholder because the Clip Art task pane already is displayed. The following steps add a photograph to Slide 3.

1 Click the Next Slide button to display Slide 3.

2 Click the Search for text box in the Clip Art task pane and then delete the letters in the text box.

3 Type credit card and then click the Go button.

4 If necessary, scroll down the list to display the picture of a credit card shown in Figure 2–16 and then click the photograph to insert it into Slide 3 (Figure 2–16).

Q&A Why is my photograph so large on the slide?

The photograph was inserted into the slide and not into a content placeholder. You will resize the picture later in this chapter.

clicking Close button closes task pane

Clip Art   Go button

type photograph keyword in Search for text box

Search for:
credit card   Go

Search in:
All collections

Results should be:
Selected media file types

desired photograph inserted in Slide 3

Figure 2–16

To Insert a Photograph from a File into a Slide

The final image to insert in the presentation is a photograph on Slide 4. This slide uses the Picture with Caption layout, so the picture will display in the top placeholder. The following steps add a picture from the Data Files for Students. See the inside back cover of this book for instructions on downloading the Data Files for Students, or contact your instructor for more information on accessing the required files. The following steps insert a photograph of a student using an automatic teller machine (ATM).

Note: If you are using Windows XP, see Appendix F for alternate steps.

- Click the Next Slide button to display Slide 4.

- Click the Close button in the Clip Art task pane so that it no longer is displayed (Figure 2–17).

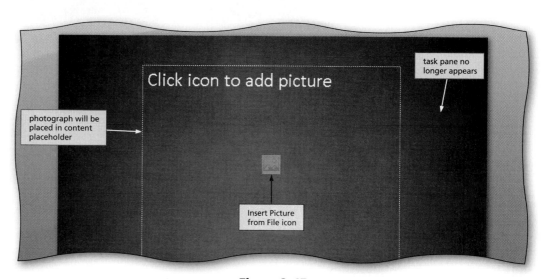

task pane no longer appears

Click icon to add picture

photograph will be placed in content placeholder

Insert Picture from File icon

Figure 2–17

- Click the Insert Picture from File icon in the content placeholder to display the Insert Picture dialog box.

- If the Folders list is displayed below the Folders button, click the Folders button to remove the Folders list.

- With your USB flash drive connected to one of the computer's USB ports, if necessary, click Computer in the Favorite Links section and then scroll until UDISK 2.0 (E:) appears in the list of available drives.

- Double-click UDISK 2.0 (E:) to select the USB flash drive, Drive E in this case, as the device that contains the picture.

- Click ATM to select the file name (Figure 2–18).

Q&A What if the photograph is not on a USB flash drive?

Use the same process, but select the device containing the photograph in the Favorite Links section.

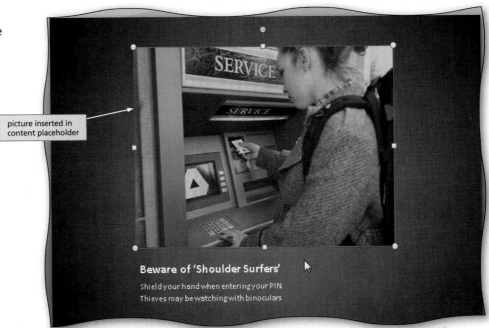

Figure 2–18

- Click the Insert button in the dialog box to insert the picture into Slide 4 (Figure 2–19).

Figure 2–19

Resizing Clip Art and Photographs

Sometimes it is necessary to change the size of clip art. **Resizing** includes both enlarging and reducing the size of a clip art graphic. You can resize clip art using a variety of techniques. One method involves changing the size of a clip by specifying exact dimensions in a dialog box. Another method involves dragging one of the graphic's sizing handles to the desired location. A selected graphic appears surrounded by a **selection rectangle**, which has small squares and circles, called **sizing handles** or move handles, at each corner and middle location.

To Resize Clip Art

On Slide 2, much space appears around the clip, so you can increase its size. The photograph on Slide 3 is too large for the slide, so you should reduce its size. To change the size, drag the corner sizing handles to view how the clip will look on the slide. Using these corner handles maintains the graphic's original proportions. Dragging the square sizing handles alters the proportions so that the graphic becomes more or less high or more or less wide. The following steps increase the size of the Slide 2 clip using a corner sizing handle.

- Click the Previous Slide button two times to display Slide 2.

- Click the shredder clip to select it and display the selection rectangle.

- Point to the upper-left corner sizing handle on the clip so that the mouse pointer shape changes to a two-headed arrow (Figure 2–20).

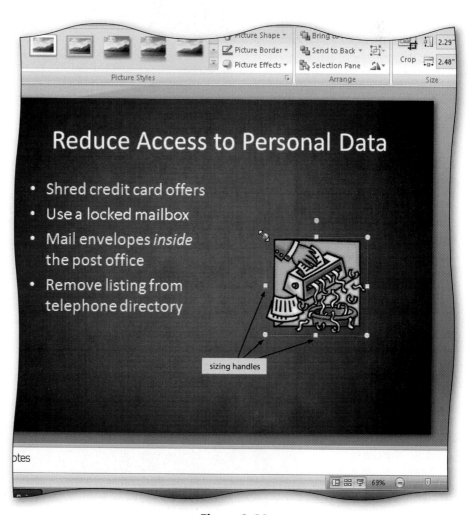

Figure 2–20

- Drag the sizing handle diagonally toward the center of the slide until the mouse pointer is positioned approximately as shown in Figure 2–21.

Q&A

What if the clip is not the same size shown in Figure 2–21?

Repeat Steps 1 and 2.

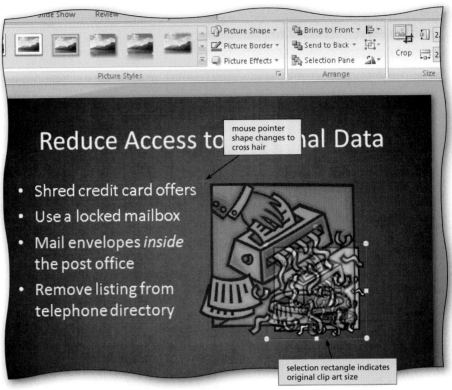

Figure 2–21

3

- Release the mouse button to resize the clip. If necessary, select the clip and then use the ARROW keys to position the clip as shown in Figure 2–21.

4

- Click outside the clip to deselect it (Figure 2–22).

Q&A

What happened to the Picture Tools and Format tabs?

When you click outside the clip, PowerPoint deselects the clip and removes the Picture Tools and Format tabs from the screen.

Q&A

What if I want to return the clip to its original size and start again?

With the graphic selected, click the Reset button in the Slides group on the Home tab.

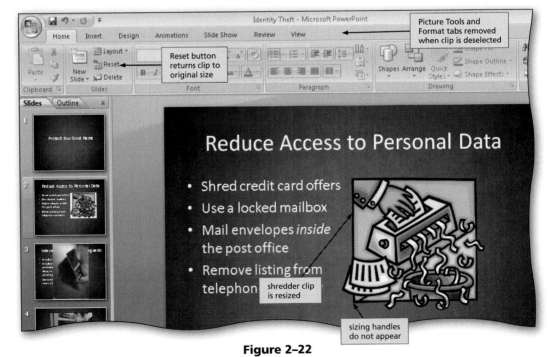

Figure 2–22

To Resize a Photograph

The credit card picture in Slide 3 fills the middle of the slide and covers some text, so you should reduce its size. The following steps resize this photograph using a sizing handle.

1 Click the Next Slide button to display Slide 3.

2 Click the credit card photograph to select it.

3 Drag the upper-left corner sizing handle on the photograph diagonally inward until the photograph is resized approximately as shown in Figure 2–23.

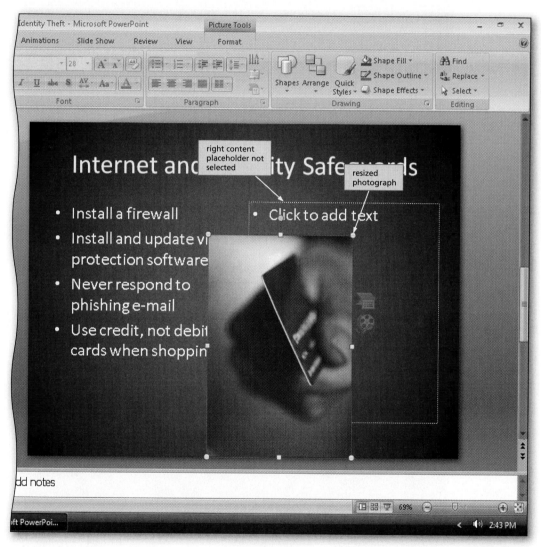

Figure 2–23

To Delete a Placeholder

The credit card photograph was inserted into the slide and not into a content placeholder. The right content placeholder, therefore, is not needed, so you can delete it from the slide. The following steps delete this placeholder.

1

- Click the right content placeholder to select it.

- Click the edge of the placeholder so the border is displayed as a solid line (Figure 2–24).

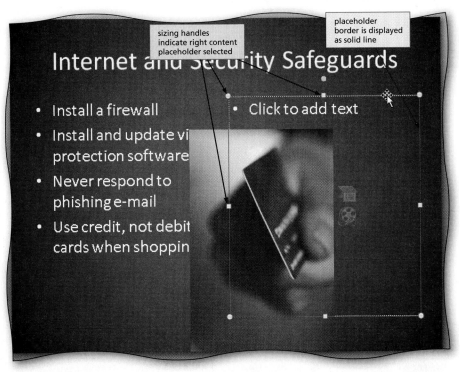

Figure 2–24

2

- Press the DELETE key to delete the placeholder from Slide 2 (Figure 2–25).

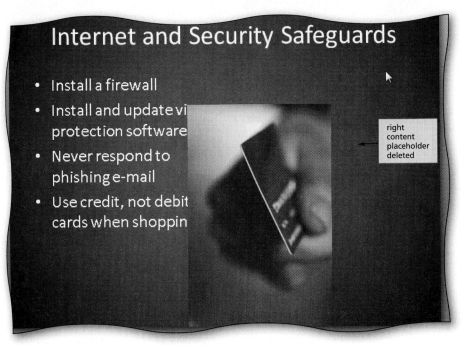

Figure 2–25

To Move Clips

After you insert clip art or a picture on a slide, you may want to reposition it. The credit card photograph on Slide 3 and the shredder clip on Slide 2 could be centered in the spaces between the bulleted text and the right edge of the slide. The following steps move these graphics.

- Click the credit card photograph on Slide 3 to select it and then press and hold down the mouse button.

- Drag the photograph diagonally upward toward the word, Safeguards (Figure 2–26).

Figure 2–26

2

- Click the Previous Slide button to display Slide 2.

- Click the shredder clip to select it, press and hold down the mouse button, and then drag the photograph toward the right side of the slide (Figure 2–27).

Figure 2–27

BTW

Inserting Special Characters
You can insert characters not found on your keyboard, such as the Euro sign (€), the copyright sign (©), and Greek capital letters (e.g., Δ, E, Θ). To insert these characters, click the Insert tab on the Ribbon, and then click the Symbol button in the Text group. When the Symbol dialog box is displayed, you can use the same font you currently are using in your presentation, or you can select another font. The Webdings, Webdings 2, and Webdings 3 fonts have a variety of symbols.

To Save an Existing Presentation with the Same File Name

You have made several changes to your presentation since you last saved it. Thus, you should save it again. The following step saves the presentation again.

1 Click the Save button on the Quick Access Toolbar to overwrite the previous Identity Theft file on the USB flash drive.

Formatting Title and Content Text

Choosing well-coordinated colors and styles for text and objects in a presentation is possible by using **Quick Styles**, which are defined combinations of formatting options. The styles in the Quick Styles Gallery have a wide variety of font, background, and border colors. You even can create a custom Quick Style and give it a unique name. Once you select a particular Quick Style and make any other font changes, you then can copy these changes to other text using the **Format Painter**. The Format Painter allows you to copy all formatting changes from one object to another.

To Format Title Text Using Quick Styles

The 42 Quick Styles are displayed in thumbnails in the Quick Style gallery. When you place your mouse pointer over a Quick Style thumbnail, PowerPoint changes the text and shows how the Quick Style affects the formatting. The title text in this presentation will have a light orange background, a dark orange border, and black letters. The following steps apply a Quick Style to the title text.

1

- Click the Slide 2 title text placeholder to select it.

- Click the Quick Styles button in the Drawing group on the Home tab to display the Quick Styles gallery. Point to the Subtle Effect – Accent 6 Quick Style (row 4, column 7) to display a live preview of the style (Figure 2–28).

Experiment

- Point to various styles in the Quick Styles gallery and watch the format of the text, backgrounds, and borders change in the placeholder.

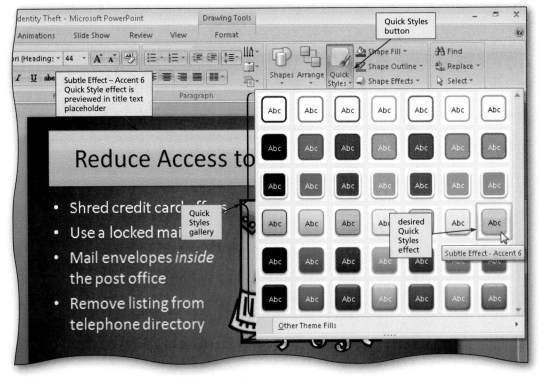

Figure 2–28

2

- Click the Subtle
Effect – Accent 6
Quick Style (row 4,
column 7) to apply
this format to the
title text placeholder
(Figure 2–29).

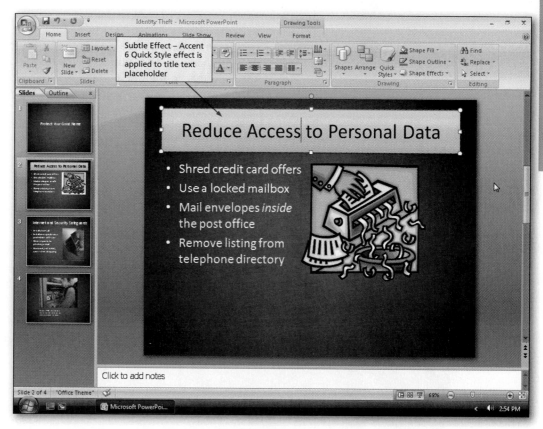

Figure 2–29

To Format Remaining Title Text Using Quick Styles

Once you have applied a Quick Style to one title text placeholder, it is a good idea to use the same style for consistency. The following steps apply the Subtle Effect – Accent 6 Quick Style to the title text placeholder on Slides 3 and 4.

1 Click the Next Slide button to display Slide 3. Click the title text placeholder and then click the Quick Styles button in the Drawing group to display the Quick Styles gallery.

2 Click the Subtle Effect – Accent 6 Quick Style (row 4, column 7) to apply this format to the title text placeholder.

3 Click the Next Slide button to display Slide 4. Click the title text placeholder, click the Quick Styles button, and then click the Subtle Effect – Accent 6 Quick Style (row 4, column 7) to apply this format to the title text placeholder (Figure 2–30).

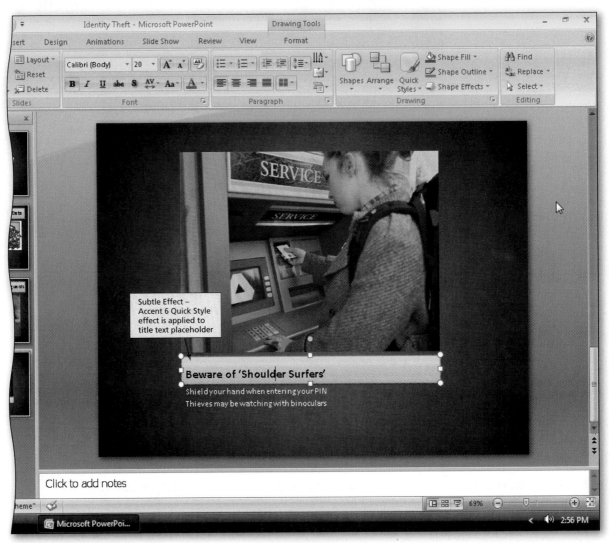

Figure 2–30

Use serif fonts for titles.
The design guidelines for title text differ from the guidelines for content body text. You would like your audience members to remember the main points of your presentation, and you can help their retention by having them read the title text more slowly than they read the words in the content text placeholder. The uneven lines in serif typefaces cause eye movement to slow down. Designers, therefore, often use serif fonts for the slide title text.

To Change the Heading Font

The default Office Theme heading and body text font is Calibri with a font size of 28 point. Calibri is a sans serif font, and designers recommend using a serif font to draw more attention to the slide title text. The following steps change the font from Calibri to Cambria.

- Click the Previous Slide button two times to display Slide 2. Triple-click the title text paragraph. With the text selected, click the Font box arrow in the Font group on the Home tab to display the Font gallery (Figure 2–31).

Q&A

Will the fonts in my Font gallery be the same as those in Figure 2–31?

Your list of available fonts may differ, depending on the type of printer you are using.

- Scroll through the Font gallery, if necessary, and then point to Cambria (or a similar font) to display a live preview of the title text in Cambria font.

Experiment

- Point to various fonts in the Font gallery and watch the font of the title text change in the document window.

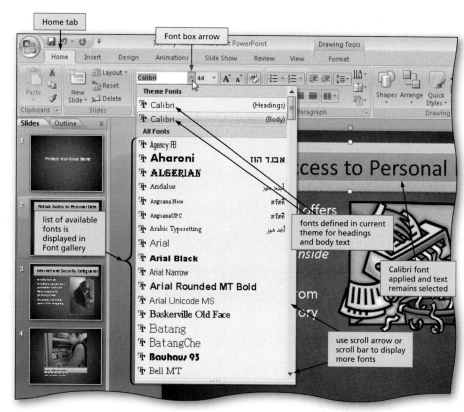

Figure 2–31

❸

- Click Cambria (or a similar font) to change the font of the selected text to Cambria (Figure 2–32).

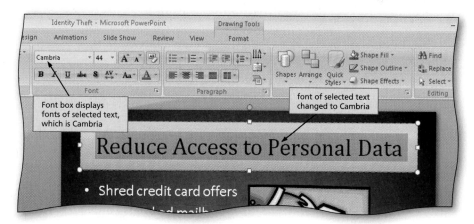

Figure 2–32

Other Ways

1. Click Font box arrow on Mini toolbar, click desired font in Font gallery
2. Right-click selected text, click Font on shortcut menu, click Font tab, select desired font
3. Click Dialog Box Launcher in Font group, click Font tab, select desired font in Font list or type a font in Font box, click OK button
4. Press CTRL+SHIFT+F, click Font tab, select desired font in the Font list, click OK button

To Shadow Text

A **shadow** helps the letters display prominently by adding a shadow behind the text. The following step adds a shadow to the selected title text, Reduce Access to Personal Data.

- With the text selected, click the Text Shadow button in the Font group on the Home tab to add a shadow to the selected text (Figure 2–33).

Q&A

How would I remove a shadow?

You would click the Shadow button a second time, or you immediately could click the Undo button on the Quick Access Toolbar.

Figure 2–33

To Change Font Color

Color is used to emphasize or draw attention to specific text. The following step changes the title text font color from black to dark red.

- With the text selected, click the Font Color box arrow in the Font group on the Home tab to display the Font Color gallery (Figure 2–34).

Q&A

What is the difference between the colors shown in the Theme Colors area and the Standard Colors?

The ten colors in the top row of the Theme Colors area are two text, two background, and six accent colors in the Office Theme; the five colors in each column under the top row display different transparencies. The ten standard colors are available in every document theme.

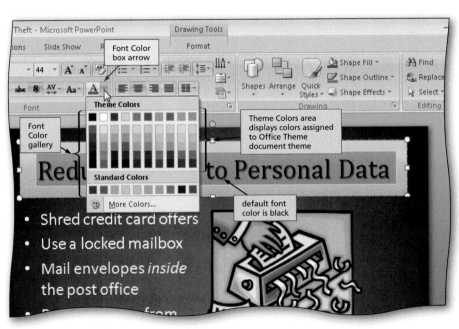

Figure 2–34

2

- Point to the Dark Red color in the Standard Colors row to display a live preview of the title text in a Dark Red color (Figure 2–35).

Experiment

- Point to various colors in the Font Color gallery and watch the title text color change in the slide.

3

- Click Dark Red to change the title text font color.

Q&A

How would I change a color?

You would click the Font Color box arrow and then select another color in the Font Color gallery.

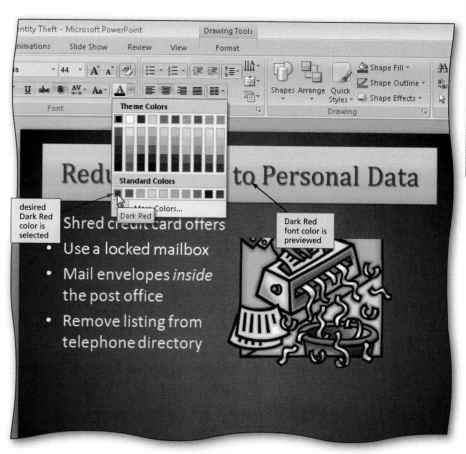

Figure 2–35

Other Ways
1. Click Font color box arrow on Mini toolbar, click desired color in Font Color gallery
2. Right-click selected text, click Font on shortcut menu, click Font tab, select desired color in Font color list, click OK button
3. Click Dialog Box Launcher in Font group, click Font tab, select desired color in Font color list, click OK button
4. Press CTRL+SHIFT+F, click Font tab, select desired color in Font color list, click OK button

Format Painter

To save time and avoid formatting errors, you can use the Format Painter to apply custom formatting to other places in your presentation quickly and easily. You can use this feature in three ways:

- To copy only character attributes, such as font and font effects, select text that has these qualities.
- To copy both paragraph attributes, such as alignment and indentation and character attributes, select the entire paragraph.
- To apply the same formatting to multiple words, phrases, or paragraphs, double-click the Format Painter button and then select each item you want to format. You then can press the ESC key or click the Format Painter button to turn off this feature.

BTW

Deleting WordArt
If you decide you no longer want the WordArt text to display on your slide, select this text, click the Format tab on the Ribbon, click the Quick Styles button, and then click Clear WordArt.

To Format Slide 3 Text Using the Format Painter

To save time and duplicated effort, you quickly can use the Format Painter to copy formatting attributes from the Slide 2 title text and apply them to Slides 3. The following steps use the Format Painter to copy formatting features.

- With the Slide 2 title text still selected, double-click the Format Painter button in the Clipboard group in the Home tab (Figure 2–36).

- Move the mouse pointer off the Ribbon.

Q&A Why did my mouse pointer change shape?

The mouse pointer changed shape by adding a paint brush to indicate that the Format Painter function is active.

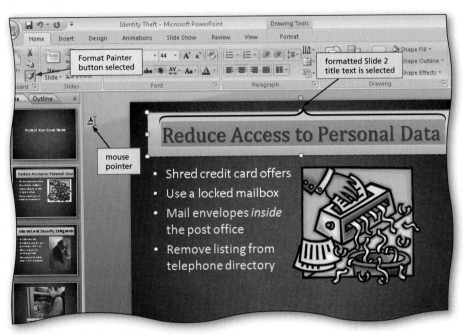

Figure 2–36

- Click the Next Slide button to display Slide 3. Triple-click the title text placeholder to apply the format to all the title text (Figure 2–37).

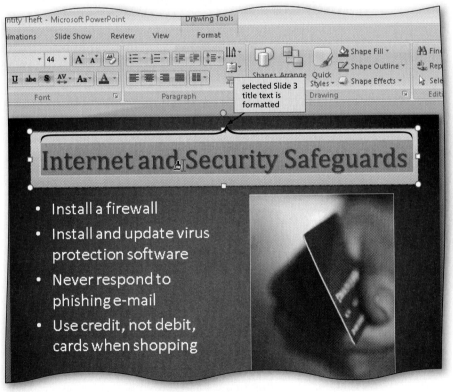

Figure 2–37

To Format Remaining Title Text

Once you have applied formatting characteristics to one text placeholder, you should maintain consistency and apply the same formats to the other title text characters. The following steps use the Format Painter to change the font and font color and apply a shadow to the Slide 4 and Slide 1 title text.

1 Click the Next Slide button to display Slide 4. Triple-click the title text placeholder to apply the format to all title text characters.

Q&A What happened to all the letters in my title?

The Format Painter applied a style that does not fit in the current placeholder. You will adjust the font size so that all the words are displayed.

2 Click the Previous Slide button three times to display Slide 1. Triple-click the title text placeholder to apply the format to all title text characters.

3 Press the ESC key to turn off the Format Painter feature (Figure 2–38).

Other Ways

1. Click Format Painter button on Mini toolbar

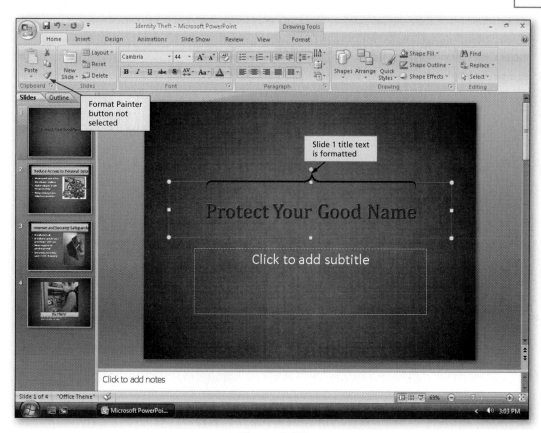

Figure 2–38

To Size Slide 4 Text

The Slide 4 title text placeholder is too small to accommodate the formatting characteristics you applied to the text. The text will fit if you reduce the font size. In addition, the body text should be enlarged for readability. The following steps adjust the size of the Slide 4 title and body text.

1 Click the Next Slide button three times to display Slide 4.

2 Select both body text paragraphs in the content text placeholder and then click the Increase Font Size button on the Mini toolbar four times to increase the font size to 24 point.

3 Triple-click the title text placeholder and then click the Decrease Font Size button on the Mini toolbar three times to reduce the font size to 32 point.

4 Click the slide anywhere outside the placeholders to deselect it (Figure 2–39).

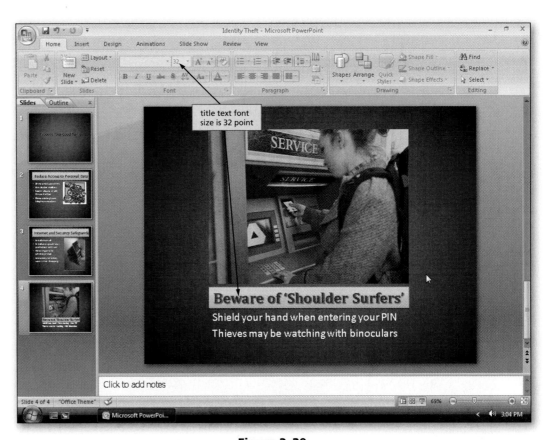

Figure 2–39

Adding and Formatting a Shape

One method of getting the audience's attention at the start of a slide show is to have graphical elements on the title slide. PowerPoint provides a wide variety of shapes that can add visual interest to a slide. Shape elements include lines, basic geometrical shapes, arrows, equation shapes, flowchart symbols, stars, banners, and callouts.

Slide 1 in this presentation is enhanced in a variety of ways. First, the title text font size is increased to aid readability and to catch the audience's attention. Then a shape is inserted below the title text with additional formatted text. Finally, the subtitle text placeholder is deleted because it no longer is needed.

To Increase Title Slide Font Size

The title on a slide should be large enough to stimulate the audience's interest and announce the topic of the presentation. The following steps increase the Slide 1 title text.

1 Click the Previous Slide button three times to display Slide 1.

2 Select the Slide 1 title text, Protect Your Good Name. Click the Increase Font Size button on the Mini toolbar six times until the font size is 80 point (Figure 2–40).

3 Click the slide anywhere outside the title text placeholder to deselect it.

Figure 2–40

To Add a Shape

After adding a shape to a slide, you can change its default characteristics by adding text, bullets, numbers, and Quick Styles. You also can combine multiple shapes to create a more complex graphic. The following steps add a banner shape to Slide 1.

- Click the Shapes button in the Drawing group on the Home tab to display the Shapes gallery. Point to the Wave banner shape in the Stars and Banners area (Figure 2–41).

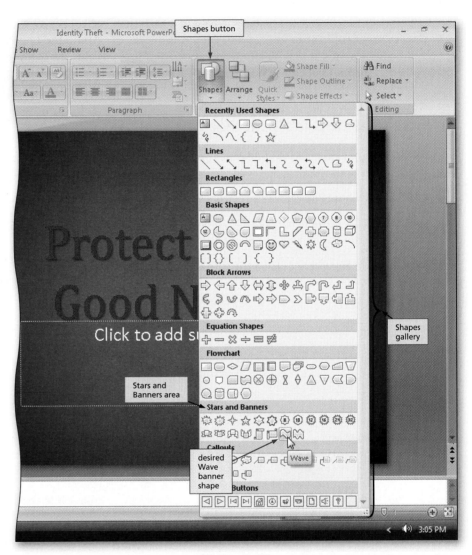

Figure 2–41

- Click the Wave shape (Figure 2–42).

Q&A

Why did my pointer change shape?

The pointer changed to a plus shape to indicate the Wave shape has been added to the Clipboard.

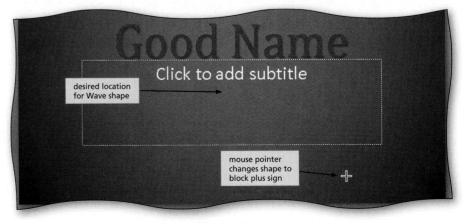

Figure 2–42

3

- Click Slide 1 anywhere below the title text to insert the Wave shape (Figure 2–43).

Figure 2–43

To Resize a Shape

The next step is to resize the Wave shape. The shape should be enlarged so that it appears prominently on the slide and can hold the subtitle text. The following steps resize the selected Wave shape.

1

- With the Wave shape still selected, point to the lower-right corner sizing handle on the picture so that the mouse pointer shape changes to a two-headed arrow (Figure 2–44).

Q&A
What if my shape is not selected?
To select a shape, click it.

Figure 2–44

- Drag the sizing handle diagonally outward and downward until the Wave shape is the approximate size of the one shown in Figure 2–45.

Figure 2–45

- Release the mouse button to resize the shape (Figure 2–46).

Q&A What if the shape is the wrong size?

Repeat Steps 1 and 2.

Q&A What if I want to move the shape to a different location on the slide?

With the shape selected, press the ARROW keys or drag the shape to the desired location.

Other Ways

1. Enter shape height and width in Height and Width text boxes in Size group on Format tab in Drawing Tools contextual tabs

2. Click Dialog Box Launcher in Size group on Format tab in Drawing Tools contextual tabs, click Size tab, enter desired height and width values in text boxes, click Close button

Figure 2–46

To Add Text to a Shape

The banner shape is displayed on Slide 1 in the correct location. The next step is to add text stating that the presentation will cover strategies to help prevent identity theft. The following step describes how to add this information to the shape.

- With the Wave banner shape selected, type Reduce Your Risk of Identity Theft in the shape (Figure 2–47).

Figure 2–47

To Format Shape Text and Add a Shape Quick Style

Formatting text in a shape follows the same techniques as formatting text in a placeholder. You can change font, font color and size, and alignment, and you also can apply a Shape Quick Style. The following steps describe how to format the shape text by increasing the font size and adding a Shape Quick Style.

- Triple-click the Wave shape text to select it and then click the Increase Font Size button on the Mini toolbar five times until the font size is 36 point (Figure 2–48).

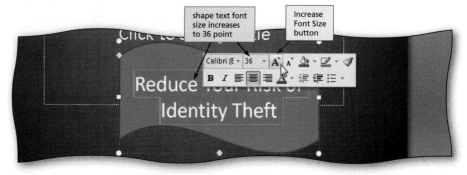

Figure 2–48

2

- Click the Shape Quick Styles button in the Drawing group on the Home tab to display the Quick Styles gallery (Figure 2–49).

- Point to the Subtle Effect – Accent 6 Shape Quick Style (row 4, column 7) to display a live preview of the style.

Experiment

- Point to various styles in the Quick Styles gallery and watch the format of the text, backgrounds, and borders change in the Wave shape.

3

- Click the Subtle Effect – Accent 6 Shape Quick Style (row 4, column 7) to apply this format to the shape.

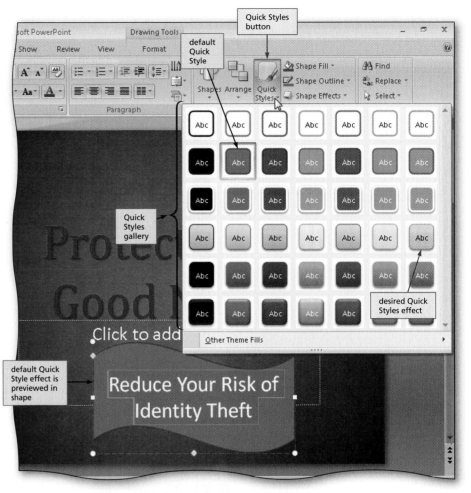

Figure 2–49

4

- Click outside the shape to deselect it (Figure 2–50).

Figure 2–50

To Delete a Placeholder

The subtitle placeholder no longer is necessary on Slide 1 because the shape fills the area below the title text. The following steps delete the Slide 1 subtitle placeholder.

1

• Click the subtitle text placeholder border two times to change the border to a solid line (Figure 2–51).

Figure 2–51

2

• Press the DELETE key to delete the placeholder. If necessary, select the shape and then use the ARROW keys to center the shape under the title text (Figure 2–52).

Figure 2–52

Plan
Ahead

> **Use simple transitions.**
> Transitions help segue one slide into the next seamlessly. They should not be used decoratively or be something on which an audience member focuses. For consistency, use the same transition throughout the presentation unless you have a special circumstance that warrants a different effect.

BTW

Certification
The Microsoft Certified Application Specialist (MCAS) program provides an opportunity for you to obtain a valuable industry credential – proof that you have the PowerPoint 2007 skills required by employers. For more information see Appendix G or visit the PowerPoint 2007 Certification Web page (scsite.com/ppt2007/cert).

Adding a Transition

PowerPoint provides many animation effects to add interest and make a slide show presentation look professional. **Animation** includes special visual and sound effects applied to text or content. A **slide transition** is a special animation effect used to progress from one slide to the next in a slide show. You can control the speed of the transition effect and add a sound.

PowerPoint provides more than 50 different transitions in the Quick Styles group. They are arranged into five categories that describe the types of effects:

- Fades and Dissolves - Blend one slide seamlessly into the next slide
- Wipes - Gently uncover one slide to reveal the next
- Push and Cover - Appear to move one slide off the screen
- Stripes and Bars – Use blinds and checkerboard patterns
- Random – Use vertical and horizontal bars or an arbitrary pattern that changes each time you run the presentation.

To Add a Transition between Slides

In this presentation, you apply the Uncover Right transition in the Wipes category to all slides and change the transition speed to Medium. The following steps apply this transition to the presentation.

1

- Click the Animations tab on the Ribbon and then point to the More button in the Transition to This Slide group (Figure 2–53).

Q&A

Is a transition applied now?

No. The first slide icon in the Transitions group has an orange border, which indicates no transition has been applied.

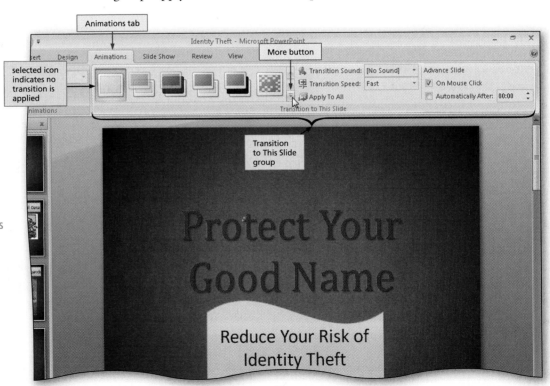

Figure 2–53

2

- Click the More button to expand the Transitions gallery.

- Point to the Uncover Right transition (row 2, column 2) in the Wipes category in the Transitions gallery to display a live preview of this transition (Figure 2–54).

 Experiment

- Point to various styles in the Transitions gallery and watch the transitions on the slide.

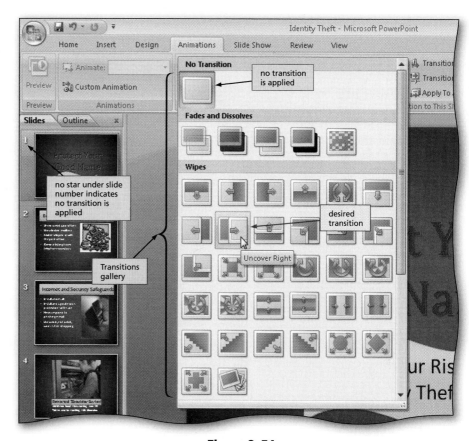

Figure 2–54

3

- Click Uncover Right in the Wipes category in the Transitions gallery to apply the Uncover Right transition to the title slide.

Q&A Why does a star appear next to Slide 1 in the Slides tab?

The star indicates that a transition animation effect is applied to that slide.

- Click the Transition Speed arrow in the Transition to This Slide group on the Animations tab to display three possible speeds: Slow, Medium, and Fast (Figure 2–55).

Figure 2–55

- Click Medium to change the transition speed for Slide 1 to Medium.

- Click the Apply to All button in the Transition to This Slide group on the Animations tab to apply the Uncover Right transition and Medium speed to all four slides in the presentation (Figure 2–56).

Q&A What if I want to apply a different transition and speed to each slide in the presentation?

Repeat Steps 2 through 5 for each slide individually.

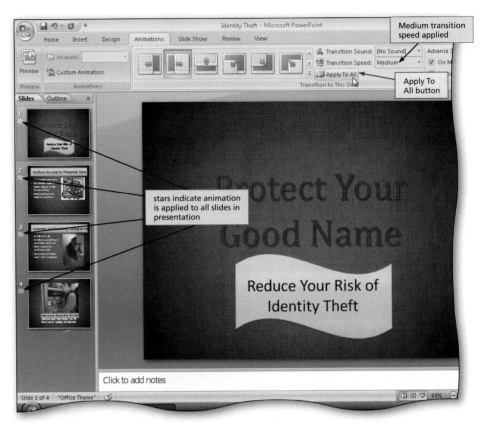

Figure 2–56

To Change Document Properties

Before saving the presentation again, you want to add your name, class name, and some keywords as document properties. The following steps use the Document Information Panel to change document properties.

1 Click the Office Button to display the Office Button menu, point to Prepare on the Office Button menu, and then click Properties on the Prepare submenu to display the Document Information Panel.

2 Click the Author text box, if necessary, and then type your name as the Author property. If a name already is displayed in the Author text box, delete it before typing your name.

3 Click the Subject text box, if necessary delete any existing text, and then type your course and section as the Subject property.

4 Click the Keywords text box, if necessary delete any existing text, and then type `identity theft, Internet safeguards, PIN` as the Keywords properties.

5 Click the Close the Document Information Panel button so that the Document Information Panel no longer is displayed.

To Save an Existing Presentation with the Same File Name

You have made several changes to the presentation since you last saved it. Thus, you should save it again. The following step saves the document again.

Note: If you are using Windows XP, see Appendix F for alternate steps.

1 Click the Save button on the Quick Access Toolbar to overwrite the previous Identity Theft file on the USB flash drive.

To Run an Animated Slide Show

All changes are complete, and the presentation is saved. You now can view the Identity Theft presentation. The following step starts Slide Show view.

1 Click the Slide Show button to display the title slide (Figure 2–57).

2 Click each slide and view the transition effect and slides.

Figure 2–57

Printing a Presentation as an Outline and Handouts

During the development of a lengthy presentation, it often is easier to review an outline in print rather than on the screen. Printing an outline also is useful for audience handouts or when your supervisor or instructor wants to review your subject matter before you develop the presentation fully. In addition, printing two or more slides on one page helps audience members see relationships between slides and also conserves paper. You can preview your print selections to see how your printout will look.

The **Print What list** in the Page Setup group or in the Print dialog box contains options for printing slides, handouts, notes, and an outline. If you want to print handouts, you can specify whether you want one, two, three, four, six, or nine slide images to display on each page. The next two sections preview and then print the presentation outline and the presentation slides as a handout.

To Preview and Print an Outline

Recall that in Chapter 1 each slide printed on a separate page when you clicked Quick Print on the Print submenu. When you want to print other materials, such as an outline, notes, or handouts, you click Print on the Print submenu and select what form of output you desire. The following steps preview and print an outline.

1
- Click the Office Button to display the Office Button menu.

- Point to Print on the Office Button menu to display the Print submenu (Figure 2–58).

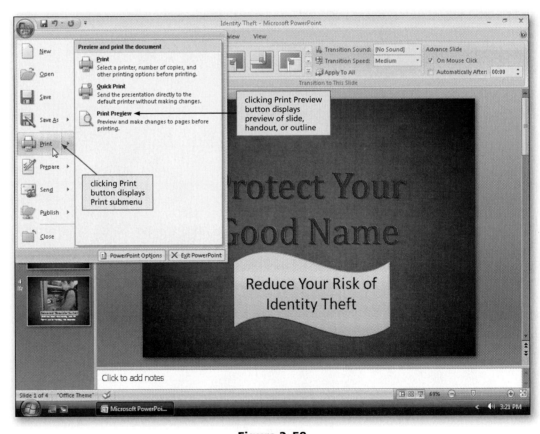

Figure 2–58

2

- Click Print Preview on the Print submenu to display a preview of a slide, handout, or outline of the presentation.

 Q&A

Why does the slide preview image vary among slides, handouts, and outlines?

PowerPoint retains the settings last specified for previewing and printing. If, for example, you last specified to print in Grayscale, the current document will print in Grayscale unless you change the setting.

- If an outline is not previewed, click the Print What box arrow in the Page Setup group on the Print Preview tab to display a list of output types in the Print What list (Figure 2–59).

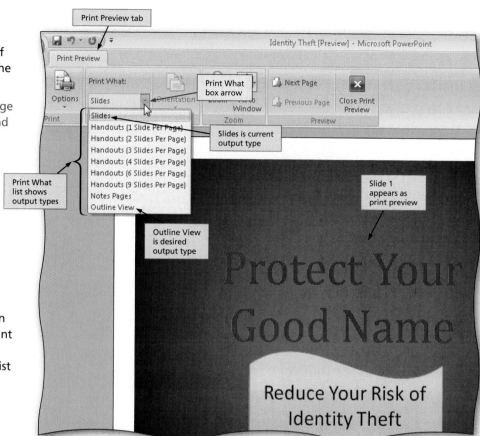

Figure 2–59

3

- Click Outline View in the Print What list if this choice is not already selected.

- Click the Zoom button in the Zoom group on the Print Preview tab to open the Zoom dialog box.

- Click 100% in the Zoom dialog box to change the zoom so that you can read the outline easily on the screen (Figure 2–60).

Q&A

If I change the zoom percentage, will the document print differently?

Changing the zoom has no effect on the printed document.

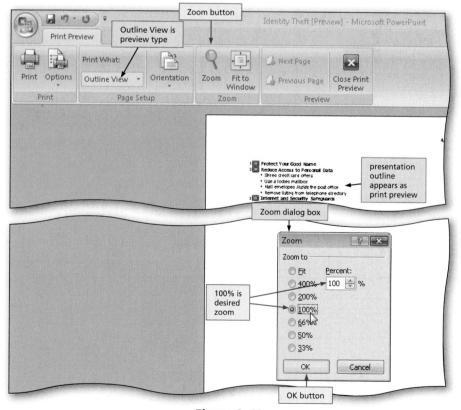

Figure 2–60

4

- Click the OK button in the Zoom dialog box to zoom the outline.

- Drag the scroll box on the vertical scroll bar up or down to move through the outline text (Figure 2–61).

Q&A

If I do not want to print my outline now, can I cancel this print request?

Yes. Click the Close Print Preview button in the Print Preview window to return to Normal view.

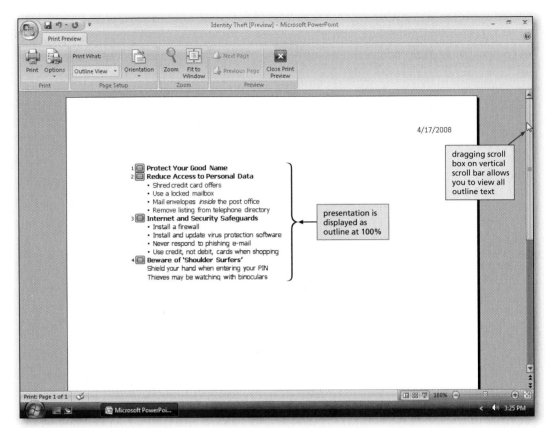

Figure 2–61

5

- Click the Print button in the Print group on the Print Preview tab to display the Print dialog box (Figure 2–62).

Q&A

What if my Print dialog box displays a different printer name?

It is likely a different printer name will display. Just ensure that the printer listed is the correct device you want to use to print your outline.

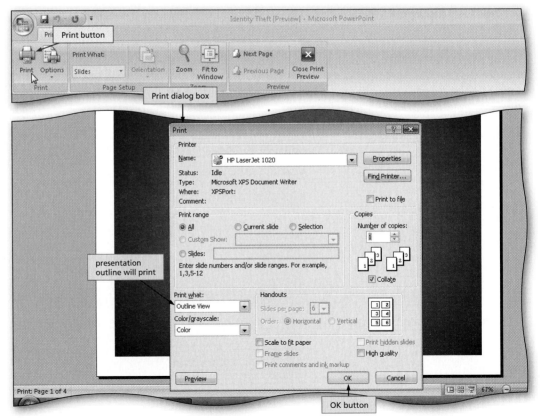

Figure 2–62

6
- Click the OK button to print the outline (Figure 2–63).

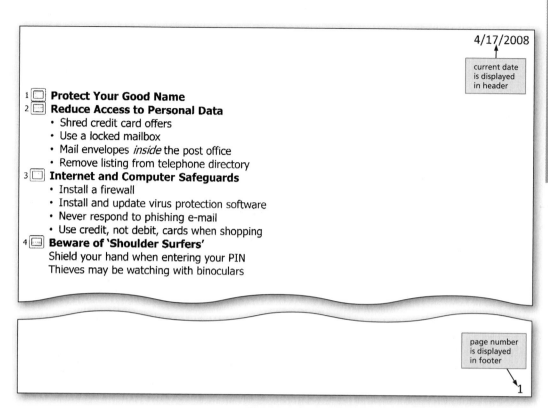

Figure 2–63

To Preview and Print Handouts

Printing handouts is useful for reviewing a presentation because you can analyze several slides displayed simultaneously on one page. Additionally, many businesses distribute handouts of the slide show before a presentation so the attendees can refer to a copy.

The default slide print order is Horizontal so that Slides 1 and 2, and 3 and 4 are adjacent to each other. You can change this order to Vertical, which shows Slides 1 and 4, and 2 and 3 adjacent to each other, by clicking Options in the Print group on the Print Preview tab and then changing the printing order.

The following steps preview and print presentation handouts.

1 Click the Print What box arrow in the Page Setup group.

2 Click Handouts (4 Slides Per Page) in the Print What list. Drag the scroll box on the vertical scroll bar up or down to move through the page.

3 Click the Print button in the Print group.

4 Click the OK button in the Print dialog box to print the handout (Figure 2–64).

5 Click the Close Print Preview button in the Preview group on the Print Preview tab to return to Normal view.

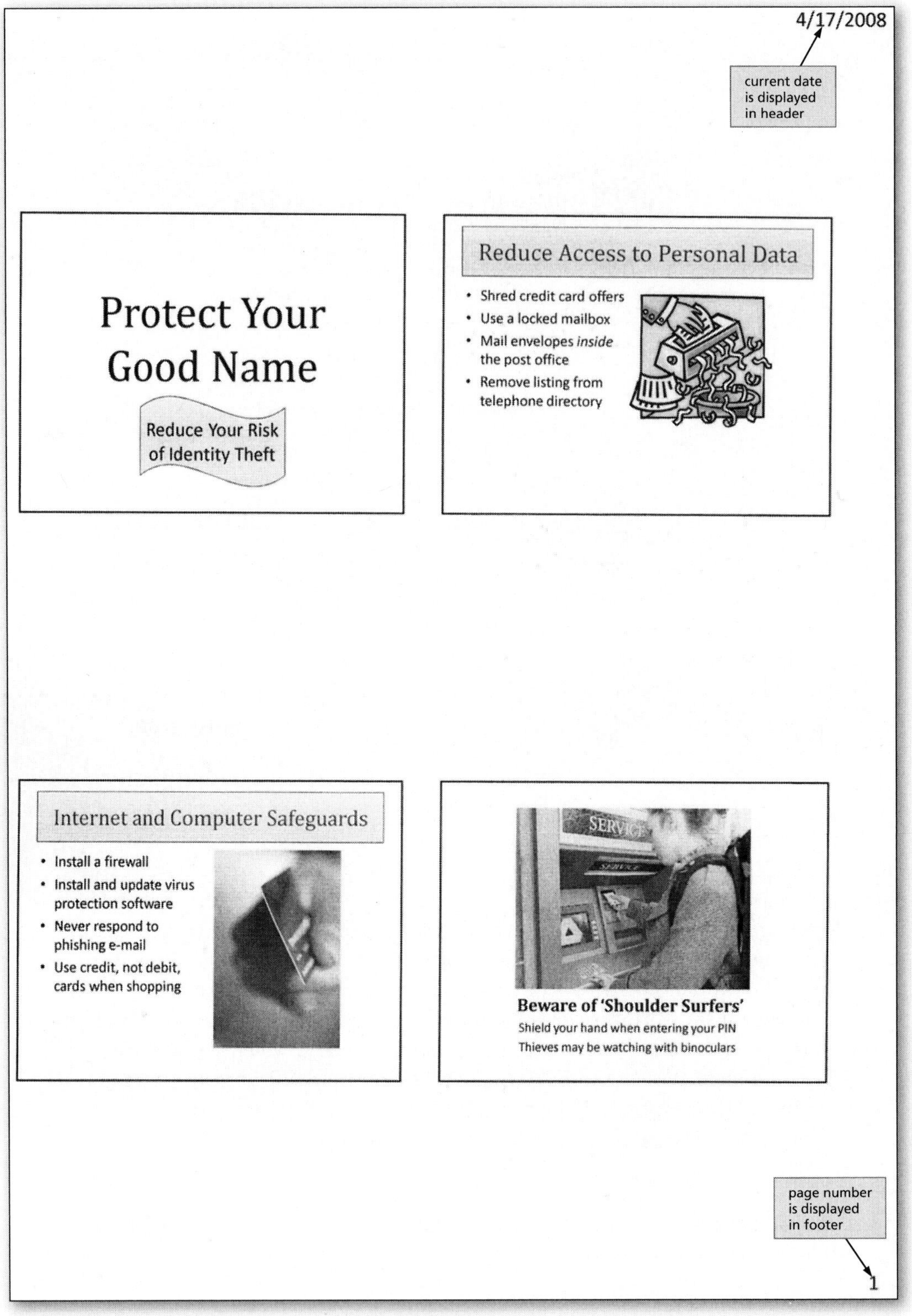

Figure 2–64

Saving and Quitting PowerPoint

If you made any changes to your presentation since your last save, you should save it again before quitting PowerPoint. The following steps save changes to the presentation and quit PowerPoint.

To Quit PowerPoint

This project is complete. The following steps quit PowerPoint.

1 Click the Office Button and then click the Exit PowerPoint button.

2 If necessary, click the Yes button in the Microsoft Office PowerPoint dialog box so that any changes you have made are saved.

Chapter Summary

In this chapter you have learned how to create slides from a blank presentation, change slide layouts, add a background style, insert clip art and pictures, size graphic elements, apply Quick Styles, select slide transitions, and preview and print an outline and handout. The items listed below include all the new PowerPoint skills you have learned in this chapter.

1. Choose a Background Style (PPT 89)
2. Change the View to Slide Sorter View (PPT 91)
3. Change the View to Normal View (PPT 91)
4. Change the Slide Layout to Two Content (PPT 92)
5. Change the Slide Layout to Picture with Caption (PPT 94)
6. Insert a Clip from the Clip Organizer into a Content Placeholder (PPT 96)
7. Insert a Photograph from the Clip Organizer into a Slide (PPT 98)
8. Insert a Photograph from a File into a Slide (PPT 99)
9. Resize Clip Art (PPT 100)
10. Resize a Photograph (PPT 103)
11. Delete a Placeholder (PPT 104)
12. Move Clips (PPT 105)
13. Format Title Text Using Quick Styles (PPT 106)
14. Format Remaining Title Text Using Quick Styles (PPT 107)
15. Change the Heading Font (PPT 109)
16. Shadow Text (PPT 110)
17. Change Font Color (PPT 110)
18. Format Text Using the Format Painter (PPT 112)
19. Format Remaining Title Text (PPT 113)
20. Add a Shape (PPT 116)
21. Resize a Shape (PPT 117)
22. Add Text to a Shape (PPT 119)
23. Format Shape Text and Add a Shape Quick Style (PPT 119)
24. Add a Transition between Slides (PPT 122)
25. Preview and Print an Outline (PPT 122)
26. Preview and Print Handouts (PPT 129)

 If you have a SAM user profile, you may have access to hands-on instruction, practice, and assessment. Log in to your SAM account (http://sam2007.course.com) to launch any assigned training activities or exams that relate to the skills covered in this chapter.

Learn It Online

Test your knowledge of chapter content and key terms.

Instructions: To complete the Learn It Online exercises, start your browser, click the Address bar, and then enter the Web address `scsite.com/ppt2007/learn`. When the Office 2007 Learn It Online page is displayed, click the link for the exercise you want to complete and then read the instructions.

Chapter Reinforcement TF, MC, and SA
A series of true/false, multiple choice, and short answer questions that test your knowledge of the chapter content.

Flash Cards
An interactive learning environment where you identify chapter key terms associated with displayed definitions.

Practice Test
A series of multiple choice questions that test your knowledge of chapter content and key terms.

Who Wants To Be a Computer Genius?
An interactive game that challenges your knowledge of chapter content in the style of a television quiz show.

Wheel of Terms
An interactive game that challenges your knowledge of chapter key terms in the style of the television show *Wheel of Fortune*.

Crossword Puzzle Challenge
A crossword puzzle that challenges your knowledge of key terms presented in the chapter.

Apply Your Knowledge

Reinforce the skills and apply the concepts you learned in this chapter.

Changing the Background and Adding Photographs and a Quick Style
Instructions: Start PowerPoint. Open the presentation, Apply 2-1 Lifestyle, from the Data Files for Students. See the inside back cover of this book for instructions on downloading the Data Files for Students, or contact your instructor for more information about accessing the required files.

The four slides in the presentation present basic guidelines for maintaining a healthy lifestyle and focus on proper weight, exercise, and food choices. The document you open is an unformatted presentation. You are to add and size photographs, change the background style, change slide layouts, apply a transition, and use the Format Painter so the slides look like Figure 2-65.

Perform the following tasks:
1. Change the background style to Style 11 (row 3, column 3). On the title slide, use your name in place of Student Name and bold and italicize your name and change the font color to orange. Increase the title text font size to 72 point, change the font to Baskerville Old Face, and change the font color to Dark Blue.
2. On Slides 2 and 4, change the layout to Two Content and then insert the photographs shown in Figure 2-65b and 2-65d from the Microsoft Clip Organizer.
3. On Slide 3, change the layout to Picture with Caption and then insert the picture shown in Figure 2-65c from the Microsoft Clip Organizer. Delete the text placeholder. Change the title text font size to 44 point, center this text, and then add the italic font style and shadow effect. Use the Format Painter to format the title text on Slides 2 and 4.
4. Apply the Subtle Effect – Accent 1 Quick Style (row 4, column 2) to the Slides 2, 3, and 4 title text placeholders. Apply the Uncover Left wipe transition (row 2, column 1) to all slides.

5. Check the spelling, and then display the revised presentation in Slide Sorter view.

6. Change the document properties, as specified by your instructor. Save the presentation using the file name, Apply 2–1 Healthy Lifestyle. Submit the revised document in the format specified by your instructor.

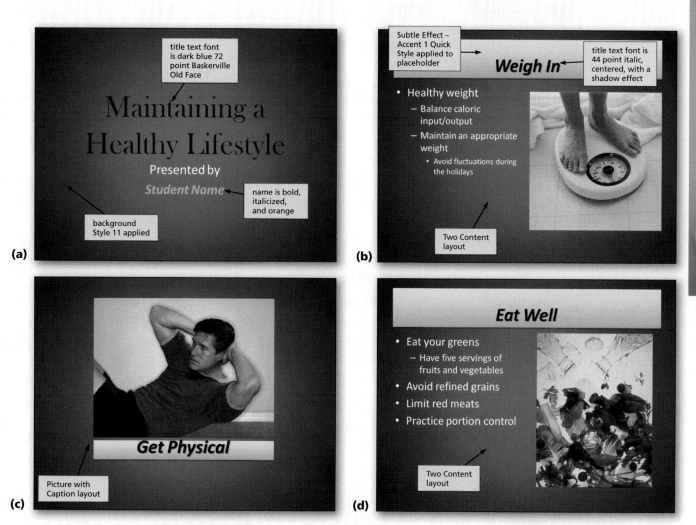

Figure 2–65

Extend Your Knowledge

Extend the skills you learned in this chapter and experiment with new skills. You may need to use Help to complete the assignment.

Changing Slide Layouts and Moving Clips

Instructions: Start PowerPoint. Open the presentation, Extend 2-1 Fats, from the Data Files for Students. See the inside back cover of this book for instructions on downloading the Data Files for Students, or contact your instructor for more information on accessing the required files.

You will choose a background, format slides, and copy clips (Figure 2–66).

Perform the following tasks:

1. Add an appropriate background style.

2. On Slide 1, use your name in place of Student Name. Format the text using techniques you learned and applied in this chapter, such as changing the font size and color and also bolding and italicizing words.

3. Slide 7 contains a variety of clips downloaded from the Microsoft Clip Organizer. Review the slides in the presentation and then move clips from Slide 7 to the appropriate slides. You do not need to use all the clips. Delete Slide 7 when you have finished moving the desired clips to the slides.

4. Change the slide layouts to accommodate the clips. Size the clips when necessary. Edit the text so that each slide meets the 7 × 7 rule, which states that each line should have a maximum of seven words, and each slide should have a maximum of seven lines.

5. Apply an appropriate transition to all slides.

6. Change the document properties, as specified by your instructor. Save the presentation using the file name, Extend 2-1 Enhanced Fats.

7. Submit the revised document in the format specified by your instructor.

variety of clips to consider moving to previous slides in presentation

Figure 2–66

Make It Right

Analyze a presentation and correct all errors and/or improve the design.

Applying Background and Quick Styles

Instructions: Start PowerPoint. Open the presentation, Make It Right 2-1 Safety, from the Data Files for Students. See the back inside cover of this book for instructions on downloading the Data Files for Students, or contact your instructor for more information on accessing the required files.

Correct the formatting problems and errors in the presentation while keeping in mind the guidelines presented in this chapter.

Perform the following tasks:

1. Change the document theme from Verve, shown in Figure 2–67, to Paper. Apply the Style 7 background style (row 2, column 3).

2. On Slide 1, replace the words, Student Name, with your name. Apply a Quick Style to your name and the title text so that they display prominently on the slide.

3. Move Slide 2 to the end of the presentation so that it becomes the new Slide 5.

4. Use the spell checker to correct the misspellings. Analyze the slides for other word usage errors that the spell checker did not find.

5. Adjust the clip art sizes so they do not overlap text and are the appropriate dimensions for the slide content.

6. Select a Quick Style to apply to the Slides 2 through 5 title text. Center the title text and apply a shadow.

7. Apply an appropriate transition to all slides. Change the speed to Slow.

8. Change the document properties, as specified by your instructor. Save the presentation using the file name, Make It Right 2-1 Home Safety.

9. Submit the revised document in the format specified by your instructor.

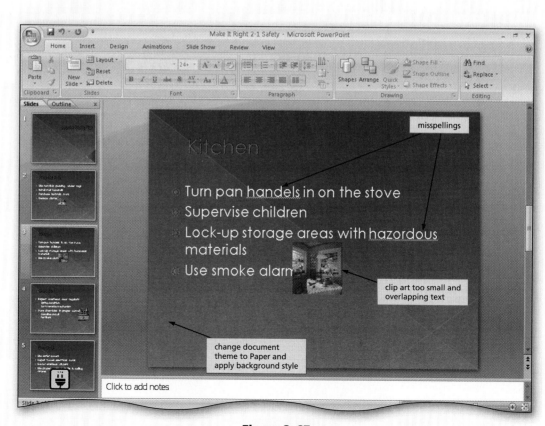

Figure 2–67

In the Lab

Design and/or create a presentation using the guidelines, concepts, and skills presented in this chapter. Labs 1, 2, and 3 are listed in order of increasing difficulty.

Lab 1: Creating a Presentation with a Clip and Shapes

Problem: The ear affects balance while it enables us to hear. This organ can be divided into three parts for analysis: outer, middle, and inner. The outer ear is composed of a flap and the auditory canal. The middle ear has three tiny bones called the auditory ossicles and the eustachian tube, which links the ear to the nose. The inner ear contains the spiral-shaped cochlea and also the semicircular canals and the vestibule, which control balance. You are studying the ear as a unit in your health class, so you decide to develop a PowerPoint slide that names these parts to help you study for a quiz. Create the slide shown in Figure 2–68 from a blank presentation.

Instructions: Perform the following tasks.

1. Apply the Style 6 background style (row 2, column 2) to the slide. Change the layout to Content with Caption. Import the ear diagram clip from the Microsoft Clip Organizer.

2. Type the slide title and caption body text shown in Figure 2–68. Use your name in place of Bill Tracy, and then italicize this text and change the font color to Blue (color 8 in the Standard Colors row). Change the color of the title text to Dark Red (color 1 in the Standard Colors row) and increase the font size to 24.

3. Use the Right Arrow, Left Arrow, Up Arrow, and Down Arrow shapes in the Block Arrow section to point to the parts of the ear shown in Figure 2–68. Add the number to each arrow. Apply the Subtle Effect – Accent 3 Quick Style (row 4, column 4) to each arrow. Change the font size of each arrow text to 24 point and bold these numbers.

4. Check the spelling and correct any errors.

5. Change the document properties, as specified by your instructor. Save the presentation using the file name, Lab 2-1 Ear.

6. Submit the revised document in the format specified by your instructor.

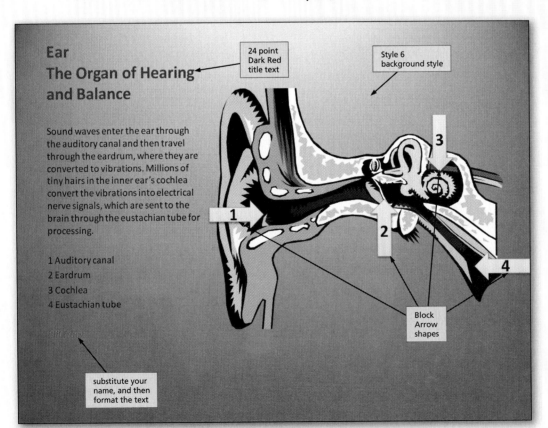

Figure 2–68

In the Lab

Lab 2: Creating a Presentation with Photographs Inserted from a File

Problem: Destructive insects damage specific species of trees throughout the world. You have learned in your Botany 202 class that the Asian Longhorn Beetle, the Emerald Ash Borer, the Gypsy Moth, and the Western Pine Beetle are among trees' biggest pests. One of your assignments in your botany class is to give a speech about common tree pests. You develop the outline shown in Figure 2–69 and then prepare the PowerPoint presentation shown in Figures 2–70a through 2–70f. You have obtained permission from the U.S. Forestry Department to copy photographs from its Web site to your slide show; these photographs are on your Data Files for Students.

Tree Pests
Creatures That Bug Our Trees
Jim DeYoung
Botany 202

Asian Longhorn Beetle
- Native to China
- Transported to United States in infested packing material

Emerald Ash Borer
- Killed 20 million trees in Michigan, Ohio, and Indiana
- Firewood quarantines to prevent new infestations

Gypsy Moth
- Spread to U.S. in 1870
- Oaks and Aspens are most common hosts
- Larva defoliate trees
- Small mammals and birds are predators

Western Pine Beetle
- Infest Ponderosa and Coulter pine trees
  - Mainly Western states
- Tree loss considered normal ecological process

Acknowledgements
- Photos and information courtesy of the USDA Forest Service
  - forestry.about.com

Figure 2–69

Continued >

In the Lab *continued*

Instructions: Perform the following tasks.

1. Create a new presentation using the Foundry document theme. Apply the Style 7 background style (row 2, column 3).

2. Using the typed notes illustrated in Figure 2–69, create the title slide shown in Figure 2–70a using your name in place of Jim DeYoung. Bold your name and apply a shadow.

3. Insert the Isosceles Triangle shape (row 1, column 3 in the Basic Shapes category) in the top center of Slide 1. Size the shape so that the top and bottom align with the edges of the brown area of the slide, as shown in Figure 2–70a.

4. Using the typed notes in Figure 2–69, create the five text slides with bulleted lists shown in Figures 2–70b through 2–70f. Use the Two Content slide layout for Slides 2 through 5 and the Title and Content slide layout for Slide 6.

5. Insert the appropriate pictures from your Data Files for Students on Slides 2 through 5.

6. Apply the Wedge transition (row 1, column 5 in the Wipes category) to all slides. Change the speed to Medium. Check the spelling and correct any errors.

7. Review the slides in Slide Sorter view to check for consistency, and then change the view to Normal.

8. Drag the scroll box to display Slide 1. Click the Slide Show button to start Slide Show view. Then click to display each slide.

9. Change the document properties, as specified by your instructor. Save the presentation using the file name, Lab 2-2 Tree Pests.

10. Submit the document in the format specified by your instructor.

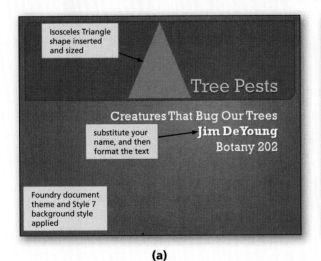

(a)

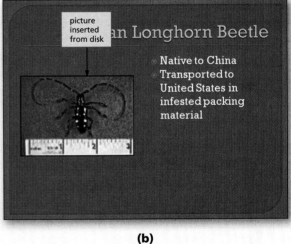

(b)

Figure 2–70

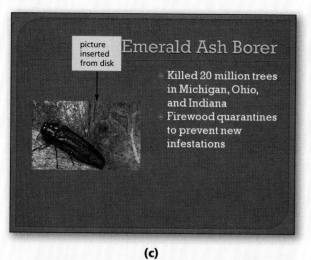

(c)

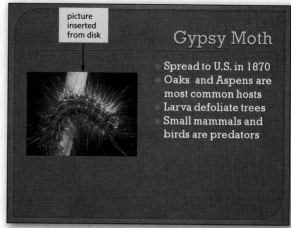

(d)

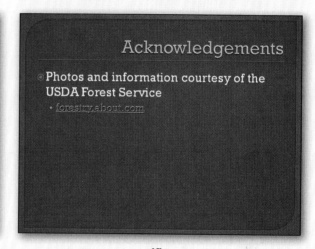

(e)

(f)

Figure 2–70

In the Lab

Lab 3: Creating a Presentation with Clips and Shapes

Problem: Snowboarding's popularity has soared in recent years; even Cameron Diaz and Space Shuttle astronauts have a passion for the sport. But with this increase in snowboarders has come a corresponding increase in injuries. The most common injuries are caused by a failure to follow common sense precautions. In order to maximize the time on the slopes, snowboarders need to prepare for the sport by wearing proper equipment, getting into condition, and snowboarding under control. Bryan Howell owns a local ski and snowboard shop in your town and has asked you to prepare a PowerPoint presentation that he can share with equipment buyers and renters. He hands you the outline shown in Figure 2–71 and asks you to create the presentation shown in Figures 2–72a through 2–72d.

Prepare for Snowboarding Season
  Vertical Slope Shop
  Bryan Howell, Owner

Dress for the Ride
- Loose fitting layers
  - Moisture wicking inner
  - Insulating middle
  - Waterproof outer shell
- Goggles
- Helmet, wrist guards

Get into Condition
- Stretch for 10 minutes
  - Do lateral squats, hops
- Eat complex carbohydrates
- Drink plenty of water
  - Dehydration is common

Snowboard under Control
- Be aware of traffic
  - Where trails merge
- Stick to slopes designed for your ability
- Be aware of changing conditions

Figure 2–71

Instructions: Perform the following tasks.

1. Use the typed notes illustrated in Figure 2–71 to create four slides shown in Figures 2–72a through 2–72d from a blank presentation. Apply the Style 7 background style (row 2, column 3). Use your name in place of Bryan Howell on the title slide shown in Figure 2–72a. Bold your name.

2. Insert the Right Triangle shape (row 1, column 4 in the Basic Shapes category) on Slide 1. With the shape selected, click the Arrange button in the Drawing group on the Home tab, point to Rotate in the Position Objects group, and then click Flip Horizontal to turn the triangle shape. Drag the shape to the lower-right corner of the slide, increase the size to that shown in Figure 2–72a, and apply the Colored Outline - Accent 3 Quick Style (row 1, column 4).

3. Italicize the Slide 1 title text, Prepare for Snowboarding Season, align the text left, and change the font color to Black. Align the subtitle text left and change the font color to Green (color 6 in the Standard Colors row).

4. Add the photographs and clip art shown in Figures 2–72a through 2–72d from the Microsoft Clip Organizer. Adjust the clip sizes when necessary.

5. Change the Slide 2 title text font size to 54 point, change the font to Forte, and then change the color to Green. Use the Format Painter to format the title text on Slides 3 and 4 with the same features as on Slide 2.

6. Apply the Newsflash transition (row 6, column 2 in the Wipes category) to all slides. Change the speed to Medium. Check the spelling and correct any errors.

7. Click the Slide Sorter button, view the slides for consistency, and then click the Normal button.

8. Change the document properties, as specified by your instructor. Save the presentation using the file name, Lab 2-3 Snowboarding.

9. Submit the revised document in the format specified by your instructor.

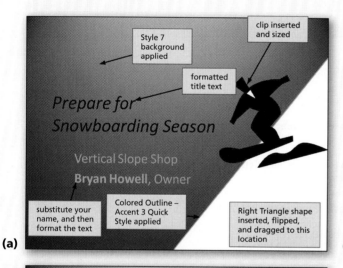

(a)

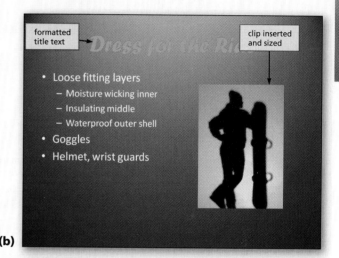

(b)

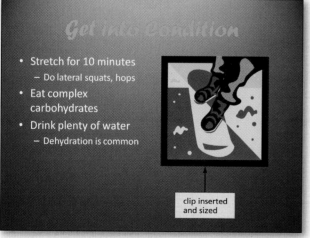

(c)

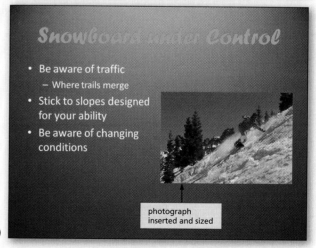

(d)

Figure 2–72

Cases and Places

Apply your creative thinking and problem solving skills to design and implement a solution.

• EASIER   •• MORE DIFFICULT

Note: Remember to use the 7×7 rule as you design the presentations: a maximum of seven words on a line and a maximum of seven lines on one slide.

• 1: Design and Create an Energy Efficiency Presentation

Global demand, industry deregulation, and regional conflicts have increased energy prices. The United States Department of Energy predicts energy use will grow 33 percent by 2030. Despite these staggering numbers, homeowners can undertake relatively simple measures to be energy efficient. Create a presentation using the outline in Figure 2–73. Apply at least three objectives found at the beginning of this chapter to develop the presentation. Add a title slide with a shape and a closing slide that cites your references. Be sure to check spelling.

Home Energy Savings Tips

Save Money While You Help the Environment

Bright Ideas
- Lighting accounts for more than 10 percent of electric bill
- Change to compact florescent lights (CFLs)
    - Use 50-75 percent less energy
    - Last up to ten times longer than conventional bulbs

Keep It Clean
- Wash only *full* loads of clothes and dishes
- Keep dryer vents clean
- Air dry dishes when possible
- Use ENERGY STAR products

Stay Out of Hot Water
- Heating water accounts for 13 percent of energy bill
- Use low-flow fixtures
- Repair leaks
- Lower thermostat
- Insulate heater

References
- www1.eere.energy.gov/consumer/tips/save_energy.html
- www.exeloncorp.com/comedcare/
- www.energystar.gov/\

Figure 2–73

• 2: Design and Create a Hypertension Presentation

According to the National Heart, Lung, and Blood Institute, nearly one-third of American adults are inflicted by the "silent killer," high blood pressure. This disease affects people of all ages and ethnicities. Use the concepts and techniques presented in this chapter to create a presentation following the outline in Figure 2–74, which includes the definition of hypertension and hypertension categories, has tips on controlling high blood pressure, and lists Web sites to view for further information. Insert photographs and clips, and apply a subtle slide transition to all slides. Be sure to check spelling.

Blood Pressure 101
Taking Control of the Silent Killer

Blood Pressure Definition
- Force of blood on vein walls
    - Pressure units: milligrams of mercury (mgHg)
- Defined by two numbers
    - Systolic: Pressure during beats
    - Diastolic: Pressure between beats
- Read as the systolic over diastolic level
    - Example: 125 over 74

Adult Blood Pressure Categories
- Normal
    - Systolic < 120
    - Diastolic < 80
- Prehypertension
    - Systolic 120 – 139
    - Diastolic 80 – 89
- Hypertension
    - Systolic > 140
    - Diastolic > 90

Detection
- No symptoms
- Person must be tested
    - Sphygmomanometer and stethoscope used

Hypertension Prevention Tips
- Eat healthy
    - Fruits, vegetables
    - Low fat diet
- Maintain weight
- Exercise regularly

References
- National Heart, Lung, and Blood Institute
    - www.nhlbi.nih.gov
- American Heart Association
    - www.americanheart.org/presenter.jhtml

Figure 2–74

Continued >

Cases and Places *continued*

•• 3: Design and Create a Portable Media Player Presentation

Video tape recorders were immensely popular more than three decades ago with several competing standards introduced in the market. Each technology touted different features. Today, the situation is similar with portable media players and cellular telephones that can download music from the Internet or rip files from your computer. Your supervisor at NextPhase Electronics recognizes buyers need assistance learning about these devices. She has asked you to prepare a presentation summarizing one of these players for next month's Saturday Seminar Series at the store. Research a specific portable media player and create a slide for each of the following attributes: featured model, user interface, and finding and loading songs. Select art and photographs from the Microsoft Clip Organizer, and add a title slide and summary slide to complete your presentation. Format the title slide with a shape and the text with colors and bolding where needed for emphasis.

•• 4: Design and Create a Campus Orientation Presentation

Make It Personal

Feedback from new students at your school cites difficulties navigating your campus. Incoming students mention the library, registrar, and health services as locations most often sought. To address these concerns, you volunteered as a member of the New Student Orientation Team to create a presentation and distribute a handout showing frequently accessed areas of the school. Use the concepts and techniques presented in this chapter to develop and format a slide show with a title slide and at least three text slides with bulleted lists. Create a slide for each landmark that briefly describes its location, and use clips and text to annotate it. Obtain a map of your campus and import it as a picture into your presentation. Select slide layouts that permit both the map and a bulleted list to appear on each slide. Use the arrow shapes to indicate the location of the landmark on the map. Add a background style and slide transitions. Be sure to check spelling. Print a handout with two slides on each page to distribute to new students on campus.

•• 5: Design and Create a Wellness Program Presentation

Working Together

Health care costs continue to rise at nearly double the inflation rate. Many health insurance companies are becoming proactive in containing those costs by offering reimbursement for wellness programs. Have each member of your team visit, telephone, or view Web sites of three health insurance companies. Gather information about:

1) Health screenings

2) Fitness center amenities

3) Self-Improvement classes

4) Wellness program benefits

After coordinating the data, create a presentation with a least one slide showcasing each topic. As a group, critique each slide. Submit your assignment in the format specified by your instructor.

Web Feature
Creating Web Pages Using PowerPoint

Objectives

You will have mastered the material in this Web feature when you can:

- Preview and save a presentation as a Web page
- Customize the Quick Access Toolbar
- Display Web pages created in PowerPoint in a browser
- Complete file management tasks within PowerPoint

Web Feature Introduction

The graphic design power of PowerPoint allows you to create vibrant presentations that convey information in a clear, interesting manner. Some of these presentations are created for small, specific audiences, such as student club members planning a fundraising activity. In this case, the presentation may be shown in an office. Other presentations are designed for large, general audiences, such as potential students planning a campus visit. These students can view the presentation on their school's **intranet**, which is an internal network that uses Internet technologies. On a grand scale, you can inform the entire world about the contents of your presentation by posting your slide show to the World Wide Web.

Planning Web Pages
If your slide show will be shown only as a Web page, you can use smaller font sizes than you generally would use in slides designed to accompany a lecture. Also, attempt to minimize the number of graphic elements on your slides so the pages load quickly. Audience members viewing your PowerPoint presentation using a browser generally prefer light colors for slide backgrounds and dark colors for fonts.

Project — Web Page

Figure 1a shows the presentation describing yoga fundamentals in Slide Sorter view. The Fitness Center director at your school requests that the information in the slide be made available on the school's intranet for employees and student workers to view. In order to accomplish this task, you must save the presentation as a Web page.

You can save a presentation, or a portion of a presentation as a Web page. The saved **Web page** is a snapshot of the presentation. It is similar to a running slide show in that you can view it, but you cannot modify it. In the browser window, the presentation appears as it would in Microsoft PowerPoint, including a Next Slide button you can click to advance the slides. As illustrated in Figure 1, this Web feature shows you how to save a presentation (Figure 1a) as a Web page (Figures 1b through 1e) and view it using your browser.

PowerPoint allows you to **publish presentations**, which is the process of making existing presentations available to others on the World Wide Web or on a company's intranet, when you use the Save As command on the Office Button menu and choose to save a presentation as a Web page. If you have access to a Web server, you can publish Web pages by saving them on a Web server or on an FTP location. To learn more about publishing Web pages on a Web server or on an FTP location using Microsoft Office applications, refer to Appendix D.

This Web feature illustrates how to create and save the Web pages on a USB flash drive, rather than on a Web server. This feature also demonstrates how to preview a presentation as a Web page and create a new folder using the Save As dialog box.

Checking Your Web Page
Be certain to verify that your presentation displays correctly using a variety of Web browsers. Check it in current and previous versions of Internet Explorer, Mozilla Firefox, and Netscape Navigator, and also view it using the PC and Apple computers.

Overview

As you read through this feature, you will learn how to create the yoga Web pages shown in Figures 1b, 1c, 1d, and 1e by performing these general tasks:

- Preview and save PowerPoint presentations as Web pages.
- Add a button to the Quick Access Toolbar.
- Use Windows Explorer to view Web pages.

Using Web Page Preview and Saving a PowerPoint Presentation as a Web Page

At any time during the construction of a presentation, PowerPoint makes it easy to preview how it will display on an intranet or on the World Wide Web by using the Web Page Preview command. When you invoke the Web Page Preview command, it starts your browser and displays the active slide in the presentation as a Web page without saving files. By previewing your slide show, you can decide which features look good and which need modification. The left side of the window includes the navigation frame, which is the outline of the presentation. The outline contains a table of contents consisting of each slide's title text. You can click the Expand/Collapse Outline button below the navigation frame to view the complete slide text. The right side of the window shows the complete slide in the slide frame. The speaker notes, if present, are displayed in the notes frame below the slide frame. Once the preview is acceptable, you then can save the presentation as a Web page. The Web Page Preview command is not available on the Ribbon, but you can add the command to the Quick Access Toolbar.

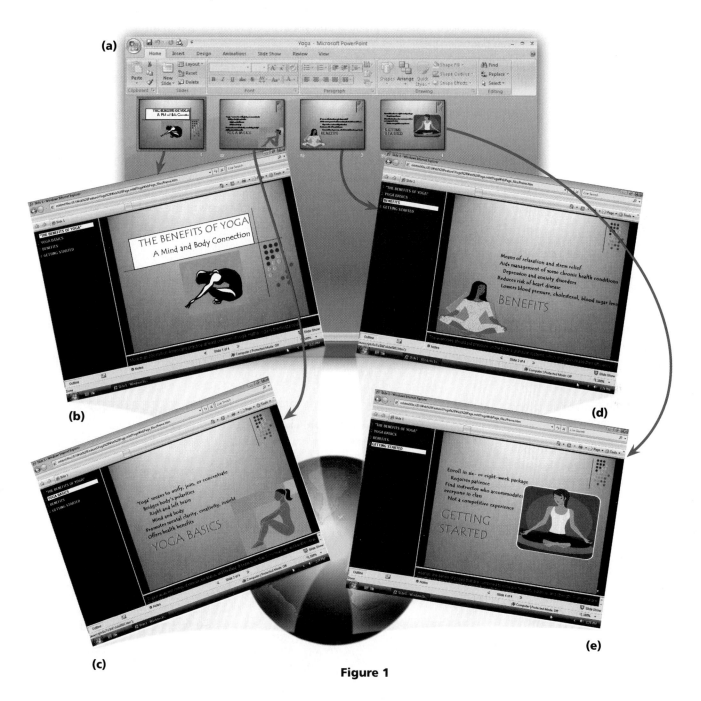

(a)

(b)

(c)

(d)

(e)

Figure 1

Plan
Ahead

General Project Guidelines

When creating the yoga Web pages, the actions you perform and decisions you make will affect the appearance and characteristics of the finished presentation. As you create Web pages, such as the project shown in Figure 1, you should follow these general guidelines:

1. **Develop an effective presentation.** Your slide show should provide essential information to a specific audience. Text should be succinct and meaningful. Graphics, such as illustrations, and color should add visual appeal and promote understanding. Ask someone else to view your presentation and give you suggestions for improvements.

2. **Preview and review the Web pages created from your PowerPoint presentation.** Preview the Web page to assess readability and visual interest. Be certain to test your finished Web page document in at least one browser program to check if it looks and works as you intended.

3. **Publish your Web page.** Once you have created a Web page, you can publish it, which makes it available to others on a network, such as the World Wide Web or a company's intranet. Many Internet service providers offer storage space on their Web servers at no cost to their subscribers. The procedures for using Microsoft Office to publish a Web page are discussed in Appendix D.

   This Web Feature focuses on the second guideline, identifying the actions you perform and the decisions you make during the creation of the Web pages shown in Figure 1. Chapters 1 and 2 presented details about how to accomplish the goals of the first guideline listed above, and Appendix D presents details about how to achieve the goals of the last guideline.

To Add a Button to the Quick Access Toolbar

Many commands available in PowerPoint are not included on any of the tabs on the Ribbon. You can, however, add such commands to the Quick Access Toolbar. One such command allows you to preview a document in a Web browser. This command, Web Page Preview, needs to be added to the Quick Access Toolbar so that the Web page can be previewed. The following steps add the Web Page Preview command to the Quick Access Toolbar.

- Connect a USB flash drive to one of the computer's USB ports.

- Start PowerPoint and then open the presentation, Yoga, from the Data Files for Students.

- Click the Customize Quick Access Toolbar button to display the Customize Quick Access Toolbar menu (Figure 2).

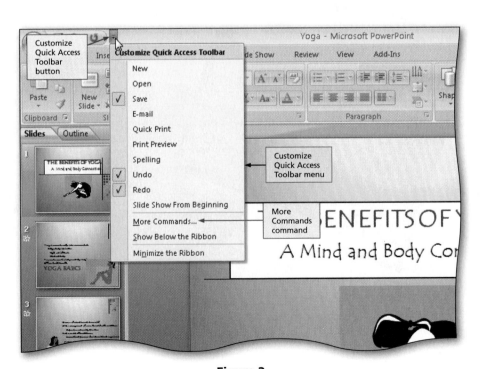

Figure 2

- Click the More Commands command on the Customize Quick Access Toolbar menu.

- When the PowerPoint Options dialog box is displayed, click the 'Choose commands from' box arrow to display the 'Choose commands from' list (Figure 3).

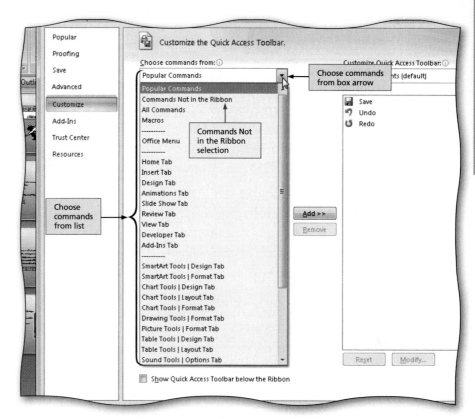

Figure 3

- Click Commands Not in the Ribbon in the 'Choose commands from' list to display a list of commands not in the Ribbon (Figure 4).

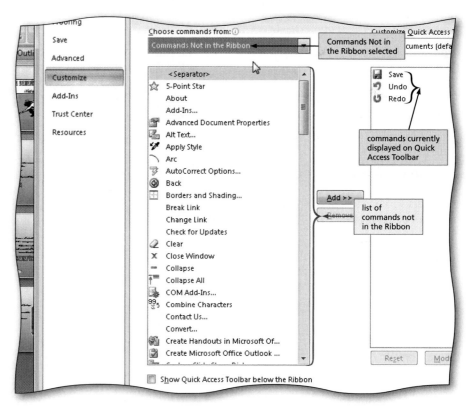

Figure 4

5

- Scroll to the bottom of the list, click Web Page Preview, and then click the Add button to add the button to the Quick Access Toolbar (Figure 5).

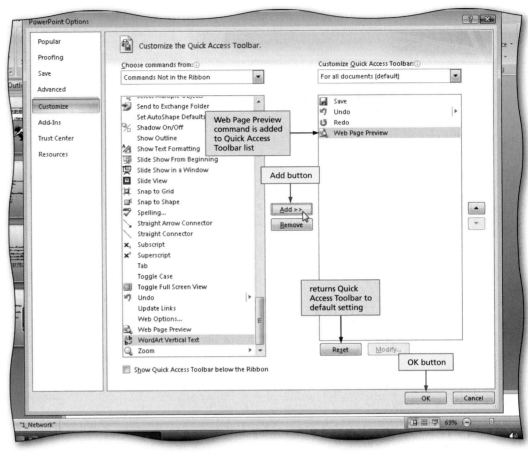

Figure 5

6

- Click the OK button to close the PowerPoint Options dialog box and display the Quick Access Toolbar with the Web Page Preview button added to it (Figure 6).

 Q&A

Will the Web Page Preview command be in the Quick Access Toolbar the next time I start PowerPoint?

Yes. When you change the Quick Access Toolbar, the changes remain even after you restart PowerPoint. If you share a computer with somebody else or if the Quick Access Toolbar becomes cluttered, PowerPoint allows you to remove commands from the Quick Access Toolbar. You will remove the Web Page Preview button from the Quick Access Toolbar later in this Web feature.

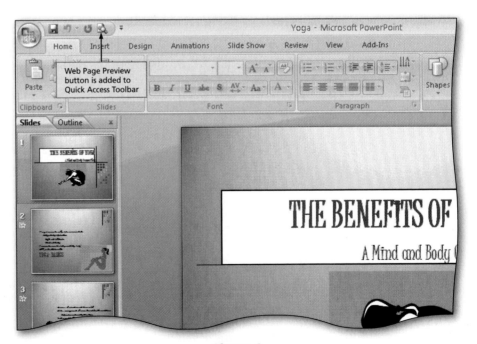

Figure 6

To Preview the Web Page

The following steps preview the presentation in a browser.

1

- Click the Web Page Preview button on the Quick Access Toolbar to display the Web page in your browser. If the Information Bar dialog box appears, click the Close button. If the security warning appears in the Information bar at the top of the Web page, click it and then click 'Allow Blocked Content' to run the ActiveX controls. If the Information Bar appears asking for an add-on from Microsoft, see your instructor.

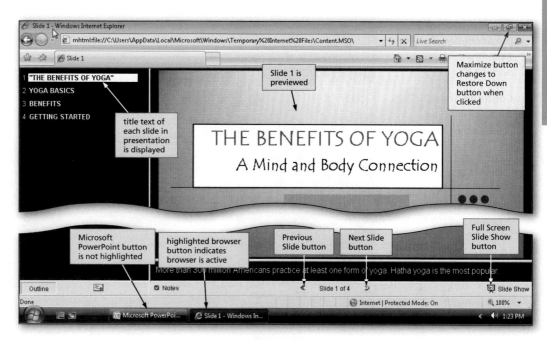

Figure 7

- If necessary, click the Maximize button on your browser's title bar (Figure 7).

Q&A What happens when I click the Web Page Preview button?

PowerPoint starts your browser and it displays a preview of how Slide 1 will appear as a Web page (Figure 7). The Web page preview is nearly identical to the display of the slide in PowerPoint.

2

- Click the Full Screen Slide Show button to have Slide 1 fill the entire screen (Figure 8).

Must I always view the full screen of each slide?

Q&A No. Viewing the slides in a full screen helps you review their style and spelling easily and allows you to see how the slides will be displayed when viewed in a browser.

Figure 8

3

- Press the SPACEBAR to display the Slide 2 title text. Continue pressing the SPACEBAR to view each line of Slide 2 body text.

- Continue pressing the SPACEBAR to view each slide in the presentation.

- When the black slide is displayed, press the SPACEBAR again to return to Web Page preview of Slide 1 in the browser window (Figure 9).

- Click the Close button on the right side of the browser title bar to close the browser and make PowerPoint active again.

Figure 9

BTW

Viewing Transitions
If slide transitions do not appear when you are previewing your Web Page, you should check your Web Options settings. To do this, click the Office Button, click the PowerPoint Options button, click Advanced, scroll down and then click the Web Options button in the PowerPoint Options dialog box, if necessary click the General tab in the Web Options dialog box, and then click Show slide animation while browsing if it is not selected already.

Web Page Format Options

Once the preview of the presentation as a Web page is acceptable, you can save the presentation as a Web page so that others can view it using a Web browser, such as Internet Explorer or Mozilla Firefox.

You can save the presentation in one of two Web page formats. Both formats convert the contents of the presentation into HTML (HyperText Markup Language), which is a language browsers can interpret. One format is called **Single File Web Page format,** which saves all of the components of the Web page in a single file with an .mht extension. This format is useful particularly for e-mailing presentations in HTML format. The second format, called **Web Page format,** saves the Web page in a file and some of its components in a folder. This format is useful if you need access to the components, such as illustrations, that comprise the Web page.

To Save a PowerPoint Presentation as a Web Page in a Newly Created Folder

Experienced users organize the files saved on a storage medium, such as a USB flash drive or hard disk, by creating folders. They then save related files in a common folder. PowerPoint allows you to create folders before saving a file using the Save As dialog box. The following steps create a new folder on the USB flash drive and then save the Yoga presentation as a Web page in the new folder.

• With the Yoga presentation open, click the Office Button.

• Click Save As on the Office Button menu to display the Save As dialog box (Figure 10).

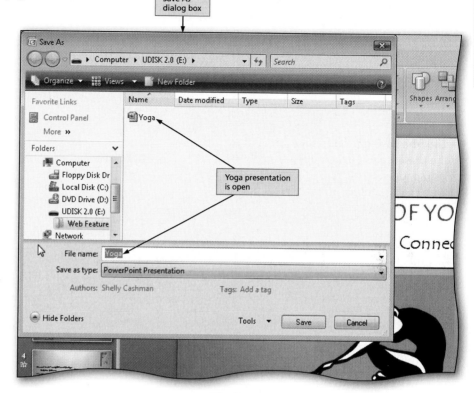

Figure 10

• Type Yoga Web Page in the File name text box.

• Click the 'Save as type' box arrow and then scroll down and click Single File Web Page.

• If the name of your USB flash drive does not appear in the Favorite Links section, click Computer in the Favorite Links section and then double-click UDISK 2.0 (E:) (your USB flash drive name and letter may be different).

• Click the New Folder button to create a new folder.

• When PowerPoint displays the new folder named New Folder, type Web Feature in the text box (Figure 11).

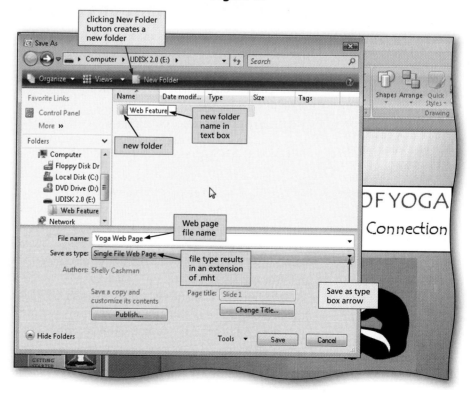

Figure 11

3
- Press the ENTER key. If the Microsoft Office PowerPoint dialog box appears, click the Yes button.

Q&A

What does PowerPoint do when I press the ENTER key?

PowerPoint automatically selects the new folder Web Feature in the Address bar. PowerPoint saves all slides in the presentation as Web pages.

4
- Click the Save button to save the presentation in a single file Web page in HTML format in the Web Feature folder on the USB flash drive (Figure 12).

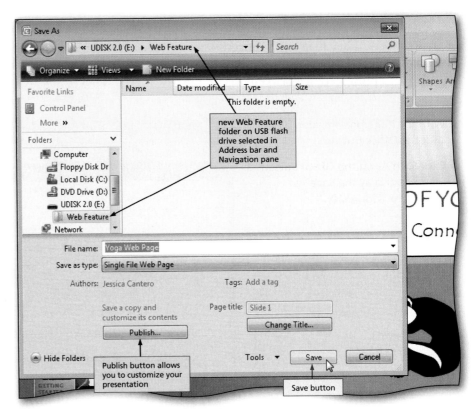

Figure 12

BTW

Certification
The Microsoft Certified Application Specialist (MCAS) program provides an opportunity for you to obtain a valuable industry credential – proof that you have the PowerPoint 2007 skills required by employers. For more information see Appendix G or visit the PowerPoint 2007 Certification Web page (scsite.com/ppt2007/cert).

Publishing Presentations as Web Pages

The Save As dialog box changes when you select Single File Web Page in the 'Save as type' box. When you use the Single File Web Page format, a Save area appears in the dialog box. Within the Save area is a Publish button (Figure 12). Some publishing options allow you to select particular slides for your presentation, display speaker notes, and select which browsers will support your presentation.

In the previous set of steps, the Save button was used to save the PowerPoint presentation as a Web page. The Publish button in the Save As dialog box shown in Figure 12 is an alternative to the Save button. It allows you to customize the Web page further.

If you have access to a Web server that allows you to save files in a Web folder, then you can save the Web page directly on the Web server by clicking the Network folder in the Save in bar of the Save As dialog box (Figure 12). If you have access to a Web server that allows you to save on an FTP site, then you can select the FTP site below FTP locations in the Save in box just as you select any folder on which to save a file. To learn more about publishing Web pages in a Web folder or on an FTP location using Office applications, refer to Appendix D.

After PowerPoint saves the presentation in Step 4, it displays the MHTML file – not the presentation – in the PowerPoint window. PowerPoint can continue to display the presentation in HTML format, because within the MHTML file that it created, it also saved the PowerPoint formats that allow it to display the MHTML file in PowerPoint. This is referred to as **round tripping** the MHTML file back to the application in which it was created.

To Reset the Quick Access Toolbar and Quit PowerPoint

Your work with the PowerPoint presentation is complete. The following steps remove the Web Page Preview button from the Quick Access Toolbar and quit PowerPoint.

1 Click the Customize the Quick Access Toolbar button on the Ribbon.

2 Click the More Commands command.

3 When the PowerPoint Options dialog box is displayed, click the Reset button. If the Reset Customizations dialog box is displayed, click the Yes button.

4 Click the OK button on the PowerPoint Options dialog box to close it.

5 Click the Close button on the Microsoft PowerPoint title bar.

Q&A Do I need to remove the button from the Quick Access Toolbar?

No. For consistency, the Quick Access Toolbar is reset after the added buttons are no longer needed. If you share a computer with others, you should reset the Quick Access Toolbar.

File Management Tools in PowerPoint

In the previous set of steps, PowerPoint automatically navigates to the new folder name in the Save in box when you press the ENTER key after typing the new folder name (Figure 12). It was not necessary to create a new folder earlier in this Web feature. You nevertheless could have saved the Web page on the USB flash drive in the same manner in which you saved files on the USB flash drive in the previous projects. Creating a new folder, however, allows you to organize your work.

Finally, once you create a folder, you can right-click it while the Save As dialog box is active and perform many file management tasks directly in PowerPoint (Figure 13). For example, once the shortcut menu appears, you can rename the selected folder, delete it, copy it, display its properties, and perform other file management functions.

BTW

Quick Reference
For a table that lists how to complete the tasks covered in this book using the mouse, Ribbon, shortcut menu, and keyboard, see the Quick Reference Summary at the back of this book, or visit the PowerPoint 2007 Quick Reference Web page (scsite.com/ppt2007/qr).

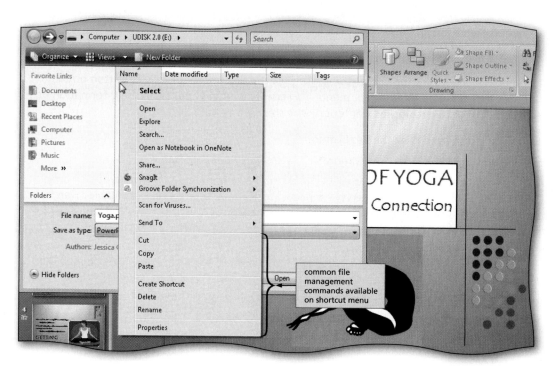

Figure 13

To View the Web Page Using a Browser

With the Web page saved in the Web Feature folder on the USB flash drive, you now can view it using a browser. If you want to display or hide the navigation frame, click the Show/Hide Outline button below the outline. Later, if you want to redisplay the navigation frame, click the Show/Hide Outline button again. Similarly, the Show/Hide Notes button below the slide frame allows you to display or conceal the speaker notes, if present, on a particular slide. To review a slide you have seen already, click the Previous Slide button. The following steps view the Yoga Web page using your browser.

- If necessary, connect the USB flash drive to one of the computer's USB ports.

- Click the Start button on the Windows Vista taskbar, click All Programs on the Start menu, and then click Internet Explorer on the All Programs list.

- When the Internet Explorer window appears, type `E:\Web Feature\ Yoga Web Page.mht` in the Address bar and then press the ENTER key to display the Web page in your browser (Figure 14). (Your USB flash drive may have a different name and letter).

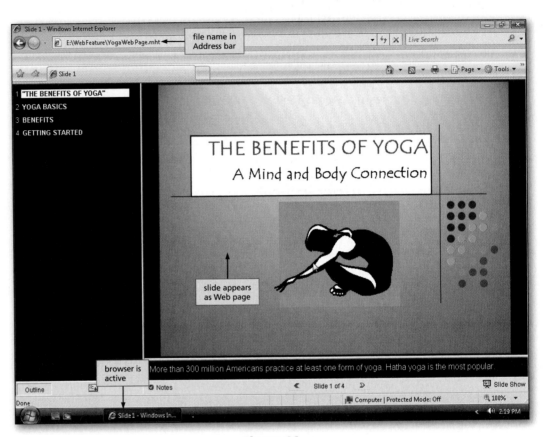

Figure 14

- If the Internet Explorer dialog box appears, click the OK button, right-click the first Internet Explorer button on the Windows Vista taskbar, and then click Close on the shortcut menu. If a security warning appears in the Information Bar, click it to view the options and then click Allow Blocked Content on the shortcut menu.

- If the Security Warning dialog box is displayed, click the Yes button.

Q&A | What are the benefits of using a browser to view a presentation?

You can see from Figures 14 and 15 that a Web page is an ideal way to distribute information to a large group of people. For example, the Web page could be published on a Web server connected to the Internet and made available to anyone with a computer, browser, and the address of the Web page. It also can be e-mailed easily, because the Web page resides in a single file, rather than in a file and folder. Publishing a Web page of a presentation, thus, is an excellent alternative to distributing printed copies of the presentation.

Q&A | Can I review a slide I have seen already?

Yes. Click the Previous Slide button.

2

- Click the Expand/Collapse Outline button at the bottom of the window to display the text of each slide in outline form in the navigation frame.

- Click the Next Slide button three times to view all four slides in your browser (Figure 15).

Q&A What if I want to display or hide the navigation and notes frames?

To hide the navigation frame, click the Show/Hide Outline button below the outline. Later, if you want to redisplay the navigation frame, click the Show/Hide Outline button again. Similarly, the Show/Hide Notes button below the slide frame allows you to display or conceal the speaker notes, if present, on a particular slide.

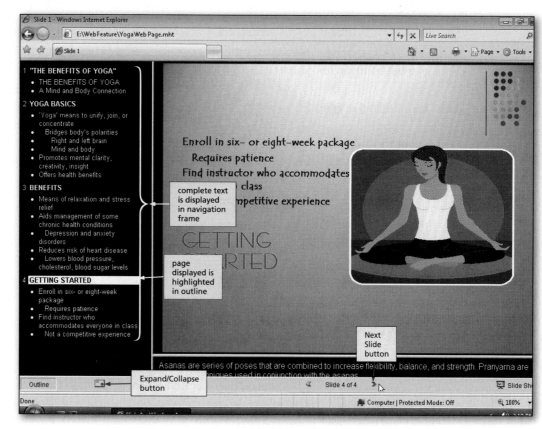

Figure 15

3

- Click the Close button on the right side of the browser title bar to close the browser.

Feature Summary

This Web feature introduced you to customizing the Quick Access Toolbar, previewing a presentation as a Web page, creating a new folder on a USB flash drive, and viewing a Web page. The items listed below include all the new Office 2007 skills you have learned in this Web feature.

1. Add a Button to the Quick Access Toolbar (PPT 148)
2. Preview the Web Page (PPT 151)
3. Save a PowerPoint Presentation as a Web Page in a Newly Created Folder (PPT 153)
4. Reset the Quick Access Toolbar and Quit Power Point (PPT 155)
5. View the Web Page Using a Browser (PPT 156)

If you have a SAM user profile, you may have access to hands-on instruction, practice, and assessment. Log in to your SAM account (http://sam2007.course.com) to launch any assigned training activities or exams that relate to the skills covered in this feature.

In the Lab

Create a Web page using the guidelines, concepts, and skills presented in this Web feature. Labs are listed in order of increasing difficulty.

Lab 1: Creating a Web Page from the A World Beneath the Waves Presentation

Problem: Dave Ehlin, the Student Government Association (SGA) president, wants to expand the visibility of the A World Beneath the Waves presentation you created in Chapter 1. He believes a Web page would be an excellent vehicle to help promote the spring break trip to Cabo San Lucas, Mexico and has asked you to help transfer the presentation to the Internet.

Instructions:

1. Open the Cabo Package presentation shown in Figure 1–1 on page PPT 5 that you created in Chapter 1. (If you did not create this presentation, see your instructor for a copy.)

2. Add the Web Page Preview command to the Quick Access Toolbar.

3. Review the five slides in the Cabo Package presentation, and then preview the presentation as a Web page. Close the browser.

4. Save the presentation as a single file Web page in a new folder titled Web Feature Exercises using the file name, Lab WF-1 Cabo Package Web Page. Reset the Quick Access Toolbar and then quit PowerPoint.

5. Start your browser. With the Web page located on the USB flash drive, type `E:\Web Feature Exercises\Lab WF-1 Cabo Package Web Page.mht` in the Address bar (your USB flash drive may have a different name and letter). When the browser displays the Web page, click the Expand/Collapse Outline button at the bottom of the window to display the text of each slide in outline form.

6. Click the Next Slide button at the bottom of the window to view the slides. Close the browser. Submit the assignment as requested by your instructor.

In the Lab

Lab 2: Creating and Printing a Web Page from the Identity Theft Presentation

Problem: The Identity Theft presentation you developed in Chapter 2 could provide useful information for consumers, so you want to save this presentation as a Web page and post it to the Internet.

Instructions:

1. Open the Identity Theft presentation shown in Figure 2–1 on page PPT 83 that you created in Chapter 2. (If you did not create this presentation, see your instructor for a copy.)

2. Add the Web Page Preview command to the Quick Access Toolbar.

3. Review the four slides in the Identity Theft presentation, and then preview the presentation as a Web page. Close the browser.

4. Save the presentation as a Web page (select Web Page in the Save as type box) in the Web Feature Exercises folder using the file name, Lab WF-2 Identity Theft Web Page. Reset the Quick Access Toolbar and then quit PowerPoint. Saving the presentation as a Web page, rather than a single file Web page, will result in an additional folder being added to the Web Feature Exercises folder.

5. Start your browser. With the Web page located on the USB flash drive, type
`E:\Web Feature Exercises\Lab WF-2 Identity Theft Web Page.mht` in the Address bar (your USB flash drive may have a different name and letter). When the browser displays the Web page, click the Next Slide button at the bottom of the window to view the slides.

6. Print the Web page by clicking the Print button on the Toolbar.

7. Close the browser. Submit the assignment as requested by your instructor.

Continued >

In the Lab

Lab 3: File Management within PowerPoint

Problem: One of your classmates has asked you to teach him how to perform basic file management tasks from within PowerPoint.

Instructions:

1. Start PowerPoint and then click the Open command on the Office Button menu. When PowerPoint displays the Open dialog box, create a new folder called In the Lab 3 on your USB flash drive.

2. Use the shortcut menu to complete the following tasks: (1) rename the In the Lab 3 folder to In the Lab 3A; (2) show the properties of the In the Lab 3A folder; and (3) delete the In the Lab 3A folder.

3 Creating a Presentation with Custom Backgrounds and SmartArt Diagrams

Objectives

You will have mastered the material in this chapter when you can:

- Create a presentation from a Microsoft Office Word 2007 outline

- Add a picture to create a custom background

- Add background graphics to slide masters

- Add slide numbers and the date to slide masters

- Apply a WordArt style

- Format WordArt

- Apply effects to pictures

- Insert and modify text boxes

- Apply effects to shapes

- Create a SmartArt graphic

- Use the Text pane to enter placeholder text

- Apply a SmartArt style to a graphic

3

Creating a Presentation with Custom Backgrounds and SmartArt Diagrams

Introduction

Today's audiences quickly become bored with basic graphics and single-level bulleted lists that are the starting point for most presentations. They often find slide shows visually unappealing and yearn for presentations filled with meaningful content. Currently, PowerPoint commands 95 percent of the presentations graphic software market, and with PowerPoint 2007, it is easy to develop impressive presentations by modifying slide backgrounds, creating diagrams, inserting and modifying tables, and developing new graphics.

Project — Presentation with Custom Backgrounds and SmartArt Diagrams

BTW

Copying SmartArt Graphics
The SmartArt feature is part of Microsoft Office Excel, Word, Outlook, and PowerPoint. You can create graphics in one of these programs and then copy and paste them into another Microsoft Office 2007 program.

The project in this chapter follows visual content guidelines and uses PowerPoint to create the presentation shown in Figure 3–1. This slide show, which discusses electives available in the science curriculum, has a variety of visual elements. This project introduces several techniques to make your presentations more exciting, including WordArt and SmartArt diagrams. A picture is inserted and then given a particular shape, border, and glow effect. The slide backgrounds consist of a picture on the title slide and a custom background on the remaining slides. The slide number and current date are added to the slide master.

Overview

As you read through this chapter, you will learn how to create the presentation shown in Figure 3–1 by performing these general tasks:

- Create a new presentation from an outline created in Microsoft Office Word 2007.
- Format slide master backgrounds.
- Format pictures by applying styles and effects.
- Insert and format SmartArt graphics.
- Change clip art elements.

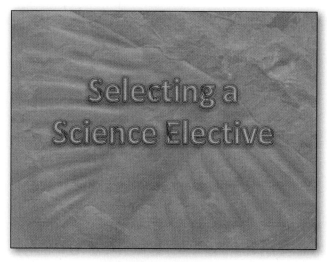

(a) Slide 1 (Title Slide)

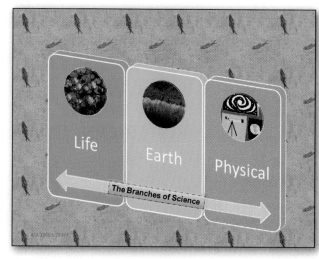

(b) Slide 2 (SmartArt Graphic and Text Box)

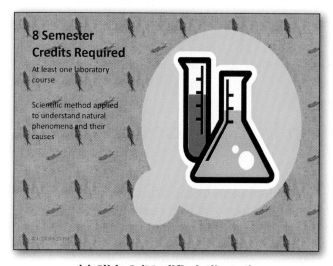

(c) Slide 3 (Modified Clip Art)

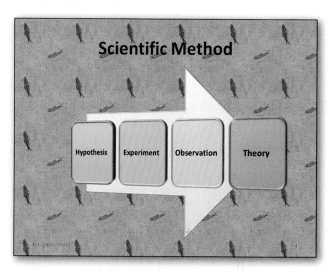

(d) Slide 4 (SmartArt Graphic)

Figure 3–1

General Project Guidelines

Plan
Ahead

When creating a PowerPoint presentation, the actions you perform and decisions you make will affect the appearance and characteristics of the finished document. As you create a presentation with WordArt and SmartArt, such as the project shown in Figure 3–1, you should follow these general guidelines:

1. **Use WordArt in moderation.** Used correctly, the graphical nature of WordArt can add interest and set a tone. Format text with a WordArt style only when needed for special emphasis.

2. **Choose an Appropriate SmartArt Layout.** SmartArt illustrations represent ideas and concepts graphically. Audiences can grasp these visual concepts and recall them more quickly and accurately than viewing text alone. Many SmartArt layouts are available, so select the one that best represents the concept you are attempting to present.

   • List

   • Process

   • Cycle

(continued)

<table>
<tr><td>

Plan
Ahead

</td><td>

(continued)

- Hierarchy

- Relationship

- Matrix

- Pyramid

3. **Consider the Verbal Message to Accompany Your Slides.** Slide shows generally accompany a speaker's presentation. They should assist the speaker by providing information presented more effectively visually rather than verbally. As you develop your slides, plan a script for the speaker.

4. **Be Certain You Have Permission to Modify Clips.** Some graphics are protected by trademarks and service marks, so they cannot be modified without permission.

5. **Use Left-Brain / Right-Brain Content Concepts.** Your brain's left hemisphere processes analytical information, such as a mathematical equation or chemical formula. Your brain's right hemisphere, in contrast, responds to sensory information, such as images and music. Construct your PowerPoint slides so the message appeals to the appropriate side of the brain.

   When necessary, more specific details concerning the above guidelines are presented at appropriate points in the chapter. The chapter also will identify the actions you perform and decisions you made regarding these guidelines during the creation of the presentation shown in Figure 3–1.

</td></tr>
</table>

BTW

Defining Outline Levels
Imported outlines can contain up to nine outline levels, whereas PowerPoint outlines are limited to six levels (one for the title text and five for body paragraph text). When you import an outline, all text in outline levels six through nine is treated as a fifth-level paragraph.

Note: If you are using Windows XP, see Appendix F for alternate steps.

Creating a Presentation from a Microsoft Office Word 2007 Outline

Many writers begin composing reports and documents by creating an outline. Others review their papers for consistency by saving the document with a new file name, removing all text except the topic headings, and then saving the file again. An outline created in Microsoft Word or another word-processing program works well as a shell for a PowerPoint presentation. Instead of typing text in PowerPoint, as you did in Projects 1 and 2, you can import this outline; add visual elements such as clip art, photos, and graphical bullets, and ultimately create an impressive slide show.

To Start PowerPoint

If you are using a computer to step through the project in this chapter and you want your screens to match the figures in this book, you should change your computer's resolution to 1024×768. For information about how to change a computer's resolution, read Appendix E.

The following steps, which assume Windows Vista is running, start PowerPoint based on a typical installation. You may need to ask your instructor how to start PowerPoint for your computer.

1. Click the Start button on the Windows Vista taskbar, click All Programs at the bottom of the left pane on the Start menu, click Microsoft Office in the All Programs list, and then click Microsoft Office PowerPoint 2007.

2. If the PowerPoint window is not maximized, click the Maximize button next to the Close button on its title bar to maximize the window.

Converting Documents for Use in PowerPoint

PowerPoint can produce slides based on an outline created in Microsoft Word, a word-processing program, or a Web page if the text was saved in a format that PowerPoint can recognize. Microsoft Word 2007 files use the file extension **.docx** in their file names. Text originating in other word-processing programs for later use with PowerPoint should be saved in Rich Text Format (.rtf) or plain text format (.txt). Web page documents that use an HTML extension (.htm) can also be imported.

PowerPoint automatically opens Microsoft Office files, and many other types of files, in the PowerPoint format. The **rich text format** file type is used to transfer formatted documents between applications, even if the programs are running on different platforms, such as PC compatible and Macintosh. When a Word or Rich Text Format document is inserted into a presentation, PowerPoint creates an outline structure based on heading styles in the document. A Heading 1 in a source document becomes a slide title in PowerPoint, a Heading 2 becomes the first level of body text on the slide, a Heading 3 the second level of text on the slide, and so on.

If the original document contains no heading styles, PowerPoint creates an outline based on paragraphs. For example, in a .doc or .rtf file, for several lines of text styled as Normal and broken by paragraphs, PowerPoint turns each paragraph into a slide title.

To Open a Microsoft Word Outline as a Presentation

The text for the Science presentation is contained in a Microsoft Word 2007 file. The following steps open this Microsoft Word outline as a presentation from the Data Files for Students. See the inside back cover of this book for instructions on downloading the Data Files for Students, or contact your instructor for more information about accessing the required files.

• Click the Delete button in the Slides group on the Home tab to delete Slide 1 (Figure 3–2).

Must I delete Slide 1 now?

No. PowerPoint will create new slides from the Science Outline, so this current Slide 1 will be blank. You could delete it after you insert the Word outline.

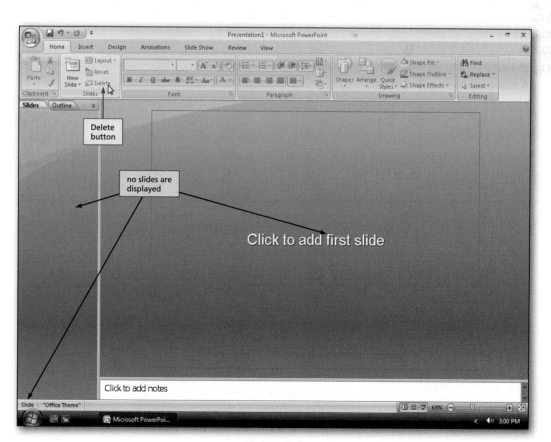

Figure 3–2

2

- Connect a USB flash drive with the Data Files for Students to one of the computer's USB ports.

- Click the New Slide button arrow to display the Office Theme Layout gallery (Figure 3–3).

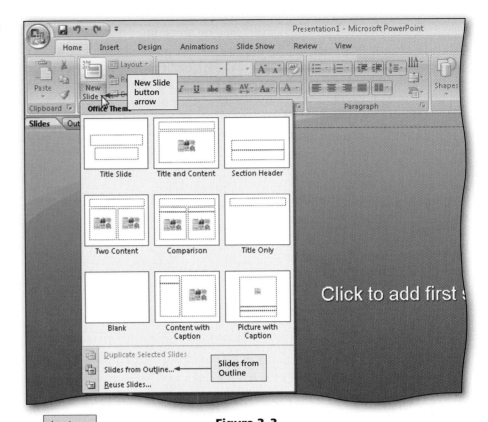

Figure 3–3

3

- Click Slides from Outline in the Office Theme Layout gallery to display the Insert Outline dialog box.

- If the Folders list is displayed below the Folders button, click the Folders button to remove the Folders list.

- If necessary, click Computer in the Favorite Links section to display a list of available drives and then double-click UDISK 2.0 (E:) to select the USB flash drive. (Your USB flash drive may have a different name and letter.)

- Click Science Outline in the File list (Figure 3–4).

 Q&A

What if the outline file is not on a USB flash drive?

Use the same process, but be certain to select the device containing the outline in the Look in list.

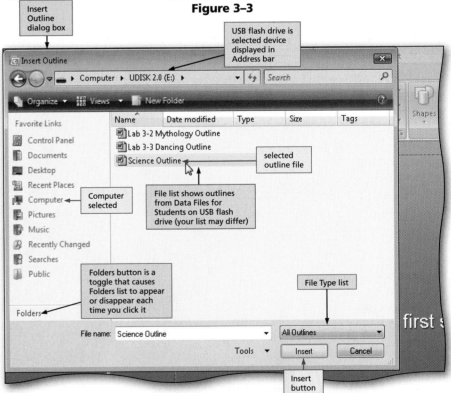

Figure 3–4

4

- Click the Insert button to open the Science Outline and create three slides in your presentation.

- Click the Outline tab in the Tabs pane to view the outline (Figure 3–5).

Q&A

Do I need to see the text as an outline in the Outline tab now?

No, but sometimes it is helpful to view the content of your presentation in this view before looking at individual slides.

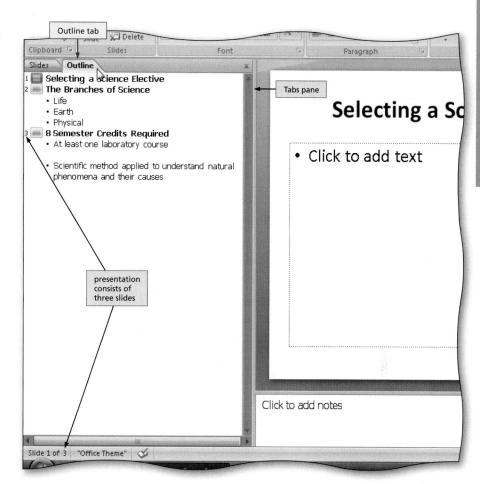

Figure 3–5

To Change the Slide 1 Layout to Title Slide

When you started the new presentation, PowerPoint applied the Title and Text slide layout to all slides. You want to apply the Title Slide slide layout to Slide 1 to introduce the presentation. The following steps change the Slide 1 slide layout.

1 Click the Layout button in the Slides group.

2 Click Title Slide to apply that layout to Slide 1.

To Save the Presentation

With all the text for your slides created, you should save the presentation. For a detailed example of the procedure summarized below, refer to pages PPT 28 through PPT 31 in Chapter 1.

1 Connect a USB flash drive to one of the computer's USB ports and then click the Save button on the Quick Access Toolbar.

2 Type Science in the File name text box. Do not press the ENTER key after typing the file name.

Note: If you are using Windows XP, see Appendix F for alternate steps.

3 Click Computer in the Favorite Links section to display a list of available drives and then double-click UDISK 2.0 (E:) to select the USB flash drive.

4 Click the Save button in the Save As dialog box.

Formatting Slide Backgrounds

Resetting Backgrounds
If you have made many changes to the background and want to start the process over, click the Reset Background button in the Format Background dialog box.

A slide's background is an integral part of a presentation because it can generate audience interest. Every slide can have the same background, or different backgrounds can be used in a presentation. This background is considered **fill**, which is the interior of a shape, line, or character. Three fills are available: solid, gradient, and picture or texture. **Solid fill** is one color used throughout the entire slide. **Gradient fill** is one color shade gradually progressing to another shade of the same color or one color progressing to another color. **Picture or texture fill** uses a specific file or an image that simulates a material, such as cork, granite, marble, or canvas.

Once you add a fill, you can adjust its appearance. For example, you can adjust its **transparency**, which allows you to see through the background, so that any text on the slide is visible. You also can select a color that is part of the theme or a custom color. You can use **offsets**, another background feature, to move the background from the slide borders in varying percentage distances. **Tiling options** repeat the background image many times vertically and horizontally on the slide; the smaller the tiling percentage, the greater the number of times the image is repeated.

To Insert a Texture Fill

A wide variety of texture fills are available to give your presentation a unique look. The 24 pictures in the Textures gallery give the appearance of a physical object, such as water drops, sand, tissue paper, and a paper bag. You also can use your own texture pictures for custom backgrounds. When you insert a fill, PowerPoint assumes you want this custom background on only the current slide displayed. To make this background appear on all slides in the presentation, click the Apply to All button in the Format Background dialog box. The following steps insert the Fish fossil fill on all four slides in the presentation.

1

- Click the Slides tab in the Tabs pane to view the slide thumbnails.

- Right-click anywhere on Slide 1 except the title or subtitle text placeholders to display the shortcut menu (Figure 3–6).

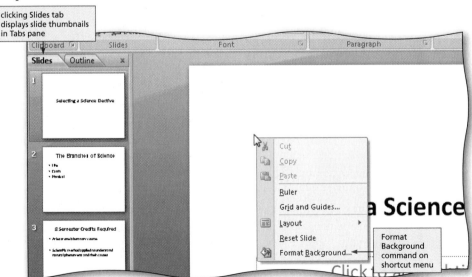

Figure 3–6

2

- Click Format Background on the shortcut menu to display the Format Background dialog box.

- With the Fill pane displaying, click 'Picture or texture fill' to expand the fill options (Figure 3–7).

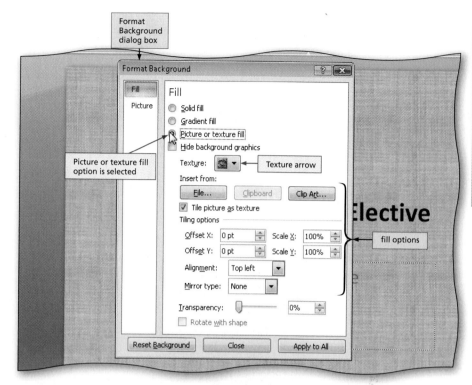

Figure 3–7

3

- Click the Texture arrow to display the Texture gallery (Figure 3–8).

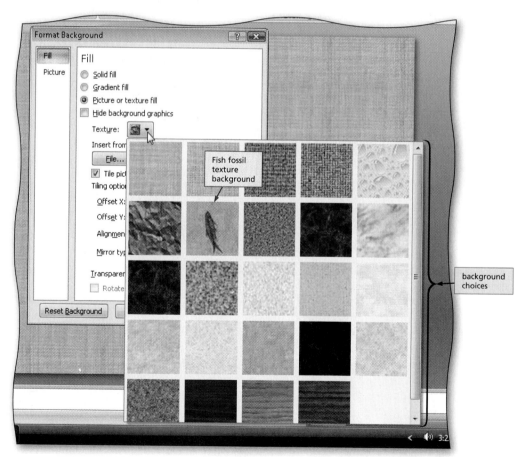

Figure 3–8

4

- Click the Fish fossil background to insert this background on Slide 1 (Figure 3–9).

Q&A

The Format Background dialog box is covering part of the slide. Can I move this box?

Yes. Click the dialog box title and drag it to a different location so that you can view the slide.

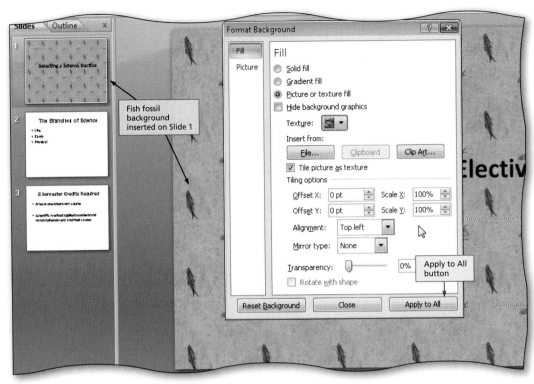

Figure 3–9

5

- Click the Apply to All button to insert the Fish fossil background on all slides (Figure 3–10).

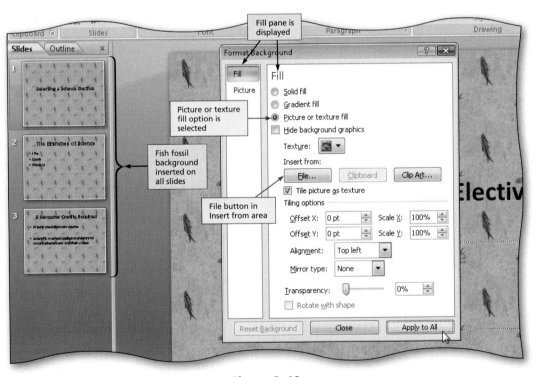

Figure 3–10

Other Ways

1. Click Design tab, click Background Styles in Background group, click Format Background

To Insert a Picture to Create a Background

For variety and interest, you want to use a fossil photograph as the Slide 1 background. This picture is stored on the Data Files for Students. PowerPoint will stretch the height and width of this picture to fill the slide area. The following steps insert the file, Fossil, on only Slide 1.

1

- If it is not already selected, click the Slide 1 thumbnail in the Tabs pane to select it.

- With the Fill pane displaying and the Picture or texture fill option selected in the Format Background dialog box, click the File button in the Insert from area to display the Insert Picture dialog box.

- If necessary, click Computer in the Favorite Links section and then double-click UDISK 2.0 (E:) to select the USB flash drive.

- Click Fossil to select the file name (Figure 3–11).

Q&A What if the photograph file is not in the file name list?

Use the same process, but be certain to select the location containing the file in the Previous Locations list.

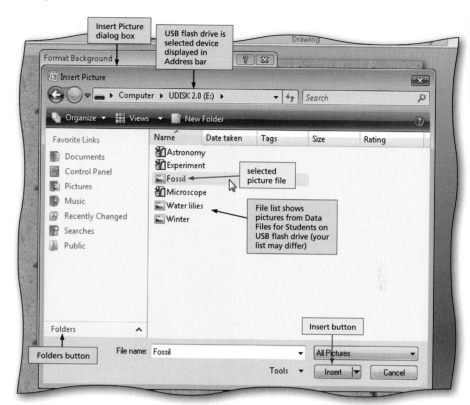

Figure 3–11

2

- Click the Insert button to insert the Fossil picture as the Slide 1 background (Figure 3–12).

Q&A What if I do not want to use this picture?

Click the Undo button on the Quick Access Toolbar.

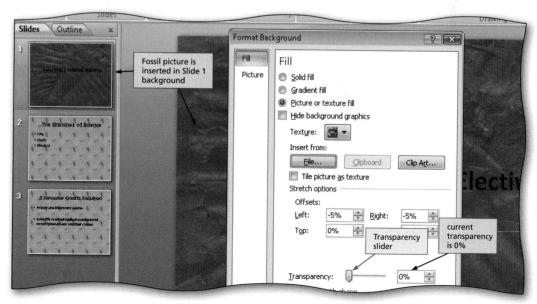

Figure 3–12

To Format the Background Picture Fill Transparency

The Fossil picture on Slide 1 has a rich color and may conflict with text you will add to the title slide. One method of reducing this brightness is to change the transparency. The **Transparency slider** indicates the amount of opaqueness. The default setting is 0, which is fully opaque. The opposite extreme is 100%, which is fully transparent. To change the transparency, you can move the Transparency slider or enter a number in the text box next to the slider. The following step adjusts the transparency to 40%.

- Click the Transparency slider and drag it to the right until 40% is displayed in the Transparency text box (Figure 3–13).

Q&A Why do the Left and Right offsets in the Stretch options area show a −5 value?

PowerPoint automatically expanded the photograph slightly so that it fills the entire slide.

2

- Click the Close button to close the Format Background dialog box.

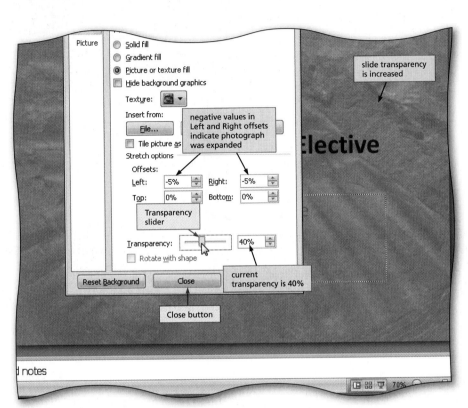

Figure 3–13

To Add Slide Numbers, Date, and Time

Slides can contain information at the top or bottom. The area at the top of a slide is called a header, and the area at the bottom is called a footer. As a default, no information is displayed in the header or footer. You can choose to apply only a header, only a footer, or both a header and footer. In addition, you can elect to have the header or footer display on single slides, all slides, or all slides except the title slide.

Slide numbers help a presenter organize a talk. While few audience members are cognizant of this aspect of a slide, the presenter can glance at the number and know which slide contains particular information. If an audience member asks a question pertaining to information contained on a slide that had been displayed previously or is on a slide that has not been viewed yet, the presenter can jump to that slide in an effort to answer the question. In addition, the slide number helps pace the slide show. For example, a speaker could have the presentation timed so that Slide 4 is displaying three minutes into the talk. The following steps add this number to a slide and also add the current date and time.

1

- Click Insert on the Ribbon to display the Insert tab.

- Click the Slide Number button in the Text group to display the Header and Footer dialog box.

- If necessary, click the Slide tab to display the Slide sheet (Figure 3–14).

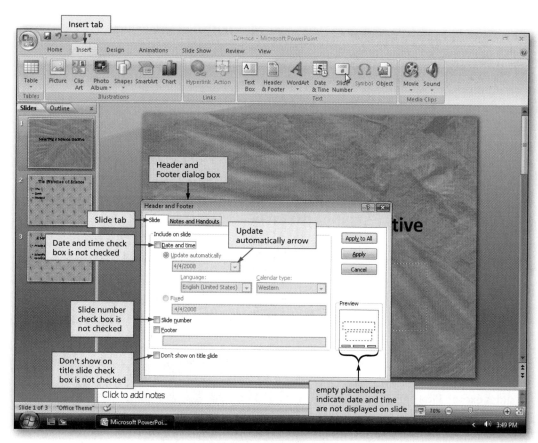

Figure 3–14

2

- Click 'Date and time' to select this check box.

- Click Slide number to select this check box.

- Click 'Don't show on title slide' to select this check box.

- Click the Update automatically arrow in the Date and time area to display the Date and time list (Figure 3–15).

 Q&A

What are the black boxes in the Preview area?

The black box in the left footer placeholder indicates the current date and time will appear on the slide; the black box in the right footer placeholder indicates the page number will appear.

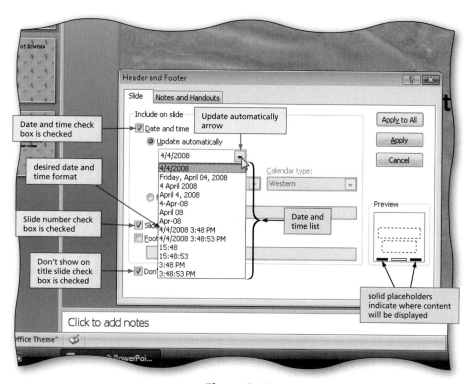

Figure 3–15

• Click the current date and time that are displayed in the format shown in Figure 3–16.

Q&A

What if I want a specific date and time to appear?

Click Fixed in the Date and time area and type the actual information you want your audience to see.

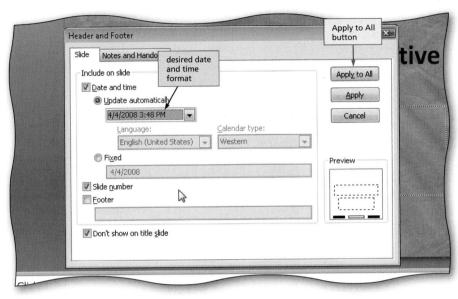

Figure 3–16

• Click the Apply to All button to display the slide number on all slides except Slide 1 (Figure 3–17).

Q&A

When would I click the Apply button instead of the Apply to All button?

Click the Apply button when you want the slide number to appear only on the slide currently selected.

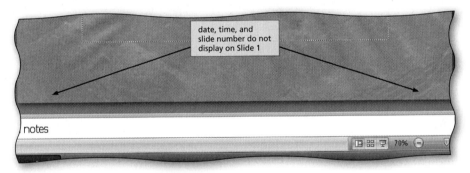

Figure 3–17

Using WordArt

One method of adding appealing visual elements to a presentation is by using **WordArt** styles. This feature is found in other Microsoft Office applications, including Word and Excel. This gallery of decorative effects allows you to type new text or convert existing text to WordArt. You then can add elements such as fills, outlines, and effects.

As with slide backgrounds, WordArt fill in the interior of a letter can consist of a solid color, texture, picture, or gradient. The WordArt **outline** is the exterior border surrounding each letter or symbol. PowerPoint allows you to change the outline color, weight, and style. You also can add an **effect**, which helps add emphasis or depth to the characters. Some effects are shadows, reflections, glows, bevels, and 3–D rotations.

Plan Ahead

> **Use WordArt in moderation.**
> Some WordArt styles are bold and detailed, and they can detract from the message you are trying to present if not used carefully. Select a WordArt style when needed for special emphasis, such as a title slide that audience members will see when they enter the room. WordArt can have a powerful effect, so do not overuse it.

To Apply a WordArt Style

The Slide 1 title text imported from the Microsoft Word outline has the default Calibri font with a font size of 44. You quickly can add visual elements to these letters by selecting a text style in the WordArt Quick Style gallery. The following steps apply a WordArt style to the Slide 1 title text.

1

• With Slide 1 displaying, select the title text, Selecting a Science Elective.

• Click Format on the Ribbon under Drawing Tools to display the Format tab.

• Click the More button in the WordArt Styles gallery on the Format tab to display the WordArt Styles gallery (Figure 3–18).

Q&A

Why did the Format tab appear automatically on the Ribbon?

It appears when you select text to which you could add a WordArt style or other effect.

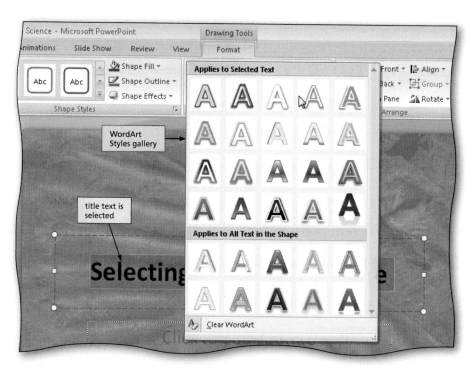

Figure 3–18

2

• Point to Fill – Accent 2, Double Outline – Accent 2 in the Applies to Selected Text area (row 3, column 5) to display a live preview of this style in the title text (Figure 3–19).

 Experiment

• Point to various styles in the WordArt Styles gallery and watch the format of the text and borders change.

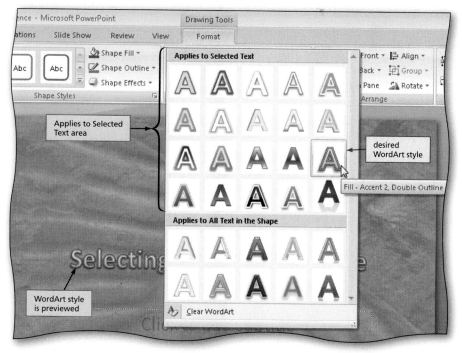

Figure 3–19

- Click Fill – Accent 2, Double Outline – Accent 2 to apply this style to the title text (Figure 3–20).

Q&A

What is a matte bevel style that is part of some of the styles in the gallery?

A matte finish gives a dull and rough effect. A bevel edge is angled or sloped and gives the effect of a three-dimension object.

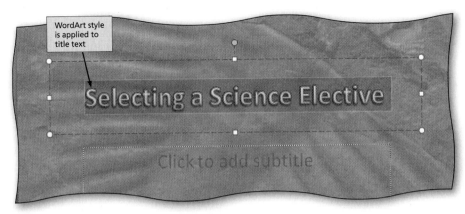

Figure 3–20

To Format the WordArt Text Fill

The Fish fossil image is integral in this presentation on the slide backgrounds, so adding it to the title text WordArt would help reinforce this graphic. The following steps add the Fish fossil as a fill for the WordArt characters on Slide 1.

- With the Slide 1 title text still selected, right-click the text to display the Mini toolbar.

- Click the Increase Font size button on the Mini toolbar repeatedly until the font size increases to 80 point.

- With the Format tab displaying, click the Text Fill arrow in the WordArt Styles group to display the Fill menu (Figure 3–21).

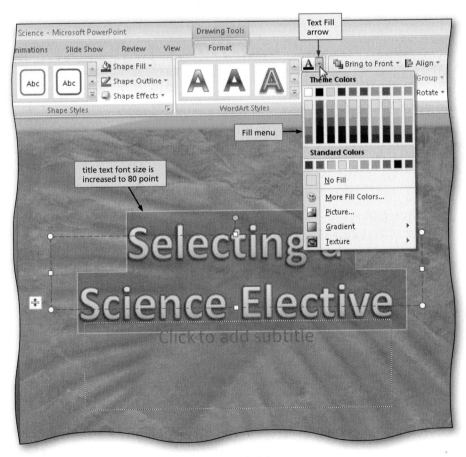

Figure 3–21

2

- Point to Texture on the Fill menu to display the Texture Fill gallery.

- Point to the Fish fossil texture to display a live preview of this texture as the fill for the title text (Figure 3–22).

 Experiment

- Point to various styles in the WordArt Styles gallery and watch the format of the text and borders change.

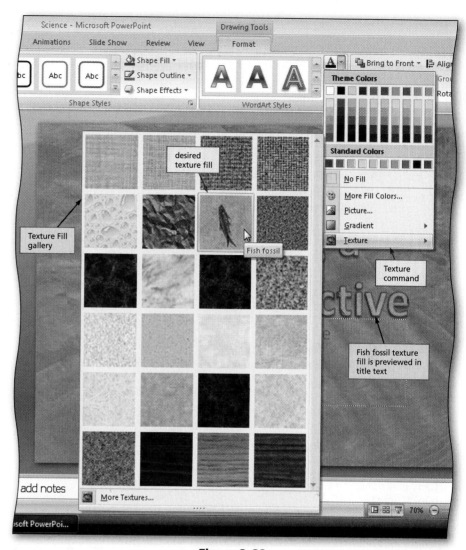

Figure 3–22

3

- Click the Fish fossil texture to apply this texture as the fill for the title text (Figure 3–23).

Q&A Can I apply this texture simultaneously to text that appears in more than one place on my slide?

Yes. Select one area of text, press and then hold the CTRL key while you select the other text, and then apply the texture.

Figure 3–23

To Change the Weight of the WordArt Outline

The WordArt style just applied to this text has a double outline. To emphasize this characteristic, you can increase the width of the lines. As with font size, lines also are measured in point size, and PowerPoint gives you the option to change the line **weight**, or thickness, starting with ¼ point (pt) and increasing in one-fourth-point increments. Other outline options include changing the color and the line style, such as dots or dashes or a combination of dots and dashes. The following steps change the title text outline weight to 4½ pt.

- With the Slide 1 title text still selected and the Format tab displaying, click the Text Outline arrow in the WordArt Styles group to display the Text Outline menu.

- Point to Weight on the Text Outline menu to display the Weight list.

- Point to 4½ pt to display a live preview of this line weight on the title text outline (Figure 3–24).

Experiment

- Point to various line weights in the Weight list and watch the line thickness change.

Q&A Can I make the line width more than 6 pt?

Yes. Click More Lines and increase the amount in the Width box.

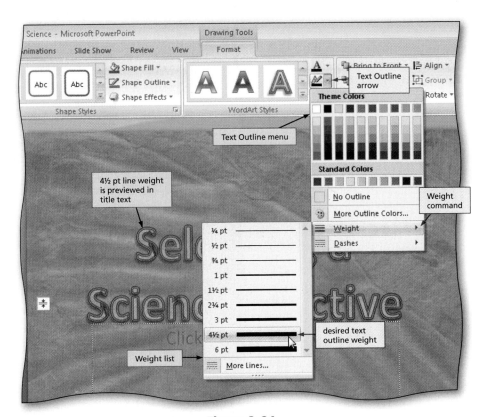

Figure 3–24

- Click 4½ pt to apply this line weight to the title text outline (Figure 3–25).

Q&A Must my text have an outline?

No. To delete the outline, click No Outline in the Text Outline menu.

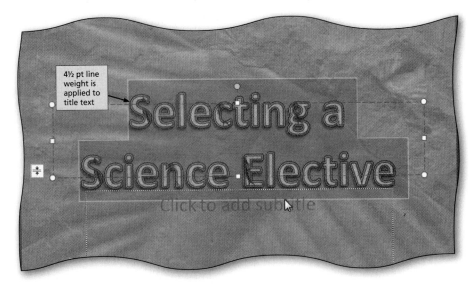

Figure 3–25

To Add a WordArt Text Effect

The Fish fossil fill and thick outline call attention to the Slide 1 title text. For further emphasis, you can add one or more effects. For example, you can add a reflection, which reverses the letters below the text, or a glow, which adds a color around each letter. Once an effect is applied, you often can modify it. For example, you can enhance a shadow effect by changing such elements as its color, size, and angle. The following steps add a glow effect to the WordArt characters on Slide 1.

1

- With the Slide 1 title text still selected and the Format tab displaying, click the Text Effects button in the WordArt Styles group to display the Text Effects list.

- Point to Glow on the Text Effects list to display the Glow gallery (Figure 3–26).

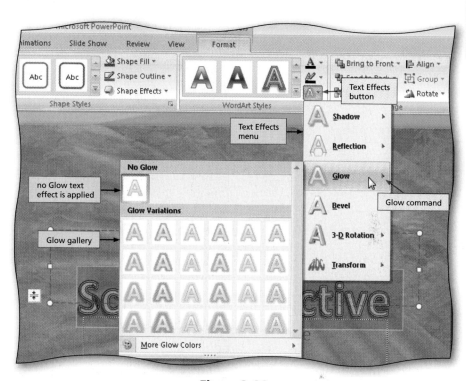

Figure 3–26

2

- Point to Accent color 6, 11 pt glow (row 3, column 6) in the Glow Variations area of the Glow gallery to display a live preview of this effect on the title text (Figure 3–27).

Experiment

- Point to various Glow Variations in the Glow gallery and watch the colors and sizes change.

 Can I select a color other than the six colors shown in the gallery?

Yes. Click More Glow Colors and then choose a standard or theme color. You also can select a custom color.

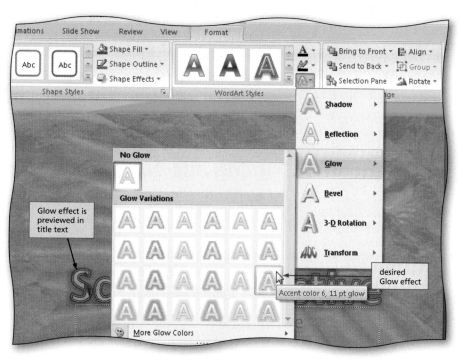

Figure 3–27

- Click Accent color 6, 11 pt glow to apply this effect to the title text (Figure 3–28).

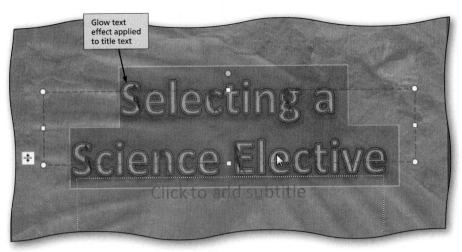

Figure 3–28

To Delete the Subtitle Placeholder

The Slide 1 subtitle placeholder will not be used in this presentation. The following steps delete this placeholder.

1 Click the subtitle text placeholder border two times to change the border to a solid line.

2 Press the DELETE key to delete the placeholder.

To Save an Existing Presentation with the Same File Name

You have made several changes to your presentation since you last saved it. Thus, you should save it again. The following step saves the presentation again.

1 Click the Save button on the Quick Access Toolbar to overwrite the previous Science file on the USB flash drive.

Creating and Formatting a SmartArt Graphic

BTW

Reading SmartArt Descriptions
Deciding which of the various shape combinations to use can be confusing. Read the informative descriptions in the Choose a SmartArt Graphic dialog box to learn the best use for each type of graphic.

An illustration often can help convey relationships between key points in your presentation. Numerous studies have shown that audience members recall information more readily and accurately when it is presented graphically rather than textually. Microsoft Office 2007 includes **SmartArt graphics**, which are visual representations of your ideas. The SmartArt layouts have a variety of shapes, arrows, and lines to correspond to the major points you want your audience to remember.

You can create a SmartArt graphic in two ways: select a type and then add text, or convert text already present on a slide to a graphic. Once the SmartArt graphic is present, you can customize its look by changing colors, adding and deleting shapes, adding fill and effects, and including animation. The following table lists some of the popular SmartArt types and their uses:

Table 3–1 SmartArt Graphic Layout Types and Purposes

Type	Purpose
List	Show nonsequential information
Process	Show steps in a process or timeline
Cycle	Show a continual process
Hierarchy	Create an organizational chart
Relationship	Illustrate connections
Matrix	Show how parts relate to a whole
Pyramid	Show proportional relationships with the largest component at the top or bottom

Plan Ahead

Choose an appropriate SmartArt layout.
If a slide contains key points that show a process or relationship, consider using a SmartArt graphic to add visual appeal and enhance audience comprehension. As you select a layout, determine the number of ideas you need to present and then select a graphic that contains the same number of shapes. For example, the Counterbalance Arrows layout resembles a teeter-totter; it represents the notion that one concept conversely affects another concept, such as the economic principle that supply has an inverse relationship to demand.

To Convert Text to a SmartArt Graphic

You quickly can convert small amounts of slide text into a SmartArt graphic. Once you determine the type of graphic, such as process or cycle, you then have a wide variety of styles from which to choose in the SmartArt Graphic gallery. As with other galleries, you can point to the samples and view a live preview if you desire. The following steps convert the Slide 2 text to the Continuous Picture List graphic, which is part of the List, Process, and Relationship categories.

1
- Click the Next Slide button to display Slide 2.

- Select the three bulleted list items and then right-click the text to display the shortcut menu.

- Point to Convert to SmartArt in the shortcut menu to display the SmartArt Graphics gallery (Figure 3–29).

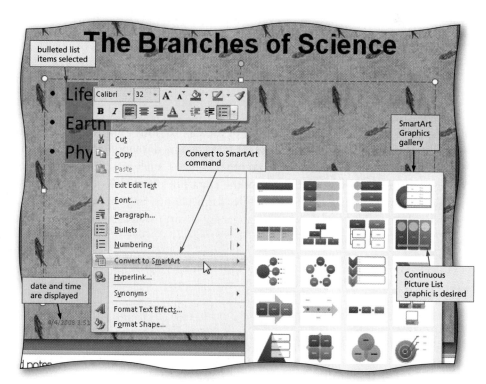

Figure 3–29

2

- Click the Continuous Picture List graphic (row 2, column 4) to apply this shape and convert the text (Figure 3–30).

Q&A

How can I edit the text that displays in the three shapes?

The text also appears in the Text pane displayed to the left of the graphic. Click the text you want to change and make your desired edits.

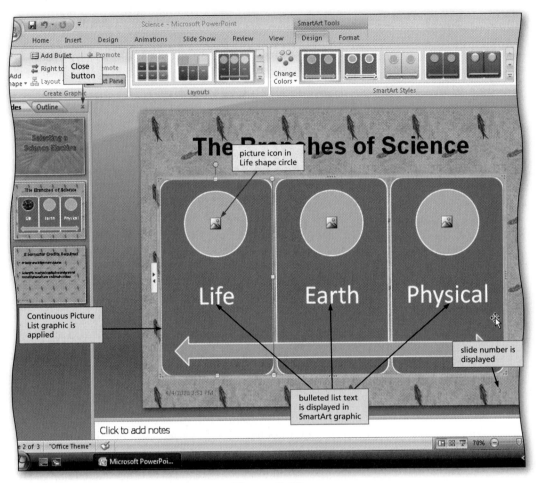

Figure 3–30

To Insert Images from a File into the SmartArt Graphic

The **Text pane** consists of two areas: the top portion has the text that will appear in the SmartArt graphic; the bottom portion gives the name of the graphic and suggestions of what type of information is best suited for this type of visual. The information at the bottom of the Continuous Picture List Text pane indicates that the three circular shapes in the Continuous Picture List graphic are designed to hold images. You can select files from the Clip Organizer or from images you have obtained from other sources, such as a photograph taken with your digital camera. In this presentation, you will add files from the Data Files for Students. See the inside back cover of this book for instructions on downloading the Data Files for Students, or contact your instructor for more information about accessing the required files. The following steps insert three images into the SmartArt graphic.

1

- Double-click the circle picture icon in the Life shape to display the Insert Picture dialog box.

- With your USB flash drive connected to one of the computer's USB ports, double-click UDISK 2.0 (E:) to select the USB flash drive, Drive E in this case, as the device that contains the picture.

- Click Water lilies to select the file name (Figure 3–31).

Q&A

What if the photograph is not on a USB flash drive?

Use the same process, but be certain to select the location containing the photograph in the File list.

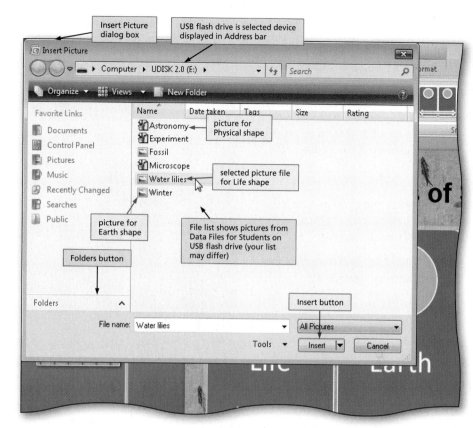

Figure 3–31

2

- Click the Insert button in the dialog box to insert the Water lilies picture into the Life shape circle (Figure 3–32).

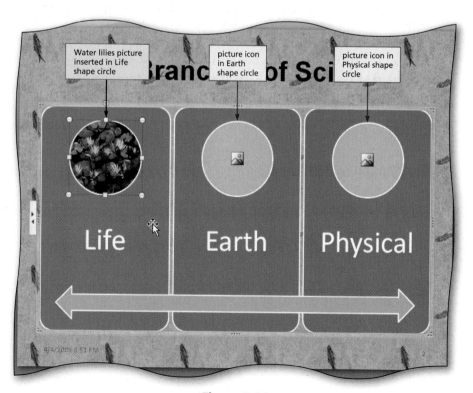

Figure 3–32

3

- Double-click the circle picture icon in the Earth shape to display the Insert Picture dialog box.

- Click Winter to select the file name.

- Click the Insert button to insert the picture into the Earth shape circle.

4

- Double-click the circle picture icon in the Physical shape to display the Insert Picture dialog box.

- Click Astronomy and then click the Insert button (Figure 3–33).

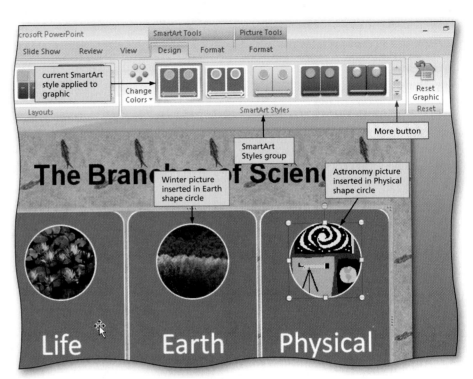

Figure 3–33

To Add a SmartArt Style to the Graphic

You can change the look of your SmartArt graphic easily by applying a **SmartArt Style**. These professionally designed effects have a variety of shape fills, edges, shadows, line styles, gradients, and three-dimensional graphics that allow you to customize the appearance of your presentation. The following steps add the Brick Scene style to the Slide 2 SmartArt graphic.

1

- With the SmartArt graphic still selected and the Design tab active, click the More button in the SmartArt Styles group to expand the SmartArt Styles gallery (Figure 3–34).

Q&A How do I select the graphic if it is no longer selected?

Click the graphic anywhere except the images you just added.

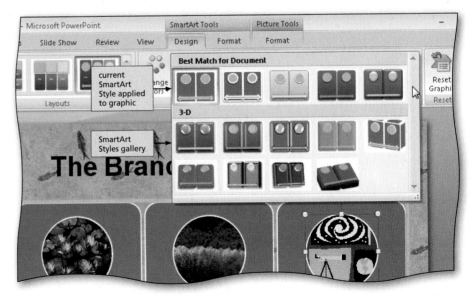

Figure 3–34

2

- Point to the Brick Scene style (row 2, column 5) in the 3-D category in the SmartArt gallery to display a live preview of this style (Figure 3–35).

Experiment

- Point to various styles in the SmartArt gallery and watch the Continuous Picture List graphic change styles.

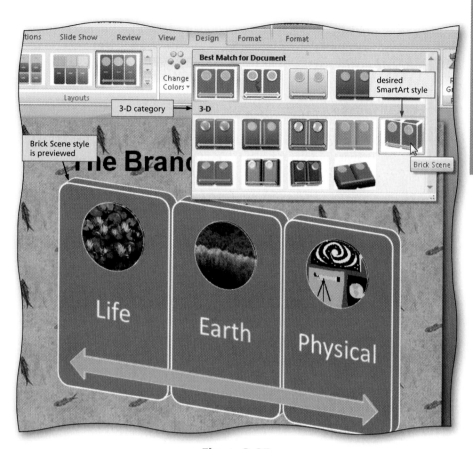

Figure 3–35

3

- Click Brick Scene to apply this style to the graphic (Figure 3–36).

Figure 3–36

To Change the SmartArt Color

Another modification you can make to your SmartArt graphic is to change its color. As with the WordArt Style gallery, PowerPoint provides a gallery of color options you can preview and evaluate. The following steps change the SmartArt graphic color to a Colorful range.

1

- With the SmartArt graphic still selected and the Design tab active, click the Change Colors button in the SmartArt Styles group to display the Change Colors gallery (Figure 3–37).

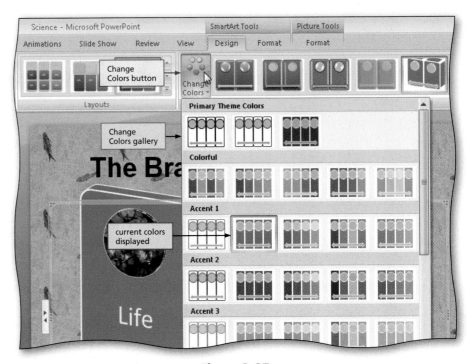

Figure 3–37

2

- Point to Colorful Range – Accent Colors 5 to 6 (row 2, column 5) in the Colorful category to display a live preview of these colors (Figure 3–38).

 Experiment

- Point to various colors in the Change Colors gallery and watch the shapes change colors.

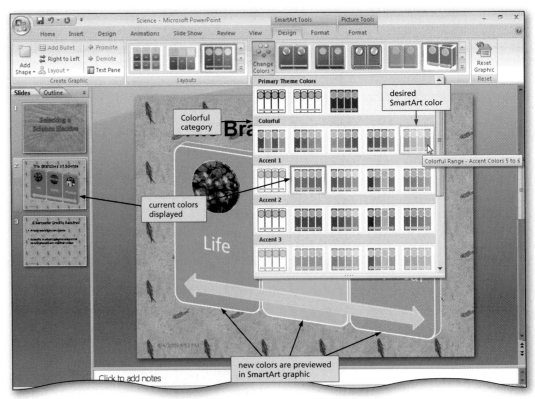

Figure 3–38

3

- Click Colorful Range – Accent Colors 5 to 6 to apply this color variation to the graphic (Figure 3–39).

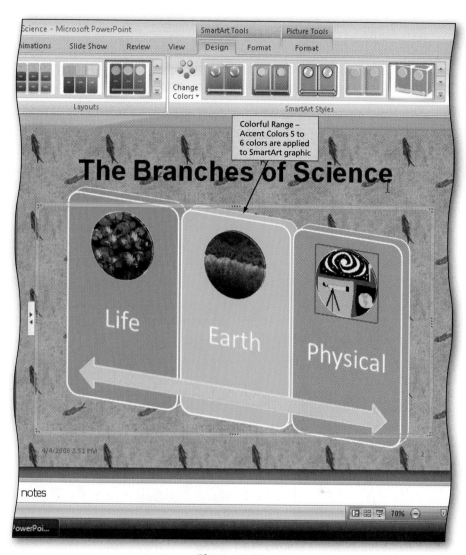

Figure 3–39

Plan Ahead	**Consider the verbal message to accompany your slides.**
	As you design each screen, think about the spoken words that the presenter will use. Audience members want to hear a motivated, passionate speaker who does more than read the text on a screen. Each slide should generate interest, and the speaker should give additional information in an enthusiastic manner. Some speech coaches abide by the principle that a speaker should not say any word that appears on a screen. You should, consequently, make notes as you assemble the slides so that they and the presenter make a unified packaged presentation.

To Insert a Text Box

The arrow in the SmartArt graphic spans across the three shapes. You can add meaningful text to this shape by inserting a **text box**, which is a movable, resizable container. Once you insert this text box, you can add text and graphics and then format these characters and shapes. The following steps cut the text from the slide title, insert a text box on the SmartArt graphic, and then paste the title text in the text box.

- Select the Slide 2 title text, The Branches of Science.

- Right-click the selected text to display the shortcut menu (Figure 3–40).

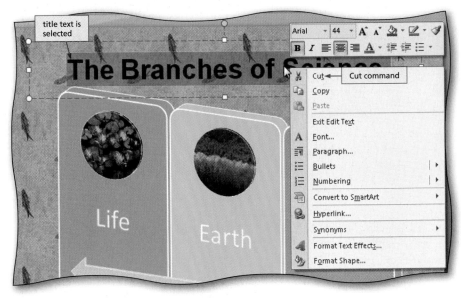

Figure 3–40

- Click Cut on the shortcut menu to delete the title text.

- Click Insert on the Ribbon to display the Insert tab.

- Click the Text Box button on the Insert tab.

- Position the mouse pointer on the arrow at the bottom of the three shapes (Figure 3–41).

Q&A

Why did my mouse pointer change shape?

The different shape indicates that PowerPoint is ready to create the text box where you click.

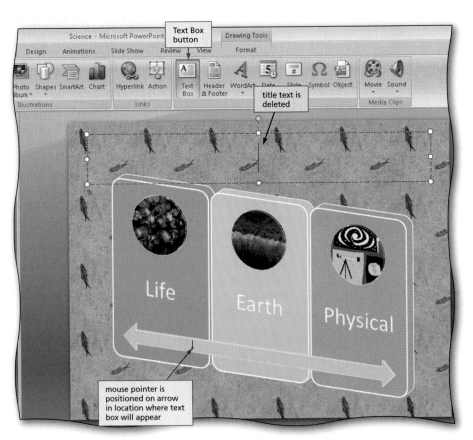

Figure 3–41

3

- Click the arrow to insert a text box.

- Click the Paste button in the Clipboard group on the Home tab to insert the title text in the text box (Figure 3–42).

Q&A Why does a clipboard icon display near the inserted text box?

The clipboard is the Paste Options button, which presents a variety of methods for inserting the text.

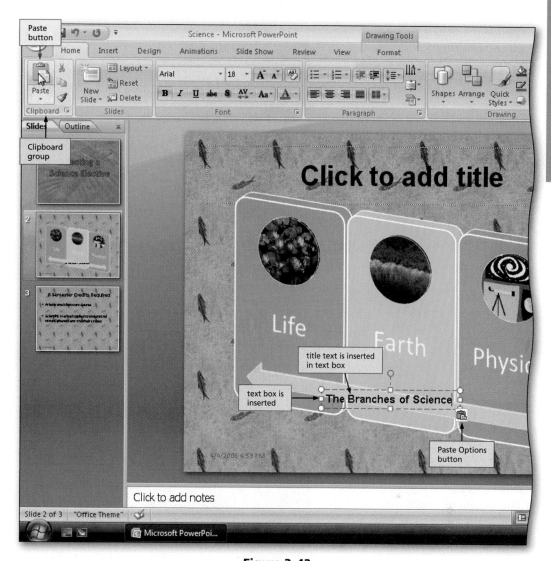

Figure 3–42

To Rotate a Text Box

Once the text box is inserted, you can move it to various locations on the slide. If you need to move it a large distance, select it and drag it to the desired place. In contrast, if you need to move it only a slight increment, use the UP ARROW and DOWN ARROW keys. The text box's orientation on the slide also can change by rotating to the left or right or by flipping horizontally or vertically. Dragging the green **rotation handle** above a selected object allows you to rotate an object in any direction. The steps on the following page rotate the text box.

1

- Position the mouse pointer over the text box rotation handle so that it changes to a Free Rotate pointer (Figure 3–43).

- Drag the text box clockwise so that it is parallel with the arrow on the SmartArt graphic.

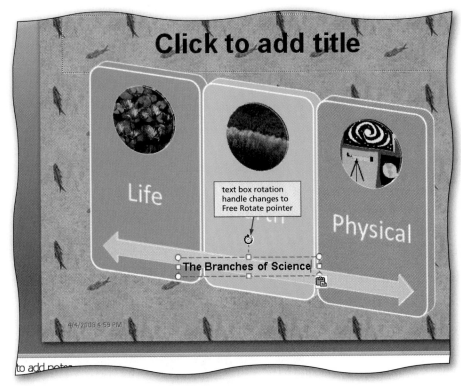

Figure 3–43

2

- If necessary, click an edge of the text box to select the box and then press the UP ARROW or DOWN ARROW keys to position the text box as shown in Figure 3–44.

Q&A

How do I move the text box in small, predefined increments?

To move or nudge the text box shape in very small increments, hold down the CTRL key while pressing the UP ARROW, DOWN ARROW, RIGHT ARROW, or LEFT ARROW keys.

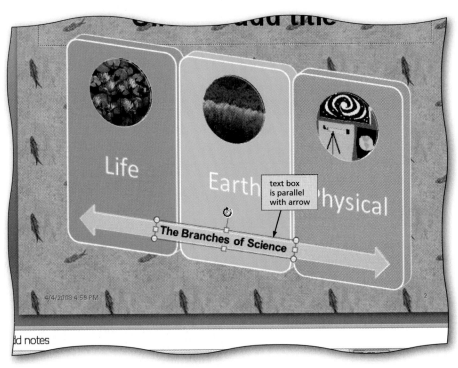

Figure 3–44

Other Ways
1. Click Rotate button in Arrange group on Format tab of Drawing Tools contextual tab

To Format the Text Box

The text box can be formatted in the same manner that shapes are formatted. You can change the fill and outline and also add effects. The following steps add a gradient fill, an outline with dashes and dots, and a glow effect.

- With the text box selected, click Format on the Ribbon to display the Format tab under Drawing Tools.

- Click the Shape Fill button in the Shape Styles group on the Format tab to display the Shape Fill menu (Figure 3–45).

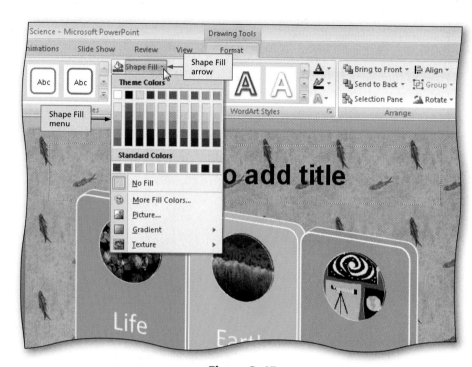

Figure 3–45

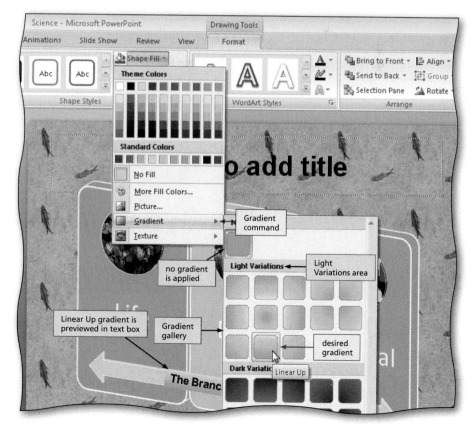

2

- Point to Gradient on the Shape Fill menu to display the Gradient gallery.

- Point to Linear Up in the Light Variations area (row 3, column 2) to display a live preview of this gradient in the text box (Figure 3–46).

Experiment

- Point to various Light and Dark variations in the Gradient gallery and watch the text box fill change.

Figure 3–46

- Click Linear Up to apply this gradient to the text box.

- Click the Shape Outline button in the Shape Styles group on the Format tab to display the Shape Outline menu.

- Point to Dashes on the Shape Outline menu to display the Dashes list (Figure 3–47).

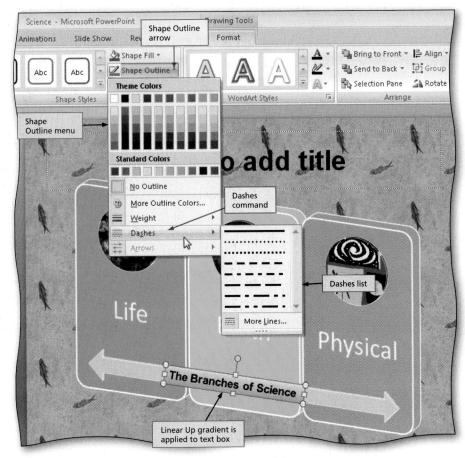

Figure 3–47

- Point to the Long Dash Dot Dot dash to display a live preview of this dash outline in the text box (Figure 3–48).

🔍 **Experiment**

- Point to various dashes and watch the text box outline change.

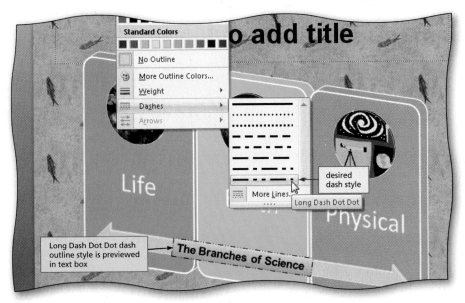

Figure 3–48

5

- Click the Long Dash Dot Dot dash to apply this dash to the text box.

- Click the Shape Effects button in the Shape Styles group on the Format tab to display the Shape Effects list.

- Point to Glow on the Shape Effects list to display the Glow gallery.

- Point to the green Accent color 3, 11 pt glow variation (row 3, column 3) to display a live preview of this glow shape effect in the text box (Figure 3–49).

 Experiment

- Point to various glow variations and watch the text box effects change.

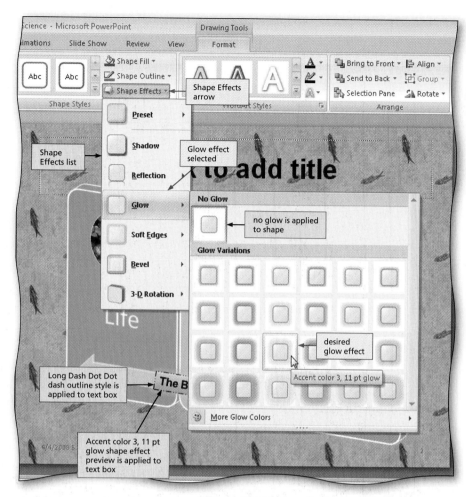

Figure 3–49

6

- Click the Accent color 3, 11 pt glow variation to apply this glow shape effect to the text box (Figure 3–50).

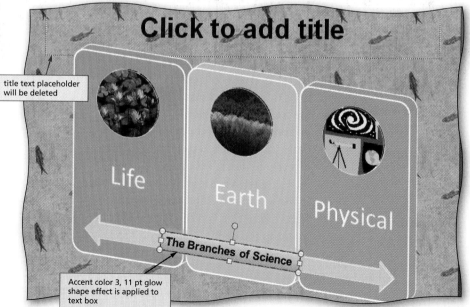

Figure 3–50

To Delete the Title Placeholder

The Slide 2 title placeholder will not be used in this presentation. The following steps delete this placeholder.

1 Double-click the title text placeholder border to change the border to a solid line.

2 Press the DELETE key to delete the placeholder.

To Save an Existing Presentation with the Same File Name

Now that Slide 2 is complete, you should save the presentation. The following step saves the presentation again.

1 Click the Save button on the Quick Access Toolbar to overwrite the previous Science file on the USB flash drive.

Graphic Formats: Vector and Bitmap

A clip art picture is composed of many objects grouped together to form one object. PowerPoint allows you to modify and enhance the clip by disassembling it into the objects. **Disassembling** a clip art picture, also called **ungrouping**, separates one object into multiple objects. Once ungrouped, you can manipulate the individual objects as needed to form a new object. When you ungroup a clip art picture in PowerPoint, it becomes a **drawing object** and loses its link to the Microsoft Clip Organizer. In addition to clips, other drawing objects are curves, lines, arrows, and stars.

Vector Graphics

Objects usually are saved in one of two **graphic formats**: vector or bitmap. A **vector graphic** is a piece of art that has been created by a drawing program such as CorelDRAW or Adobe Illustrator. The clip art pictures used in this project are vector graphic objects and are created as a collection of lines. Vector graphic files store data either as picture descriptions or as calculations. These files describe a picture mathematically as a set of instructions for creating the objects in the picture. These mathematical descriptions determine the position, length, and direction in which the lines are drawn. These calculations allow the drawing program to re-create the picture on the screen as necessary. Because vector graphic objects are described mathematically, they also can be layered, rotated, and magnified with relative ease. Vector graphics also are known as **object-oriented pictures**. Clip art pictures in the Microsoft Clip Organizer that have the file extension of **.wmf** are examples of vector files. Vector files can be ungrouped and manipulated by their component objects. You will ungroup the clip used on Slide 3 in this project.

Bitmap Graphics

A **bitmap graphic** is the other major format used to store objects. These art pieces are composed of a series of small dots, called pixels, which form shapes and lines. A **pixel**, short for **picture element**, is one dot in a grid. A picture that is produced on the computer screen or on paper by a printer is composed of thousands of these dots. Just as a bit is the smallest unit of information a computer can process, a pixel is the smallest element that can display or that printing hardware and software can manipulate in creating letters, numbers, or graphics.

Bitmap graphics are created by digital cameras or in paint programs such as Microsoft Paint. Bitmap graphics also can be produced from **digitizing** art, pictures, or photographs by passing the artwork through a scanner. A **scanner** is a hardware device that converts lines and shading into combinations of the binary digits 0 and 1 by sensing different intensities of light and dark. The scanner shines a beam of light on the picture being scanned. The beam passes back and forth across the picture, sending a digitized signal to the computer's memory. A **digitized signal** is the conversion of input, such as the lines in a drawing, into a series of discrete units represented by the binary digits 0 and 1. **Scanned pictures** are bitmap pictures and have jagged edges. The jagged edges are caused by the individual pixels that create the picture. Bitmap graphics also are known as **raster images**. Pictures in the Microsoft Clip Organizer that have the file extensions of **.jpg** (Joint Photographic Experts Group), **.bmp** (Windows Bitmap), **.gif** (Graphics Interchange Format), and **.png** (Portable Network Graphics) are examples of bitmap graphic files. Bitmap files cannot be ungrouped and converted to smaller PowerPoint object groups. They can be manipulated, however, in an imaging program such as Microsoft Photo Editor. This program allows you to rotate or flip the pictures and then insert them in your slides.

Plan Ahead

Be certain you have permission to modify clips.
If you change a clip, be certain you have the legal right to do so. For example, corporate logos are designed using specific colors and shapes and often cannot be altered. In addition, you cannot use photographs and illustrations to damage people's reputations by representing them falsely. For instance, you cannot insert a photograph of your former boyfriend or girlfriend, who has made the Dean's List every semester, in a slide that gives information about students who have been placed on academic probation.

Inserting and Modifying Clips

Slide 3 (shown in Figure 3–1c on PPT 163) contains a modified version of a beaker. This clip is from the Microsoft Clip Organizer. You may want to modify a clip art picture for various reasons. Many times you cannot find a clip art picture that precisely illustrates your topic. For example, you want a picture of a man and woman shaking hands, but the only available clip art picture has two men and a woman shaking hands.

Occasionally you may want to remove or change a portion of a clip art picture or you might want to combine two or more clip art pictures. For example, you can use one clip art picture for the background and another picture as the foreground. Still other times, you may want to combine a clip art picture with another type of object. The types of objects you can combine with a clip art picture depend on the software installed on your computer. The **Object type list** in the Insert Object dialog box identifies the types of objects you can combine with a clip art picture. In this presentation, the picture with a beaker contains a green background that is not required to display on the slide, so you will ungroup the clip art picture and remove the background.

BTW

Locating Clip Art
Microsoft Office 2007 includes more then 1,600 clip art images, bullets, lines, and sound files. They were placed in the Office Collections group when the software was installed. Each clip has a variety of keywords that help identify the file; you cannot edit these keywords.

BTW

Cropping Pictures
Use the Crop command to cut unwanted areas from any picture except an animated GIF picture. Select the picture, click the Crop button on the Picture toolbar, position the cropping tool over a center cropping handle, and then drag the handle inward. Click the Crop button again to turn off the cropping command.

Modifying the clip on Slide 3 requires several steps. First, you display Slide 3 and change the slide layout. Then, you insert the beaker picture into the slide. In the next step, you scale the picture to increase its size. Finally, you ungroup the clip, change the color of the liquid in the beaker, and then regroup the component objects. The following steps explain in detail how to insert, scale, ungroup, modify, and regroup a clip art image.

To Change the Slide Layout

For aesthetic reasons, you want the clip art to display prominently on the right side of the slide. The following steps change the slide layout to Content with Caption.

1 Click the Next Slide button to display Slide 3.

2 Click the Layout button in the Slides group on the Ribbon.

3 Click Content with Caption to apply that layout to Slide 3 (Figure 3–51).

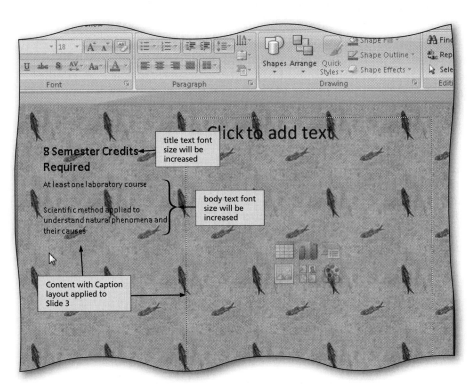

Figure 3–51

To Increase the Font Size

The imported Microsoft Word text can be enlarged to enhance readability. The following steps enlarge the title and body text for Slide 3.

1 Drag through the title text, 8 Semester Credits Required, to select the text and display the Mini toolbar.

2 Move the mouse pointer into the transparent Mini toolbar so that it changes to a bright toolbar and then click the Increase Font Size button on the Mini toolbar three times to change the font size to 32 point.

3 Drag through the two body text paragraphs.

4 Click the Increase Font Size button on the Mini toolbar three times to change the font size to 20 point (Figure 3–52).

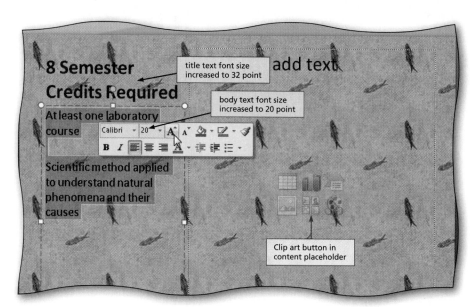

Figure 3–52

To Insert a Clip into a Content Placeholder

The first step in modifying a clip is to insert the picture into a slide. In later steps, you modify the clip. The following steps insert the beaker clip from the Microsoft Clip Organizer. See your instructor if this clip is not available on your system.

1 Click the Clip Art button in the content placeholder (row 2, column 2).

2 Type beaker in the Search for text box and then click the Go button.

3 If necessary, scroll down the list to display the desired clip shown in Figure 3–53 and then click the clip to insert it into the Slide 3 content placeholder.

4 Click the Close button in the Clip Art task pane.

5 If a bullet and the Click to add text paragraph displays behind the clip, click the paragraph and then press the DELETE key to delete the paragraph.

6 If necessary, increase the beaker clip art size by dragging one of the corner sizing handles outward until the clip is the size shown in Figure 3–53. Drag the clip to the location shown in this figure.

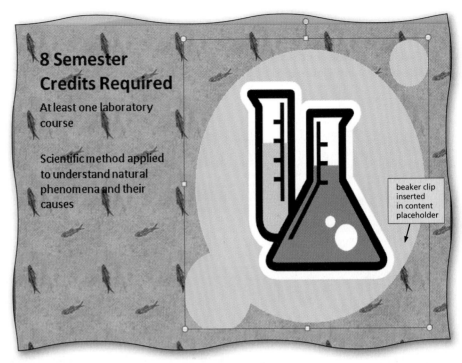

Figure 3–53

To Ungroup a Clip

The next step is to ungroup the beaker clip on Slide 3. When you **ungroup** a clip art picture, PowerPoint breaks it into its component objects. A clip may be composed of a few individual objects or several complex groups of objects. These groups can be ungrouped repeatedly until they decompose into individual objects. Because a clip art picture is a collection of complex groups of objects, you may need to ungroup a complex object into less complex objects before being able to modify a specific object. When you ungroup a clip and click the Yes button in the Microsoft Office PowerPoint dialog box, PowerPoint converts the clip to a PowerPoint object. Recall that a PowerPoint object is an object not associated with a supplementary application. The following steps ungroup a clip.

1

- With the beaker clip selected, click the Format tab under Picture Tools on the Ribbon.

- Click the Group button in the Arrange group on the Format tab (Figure 3–54).

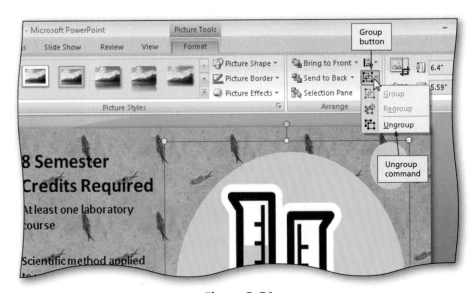

Figure 3–54

2

- Click Ungroup to display the Microsoft Office PowerPoint dialog box.

- Click the Yes button in the Microsoft Office PowerPoint dialog box to convert the clip to a Microsoft Office drawing.

- On the Format tab, click the Group button in the Arrange group and then click Ungroup again to display the objects that comprise the beaker clip (Figure 3–55).

Q&A What if I click the No button?

The clip art picture is displayed on the slide as a clip art picture.

Q&A Why does the Format tab show different options this time?

The clip has become a drawing object, so tools related to drawing now display.

Other Ways

1. Right-click clip, point to Group on shortcut menu, click Ungroup

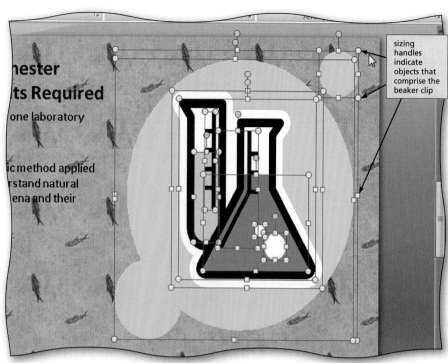

Figure 3–55

To Change the Color of PowerPoint Objects

Now that the beaker picture is ungrouped, you can change the color of the objects. The clip is composed of hundreds of objects, so you must exercise care when selecting the correct object to modify. The following steps change the color of the beaker and test tube liquids.

1

- Click outside the clip area to display clip without the sizing handles around the objects.

- Click the medium blue beaker liquid to display sizing handles around the colored area (Figure 3–56).

Q&A What if I selected a different area?

Click outside the clip and retry.

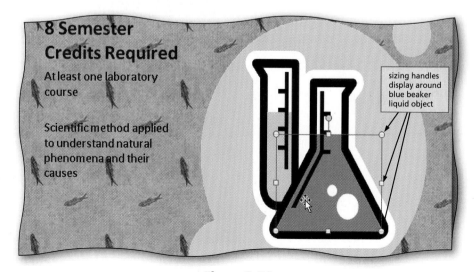

Figure 3–56

2

- Click the Shape Fill arrow in the Shape Styles group to display the Shape Fill menu.

- Point to the color Orange in the Standard Colors area (third color) to display a live preview of the color of the selected liquid in the graphic (Figure 3–57).

 Experiment

- Point to various colors and watch the beaker liquid color change.

Q&A Why do those specific colors display in the Standard Colors area?

They are the default colors associated with the Office Theme.

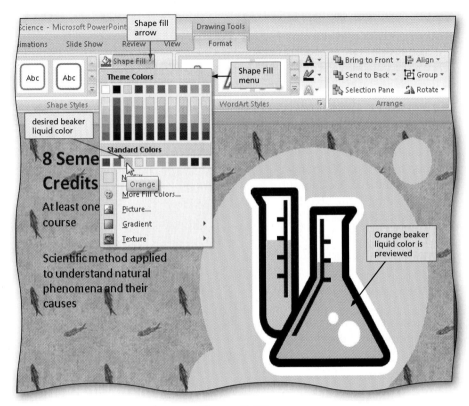

Figure 3–57

3

- Click the color Orange to change the beaker liquid color.

- Click the test tube liquid to display the sizing handles around the colored area (Figure 3–58).

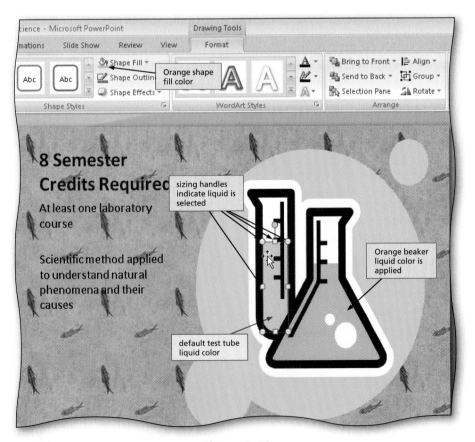

Figure 3–58

- Click the Shape Fill button in the Shape Styles group and then point to the Blue color in the Standard Colors area (eighth color) to display a live preview of the color of the selected liquid in the graphic (Figure 3–59).

Experiment

- Point to various colors and watch the test tube color change.

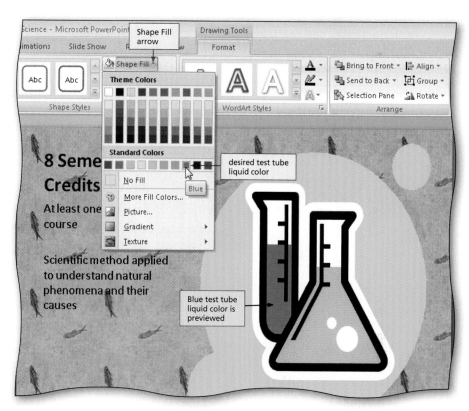

Figure 3–59

- Click the Blue color to change the test tube liquid (Figure 3–60).

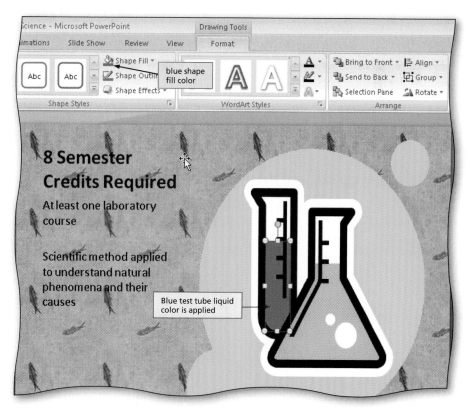

Figure 3–60

Other Ways

1. Right-click object, click Format Shape on shortcut menu, click Color button

To Delete a PowerPoint Object

With the beaker and test tube liquid color changes, you want to delete the green circle in the upper-right corner of the clip. The following steps delete this object.

1
• Click the green circle in the upper-right corner to select it (Figure 3–61).

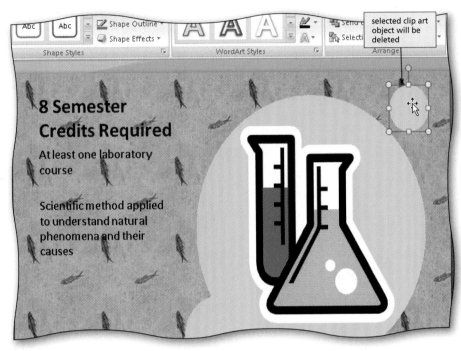

Figure 3–61

2
• Press the DELETE key to delete this object (Figure 3–62).

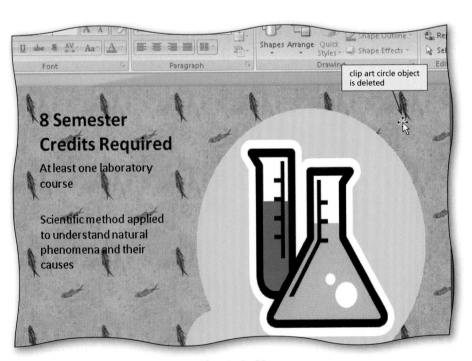

Figure 3–62

To Regroup Objects

Recall that a clip art picture is an object imported from the Microsoft Clip Organizer. Disassembling imported, embedded, or linked objects eliminates the embedding data or linking information the object contains that ties it back to its original source. Use caution when objects are not completely regrouped. Dragging or scaling affects only the selected object, not the entire collection of objects. All of the ungrouped objects in the beaker picture must be regrouped so they are not accidentally moved or manipulated. The following steps regroup these objects into one object.

1

- Click just outside the clip to display the clip placeholder.

Q&A

How do I know if I have clicked the correct area?

The Group button should be available in the Arrange group.

- Click the Format tab under Drawing Tools, if necessary, and then click the Group button in the Arrange group (Figure 3–63).

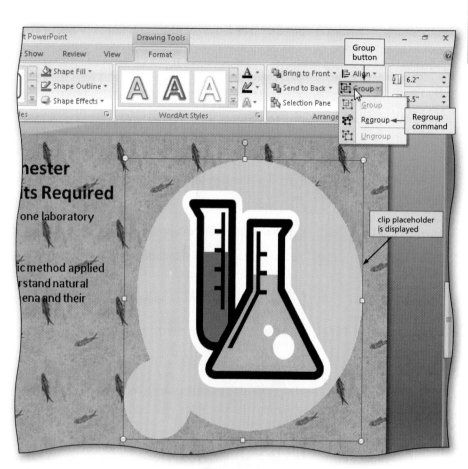

Figure 3–63

2

- Click Regroup to combine all the objects.

Other Ways

1. Right-click clip, point to Group on shortcut menu, click Regroup

---

Use left-brain / right-brain content concepts.
The left side of your brain screens material analytically and filters out most of the information presented. At best, this text is transferred to your short-term memory. If you have critical text on your slides, therefore, you need to make it stand out by making it visually appealing. This graphic information gets processed by your right brain, which responds to sensory information and stores the images in long-term memory.

Plan Ahead

Creating and Modifying a SmartArt Diagram

The wide variety of SmartArt layouts and styles adds visual interest to your slides. The Microsoft Word outline you imported had bulleted text on Slide 2 that you converted into a SmartArt graphic. You also can create a graphic by selecting a graphic type and then adding text. The second text paragraph on Slide 3 mentions the scientific method, so Slide 4 will explain the steps used in this methodology. The Continuous Block Process SmartArt graphic is an appropriate type to help visualize the scientific method. This graphic type is found in the Process category.

To Insert a Slide and Add Title Text

The final slide in this presentation will use a SmartArt layout. The following steps add a new slide (Slide 4) and then create the title text.

1 Click Home on the Ribbon and then click the New Slide button in the Slides group.

2 Click the Layout button in the Slides group and then click the Title Only layout.

3 Type Scientific Method in the title text placeholder.

4 Select the title text and then click the Bold button on the Mini toolbar (Figure 3–64).

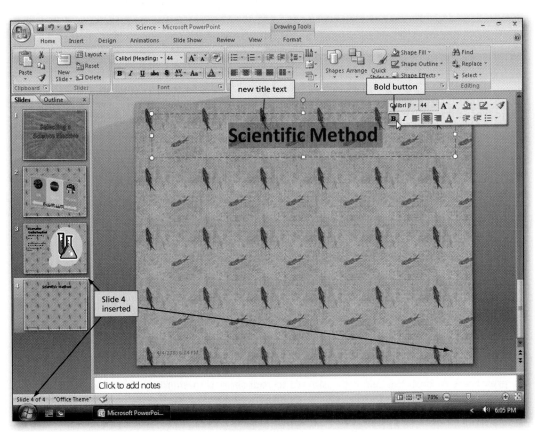

Figure 3–64

To Insert a SmartArt Graphic

The following steps insert the Continuous Block Process SmartArt graphic on Slide 4.

● Click Insert on the Ribbon to display the Insert tab.

● Click the SmartArt button in the Illustrations group to display the Choose a SmartArt Graphic dialog box.

● Click Process in the left pane to display the Process gallery.

● Click the Continuous Block Process graphic (row 2, column 1) to display a preview of this graphic in the right pane (Figure 3–65).

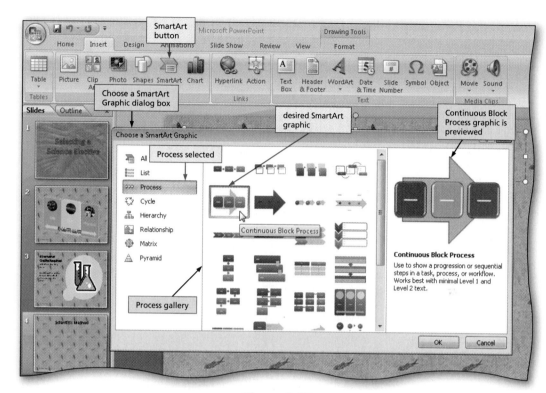

Figure 3–65

❷

● Click the OK button to insert this SmartArt graphic on Slide 4 (Figure 3–66). If necessary, click Text Pane in the Create Graphic group to open the text pane if it does not display automatically.

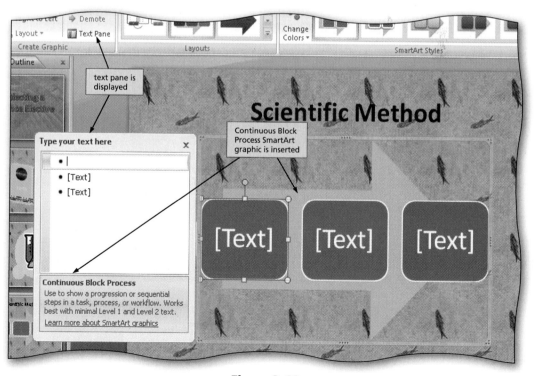

Figure 3–66

Certification
The Microsoft Certified Application Specialist (MCAS) program provides an opportunity for you to obtain a valuable industry credential — proof that you have the PowerPoint 2007 skills required by employers. For more information see Appendix G or visit the PowerPoint 2007 Certification Web page (scsite.com/ppt2007/cert).

Text Pane

The Text pane assists you in creating a graphic because you can direct your attention to developing and editing the message without being concerned with the actual graphic. Each SmartArt graphic has an associated Text pane with bullets that function as an outline and map directly to the image. You can create new lines of bulleted text and then indent and demote these lines. You also can check spelling. The following table shows the character shortcuts you can use to enter Text pane characters.

Table 3–2 Text Pane Keyboard Shortcuts	
Activity	**Shortcut**
Indent text	TAB or ALT+SHIFT+RIGHT ARROW
Demote text	SHIFT+TAB or ALT+SHIFT+LEFT ARROW
Add a tab character	CTRL+TAB
Create a new line of text	ENTER
Check spelling	F7
Merge two lines of text	DELETE at the end of the first text line
Display the shortcut menu	SHIFT+F10
Switch between the Text pane top and the Learn more about SmartArt graphics link at the bottom	CTRL+SHIFT+F
Switch between the SmartArt graphic and the Text pane	CTRL+SHIFT+F2
Close the Text pane	ALT+F4
Switch the focus from the Text pane to the SmartArt graphic border	ESC

To Enter Text in the SmartArt Graphic

The following steps insert four lines of text in the Text pane and in the corresponding SmartArt shapes on Slide 4.

1

- Type Hypothesis in the first bullet line and then press the RIGHT ARROW key to move the insertion point to the second bullet line (Figure 3–67).

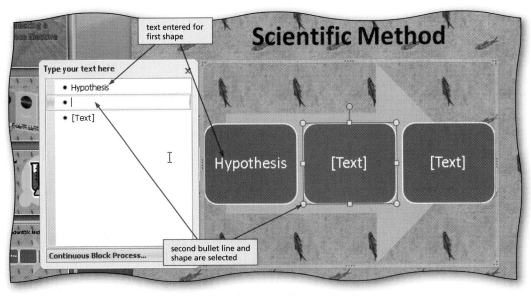

Figure 3–67

- Type Experiment in the second bullet line and then press the RIGHT ARROW key.

- Type Observation in the third bullet line and then press the ENTER key to create a fourth bullet line and shape.

- Type Theory in the fourth bullet line. Do not press the ENTER or RIGHT ARROW keys (Figure 3–68).

Q&A I mistakenly pressed the ENTER key. How can I delete the bullet line I just added?

Press the BACKSPACE key to delete the line.

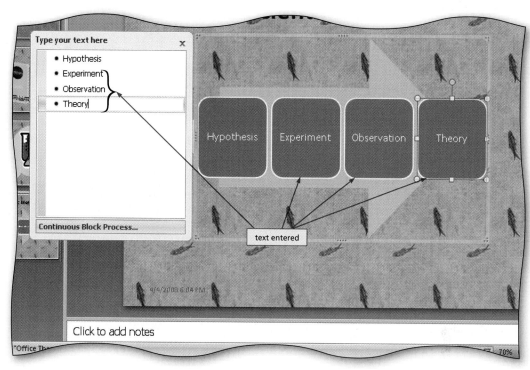

Figure 3–68

To Format the Text Pane Characters

Once the desired characters are entered in the Text pane, you can change the font size, and apply formatting features, such as bold, italic, and underlined text. The following steps format the text by changing the shape text font color and bolding the letters.

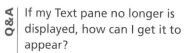

- With the Text pane open, drag through all four bulleted lines to select the text and display the Mini toolbar (Figure 3–69).

Q&A If my Text pane no longer is displayed, how can I get it to appear?

Click the control, which is the tab with two arrows pointing to the right and left, on the left side of the SmartArt graphic.

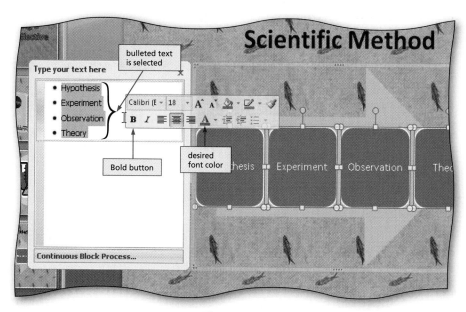

Figure 3–69

● Click the Font Color button to change the color of the shape text to the red displayed on the button.

● Click the Bold button on the Mini toolbar to bold the text (Figure 3–70).

Q&A

These two formatting changes did not appear in the Text pane. Why?

Not all the formatting changes are evident in the Text pane, but they will appear in the corresponding shape.

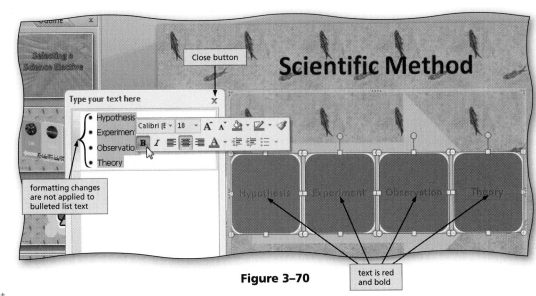

Figure 3–70

To Add a SmartArt Style to the Graphic

With the text entered in the Text pane, you can close it and then add a style to the four SmartArt shapes. The following steps add the Metallic Scene style to the Slide 4 SmartArt graphic.

1 Click the Close button in the SmartArt Text pane so that it no longer is displayed.

2 With the SmartArt graphic still selected, click the More button in the SmartArt Styles group to expand the SmartArt Styles gallery.

3 Click the Metallic Scene style (row 2, column 2) in the 3-D category in the SmartArt gallery to apply this style to the graphic (Figure 3–71).

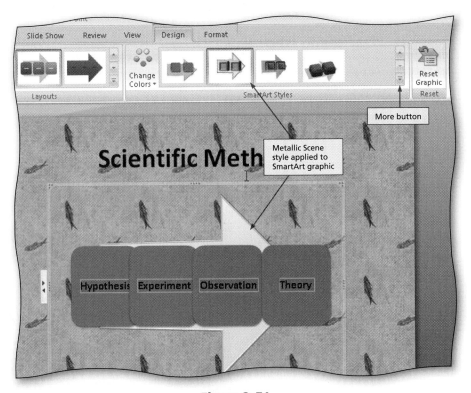

Figure 3–71

To Change the SmartArt Color

A final modification you can make is to change the graphic's color. The following steps change the SmartArt graphic color to the same Colorful range used in the SmartArt graphic in Slide 2.

1 With the SmartArt graphic still selected, click the Change Colors button in the SmartArt Styles group to display the Change Colors gallery.

2 Click the Colorful Range – Accent Colors 5 to 6 (row 2, column 5) in the Colorful category to apply this color variation to the graphic (Figure 3–72).

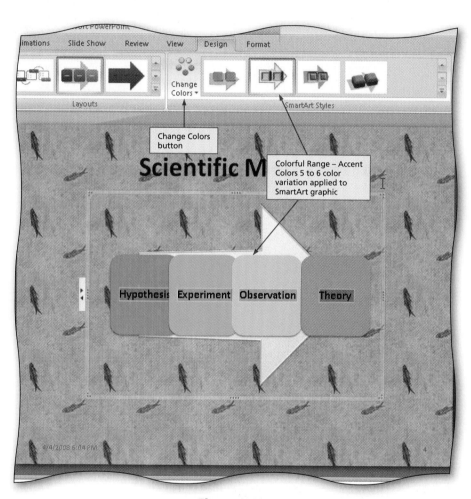

Figure 3–72

To Adjust the SmartArt Graphic Size

When you view the completed graphic, you may decide that individual shapes or the entire art needs to be enlarged or reduced. If you change the size of one shape, the other shapes also may change size to maintain proportions. Likewise, the font size may change in all the shapes if you increase or decrease the font size of one shape. On Slide 4, the SmartArt graphic size can be increased to fill the space and add readability. All the shapes will enlarge proportionally when you adjust the graphic's height and width. The following steps increase the SmartArt graphic size.

- With the SmartArt graphic still selected, press and hold the left mouse button and then drag the bottom-right corner sizing handle diagonally to the location shown in Figure 3–73.

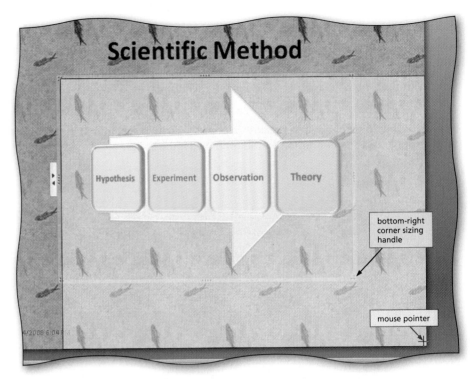

Figure 3–73

- Release the mouse button

- Press the UP and LEFT ARROW keys to position the graphic in the center of the slide below the title text (Figure 3–74).

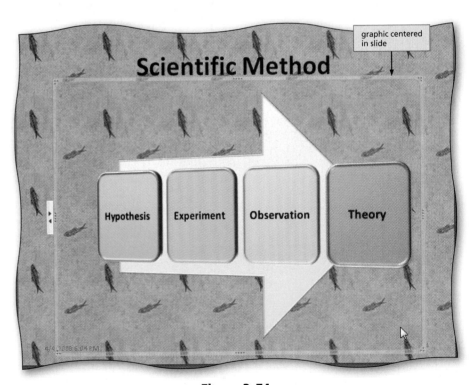

Figure 3–74

To Save an Existing Presentation with the Same File Name

Now that Slide 4 is complete, you should save the presentation. The following step saves the presentation again.

1 Click the Save button on the Quick Access Toolbar to overwrite the previous Science file on the USB flash drive.

To Add a Transition between Slides

A final enhancement you will make in this presentation is to apply the Shape Diamond transition in the Wipes category to all slides and change the transition speed to Slow. The following steps apply this transition to the presentation.

1 Click Animations on the Ribbon to display the Animations tab and then click the More button in the Transition to This Slide group to expand the Transitions gallery.

2 Click the Shape Diamond transition (row 5, column 6) in the Wipes category in the Transitions gallery to apply this transition to Slide 4.

3 Click the Transition Speed arrow in the Transition to This Slide group and then click Slow to change the transition speed for Slide 4.

4 Click the Apply To All button in the Transition to This Slide group to apply this transition and speed to all four slides in the presentation (Figure 3–75).

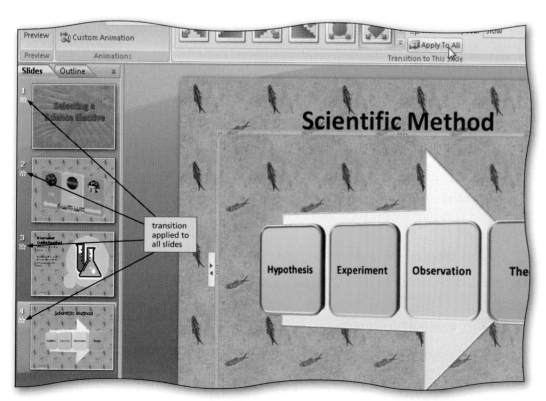

Figure 3–75

To Change Document Properties and Save the Presentation

Before saving the presentation again, you want to add your name, class name, and some keywords as document properties. The following steps use the Document Information Panel to change document properties and then save the project.

1 Click the Office Button to display the Office Button menu, point to Prepare on the Office Button menu, and then click Properties on the Prepare submenu to display the Document Information Panel.

2 Click the Author text box, if necessary, and then type your name as the Author property. If a name already is displayed in the Author text box, delete it before typing your name.

3 Click the Subject text box, if necessary delete any existing text, and then type your course and section as the Subject property.

4 Click the Keywords text box, if necessary delete any existing text, and then type `science electives, required credits, scientific method` as the Keywords property.

5 Click the Close the Document Information Panel button so that the Document Information Panel no longer is displayed.

6 Click the Save button on the Quick Access Toolbar to overwrite the previous Science file on the USB flash drive.

BTW

Quick Reference
For a table that lists how to complete the tasks covered in this book using the mouse, Ribbon, shortcut menu, and keyboard, see the Quick Reference Summary at the back of this book, or visit the PowerPoint 2007 Quick Reference Web page (scsite.com/ppt2007/qr).

To Run an Animated Slide Show

All changes are complete, and the presentation is saved. You now can view the Science presentation. The following step starts Slide Show view.

1 Click Slide 1 in the Slides pane to display the title slide and then click the Slide Show button to display the title slide.

2 Click each slide and view the transition effect and slides.

To Preview and Print Handouts

All changes are complete, and the presentation is saved. You now can create handouts to accompany the slide show. The following steps preview and then print the presentation.

1 Click the Office Button, point to Print, and then click Print Preview on the Print submenu.

2 Click the Print What arrow in the Page Setup group and then click Handouts (4 Slides Per Page) in the Print What list.

3 Click the Print button in the Print group.

4 Click the OK button in the Print dialog box to print the handout (Figure 3–76).

5 Click the Close Print Preview button in the Preview group on the Print Preview tab to return to Normal view.

4/24/2008

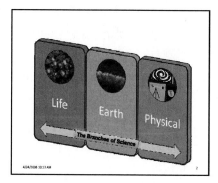

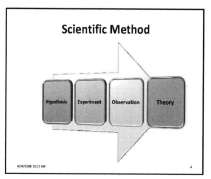

1

Figure 3–76

To Quit PowerPoint

This project is complete. The following steps quit PowerPoint.

1 Click the Close button on the right side of the title bar to quit PowerPoint.

2 If necessary, click the No button in the Microsoft Office PowerPoint dialog box so that any changes you have made are not saved.

Chapter Summary

In this chapter you have learned how to open a Microsoft Word document as a PowerPoint presentation, format a slide background, convert text to a WordArt and to a SmartArt graphic, modify clip art, and insert a SmartArt graphic and then add text. The items listed below include all the new PowerPoint skills you have learned in this chapter.

1. Open a Microsoft Word Outline as a Presentation (PPT 165)
2. Insert a Texture Fill (PPT 168)
3. Insert a Picture to Create a Background (PPT 171)
4. Format the Background Picture Fill Transparency (PPT 172)
5. Add Slide Numbers, Date, and Time (PPT 172)
6. Apply a WordArt Style (PPT 175)
7. Format the WordArt Text Fill (PPT 176)
8. Change the Weight of the WordArt Outline (PPT 178)
9. Add a WordArt Text Effect (PPT 179)
10. Delete the Subtitle Placeholder (PPT 180)
11. Convert Text to a SmartArt Graphic (PPT 181)
12. Insert Images from a File into a SmartArt Graphic (PPT 182)
13. Add a SmartArt Style to the Graphic (PPT 184)
14. Change the SmartArt Color (PPT 186)
15. Insert a Text Box (PPT 188)
16. Rotate a Text Box (PPT 189)
17. Format the Text Box (PPT 191)
18. Insert a Clip into a Content Placeholder (PPT 197)
19. Ungroup a Clip (PPT 198)
20. Change the Color of PowerPoint Objects (PPT 199)
21. Delete a PowerPoint Object (PPT 202)
22. Regroup Objects (PPT 203)
23. Insert a SmartArt Graphic (PPT 205)
24. Enter Text in the SmartArt Graphic (PPT 206)
25. Format the Text Pane Characters (PPT 207)
26. Add a SmartArt Style to the Graphic (PPT 208)
27. Change the SmartArt Color (PPT 209)
28. Adjust the SmartArt Graphic Size (PPT 209)
29. Save an Existing Presentation with the Same File Name (PPT 211)
30. Add a Transition between Slides (PPT 211)

If you have a SAM user profile, you may have access to hands-on instruction, practice, and assessment. Log in to your SAM account (http://sam2007.course.com) to launch any assigned training activities or exams that relate to the skills covered in this chapter.

Learn It Online

Test your knowledge of chapter content and key terms.

Instructions: To complete the Learn It Online exercises, start your browser, click the Address bar, and then enter the Web address `scsite.com/ppt2007/learn`. When the Office 2007 Learn It Online page is displayed, click the link for the exercise you want to complete and then read the instructions.

Chapter Reinforcement TF, MC, and SA
A series of true/false, multiple choice, and short answer questions that test your knowledge of the chapter content.

Flash Cards
An interactive learning environment where you identify chapter key terms associated with displayed definitions.

Practice Test
A series of multiple choice questions that test your knowledge of chapter content and key terms.

Who Wants To Be a Computer Genius?
An interactive game that challenges your knowledge of chapter content in the style of a television quiz show.

Wheel of Terms
An interactive game that challenges your knowledge of chapter key terms in the style of the television show *Wheel of Fortune*.

Crossword Puzzle Challenge
A crossword puzzle that challenges your knowledge of key terms presented in the chapter.

Apply Your Knowledge

Reinforce the skills and apply the concepts you learned in this chapter.

Changing the Backgrounds, Modifying a Clip, and Applying WordArt
Instructions: Start PowerPoint. Open the presentation, Apply 3–1 Tidal Wave, from the Data Files for Students. See the inside back cover of this book for instructions for downloading the Data Files for Students, or contact your instructor for more information about accessing required files.

The two slides in the presentation present general information about tidal waves. The document you open is an unformatted presentation. You are to insert a texture fill, insert a picture to create a background, modify clip art, and add a WordArt text effect so the slides look like Figure 3–77.

Perform the following tasks:

1. Insert the Water droplets texture fill on the Slide 1 background (row 1, column 5) and change the transparency to 20%. Use your name in place of Student Name and bold and underline your name.

2. On Slide 2, insert the Wave picture from the Microsoft Clip Organizer to create the background and change the transparency to 5%.

3. On Slide 1, apply the WordArt style Fill – Accent 1, Metal Bevel, Reflection (row 6, column 5) to the title text and increase the font size to 80.

4. On Slide 2, apply the WordArt style Fill – Accent 1, Inner Shadow – Accent 1 (row 2, column 4) shown in Figure 3–77b to the text paragraphs. Apply the Glow Variation Accent color 3, 5 pt glow (row 1, column 3).

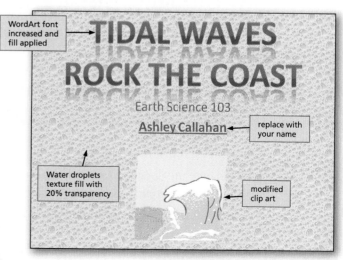

Figure 3–77 (a)

Continued >

Apply Your Knowledge *continued*

5. On Slide 1, ungroup the wave clip and then delete the red and black borders. Regroup the clip.

6. Apply the Wedge wipe transition (row 1, column 5) to all slides.

7. Check the spelling, and then display the revised presentation in Slide Sorter view to check for consistency.

8. Change the document properties, as specified by your instructor. Save the presentation using the file name, Apply 3–1 Sea. Submit the revised document in the format specified by your instructor.

Figure 3–77 (b)

Extend Your Knowledge

Extend the skills you learned in this chapter and experiment with new skills. You may need to use Help to complete the assignment.

Formatting Slide Backgrounds and Converting Text to SmartArt

Instructions: Start PowerPoint. Open the presentation, Extend 3-1 Food Pyramid, from the Data Files for Students. See the inside back cover of this book for instructions for downloading the Data Files for Students, or contact your instructor for more information about accessing required files. The images for the slides were obtained with permission from the MyPyramid.gov Web site, which is sponsored by the United States Department of Agriculture.

You will format slide backgrounds and add your name and slide number to the slide footers. You then will convert bulleted text to a SmartArt graphic.

Perform the following tasks:

1. On Slide 1, insert a texture fill on the background. On Slides 2 through 6, insert a different fill on the backgrounds and change the transparency.

2. On all slides, add slide numbers and your name (Figure 3–78a). To insert your name, click the Footer box on the Slide tab in the Header and Footer dialog box and then type your name in the Footer text box.

3. Convert the bulleted lists on Slides 2 through 6 to the Vertical Block List layout (row 4, column 3 in the List category) SmartArt graphic. Change the color.

4. Apply a fill to the title text on Slides 2 through 6. Change the text outline color to an appropriate color and bold the text.

5. Apply a transition to all slides.

6. Change the document properties, as specified by your instructor. Save the presentation using the file name, Extend 3-1 Revised Pyramid.

7. Submit the revised document in the format specified by your instructor.

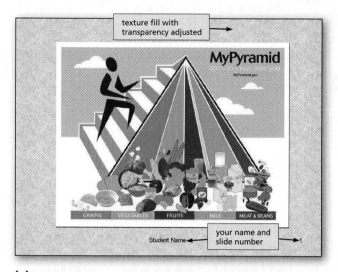

(a)

(b)

(c)

(d)

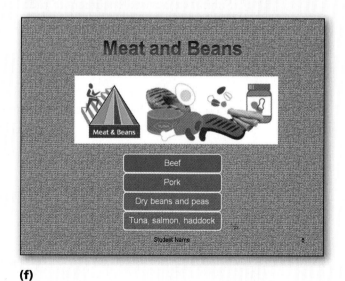

(e)

(f)

Figure 3–78

Make It Right

Analyze a presentation and correct all errors and/or improve the design.

Applying Background and Quick Styles

Instructions: Start PowerPoint. Open the presentation, Make It Right 3-1 Money, from the Data Files for Students. See the inside back cover of this book for instructions for downloading the Data Files for Students, or contact your instructor for more information about accessing required files.

Correct the formatting problems and errors in the presentation while keeping in mind the guidelines presented in this chapter.

Perform the following tasks:

1. Insert the Oak texture fill and change the transparency to 10%.

2. Replace the words, Student Name, in the text box with your name. Rotate the text box 90 degrees to the right and then move the text box to the left of the title and subtitle placeholders. Delete the subtitle placeholder.

3. Ungroup the money clip and then delete the green background. Recolor the dollar sign to Green (color 6 in the Standard Colors row). Regroup the clip and adjust its size.

4. Use the spell checker to correct the misspellings.

5. Apply the Wipe Right transition. Change the speed to Slow.

6. Change the document properties, as specified by your instructor. Save the presentation using the file name, Make It Right 3-1 Manage.

7. Submit the revised document in the format specified by your instructor.

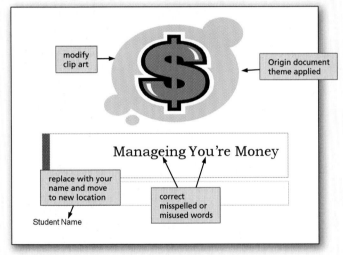

Figure 3–79

In the Lab

Design and/or create a presentation using the guidelines, concepts, and skills presented in this chapter. Labs 1, 2, and 3 are listed in order of increasing difficulty.

Lab 1: Modifying and Grouping Two Clips

Problem: Often you need to insert several clips on one slide to create the desired visual message. If these clips work together to form one new picture, you can group them so their proportions and distance from each other will not change if you modify the slide. You decide to develop a PowerPoint slide with two clips of a dog and a bone in a dish. You insert these clips, modify them to meet your intended message, and then group them together to create the slide shown in Figure 3–80 from a blank presentation.

Instructions: Perform the following tasks.

1. Apply the Opulent document theme, change the layout to Blank, and then change the slide orientation to Portrait by clicking Design on the Ribbon to display the Design tab, clicking Slide Orientation in the Page Setup group, and then clicking Portrait. Insert the Pink tissue paper texture fill and change the transparency to 50%.

2. Import and size the dog clip shown in Figure 3–80. Ungroup the picture. Delete the bone under the dog's left paw. Delete the three triangles beside the dog's right paw.

3. Insert and size the bowl with a dog bone clip. Ungroup this clip and delete the green background. Recolor the two green parts of the bowl to Purple (color 10 in the Standard Colors row).

4. Regroup both clips together as one object by clicking the edge of one clip, holding down the SHIFT key, clicking the edge of the other object, right-clicking one object, pointing to Group on the shortcut menu, and then clicking Group.

5. Apply the Box Out wipe transition (row 3, column 3).

6. Add the current date and time and your name to the slide footer. To insert your name, click the Footer box on the Slide tab in the Header and Footer dialog box and then type your name in the Footer text box.

7. Change the document properties, as specified by your instructor. Save the presentation using the file name, Lab 3-1 Dog.

8. Submit the revised document in the format specified by your instructor.

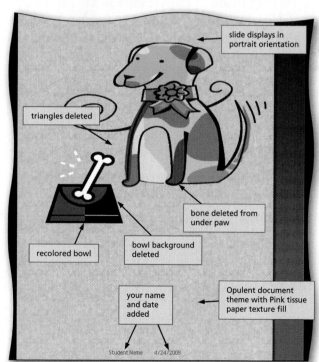

Figure 3-80

In the Lab

Lab 2: Creating a Presentation by Inserting an Outline and SmartArt

Problem: Thousands of years ago, myths were considered true. They were developed to explore the world's mysteries and to explain human nature. The twelve Greek gods ruled from atop Mount Olympus in Greece. Other gods and goddesses ruled from Egypt, Mexico, Guatemala, and Scandinavia. One of the assignments in your literature class is to give a speech about gods and goddesses. You develop an outline in Microsoft Word and then import it to prepare the PowerPoint presentation shown in Figures 3–81a through 3–81e to accompany your talk.

Instructions: Perform the following tasks.

1. Import the outline, Lab 3-2 Mythology Outline, from the Data Files for Students to a new presentation. Apply the Median document theme to the presentation.

2. On Slide 1, change the layout to Title Slide. Apply the Fill – Accent 1, Plastic Bevel, Reflection WordArt style (row 1, column 5 in the Applies to All Text in the Shape category) to the title text. Change the text fill color to Dark Blue (color 9 in the Standard Colors row) and change the outline line to 3 pt.

3. Insert the Goddess picture shown in Figure 3–81a to create the Slide 1 background and change the transparency to 70%.

4. On Slides 2 through 5, change the layout to Title and Text and then insert the Stationery texture fill. Apply the WordArt Offset Diagonal Top Left shadow text effect (row 3, column 3 in the Outer category) to the title text on each of these slides.

5. On Slide 2, import and size the Icarus clip shown in Figure 3–81b. Ungroup the picture. Delete the red tie and then regroup the clip.

6. On Slides 4 and 5, convert the bulleted lists to the Target List layout (row 3, column 3 in the Relationship category) SmartArt graphic. Apply the Powder design (row 1, column 4 in the 3-D category). Change the color to Colorful Range – Accent Colors 4 to 5 (column 4 in the Colorful category).

7. Insert your name in the footer on all slides except the title slide. Apply the Strips Left-Up transition (row 5, column 2 in the Wipes category) to all slides. Change the speed to Medium. Check the spelling and correct any errors.

8. Click the Slide Sorter view button, view the slides for consistency, and then click the Normal view button.

9. Change the document properties, as specified by your instructor. Save the presentation using the file name, Lab 3-2 Mythology.

10. Submit the revised document in the format specified by your instructor.

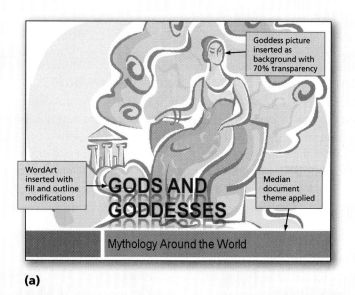

(a)

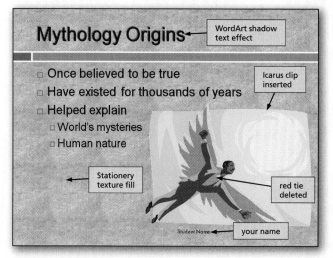

(b)

(c)

(d)

(e)

Figure 3–81

In the Lab

Lab 3: Creating a Presentation with a Text Box and WordArt

Problem: Today's ballroom dancing popularity is riding on the nostalgia of the 1950s' movies where Fred Astaire and Ginger Rogers showcased their ballroom dancing finesse. Television, motion picture, and Internet audiences are enthralled with watching stars, amateurs, and athletes perform their routines. Group dancing lessons are gaining popularity as a fun and energetic way to keep in shape and meet new people with similar interests. A new dance studio has opened in your town, and the owner has asked you to develop a PowerPoint presentation that she can share with potential customers. She hands you a Microsoft Word outline and asks you to create the presentation shown in Figures 3–82a through 3–82d.

Instructions: Perform the following tasks.

1. Import the outline, Lab 3–3 Dance Outline, from the Data Files for Students. Apply the Module document theme to the presentation. Change the font color of all title text to Yellow. On Slides 2, 3, and 4, center the title text and insert the Parchment texture fill.

2. On Slide 1, change the layout to Title Slide. Insert a text box in the gray area at the bottom of the slide, type your name, and then type Dance Studio in the text box. Bold your name, change the font color of the box text to Yellow, change the font size to 24, and then center the text box in the gray area.

3. Change the Slide 1 title text font size to 54 and then apply the Perspective Contrasting Right 3-D Rotation text effect (row 3, column 1 in the Perspective category). Delete the Subtitle placeholder.

4. Add the photograph and clip art shown in Figures 3–82a, 3–82c, and 3–82d from the Microsoft Clip Organizer. Adjust the clip sizes when necessary.

5. On Slide 2, change the layout to Title Only. Insert the Trapezoid List layout (row 5, column 2 in the List category) SmartArt graphic. Apply the Metallic Scene design (row 2, column 2 in the 3-D category). Change the color to Gradient Loop – Accent 1 (column 4 in the Accent 1 category). Add the text shown in Figure 3–82b in the Text pane. (To delete the second bullet in each group, select the line with that bullet and then press the BACKSPACE key twice. To create the Native American shape, position the insertion point in the last bullet line, press the SHIFT+TAB keys to promote the line, and then press the TAB key to demote the line.) Adjust the SmartArt graphic size and center it on the parchment portion of the slide.

6. Insert the slide number and date to Slides 2, 3, and 4. Apply the Shape Circle transition (row 5, column 5 in the Wipes category) to all slides. Change the speed to Medium. Check the spelling and correct any errors.

7. Click the Slide Sorter view button, view the slides for consistency, and then click the Normal view button.

8. Change the document properties, as specified by your instructor. Save the presentation using the file name, Lab 3-3 Dancing.

9. Submit the revised document in the format specified by your instructor.

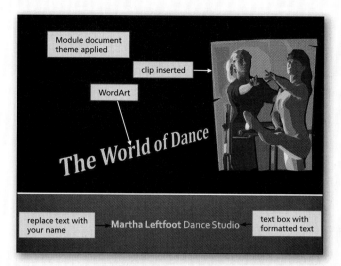

Figure 3–82

Cases and Places

Apply your creative thinking and problem solving skills to design and implement a solution.

● Easier ●● More Difficult

Note: Remember to use the 7 × 7 rule as you design the presentations: a maximum of seven words on a line and a maximum of seven lines on one slide.

● 1: Design and Create a National Parks Presentation

The United States Park Service establishes and preserves America's natural resources. Approximately 400 protected areas are part of the system, including the Grand Canyon, the Statue of Liberty, and Gettysburg. The National Park Service, part of the U.S. Department of the Interior, also works with local communities to help them preserve and manage their own local heritage and recreational areas. You and your friends have visited several National Park Service sites and have photos of the landscapes and animals you have seen. These digital photos are in the National Parks Photos folder on the Data Files for Students. Create a presentation using these photos. Apply at least three objectives found at the beginning of this chapter to develop the presentation. Add a title slide with SmartArt. Be sure to check spelling.

Continued >

Cases and Places *continued*

• 2: Design and Create a Solar System Presentation

In your Astronomy 101 class, you are studying the solar system, concentrating on the planets Mercury and Venus. For extra credit, you create a presentation with a slide featuring each planet. Begin the presentation with a title slide showing one aspect of the solar system as the slide background. Slide 2 should use the Basic Target SmartArt graphic in the Relationships category with the innermost circle representing the Sun, the middle circle representing Mercury, and the outer circle representing Venus. Use the files in the Inner Solar System folder on the Data Files for Students as backgrounds for each slide. Place the information in Table 3–3 in SmartArt diagrams. Apply slide transitions and a footer with page numbers and your name on all slides. Be sure to check spelling.

Table 3–3 Inner Solar System		
Planet	**Features**	**Distance from Sun**
Mercury	Temperature: 950°F sunlit side; −346°F dark side	36 million miles
Venus	Temperature: 55°F to 396°F Atmosphere: Carbon dioxide, nitrogen, and sulfuric acid	67 million miles

•• 3: Design and Create an Exercise Variety Presentation

In January of every year, people make resolutions to exercise on a regular basis. They faithfully begin working out for a few weeks, but then many quit because they become bored with the routine. In an effort to retain members, the fitness center in your community wants to persuade members to participate in a variety of activities to remain motivated. The director has asked you to prepare a presentation showcasing at least four activities and the number of calories burned per hour. You begin by writing an outline of your presentation in Microsoft Word and then show this document to her for approval. Import this document into a PowerPoint presentation and create a slide show. Convert text into a SmartArt graphic. Insert a text box and WordArt on the title slide, and use at least one modified clip from the Microsoft Clip Organizer. Apply a slide transition to all slides.

•• 4 Design and Create a Career Presentation

Make It Personal

Choosing a college major often is difficult. Most students change their major at least twice during their college careers, and many students return to campus to train for a new career after having worked for many years or raised a family. To gain information about a possible career, obtain a copy of the *Occupational Outlook Handbook* in your library, or view the publication online at www.bls.gov/oco/home.htm, and read about your intended field of study. Use the concepts and techniques from this chapter to develop and format a slide show with a title slide and a slide about training requirements, occupational duties, compensation, and employment prospects. Add at least one clip, a texture fill for the background, and a SmartArt graphic. Be sure to check spelling. Print a handout with two slides on each page.

•• 5: Design and Create a Large Deciduous Trees Presentation

Working Together

Homeowners often desire trees as part of their landscaping plans. Many deciduous trees, which drop their leaves in the fall, grow taller than 40 feet. If a tree is going to survive transplanting and grow properly, it must be planted in the proper location. Have each member of your team visit a local nursery or arboretum, or conduct online research and each select one large deciduous tree that is well suited for your environment. Gather information about each tree's botanical and common name, height, and spread. After coordinating the data, create a presentation with a least one slide showcasing each tree, including a photograph and SmartArt. As a group, critique each slide. Submit your assignment in the format specified by your instructor.

4 Working with Information Graphics

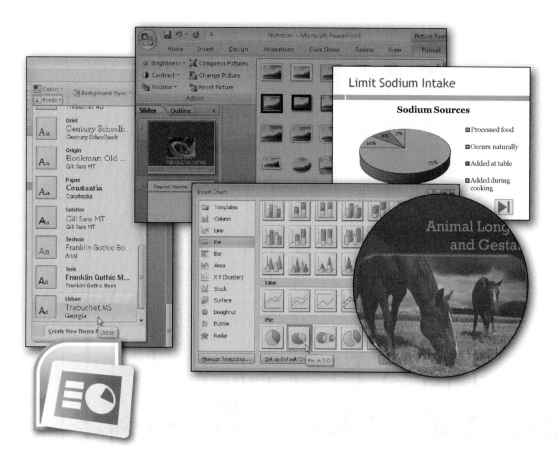

Objectives

You will have mastered the material in this chapter when you can:

- Modify an entire presentation by changing the theme colors and fonts
- Insert pictures and clips into slides without content placeholders
- Format pictures and clips by applying styles and adding borders
- Apply effects to pictures and clips
- Add hyperlinks to a slide
- Create and format a table

- Create a chart
- Find synonyms using the thesaurus
- Add action buttons and action settings
- Display guides to position slide elements
- Hide slides
- Run a slide show with hyperlinks

4 | Working with Information Graphics

Introduction

Audiences generally focus first on the visual elements displayed on a slide. Graphical elements increase **visual literacy**, which is the ability to examine and assess these images. They can be divided into two categories: images and information graphics. Images are the clips and photographs you have used in Chapters 2 and 3, and information graphics are tables, charts, graphs, and diagrams. Both sets of visuals help audience members interpret and retain material, so they should be designed and presented with care.

Project — Presentation with a Chart, Table, and Hyperlinks

BTW

Enhancing Speaker Confidence
Using information graphics can help increase your confidence as a speaker. When you rehearse your speech with your PowerPoint charts and tables, you should become confident knowing that these visuals support your verbal message. While you will burn nervous energy as you move toward the screen and point to specific information on these graphics, you should be relieved to know that your audience will be studying your charts and graphs and not focusing on you.

The project in this chapter follows visual content guidelines and uses PowerPoint to create the presentation shown in Figure 4–1. The slide show uses several visual elements to help audience members understand which vitamins are important in their diet and where sodium is added to food. The three-column table lists six essential vitamins, their sources, and how the body uses them. The three-dimensional pie chart shows four sources of sodium and emphasizes that the largest amount enters the body through processed food. The title slide picture is inserted and then given a particular effect. The document theme's color scheme is changed for visual interest. Action buttons on Slides 2, 3, and 4 help a presenter navigate from one slide to another. In addition, hyperlinks display specific Web sites when clicked during a presentation.

Overview

As you read through this chapter, you will learn how to create the presentation shown in Figure 4–1 by performing these general tasks:

- Format a picture by applying an effect.
- Create a table and chart.
- Change the document theme color scheme.
- Find and replace words.
- Run a slide show with action buttons and hyperlinks.

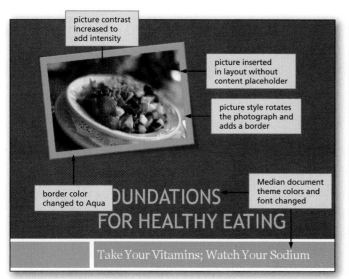

(a) Slide 1 (Title Slide)

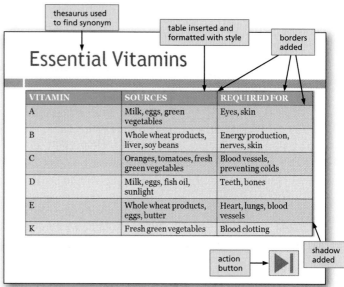

(b) Slide 2

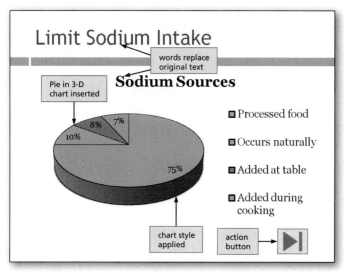

(c) Slide 3

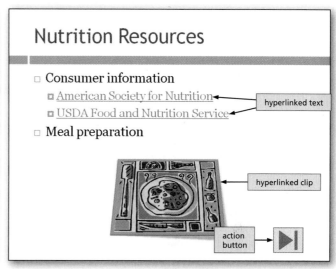

(d) Slide 4

Figure 4–1

General Project Guidelines

When creating a PowerPoint presentation, the actions you perform and decisions you make will affect the appearance and characteristics of the finished document. As you create a presentation with information graphics, such as the project shown in Figure 4–1, you should follow these general guidelines:

1. **Select an appropriate font.** All letters in a particular font are constructed from lines, which are called strokes. The weight, or thickness, of these strokes and their slant, or direction, determine the structure of the font. Some fonts are suited best for titles, and others are most appropriate for the body of the slide.

2. **Choose outstanding hyperlink text or images.** Make the hypertext letters or graphics large so a speaker is prompted to click them during a speaking engagement.

3. **Consider the graphic's function.** Decide precisely what message you want the chart, table, or illustration to convey to the audience. Determine its purpose.

(continued)

Plan Ahead

(continued)

4. **Choose the appropriate chart style.** Most audience members like charts to help them understand the relationships between groups of data. Charts express numbers visually, but you must decide which chart type best conveys the points you are attempting to make in your presentation. PowerPoint presents a variet y of chart layouts, and you must decide which one is effective in presenting the relationships between numbers and to indicate important trends.

5. **Obtain information for the graphic from credible sources.** The text or numbers in the graphics should be current and correct. Verify the sources of the information and be certain you have typed the data correctly. On the slide or during your presentation, acknowledge the source of the information. Give credit to the person or organization that supplied the information for your graphics, if necessary.

6. **Test your visual elements.** Show your slides to several friends or colleagues and ask them to interpret what they see. Time the duration they studied each slide. Have them verbally summarize the information they perceived.

When necessary, more specific details concerning the above guidelines are presented at appropriate points in the chapter. The chapter also will identify the actions you perform and decisions you made regarding these guidelines during the creation of the presentation shown in Figure 4–1.

To Start PowerPoint and Apply a Document Theme

Note: If you are using Windows XP, see Appendix F for alternate steps.

If you are using a computer to step through the project in this chapter and you want your screens to match the figures in this book, you should change your computer's resolution to 1024 × 768. For information about how to change a computer's resolution, read Appendix E.

The following steps start PowerPoint and apply a document theme.

1 Start PowerPoint.

2 If the PowerPoint window is not maximized, click its Maximize button.

3 Apply the Median document theme.

BTW

Increasing Audience Retention
Researchers unanimously conclude that well-constructed information graphics help audience members retain the information you are presenting. Although the exact amount of measured retention varies, one study found that an audience recalled five times more material when it was presented both verbally and visually. These audience members needed to use both senses of sight and hearing to engaged in the presentation and tune out distractions. Their retention ultimately is enhanced.

Developing the Core Presentation Slides

The four slides in your presentation give details about healthy eating. The title slide introduces the topic, Slides 2 and 3 give information about vitamins and sodium, and the final slide contains information about Internet sources for nutritional information. You will enhance all four slides with visual elements, including a photograph, table, chart, and clip.

To Create a Title Slide

The title slide in the project uses a large photograph of a salad bowl to gain the viewers' attention and to express the concept that they can make healthy food choices. The title and subtitle text reinforce the food concept by mentioning that the slide show will focus on taking vitamins and limiting salt to promote healthy eating. The following steps create the text for the title slide.

1 Click the title text placeholder.

2 Type foundations in the title text placeholder and then press the ENTER key.

3 Type for healthy eating in the second line of the title text placeholder.

4 Press CTRL+ENTER to move the insertion point to the subtitle text placeholder.

5 Type Take Your Vitamins; Watch Your Salt but do not press the ENTER key (Figure 4–2).

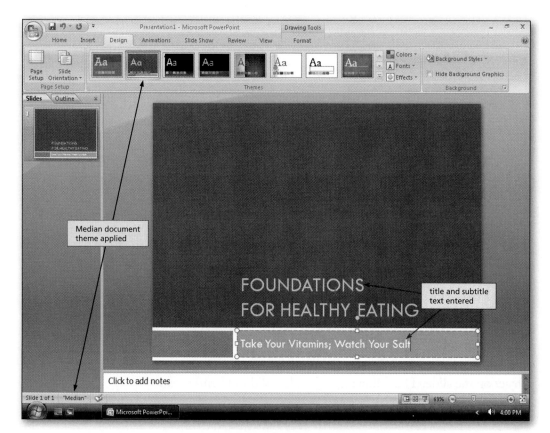

Figure 4–2

To Create Slide 2

An information graphic will be the primary content of Slide 2. The table on Slide 2 will give viewers details on which vitamins are necessary for healthy living. The title text of this slide will introduce this topic. The following steps create the title text for Slide 2.

1 Click the New Slide button on the Home tab.

2 Type Required Vitamins in the title text placeholder (Figure 4–3).

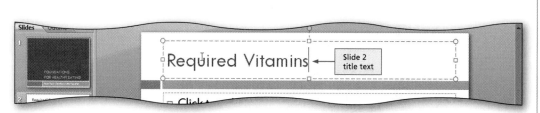

Figure 4–3

BTW

Rehearsing with Your Graphics
As you practice your speech, rehearse transitioning from your speech to your graphic and then from your graphic to your speech. Consider the points where you introduce the material, unveil the slide, walk to the screen, point to pertinent material, and then walk away from the screen. Know precisely where material is displayed on the screen; you should not need to examine the slides to locate the statistics or pictures that coordinate with your verbal message.

To Create Slide 3

Slide 3 will give information about sources of salt in the diet. The chart you will create will show where salt is found in the foods we ingest. The following steps create the title text for this slide.

1 Click the New Slide button on the Home tab.

2 Type Limit Salt Intake in the title text placeholder (Figure 4–4).

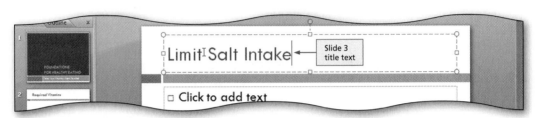

Figure 4–4

To Create Slide 4

Slide 4 in the presentation gives resources for additional information. Audience members can refer to these sources to learn more about the topics presented in the slide show or to obtain specific information that would benefit them personally.

Part of this slide will contain hyperlinks. A **hyperlink**, also called a **link**, is a connection from one slide to a Web page, another slide, a custom show consisting of specific slides in a presentation, or a file. Hyperlinks can be text or an object, such as a picture, graph, shape, or WordArt. The first step in creating hyperlinks is typing the text or inserting an object on the slide. The following steps add a slide and enter text.

1 Click the New Slide button on the Home tab.

2 Type Nutrition Resources in the title text placeholder.

3 Press CTRL+ENTER to move the insertion point to the body text placeholder.

4 Type Consumer information and then press the ENTER key.

5 Press the Tab key. Type American Society for Nutrition and then press the ENTER key.

6 Type USDA Food and Nutrition Service and then press the ENTER key.

7 Press SHIFT+TAB to demote the paragraph. Type Meal planning but do not press the ENTER key (Figure 4–5).

Figure 4–5

To Save the Presentation

You applied a design template and created four slides. The next step is to save the presentation.

Note: If you are using Windows XP, see Appendix F for alternate steps.

1 With a USB flash drive connected to one of the computer's USB ports, click the Save button on the Quick Access Toolbar to display the Save As dialog box.

2 Type `Nutrition` in the File name text box to change the file name.

3 Close the Folders list. If Computer is not displayed in the Favorite Links section, drag the top or bottom edge of the Save As dialog box until Computer is displayed.

4 Click Computer in the Favorite Links section, and then double-click your USB flash drive in the list of available drives.

5 Click the Save button in the Save As dialog box to save the document on the USB flash drive with the file name, Nutrition.

Customizing Entire Presentation Elements

With the basic elements of the slide show created, you can modify two default elements that display on all slides in the presentation. First, you will modify the template by changing the color scheme. Then, you will change the font.

Presentation Template Color Scheme

Each presentation template has twelve complementary colors, which are called the **color scheme**. You can apply these colors to all slides, an individual slide, notes pages, or audience handouts. A color scheme consists of four colors for a background and text, six accent colors, and two hyperlink colors. The Theme Colors button on the Design tab contains a square with four colors; the top two colors indicate the primary text and background colors, and the bottom two colors indicate the accent colors. You also can customize the theme colors to create your own set and give them a unique name. Table 4–1 explains the components of a color scheme.

BTW

Choosing Contrasting Colors
Researchers have determined that black or dark blue type on a white screen is an extremely effective color combination. The contrast increases readability. If you add a background color, be certain it has sufficient contrast with the font color. This contrast is especially important if your presentation will be delivered in a room with bright lighting that washes out the screen.

Table 4–1 Color Scheme Components

Component	Description
Background color	The background color is the fundamental color of a PowerPoint slide. For example, if the background color is black, you can place any other color on top of it, but the fundamental color remains black. The black background shows everywhere you do not add color or other objects.
Text color	The text color contrasts with the background color of the slide. As a default, the text border color is the same as the text color. Together with the background color, the text and border colors set the tone for a presentation. For example, a gray background with black text and border sets a dramatic tone. In contrast, a red background with yellow text and border sets a vibrant tone.
Accent colors	Accent colors are designed as colors for secondary features on a slide. They often are used as fill colors on graphs and as shadows.
Hyperlink colors	The default hyperlink color is set when you type the text. When you click the hyperlink text during a presentation, the color changes to the Followed Hyperlink color.

To Change the Presentation Theme Colors

The first modification to make is to change the color scheme throughout the presentation. The following steps change the color scheme for the template from a brown title slide background with orange and blue accent to a gray background with blue and gold accents.

1

- Click Design on the Ribbon to display the Design tab.

- Click the Theme Colors button in the Themes group to display the Theme Colors gallery.

- Point to the Module built-in theme to display a live preview of this color scheme (Figure 4–6).

 Experiment

- Point to various themes in the Theme Colors gallery and watch the colors change on Slide 4.

Q&A Why does an orange circle surround the Median color scheme in the Themes Colors gallery?

It shows the Median document theme is applied, and those eight colors are associated with that theme.

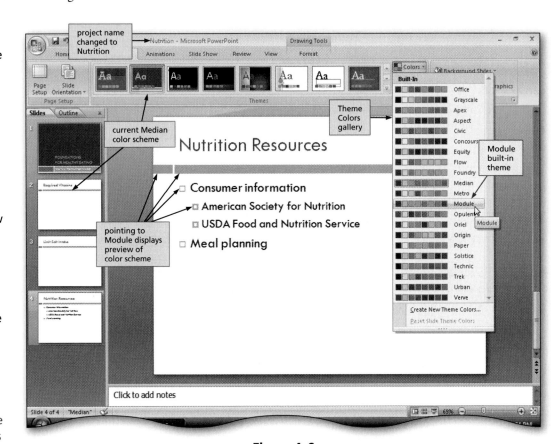

Figure 4–6

2

- Click Module in the Theme Colors gallery to change the presentation theme colors to Module (Figure 4–7).

Q&A What if I want to return to the original theme color?

You would click the Theme Colors button and then click Median in the Theme Colors gallery.

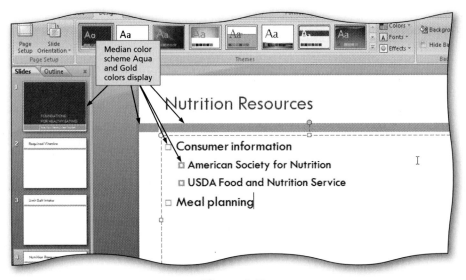

Figure 4–7

Plan
Ahead

Select an appropriate font.

Complex messages and formal settings call for simple fonts. If the topic of your presentation is to discuss corporate downsizing or elimination of a company pension, then a script or playful font, such as Comic Sans, sends a mixed message. This sentence uses the Comic Sans font. Some fonts are mono-spaced, which means the spacing for each letter is the same. Courier is a mono-spaced font. Most fonts are proportionally spaced, such as the font used in this sentence, so that different letters have varying spacing between them. Proportionally spaced fonts generally are easier to read than mono-spaced fonts.

PowerPoint designers often set their own guidelines on type usage. Some never use italic type or fancy fonts, such as **Broadway Engraved** or UMBRA. Some fonts, such as *Blackadder*, look good on a computer monitor but look distorted when they are projected on a screen, and others, such as *Vivaldi*, look better when they are projected. Use a maximum of four fonts in an entire presentation: one for title text, a second for body text, and one or two other fonts for emphasis.

To Change the Theme Fonts

The second modification to make is to change the theme fonts. Each document theme uses at least one font and several font sizes for the heading and body text. The Theme Fonts button displays a capital letter A with the current heading font associated with the document theme. When you click the Theme Fonts button, names and samples of the fonts are displayed for each document theme. As with the default document color scheme, you also can customize the theme fonts. The following steps change the theme heading and body fonts from Twentieth Century MT to Trebuchet MS and Georgia, which are associated with the Urban document theme.

- Click the Theme Fonts button in the Themes group to display the Theme Fonts gallery.

- Scroll through the Theme Fonts gallery until Urban is displayed and then point to Urban to display a live preview of the Urban font set (Figure 4–8).

🔍 **Experiment**

- Point to various font sets in the Theme Fonts gallery and watch the title text and body text fonts change in Slide 4.

Q&A What elements are selected in the Urban theme font set?

The capital letter A in the square shows a sample of the heading font (Trebuchet MS); the lowercase letter a shows the body font (Georgia). The names of these fonts display to the right of the button.

Figure 4–8

2

• Click Urban in the Theme Fonts gallery to change the presentation theme fonts to Urban (Figure 4–9).

Q&A

What if I want to return to the original font set?

You would click the Theme Fonts button and then click Median in the Theme Fonts gallery.

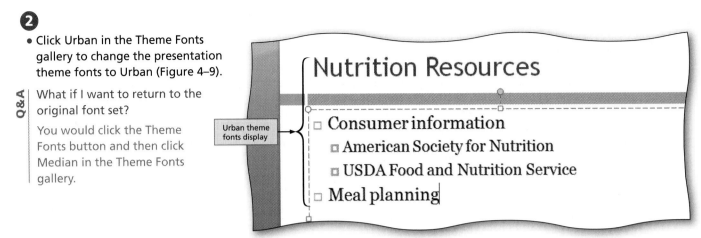

Figure 4–9

Inserting and Formatting a Picture and a Clip into Slides Without Content Placeholders

PowerPoint does not require you to use a content placeholder to add pictures and clips to a slide. You can insert these graphical elements on any slide regardless of its slide layout. The Slide 1 and Slide 4 layouts do not have a content placeholder for graphics, but you can insert files from the Microsoft Clip Organizer or from your Data Files for Students. Once these visuals are inserted, you can format them by applying a style, applying and coloring borders, recoloring, and changing the brightness or contrast.

To Insert a Picture into a Slide without a Content Placeholder

The next step in creating the presentation is to insert a picture of a salad bowl into Slide 1, which does not have a content placeholder. This picture is found in the Microsoft Clip Organizer and also on the Data Files for Students. See the inside back cover of this book for instructions on downloading the Data Files for Students, or contact your instructor for more information about accessing the required files. The following steps insert this picture.

1

• Click the Previous Slide button three times to display Slide 1.

• Click Insert on the Ribbon to display the Insert tab (Figure 4–10).

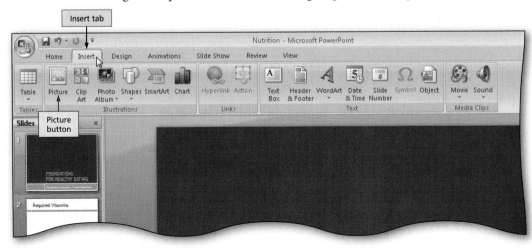

Figure 4–10

2

- With your USB flash drive connected to one of the computer's USB ports, click the Picture button to display the Insert Picture dialog box.

- If the Folders list is displayed below the Folders button, click the Folders button to remove the Folders list.

- Click the Previous Locations arrow on the Address bar and then click Computer in the Favorite Links section. Double-click UDISK 2.0 (E:) to select the USB flash drive, Drive E in this case, as the device that contains the picture.

- Click Salad to select the file name (Figure 4–11).

Q&A What if the picture is not on a USB flash drive?

Use the same process, but select the device containing the picture in the Favorite Links section. Another option is to locate the picture in the Microsoft Clip Organizer.

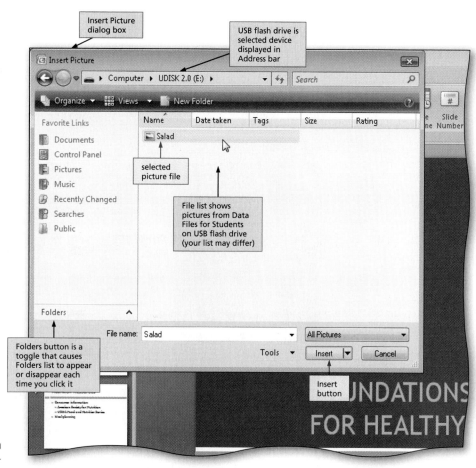

Figure 4–11

3

- Click the Insert button in the dialog box to insert the picture into Slide 1 (Figure 4–12).

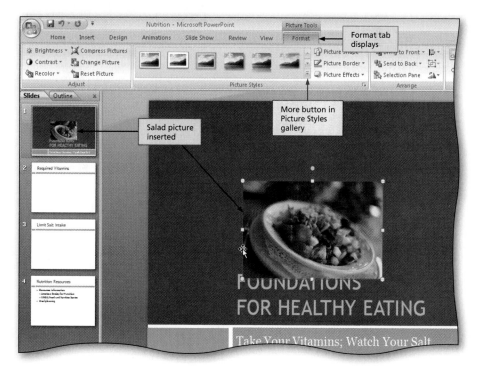

Figure 4–12

To Apply a Picture Style

A title slide should grasp the audience's attention, and one method of creating interest is by modifying graphical images. The salad picture is colorful, but you can increase its visual appeal by adding a style. PowerPoint has a wide variety of more than 25 styles to alter the rectangular shape. These styles include borders, shadows, reflections, and various shapes. The following steps apply a picture style with an angle and a reflection to the salad picture in Slide 1.

1

- With the salad picture selected, click the More button in the Picture Styles gallery to expand the gallery.

- Point to the Rotated, White style in the Picture Styles gallery (row 3, column 5) to display a live preview of that style applied to the picture in the slide (Figure 4–13).

Experiment

- Point to various picture styles in the Picture Styles gallery and watch the format of the picture change in the slide.

2

- Click the Rotated, White style to apply this selected style to the picture.

3

- Drag the picture to the location shown in Figure 4–1a on page PPT 227.

Figure 4–13

To Change a Picture Border Color

The Module presentation theme colors can be used to enhance the salad picture border. The area under the Picture Border button indicates the current border color, which is tan. To coordinate the colors on the slide, you can apply the Aqua color located in the lower-left corner of Slide 1 to the picture border. The theme colors associated with the Module document theme are displayed in the first row of the Picture Border color palette. The following steps change the border color.

1

- With the salad picture selected, click the Picture Border button on the Format tab to display the Picture Border color palette.

- In the Theme Colors area, point to the Aqua, Accent 2 color (row 1, column 6) to display a live preview of this color on the picture border (Figure 4–14).

Experiment

- Point to various colors in the Picture Border gallery and watch the border color on the picture change in Slide 1.

2

- Click the Aqua, Accent 2 color to apply this color to the salad picture border.

Q&A If I had other pictures with borders, could I change their borders to Aqua easily?

Yes. Every picture border color will change to Aqua when you select the picture and then click the Picture Border icon.

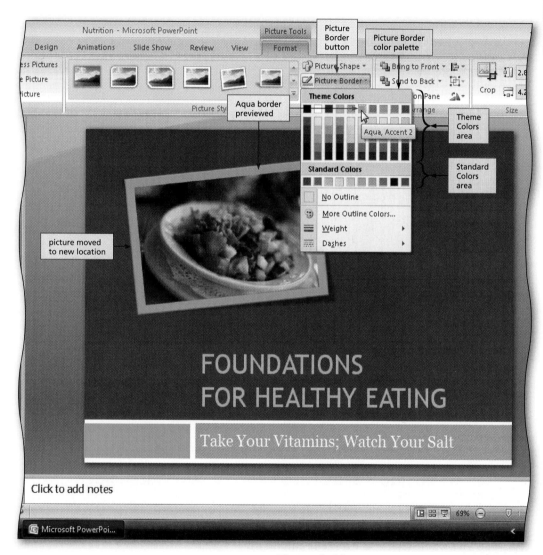

Figure 4–14

To Change a Picture Contrast

A photograph's color intensity can be modified by changing the brightness and contrast. **Brightness** determines the overall lightness or darkness of the entire image, whereas **contrast** is the difference between the darkest and lightest areas of the image. The brightness and contrast are changed in predefined percentage increments. The following steps increase the contrast to intensify the picture colors.

- With the salad picture still selected, click the Contrast button in the Adjust group to display the Contrast gallery.

- Point to +20 % to display a live preview of this contrast on the picture (Figure 4–15).

🔍 **Experiment**

- Point to various percentages in the Contrast gallery and watch the contrast change on the picture in Slide 1.

❷

- Click +20 % to apply this contrast to the salad picture.

Q&A
How can I remove all effects from the salad picture?

Click the Reset Picture button in the Adjust group.

Figure 4–15

Other Ways
1. In Format Picture dialog box, move Contrast slider or   enter number in box next to slider

To Insert a Clip into a Slide without a Content Placeholder

Slide 4 does not have a content placeholder, but you want to insert a clip of a placemat and utensils into this slide. This clip is found in the Microsoft Clip Organizer. Contact your instructor if you have difficulty locating this clip. The following steps insert this clip into Slide 4.

- Click the Next Slide button three times to display Slide 4.

- Click Insert on the Ribbon to display the Insert tab (Figure 4–16).

Figure 4–16

2

- Click the Clip Art button in the Illustrations group to display the Clip Art task pane.

- Type utensils in the Search for text box and then click the Go button.

- If necessary, scroll down the list to display the utensils clip shown in Figure 4–17.

- Click the clip shown in Figure 4–17 to insert it into Slide 4 (Figure 4–17).

Q&A

What if the utensils image displayed in Figure 4–17 is not shown in my Clip Art task pane?

Select a similar clip. Your clips may be different depending on the clips installed on your computer and if you have an open connection to the Internet.

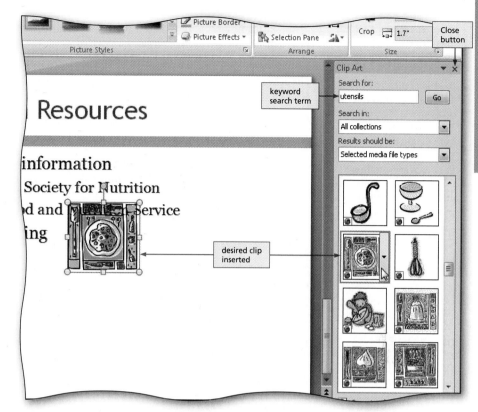

Figure 4–17

3

- Click the Close button on the Clip Art task pane title bar.

- Drag a corner sizing handle to increase the clip's size to approximately the size shown in Figure 4–18.

- Drag the clip to the location shown in Figure 4–18.

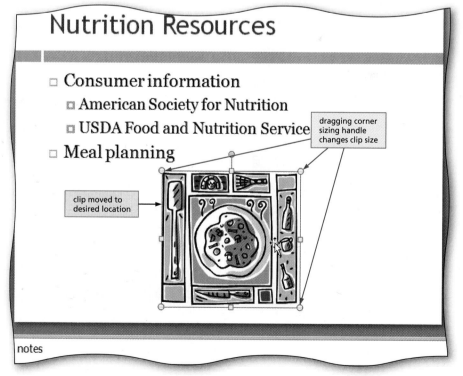

Figure 4–18

To Apply a Picture Style to a Clip

BTW

Importing Pictures from Scanners and Cameras
Previous PowerPoint versions allowed users to import pictures directly from a scanner or a camera. PowerPoint 2007, however, does not include this feature. You must download the pictures from these sources to your computer and then insert them into your presentation.

Adding a style to a clip helps add visual interest. To enhance the clip in this manner, you follow the same procedure used with applying a style to a picture. The same styles available for pictures can be used for clips, including shapes, borders, reflection, and shadows. The following steps apply a picture style with an angle and border to the clip in Slide 4.

1 With the utensils clip selected, click Format on the Ribbon to display the Format tab, if necessary. Click the More button in the Picture Styles gallery to expand the gallery.

2 Preview the various picture styles and then click the Relaxed Perspective, White style in the Picture Styles gallery (row 4, column 1) to apply this selected style to the clip (Figure 4–19).

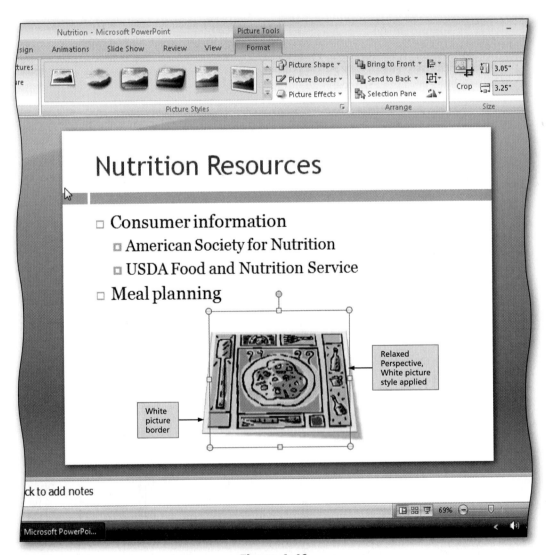

Figure 4–19

To Change the Border Color of a Clip

The Module presentation theme colors again can be used to enhance the utensils clip border color. For consistency, apply the Aqua color to this border. The Picture Border button is displaying with the Aqua color below the icon, so that color is the active color. If you select the clip and then click the Picture Border button, the active color will be added to the clip border. The following steps change the clip's border color.

1 With the utensils clip selected, click the Picture Border icon to apply the Aqua color to the clip border (Figure 4–20).

Q&A Can I select another color for the border?

Yes. Click the Picture Border button arrow and select one of the colors in the Theme Colors or Standard Colors areas.

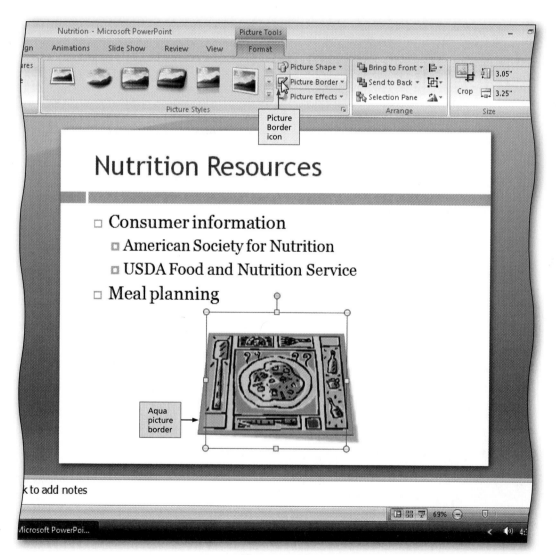

Figure 4–20

To Change the Brightness of a Clip

The final format change you will make is to increase the clip's brightness. The same steps used to modify a picture's contrast are used to modify a clip's brightness. The following steps increase the brightness.

1 With the utensils clip still selected, click the Brightness button in the Adjust group to display the Brightness gallery (Figure 4–21).

2 Preview the various percentages in the Brightness gallery and then click -10 % to apply this brightness to the utensils clip.

Q&A Do I remove all effects from a clip in the same manner as I would remove them from a picture?

Yes. Click the Reset Picture button in the Adjust group.

Other Ways

1. In Format Picture dialog box, move Brightness slider or enter number in box next to slider

Figure 4–21

**Plan
Ahead**

> **Choose outstanding hyperlink text or images.**
> Outstanding speakers are aware of their audiences and know their speech material well. They have rehearsed their presentations and know where the hypertext is displayed on the slides. During a presentation, however, they sometimes need to divert from their planned material. Audience members may interrupt with questions, the room may not have optimal acoustics or lighting, or the timing may be short or long. It is helpful, therefore, to make the slide hyperlinks as large and noticeable to speakers as possible. The presenters can glance at the slide and receive a visual cue that it contains a hyperlink. They then can decide whether to click the hyperlink to display a Web page.

Adding Hyperlinks

Many speeches are presented in rooms with Internet access. Showing Web sites during a presentation can add much visual imagery, and this content can greatly enhance the overall message.

Hyperlinks

PowerPoint includes a hyperlink feature that allows you to access a specific Uniform Resource Locator (URL) from within your presentation if you are connected to the Internet. **Hyperlinks**, also called **links**, connect one slide to a Web page, another slide, a custom show consisting of specific slides in a presentation, or a file.

When you point to a hyperlink, the mouse pointer becomes the shape of a hand to indicate the text or object contains a hyperlink. A hyperlink can be any element of a slide. This includes a single letter, a word, a paragraph, or any graphical image. By default, hyperlinked text is displayed underlined and in a color that is part of the color scheme. When you click a hyperlink during a presentation, the Web browser will open a new window and display the Web address you specified when you created the presentation.

Slide 4 contains three hyperlinks to organizations' Web pages: two are text, and one is the utensils clip art. The following sections explain how to create the hyperlinks.

BTW

**Customizing
ScreenTips**
You can create a custom screen tip that displays when you hover your mouse over a hyperlink. Click the ScreenTip button in the Insert Hyperlink dialog box, type the desired ScreenTip text in the Set Hyperlink ScreenTip dialog box, and then click the OK button.

To Add a Hyperlink to a Slide

On Slide 4, each second-level paragraph will be a hyperlink to a nutrition organization's Web page. If you are connected to the Internet when you run the presentation, you can click each of these paragraphs. Your browser will display the corresponding Web page for each paragraph. The following steps create the first hyperlink.

- Triple-click the first second-level paragraph, American Society for Nutrition, to select the text.

- Click Insert on the Ribbon to display the Insert tab (Figure 4–22).

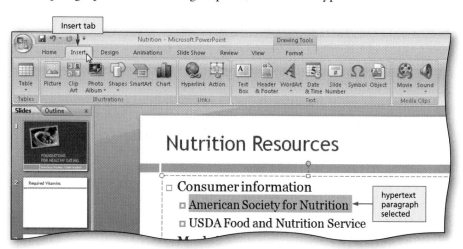

Figure 4–22

- Click the Insert Hyperlink button in the Links group to display the Insert Hyperlink dialog box.

- If necessary, click the Existing File or Web Page button in the Link to area.

- Type www.nutrition.org in the Address text box (Figure 4–23).

Q&A

I did not type http://, but those letters displayed automatically in the Address text box. Why?

PowerPoint realizes you typed a URL and consequently inserted those letters automatically.

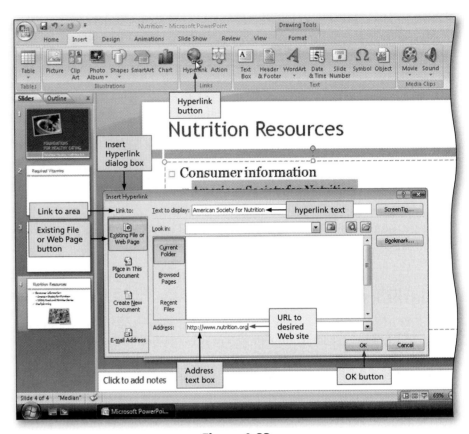

Figure 4–23

- Click the OK button to insert the hyperlink.

- Click Slide 4 anywhere except the text placeholder (Figure 4–24).

Q&A

Why is this paragraph now displaying underlined and with a new font color?

The default style for hyperlinks is underlined text. The Module hyperlink color is Aqua, so PowerPoint formatted the paragraph to that color automatically.

Q&A

I clicked the hyperlink, but the Web page did not display. Why?

Hyperlinks are active only when you run the presentation, not when you are creating it in Normal or Slide Sorter view.

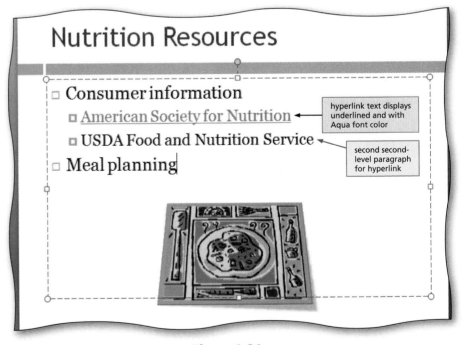

Figure 4–24

Other Ways

1. Right-click selected text, click Hyperlink, type address, click OK button

2. Press CTRL+K, type address, press ENTER

To Add a Hyperlink to the Second Paragraph

The hyperlink for the first second-level paragraph is complete. The next task is to create the hyperlink for the other second-level paragraph on Slide 4.

1 Triple-click the second second-level paragraph, USDA Food and Nutrition Service.

2 Click the Insert Hyperlink button and then type `www.fns.usda.gov/nutritionlink/` in the Address text box. Click the OK button.

3 Click Slide 4 anywhere except the text placeholder.

To Add a Hyperlink to a Clip

Pictures, shapes, and objects also can serve as hyperlinks. The next step is to create the hyperlink for the utensils clip on Slide 4.

1 Click the utensils clip to select it.

2 Click the Insert Hyperlink button and then type `www.mealsmatter.org/` in the Address text box. Click the OK button.

3 Click Slide 4 anywhere except the text placeholder (Figure 4–25).

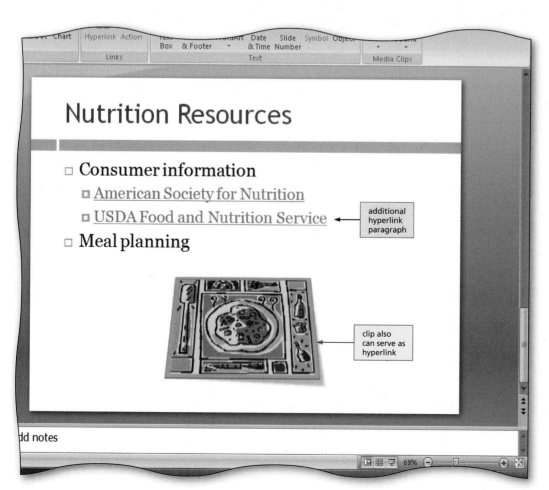

Figure 4–25

Plan
Ahead

Consider the graphic's function.
Determine why you are considering using an information graphic. The chart or graph should introduce meaningful information, support information in your speech, and help you convey details. If you are inserting the graphic simply for the sake of enlivening the presentation, then do not use it. Graphics should help your audience understand and retain information and should not merely repeat details they have seen or heard up to this point in the slide show. Take care in placing a manageable amount of information in your chart or table. Avoid overwhelming your audience with numerous slices or bars in your chart or lines in your table. If your audience is confused or struggling with comprehending the graphic, chances are they simply will abandon the task and wait for you to display the next slide.

Adding a Table to a Slide and Formatting

BTW

Copying Tables to and from Excel and Word
In this project you create a table, but you also can copy a table created in Microsoft Excel or Word to the Office Clipboard and then paste it into your slide. Similarly, you can copy a table you create in PowerPoint to an Excel worksheet or a Word document.

One effective method of organizing information on a slide is to use a **table**, which is a grid consisting of rows and columns. You can enhance a table with formatting, including adding colors, lines, fonts, and backgrounds. In this project you will create the table and then add borders and a shadow effect.

Tables

The table on Slide 2 (shown in Figure 4–1b on page PPT 227) contains information about specific vitamins, what food products contain them, and what part of the body they affect. This data is listed in three columns and seven rows. The intersections of these rows and columns are **cells**.

To begin developing this table, you first must create an empty table and insert it into the slide. You must specify the table's **dimension**, which is the total number of rows and columns. This table will have a 3 × 7 dimension; the first number indicates the number of columns, and the second specifies the number of rows. You will fill the cells with data pertaining to vitamins. Then you will format the table using a table style.

To Insert an Empty Table

The next step in developing the presentation is to insert an empty table into Slide 2. The following steps insert a table with three columns and seven rows into Slide 2.

1
• Click the Previous Slide button two times to display Slide 2 (Figure 4–26).

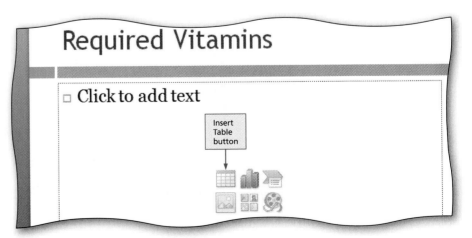

Figure 4–26

2

- Click the Insert Table button in the content placeholder to display the Insert Table dialog box.

- Click the down arrow to the right of the Number of columns text box two times so that the number 3 appears in the box.

- Click the up arrow to the right of the Number of rows text box five times so that the number 7 appears in box (Figure 4–27).

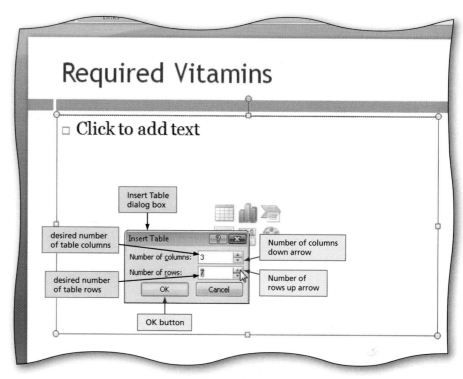

Figure 4–27

3

- Click the OK button to insert the table into Slide 2 (Figure 4–28).

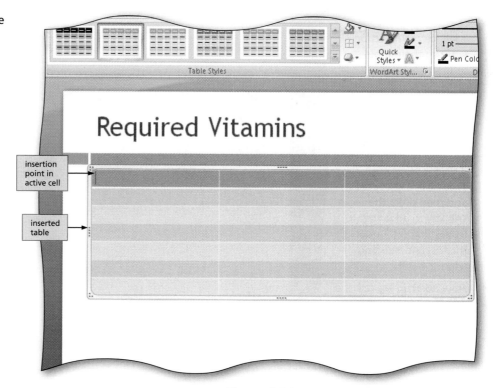

Figure 4–28

Other Ways

1. Click Table on Insert tab, drag to select columns and rows, press ENTER

To Enter Data in a Table

The Slide 2 table consists of three columns: one for the vitamin name, one for the vitamin source, and the third for how the body uses the vitamin. A **heading** identifies each column. The next step is to enter the data in the cells of the empty table. To place data in a cell, you click the cell and then type. Table 4–2 shows the three column headings and the corresponding data.

Table 4–2 Required Vitamins Data		
Vitamin	**Sources**	**Required for**
A	Milk, eggs, green vegetables	Eyes, skin
B	Whole wheat products, liver, soy beans	Energy production, nerves, skin
C	Oranges, tomatoes, fresh green vegetables	Blood vessels, preventing colds
D	Milk, eggs, fish oil, sunlight	Teeth, bones
E	Whole wheat products, eggs, butter	Heart, lungs, blood vessels
K	Fresh green vegetables	Blood clotting

The following steps enter the headings and data in the table.

1

- With the insertion point in the left cell of the table, type VITAMIN and then press the TAB key to advance the insertion point to the middle column heading cell.

- Type SOURCES and then press the TAB key to advance to the rightmost column heading cell.

- Type REQUIRED FOR and then press the TAB key to advance to the first cell under the Vitamin heading (Figure 4–29).

Q&A

How do I correct cell contents if I make a mistake?

Click the cell and then correct the text.

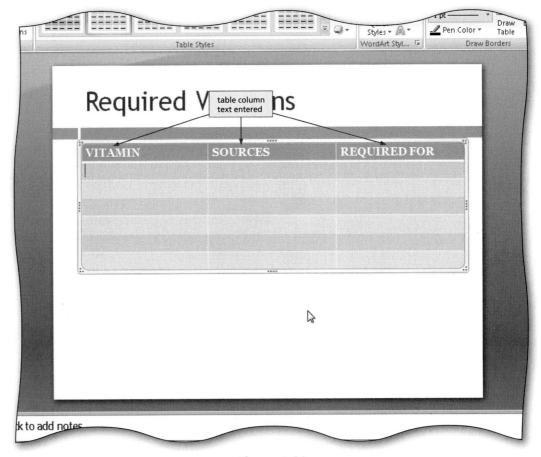

Figure 4–29

2

- Repeat Step 1 to enter the remaining table cells by using Table 4-2 as a guide (Figure 4–30).

Q&A How can I add more rows to the table?

When the insertion point is positioned in the bottom-right cell, press the TAB key.

Q&A What if I pressed TAB after filling in the last cell and added another row?

Right-click the unnecessary row and then click Delete Rows in the shortcut menu.

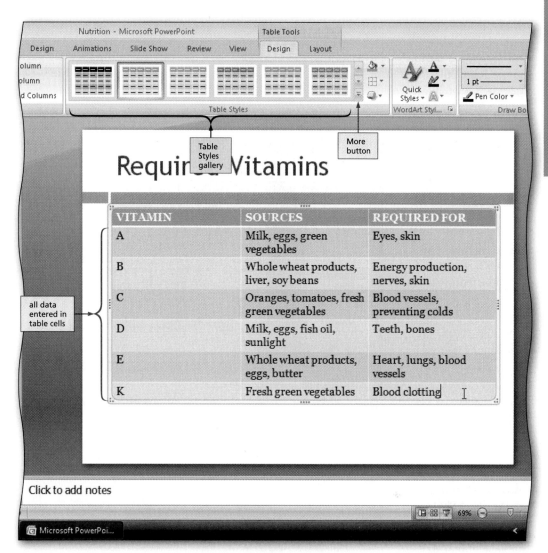

Figure 4–30

To Apply a Table Style

A table Quick Style is a combination of formatting options that use the theme colors applied to the presentation. When you inserted the table, PowerPoint automatically applied a style. Thumbnails of this style and others are displayed in the Table Styles gallery. These styles use a variety of colors and shading and are grouped in the categories of Best Match for Document, Light, Medium, and Dark. You want the Slide 2 table to coordinate with the Aqua border you applied to the photograph and clip in Slides 1 and 4, so you will select a table style that uses both the Aqua and Gold accent colors that are part of the Module color scheme. The steps on the following page apply a table style to the Slide 2 table.

- With the insertion point in the table, click the More button in the Table Styles gallery (shown in Figure 4–30) to expand the Table Styles gallery.

- Scroll down and then point to Dark Style 2 - Accent 1/Accent 2 in the Dark area (row 2, column 2) (Figure 4–31).

Q&A

Does the Table Styles gallery have a live preview feature?

Yes, but the gallery is covering most the table, greatly limiting your ability to preview table styles.

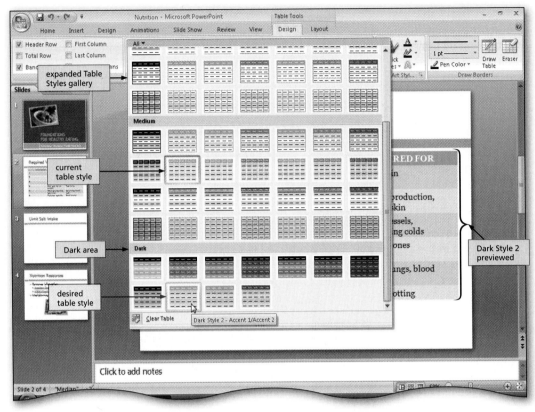

Figure 4–31

- Click Dark Style 2 - Accent 1/Accent 2 in the Table Styles gallery to apply the selected style to the table (Figure 4–32).

Q&A

Can I resize the columns and rows or the entire table?

Yes. To resize columns or rows, drag a **column boundary** (the border to the right of a column) or the **row boundary** (the border at the bottom of a row) until the column or row is the desired width or height. To resize the entire table, drag a **table resize handle**.

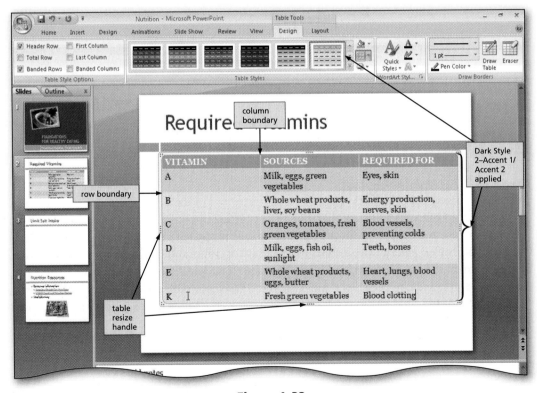

Figure 4–32

To Add Borders to a Table

The Slide 2 table does not have borders around the entire table or between the cells. The following steps add borders to the entire table.

1

- Click the edge of the table so that the insertion point does not appear in any cell.

- Click the No Border button arrow in the Table Styles group to display the Border gallery (Figure 4–33).

Q&A

Why is the button called No Border?

The button name will change based on the type of border, if any, present in the table. Currently no borders are applied.

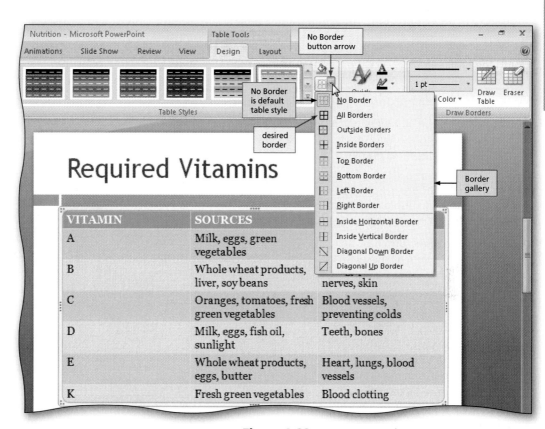

Figure 4–33

2

- Click All Borders in the Border gallery to add borders around the entire table and to each table cell (Figure 4–34).

Q&A

Can I apply any of the border options in the Border gallery?

Yes. You can vary the look of your table by applying borders only to the cells, around the table, or in such combinations as the top, bottom, or left and right edges.

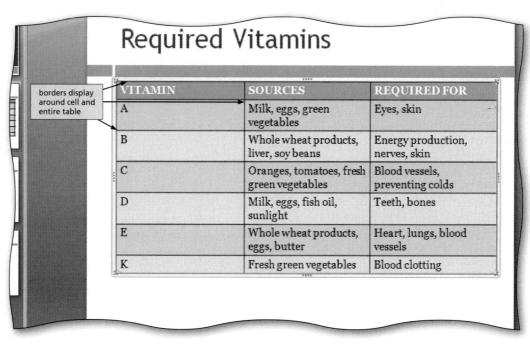

Figure 4–34

To Add an Effect to a Table

To enhance the visual appeal of the table, you can add an effect. PowerPoint gives you the option of applying a bevel to specified cells so they have a three-dimensional appearance. You also can add a shadow or reflection to the entire table. The following steps add a shadow similar to the shadow in the lower-right corner of the Slide 1 salad photograph and give a three-dimensional appearance to the entire table.

1

- With the table selected, click the Effects button in the Table Styles group to display the Effects list.

Q&A What is the difference between a shadow and a reflection?

A shadow gives the appearance that a light is displayed on the table, which causes a shadow behind the graphic. A reflection gives the appearance that the table is shiny, so a mirror image appears below the actual graphic.

2

- Point to Shadow to display the Shadow gallery (Figure 4–35).

Q&A How do the shadows differ in the Outer, Inner, and Perspective categories?

The Outer shadows are displayed on the outside of the table, while the Inner shadows are displayed in the interior cells. The Perspective shadows give the illusion that a light is shining from the right or left sides of the table or from above, and the table is casting a shadow.

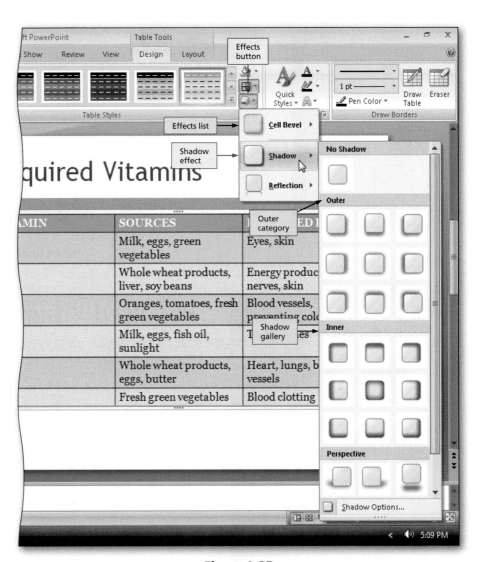

Figure 4–35

3

- Point to Offset Right in the Outer category (row 2, column 1) to display a live preview of this shadow (Figure 4–36).

Experiment

- Point to the various shadows in the Shadow gallery and watch the shadows change in the table.

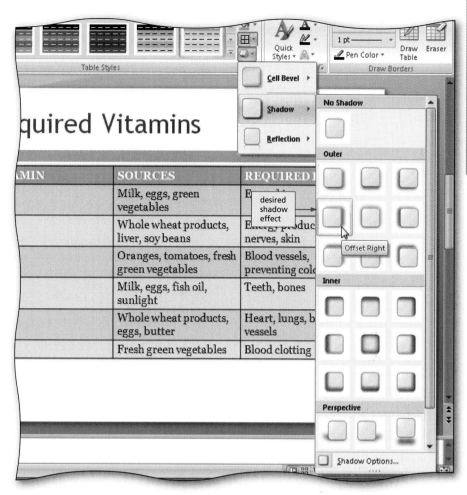

Figure 4–36

4

- Click Offset Right to apply this shadow to the table (Figure 4–37).

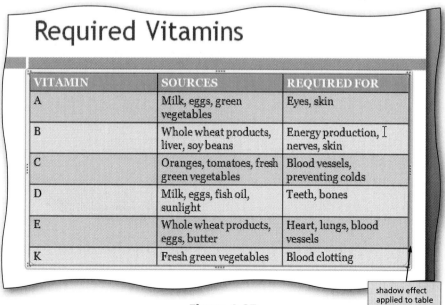

Figure 4–37

Plan
Ahead

Choose the appropriate chart style.
General adult audiences are familiar with bar and pie charts, so those chart types are good choices. Specialized audiences, such as engineers and architects, are comfortable reading scatter and bubble charts.

Common chart types and their purposes are:

- Column – vertical bars compare values over a period of time

- Bar – horizontal bars compare two or more values to show how the proportions relate to each other

- Line – shows trends, increases and decreases, levels, and costs during a continuous period of time

- Pie – divides a single total into parts to illustrate how the segments differ from each other and the whole

- Scatter – displays the effect on one variable when another variable changes

In general, three-dimensional charts are more difficult to comprehend than two-dimensional charts. The added design elements in a three-dimensional chart add clutter and take up space. Also, legends help keep the chart clean, so use them prominently on the slide.

BTW

Entering Data
The Microsoft Excel spreadsheet contains sample data. To enter your own data, you can move from cell to cell and replace the numbers and letters. You also can delete all the sample data by clicking the box in the upper-left corner of the spreadsheet that is above the column of numbers and left of the row of letters and then pressing the DELETE key.

Adding a Chart to a Slide and Formatting

The chart on Slide 3 shows the four major sources of salt in our diets. The largest amount of salt ingested is by eating processed food, and you want to emphasize this fact by creating a chart. You will build the chart on Slide 3, shown in Figure 4–38, directly within the PowerPoint presentation.

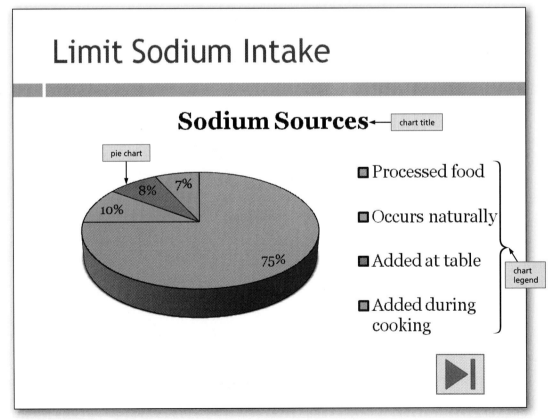

Figure 4–38

Microsoft Excel and Microsoft Graph

PowerPoint uses one of two programs to develop a chart. It opens Microsoft Excel if that software is installed on your system. It opens Microsoft Graph if Excel is not installed and displays a chart with its associated data in a table called a datasheet. Microsoft Graph does not have the advanced features found in Excel. In the chapter, the assumption that Microsoft Excel has been installed is made. When you start to create a chart, Excel opens and displays a chart in the PowerPoint slide. The default chart type is a **Clustered Column chart**. The Clustered Column chart is appropriate when comparing two or more items in specified intervals, such as comparing how inflation has risen during the past 10 years. Other popular chart types are line, bar, and pie, the latter of which you will use in Slide 3.

The figures for the chart are entered in a corresponding **Microsoft Excel worksheet**, which is a rectangular grid containing vertical columns and horizontal rows. Column letters display above the grid to identify particular **columns**, and row numbers display on the left side of the grid to identify particular **rows**. **Cells** are the intersections of rows and columns, and they are the locations for the chart data and text labels. For example, cell A1 is the intersection of column A and row 1. Numeric and text data are entered in the **active cell**, which is the one cell surrounded by a heavy border. You will replace the sample data in the worksheet by typing entries in the cells, but you also can import data from a text file, import a Microsoft Excel worksheet or chart, or paste data obtained in another program. Once you have entered the data, you can modify the appearance of the chart using menus and commands.

BTW

Linking to an Excel File
In this project you create a new spreadsheet and chart. If, however, you have an Excel chart completed already, you can link to this chart instead of copying it into your slide or developing a new chart. Linking is particularly useful when the data changes frequently, such as displaying stock quotes or real-time sales figures. When the Excel chart is updated, the corresponding linked chart in PowerPoint also is updated.

To Insert a Chart

The next step in developing the presentation is to insert a chart into Slide 3. The following steps insert a chart with sample data into Slide 3.

- Click the Next Slide button to display Slide 3 (Figure 4–39).

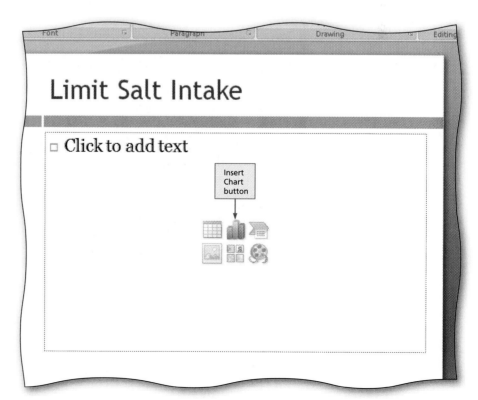

Figure 4–39

2

- Click the Insert Chart button in the content placeholder to display the Insert Chart dialog box.

- Scroll down and then click the Pie in 3-D chart button in the Pie area to select that chart style (Figure 4–40).

Q&A Can I change the chart style after I have inserted a chart?

Yes. Click the Change Chart Type button in the Type group on the Design tab to display the Change Chart Type dialog box and then make another selection.

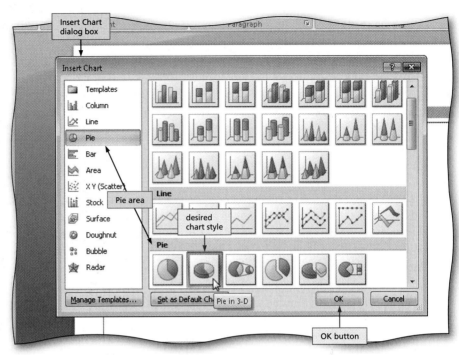

Figure 4–40

3

- Click the OK button to start the Microsoft Excel program and open a worksheet tiled on the right side of your Nutrition presentation (Figure 4–41).

Q&A What do the numbers in the worksheet and the chart represent?

Microsoft Excel places sample data in the worksheet and charts the sample data in the default chart type.

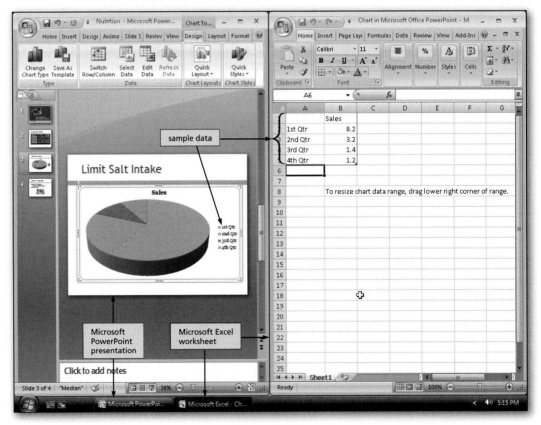

Figure 4–41

Other Ways

1. Click Chart button on Insert tab

**Plan
Ahead**

Obtain information for the graphic from credible sources.
At times you are familiar with the data for your chart or graph because you have conducted in-the-field, or primary, research by interviewing experts or taking measurements. Other times, however, you have gathered the data from secondary sources, such as magazine or newspaper articles or from Web sites. General circulation magazines and newspapers, such as *Newsweek* and the *Wall Street Journal*, use experienced journalists and editors to verify their information. Also, online databases, such as EBSCO, OCLC FirstSearch, LexisNexis Academic, and NewsBank Info Web contain articles from credible sources.

On the other hand, some sources have particular biases and present information that supports their causes. Political, religious, and social publications and Web sites often are designed for specific audiences who share a common point of view. You should, therefore, recognize that data from these sources can be skewed and edited to support a cause.

If you did not conduct the research yourself, you should give credit to the source of your information. You are acknowledging that someone else provided the data and giving your audience the opportunity to obtain the same materials you used. Type the source at the bottom of your chart or graph, especially if you are distributing handouts of your slides. At the very least, state the source during the body of your speech.

To Replace the Sample Data

The next step in creating the chart is to replace the sample data, which will redraw the chart. The sample data is displayed in two columns and five rows. The first row and left column contain text labels and will be used to create the chart title and legend. A **legend** is a box that identifies each slice of the pie chart and coordinates with the colors assigned to the slice categories. The other cells contain numbers that are used to determine the size of the pie slices. The following steps replace the sample data in the worksheet.

1
- Click cell B1, which is the intersection of column B and row 1, to select it (Figure 4–42).

Q&A

Why did my mouse pointer change shape?

The mouse pointer changes to a block plus sign to indicate a cell is selected.

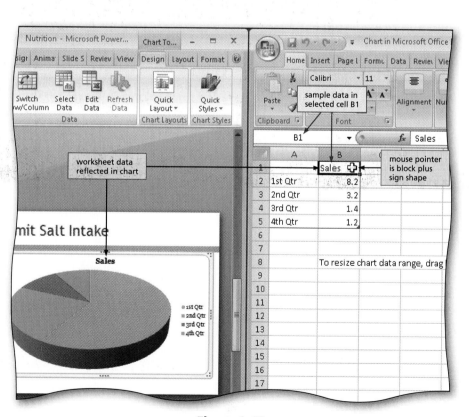

Figure 4–42

2

- Type Salt Sources in cell B1 to replace the sample chart title.

- Click cell A2 to select that cell (Figure 4–43).

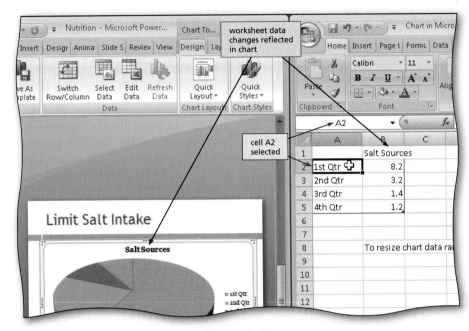

Figure 4–43

3

- Type Processed food in cell A2 and then press the DOWN ARROW key to move the mouse pointer to cell A3.

Q&A Why did some of the letters disappear in cell A2 when I moved the mouse pointer?

The default cell width is not wide enough to display the entire cell contents in the worksheet. The entire cell contents are displayed in the chart legend in the PowerPoint presentation.

- Type Occurs naturally in cell A3 and then press the DOWN ARROW key.

- Type Added at table in cell A4 and then press the DOWN ARROW key.

- Type Added during cooking in cell A5 (Figure 4–44).

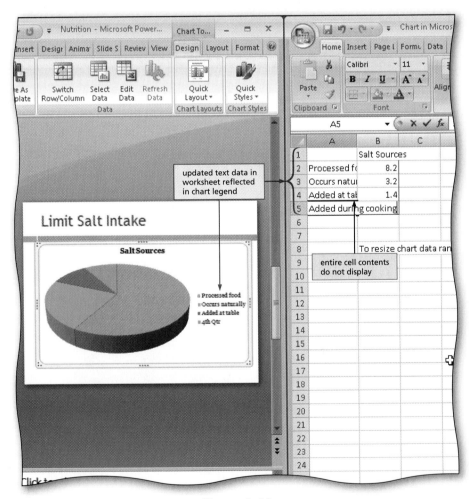

Figure 4–44

4

- Click cell B2, type 75% in that cell, and press the DOWN ARROW key to move the mouse pointer to cell B3.

- Type 10% in cell B3 and then press the DOWN ARROW key.

- Type 8% in cell B4 and then press the DOWN ARROW key.

- Type 7% in cell B5 and then press the DOWN ARROW key (Figure 4–45).

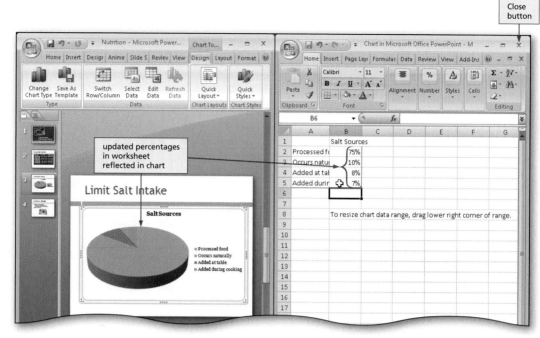

Figure 4–45

5

- Close Microsoft Excel by clicking its Close button (Figure 4–46).

 Can I open the Excel spreadsheet once it has been closed?

Yes. Click the chart to select it and then click the Edit Data button in the Data group on the Design tab under Chart Tools.

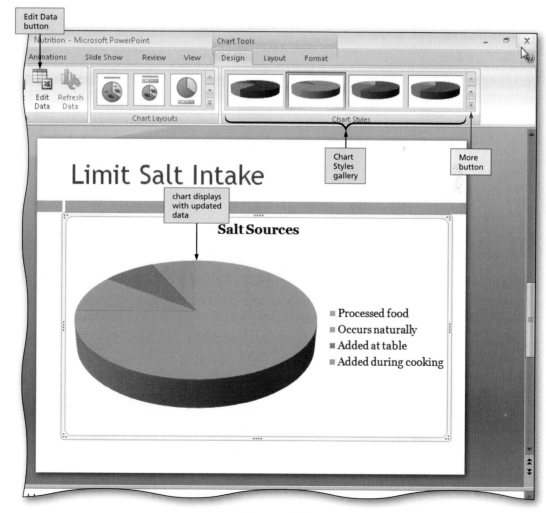

Figure 4–46

To Apply a Chart Style

Each chart type has a variety of styles that can change the look of the chart. If desired, you can change the chart from two dimensions to three dimensions, add borders, and vary the colors of the slices, lines, and bars. When you inserted the Pie in 3-D, a style was applied automatically. Thumbnails of this style and others are displayed in the Chart Styles gallery. The following steps apply a chart style to the Slide 3 pie chart.

1

- With the chart still selected, click the More button in the Chart Styles gallery (shown in Figure 4–46) to expand the Table Styles gallery.

- Point to Style 10 (row 2, column 2) (Figure 4–47).

Q&A

Does the Table Styles gallery have a live preview feature?

This feature is not available.

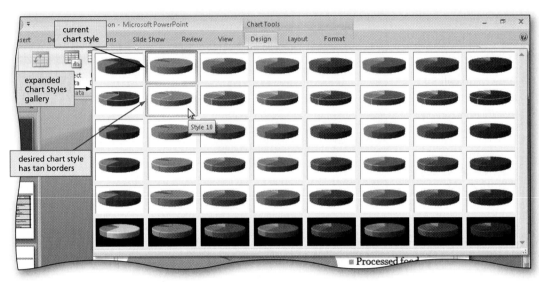

Figure 4–47

2

- Click Style 10 in the Table Styles gallery to apply the selected style to the table (Figure 4–48).

Q&A

Can I change the chart type?

If you want to change the chart type, click the Change Chart Type button in the Type group on the Design tab and then select a different type.

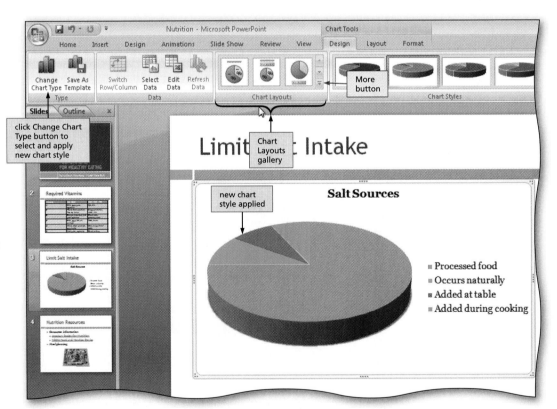

Figure 4–48

To Change the Chart Layout

Once you have selected a chart style, you can modify the look of the chart elements by changing its layout. The various layouts move the legend above or below the chart or move some or all of the legend data directly onto the individual chart pieces. For example, in the pie chart type, seven different layouts display only percentages on the pie slices, only the identifying information, such as the words Processed food, or combinations of this data. The following steps apply a chart layout with percentages to the Slide 3 pie chart.

1

- With the chart still selected, click the More button in the Chart Layouts gallery (shown in Figure 4–48) to expand the Chart Layouts gallery.

- Point to Layout 6 (row 2, column 3) (Figure 4–49).

Q&A Does the Chart Layouts gallery have a live preview feature?

This feature is not available.

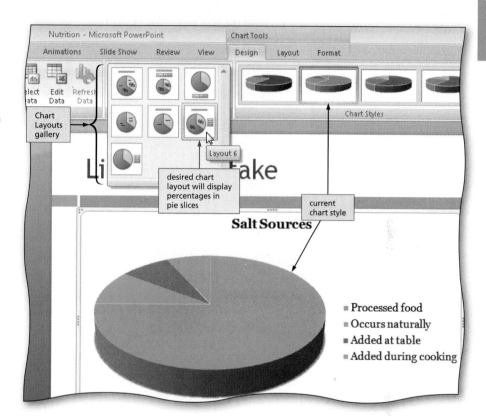

Figure 4–49

2

- Click Layout 6 in the Chart Layouts gallery to apply the selected layout to the chart (Figure 4–50).

Q&A Can I change the chart layout?

Because a live preview is not available, you may want to sample the various layouts to evaluate their effectiveness. To change these layouts, repeat Steps 1 and 2.

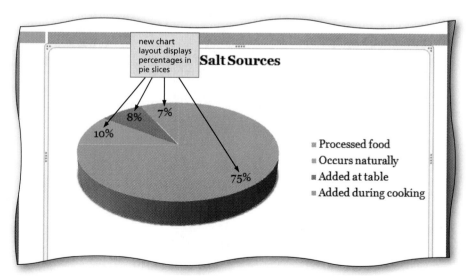

Figure 4–50

To Change the Shape Outline Weight

The new Style 10 has thin white outlines around each pie slice and around each color square in the legend. You can change the weight of these lines to accentuate each slice. The following steps change the outline weight.

- Click Format on the Ribbon to display the Format tab.

- Click the pie chart to select it and display the sizing handles.

- Click the Shape Outline button arrow in the Shape Styles group to display the Shape Outline color palette.

- Point to Weight in the Shape Outline menu to display the Weight submenu (Figure 4–51).

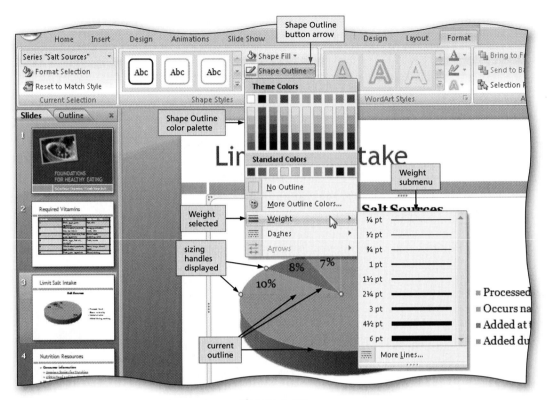

Figure 4–51

- Point to 3 pt to display a live preview of this outline line weight (Figure 4–52).

🔍 **Experiment**

- Point to various weights on the submenu and watch the border weights on the pie slices change.

Q&A What does pt mean after each number in the Weight submenu?

Pt is the abbreviation for point, which is the unit of measure used in the graphic arts industry.

- Click 3 pt to increase the border around each slice to that width.

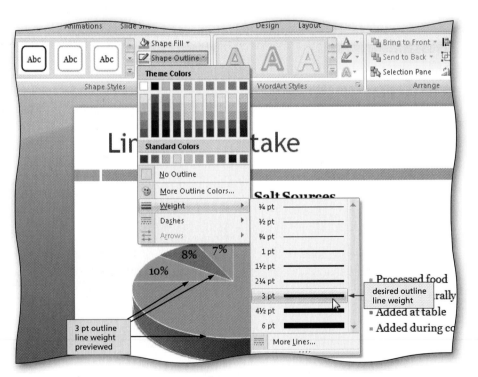

Figure 4–52

To Change the Shape Outline Color

The new Style 10 has white outlines around each pie slice and around each color square in the legend. You can change this color to add contrast to each slice and legend color square. The following steps change the border color.

1

- Click the Shape Outline button arrow in the Shape Styles group to display the Shape Outline color palette.

- In the Theme Colors area, point to the Black, Text 1 color (row 1, column 2) to display a live preview of this color on the pie shape borders (Figure 4–53).

 Experiment

- Point to various colors in the Shape Outline gallery and watch the border color on the pie slices change.

Q&A

What color is the active outline color?

Aqua. PowerPoint retains the setting of the previous border color selected.

2

- Click Black, Text 1 to add black borders around each slice and also around the color squares in the legend.

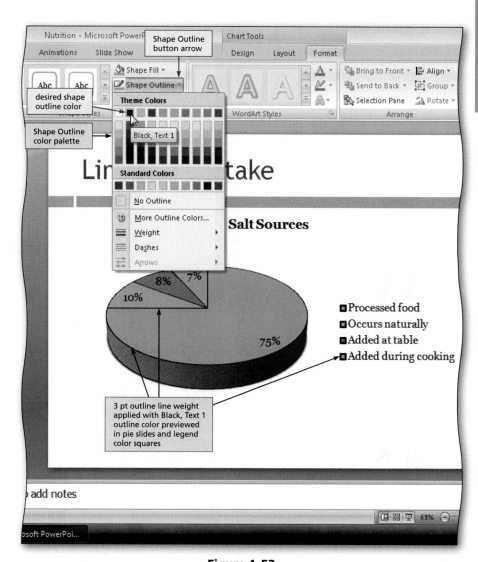

Figure 4–53

To Change the Title and Legend Font Size

Depending upon the complexity of the chart and the overall slide, you may want to increase the font size of the chart title and legend to increase readability. The steps on the following page change the font size of both of these chart elements.

- Click the chart title, Salt Sources, and then triple-click the paragraph to select the text and display the Mini toolbar.

- Click the Increase Font Size button three times to increase the font size of the selected text to 32 point (Figure 4–54).

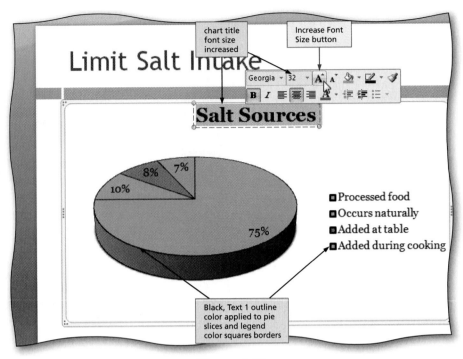

Figure 4–54

- Right-click the legend in the chart to display the Mini toolbar and a shortcut menu related to legends.

- Click the Increase Font Size button once on the Mini toolbar to increase the font size of the selected text to 20 point (Figure 4–55).

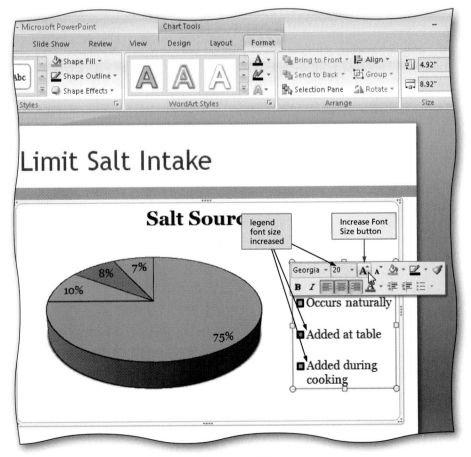

Figure 4–55

**Plan
Ahead**

Test your visual elements.
Proofread your charts and tables carefully using these guidelines:

- Verify that your charts and tables contain the correct data. It is easy to make mistakes inputting large quantities of numbers or entering many lines of text. Check that numbers are not transposed and that pie chart percentages total 100.

- Be certain graphics are clearly labeled. The slide title text or the chart title should state the graphic's purpose. Table column headings must indicate the data below. Chart legends must accompany the graphic if the data are not displayed on the chart itself. Units of measurement, such as degrees, dollars, or inches, should appear for clarity.

- Show your graphic to people unfamiliar with your topic. Ask them to explain verbally what they gather from viewing the material. Determine how long it takes them to state their interpretations. If they pause or look confused, then your graphic either has too much or too little information and needs revision.

Revising and Customizing Individual Slides

The text and information graphics for all four slides in the Nutrition presentation have been entered. Once you complete a slide show, you might decide to change elements. PowerPoint provides several tools to assist you with making changes. The following pages discuss these tools.

Hiding a Slide

Slides 2, 3, and 4 present technical information in graphical form or with hyperlinks. Depending on the audience's needs and the time constraints, you may decide not to display one or more of these slides, particularly Slide 4 because it is a supporting slide. A **supporting slide** provides detailed information to supplement another slide in the presentation. For example, in a presentation to bank officers about the increase in student loans, one slide displays a graph representing the current year's loan amounts and the previous three years' loan figures. A supporting slide might display a table showing each branch office's loan application figures for every year in the graph.

When running a slide show, you may not always want to display the supporting slide. You would want to display it when time permits and when you want to show the audience more details about a topic. You should insert the supporting slide after the slide you anticipate may warrant more detail. Then, you use the **Hide Slide command** to hide the supporting slide. The Hide Slide command hides the supporting slide from the audience during the normal running of a slide show. When you want to display the supporting hidden slide, press the H key. No visible indicator displays to show that a hidden slide exists. You must be aware of the content of the presentation to know where the supporting slide is located.

When you run your presentation, the hidden slide does not display unless you press the H key when the slide preceding the hidden slide is displaying. For example, Slide 5 does not display unless you press the H key when Slide 4 display in Slide Show view. You continue your presentation by clicking the mouse or pressing any of the keys associated with running a slide show. You skip the hidden slide by clicking the mouse and advancing to the next slide.

BTW

Showing a Range of Slides
If your presentation consists of many slides, you may want to show only a portion of them in your slide show. For example, if your 40-slide presentation is designed to accompany a 30-minute speech and you are given only 10 minutes to present, you may elect to display only the first 10 slides. Rather than have the show end abruptly after Slide 10, you can elect to show a range of slides. To specify this range, click the Slide Show tab, click the Set Up Slide Show button to display the Set Up Show dialog box, and then specify the starting and ending slide numbers in the From and To boxes in the Show slides area.

To Hide a Slide

Slide 4 is a slide that supports information presented in the entire presentation. If time permits, or if the audience requires more information, you can display Slide 4. As the presenter, you decide whether to show Slide 4. You hide a slide in Slide Sorter view so you can see the slashed square surrounding the slide number, which indicates a slide is hidden. The following steps hide Slide 4.

- Right-click the Slide 4 thumbnail in the Slides tab to display the shortcut menu (Figure 4–56).

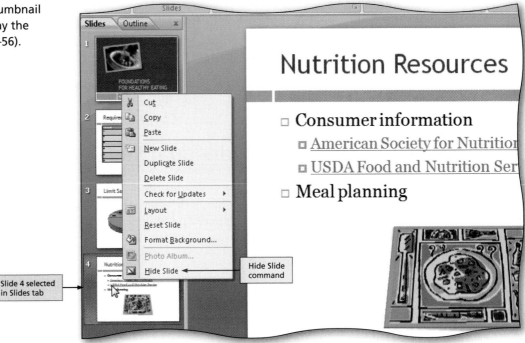

Figure 4–56

- Click the Hide Slide command on the shortcut menu to hide Slide 4 (Figure 4–57).

Q&A How do I know that Slide 4 is hidden?

The rectangle with a slash surrounds the slide number to indicate Slide 4 is a hidden slide.

Q&A What if I decide I no longer want to hide a slide?

Repeat Steps 1 and 2. The Hide Slide button is a toggle; it either hides or displays a slide.

Other Ways

1. Change view to Slide Sorter, right-click desired slide, click Hide Slide on shortcut menu
2. Click Hide Slide button on Slide Show tab

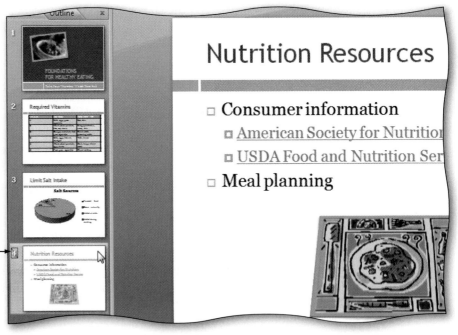

Figure 4–57

Find and Replace Dialog Box

At times you many want to change all occurrences of a word or phrase to another word or phrase. For example, a marketing representative may have one slide show to accompany a sales presentation given daily at a variety of offices, and he wants to update several sides with the name of the office where the presentation is occurring. He manually could change the words, but PowerPoint includes an efficient method of replacing one word with another. The Replace All button in the Find and Replace dialog box changes all occurrences of the Find what text with the Replace with text.

In some cases, you may want to replace only certain occurrences of a word or phrase, not all of them. To instruct PowerPoint to confirm each change, click the Find Next button in the Replace dialog box instead of the Replace All button. When PowerPoint locates an occurrence of the text, it pauses and waits for you to click either the Replace button or the Find Next button. Clicking the Replace button changes the text; clicking the Find Next button instructs PowerPoint to disregard the replacement and look for the next occurrence of the Find what text.

If you accidentally replace the wrong text, you can undo a replacement by clicking the Undo button on the Quick Access Toolbar. If you used the Replace All button to make the word changes, PowerPoint undoes all replacements. If you used the Replace button, PowerPoint undoes only the most recent replacement.

BTW

Finding Whole Words
The Replace dialog box contains an option to search for whole words. This feature is useful when your search term is embedded in unrelated words that are used frequently. For example, you may want to search for the word, use. PowerPoint will locate this combination of letters in other words, such as mouse and useful. To instruct PowerPoint to find only the word, use, click 'Find whole words only'.

To Find and Replace Text

While reading a nutrition label, you notice that food companies list sodium rather than salt content. You decide to use the term your audience members will see on their food packages and want to change all occurrences of salt to sodium. To perform this action, you can use PowerPoint's Find and Replace feature, which automatically locates each occurrence of a word or phrase and then replaces it with specified text. The following steps use Find and Replace to replace all occurrences of the word, salt, with the word, sodium.

- If necessary, click Home on the Ribbon to display the Home tab. Click the Replace button in the Editing group to display the Replace dialog box.

- Type `Salt` in the Find what text box.

- Press the TAB key. Type `Sodium` in the Replace with text box (Figure 4–58).

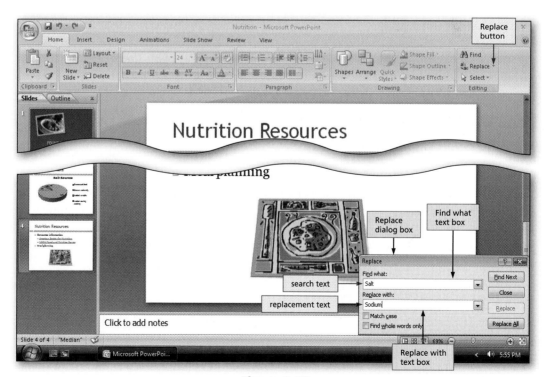

Figure 4–58

2

● Click the Replace All button in the Replace dialog box to instruct PowerPoint to replace all occurrences of the search for word, salt, with the replace with word, sodium (Figure 4–59).

3

● Click the OK button in the Microsoft Office PowerPoint dialog box.

● Click the Close button in the Replace dialog box.

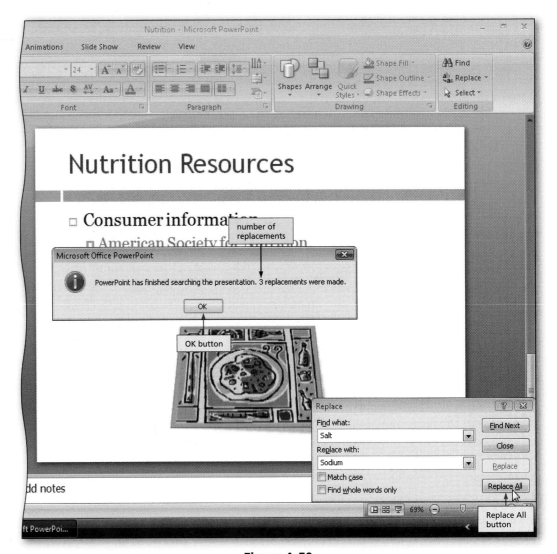

Figure 4–59

Other Ways

1. Press CTRL+H

To Use the Thesaurus

When reviewing your slide show, you may decide that a particular word does not express the exact usage you intended or that you used the same word on multiple slides. In these cases, you could find a **synonym**, or word similar in meaning, to replace the inappropriate or duplicate word. PowerPoint provides a **thesaurus**, which is a list of synonyms, to help you find a replacement word.

In this project, you want to find a synonym to replace the word, Required, on Slide 2. The following steps locate an appropriate synonym and replace the words.

1

- Click the Previous Slide button twice to display Slide 2. Right-click the word, Required, to display a shortcut menu.

- Point to Synonyms on the shortcut menu to display a list of synonyms (Figure 4–60).

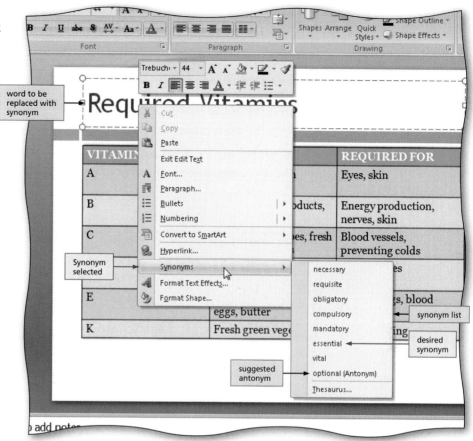

Figure 4–60

2

- In the Synonyms submenu, click the word, essential, which is the synonym you want to replace the word, Required.

Q&A

What if a suitable word does not display in the Synonyms submenu?

You can display the thesaurus in the Research task pane by clicking Thesaurus on the Synonyms submenu. A complete thesaurus with synonyms displays in the Research task pane along with an **antonym**, which is a word with an opposite meaning.

- Change the lowercase letter e in the word, essential, to a capital letter E (Figure 4–61).

VITAMIN	SOURCES	REQUIRED FOR
A	Milk, eggs, green vegetables	Eyes, skin
B	Whole wheat products, liver, soy beans	Energy production, nerves, skin
C	Oranges, tomatoes, fresh green vegetables	Blood vessels, preventing colds
D	Milk, eggs, fish oil, sunlight	Teeth, bones
E	Whole wheat products,	Heart, lungs, blood

Figure 4–61

Other Ways

1. Click Thesaurus on Review tab
2. Press SHIFT+F7

To Find a Second Synonym

Now that you have found a synonym for the word, Required, you want to find a synonym for the word, planning, on Slide 4. The following steps replace that word with a more appropriate one.

1 Click the Find button in the Editing group on the Home tab to display the Find dialog box.

2 Type planning in the Find what text box and then click the Find Next button.

3 With the word, planning, selected on Slide 4, click the Close button in the Find dialog box.

4 Right-click the word, planning, point to Synonyms on the shortcut menu, and then click the word, preparation, in the Synonyms submenu (Figure 4–62).

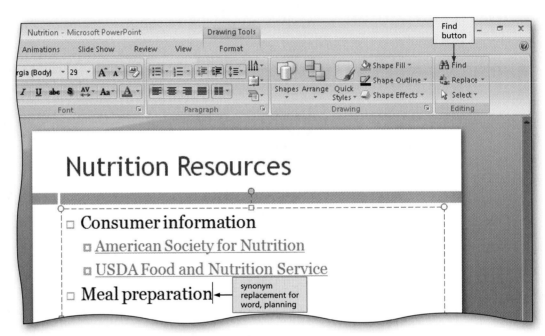

Figure 4–62

Adding and Formatting Action Buttons

When presenting the Nutrition slide show and discussing information on Slides 1, 2, or 3, a speaker might want to skip to the last slide in the presentation and then access a Web site for further information. Or the presenter may be discussing information on Slide 4 and want to display Slide 2 or 3 to re-emphasize information on the table or chart. One method of jumping non-sequentially to slides is by clicking an action button on a slide. An **action button** is a built-in 3-D button that can perform specific tasks such as display the next slide, provide help, give information, and play a sound. In addition, the action button can activate a hyperlink that allows users to jump to a specific slide in the presentation.

In the Nutrition slide show, you will insert and format the action button shape on Slides 2 and 3 and create a link to Slide 4 so that you will be able to display Slide 4 at any point in the presentation by clicking the action button. When you click the action button, a chime sound will play.

To Insert an Action Button

PowerPoint provides 12 built-in action buttons. You can customize one of them with a photograph, clip, logo, or any graphic you desire. The following steps insert an action button on Slide 2 and link it to Slide 4.

1

- Click the Previous Slide button two times to display Slide 2.

- Click Insert on the Ribbon to display the Insert tab. Click the Shapes button in the Illustrations group to display the Shapes gallery.

- Point to the Action Button: End shape in the Action Buttons area (column 4) (Figure 4–63).

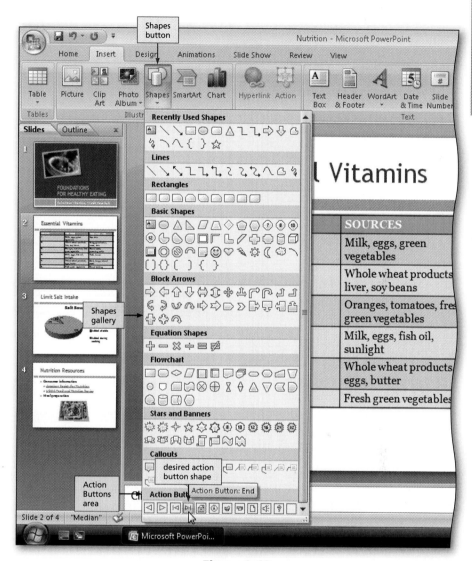

Figure 4–63

- Click the Action Button: End shape.

- Click the bottom-right corner of the slide to insert the action button and to display the Action Settings dialog box.

- If necessary, click the Mouse Click tab in the Action Settings dialog box (Figure 4–64).

Q&A Why is the default setting the action to hyperlink to the last slide?

The shape you selected, Action Button: End, establishes a hyperlink to the last slide in a presentation.

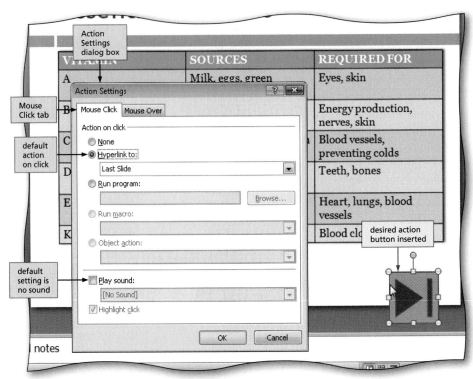

Figure 4–64

- Click the Play sound check box, click the Play sound arrow, and then scroll down and click Chime to select that sound (Figure 4–65).

Q&A I did not hear the chime when I selected that sound. Why not?

The chime sound will play when you run the slide show and click the action button.

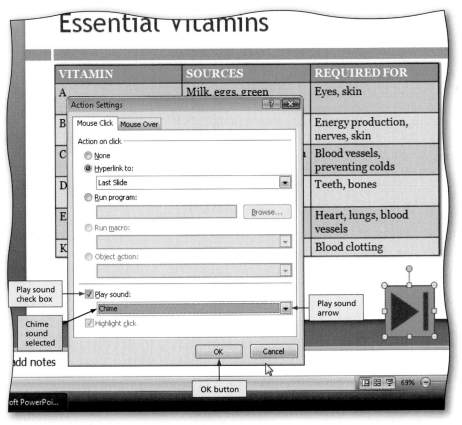

- Click the OK button to apply the hyperlink setting and sound to the action button.

Figure 4–65

To Size an Action Button

The action button size can be decreased to make it less obvious on the slide. The following step resizes the selected action button.

1 With the action button still selected, point to the lower-right corner sizing handle on the button and then drag the sizing handle diagonally upward and inward until the button is the approximate size of the one shown in Figure 4–66.

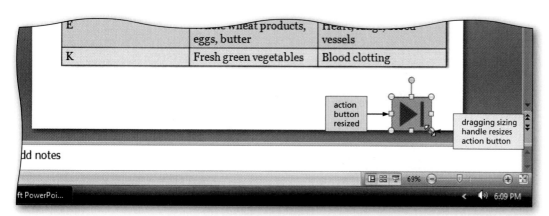

Figure 4–66

To Change the Action Button Fill Color

The action button's gold interior color is bright. To soften the hue, you can select a new fill color. The following steps change the fill to a lighter gold color.

1

• Right-click the action button to display the shortcut menu associated with the shape and the Mini toolbar (Figure 4–67).

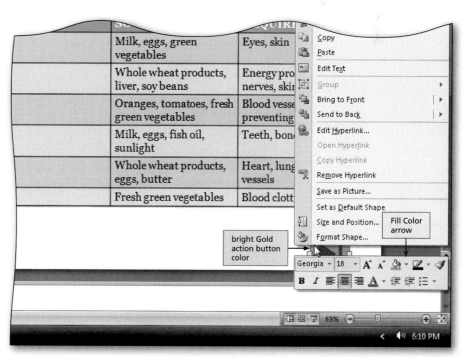

Figure 4–67

- Click the Fill Color arrow on the Mini toolbar and then point to Gold, Accent 1, Lighter 80% in the Theme Colors palette (row 2, column 5) (Figure 4–68).

- Click Gold, Accent 1, Lighter 80% to apply this color to the action button.

- Click the slide to hide the Mini toolbar.

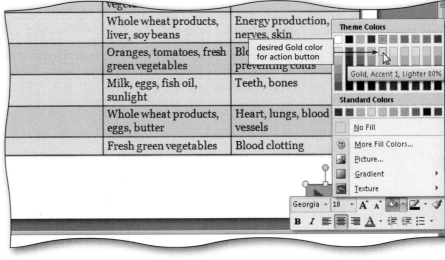

Figure 4–68

Other Ways

1. Click Shape Fill button on Format tab

Guides

The PowerPoint guides help position shapes and objects on slides. **Guides** are two straight dotted lines, one horizontal and one vertical. When an object is close to a guide, its corner or its center (whichever is closer) **snaps**, or attaches itself, to the guide. You can drag a guide to a new location to meet your alignment requirements.

When you point to a guide and then press and hold the mouse button, PowerPoint displays a box containing the exact position of the guide on the slide in inches. The center of a slide is 0.00 on both the vertical and the horizontal guides. An arrow is displayed below the guide position to indicate the vertical guide either left or right of center. An arrow is displayed to the right of the guide position to indicate the horizontal guide either above or below center.

To Position the Action Button Using Guides

The action buttons should be displayed in precisely the same location on Slides 2, 3, and 4 so they appear static as you transition from one slide to the next during the slide show. Guides help you align objects on slides. The following steps display the guides and position the action button on Slide 2.

1

- Right-click Slide 2 anywhere except the chart and the title text to display the shortcut menu (Figure 4–69).

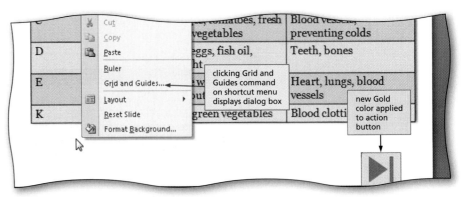

Figure 4–69

● Click Grid and Guides on the shortcut menu to display the Grid and Guides dialog box.

● Click the 'Display drawing guides on screen' check box in the Guide settings area (Figure 4–70).

Q&A Why does a check mark display in the Snap objects to grid check box?

The check mark indicates the action button and other shapes will snap to drawing guides that appear on the screen. This check mark is a default setting.

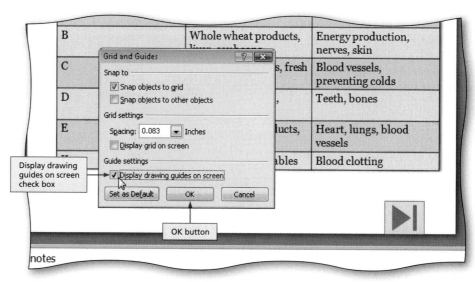

Figure 4–70

● Click the OK button to display the grids and the horizontal and vertical guides.

● Point to the horizontal guide anywhere except the table.

Q&A Why does 0.00 display when I hold down the mouse button?

The ScreenTip displays the horizontal guide's position. A 0.00 setting means that the guide is precisely in the middle of the slide and is not above or below the center.

● Click and then drag the horizontal guide to 2.75 inches below center. Do not release the mouse button (Figure 4–71).

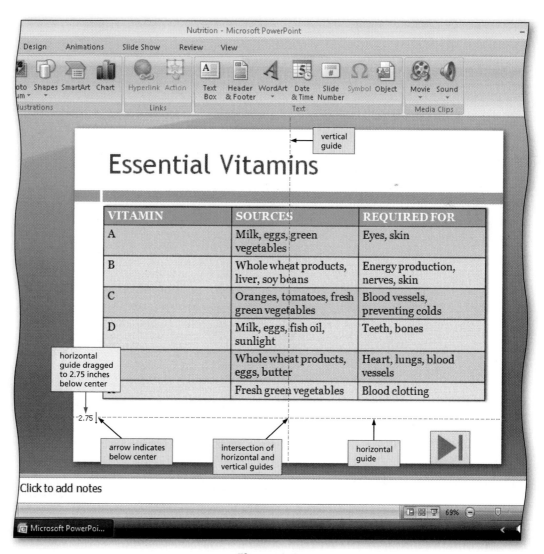

Figure 4–71

- Release the mouse button to position the horizontal guide at 2.75, which is the intended location of the action button's top border.

- Point to the vertical guide anywhere except the table.

- Click and then drag the vertical guide to 3.25 inches right of center.

- Drag the action button to the intersection of the vertical and horizontal guides to position the shape in the desired location (Figure 4–72).

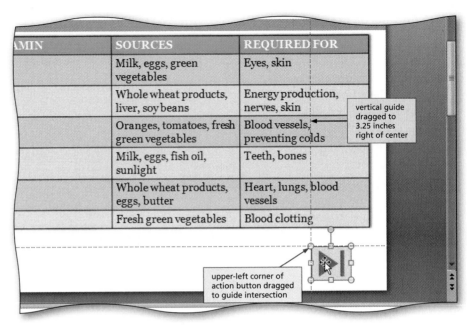

Figure 4–72

To Copy the Action Button

The Slide 2 action button is formatted and positioned correctly. You can copy this shape to Slides 3 and 4. The following steps copy the Slide 2 action button to the next two slides in the presentation.

1

- Right-click the action button on Slide 2 to display the shortcut menu (Figure 4–73).

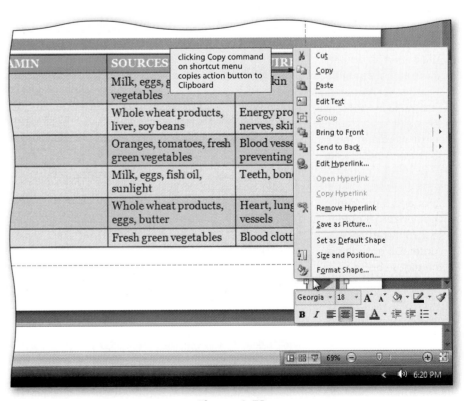

Figure 4–73

2

- Click Copy on the shortcut menu to copy the action button to the Clipboard.

- Click the Next Slide button to display Slide 3.

- Right-click Slide 3 anywhere except the chart and the title text to display the shortcut menu (Figure 4–74).

Why does my shortcut menu have different commands?

Depending upon where you right-clicked, you might see a different shortcut menu. As long as this menu displays the Paste command, you can use it. If the Paste command is not visible, click the slide again to display another shortcut menu.

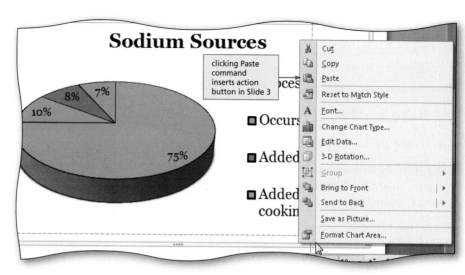

Figure 4–74

3

- Click Paste on the shortcut menu to paste the action button in the lower-right corner of Slide 3 (Figure 4–75).

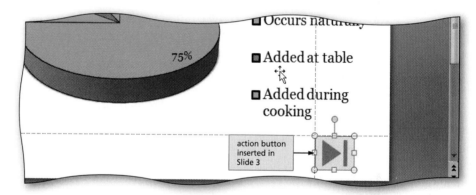

Figure 4–75

4

- Click the Next Slide button to display Slide 4.

- Right-click Slide 4 anywhere except the body text, title text, and clip to display the shortcut menu.

- Click Paste on the shortcut menu to paste the action button in the lower-right corner of Slide 4 (Figure 4–76).

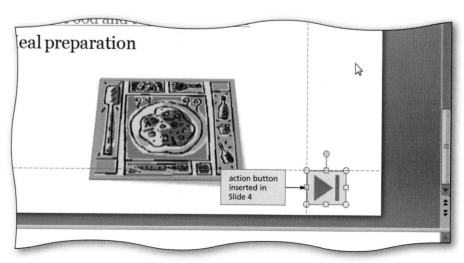

Figure 4–76

To Edit the Action Button Hyperlink Setting

When you copied the action button, PowerPoint retained the settings to hyperlink to the last slide and to play the Chime sound. These settings are correct for Slide 3, but you want the Slide 4 action button to hyperlink to Slide 2. The following steps edit the Slide 4 hyperlink setting to Slide 2.

- Right-click the action button on Slide 4 to display the shortcut menu and the Mini toolbar.

- Click Edit Hyperlink on the shortcut menu to display the Action Settings dialog box.

- Click the Hyperlink to arrow to display the Hyperlink to menu (Figure 4–77).

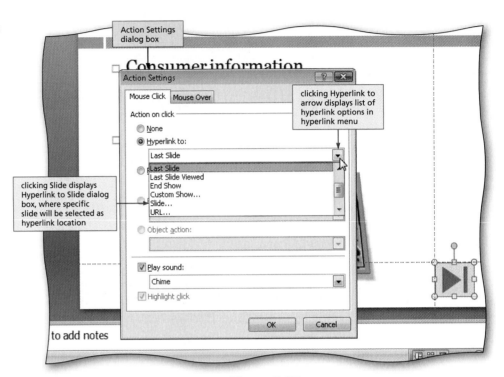

Figure 4–77

- Click Slide on the Hyperlink to menu and then click '2. Essential Vitamins' in the Slide title list to select Slide 2 as the hyperlink (Figure 4–78).

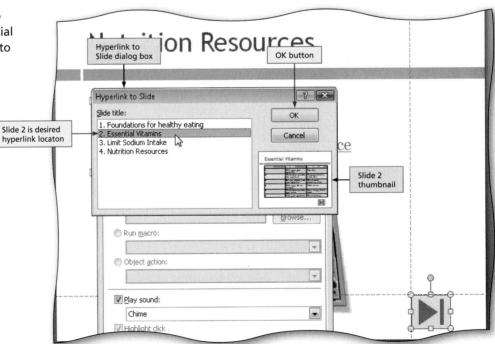

Figure 4–78

3

- Click the OK button in the Hyperlink to Slide dialog box to display the Action Settings dialog box (Figure 4–79).

4

- Click the OK button in the Action Settings dialog box to apply the new hyperlink settings to the Slide 4 action button.

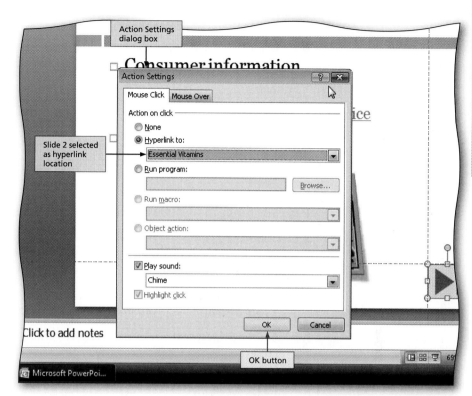

Figure 4–79

To Hide Guides

The three action buttons are copied and formatted, so the guides no longer are needed to display. The following steps hide the guides.

1 Right-click Slide 4 anywhere except the text, clip, or action button to display the shortcut menu.

2 Click Grid and Guides on the shortcut menu and then click the 'Display drawing guides on screen' check box in the Guide settings area so that the box is not selected.

3 Click the OK button to hide the guides.

To Add a Transition between Slides

A final enhancement you will make in this presentation is to apply the Split Vertical Out transition in the Wipes category to all slides and change the transition speed to Slow. The following steps apply this transition to the presentation.

1 Click Animations on the Ribbon to display the Animations tab and then click the More button in the Transition to This Slide group to expand the Transitions gallery.

2 Click the Split Vertical Out transition (row 4, column 6) in the Wipes category in the Transitions gallery to apply this transition to Slide 4.

③ Click the Transition Speed arrow in the Transition to This Slide group and then click Slow to change the transition speed for Slide 4.

④ Click the Apply To All button in the Transition to This Slide group to apply this transition and speed to all four slides in the presentation.

To Change Document Properties and Save the Presentation

Before saving the presentation again, you want to add your name, class name, and some keywords as document properties. The following steps use the Document Information Panel to change document properties and then save the project.

① Click the Office Button to display the Office Button menu, point to Prepare on the Office Button menu, and then click Properties on the 'Prepare the document for distribution' submenu to display the Document Information Panel.

② Click the Author text box, if necessary, and then type your name as the Author property. If a name already is displayed in the Author text box, delete it before typing your name.

③ Click the Subject text box, if necessary delete any existing text, and then type your course and section as the Subject property.

④ Click the Keywords text box, if necessary delete any existing text, and then type `nutrition, vitamins, sodium, Web links` as the Keywords property.

⑤ Click the Close the Document Information Panel button so that the Document Information Panel no longer is displayed.

⑥ Click the Save button on the Quick Access Toolbar to overwrite the previous Nutrition file on the USB flash drive.

BTW

Certification
The Microsoft Certified Application Specialist (MCAS) program provides an opportunity for you to obtain a valuable industry credential – proof that you have the PowerPoint 2007 skills required by employers. For more information see Appendix G or visit the PowerPoint 2007 Certification Web page (scsite.com/ppt2007/cert).

Running a Slide Show with Hyperlinks and Action Buttons

The Nutrition presentation contains a variety of useful features that provide value to an audience. The vitamin table and the sodium chart graphics should help viewers understand and recall the information being presented. The hyperlinks on Slide 4 show useful Web sites that give current nutritional information. In addition, the action button allows a presenter to jump to Slide 4 while Slides 2 or 3 are being displayed. If an audience member asks a question or if the presenter needs to answer specific questions regarding nutrition, the information on Slide 4 can be accessed immediately by clicking the action button.

To Run a Slide Show with a Hidden Slide and Hyperlinks

Running a slide show that contains hyperlinks is the same as running any other slide show. When a presentation contains hyperlinks and you are connected to the Internet, you can click the hyperlink text to command your default browser to locate the hyperlink file. The following steps run the Nutrition presentation.

1 Click Slide 1 on the Slides tab. Click the Slide Show button to run the slide show and display Slide 1.

2 Press the ENTER key to display Slide 2.

3 Press the ENTER key to display Slide 3.

4 Press the H key to display Slide 4.

5 Click the first hyperlink to start your browser and view The American Society for Nutrition Web page. If necessary, maximize the Web page window when the page is displayed. Click the Close button on the Web page title bar to close the browser.

6 Repeat Step 5 for the second hyperlink.

7 Click the ENTER key twice to display the black slide and then end the slide show.

To Run a Slide Show with Action Buttons

Once you have run the presentation and have seen all slides display, you should run the presentation again to use the action buttons. When you click the action buttons on Slides 2 and 3, PowerPoint will display Slide 4 because you hyperlinked the button to the last slide in the presentation. When Slide 4 is displayed and you view the information and Web sites, you want to return to Slide 2 in the presentation. The following steps run the slide show using the action buttons.

1 Click Slide 1 on the Slides tab, if necessary. Click the Slide Show button to run the slide show, and then display Slide 2.

2 Click the Slide 2 action button to display Slide 4.

3 When Slide 4 is displayed, click the action button to return to Slide 2.

4 Continue advancing through the slide show and using the action buttons until you have viewed all slides in the presentation and then ended the presentation.

BTW

Quick Reference
For a table that lists how to complete the tasks covered in this book using the mouse, Ribbon, shortcut menu, and keyboard, see the Quick Reference Summary at the back of this book, or visit the PowerPoint 2007 Quick Reference Web page (scsite.com/ppt2007/qr).

To Preview and Print Handouts

All changes are complete, and the presentation is saved. You now can create handouts to accompany the slide show. The following steps preview and then print the presentation.

1 Click the Office Button, point to Print, and then click Print Preview on the 'Preview and print the document' submenu.

2 Click the Print What arrow in the Page Setup group and then click Handouts (4 Slides Per Page) in the Print What list.

3 Click the Print button in the Print group.

4 Click the OK button in the Print dialog box to print the handout (Figure 4–80).

5 Click the Close Print Preview button in the Preview group on the Print Preview tab to return to Normal view.

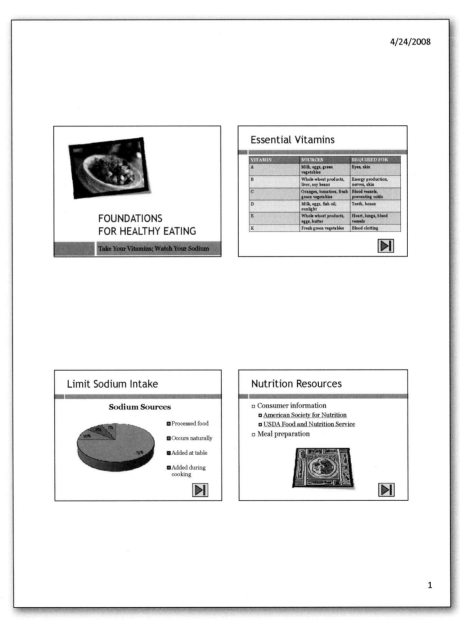

Figure 4–80

To Quit PowerPoint

This project is complete. The following steps quit PowerPoint.

1 Click the Close button on the right side of the title bar to quit PowerPoint.

2 If necessary, click the No button in the Microsoft Office PowerPoint dialog box so that any changes you have made are not saved.

Chapter Summary

In this chapter you have learned how to create and format a table, create a chart, develop a slide with hyperlinks to Web sites containing additional nutritional information, change the entire presentation color scheme and fonts, use the Thesaurus to change slide wording, and insert and format action buttons. The items listed below include all the new PowerPoint skills you have learned in this chapter.

1. Change the Presentation Theme Colors (PPT 232)
2. Change the Theme Fonts (PPT 233)
3. Insert a Picture into a Slide without a Content Placeholder (PPT 234)
4. Apply a Picture Style (PPT 236)
5. Change the Border Color of a Picture (PPT 237)
6. Change a Picture Contrast (PPT 238)
7. Insert a Clip into a Slide without a Content Placeholder (PPT 238)
8. Change the Border Color of a Clip (PPT 241)
9. Change the Brightness of a Clip (PPT 242)
10. Add a Hyperlink to a Slide (PPT 243)
11. Insert an Empty Table (PPT 246)
12. Enter Data in a Table (PPT 248)
13. Apply a Table Style (PPT 249)
14. Add Borders to a Table (PPT 251)
15. Add an Effect to a Table (PPT 252)
16. Insert a Chart (PPT 255)
17. Replace the Sample Data (PPT 257)
18. Apply a Chart Style (PPT 260)
19. Change the Chart Layout (PPT 261)
20. Change the Shape Outline Weight (PPT 262)
21. Change the Shape Outline Color (PPT 263)
22. Change the Title and Legend Font Size (PPT 263)
23. Hide a Slide (PPT 266)
24. Find and Replace Text (PPT 267)
25. Use the Thesaurus (PPT 268)
26. Find a Second Synonym (PPT 270)
27. Insert an Action Button (PPT 271)
28. Size an Action Button (PPT 273)
29. Change the Action Button Fill Color (PPT 273)
30. Position the Action Button Using Guides (PPT 274)
31. Copy the Action Button (PPT 276)
32. Edit the Action Button Hyperlink Settings (PPT 278)
33. Hide Guides (PPT 279)
34. Run a Slide Show with a Hidden Slide and Hyperlinks (PPT 281)
35. Run a Slide Show with Action Buttons (PPT 281)

 If you have a SAM user profile, you may have access to hands-on instruction, practice, and assessment. Log in to your SAM account (http://sam2007.course.com) to launch any assigned training activities or exams that relate to the skills covered in this chapter.

Learn It Online

Test your knowledge of chapter content and key terms.

Instructions: To complete the Learn It Online exercises, start your browser, click the Address bar, and then enter the Web address scsite.com/ppt2007/learn. When the Office 2007 Learn It Online page is displayed, click the link for the exercise you want to complete and then read the instructions.

Chapter Reinforcement TF, MC, and SA
A series of true/false, multiple choice, and short answer questions that test your knowledge of the chapter content.

Flash Cards
An interactive learning environment where you identify chapter key terms associated with displayed definitions.

Practice Test
A series of multiple choice questions that test your knowledge of chapter content and key terms.

Who Wants To Be a Computer Genius?
An interactive game that challenges your knowledge of chapter content in the style of a television quiz show.

Wheel of Terms
An interactive game that challenges your knowledge of chapter key terms in the style of the television show *Wheel of Fortune*.

Crossword Puzzle Challenge
A crossword puzzle that challenges your knowledge of key terms presented in the chapter.

Apply Your Knowledge

Reinforce the skills and apply the concepts you learned in this chapter.

Changing Theme Colors, Applying a Picture Style, Changing a Picture Border and Contrast, and Adding a Hyperlink
Instructions: Start PowerPoint. Open the presentation, Apply 4-1 Oral Hygiene, from the Data Files for Students. See the inside back cover of this book for instructions for downloading the Data Files for Students, or contact your instructor for more information about accessing required files.

The two slides in the presentation present general information about proper oral hygiene. The document you open is an unformatted presentation. You are to select a document theme and change the theme colors, add a style to the pictures on both slides, change the pictures' borders and contrast, and change the Slide 2 text to hyperlinks so the slides look like Figure 4–81.

Perform the following tasks:
1. Add the Solstice document theme and change the presentation theme colors to Flow. Move the subtitle text placeholder upward so that it is positioned under the title text placeholder, as shown in Figure 4–81a.
2. Apply the Reflected Bevel, Black picture style (row 5, column 1) to the Slide 1 picture and the Metal Oval picture style (row 5, column 4) to the Slide 2 picture. Change both picture borders to Bright Green, Accent 4, Lighter 60% (row 3, column 8 in the Theme Colors area). Change the contrast for both photographs to -30%.
3. Display the drawing guides. On Slide 1, set the horizontal guide to .50 above center and the vertical guide to 1.75 left of center. Move the picture so that its upper-left sizing handle aligns with the intersection of the guides. On Slide 2, set the horizontal guide to .08 below center and the vertical guide to 1.50 left of center, and then move the picture so that its upper-left sizing handle aligns with the intersection of the guides. Hide the guides.

4. On Slide 2, create hyperlinks for the two bullets. The American Dental Hygienists' Association bullet should be hyperlinked to adha.org/oralhealth, and the Amercian Dental Association's bullet should be hyperlinked to ada.org.

5. Apply the Wipe Down wipe transition (row 1, column 1) to both slides and change the transition speed to Slow.

6. Check the spelling, and then display the revised presentation in Slide Sorter view to check for consistency.

7. Use your name in place of Student Name in the footer. Change the document properties, as specified by your instructor. Save the presentation using the file name, Apply 4-1 Dental. Submit the revised document in the format specified by your instructor.

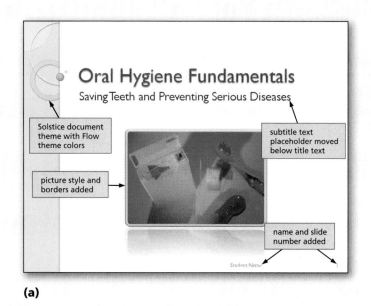

(a)

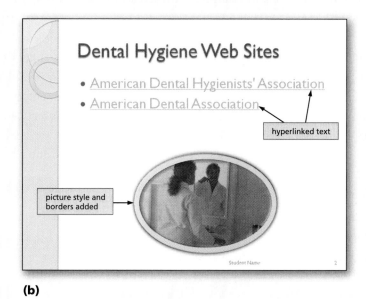

(b)

Figure 4–81

Extend Your Knowledge

Extend the skills you learned in this chapter and experiment with new skills. You may need to use Help to complete the assignment.

Inserting a Photograph and Creating a Table

Instructions: Start PowerPoint. Open the presentation, Extend 4-1 Animals, from the Data Files for Students. See the inside back cover of this book for instructions for downloading the Data Files for Students, or contact your instructor for more information about accessing required files.

You will add and format a picture on the title slide, add your name and slide number to the Slide 2 footer, insert an empty table, enter the data in Table 4–3, and add borders and an effect (Figure 4–82).

Table 4–3 Animal Longevity and Gestation

Animal	Longevity (Years)	Gestation (Days)
Hamster	2	14-17
Guinea Pig	3	58-75
Kangaroo	4-6	32-39
Rabbit	6-8	30-35
Parakeet	8	17-20
Horse	20-25	329-345
Hippopotamus	30	220-255

Perform the following tasks:

1. Add the Verve document theme and change the presentation theme colors to Origin. Change the theme font to Foundry.

2. Insert the Horses photograph from the Data Files for Students into Slide 1. Apply a picture style similar to the one shown in Figure 4–82a and a Glow picture effect. Change the border color and reduce the picture contrast.

3. In Slide 2, add the slide number and your name to the footer. Insert an empty table and enter the data shown in Table 4–2. Apply a table style and add borders around the outside of the table. Add a shadow effect from the Perspective category.

4. Center all text in the table by selecting all cells and then clicking the Center button in the Paragraph group on the Home tab.

5. Apply a transition to all slides.

6. Change the document properties, as specified by your instructor. Save the presentation using the file name, Extend 4-1 Revised Animals.

7. Submit the revised document in the format specified by your instructor.

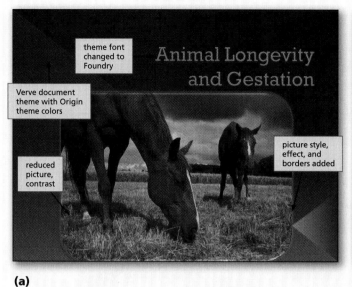

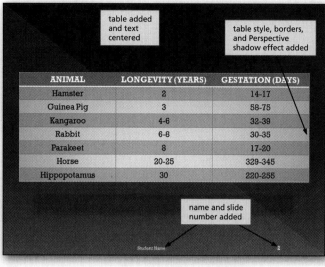

(a)

(b)

Figure 4–82

Make It Right

Analyze a presentation and correct all errors and/or improve the design.

Modifying a Table and Clips

Instructions: Start PowerPoint. Open the presentation, Make It Right 4-1 Birthstones, from the Data Files for Students. See the inside back cover of this book for instructions for downloading the Data Files for Students, or contact your instructor for more information about accessing required files.

Correct the formatting problems and errors in the presentation while keeping in mind the guidelines presented in this chapter.

Perform the following tasks:

1. Change the theme font to Origin. Increase the size of both gem clips at the top of the slide to 160% by right-clicking a clip, clicking Size and Position on the shortcut menu, changing the Height text box value in the Scale area to 160, and then clicking the Close button in the Size and Position dialog box. Rotate the right clip 90 degrees to the right. Apply the 25 Point Soft Edges picture effect to both gem photographs.

2. Display the drawing guides and set the horizontal guide to 4.75 above center and the vertical guide to 3.50 left of center. Move the left gem picture so that its upper-left corner aligns with the intersection of the guides. Set the vertical guide to 3.50 right of center and move the right gem picture so that its upper-right corner aligns with the intersection of the guides.

3. Replace the words, Student Name, in the text box with your name. Set the horizontal guide to 4.25 below center and the vertical guide to 3.50 left of center. Move the text box so that its upper-left corner aligns with the intersection of the guides.

4. Select the table and then apply the Medium Style 3 - Accent 1 table style (row 3, column 2 in the Medium area). Add borders to all table elements. Delete the empty rightmost column by right-clicking that column and then clicking Delete Columns on the shortcut menu. Set the horizontal guide to 3.00 above center and the vertical guide to 2.25 left of center. Move the table so that its upper-left corner aligns with the intersection of the guides. Hide the guides.

Continued >

Make It Right *continued*

5. Add a row for April by right-clicking either cell in the March row, pointing to Insert on the shortcut menu, and then clicking Insert Rows Below. Add the word, April, in the new left cell and the word, Diamond, in the new right cell. Add a row for September and add the gemstone Sapphire.

6. Use the spell checker to correct the misspellings.

7. Change the document properties, as specified by your instructor. Save the presentation using the file name, Make It Right 4-1 Gems.

8. Submit the revised document in the format specified by your instructor.

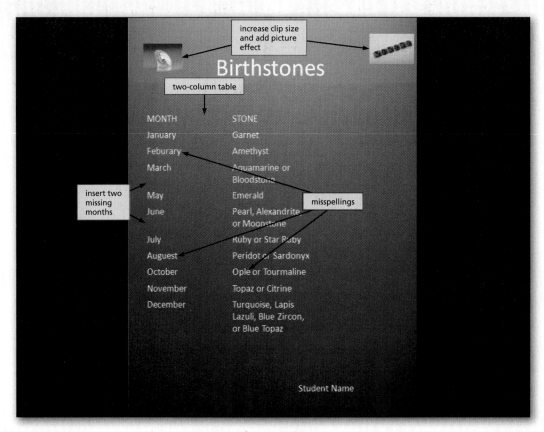

Figure 4–83

In the Lab

Design and/or create a presentation using the guidelines, concepts, and skills presented in this chapter. Labs 1, 2, and 3 are listed in order of increasing difficulty.

Lab 1: Inserting and Formatting a Clip and Chart

Problem: More than 50 million people travel throughout the United States each year to view natural land formations. Whether they trek to Niagara Falls, the rolling countrysides, the fertile plains, the lush forests, or the vast deserts, the country's physical features provide a variety of sights. You have been studying this country in your geography class and decide to begin a PowerPoint presentation with a clip of the United States and a chart of the land types. You insert this clip on Slide 1, create a chart on Slide 2 using the data in Table 4–4, and then modify these information graphics to enhance the visual message to create the slides shown in Figure 4–84 from a blank presentation.

Perform the following tasks.

Table 4–4 U.S. Land Types	
Type	**Percent**
Forest	37.5
Farmland	29.5
Desert	12
Grassland	9.5
Tundra	5
Barren	3.5
Wetland	2.5
Built-up	.5

1. Create a new presentation using the Technic document theme, and then change the presentation theme colors to Concourse. Delete the Slide 1 subtitle placeholder, type the slide title text shown in Figure 4–84a, and insert the United States clip from the Data Files for Students. Adjust the clip size and then add a text box with your name on the United States clip.

2. Apply the Bevel Perspective Left, White picture style (row 4, column 6) to the clip and change the border to Blue, Accent 4 (row 1, column 8 in the Theme Colors area). Apply the Accent color 2, 11 pt glow (row 3, column 2) glow variation picture effect, and change the brightness to -20%. Size and position the clip as shown in Figure 4–84a.

3. Insert a new slide and delete the title text placeholder. Create the chart shown in Figure 4–84b using the 'Exploded pie in 3-D' chart style. Use the data from Table 4–4. After you have replaced the sample data, you may need to drag the lower-right corner of the blue Excel box downward to select all the cells and consequently resize the chart data range.

4. Apply the Style 10 (row 2, column 2) chart style, increase the line weight to 2¼ pt, and change the line color to Blue. Change the chart layout to Layout 5. Increase the chart title font size to 24 and change the font color to Turquoise, Accent 1 (row 1, column 5 in the Theme Colors area).

5. Apply the Shape Circle wipe transition (row 5, column 5) and change the speed to Medium for both slides.

6. Change the document properties, as specified by your instructor. Save the presentation using the file name, Lab 4-1 United States Land.

7. Submit the revised document in the format specified by your instructor.

In the Lab *continued*

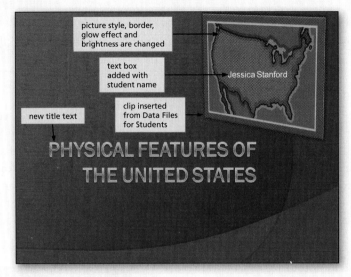

(a)

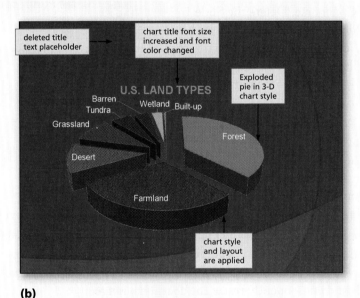

(b)

Figure 4–84

In the Lab

Lab 2: Creating a Presentation by Inserting a Table and Chart

Problem: Your college expanded its fitness center four years ago by adding a lap pool and aquatic exercise classes. At first, interest in the aquatic facilities and classes was high, but during the past two years the number of swimmers has declined. The receptionists at the front desk have recorded data about the people who have entered the facility during that time to use the pool, including whether the person was a student or a staff member. Those figures are indicated in Table 4–5. In an attempt to increase awareness of the decline in swimmers and the availability of aquatic classes, the fitness center director has asked you to create the PowerPoint presentation shown in Figures 4–85a through 4–85d. The 3-D bar chart uses the data in Table 4–5. The other slides show the current aquatic class schedule and give hyperlinks to fitness Web sites showing the health benefits of aquatic exercise.

Table 4–5 Fitness Center Members				
	4 years ago	**3 years ago**	**2 years ago**	**1 year ago**
Students	3,456	4,573	2,984	2,210
Staff	478	743	603	588

Instructions: Perform the following tasks.

1. Create a new presentation using the Concourse document theme, and then change the theme font to Flow. Create the four core presentation slides by typing the Slide 1 title and subtitle text, the Slide 2 and 3 title text, and the Slide 4 title and body text.

2. On Slide 2, create the 3-D Clustered Column (row 1, column 4 in the Column area) chart shown in Figure 4–85b. When you have replaced the sample data with the data in Table 4–5, drag the lower-right corner of the blue Excel box upward to select all the cells and consequently resize the chart data range. Apply chart design Style 26 (row 4, column 2) and change the chart layout to Layout 3. Select the chart title text (Chart Title) and press the DELETE key to delete this text.

3. On Slide 3, create the table shown in Figure 4–85c. Apply the Medium Style 3 - Accent 1 table style (row 3, column 2 in the Medium area) and the Inside Bottom shadow (row 3, column 2 in the Inner area).

4. On Slide 4, create hyperlinks for the two URLs in the body paragraphs. That is, usms.org/fitness should be the hyperlink text for United States Masters Swimming, Inc., and usoc.org/132_51527. htm should be the hyperlink text for the U.S. Olympic Team.

5. On Slide 4, insert the Swimming photograph from the Data Files for Students. Apply the Bevel Perspective Left, White picture style (row 4, column 6) to the photograph, change the picture border to Turquoise, Accent 1 (row 1, column 5 in the Theme Colors area), apply the Circle (row 1, column 1) Bevel picture effect, and change the brightness to +10%.

6. Insert your name and the slide number in the footer on all slides except the title slide. Apply the Wheel Clockwise, 2 Spokes transition (row 3, column 5 in the Wipes category) to all slides. Change the speed to Medium. Check the spelling and correct any errors.

7. Change the document properties, as specified by your instructor. Save the presentation using the file name, Lab 4-2 Fitness Center.

8. Submit the revised document in the format specified by your instructor.

Continued >

In the Lab *continued*

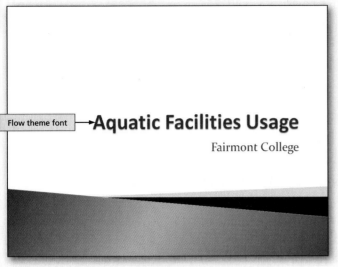

(a)

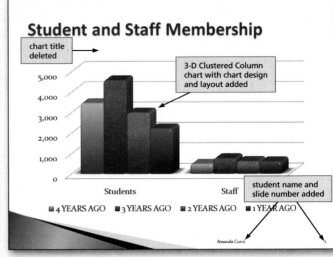

(b)

Aquatic Exercise Schedule

Monday	Tuesday	Wednesday	Thursday	Friday
9 a.m. Aqua Motion	10 a.m. New Wave Strength	11 a.m. Water Bootcamp	10 a.m. Aqua Motion	9 a.m. Generation Aqua
6 p.m. New Wave Strength	7 p.m. Generation Aqua	5 p.m. Water Bootcamp	6 p.m. New Wave Strength	4 p.m. Aqua Motion

(c)

(d)

Figure 4–85

In the Lab

Lab 3: Creating a Presentation with Action Buttons and a Hidden Slide

Problem: Your public speaking instructor has assigned an informative speech, and you have decided to discuss orchestra instruments. You create the presentation in Figure 4–86 that consists of six slides and decide to hide one slide in case your speech runs longer than expected. The table on Slide 2 contains hyperlinks to Slides 3, 4, 5, and 6, and those slides contain hyperlinks to Slide 2.

Perform the following tasks.

1. Create a new presentation using the Civic document theme, and then change the theme font and the theme colors to Metro. Using Figure 4–86, create the six core presentation slides by typing the Slide 1 title and subtitle text, the Slide 2 title text, and the Slide 3, 4, 5, and 6 title and body text. Apply the Two Content layout to Slides 3 – 6

2. On Slide 2, create the table shown in Figure 4–86b. Apply the Dark Style 2 – Accent 1/Accent 2 table style (row 2, column 2 in the Dark area) and the Inside Diagonal Bottom Left Inner shadow (row 3, column 1 in the Inner area).

3. Insert the pictures from your Data Files for Students on all slides. Apply the 10 Point Soft Edges picture effect to each picture.

4. Insert a Sound action button to the right of each category on Slide 2. Hyperlink each button to the corresponding slide. For example, the Strings action button should hyperlink to Slide 3. Play the Push sound when the Strings button is clicked, the Wind sound for the Woodwind button, the Breeze sound for the Brass button, and the Drum Roll for the Percussion button. Size the buttons to fit in each table row and change the fill color to Turquoise, Accent 4 (row 1, column 8 in the Theme Colors area).

5. Insert a Back or Previous action button in the lower-left corner of Slides 3 – 6, and hyperlink the buttons to Slide 2. Change the action button fill color to Pink, Accent 2, Lighter 40% (row 4, column 6 in the Theme Colors area). Do not play a sound. Size and move the buttons as shown in Figures 4–86c through 4–86f.

6. Use the thesaurus to find a synonym for the word, Category, in the Slide 2 table. Hide Slide 2.

7. Insert the slide number in all slides except the title slide. Apply the Uncover Right-Up transition (row 3, column 1 in the Wipes category) to all slides. Change the speed to Medium. Check the spelling and correct any errors.

8. Click the Slide Sorter view button, view the slides for consistency, and then click the Normal view button.

9. Change the document properties, as specified by your instructor. Save the presentation using the file name, Lab 4-3 Orchestra Instruments.

10. Submit the revised document in the format specified by your instructor.

Continued >

In the Lab *continued*

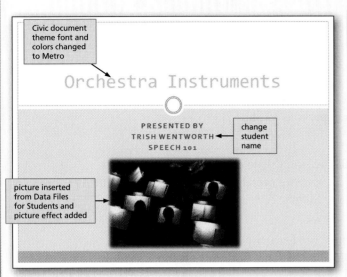

(a)

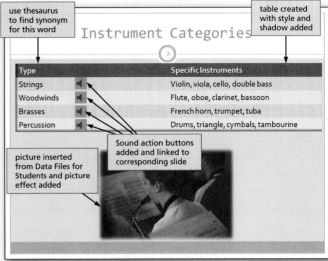

(b)

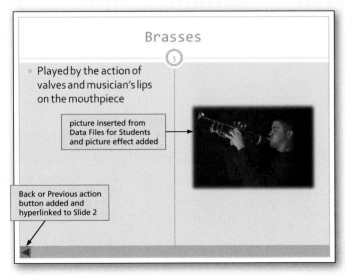

(c)

(d)

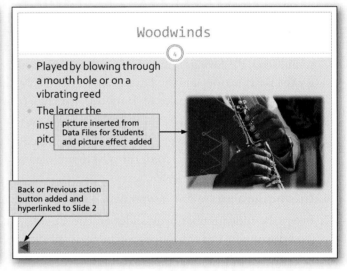

(e)

(f)

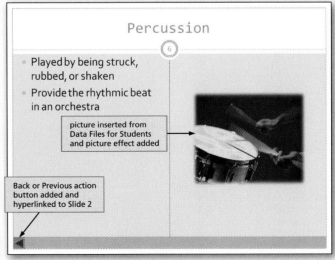

Figure 4–86

Cases and Places

Apply your creative thinking and problem solving skills to design and implement a solution.

• Easier •• More Difficult

Note: Remember to use the 7 × 7 rule as you design the presentations: a maximum of seven words on a line and a maximum of seven lines on one slide.

• 1: Design and Create an English Dialects Presentation

Much of the world speaks English as a primary language, but the grammar—vocabulary and pronunciation, or dialect—varies greatly. Linguists study the nature and structure of speech and focus on how language varies among countries and different regions within each country. Members of the American Dialect Society (www.americandialect.org) study English language use among people living in North America. They analyze how other languages influence English-speaking North Americans and how, in turn, North Americans influence speakers of other languages. Dialect numbers among native English speakers in America, Britain, Canada, and Australia are shown in Table 4–6.

Using the information in Table 4–6 create a chart and a hyperlink to the American Dialect Society as part of a presentation on dialects. Apply at least three objectives found at the beginning of this chapter to develop the presentation. Add a title slide with at least one clip to which you add an effect. Be sure to check spelling.

Table 4–6 English Dialects	
Native Speakers	**Number of Dialects**
American	226,710
British	156,990
Canadian	19,700
Australian	15,316
Other	18,581

• 2: Design and Create a Gods and Goddesses Presentation

People have worshipped gods and goddesses since prehistoric times, thinking these spirits affect the destinies of humans and nature. These deities are believed to control forces beyond human power, and the rituals associated with worshipping them have held societies together. Some of these figures resemble humans, while others have part-human or part-animal forms. Many of the Roman gods are equivalent to earlier Greek versions, and their names and roles are listed in Table 4–7. Create a presentation about gods and goddesses, and include a table with the data in Table 4–7. Apply a table style and borders. Use clips from the Clip Organizer and add effects. Apply slide transitions and a footer with page numbers and your name on all slides. Be sure to check spelling.

Table 4–7 Gods and Goddesses		
Role	**Greek Name**	**Roman Name**
Goddess of love	Aphrodite	Venus
God of the arts and medicine	Apollo	Apollo
God of war	Ares	Mars
God of travel, roads, and trade	Hermes	Mercury
God of the sea	Poseidon	Neptune
Ruler of the gods	Zeus	Jupiter

•• 3: Design and Create a Body Mass Index Presentation

The body mass index (BMI) is a tool used in assessing an individual's ideal weight. To calculate a person's BMI, multiply his height in inches by his height in inches and then divide that number into his weight. Multiply the result of that computation by 703. Compare the final number to the BMI Classification Table 4–8 to determine if he is healthy, overweight, obese, or very obese. Your campus fitness center director has asked you to prepare a presentation showing the formula, the data in Table 4–8, sample BMIs using a person with a height of 5' 7" and weights of 100, 125, 150, 175, and 200 pounds, and hyperlinks to the American Heart Organization and the National Institutes of Health Web sites. Create this slide show, and hide the BMI example slide. Use an action button to jump from the BMI formula slide to the slide containing the BMI classification table and a second action button to return to the formula slide from the table slide. Use at least one formatted clip from the Clip Organizer, apply a slide transition to all slides, and insert your name in a footer on all slides.

Table 4–8 Body Mass Index		
Range	**Condition**	**Risk Classification**
19 to 24.9	Healthy weight	Desirable
25 t0 29.9	Overweight	Borderline high
30 to 39.9	Obese	High
40 to 54	Very obese	Very high

•• 4 Design and Create an Energy Drinks Presentation

Make It Personal

Energy drinks are a popular alternative to coffee and caffeinated beverages. In this $4 billion industry, some energy drinks have up to four times the caffeine contained in popular colas. Visit your local grocery store and compare the ingredients in at least three different energy drinks, including the ones you or your friends drink regularly. Compare price, serving size, calories, sodium, carbohydrates, niacin, and B-group vitamins. Then read articles or search the Internet to find nutrition experts' reviews and opinions of these drinks' taste and effect. Then use the concepts and techniques presented in this chapter to develop and format a slide show reporting your findings. Include a formatted table comparing the energy drinks. Enhance the presentation with at least one formatted clip. Include hyperlinks to three of the drinks' Web sites. Be sure to check spelling. Print a handout with two slides on each page.

•• 5: Design and Create a Staging Presentation

Working Together

Homeowners attempting to sell their homes are turning to Staging, a trademarked term of Stagedhomes.com. Stagers prepare a home for sale by rearranging furniture, removing clutter, and accentuating the house's positive features. Have each member of your team call or visit a local Stager or conduct online research and gather information about how long the average staged home remains on the market compared to a non-staged home. Also find out the average increase in sale price between a staged and non-staged home. After coordinating the data, create a presentation with charts showing both these sets of statistics. As a group, critique each slide. Submit your assignment in the format specified by your instructor.

Collaboration Feature

Collaborating on and Delivering Presentations

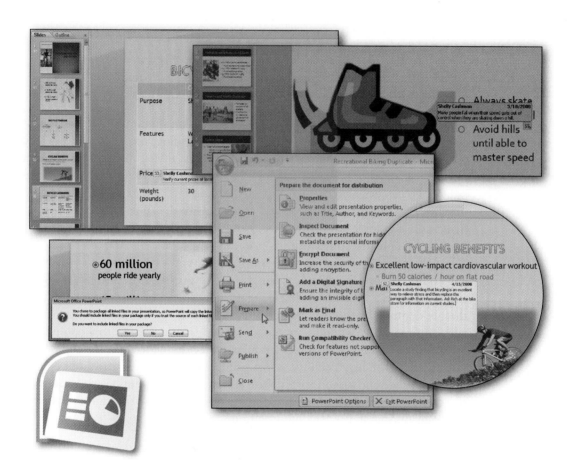

Objectives

You will have mastered the material in this Collaboration feature when you can:

- Insert, delete, and modify comments
- Inspect and protect files
- Compress files and mark them as final

- Create a digital signature
- Save files as a PowerPoint show
- Run shows with pens and highlighters
- Package presentations for a CD

Collaboration Feature Introduction

Often presentations are enhanced when individuals collaborate to fine-tune text, visuals, and design elements on the slides. A **review cycle** occurs when a slide show designer e-mails a file to multiple reviewers so they can make comments and changes to their copies of the slides and then return the file to the designer. The designer then can display the comments, modify their content and ask the reviewers to again review the presentation, and continue this process until the slides are satisfactory. Once the presentation is complete, the designer can protect the file so no one can open it without a password, remove comments and other information, and assure that it is authentic. The designer also can compress the overall file size and then save the presentation to a compact disc. In addition, a presenter can use PowerPoint's variety of tools to run the show effectively and emphasize various elements on the screen.

Project — Presentation with Comments, Protection, and Authentication

The six slides in the Recreational Biking presentation (Figure 1) give specific information about the sport, including statistics about who is riding, the history of the bicycles, and the benefits of participating in this activity. When you are developing a presentation, it often is advantageous to ask a variety of people to review your work in progress. These individuals can evaluate the wording, art, and design, and experts in the subject can check the slides for accuracy. They can add comments to the slides in specific areas, such as a paragraph, a graphic, or a table. You then can review their comments and use them to modify and enhance your work.

Once you develop the final set of slides, you can finalize the file by removing any comments and personal information, compressing the file size to aid in e-mailing and posting to a Web site, adding a password so that unauthorized people cannot see the file contents without your permission, saving the file as a PowerPoint show so it runs automatically when you open a file, and saving the file to a compact disc.

When running your presentation, you may decide to show the slides nonsequentially. For example, you may need to review a slide you discussed already, or you may want to skip some slide and jump forward. You also may want to emphasize, or **annotate**, material on the slides by highlighting text or writing on the slides. You can save your annotations to review during or after the presentation.

Overview

As you read through this chapter, you will learn how to use PowerPoint's commenting feature and presentation tools shown in Figure 1 by performing these general tasks:

- Review a presentation.
- Protect a presentation.
- Secure and share a presentation.
- Use presentation tools.
- Package presentations for a CD.

(a) Slide 1

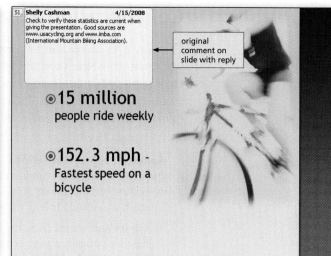

(b) Slide 2

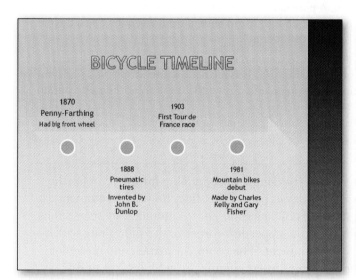

(c) Slide 3

(d) Slide 4

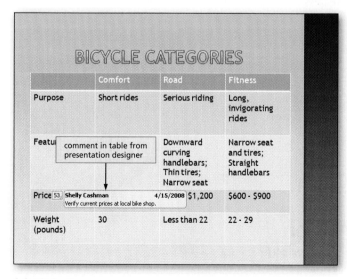

(e) Slide 5

(f) Slide 6

Figure 1

Collaborating on a Presentation

When you are developing a presentation, it often is beneficial to share your ideas and work with colleagues and friends. These people can offer suggestions on how to enhance the overall presentation and specific slide elements. While adding this step to the development process increases the overall creation time, the end result most often is worth the effort. PowerPoint makes it easy to insert, review, modify, and delete comments.

Plan Ahead

General Project Guidelines

The actions you perform and decisions you make will affect the appearance and characteristics of the finished document. As you collaborate on a presentation, such as the project shown in Figure 1, you should follow these general guidelines:

1. **Ask for and accept criticism.** Feedback, both positive and negative, that enables you to improve yourself and your work, is called **criticism**. Written and oral comments from others can help reinforce the positive aspects and also identify the flaws. Seek comments from a variety of people who genuinely want to help you develop an effective slide show.

2. **Select an appropriate password.** A **password** is a private combination of characters that allows users to open a file. To prevent unauthorized people from viewing your slides, choose a good password and keep it confidential.

When necessary, more specific details concerning the above guidelines are presented at appropriate points in the feature. The feature also will identify the actions you perform and decisions you made regarding these guidelines during the creation of the presentation shown in Figure 1.

To Insert a Comment

To prepare a presentation for review, you might want to insert a comment containing information for the reviewers. A **comment** is a description that normally does not display as part of the slide show. The comment can be used to clarify information that may be difficult to understand, to pose questions, or to communicate suggestions. PowerPoint adds a small rectangle, called a **comment marker**, to the upper-left corner of the slide along with a **comment box**, which is the area where you write or review the comment. The comment marker and box colors change depending upon your computer's settings. The following steps insert comments on Slides 2, 4, and 5.

- Start PowerPoint and then open the presentation, Recreational Biking, from the Data Files for Students.

- Click the Next Slide button to display Slide 2.

- Click Review on the Ribbon to display the Review tab.

- Click the Insert Comment button, which is labeled New Comment, in the Comments group to display a comment box at the top of Slide 2 (Figure 2).

Q&A

What is the information at the top at the comment box?

PowerPoint inserts the system date and the user's name that was entered when Microsoft Office 2007 was installed.

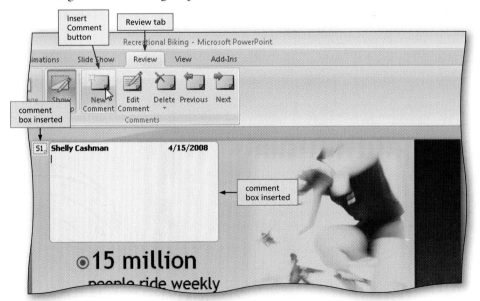

Figure 2

2

- **Type** Check to verify these statistics are current when giving the presentation. in the comment box (Figure 3).

Can I change the initials and name that display in the comment box and comment marker?

Yes. Click the Office Button, click PowerPoint Options, click Popular, and then change the information. When you are finished, click the OK button.

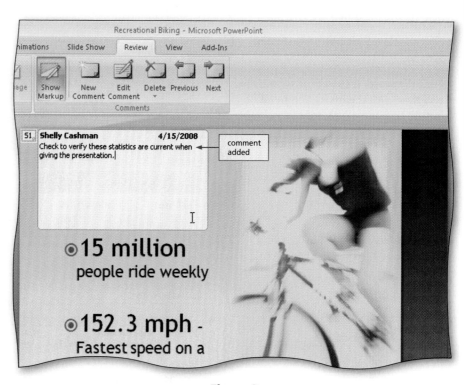

Figure 3

3

- Click anywhere outside the comment box to close the comment box.

- Click the Next Slide button twice to display Slide 4.

- Click after the second bullet and then click the Insert Comment button to display a comment box to the right of the bullet.

- **Type** Locate a study finding that bicycling is an excellent way to relieve stress and then replace this paragraph with that information. in the comment box (Figure 4).

Can I insert more than one comment on a slide?

Yes. Add the comments wherever they point out positive or negative slide elements.

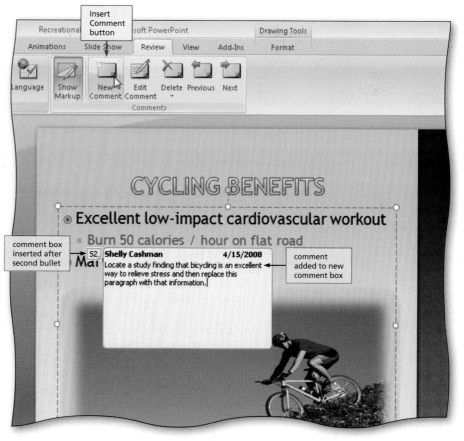

Figure 4

4

- Click anywhere outside the comment box to close the comment box.

- Click the Next Slide button to display Slide 5.

- Click the word, Price, in the table and then click the Insert Comment button to open a new comment box on the table.

- Type `Verify current prices at local bike shop.` in the comment box (Figure 5).

5

- Click anywhere outside the comment box to close the comment box.

Q&A Will the comments display if I run a presentation?

No. The comments are visible only in Normal view.

Q&A Will the comments display if I print a presentation?

Yes. If you do not want them to print, you can turn off this default setting by clearing the 'Print comments and ink markup' check box in the Print dialog box.

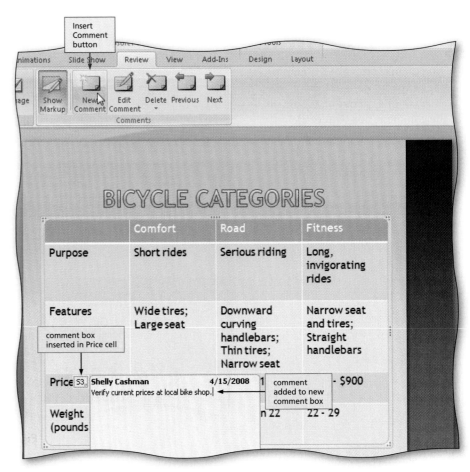

Figure 5

Plan Ahead

Ask for and accept criticism.

Receiving feedback from others ultimately should enhance your presentation. If several of your reviewers make similar comments, such as too much text appears on one slide or that a chart would help present your concept, then you should heed their criticism and modify your slides. Criticism from a variety of people, particularly if they are from different cultures or vary in age, gives a wide range of viewpoints. Some reviewers might focus on the font size, others on color and design choices, while others might single out the overall message. These individuals should make judgments on your work, such as saying that the overall presentation is good or that a particular paragraph is confusing, and then offer reasons of what elements are effective or how you can edit a paragraph.

When you receive these comments, do not get defensive. Ask yourself why your reviewers would have made these comments. Perhaps they lack a background in the subject matter. Or they may have a particular interest in this topic and can add their expertise.

If you are asked to critique a presentation, begin and end with positive comments. Give specific details about a few key areas that can be improved. Be honest, but be tactful. Avoid using the word, you. For example, instead of writing, "You need to give some statistics to support your viewpoint," write "I had difficulty understanding which departments' sales have declined in the past five months. Perhaps a chart with specific losses would help depict how dramatically revenues have fallen."

To Modify a Comment

Once a comment is added to a slide, you can review the wording and then edit the text or add more material. The following steps edit the comments on Slides 2 and 4.

1

- Display Slide 2 and then click the comment marker to display the comment on Slide 2.

- Click the Edit Comment button in the Comments group to open the comment box.

- At the end of the current text type Good sources are www.usacycling.org and www.imba.com (International Mountain Bicycling Association). in the comment box (Figure 6).

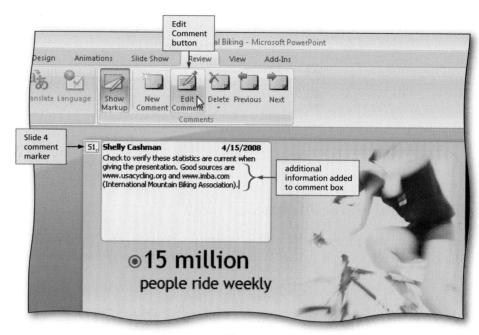

Figure 6

2

- Click the Next Comment button, which is labeled Next, in the Comments group to display the comment on Slide 4.

- Click the Edit Comment button and then type Ask Rich at the bike store for information on current studies. in the comment box (Figure 7).

Q&A

Can I move a comment on a slide?

Yes. Drag the comment marker to the desired location on the same slide.

Other Ways

1. Right-click comment marker, click Edit Comment on shortcut menu

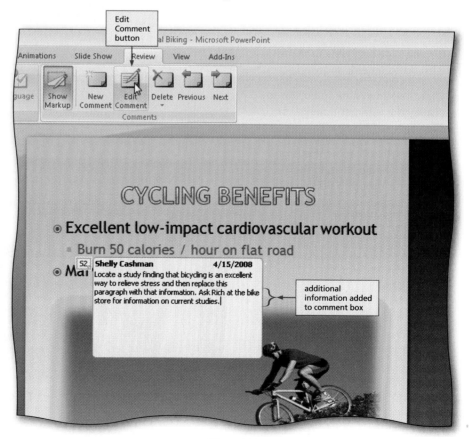

Figure 7

To Save the Presentation

You added comments to three slides. The next step is to save the presentation.

Note: If you are using Windows XP, see Appendix F for alternate steps.

1 With a USB flash drive connected to one of the computer's USB ports, click the Office Button and then display the Save As dialog box.

2 Type `Recreational Biking Revised` in the File name text box to change the file name.

3 Click Computer in the Favorite Links section, double-click your USB flash drive in the list of available drives, and then click the Save button to save the document on the USB flash drive with the new file name.

To Hide and Show Markups

The marker for each comment is displayed where you inserted it when you open the presentation. The Show Markup button is a toggle to display and hide these markers. The following steps hide and then show the markups on Slides 2, 4, and 5.

- Click the Show Markup button in the Comments group to hide the comment on Slide 4 (Figure 8).

- Display Slide 5 to view the slide with no comments showing.

- Click the Show Markup button to display the comment marker on Slide 5.

- Click the Next Comment button, which is labeled Next, in the Comments group to display the Slide 2 comment.

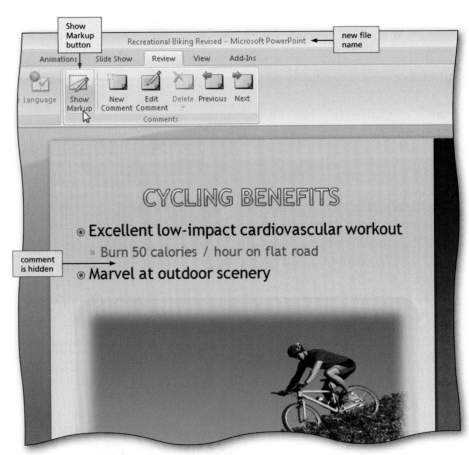

Figure 8

To Delete a Comment

If a particular comment no longer is useful, you should delete it from the slide. The following step deletes the comment from the Slide 2 table.

1

- With Slide 2 displayed, click the Delete Comment button in the Comments group to delete the comment (Figure 9).

Q&A

What options will I have if I click the Delete button arrow?

You can choose to delete just a selected comment, all comments on the current slide, or all comments in the presentation.

Figure 9

Other Ways

1. Right-click comment marker, click Delete Comment on shortcut menu

Protecting, Securing, and Sharing a Presentation

When your slides are complete, you can perform additional functions to finalize the file and prepare it for distributing to other users or running on a computer other than the one used to develop the file. For example, the Compatibility Checker reviews the file for any feature that will not work properly or display on computers running a previous PowerPoint version. In addition, the Document Inspector locates inappropriate information, such as comments, in a file and allows you to delete these slide elements. You also can reduce the overall file size to simplify sending the file as an e-mail attachment or posting to a Web page. With passwords and digital signatures, you add security levels to protect people from distributing, viewing, or modifying your slides. When the review process is complete, you can indicate this file is the final version. You also can save the file as a PowerPoint show so that it runs automatically when opened.

To Identify Presentation Features Not Supported by Previous Versions

PowerPoint 2007 has many new features not found in previous versions of PowerPoint. For example, WordArt formatted with Quick Styles is an enhancement found only in this current software. If you give your file to people who have a previous PowerPoint version installed on their computers, they will be able to open the file but may not be able to see or edit some special features and effects. You can use the **Compatibility Checker** to see which presentation elements will not function in earlier versions of PowerPoint. The following steps run the Compatibility Checker and display a summary of the elements in your Recreational Biking presentation that will be lost if your file is opened in an earlier PowerPoint version.

• Click the Office Button and then point to Prepare on the Office Button menu to display the Prepare submenu (Figure 10).

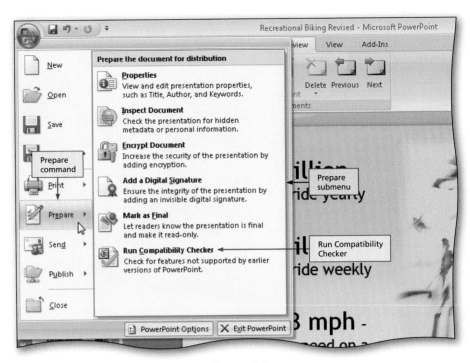

Figure 10

• Click Run Compatibility Checker to open the Microsoft Office PowerPoint Compatibility Checker dialog box.

• View the comments in the Summary area regarding the two features that are not supported by earlier versions of PowerPoint (Figure 11).

Q&A

Why do the numbers 5 and 1 display in the right side of the Summary area?

The Compatibility Checker found five shapes in your presentation that cannot be edited in previous versions. These graphics will be converted to bitmap images in older versions, so they cannot be ungrouped and modified.

Q&A

What happens if I click the Help links in the Summary area?

PowerPoint will provide additional information about the particular incompatible slide element.

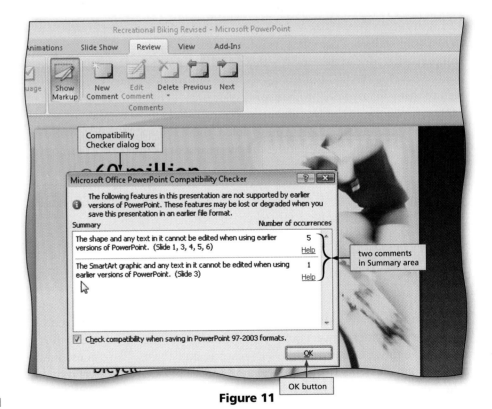

Figure 11

• Click the OK button to close the Microsoft Office PowerPoint Compatibility Checker dialog box.

To Remove Inappropriate Information

As you work on your presentation, you might add information meant only for you to see. For example, you might write comments to yourself or put confidential information in the Document Information Panel. You would not want other people to access this information if you give a copy of the presentation file to them. The Document Inspector provides a quick and efficient method of searching for and deleting inappropriate information.

If you tell the Document Inspector to delete content, such as personal information, comments, invisible slide content, or notes, and then decide you need to see those slide elements, quite possibly you will be unable to retrieve the information by using the Undo command. For that reason, it is a good idea to make a duplicate copy of your file and then inspect this new second copy. The following steps save a duplicate copy of your Recreational Biking presentation, run the Document Inspector on this new file, and then delete comments.

1

- Click the Office Button, point to Save As on the Office Button menu, and then click PowerPoint presentation.

- Type Recreational Biking Duplicate in the File name text box and then click the Save button to change the file name and save another copy of this presentation.

- Click the Office Button and then point to Prepare on the Office Button menu (Figure 12).

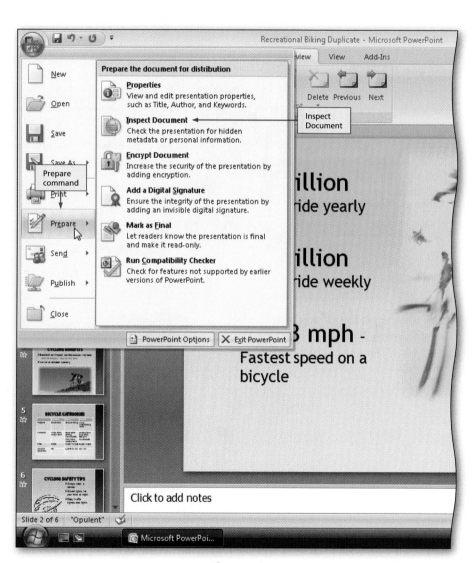

Figure 12

2

• Click Inspect Document in the Prepare submenu to display the Document Inspector dialog box (Figure 13).

Q&A

What information does the Document Inspector check?

This information includes text in the Document Information Panel, such as your name and company. Other information includes details of when the file was last saved, objects formatted as invisible, graphics and text you dragged off a slide, presentation notes, and e-mail headers.

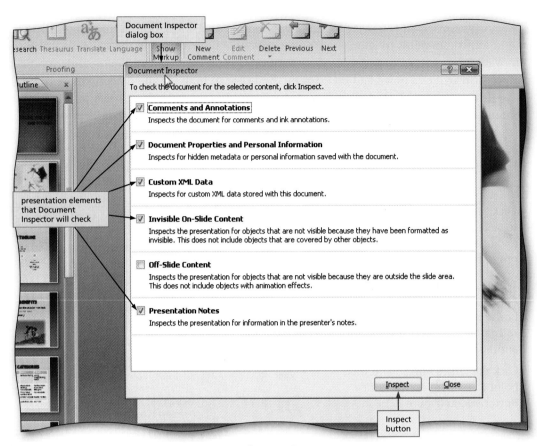

Figure 13

3

• Click the Inspect button to check the document (Figure 14).

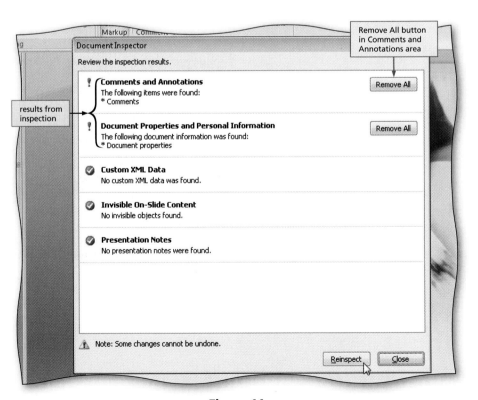

Figure 14

4

• When the inspection report is displayed, click the Remove All button in the Comments and Annotations area to remove the comments from the presentation (Figure 15).

Q&A

Should I also remove the document properties and personal information?

You might want to delete this information so that no identifying information is saved. This information includes text that displays in the Document Information Panel, such as your name and company, and also comments and other hidden data.

5

• Click the Close button to close the Document Inspector dialog box.

Figure 15

Plan Ahead	**Select an appropriate password.**
	A password should be at least six characters and contain a combination of letters and numbers. Using both uppercase and lowercase letters is advised. Do not use a password that someone could guess, such as your first or last name, spouse's or child's name, telephone number, birth date, street address, license plate number, or Social Security number.
	Once you develop this password, write it down in a secure place. Underneath your keyboard is not a secure place, nor is your middle desk drawer.

To Set a Password

You can protect your slide content on CDs by using passwords on all packaged presentations. The passwords specify whether a user can look at or modify a file. The following steps set a password for the Recreational Biking Duplicate file.

- Click the Office Button and click Save As on the Office Button menu to display the Save As dialog box.

- Click the Tools button to display the Tools menu (Figure 16).

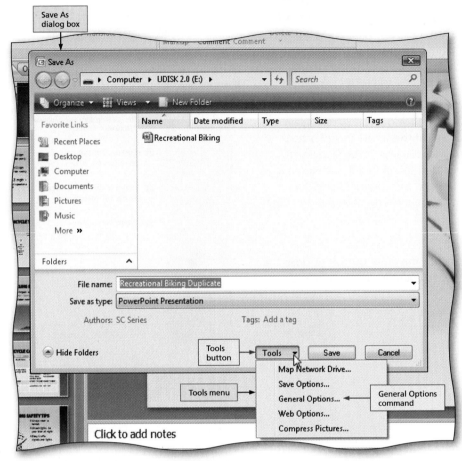

Figure 16

- Click General Options in the Tools menu to display the General Options dialog box.

- Type Biking4me in the 'Password to open' text box (Figure 17).

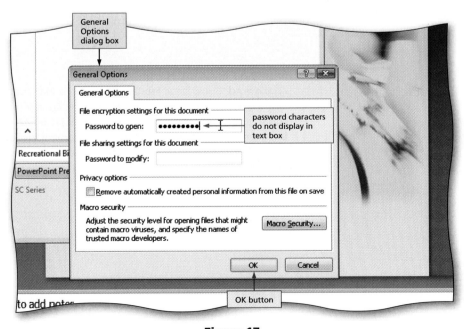

Figure 17

3

- Click the OK button to display the Confirm Password dialog box.

- Type `Biking4me` in the 'Reenter password to open' text box (Figure 18).

Q&A What if I forget my password?

You will not be able to open your file. For security reasons, Microsoft or other companies cannot retrieve a lost password.

4

- Click the OK button in the Confirm Password dialog box.

- Click the Save button in the Save As dialog box to add the password to the document.

- Click the Yes button in the Confirm Save As dialog box to replace the existing presentation.

Q&A When does the password take effect?

You will need to enter your password the next time you open your presentation.

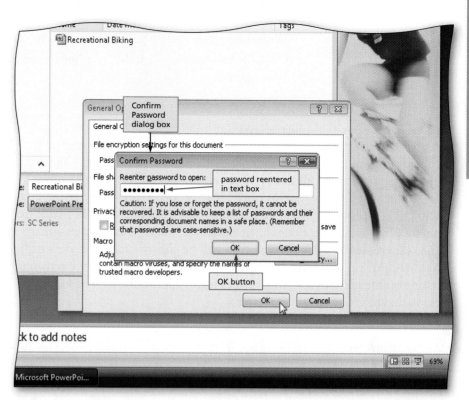

Figure 18

To Open a Presentation with a Password

To open a file that has been protected with a password, you would perform the following steps.

1. Click the Office Button and then click Open on the Office Button menu.

2. Locate the desired file and then click the Open button to display the Password dialog box.

3. When the Password dialog box appears, type the password in the Password text box and then click the OK button to display the presentation.

To Change the Password or Remove Password Protection

To change a password that you added to a file or to remove all password protection from the file, you would perform the following steps.

1. Click the Office Button and then click Open on the Office Button menu.

2. Locate the desired file and then click the Open button to display the Password dialog box.

3. When the Password dialog box appears, type the password in the Password text box and then click the OK button to display the presentation.

4. Click the Office Button and then click Save As to display the Save As dialog box. Click the Tools button and then click General Options in the Tools list.

5. Select the contents of the 'Password to modify' text box or the 'Password to open' text box. To change the password, type the new password and then click the OK button. When prompted, retype your password to reconfirm it, and then click the OK button.

6. Click the OK button, click the Save button, and then click the Yes button to resave the presentation.

To Compress a Presentation

PowerPoint file sizes can become quite large, especially if the slides contain many photographs and graphical elements. To reduce the file size, you can **compress** one or more pictures. When you compress a picture, however, some of the image's resolution or clarity may be lost. PowerPoint gives you options to decide on a particular amount of compression. The compression options are measured in **pixels per inch (ppi)**. A pixel, short for picture element, is the smallest element in an electronic image. A resolution's image quality improves when the number of pixels increases. If your presentation will be shown only on a Web page, the resolution can be low. On the other hand, if you are going to project your presentation on a large screen in a conference room, compression is not recommended because your images might appear blurry. The following steps compress all pictures in your presentation to 150 pixels per inch (ppi).

- Display Slide 4 and then click the bicycle picture to select it.

- Click Format on the Ribbon to display the Format tab under Picture Tools.

- Click the Compress Pictures button in the Adjust group to display the Compress Pictures dialog box (Figure 19).

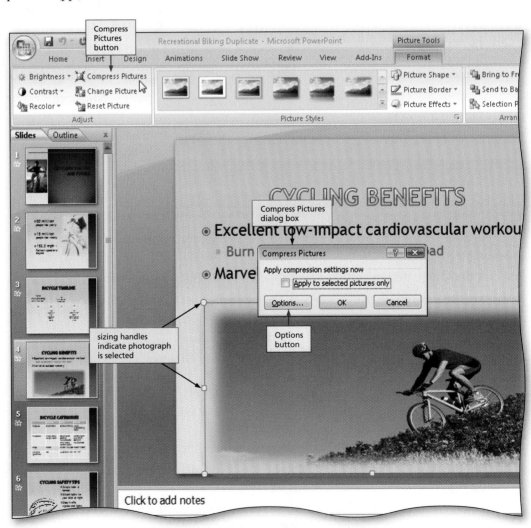

Figure 19

2

- Click the Options button in the Compress Pictures dialog box to display the Compression Settings dialog box.

- Click Screen to select the Screen (150 ppi) option (Figure 20).

Q&A What is the option to delete cropped areas of pictures?

If you have cropped photographs and know you will not want to view the complete photographs, or if you have the original picture file stored in another location, you have the option to remove the cropped areas to save space.

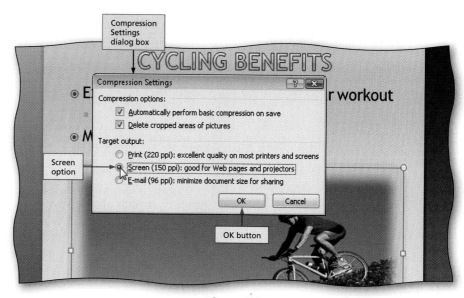

Figure 20

3

- Click the OK button to close the Compression Settings dialog box.

- Click the OK button to close the Compress Pictures dialog box and to compress all pictures in the presentation.

To Create a Digital Signature and Add It to a Document

Digital certificates, or digital IDs, verify that the file contents are authentic and valid. You can add a digital signature to files that require security, such as a presentation about a company's prototype or a patent application that will be submitted shortly. Only users with Office PowerPoint 2003 or later can view presentations protected by the digital signature. You can obtain an authentic digital certificate from a Microsoft partner, or you can create one yourself. Files protected with this certificate cannot be viewed in the PowerPoint viewer or sent as an e-mail attachment. The following steps create a digital signature and add it to the Recreational Biking Duplicate file.

1

- Click the Office Button and then point to Prepare on the Office Button menu to display the Prepare submenu (Figure 21).

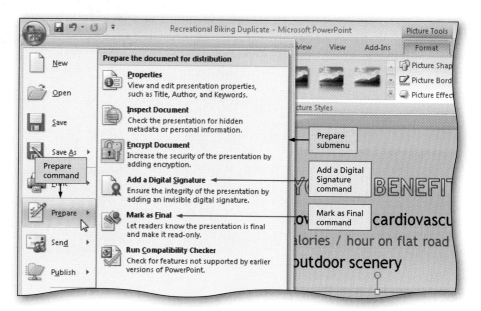

Figure 21

- Click Add a Digital Signature on the Prepare submenu to display the Microsoft Office PowerPoint dialog box (Figure 22).

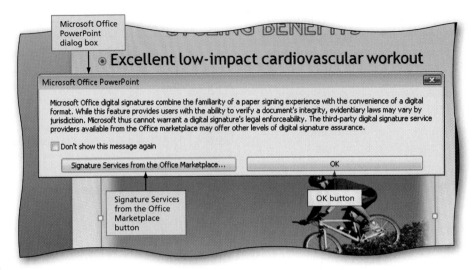

Figure 22

- Click the OK button to display the Get a Digital ID dialog box (Figure 23).

Q&A

What would have happened if I had clicked the Signature Services from the Office Marketplace button instead of the OK button?

You would have been connected to the Microsoft Office Marketplace, which is the same process that will occur if you click the 'Get a digital ID from a Microsoft partner' option button now.

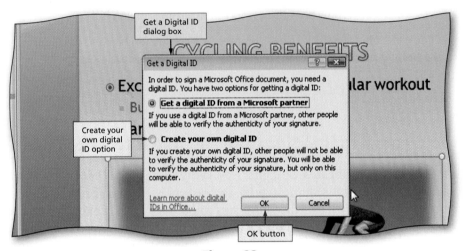

Figure 23

- Click 'Create your own digital ID' and then click the OK button to display the Create a Digital ID dialog box.

- Type Mary Halen in the Name text box.

- Type mary_halen@hotmail.com in the E-mail address text box.

- Type Mary's Bike Shop in the Organization text box.

- Type Los Angeles, CA in the Location text box (Figure 24).

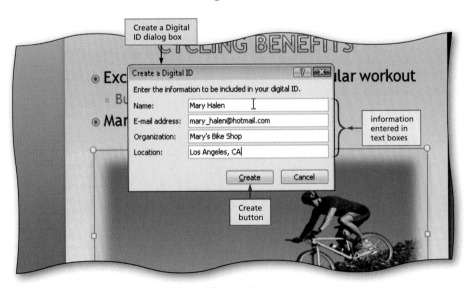

Figure 24

5

- Click the Create button to display the Sign dialog box (Figure 25).

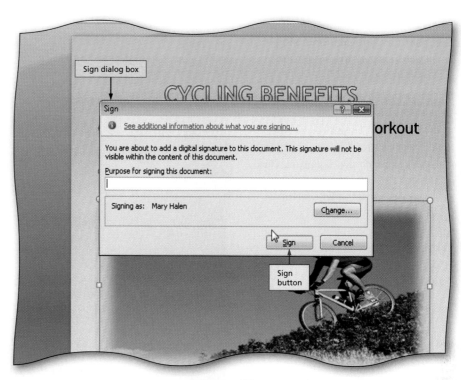

Figure 25

6

- Click the Sign button to display the Signature Confirmation dialog box (Figure 26).

Q&A

Why would a company want to add a digital signature to a document?

The publisher, who is the signing person or organization, is trusted to assure the source and integrity of the digital information. A signature confirms that the file contents have not been altered since it was signed.

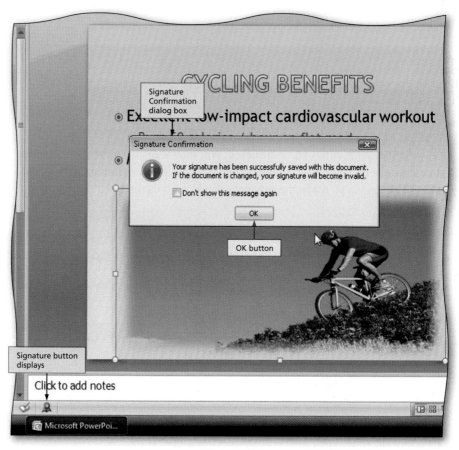

Figure 26

● Click the OK button to close the Signature Confirmation dialog box and display the Signatures task pane (Figure 27).

Q&A Can I remove a digital signature that has been applied?

Yes. Point to a signature in the Signatures task pane, click the list arrow, click Remove Signature, click the Yes button, and then, if necessary, click the OK button.

● Click the Close button in the Signatures task pane so that it no longer is displayed.

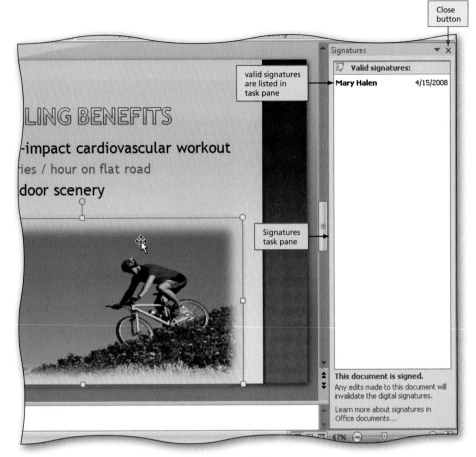

Figure 27

To Mark a Presentation as Final

When your slides are completed, you may want to prevent others or yourself from accidentally changing the slide content or features. If you use the **Mark as Final** command, the presentation becomes a read-only document. The following steps mark the presentation as a final (read-only) document.

1

● Click the Office Button and then point to Prepare on the Office Button.

● Click Mark as Final (shown in Figure 21 on PPT 313) to display the Microsoft Office PowerPoint dialog box (Figure 28).

2

● Click the Yes button to invalidate the signatures in the presentation.

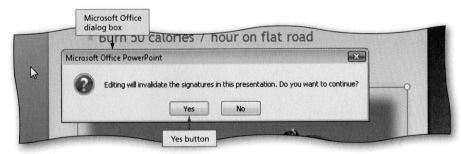

Figure 28

● If necessary, click the OK button to display a second Microsoft Office PowerPoint dialog box indicating that the presentation is final.

Q&A Can I turn off this read-only status so that I can edit the file?

Yes. Repeat Step 1 above to toggle off the read-only status.

To Save a File in .PPS Format

To simplify giving a presentation in front of an audience, you may want your slide show to start running without having to start PowerPoint, open a file, and then click the Slide Show button. When you save a presentation as a **PowerPoint show (.pps)**, it automatically begins running when opened. The following steps save the Recreational Biking Duplicate file as a PowerPoint show.

- Click the Office Button, point to Save As on the Office Button menu, and then click PowerPoint Presentation.

- Type `Recreational Biking Show` in the File name text box.

- Click the Save as type arrow to display the Save as type list (Figure 29).

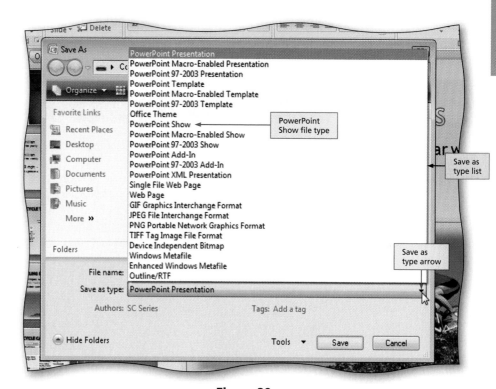

Figure 29

- Click PowerPoint Show in the Save as type list (Figure 30).

- Click the Save button to save the Recreational Biking presentation as a PowerPoint show.

- Click the Yes button in the Microsoft Office PowerPoint dialog box to remove all signatures in the presentation.

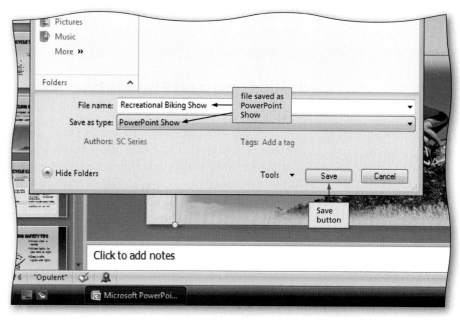

Figure 30

Using Presentation Tools to Navigate

When you click the slide show options button on the Slide Show toolbar, PowerPoint displays the Popup menu. This menu is described on page PPT 51.

When you display a particular slide and view the information, you may want to return to one of the other slides in the presentation. Jumping to particular slides in a presentation is called **navigating**. A set of keyboard shortcuts can help you navigate to various slides during the slide show. When running a slide show, you can press the F1 key to see a list of these keyboard controls. These navigational features are listed in Table 1.

Table 1 Navigation Shortcut Keys	
Keyboard Shortcut	**Purpose**
N Click SPACEBAR RIGHT ARROW DOWN ARROW ENTER PAGE DOWN	Advance to the next slide
P BACKSPACE LEFT ARROW UP ARROW PAGE UP	Return to the previous slide
Number followed by ENTER	Go to a specific slide
B PERIOD	Display a black screen Return to slide show from a black screen
W COMMA	Display a white screen Return to slide show from a white screen
ESC CTRL+BREAK HYPHEN	End a slide show

Delivering and Navigating a Presentation Using the Slide Show Toolbar

When you begin running a slide show and move the mouse pointer, the Slide Show toolbar is displayed. The **Slide Show toolbar** contains buttons that allow you to navigate to the next slide or previous slide, mark up the current slide, or change the current display. When you move the mouse, the toolbar is displayed in the lower-left corner of the slide; it disappears after the mouse has not been moved for three seconds. Table 2 describes the buttons on the Slide Show toolbar.

Table 2 Slide Show Toolbar Buttons	
Description	**Function**
previous slide	Previous slide or previous animated element on the slide
pointer arrow	Shortcut menu for arrows, pens, and highlighters
slide show options	Shortcut menu for slide navigation and screen displays
next slide	Next slide or next animated element on the slide

To Highlight Items on a Slide

You click the arrow buttons on either end of the toolbar to navigate backward or forward through the slide show. The pointer arrow button has a variety of functions, most often to add **ink** notes or drawings to your presentation to emphasize aspects of slides or make handwritten notes. This feature is available in all views except Slide Sorter view. The following steps highlight items on a slide in Slide Show view.

- Click the Slide 1 thumbnail in the Slides tab and then run the slide show.

- If the Slide Show toolbar is not visible, move the mouse pointer on the slide.

- Click the pointer arrow on the Slide Show toolbar to display the shortcut menu (Figure 31).

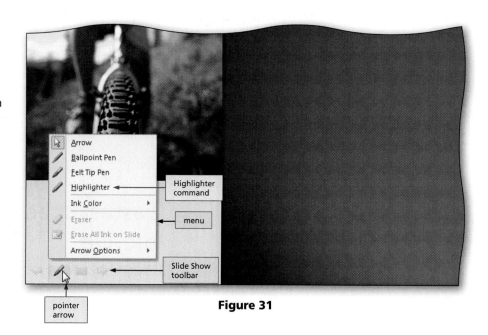

Figure 31

- Click Highlighter and then drag the mouse over the word, Fitness, until the entire word is highlighted (Figure 32).

- Move the mouse and then click to highlight any area of the slide.

Figure 32

To Change Ink Color

Instead of the Highlighter, you also can click Ballpoint Pen and Felt Tip Pen to draw or write notes on the slides. When the presentation ends, PowerPoint will prompt you to keep or discard the ink annotations. The following steps change the pointer to a ballpoint pen and change the color of ink during the presentation.

1

- Click the Next Slide button on the Slide Show toolbar to display Slide 2.

- Click the pointer arrow on the Slide Show toolbar and then click Ballpoint Pen on the shortcut menu.

- Click the pointer arrow on the Slide Show toolbar and then point to Ink Color (Figure 33).

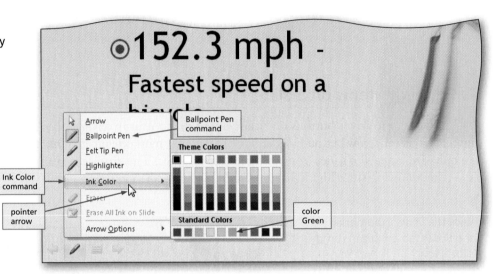

Figure 33

2

- Click the color Green in the Standard Colors row.

- Drag the mouse around the third bulleted paragraph, 152.3 mph - , to draw a line around this text (Figure 34).

Figure 34

3

- Right-click the slide to display the Popup menu.

- Click End Show to display the Microsoft Office PowerPoint dialog box (Figure 35).

4

- Click the Discard button to end the presentation without saving the annotations.

Figure 35

TO HIDE THE MOUSE POINTER AND SLIDE SHOW TOOLBAR

To hide the mouse pointer and Slide Show toolbar during the slide show, you would perform the following step.

1. Click the pointer arrow on the Slide Show toolbar, point to Arrow Options, and then click Hidden.

TO CONSTANTLY DISPLAY THE MOUSE POINTER AND SLIDE SHOW TOOLBAR

By default, the mouse pointer and toolbar are set at Automatic, which means they are hidden after three seconds of no movement. After you hide the mouse pointer and toolbar, they remain hidden until you choose one of the other commands on the Pointer Options submenu. They are displayed again when you move the mouse.

To keep the mouse pointer and toolbar displayed at all times during a slide show, you would perform the following step.

1. Click the pointer arrow on the Slide Show toolbar, point to Arrow Options, and then click Visible.

To Package a Presentation for Storage on a Compact Disc

If your computer has compact disc (CD) burning hardware, the Package for CD option will copy a PowerPoint presentation and linked files onto a CD. Two types of CDs can be used: recordable (CD-R) and rewritable (CD-RW). You must copy all the desired files in a single operation if you use PowerPoint for this task because you cannot add any more files after the first set is copied. If, however, you want to add more files to the CD, you can use Windows Explorer to copy additional files. If you are using a CD-RW with existing content, these files will be overwritten.

The PowerPoint Viewer is included so you can show the presentation on another computer that has Microsoft Windows but does not have PowerPoint installed. The **PowerPoint Viewer** also allows users to view presentations created with PowerPoint 2003, 2000, and 97.

The Package for CD dialog box allows you to select the presentation files to copy, linking and embedding options, whether to add the Viewer, and passwords to open and modify the files. The following steps show how to save a presentation and related files to a CD using the Package for CD feature.

- Insert a CD-RW or a blank CD-R into your CD drive.

- Click the Office Button and then point to Publish on the Office Button menu (Figure 36).

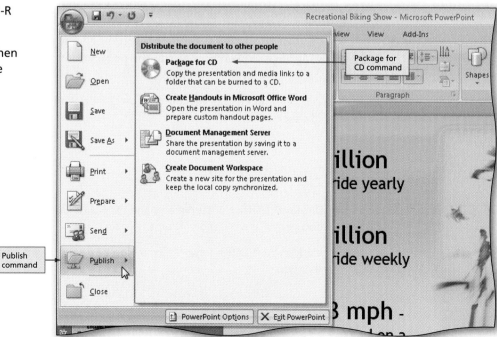

Figure 36

- Click Package for CD to display the Microsoft Office PowerPoint dialog box.

- Click the OK button to display the Package for CD dialog box.

- Type `Biking` in the Name the CD text box.

Q&A

What if I want to add more files to the CD?

Click the Add Files button and then locate the files you want to write on the CD.

- Click the Copy to CD button to package the presentation files (Figure 37).

- Click the No button in the Microsoft Office PowerPoint dialog box to not include linked files.

- When the files have been written, click the Close button in the Package for CD dialog box.

- Click the No button to not copy the files to another CD.

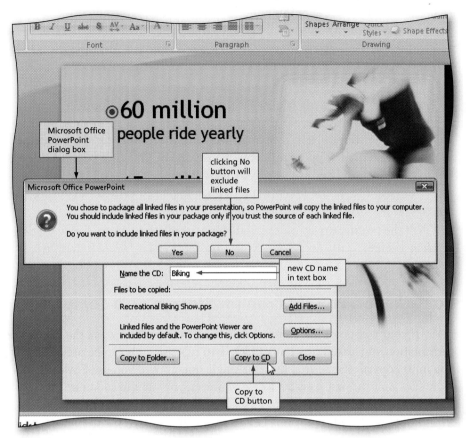

Figure 37

TO VIEW A POWERPOINT SHOW USING THE POWERPOINT VIEWER

When you arrive at a remote location, you will run the packaged presentation. The following steps explain how to run the presentation using the PowerPoint Viewer.

1. Insert your CD in the CD drive.
2. Accept the licensing agreement for the PowerPoint Viewer to open and run the slide show.

To Quit PowerPoint

1 Display the Office Button menu and then click the Exit PowerPoint button to close all open documents and quit PowerPoint.

2 If a Microsoft Office PowerPoint dialog box is displayed, click the Yes button to save the changes.

Collaboration Feature Summary

This Collaboration feature introduced you to inserting, modifying, and deleting comments, reviewing presentations for inappropriate information and features not supported in earlier versions of PowerPoint, setting a password, saving as a PowerPoint show, and adding slide annotations. The items listed below include all the new Office 2007 skills you have learned in this Collaboration feature.

1. Insert a Comment (PPT 300)
2. Modify a Comment (PPT 303)
3. Hide and Show Markups (PPT 304)
4. Delete a Comment (PPT 305)
5. Identify Presentation Features Not Supported by Previous Versions (PPT 305)
6. Remove Inappropriate Information (PPT 307)
7. Set a Password (PPT 310)
8. Open a Presentation with a Password (PPT 311)
9. Change the Password or Remove Password Protection (PPT 311)
10. Compress a Presentation (PPT 312)
11. Create a Digital Signature and Add It to a Document (PPT 313)
12. Mark a Presentation as Final (PPT 316)
13. Save a File in .PPS Format (PPT 317)
14. Highlight Items on a Slide (PPT 319)
15. Change Ink Color (PPT 321)
16. Hide the Mouse Pointer and Slide Show Toolbar (PPT 321).
17. Constantly Display the Mouse Pointer and Slide Show Toolbar (PPT 321)
18. Package a Presentation for Storage on a Compact Disc (PPT 321)
18. View a PowerPoint Show Using the PowerPoint Viewer (PPT 322)

If you have a SAM user profile, you may have access to hands-on instruction, practice, and assessment. Log in to your SAM account (http://sam2007.course.com) to launch any assigned training activities or exams that relate to the skills covered in this feature.

In the Lab

Create a presentation using the guidelines, concepts, and skills presented in this feature. Labs 1, 2, and 3 are listed in order of increasing difficulty.

Lab 1: Adding Comments to and Protecting a Presentation

Problem: Registered dietitians provide a variety of nutrition services, including personal consultations on developing appropriate eating plans and preparing healthy meals. Jen Rowley, the registered dietitian at your community center, has created a presentation she would like to use during these consultations on the topic of choosing nutritious foods, and she asks you to review it. She sends you the slides and requests comments. You add several comments, check the slides for incompatibility with previous PowerPoint versions, and then protect the presentation with a password. When you run the presentation, you add annotations. The annotated slides are shown in Figure 38.

Instructions: Perform the following tasks.

1. Open the presentation, Lab SF-1 Healthy Meals, from the Data Files for Students.

2. On Slide 1, replace Jen Rowley's name with your name. Add a comment on the photograph with the following text: I suggest you enlarge this photo and add a border.

3. On Slide 2, add a comment in the Breakfast cell with the following text: Can you add a bullet on this slide to emphasize that breakfast is the most important meal of the day? Everyone should make the time to eat a healthy breakfast.

4. On Slide 3, add a comment on the apple graphic with the following text: I would change the color of the title text to red so that it blends with the clip.

5. Run the Compatibility Checker to identify the presentation features not supported in previous PowerPoint versions. Summarize these features in a comment placed on Slide 1.

6. Protect the presentation with the password, Food4Health.

7. Change the document properties, as specified by your instructor. Save the presentation using the file name, Lab SF-1 Healthy Meals Comments.

(a)   (b)

Figure 38

8. Run the presentation. On Slide 1, click the pointer arrow in the Slide Show toolbar and use the yellow highlighter to draw a circle around the word, Healthy, in the title text. Click the Next Slide button on the toolbar, click the pointer arrow, click Felt Tip Pen in the menu, and then draw two underlines under the word, Breakfast, in the table. Click the Next Slide button on the toolbar, click the pointer arrow, and then click Ballpoint Pen in the menu. Click the pointer arrow, point to Ink Color in the menu and then click Yellow in the Standard Colors row. Draw a check mark to the left of each of the three bullets on this slide. Save the annotations. Print the slides.

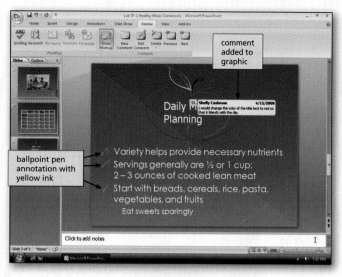

Figure 38 (c)

9. Submit the revised document in the format specified by your instructor.

In the Lab

Lab 2: Modifying and Deleting Comments in a Protected Presentation

Problem: Antibiotics are used to kill bacteria and can control infectious diseases. Some people, however, believe these drugs will help relieve the symptoms of viral infections, such as coughs and sore throats caused by colds and the flu. Many bacteria have become resistant to antibiotics because these drugs have been taken unnecessarily. You are working with a friend in your health class to develop a PowerPoint presentation on the topic of antibiotics. Your friend gives you a password-protected file that she created, and she asks you to review the slides, which are shown in Figure 39. She has inserted comments with questions, and you offer some suggestions. You modify her comments and remove inappropriate information.

Instructions: Perform the following tasks.

1. Open the presentation, Lab SF-2 Antibiotics, from the Data Files for Students. The password is Anti4Us.

2. Insert your name in the footer on all slides. On Slide 1, modify the comment on the photograph by adding the following text: No. The photo's size is great. It introduces the topic and calls attention to the presentation.

3. On Slide 2, modify the comment by adding the following text: You can leave those words in past tense, or you can change them to the present tense words you recommend. Either one is fine as long as you are consistent.

4. On Slide 3, modify the comment by adding the following text: Yes. I think it is better if you tell your audience why the drugs are prescribed rather than why they are not prescribed.

5. On Slide 4, delete the comment.

6. Print the slides and comments.

7. Inspect the document and then remove all document properties and personal information.

Continued >

In the Lab *continued*

8. Save the presentation using the file name, Lab SF-2 Antibiotics Revised.

9. Submit the revised document in the format specified by your instructor.

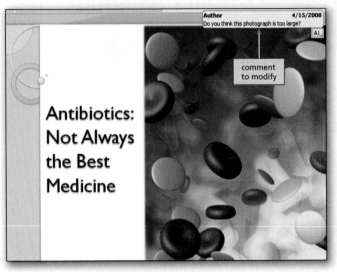

(a)

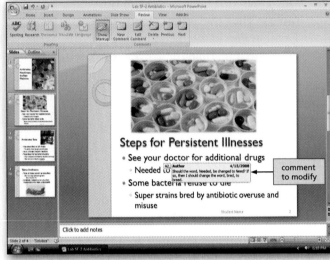

(b)

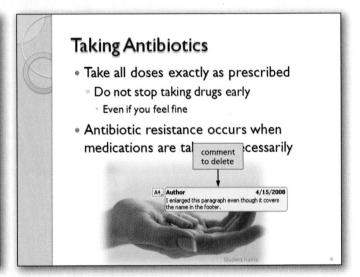

(c)

(d)

Figure 39

In the Lab

Lab 3: Compressing a Presentation, Saving in .PPS Format, and Packaging the Presentation for a CD

Problem: In-line skating is a popular method of exercising and having fun with friends and family. The owner of the sporting goods store in your town has created a presentation with skating safety tips and also with statistics about the number of people who participate in this sport. She sends you the slides shown in Figure 40. You delete her comments, compress the presentation, add a digital signature, save the file as a PowerPoint show, and then package the presentation on a CD.

Instructions: Perform the following tasks.

1. Open the presentation, Lab SF-3 Skating, from the Data Files for Students.

2. Show the markups, review the Slide 1 comment, and then click the Next Comment button in the Comments group to review the comment on Slide 2. Continue clicking the Next Comment button to review all the comments on the slides.

3. Inspect the document and then remove all comments and annotations.

4. Compress the presentation using the default settings.

5. Change the document properties, as specified by your instructor.

6. Save the presentation using the file name, Lab SF-3 Skating Revised. Protect the presentation with the password, 2Sk8.

7. Save the presentation as a PowerPoint show. Use the file name, Lab SF-3 Skating Show.

8. Mark the presentation as final.

9. Add a digital signature by creating your own digital ID. Enter your name in the Name text box, `mary_halen@hotmail.com` in the E-mail address text box, `Sarah's Skate Shop` in the Organization text box, and `Los Angeles, CA` in the Location text box.

10. Save the Skating Show presentation using the Package for CD feature.

11. Submit the revised document in the format specified by your instructor.

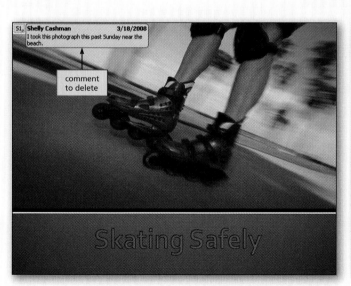

(a)

(b)

Figure 40

Continued >

In the Lab *continued*

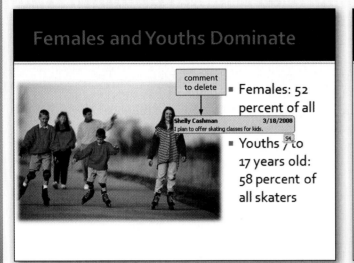

(c)

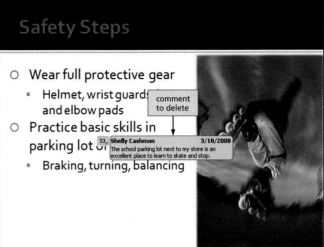

(d)

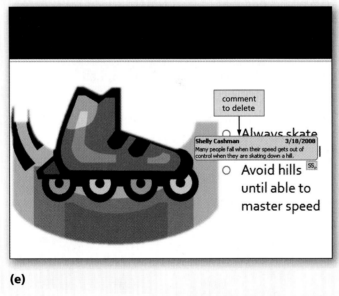

(e)

Figure 40 (continued)

5 Reusing a Presentation with Multimedia

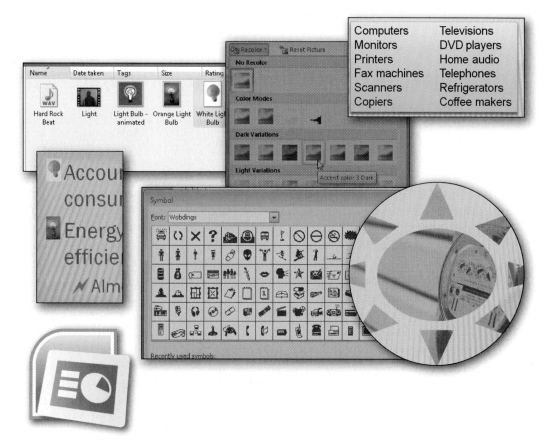

Objectives

You will have mastered the material in this chapter when you can:

- Recolor photographs
- Resize pictures
- Apply a shape to a picture
- Change a bullet character to a picture
- Change a bullet character to a symbol
- Format a bullet size

- Format a bullet color
- Add a movie file and clip
- Add a sound clip
- Create columns in a text box
- Rehearse timings
- Set slide show timings manually

5 | Reusing a Presentation with Multimedia

Introduction

At times you will need to revise a PowerPoint presentation. Changes may include inserting current figures, replacing outdated photographs, and updating visual elements displayed on a slide. Often applying a different theme, changing fonts, and substituting graphical elements give a slide show an entirely new look. Adding multimedia, including sounds, video, and music, can enhance a presentation and help audience members retain the information being presented.

Project — Presentation with Formatted Pictures, Video, and Sounds

BTW

Inserting QuickTime Movies (.mov)
Many movie files are saved as an Apple QuickTime movie (.mov) file. These files, however, cannot be inserted into a PowerPoint presentation. To play a QuickTime movie during your presentation, you must create a hyperlink to your presentation or convert the file to a Microsoft Windows video (.avi) file or another compatible multimedia file format.

The project in this chapter follows visual content guidelines and uses PowerPoint to create the presentation shown in Figure 5–1. The slide show uses several visual and audio elements to introduce the concept that saving electricity is easy to accomplish and necessary in today's world. Using Energy Star appliances, equipment, and light bulbs at home and at work can reduce electricity consumption by as much as 90 percent. The four slides in this presentation use a variety of visual elements to draw the audience into the topic. The speaker's role is to provide specific details of the amount of energy, and, in turn, the amount of money that can be saved by shopping wisely and practicing energy conservation. The presentation begins with upbeat music that should stimulate the audience's interest and help set the mood for energy enlightenment. The electric meter on Slide 1 is colored gold and transformed into a sun shape. The paragraphs on Slide 2 are embellished with formatted graphical bullets in the shape of electric bulbs and a lightning bolt. The power lines on Slide 3 are graphically altered and changed to the shape of a curved arrow. A speaker in a short video clip inserted on that slide shows a compact fluorescent light and describes the cost savings realized by using this bulb. The two-column list on Slide 4 provides a few of the common appliances and office products used daily that can have an Energy Star rating.

Overview

As you read through this chapter, you will learn how to create the presentation shown in Figure 5–1 by performing these general tasks:

• Format pictures by recoloring.
• Add shapes to pictures.
• Add multimedia to a presentation.
• Prepare and print speaker notes.
• Add and adjust slide timings.

(a)

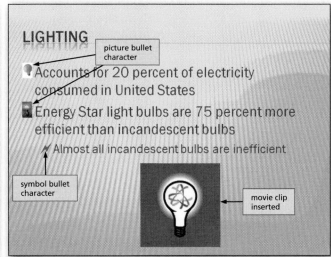

(b)

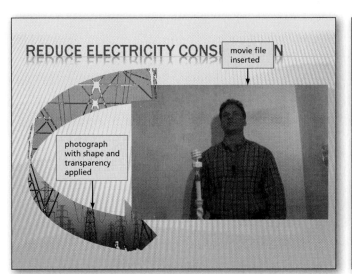

(c)

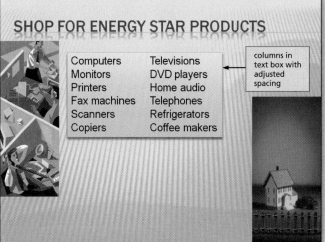

(d)

Figure 5–1

Plan
Ahead

General Project Guidelines

When creating a PowerPoint presentation, the actions you perform and decisions you make will affect the appearance and characteristics of the finished document. As you create a presentation with information graphics, such as the project shown in Figure 5–1, you should follow these general guidelines:

1. **Use multimedia selectively.** Video, music, and sound files can add interest to your presentation. Use these files only when necessary, however, because they draw the audience's attention away from the presenter and toward the slides. Using many multimedia files can be overwhelming.

2. **Coordinate your verbal message with the PowerPoint slides.** Effective speakers take much time to prepare their verbal message that will accompany each slide. They practice their speeches and decide how to integrate the material displayed.

(continued)

Plan
Ahead

> *(continued)*
>
> 3. **Evaluate your presentation.** As soon as you finish your presentation, critique your performance. You will improve your communication skills by eliminating the flaws and accentuating the positives.
>
> When necessary, more specific details concerning the above guidelines are presented at appropriate points in the chapter. The chapter also will identify the actions you perform and decisions you make regarding these guidelines during the creation of the presentation shown in Figure 5–1.

To Start PowerPoint and Apply a Document Theme

If you are using a computer to step through the project in this chapter and you want your screens to match the figures in this book, you should change your computer's resolution to 1024 × 768. For information about how to change a computer's resolution, read Appendix E.

The following steps start PowerPoint, open a presentation, and apply a document theme and color scheme.

1 Start PowerPoint and then open the presentation, Energy Efficiency, from the Data Files for Students.

2 Maximize the PowerPoint window, if necessary.

3 Apply the Trek document theme.

4 Apply the Metro color scheme.

Formatting Pictures and Text

The slides in your presentation give tips on saving energy. The title slide introduces the topic with a recolored picture in the shape of the sun. The power lines on Slide 3 are transparent and reveal the background. Bullet characters are formed by substituting pictures and symbols for the default bullets. Another visual slide enhancement is to create columns from a list in a text box.

BTW

Creating a Photo Album
The photo album tool allows you to set up a series of photos and captions that can be shown as a stand-alone presentation or inserted into a PowerPoint presentation. To start a photo album, click the Photo Album button on the Insert tab, click the File/Disk button, select a picture, and then click the Insert button. You can use photo editing tools to change the brightness or contrast or to rotate these photos. Click the New Text Box button to include a text slide.

To Recolor a Photograph

To match your document's color scheme or to add interest, you can **recolor** pictures, graphics, and clip art. The Recolor gallery can turn a color picture to pure black and white or grayscale, give it an old-fashioned look by applying a sepia tone, or apply light and dark color variations in such colors as purple, green, pink, and gold. The following steps recolor the Slide 1 electric meter photograph.

1

- Select the Slide 1 electric meter photograph.

- Click Format on the Ribbon under Picture Tools to display the Format tab.

- Click the Recolor button in the Adjust group to display the Recolor gallery (Figure 5–2)

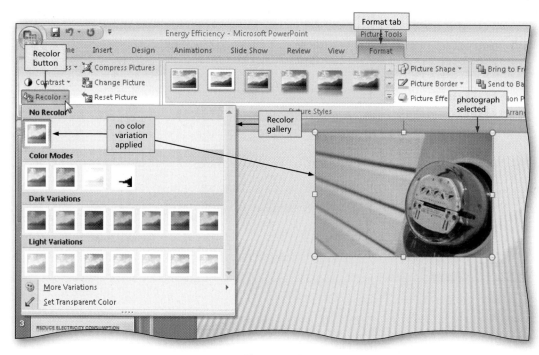

Figure 5–2

2

- Point to Accent color 3 Dark in the Dark Variations area to display a live preview of this color (Figure 5–3).

 Experiment

- Point to various colors in the Recolor gallery and watch the colors change on the meter photograph.

Q&A | Are more color variations available?

Yes. If you click More Variations in the Recolor gallery, the Theme Colors palette is displayed. You can select any color shown or click More Colors to choose a Standard or Custom color.

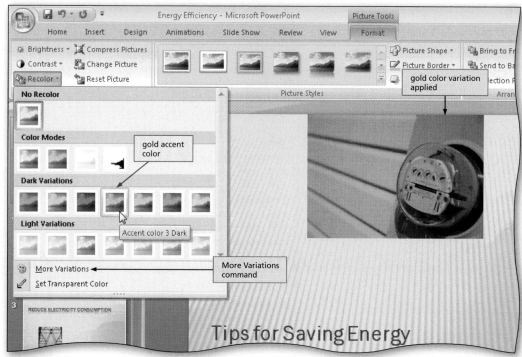

Figure 5–3

● Click Accent color 3 Dark to change the color of the electric meter photograph (Figure 5–4).

Q&A

How can I delete this color variation from my picture?

With the picture selected, you would click the Reset Picture button in the Adjust group on the Format tab.

Other Ways

1. Right-click photograph, click Format Picture on shortcut menu, click Picture in left pane, click Recolor button, select color, click Close button

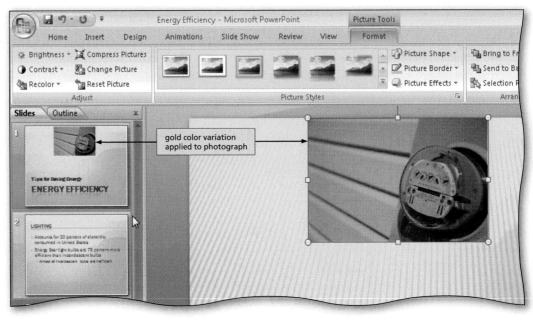

Figure 5–4

To Set a Transparent Color in a Photograph

You can make one color in the picture transparent so that the slide's background is visible through the recolored object. The following steps set a transparent color for the Slide 3 photograph.

1

● Display Slide 3 and then select the power lines photograph.

● Click the Recolor button in the Adjust group on the Format tab to display the Recolor gallery (Figure 5–5).

Figure 5–5

2
- Click Set Transparent Color in the Recolor gallery to display a pen mouse pointer in the document window.

- Position the pen mouse pointer in the black area at the bottom of the photograph where you want to make the color transparent (Figure 5–6).

Q&A Can I point to any black area of the picture?

Yes. Any color on the photograph can become transparent. It is easy to select a particular color when it fills a large area of a graphic.

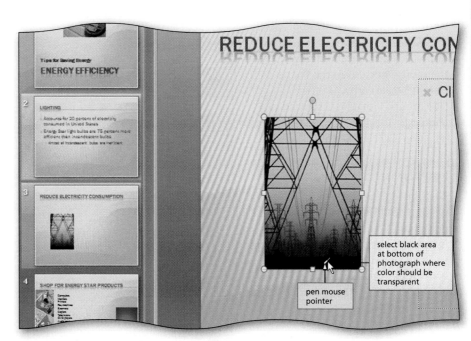

Figure 5–6

3
- Click the black area to delete the black lines from the photograph and allow the Trek background to show through the photograph (Figure 5–7).

Q&A Can I also apply a color variation to this photograph?

Yes. You can combine recoloring effects on one picture.

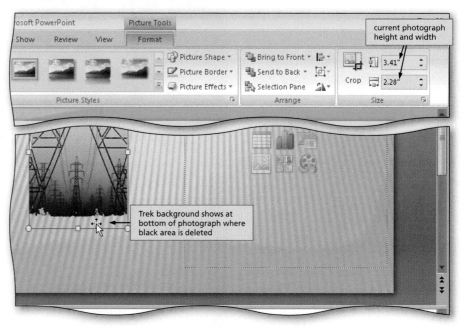

Figure 5–7

To Resize a Picture

Sometimes it is necessary to change the size of photographs and clip art. For example, on Slides 1 and 3, much space appears around the photographs. To make these objects fit onto the slides, you increase their sizes. To change the size of a clip by an exact percentage, enter a height or width in the Shape Height or Shape Width text boxes in the Size area on the Format tab. The steps on the following page describe how to increase the size of the power lines and electric meter photographs.

- With the power lines photograph selected and the Format tab displayed, click and hold down the mouse button on the Shape Height box up arrow in the Size group until 6" is displayed (Figure 5–8).

Q&A

Why did the Shape Width value change when I was increasing the height value?

The photograph's **aspect ratio**, or the relationship between the object's height and width, is locked. When you change the value of one measurement, the other measurement changes proportionally so that the image retains its original shape.

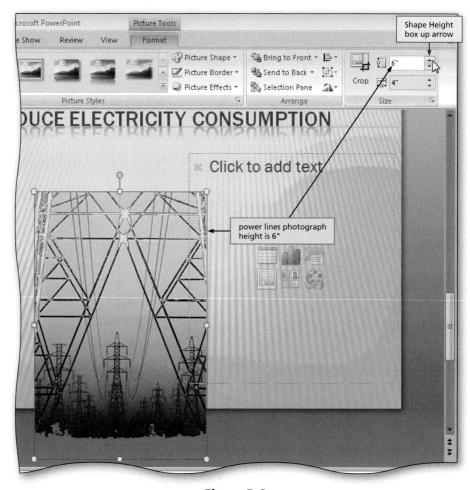

Figure 5–8

- Drag the photograph to the location shown in Figure 5–9 (Figure 5–9).

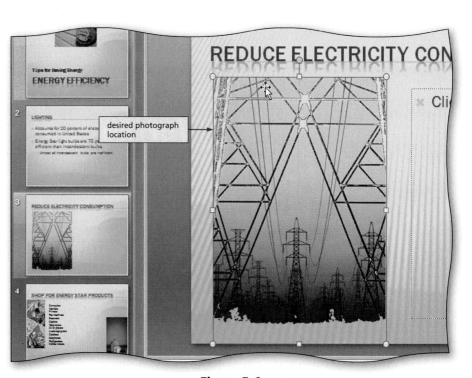

Figure 5–9

- Display Slide 1 and then select the electric meter photograph.

- With the Format tab displayed, click and hold down the mouse button on the Shape Height box up arrow in the Size group until 4" is displayed (Figure 5–10).

Figure 5–10

Other Ways

1. Right-click photograph, click Size and Position on shortcut menu, click Size tab, click and hold down mouse button on Height box up or down arrow in Scale area until desired size is reached, click OK button

2. Click clip, drag a sizing handle until clip is desired shape and size

To Apply a Shape to a Picture

Adding visual interest to a graphic is possible by applying a shape. Any of the shapes in the Picture Shapes gallery can be inserted in a picture, and the picture then will match this form. Arrows, shapes, stars, and banners often are used to create an appealing slide element. The following steps apply a sun shape to the Slide 1 electric meter photograph and a block arrow shape to the Slide 3 photograph.

- With the electric meter photograph selected on Slide 1 and the Format tab displayed, click the Picture Shape button in the Picture Styles group to display the Picture Shape gallery (Figure 5–11).

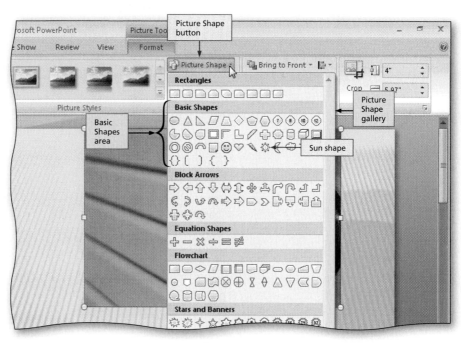

Figure 5–11

2

- Click the Sun shape in the Basic Shapes area (row 3, column 8) to apply this shape to the electric meter photograph (Figure 5–12).

Q&A

Is the live preview feature available for the Picture Shape gallery?

No. To try various shapes, you must click the Reset Picture button in the Adjust area to return the picture to its original format and then repeat Steps 1 and 2 with a different shape.

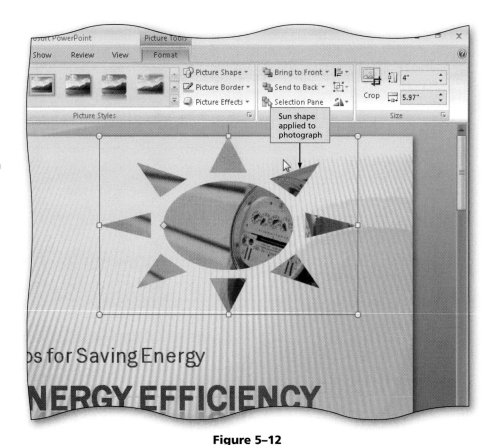

Figure 5–12

3

- Display Slide 3 and then select the power lines photograph.

- Click the Picture Shape button in the Picture Styles group to display the Picture Shape gallery (Figure 5–13).

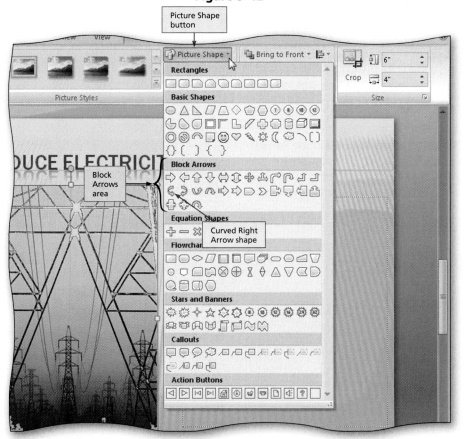

Figure 5–13

- Click the Curved Right Arrow shape in the Block Arrows area (row 2, column 1) to apply this shape to the power lines photograph (Figure 5–14).

Q&A Can I move this photograph to a different location on the slide?

Yes. Click the photograph to select it and then drag it to the desired location on the slide.

Q&A How would I resize this photograph?

Select it and then drag a sizing handle to increase or decrease the size.

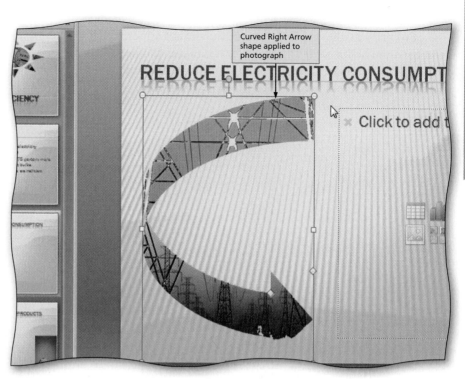

Figure 5–14

Use handouts to organize your speech.
As you develop a lengthy presentation with many visuals, handouts may help you organize your material. Print handouts with the maximum number of slides per page. Use scissors to cut each thumbnail and then place these miniature slide images adjacent to each other on a flat surface. Any type on the thumbnails will be too small to read, so the images will need to work with only the support of the verbal message you provide. You can rearrange these thumbnails as you organize your speech. When you return to your computer, you can rearrange the slides on your screen to match the order of your thumbnail printouts. Begin speaking the actual words you want to incorporate in the body of the talk. This process of glancing at the thumbnails and hearing yourself say the key ideas of the speech is one of the best methods of organizing and preparing for the actual presentation. Ultimately, when you deliver your speech in front of an audience, the images on the slides or on your note cards should be sufficient to remind you of the accompanying verbal message.

Plan Ahead

To Save the Presentation

You formatted photographs by recoloring, resizing, and applying a shape. The next step is to save the presentation.

1. With a USB flash drive connected to one of the computer's USB ports, display the Save As dialog box and type `Energy Savings` in the File name text box to change the file name.

2. Click Computer in the Favorite Links section, and then double-click your USB flash drive in the list of available drives.

3. Save the document with the file name, Energy Savings.

To Change a Bullet Character to a Picture

PowerPoint allows you to change the default appearance of bullets in a slide show. The document themes determine the bullet character. A **bullet character** can be a predefined style, a variety of fonts and characters displayed in the Symbol gallery, or a picture from a file or the Clip Organizer. You may want to change a character to add visual interest and variety. The following steps change the first paragraph bullet character to a light bulb picture with a white background.

- Click Home on the Ribbon, display Slide 2, and then click the first paragraph (Figure 5–15).

Q&A If I want to insert the same bullet character in several paragraphs, can I change all the bullets simultaneously?

Yes. Select all the paragraphs and then perform the steps below.

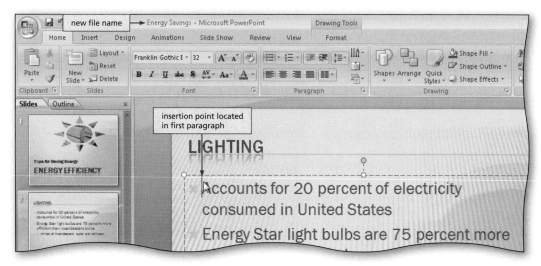

Figure 5–15

- Click the Bullets arrow in the Paragraph group to display the Bullets gallery (Figure 5–16).

Q&A Why is an orange box displayed around the three green x characters?

They are the default first-level bullet characters for the Trek document theme.

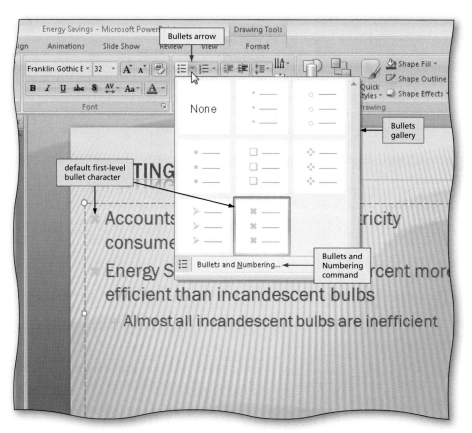

Figure 5–16

- Click Bullets and Numbering to
display the Bullets and Numbering
dialog box (Figure 5–17).

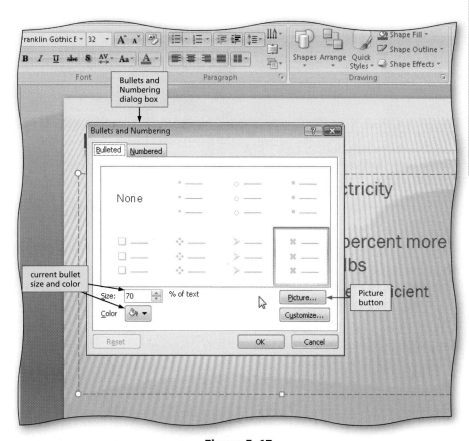

Figure 5–17

- Click the Picture button in the
Bullets and Numbering dialog box
to display the Picture Bullet dialog
box (Figure 5–18).

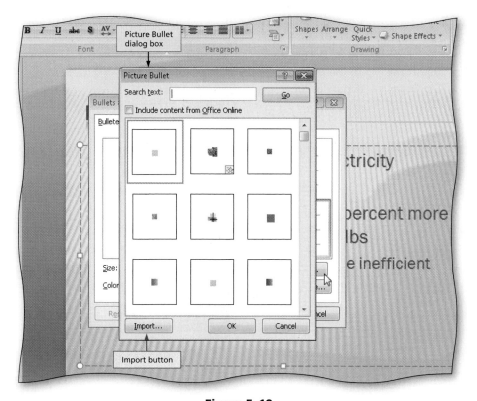

Figure 5–18

- With your USB flash drive connected to one of the computer's USB ports, click the Import button in the Picture Bullet dialog box to display the Add Clips to Organizer dialog box.

- If the Folders list is displayed below the Folders button, click the Folders button to collapse the Folders list.

- Click the Previous Locations arrow on the Address bar and then click Computer in the Favorite Links section. Double-click UDISK 2.0 (E:) to select the USB flash drive, Drive E in this case, as the device that contains the picture.

- If necessary, scroll down and then click White Light Bulb to select the file (Figure 5–19).

Figure 5–19

- Click the Add button in the Add Clips to Organizer dialog box to import the clip to the Microsoft Clip Organizer (Figure 5–20).

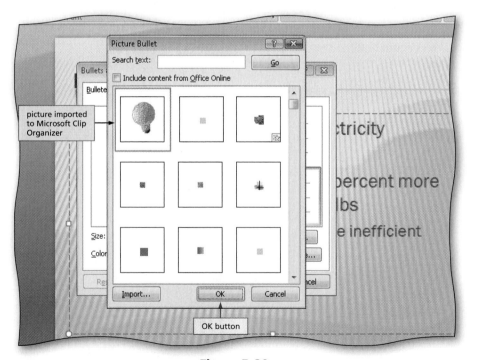

Figure 5–20

7

- Click the OK button in the Picture Bullet dialog box to insert the White Light Bulb picture as the first paragraph bullet character (Figure 5–21).

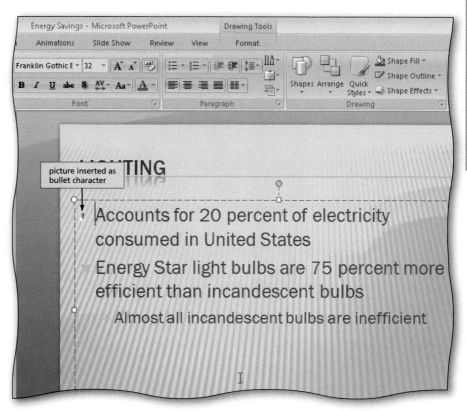

Figure 5–21

Other Ways

1. Right-click paragraph, point to Bullets on shortcut menu, click Bullets and Numbering
2. Select paragraph, click Bullets arrow on Mini toolbar, click Bullets and Numbering

To Change a Second Bullet Character to a Picture

If desired, you can change every bullet in a presentation to a unique character. The Energy Savings presentation has only one slide with bullets, so each bullet on Slide 2 can have a unique look. If your presentation has many bulleted slides, however, you would want to have a consistent look throughout the presentation. This issue will be addressed in Chapter 6 with a discussion of slide masters.

The following steps change the second first-level paragraph bullet character on Slide 2 to a light bulb picture with an orange background.

1 Click the second first-level paragraph, which begins with the words Energy Star, click the Bullets arrow in the Paragraph group to display the Bullets gallery, and then click Bullets and Numbering to display the Bullets and Numbering dialog box.

2 Click the Picture button in the Bullets and Numbering dialog box and then click the Import button in the Picture Bullet dialog box.

3 Click Orange Light Bulb to select the file name and then click the Add button in the Add Clips to Organizer dialog box to import the clip to the Microsoft Clip Organizer.

4 Click the OK button in the Picture Bullet dialog box to insert the Orange Light Bulb picture as the second first-level paragraph bullet character (Figure 5–22).

BTW

Quick Reference
For a table that lists how to complete the tasks covered in this book using the mouse, Ribbon, shortcut menu, and keyboard, see the Quick Reference Summary at the back of this book, or visit the PowerPoint 2007 Quick Reference Web page (scsite.com/ppt2007/qr).

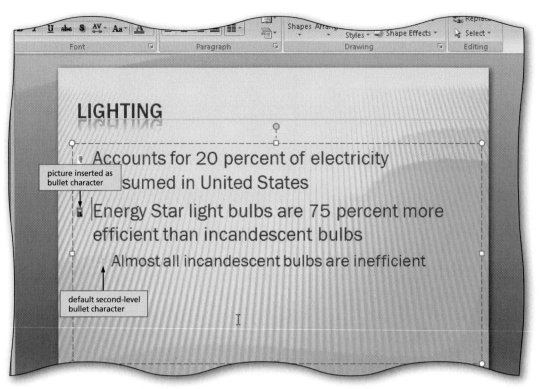

Figure 5–22

To Change a Bullet Character to a Symbol

Picture bullets add a unique quality to your presentations. Another bullet change you can make is to insert a symbol as the character. Symbols are found in several fonts, including Webdings, Wingdings, Wingdings 2, and Wingdings 3. The following steps change the second-level paragraph bullet character on Slide 2 to a lightning bolt symbol in the Webdings font.

- Click the second-level Slide 2 paragraph, which begins with the words Almost all, click the Bullets arrow, and then click Bullets and Numbering (Figure 5–23).

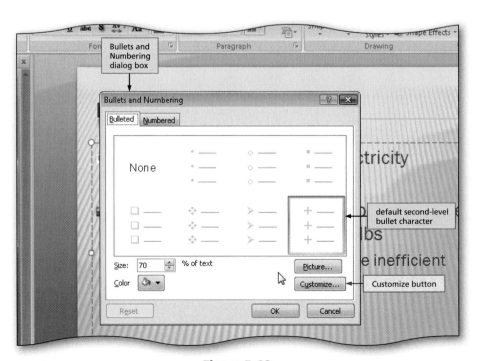

Figure 5–23

- Click the Customize button to display the Symbol dialog box.

- Click the Font box arrow in the Symbol dialog box to display the font list (Figure 5–24).

Q&A Why is a plus sign symbol selected?

That character is the default bullet character for the second-level paragraphs in the Trek document theme.

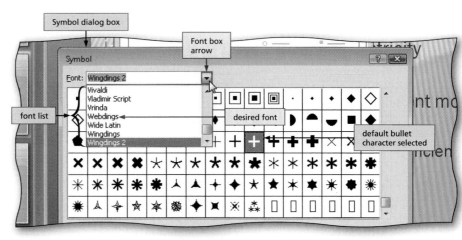

Figure 5–24

- Click Webdings in the list and then scroll up to locate the lightning bolt symbol.

- Click the lightning bolt symbol to select it (Figure 5–25).

Q&A Why does my dialog box have more rows of symbols and different fonts from which to choose?

The rows and fonts displayed depend upon how PowerPoint was installed on your system.

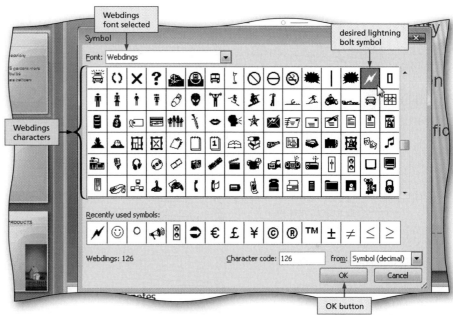

Figure 5–25

- Click the OK button in the Symbol dialog box to display the Bullets and Numbering dialog box (Figure 5–26).

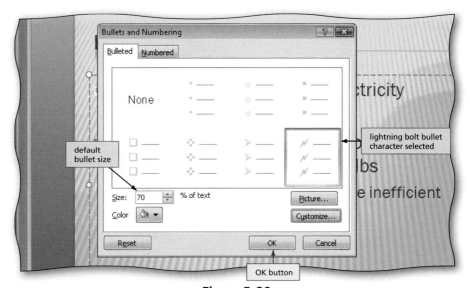

Figure 5–26

5

- Click the OK button in the Bullets and Numbering dialog box to insert the lightning bolt character as the second-level paragraph bullet (Figure 5–27).

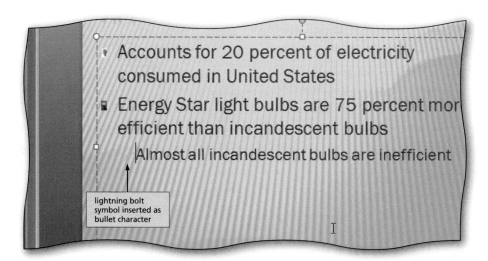

Figure 5–27

To Format a Bullet Size

Bullets have a default size determined by the design theme. **Bullet size** is measured as a percentage of the text size and can range from 25 to 400 percent. The following steps change the White Light Bulb character size.

- Click the first paragraph on Slide 2, click the Bullets arrow, and then click Bullets and Numbering in the Bullets gallery to display the Bullets and Numbering dialog box (Figure 5–28).

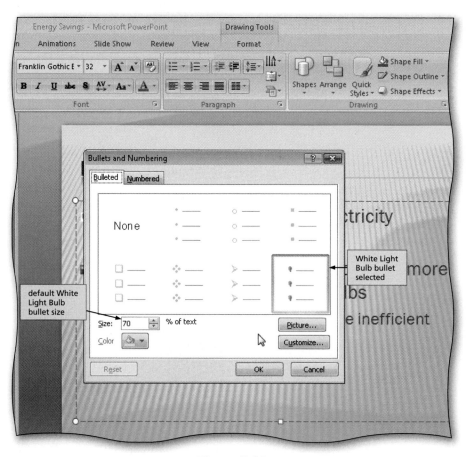

Figure 5–28

2

- Click and hold down the mouse button on the Size box up arrow until 150 is displayed (Figure 5–29).

Q&A Can I type a number in the text box instead of clicking the up arrow?

Yes. Double-click the text box and then type the desired percentage.

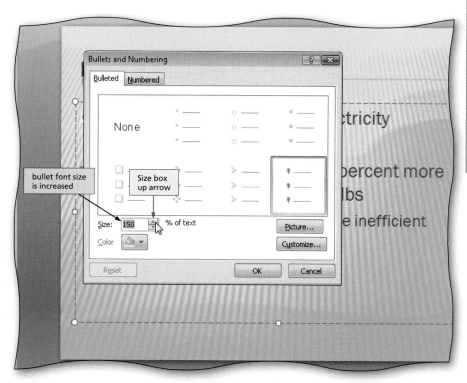

Figure 5–29

3

- Click the OK button to increase the White Light Bulb bullet size to 150 percent of its original size (Figure 5–30).

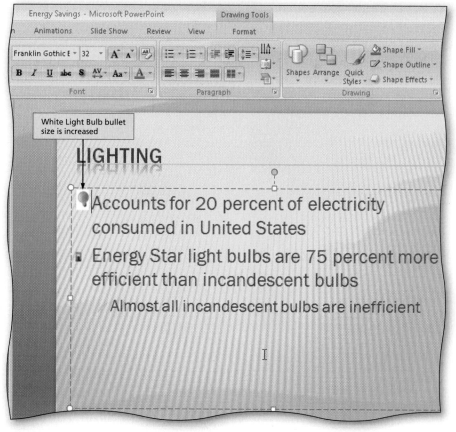

Figure 5–30

To Change the Size of Other Bullet Characters

For consistency, the bullet character in the second first-level paragraph on Slide 2 should have a similar size as that of the first paragraph. In addition, the second-level paragraph's bullet should be somewhat smaller because the paragraph font size is smaller than the first-level paragraph font size. The following steps change the sizes of the Orange Light Bulb and the lightning bolt bullets.

1 Click the second first-level paragraph, which begins with the words Energy Star, click the Bullets arrow, and then click Bullets and Numbering in the Bullets gallery to display the Bullets and Numbering dialog box.

2 Click and hold down the mouse button on the Size box up arrow until 150 is displayed and then click the OK button.

3 Click the second-level paragraph, click the Bullets arrow, and then click Bullets and Numbering in the Bullets gallery.

4 Click and hold down the mouse button on the Size box up arrow until 115 is displayed. Do not click the OK button (Figure 5–31).

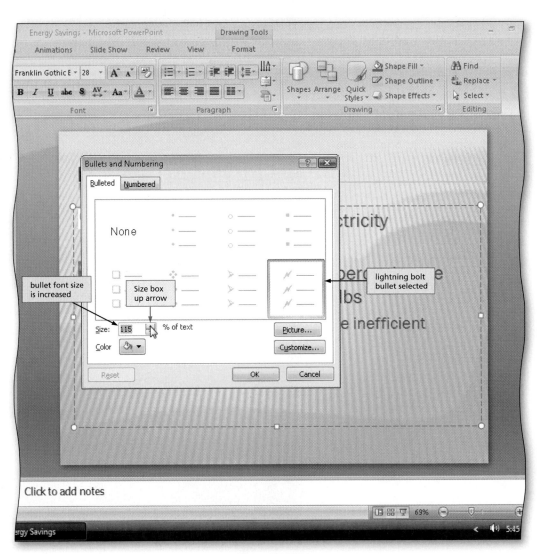

Figure 5–31

To Format a Bullet Color

A default **bullet color** is based on the eight colors in the design theme. Additional standard and custom colors also are available. The following steps change the lightning bolt bullet color from green to red.

1
- With the Bullets and Numbering dialog box displayed, click the Color arrow to display the color palette (Figure 5–32).

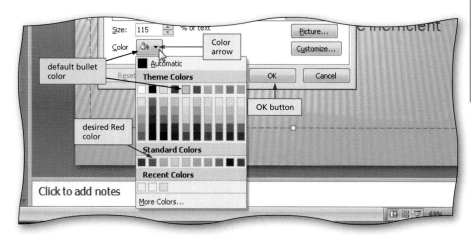

Figure 5–32

2
- Click the color Red in the Standard Colors area to change the bullet color to Red (Figure 5–33).

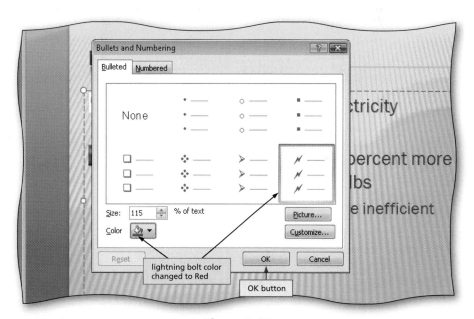

Figure 5–33

3
- Click the OK button to apply the color Red to the lightning bolt bullet (Figure 5–34).

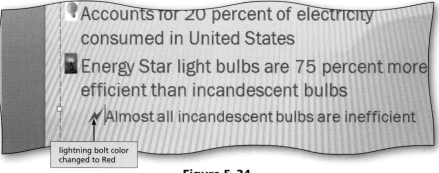

Figure 5–34

To Create Columns in a Text Box

The list of Energy Star products in the Slide 4 text box lacks visual appeal. You can change these items into two, three, or more columns and then adjust the column widths. The following steps change the text box elements into columns and then widen the columns.

- Display Slide 4 and then click the text box to select it.

- With the Home tab displayed, click the Columns button in the Paragraph group to display the Columns menu (Figure 5–35).

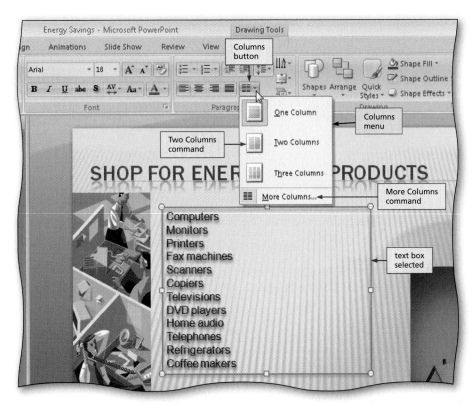

Figure 5–35

- Click Two Columns to create two columns of text.

- Drag the bottom sizing handle up to the location shown in Figure 5–36.

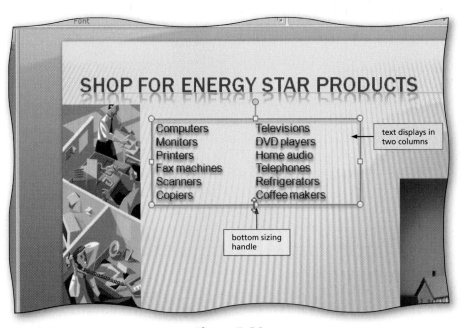

Figure 5–36

To Adjust Column Spacing

The space between the columns in each text box can be increased. The following steps increase the spacing between the columns.

1
- With the text box selected, click the Columns button, and then click More Columns.

- Click and hold down the mouse button on the Spacing box up arrow in the Columns dialog box until 0.3" is displayed (Figure 5–37).

Q&A Can I type a number in the text box instead of clicking the up arrow?

Yes. Double-click the text box and then type the desired measurement expressed in inches.

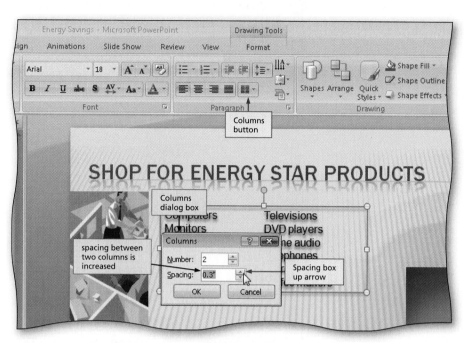

Figure 5–37

2
- Click the OK button to increase the spacing between the columns (Figure 5–38).

Q&A Can I change the text box back to one column easily?

Yes. Click the Columns button and then click One Column.

Figure 5–38

To Format the Text Box

To add interest to the text box on Slide 4, apply a Quick Style. The following steps apply a green Subtle Effect style to the text box.

1 With the text box selected and the Home tab displayed, click the Quick Styles button in the Drawing group to display the Quick Styles gallery.

2 Click Subtle Effect – Accent 6 (row 4, column 7).

3 Click the Increase Font Size button in the Font group two times to increase the font size to 24 (Figure 5–39).

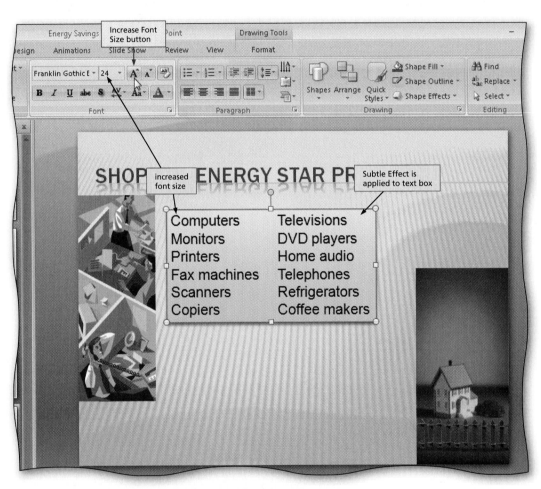

Figure 5–39

Use multimedia selectively.

PowerPoint makes it easy to add multimedia to a presentation. Well-produced video clips add value when they help explain a procedure or show movement that cannot be captured in a photograph. Music can help calm or energize an audience, when appropriate. A sound, such as applause when a correct answer is given, can emphasize an action. Before you insert these files on a slide, however, consider whether they really add any value to your overall slide show. If you are adding them just because you can, then you might want to reconsider your decision. Audiences quickly tire of extraneous sounds and movement on slides and will find these media clips annoying. Keep in mind that the audience's attention should focus primarily on the presenter, and extraneous or inappropriate media files may divert their attention, and in turn, decrease the quality of the presentation.

Adding Multimedia to Slides

Multimedia files can enrich a presentation if they are used correctly. Movies files can have two formats: digital video produced with a camera and editing software, and animated GIF (graphics interchange format) file composed of multiple images combined in a single file. Sound files can be from the Microsoft Clip Organizer, files stored on your computer, or an audio track on a CD. To hear the sounds, you need speakers and a sound card on your system.

To Add a Movie File

Slide 3 has an interesting graphic of power lines, which introduce the concept of electricity transmission. A movie clip with a suggestion of how to reduce electricity usage would complement this graphic. A brief video discussing fluorescent light bulbs is available on your Data Files for Students. The following steps add this movie clip to Slide 3.

1

- Display Slide 3. With your USB flash drive connected to one of the computer's USB ports, click the Insert Media Clip button in the content placeholder to display the Insert Movie dialog box.

- If the Folders list is displayed below the Folders button, click the Folders button to collapse the Folders list.

- Click the Previous Locations arrow on the Address bar and then click Computer in the Favorite Links section. Double-click UDISK 2.0 (E:) to select the USB flash drive, Drive E in this case, as the device that contains the picture.

- Click Light to select the file (Figure 5–40).

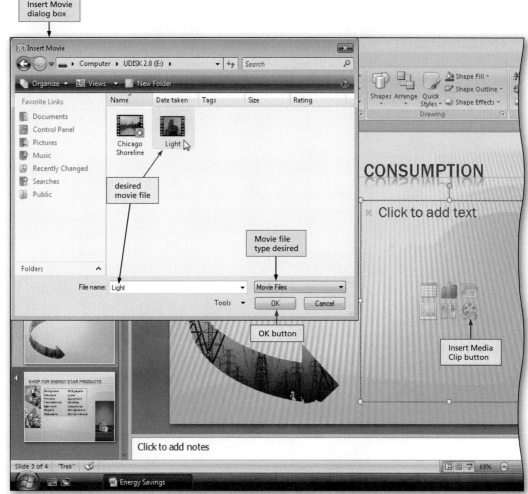

Figure 5–40

Q&A What if the movie clip is not on a USB flash drive?

Use the same process, but select the device containing the file in the Favorite Links section.

2

- Click the OK button in the dialog box to insert the movie clip into Slide 3 (Figure 5–41).

3

- When the Microsoft Office PowerPoint dialog box is displayed, click the Automatically button to specify the clip will begin playing when Slide 3 is displayed during a slide show.

Q&A

What does the When Clicked option do?

The movie clip would begin playing when a presenter clicks the slide during the slide show.

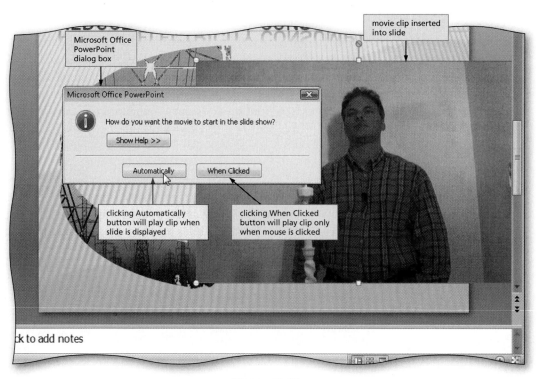

Figure 5–41

4

- With the Options tab displayed, click and hold down the mouse button on the Shape Height box down arrow in the Size group until 4" is displayed (Figure 5–42).

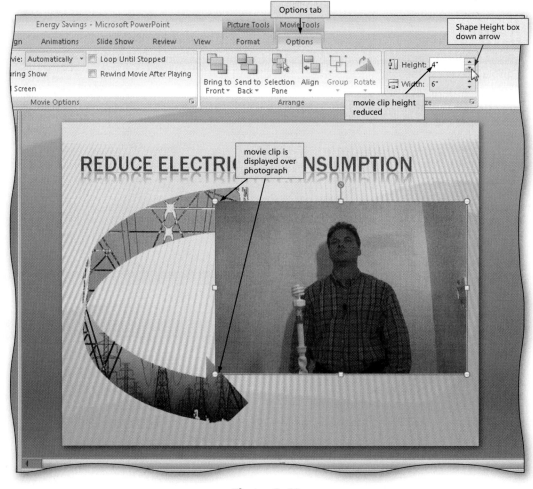

Figure 5–42

5

- Click the Send to Back button in the Arrange group to move the movie clip under the power lines photograph.

- Drag the clip to the location shown in Figure 5–43 (Figure 5–43).

Can I preview the movie clip?

Yes. Select the clip and then click Options on the Ribbon. The Options tab contains many tools that help control the video presentation. The Preview button will play the video. Other useful buttons allow you to set the movie size precisely, adjust the volume, and replay the clip continually.

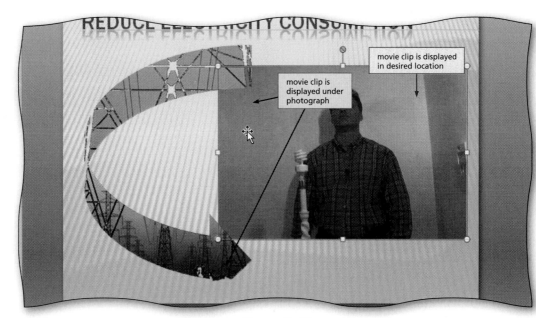

Figure 5–43

Other Ways
1. Click the Movie from File button on Insert tab

To Add a Sound Clip

When the Energy Savings presentation starts, you want a short musical sound clip to play that will add interest and help set an upbeat tempo to the slide show. This clip, Hard Rock Beat, will play for 15 seconds when Slide 1 is displayed. This clip is available on the Microsoft Office Online Clip Art Web site and is on your Data Files for Students. It is a **Windows waveform (wav)** file, which uses a standard format to encode and communicate music and sound between computers, music synthesizers, and instruments. The following steps add the music clip to Slide 1.

1

- Display Slide 1 and then click Insert on the Ribbon to display the Insert tab.

- Click the Sound from File button, which is labeled Sound, in the Media Clips group to display the Insert Sound dialog box (Figure 5–44).

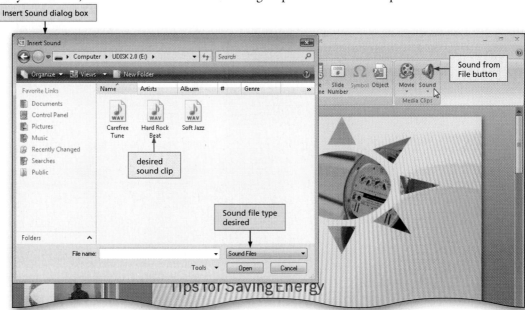

Figure 5–44

• With your USB flash drive as the active drive, click Hard Rock Beat to select the file (Figure 5–45).

Q&A What if the sound clip is not on the USB flash drive?

Use the same process, but select the device containing the file in the Favorite Links section.

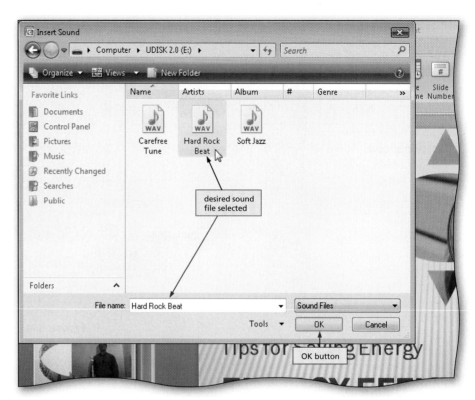

Figure 5–45

❸

• Click the OK button in the Insert Sound dialog box to insert the sound clip into Slide 1 (Figure 5–46).

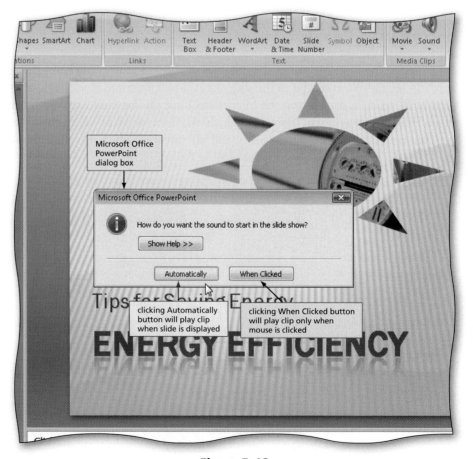

Figure 5–46

4

- When the Microsoft Office PowerPoint dialog box is displayed, click the Automatically button to specify the clip will begin playing when Slide 1 is displayed at the start of the slide show (Figure 5–47).

Q&A Does the When Clicked option function the same way for an audio clip as for a video clip?

Yes. If you were to click the When Clicked button in this dialog box, the music would begin playing only after the presenter clicks Slide 1 during a presentation.

Q&A Why is a speaker icon displayed in the middle of the slide?

The icon indicates a sound file is inserted.

Figure 5–47

5

- Drag the speaker icon off the slide to the lower-right corner of the screen (Figure 5–48).

Q&A Can I hide the speaker icon?

No. You can drag it off the slide because you specified the sound clip will play automatically when Slide 1 is displayed. If you had clicked the When Clicked option, you would need to leave the icon on the slide so that you can click it during a presentation.

Figure 5–48

To Add a Movie Clip

Animated GIF files are commonplace on Web sites. They also are found in PowerPoint presentations when you want to call attention to material on a particular slide. You can insert them into a PowerPoint presentation in the same manner that you insert movie and sound files. They play automatically when the slide is displayed. The following steps add the light bulb movie clip to Slide 2.

1

- Display Slide 2 and then, if necessary, click Insert on the Ribbon to display the Insert tab.

- Click the Insert Picture from File button, labeled Picture, in the Illustrations group to display the Insert Picture dialog box.

- With your USB flash drive as the active drive, click Light Bulb - animated to select the file (Figure 5–49).

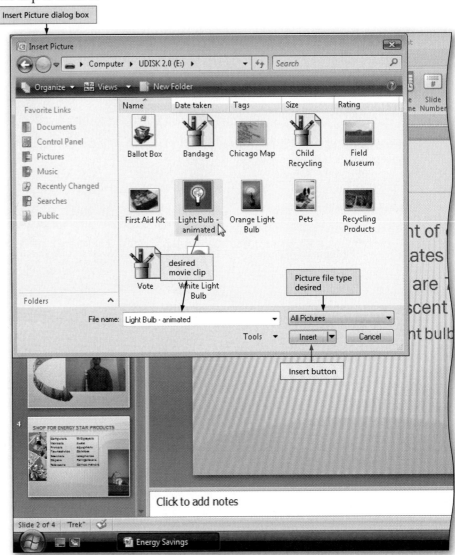

Figure 5–49

2

- Click the Insert button in the Insert Picture dialog box to insert the light bulb movie clip into Slide 2.

- With the Format tab displayed, click and hold down the mouse button on the Shape Height box up arrow in the Size group until 2.5" is displayed.

- Drag the clip to the location shown in Figure 5–50.

Q&A

Why is the animation not showing?

Animated GIF files move only in Slide Show view.

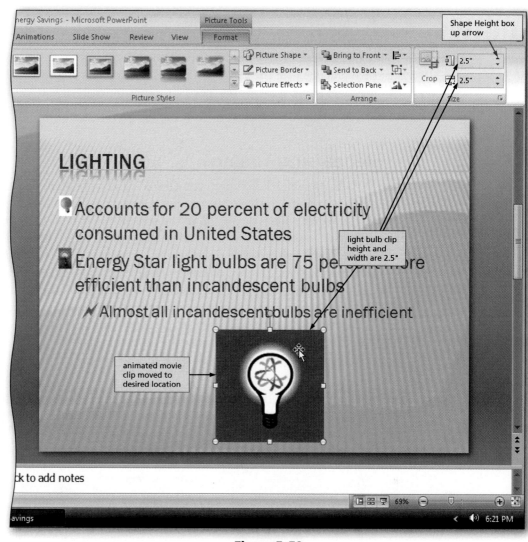

Figure 5–50

Coordinate your verbal message with the PowerPoint slides.

On average, designers spend one hour developing each slide in a presentation. They meticulously decide on effective words and visuals that convey the intended message. Many times, however, they spend so much time developing their presentations that they have insufficient time to rehearse their verbal message.

It is important, therefore, that you allocate time to practice coordinating your PowerPoint presentation with your speech. You should not need to read any material on the screen while presenting. Your notes should contain key phrases, not the exact sentences. Each time you rehearse, your wording should vary slightly because you are elaborating on each major idea.

Stand as you rehearse, preferably in front of a mirror. Speak your words out loud as you envision your audience listening intently to your message. Do not stop if you stumble over some words; just make a note to rework those rough spots later. If possible, record video or audio of your practice session.

Plan
Ahead

Preparing For and Rehearsing Delivery

Polished speakers spend much time preparing their presentations. They memorize their introductions and conclusions, practice in front of a mirror, and test their speech in front of objective colleagues and friends. When they are very familiar with the material, they then practice with the PowerPoint presentation to synchronize the slides with their verbal message. Some speakers set specific timings for each slide to display. Other presenters type notes in the Notes pane as they develop their presentations.

Rehearsing Timings

BTW

Certification
The Microsoft Certified Application Specialist (MCAS) program provides an opportunity for you to obtain a valuable industry credential — proof that you have the PowerPoint 2007 skills required by employers. For more information see Appendix G or visit the PowerPoint 2007 Certification Web page (scsite.com/ppt2007/cert).

In previous slide shows, you clicked to advance from one slide to the next. Because all slide components have been added to the slides in the presentation, you now can set the time each slide is displayed on the screen. You can set these times in two ways. One method is to specify each slide's display time manually. The second method is to use PowerPoint's **rehearsal feature**, which allows you to advance through the slides at your own pace, and the amount of time you view each slide is recorded. You will use the second technique in this chapter and then adjust the last slide's timing manually.

When you begin rehearsing a presentation, the Rehearsal toolbar is displayed. The **Rehearsal toolbar** contains buttons that allow you to start, pause, and repeat viewing the slides in the slide show and to view the times for each slide and the elapsed time. Table 5–1 describes the buttons on the Rehearsal toolbar.

Table 5–1 Rehearsal Toolbar Buttons		
Button	**Button Name**	**Description**
➡	Next	Displays the next slide or next animated element on the slide.
❚❚	Pause	Stops the timer. Click the Next or Pause button to resume timing.
0:00:00	Slide Time	Indicates the length of time a slide has been displayed. You can enter a slide time directly in the Slide Time box.
↺	Repeat	Clears the Slide Time box and resets the timer to 0:00.
0:00:00	Elapsed Time	Indicates slide show total time.

To Rehearse Timings

Table 5–2 indicates the desired timings for the five slides in the Energy Savings presentation. Slide 1 is displayed and the sound clip plays for 15 seconds. Slides 2 and 4 are displayed for 15 seconds. Slide 3 has the video clip, and its length is approximately 10 seconds.

Table 5–2 Slide Rehearsal Timings		
Slide Number	**Display Time**	**Elapsed Time**
1	0:00	0:15
2	0:15	0:30
3	0:10	0:40
4	0:15	0:55

The following steps add slide timings to the slide show.

1

- Click Slide Show on the Ribbon to display the Slide Show tab (Figure 5–51).

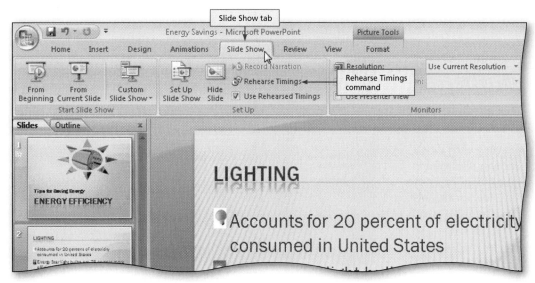

Figure 5–51

2

- Click the Rehearse Timings command in the Set Up group to start the slide show and the counter (Figure 5–52).

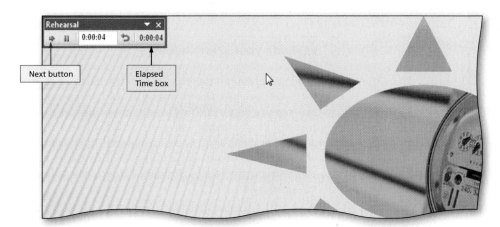

Figure 5–52

3

- When the Elapsed time displays 0:15, click the Next button to display Slide 2.

- When the Elapsed time displays 0:30, click the Next button to display Slide 3.

- When the Elapsed time displays 0:40, click the Next button to display Slide 4.

- When the Elapsed time displays 0:55, click the Next button to display the black slide (Figure 5–53).

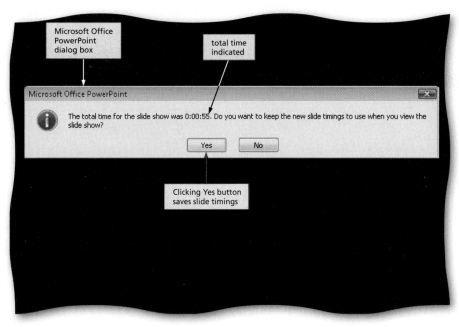

Figure 5–53

4

- Click the Yes button in the Microsoft Office PowerPoint dialog box to keep the new slide timings with an elapsed time of 0:55.

- Review each slide's timing displayed in the lower-left corner in Slide Sorter view (Figure 5–54).

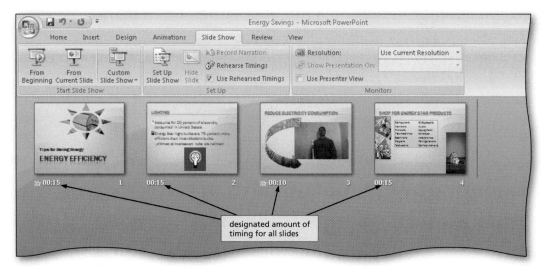

Figure 5–54

Plan Ahead	**Evaluate your presentation.** Public speaking is a skill that can improve with practice and evaluation. Immediately after making a presentation, evaluate what aspects worked well and what parts needed improvement. Ask yourself several questions: Did the speech meet the time restrictions? Did I use appropriate gestures? Did I look at my audience? If so, did they seem interested in my message? Did my audience notice my nervousness? Did I follow the intended organizational pattern, or did I forget or ad-lib material? If I were to give the presentation a second time, what qualities would I want to repeat? What aspects would I improve by practicing? If you reflect upon your performance objectively, you will gain confidence and improve your speaking style.

To Adjust Timings Manually

If the slide timings need adjustment, you manually can change the length of time each slide is displayed. In this presentation, you decide to display Slide 4 for 20 seconds instead of 15. The following steps increase the Slide 4 timing.

1

- Click Animations on the Ribbon to display the Animations tab.

- With Slide 4 selected, click and hold down the Automatically After up arrow in the Transition to This Slide group until 00:20 is displayed (Figure 5–55).

Figure 5–55

To Add Notes

Slides and handouts usually are printed to distribute to audience members. These printouts also are helpful to speakers so they can write notes that will guide them through a presentation. As you create slides, you may find material you want to state verbally and do not want to include on the slide. You can type and format notes in the **Notes pane** as you work in Normal view and then print this information as **notes pages**. Notes pages print with a small image of the slide at the top and the comments below the slide. Charts, tables, and pictures added to the Notes pane also print on these pages. You can make changes to the **Notes Master** if you want to alter the default settings, such as the font or the position of page elements, such as the slide area and notes area.

In this project, comments are added to Slides 2 and 4. After adding comments, you can print a set of speaker notes. The following steps add text to the Notes pane on these slides and then print the notes.

- Click the Normal button to display Slide 4 in Normal view.

- Click the Notes pane and then type Energy Star equipment and appliances provide dramatic reductions on

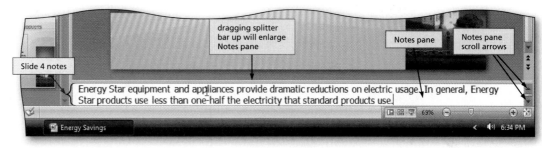

Figure 5–56

electric usage. In general, Energy Star products use less than one-half the electricity that standard products use. (Figure 5–56).

Q&A

What if I cannot see all the lines I typed?

You can drag the splitter bar up to enlarge the Notes pane. Clicking the Notes pane scroll arrows allows you to view the entire text.

- Display Slide 2, click the Notes pane, and then type CFLs now have brightness and color rendition comparable to incandescent lights. Because of the electrical

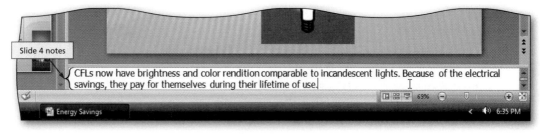

Figure 5–57

savings, they pay for themselves during their lifetime of use. (Figure 5–57).

To Print Speaker Notes

These notes give additional information that supplements the text on the slides. The following steps print the speaker notes.

1. Click the Office Button, point to Print, and then click Print Preview on the 'Preview and print the document' submenu.

2. Click the Print What arrow in the Page Setup group and then click Notes Pages in the Print What list.

3 Click the Print button in the Print group.

4 Click the OK button in the Print dialog box to print the handouts (Figure 5–58).

5 Click the Close Print Preview button in the Preview group on the Print Preview tab to return to Normal view.

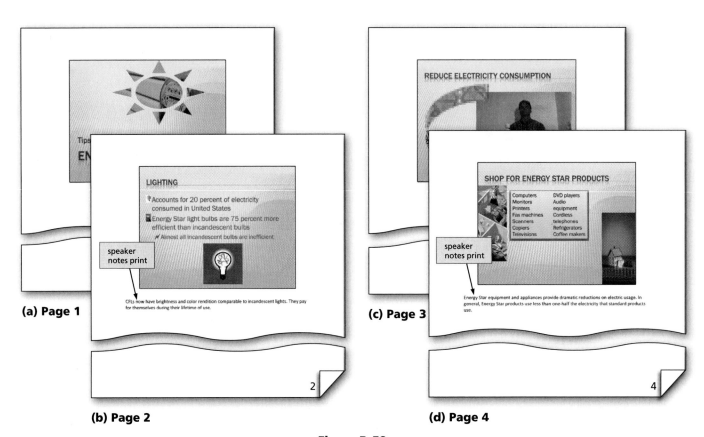

(a) Page 1

(b) Page 2

(c) Page 3

(d) Page 4

Figure 5–58

To Change Document Properties and Save the Presentation

Before saving the presentation again, you want to add your name, class name, and some keywords as document properties. The following steps use the Document Information Panel to change document properties and then save the project.

1 Click the Office Button, point to Prepare, and then click Properties on the 'Prepare the document for distribution' submenu.

2 Type your name as the Author property and your course and section as the Subject properties.

3 Type energy, lighting, energy star as the Keywords property.

4 Close the Document Information Panel.

5 Click the Save button to overwrite the previous Energy Savings file on the USB flash drive.

To Quit PowerPoint

This project is complete. The following steps quit PowerPoint.

1 Click the Close button on the right side of the title bar to quit PowerPoint; or if you have multiple PowerPoint documents open, click the Office Button and then click the Exit PowerPoint button on the Office Button menu to close all open documents and quit PowerPoint.

2 If necessary, click the No button in the Microsoft Office PowerPoint dialog box so that any changes you have made are not saved.

Chapter Summary

In this chapter you have learned how to recolor and resize a picture, apply a shape to a picture, change a bullet character to a picture or a symbol and then change its size and color, create columns and then adjust the width, add multimedia, set slide timings, and then add and print notes. The items listed below include all the new PowerPoint skills you have learned in this chapter.

1. Recolor a Photograph (PPT 333)
2. Set a Transparent Color in a Photograph (PPT 334)
3. Resize a Picture (PPT 335)
4. Apply a Shape to a Picture (PPT 337)
5. Change a Bullet Character to a Picture (PPT 340)
6. Change a Bullet Character to a Symbol (PPT 344)
7. Format a Bullet Size (PPT 346)
8. Format a Bullet Color (PPT 349)
9. Create Columns in a Text Box (PPT 350)
10. Adjust Column Spacing (PPT 351)
11. Add a Movie File (PPT 353)
12. Add a Sound Clip (PPT 355)
13. Add a Movie Clip (PPT 358)
14. Rehearse Timings (PPT 360)
15. Adjust Timings Manually (PPT 362)
16. Add Notes (PPT 363)
17. Print Speaker Notes (PPT 363)

If you have a SAM user profile, you may have access to hands-on instruction, practice, and assessment. Log in to your SAM account (http://sam2007.course.com) to launch any assigned training activities or exams that relate to the skills covered in this chapter.

Learn It Online

Test your knowledge of chapter content and key terms.

Instructions: To complete the Learn It Online exercises, start your browser, click the Address bar, and then enter the Web address scsite.com/ppt2007/learn. When the Office 2007 Learn It Online page is displayed, click the link for the exercise you want to complete and then read the instructions.

Chapter Reinforcement TF, MC, and SA
A series of true/false, multiple choice, and short answer questions that test your knowledge of the chapter content.

Flash Cards
An interactive learning environment where you identify chapter key terms associated with displayed definitions.

Practice Test
A series of multiple choice questions that test your knowledge of chapter content and key terms.

Who Wants To Be a Computer Genius?
An interactive game that challenges your knowledge of chapter content in the style of a television quiz show.

Wheel of Terms
An interactive game that challenges your knowledge of chapter key terms in the style of the television show *Wheel of Fortune*.

Crossword Puzzle Challenge
A crossword puzzle that challenges your knowledge of key terms presented in the chapter.

Apply Your Knowledge

Reinforce the skills and apply the concepts you learned in this chapter.

Resizing and Recoloring a Picture, Applying a Shape to a Picture, Creating Columns, Adding Notes, and Setting Timings

Instructions: Start PowerPoint. Open the presentation, Apply 5-1 Getting a Job, from the Data Files for Students. See the inside back cover of this book for instructions on downloading the Data Files for Students, or contact your instructor for more information about accessing required files.

The four slides in the presentation present information about preparing a resume and cover letter for a job search. The document you open is an unformatted presentation. You are to select a document theme and change the theme colors, recolor the pictures and apply shapes, create columns, and add notes so the slides look like Figure 5–59.

Perform the following tasks:

1. Add the Urban document theme and change the presentation theme colors to Concourse. On Slide 1, change the clip size to 280% and then apply the 7-Point Star shape (row 1, column 6 in the Stars and Banners area). The clip is animated, so it may appear different on your screen than it does in Figure 5–59a. Move the clip so that it is positioned as shown in Figure 5–59a.

2. On Slide 2, change the clip size to 28% and then apply the Multidocument shape (row 1, column 8 in the Flowchart group). Recolor the clip by applying the Accent color 2 Light variation (column 3 in the Light Variations area). Move the clip so that it is positioned as shown in Figure 5–59b.

3. On Slide 3, create two columns in the text box, adjust the column spacing to 0.7", and position the text box as shown in Figure 5–59c. Bold the words Chronological and Functional. Change the clip size to 30%. Move the clip so that it is positioned as shown in Figure 5–59c.

4. On Slide 4, change the clip size to 37% and then recolor the clip by applying the Accent color 2 Light variation (column 3 in the Light Variations area). Move the clip so that it is positioned as shown in Figure 5–59d.

5. Apply the Shape Plus wipe transition (row 6, column 1) to all slides and change the transition speed to Slow.

6. Set the slide timings to 15 seconds for Slide 1 and 10 seconds for the other three slides.

7. On Slide 2, type A resume should include your educational background, work experience, and contact information. Be certain to have someone read your resume to check for clarity and correct spelling and word usage. in the Notes pane.

8. On Slide 4, type Design an attractive letterhead for your cover letter. The paragraphs should give specific examples of your accomplishments in school and on the job. in the Notes pane.

9. Check the spelling, and then display the revised presentation in Slide Sorter view to check for consistency.

10. Use your name in place of Student Name on the title slide. Change the document properties, as specified by your instructor. Save the presentation using the file name, Apply 5-1 Job. Submit the revised document in the format specified by your instructor.

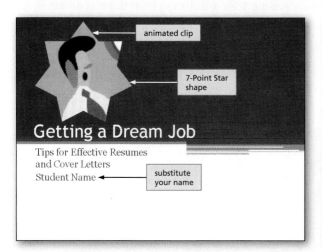

(a)

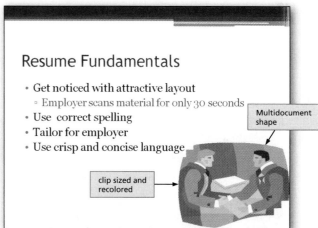

(b)

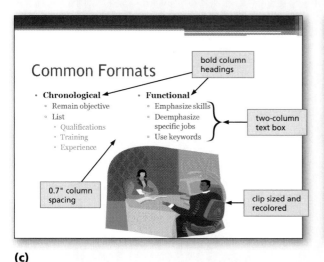

(c)

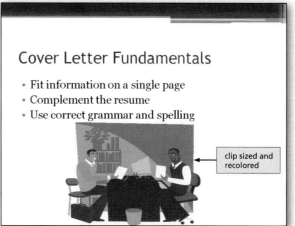

(d)

Figure 5–59

Extend Your Knowledge

Extend the skills you learned in this chapter and experiment with new skills. You may need to use Help to complete the assignment.

Recoloring a Movie File and Changing Bullet Characters

Instructions: Start PowerPoint. Open the presentation, Extend 5-1 Vote, from the Data Files for Students. See the inside back cover of this book for instructions on downloading the Data Files for Students, or contact your instructor for more information about accessing required files.

You will insert, size, and recolor a movie clip and then change both bullet characters (Figure 5–60).

Perform the following tasks:

1. Display the Insert tab, click the Picture button in the Illustrations group, select the Ballot Box file on the Data Files for Students, and then click the Insert button to insert this clip into the slide. Increase the clip size and then apply a variation to recolor the clip.

2. Change the first bullet character to the Vote picture found on the Data File for Students. Change the second bullet character to a symbol of your choice.

3. Increase the size of both bullet characters.

4. Add speaker notes discussing the importance of exercising your right to vote in the election.

5. Insert your name in a footer.

6. Change the document properties, as specified by your instructor. Save the presentation using the file name, Extend 5-1 Revised Vote.

7. Submit the revised document in the format specified by your instructor.

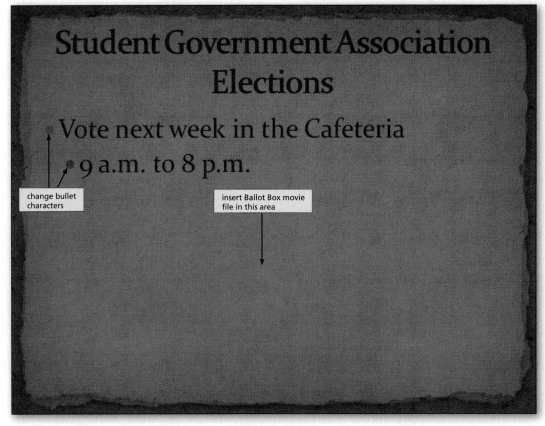

Figure 5–60

Make It Right

Analyze a presentation and correct all errors and/or improve the design.

Modifying Pictures, Bullets, and Timings

Instructions: Start PowerPoint. Open the presentation, Make It Right 5-1 Massage, from the Data Files for Students. See the inside back cover of this book for instructions on downloading the Data Files for Students, or contact your instructor for more information about accessing required files.

Correct the formatting problems and errors in the presentation while keeping in mind the guidelines presented in this chapter (Figure 5–61).

Perform the following tasks:

1. Change the title text color on both sides to a color that complements the slide background. Insert your name in a footer on Slide 2.

2. On Slide 1, replace the picture shape to a shape that shows both people. Increase the size of the picture.

3. On Slide 2, increase the bullet sizes, change the color to a color that complements the slide background, and set a transparent color. Increase the font size of the second body text paragraph so that it complies with the 7 × 7 rule.

4. Delete one of the two clips on Slide 2 because they both portray similar concepts. Recolor the remaining clip, increase the size, and center it between the third body paragraph and the footer.

5. Increase the slide timings, and change the slide transitions to a fade or dissolve.

6. Use the spell checker to correct the misspellings.

7. Change the document properties, as specified by your instructor. Save the presentation using the file name, Make It Right 5-1 Therapy.

8. Submit the revised document in the format specified by your instructor.

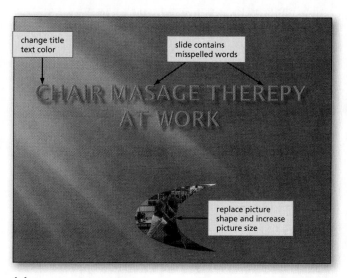

(a)

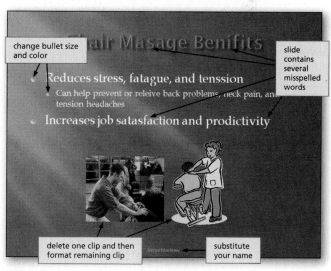

(b)

Figure 5–61

In the Lab

Design and/or create a presentation using the guidelines, concepts, and skills presented in this chapter. Labs 1, 2, and 3 are listed in order of increasing difficulty.

Lab 1: Inserting a Clip, Picture, and Sound

Problem: The "3 Rs" in the waste hierarchy are reduce, reuse, and recycle. Taken together, these three waste management strategies can help minimize garbage and toxic wastes. Children often are enthusiastic participants in the efforts to sort products for recycling and reusing household products. You work several mornings each week at the day care center at your school, and you decide to develop a PowerPoint presentation designed for these children. You begin with a clip of a child recycling newspapers on Slide 1. On the next slide, you insert a picture of three recyclable products: plastic, glass, and paper. You format these objects by resizing, recoloring, and applying a shape. You then enhance the message by adding a sound and transitions to create the slides shown in Figure 5–62 from a blank presentation.

Instructions: Perform the following tasks.

1. Create a new presentation using the Foundry document theme. Apply the Style 7 background style (row 2, column 3). Type the slide title text shown in Figure 5–62a and insert the Child Recycling clip from the Data Files for Students. Increase the clip size to 210% and position the clip as shown in the figure.

2. Insert the Carefree Tune sound clip from the Data Files for Students and have it play automatically when Slide 1 is displayed at the start of the slide show. Drag the speaker icon off the slide to the lower-right corner of the screen.

3. On Slide 2, type the slide title text shown in Figure 5–62b and insert the Recycling Products picture from the Data Files for Students. Resize the picture to 200% and position the picture as shown in the figure. Recolor the picture to Accent color 5 Dark (column 6 in the Dark Variations area). Apply the Plaque shape (row 2, column 9 in the Basic Shapes area) to the picture.

4. Set the slide timings by rehearsing the slide show. Slide 1 should display for 15 seconds and Slide 2 should display for 10 seconds.

5. Apply the Wheel Clockwise, 8 Spokes wipe transition (row 4, column 2) and change the speed to Medium for both slides.

6. Change the document properties, as specified by your instructor. Save the presentation using the file name, Lab 5-1 Recycling.

7. Submit the revised document in the format specified by your instructor.

(a)

(b)

Figure 5–62

In the Lab

Lab 2: Creating a Presentation with Columns and Pictures

Problem: Disasters can occur without warning. In preparation for emergencies, all families should have a first aid kit and an emergency supply kit filled with items that may be needed for survival for at least three days. A separate kit should be prepared for household pets. The supplies should be placed in a sturdy bag or box and checked at least twice a year. You have decided to create the PowerPoint presentation shown in Figures 5–63a through 5–63d to show in your First Aid 101 class.

Instructions: Perform the following tasks.

1. Create a new presentation using the Median document theme and then change the presentation theme colors to Aspect. Using Figure 5–63a as a guide, type the Slide 1 title and subtitle text and replace the presenter's name with your name.

2. Insert the First Aid Kit picture from your Data Files for Students, size the picture to 160%, apply the Cross shape (row 2, column 8 in the Basic Shapes area), and then reposition the picture. Recolor the picture by applying the Accent color 2 Light variation (column 3 in the Light Variations area).

3. Add three slides with the Title and Content slide layout. Format the background with the Stationery texture fill. Type the title text on all slides. Create three columns in Slide 2 and two columns in Slides 3 and 4. Type the supplies in each slide as consecutive bulleted lists. If the AutoFit Layout Options button is displayed, click Stop Fitting Text to This Placeholder to prevent PowerPoint from adjusting the font size.

4. On Slide 4, adjust the column spacing to 1" and then drag the bottom edge of the text box up to divide the columns as shown in Figure 5–63d. Insert the Pets picture from your Data Files for Students, size the picture to 110%, apply the Oval shape (row 1, column 1 in the Basic Shapes area), and then reposition the picture.

5. On Slide 2, select all the text paragraphs and then change the bullet characters to the Bandage picture found on the Data File for Students. Change the bullet size to 80% of text. On Slide 3, change the bullet characters to the ambulance symbol found in the Webdings font (row 5, column 9), change the bullet size to 80% of text, and change the color to Red.

Continued >

In the Lab *continued*

6. Insert the slide number in the footer on all slides except the title slide. Apply the Shape Plus transition (row 6, column 1 in the Wipes category) to all slides. Change the speed to Medium. Check the spelling and correct any errors.

7. Change the document properties, as specified by your instructor. Save the presentation using the file name, Lab 5-2 Supply Kit.

8. Submit the revised document in the format specified by your instructor.

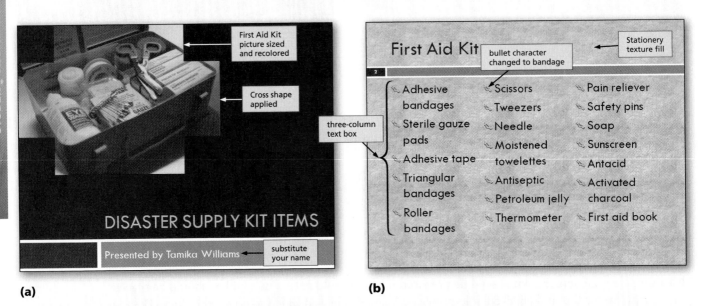

(a) (b)

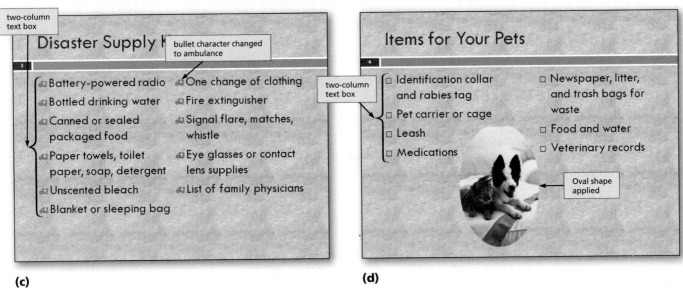

(c) (d)

Figure 5–63

In the Lab

Lab 3: Creating a Presentation with Recolored and Resized Pictures and Bullets, Columns, and a Movie Clip

Problem: This past summer you visited Chicago, and you have decided to begin creating a presentation that showcases the lakefront and attractions. You create the presentation in Figure 5–64 that consists of three slides. Slide 1 contains a resized photograph with a shape, Slide 2 contains a movie clip of the lakeshore, and Slide 3 contains columns and a photograph of the Field Museum of Natural History with a shape.

Instructions: Perform the following tasks.

1. Create a new presentation using the Solstice document theme. Apply the Two Content layout to Slide 2 and the Title and Content layout to Slide 3. Using Figure 5–64, create the three core presentation slides by typing the title and subtitle text.

2. On Slide 1, insert the Chicago Map picture from your Data Files for Students, size the picture to 80%, and then apply the Off-page Connector shape in the Flowchart area. Recolor the picture by applying the Accent color 2 Dark variation (column 3 in the Dark Variations area), and then reposition the picture.

3. On Slide 1, replace the presenter's name with your name. Insert the Soft Jazz sound clip from your Data Files for Students and start it automatically when the slide show begins. Drag the speaker icon off the slide to the lower-right corner of the screen.

4. On Slide 2, insert the Chicago Shoreline movie clip from your Data Files for Students and start it automatically in the slide show. Change the movie clip height to 3.3" and width to 4.4", and then reposition the clip.

5. On Slide 3, create two columns in the text box and adjust the column spacing to 0.1". Insert the Field Museum picture from your Data Files for Students, apply the Rounded Rectangle shape (column 2 in the Rectangles area), size the picture to 35%, and then move it to the bottom edge of the slide centered between the two columns.

6. Change the bullets to the check mark symbol shown in Figure 5–64c (column 13 in the last Wingdings row), change the color to Green, and then increase the size to 110% of text.

7. Rehearse timings for the side show. Have Slide 1 display for 15 seconds, Slide 2 for 10 seconds, and Slide 3 for 20 seconds.

8. On Slide 2, type `Every July 3, millions of people line Chicago's lakefront for an incredible fireworks show. More than 30 food vendors participate in Taste of Chicago, where hungry visitors can sample a wide variety of appetizers, entrees, and desserts.` in the Notes pane.

9. Insert the slide number in Slides 2 and 3. Apply the Wedge transition (row 1, column 5 in the Wipes category) to all slides. Change the speed to Medium. Check the spelling and correct any errors.

10. Click the Slide Sorter view button, view the slides for consistency, and then click the Normal view button.

11. Change the document properties, as specified by your instructor. Save the presentation using the file name, Lab 5-3 Chicago Travels.

12. Submit the revised document in the format specified by your instructor.

Continued >

Cases and Places *continued*

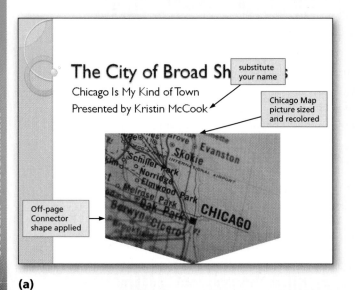

(a)

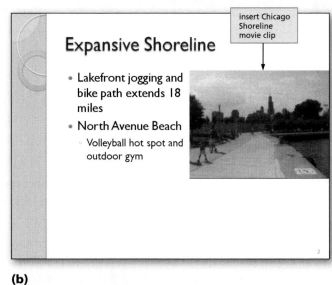

(b)

Figure 5–64

(c)

Cases and Places

Apply your creative thinking and problem solving skills to design and implement a solution.

• EASIER   •• MORE DIFFICULT

Note: Remember to use the 7×7 rule as you design the presentations: a maximum of seven words on a line and a maximum of seven lines on one slide.

• 1: Design and Create a Words Presentation

Linguists study the origin of words and how they are used. One of their interests is onomatopoeic words, which are words that sound like the noise they describe and often are seen in comic strips. Common onomatopoeic words are shown in Table 5–3.

Another interesting word or phrase is a palindrome, which reads the same backwards and forwards. Some palindromes are shown in Table 5–4.

The ten most common spoken and written words in the English language are shown in Table 5–5.

Using this information, create a presentation with a title slide introducing the topic and two text slides with columns of the onomatopoeic words and palindromes. The fourth slide should include a table with the ten most common English spoken and written words. Include at least one sized and recolored picture with a transparent color. Apply at least three objectives found at the beginning of this chapter to develop the presentation. Add speaker notes in the Notes pane of the slides with the onomatopoeic words and palindromes, giving the definitions of these word types. Apply slide transitions and a footer with your name and the page number on all slides. Be sure to check spelling.

Table 5–3 Onomatopoeic Words

Bang	Growl	Tap
Boom	Meow	Whack
Clang	Oink	Wham
Cock-a-doodle-doo	Pop	Whizz
Crack	Roar	Whoosh
Crackle	Slam	Woof
Creak	Snap	Zap
Crunch	Splash	Zoom
Gasp		

Table 5–4 Palindromes

A MAN A PLAN A CANAL PANAMA
MADAM I'M ADAM
POOR DAN IS IN A DROOP
ABLE WAS I ERE I SAW ELBA
RATS LIVE ON NO EVIL STAR
HANNAH
ANNA
NOT A TON
ROTOR

Table 5–5 Ten Most Common English Words

Spoken	Written
the	the
and	of
I	to
to	in
of	and
a	a
you	for
that	was
in	is
it	that

• 2: Design and Create a Popular Baby Names Presentation

The Social Security Administration (SSA) tracks popular baby names each year. Visit the SSA Web site (www.ssa.gov/OACT/babynames/) and view the lists of Top 10 male and female names. Scroll down, select one of the four lists (Popular Names by Birth Year, Popularity of a Name, Top 5 names by State, or Top 1000 names by decade), and enter your choice of data, such as your name or your year of birth. Using this information, create a presentation with a title slide introducing the topic and three text slides with columns of the male names, female names, and names from the list of your choice. Include at least one recolored photograph with a transparent color. Rehearse timings for the slide show. Have Slide 1 display

Continued >

Cases and Places *continued*

for 10 seconds and Slides 2, 3, and 4 display for 15 seconds. Apply at least three objectives found at the beginning of this chapter to develop the presentation. Be sure to check spelling.

•• 3: Design and Create a Most Connected Campuses Presentation

College campuses today must provide a variety of technological tools to support learning. Online classes, wireless networking, and computer labs are part of the campus environment. The Princeton Review collects data each year from more than 350 colleges and universities throughout the United States and analyzes the campuses' technologies. Review the latest report (www.forbes.com/connected/) and then create a presentation about America's most connected college campuses. Include one slide with columns showing the ten top schools and another with the methodology used to determine the rankings. Change the bullet characters to the computer monitor symbol in the Webdings font and change the color and default size. Add speaker notes in the Notes pane of two slides. Apply slide transitions and a footer with your name and the slide number on all slides. Be sure to check spelling.

•• 4: Design and Create a Recording Industry Presentation

Make It Personal

The recording industry generates more than $40 billion annually worldwide, according to the Recording Industry Association of America (RIAA). Visit at least one entertainment Web site, such as Yahoo! (http://dir.yahoo.com/Entertainment/Music/) or Information Please (www.infoplease.com/ent. html), and locate information about your favorite musical artist or group. Find a list of the most songs or CDs downloaded or sold, earnings, or concert attendance per year. Use the concepts and techniques presented in this chapter to develop and format a slide show reporting your findings. Include at least two slides with columns of the data you located. Enhance the presentation with at least one resized and recolored photograph with a shape applied. If available, add a sound clip with one of your artist's music. Include hyperlinks to your artist's Web site, and add notes on at least two slides. Be sure to check spelling. Print handouts with speaker notes.

•• 5: Design and Create a Dream Vacation Presentation

Working Together

People save their hard-earned dollars for years in hopes of one day traveling to a dream destination. An African safari, a Hawaiian holiday, and a European vacation top the lists of many students. Decide on a destination, and then have each member of your team call or visit a local travel agency or conduct online research and gather information about airfares during Spring Break, the Christmas holidays, and summer vacation. Also find hotel room rates in economy, moderate, and luxury hotels. Make a list of sightseeing activities and tours. After coordinating the data, create a presentation with pictures that you recolor and resize. Also apply a shape to these pictures. Insert tables with the airfare and hotel information, and then create columns in text boxes listing the sights and activities. Add notes to each of the text slides. Rehearse timings for each slide. As a group, critique each slide. Submit your assignment in the format specified by your instructor.

6 Creating a Self-Running Presentation Containing Animated Shapes

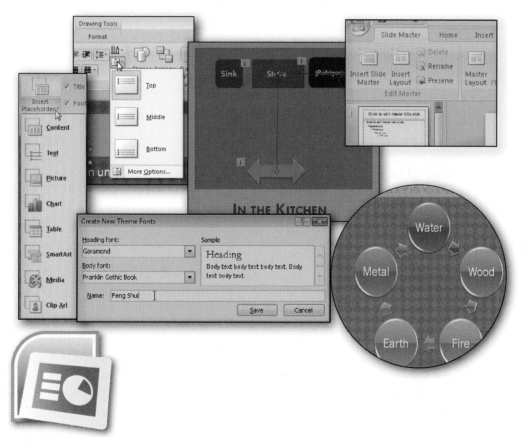

Objectives

You will have mastered the material in this chapter when you can:

- Apply themes to and format backgrounds on slide masters

- Apply Quick Styles to slide masters

- Set text direction and alignment

- Change bullet characters to numbers

- Change paragraph line spacing

- Insert entrance effects

- Change start settings

- Delete slides

- Reuse slides from an existing presentation

- Animate bulleted lists

- Animate SmartArt graphics

- Add and adjust motion paths

6 | Creating a Self-Running Presentation Containing Animated Shapes

Introduction

One method used for disseminating information is a **kiosk**. This freestanding, self-service structure is equipped with computer hardware and software and is used to provide information or reference materials to the public. Some have a touch screen or keyboard that serves as an input device and allows users to select various options to browse through or find specific information. Advanced kiosks allow customers to place orders, make payments, and access the Internet. Many kiosks have multimedia devices for playing sound and video clips.

Kiosks frequently are found in public places, such as shopping centers, hotels, museums, libraries, and airport terminals, where customers or visitors may have questions about community events, local hotels, and rental cars. Military bases have installed kiosks that allow soldiers to conduct personal business and communicate with friends and family back home by sending video clips and photographs. Governments worldwide have installed kiosks that provide Internet access to public services and information.

Project — Presentation with Animated Shapes and Customized Slide Masters

The project in this chapter follows visual content guidelines and uses PowerPoint to create the presentation shown in Figure 6–1. The slide show uses several visual elements to introduce **feng shui**, pronounced "fung shway." This Chinese art of arranging and aligning furniture, objects, and buildings has a goal of creating harmony and balance. It is based on patterns of yin and yang, where an individual's environment has opposite positive and negative, or receptive and active, forces, called chi. The wind (feng) and water (shui) distribute chi throughout the universe, and good health, prosperity, and growth are present when the forces are balanced.

Some interior designers and builders use feng shui principles when designing home and office environments. They position chairs, beds, stairs, doors, and appliances to direct the chi flow throughout the home. The presentation you develop in this chapter illustrates a few of these design concepts. It is developed to run at a kiosk in a local interior decorating store. When the last slide in the presentation is viewed, the slide show will restart at Slide 1. The presentation consists of several animated bulleted lists and an animated SmartArt graphic. The material on the text slides is complemented with three slides inserted from another presentation that illustrates basic feng shui principles in the home. Objects on these slides move to emphasize proper interior design. The presentation is customized with a unique slide master formatted with a yin and yang background graphic, background, placeholder with vertical text, and a Quick Style.

BTW

Arranging Presentation Windows
As you create one presentation, you may want to refer to another presentation and view its slides. PowerPoint allows you to view multiple presentations simultaneously on your monitor. With two or more presentations open, click the Arrange All button in the Window group on the View tab. Clicking the Switch Windows button makes a selected presentation active or current. Clicking the Cascade button overlaps the presentation windows. To close a presentation, click its Close button and then click the Maximize button on the remaining window's title bar.

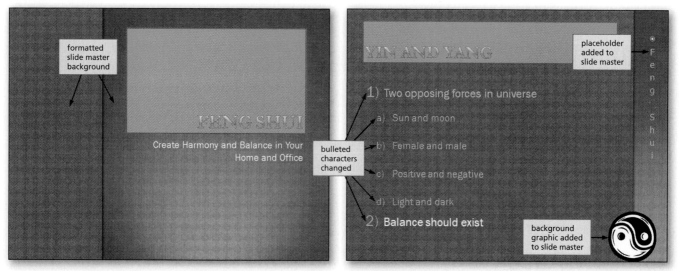

(a) Slide 1 (Title Slide)

(b) Slide 2

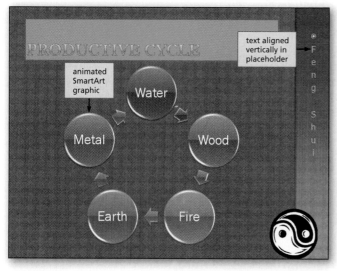

(c) Slide 3

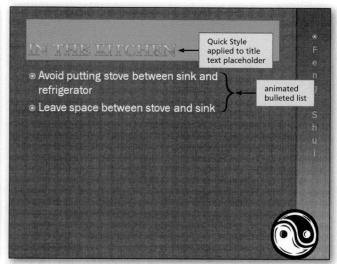

(d) Slide 4

(e) Slide 6

(f) Slide 8

Figure 6–1

Separate Presentation

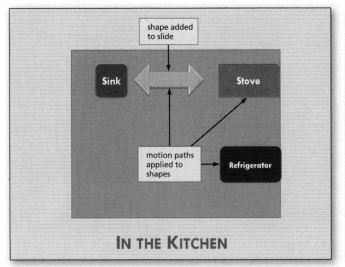

(g) Slide 5

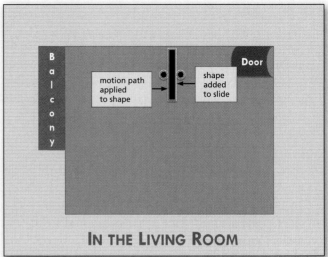

(h) Slide 7

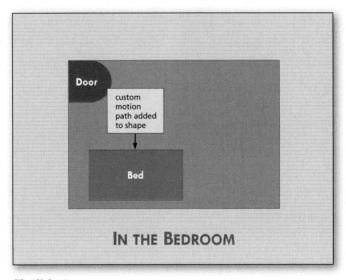

(i) Slide 9

Figure 6–1 *(continued)*

Overview

As you read through this chapter, you will learn how to create the presentation shown in Figure 6–1 by performing these general tasks:

- Customize slide masters.
- Set text orientation and alignment.
- Create custom animations.
- Insert slides.
- Set slide show options.

General Project Guidelines

When creating a PowerPoint presentation, the actions you perform and decisions you make will affect the appearance and characteristics of the finished document. As you create a presentation with information graphics, such as the project shown in Figure 6–1, you should follow these general guidelines:

1. **Plan the slide master.** Using a new slide master gives you the freedom to plan every aspect of the slide. Take care to think about the overall message you are trying to convey before you start to select the elements for this master.

2. **Use animation sparingly.** Prior to using an animation effect, think about why you need it and what effect it will have upon your presentation. Do not use animation merely for the sake of using animation.

3. **Add preset animations to your text and graphics.** PowerPoint has three preset animation effects: Fade, Wipe, and Fly In. Consider using them to save time when developing a presentation.

4. **Give your audience sufficient time to view your slides.** On average, an audience member will spend only eight seconds viewing your slides. When you are setting slide timings, keep this length of time in mind, particularly when the presentation is viewed at a kiosk without a speaker's physical presence.

When necessary, more specific details concerning the above guidelines are presented at appropriate points in the chapter. The chapter also will identify the actions you perform and decisions you make regarding these guidelines during the creation of the presentation shown in Figure 6–1.

Plan
Ahead

Delivering a Presentation on Two Monitors
Presenter view allows you to run a presentation on one monitor while your audience views the same or another presentation on another monitor. The two monitors allow you to preview your next slide on your monitor, select slides out of sequence to create a customized presentation, display your speaker's notes and use them as a script, view the elapsed time, and black out the screen during the presentation. The icons and buttons in Presenter view are large, so you can navigate easily through the presentation.

BTW

To Start PowerPoint, Open a Presentation, and Rename the Presentation

If you are using a computer to step through the project in this chapter and you want your screens to match the figures in this book, you should change your computer's resolution to 1024 × 768. For information about how to change a computer's resolution, read Appendix E.

The following steps start PowerPoint and open a presentation.

1 Start PowerPoint and then open the presentation, Feng Shui, from the Data Files for Students.

2 Maximize the PowerPoint window, if necessary.

3 Type `Revised Feng Shui` in the file name text box in the Save As dialog box.

4 Save the document on your USB flash drive.

Plan the slide master.

Using a new slide master gives you the freedom to specify every slide element. Like an artist with a new canvas or a musician with blank sheet music, only your imagination prevents you from creating an appealing master that conveys the overall look of your presentation.

Before you start developing the master, give your overall plan some careful thought. The decisions you make at this point should be reflected on every slide. A presentation can have several master layouts, but you should change these layouts only if you have a compelling need to change. Use the Plan Ahead concepts you have read throughout the chapters in this book to guide your decisions about fonts, colors, backgrounds, art, and other essential slide elements.

Plan
Ahead

Customizing Presentation Masters

BTW

Preserving a Slide Master

Normally an original slide master is deleted when a new design template is selected. To keep the original master as part of your presentation, you can preserve it. To preserve a particular slide master, click the thumbnail and then click the Preserve button in the Edit Master group. An icon in the shape of a pushpin is displayed below the slide number to indicate the master is preserved. If you decide to unpreserve a slide master, select this thumbnail and then click the Preserve button.

PowerPoint has many template files, which have the file extension .potx. Each template file has three masters: slide, handout, and notes. A **slide master** has at least one layout; you have used many of these layouts, such as Two Content and Picture with Caption, to create presentations. A **handout master** designates the placement of text, such as page numbers, on a sheet of paper intended to distribute to audience members. A **notes master** defines the formatting for speaker's notes.

Slide Master

If you select a document theme and want to change one of its components on every slide, you can override that component by changing the slide master. In addition, if you want your presentation to have a unique design, you may want to create a slide master rather than attempt to modify a current document theme. A slide master indicates the size and position of text and object placeholders, font styles, slide backgrounds, transitions, and effects. Any change to the slide master results in changing that component on every slide in the presentation. For example, if you change the second-level bullet on the slide master, each slide with a second-level bullet will display this new bullet.

One presentation can have more than one slide master. You may find two or more slide masters are necessary when your presentation reuses special slide layouts. In this feng shui presentation, for example, some slides will have text explanations, and others will display design concepts. All slides will have a yin yang symbol on the slide master.

To Display the Slide Master

To begin developing a unique design for the feng shui slides, you need to display the slide master so that you can customize the slide components. The following steps display the slide master.

1

- Click View on the Ribbon to display the View tab (Figure 6–2).

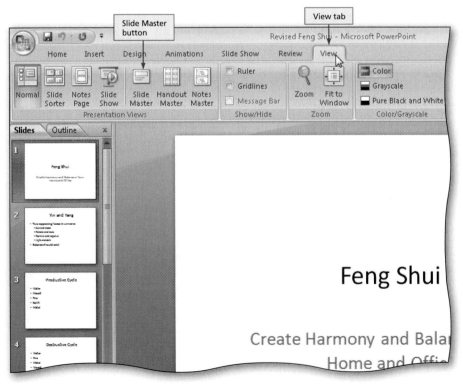

Figure 6–2

- Click the Slide Master button in the Presentation Views group to display the slide thumbnails.

- Click the Office Theme slide master (Figure 6–3).

Q&A

What are all the other thumbnails in the left pane below the slide master?

They are all the slide layouts associated with this slide master. You have used many of these layouts in the presentations you have developed for the presentations and exercises in this book.

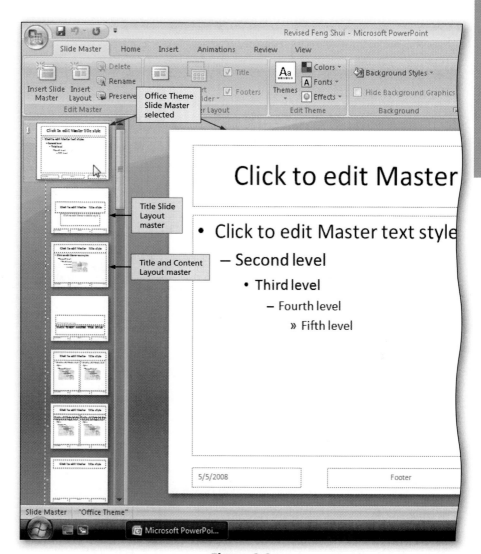

Figure 6–3

To Apply Slide and Font Themes to a Slide Master

You can change the look of an entire presentation by applying formats to the slide master in the same manner that you applied these formats to individual slides. Feng shui methods of balancing chi use natural elements, such as landscapes, crystals, and water, so you want your slides to reflect earthy tones and flowing fonts. The steps on the following page apply a theme and change the font theme.

- With the slide master displayed, click the Themes button in the Edit Theme group on the Slide Master tab to display the Themes gallery (Figure 6–4).

Experiment

- Point to various themes in the Themes gallery and watch the colors and fonts change on the slide master.

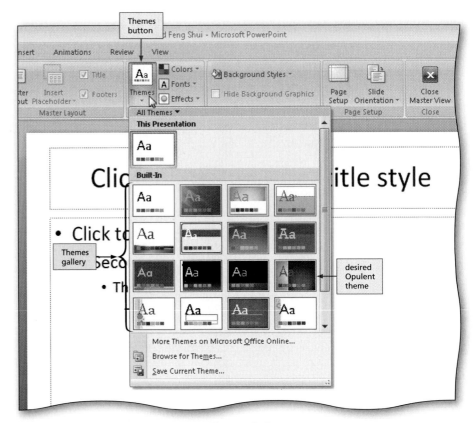

Figure 6–4

- Click the Opulent theme (row 3, column 4) to apply this theme to the slide master.

- Click the Theme Colors button in the Edit Theme group to display the Theme Colors gallery (Figure 6–5).

Experiment

- Point to various themes in the Theme Colors gallery and watch the colors change on the slide master.

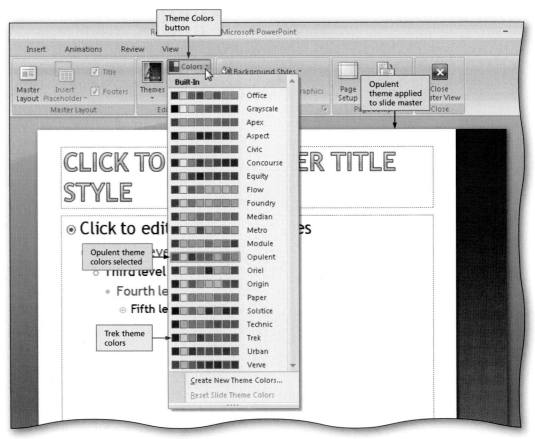

Figure 6–5

• Click Trek in the Theme Colors gallery to change the slide master colors to Trek.

• Click the Theme Fonts button in the Edit Theme group to display the Fonts gallery (Figure 6–6).

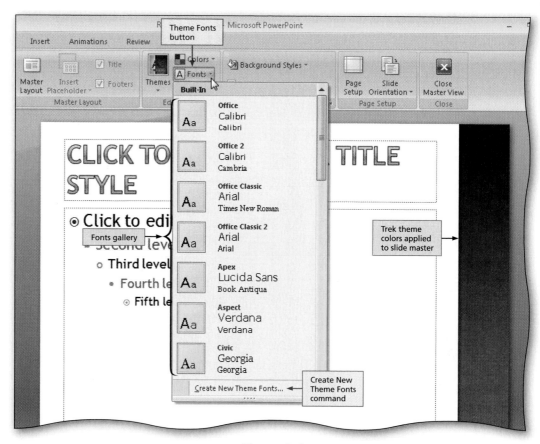

Figure 6–6

• Click Create New Theme Fonts in the Fonts gallery to display the Create New Theme Fonts dialog box.

• Click the Heading font arrow and scroll up to display Garamond in the list (Figure 6–7).

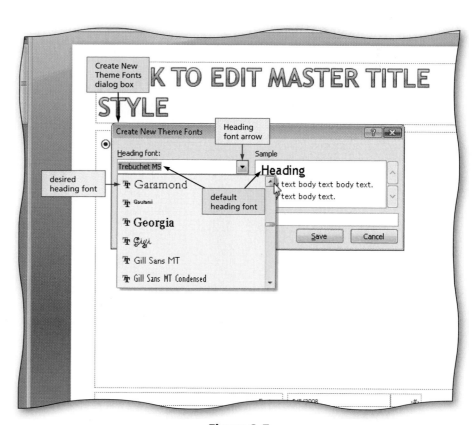

Figure 6–7

- Click Garamond to apply that font as the new heading text font.

- Click the Body font arrow and scroll up to display Franklin Gothic Book in the list (Figure 6–8).

Q&A What if the Garamond or Franklin Gothic Book fonts are not in my list of fonts?

Select fonts that resemble the fonts shown in Figure 6–8.

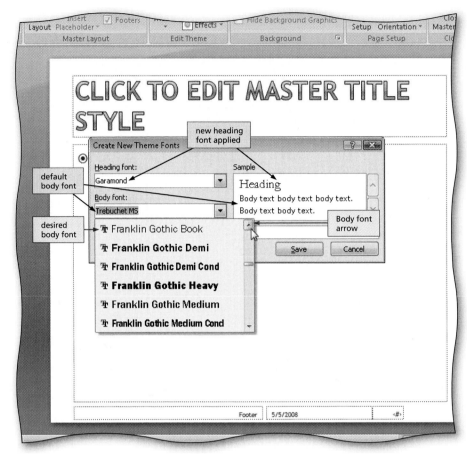

Figure 6–8

- Click Franklin Gothic Book to apply that font as the new body text font.

- Select the words, Custom 1, in the Name text box and then type Feng Shui to name the new font set (Figure 6–9).

Q&A Must I name this font set I just created?

No. In the future, however, you easily will recognize this combination in your font set if you want to use it in new presentations. It will display in the Custom area of the Fonts gallery.

- Click the Save button in the Create New Theme Fonts dialog box to save this new font set with the name, Feng Shui.

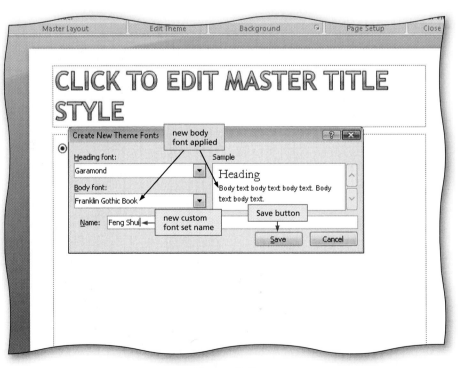

Figure 6–9

To Format a Slide Master Background and Apply a Quick Style

Once you have applied a theme to the slide master and determined the fonts for the presentation, you can further customize the presentation. The following steps format the slide master background and then apply a Quick Style.

1

- Click the title text placeholder to select it.

- Click the Background Styles button in the Background group to display the Background Styles gallery (Figure 6–10).

 Experiment

- Point to various styles themes in the Background Styles gallery and watch the backgrounds change on the slide master title text placeholder.

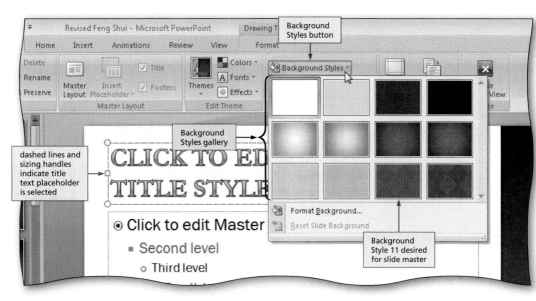

Figure 6–10

2

- Click Background Style 11 (row 3, column 3) to apply this background to the slide master (Figure 6–11).

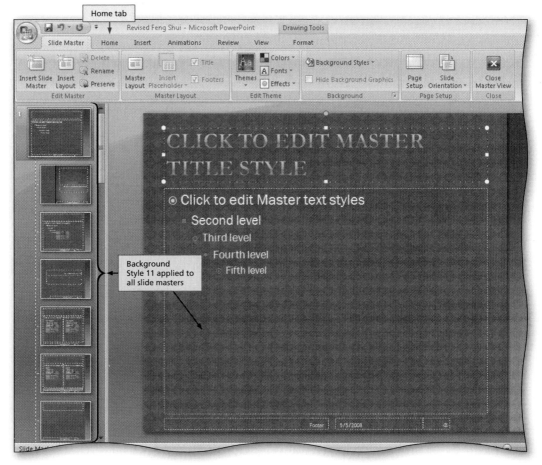

Figure 6–11

● Click Home on the Ribbon to display the Home tab. Click the Quick Styles button in the Drawing group to display the Quick Styles gallery (Figure 6–12).

Experiment

● Point to various styles in the Quick Styles gallery and watch the background and borders change on the slide master title text placeholder.

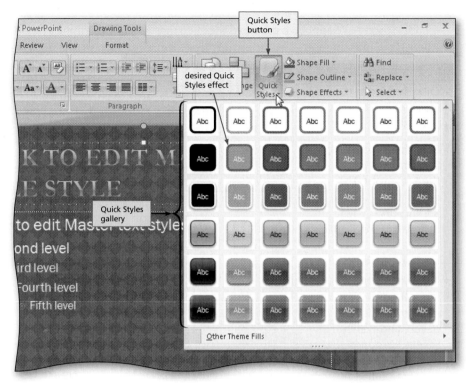

Figure 6–12

● Click the Colored Fill – Accent 1 Quick Style (row 2, column 2) to apply the format to the title text placeholder (Figure 6–13).

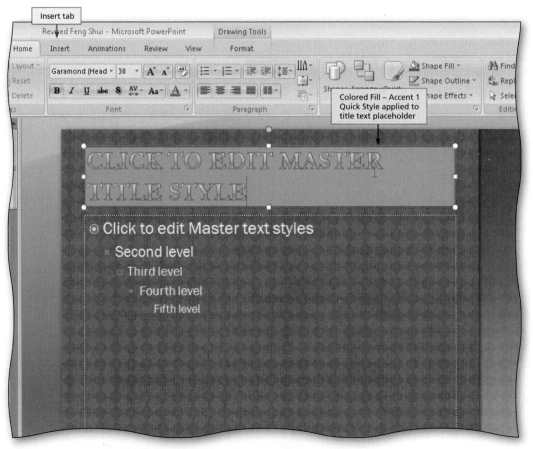

Figure 6–13

To Add a Background Graphic to a Slide Master

The theme, fonts, and background colors are set. The next step is to reinforce one of the basic feng shui concepts: yin and yang. These two opposing forces need a state of balance to keep the universe in harmony and produce chi, energy present in all objects. One technique of emphasizing this constant combination of positive and negative is to place the symbol on every slide. The following steps add the yin and yang symbol to the slide master.

1

- With the slide master displayed, click Insert on the Ribbon and then click the Insert Picture from File button, which is labeled Picture, in the Illustrations group to display the Insert Picture dialog box.

- With your USB flash drive connected to one of the computer's USB ports, select this drive, Drive E in this case, as the device that contains the picture and then click Yin Yang to select the file name (Figure 6–14).

Q&A

What if the picture is not on a USB flash drive?

Use the same process, but select the device containing the picture in the Favorite Links section. Another option is to locate this picture or a similar one in the Microsoft Clip Organizer

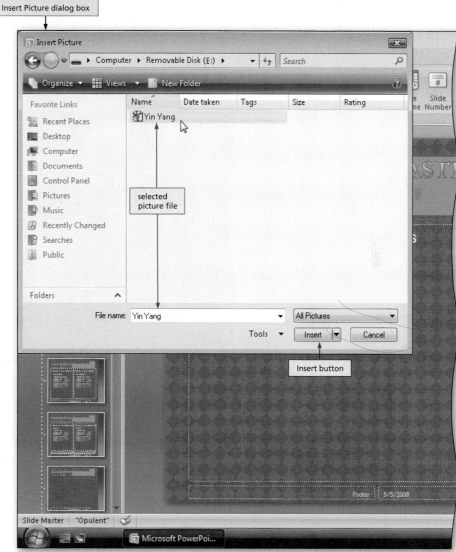

Figure 6–14

BTW

Renaming a Slide Master
PowerPoint names a new slide master, Custom Design. Once all the changes are made to this new master or to another slide master, you may want to rename it with a meaningful name that describes its function or features. To rename the slide master, click the large slide master thumbnail at the top of the left pane and then click the Rename button in the Edit Master group. The new name will be displayed on the status bar.

2

- Click the Insert button in the dialog box to insert the picture into the slide master.

- With the Format tab displayed, click the down arrow in the Size group to change the Shape Height to 1.5".

- Drag the picture to the location shown in Figure 6–15 (Figure 6–15).

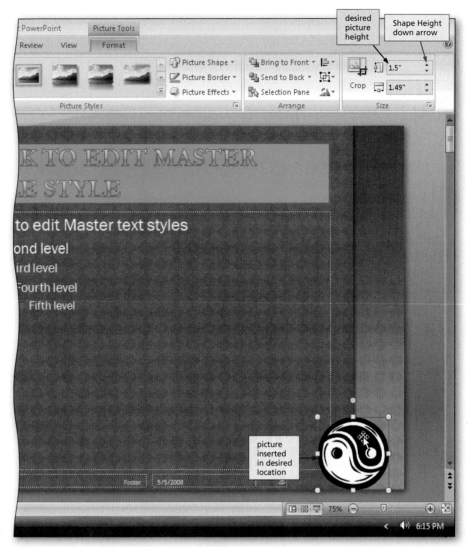

Figure 6–15

BTW

Adding Page Numbers and the Date and Time to a Slide Master
Slide numbers along with the date and time can be displayed anywhere on a slide, not just in the footer. Insert a placeholder and then click either the Slide Number or the Date & Time button in the Text group on the Insert tab. You then can format the date and time by selecting a format in the Available formats list in the Date and Time dialog box. You also can change the default font characteristics in the Font group on the Home tab.

To Insert a Placeholder into Slide Layouts

The words, feng shui, appear on the title slide. To reinforce this concept, you can add these words to every text slide. One efficient method of adding this text is to insert a placeholder, type the words, and, if necessary, format the characters. The following steps insert a placeholder into the Title and Content layout.

- Click the Title and Content Layout thumbnail in the left pane to display this layout.

- With the Slide Master tab displayed, click the Content button arrow, which shows Insert Placeholder on the button, in the Master Layout group to display the placeholder menu (Figure 6–16).

Q&A

Can I click the Insert Placeholder button instead of the Insert Placeholder button arrow?

Yes. If you click the Insert Placeholder button, the new placeholder can hold any content, including text, pictures, and tables. If you know the specific kind of content you want to place in the placeholder, it is best to select that placeholder type.

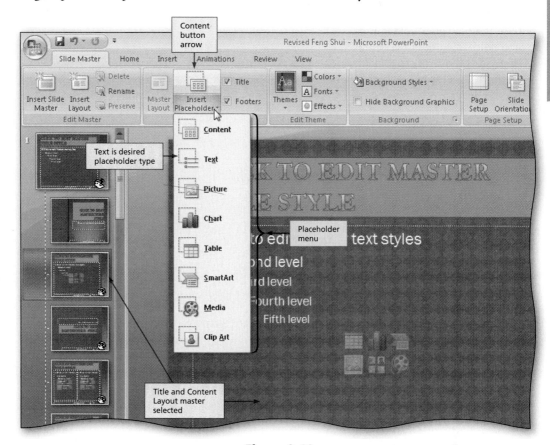

Figure 6–16

- Click Text in the menu to change the mouse pointer to a plus sign shape.

- Position the mouse pointer at the top of the green background in the location shown in Figure 6–17.

- Click to insert the new placeholder into the Title and Content layout.

Figure 6–17

To Add and Format Placeholder Text

Now that the text placeholder is positioned, you can add the desired text and then format the characters. You will need to delete the second-, third-, fourth-, and fifth-level bullets in this placeholder because they are not being used. The following steps add and format the words in the new Title and Content layout placeholder.

- Click the new placeholder, press and hold down the CTRL key, and then press the A key to select all the text in the placeholder (Figure 6–18).

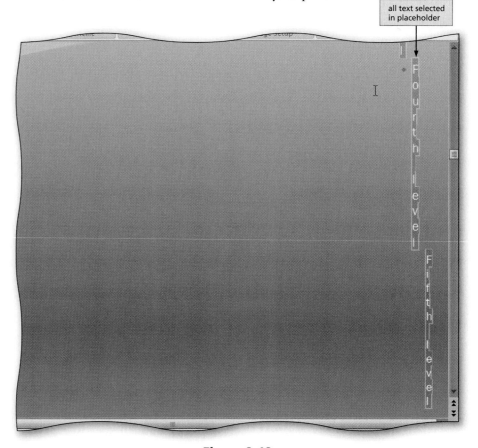

Figure 6–18

- Press the DELETE key to delete all the selected text in the placeholder.

- Type Feng Shui in the placeholder.

- Drag the bottom sizing handle down to just above the yin and yang symbol, as shown in Figure 6–19.

Figure 6–19

- Click the Home tab and then click the Text Direction button in the Paragraph group to open the Text direction gallery (Figure 6–20)

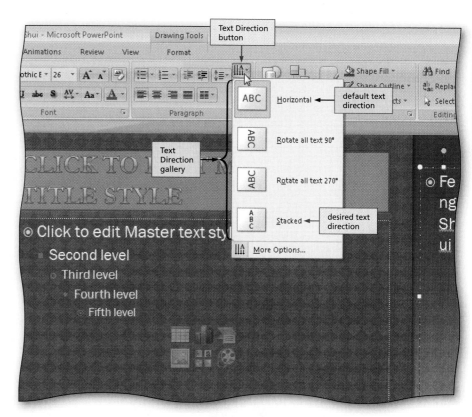

Figure 6–20

4

- Click Stacked to display the text vertically.

- Click the Align Text button in the Paragraph group to display the Align gallery (Figure 6–21).

Figure 6–21

- Click Center to display the text in the middle of the placeholder.

Q&A

What is the difference between the Center button in the Paragraph group and the Center button in the Align gallery?

The Center button in the Paragraph group positions the text between the top and bottom borders of the placeholder. The Center button in the Align gallery centers the text between the left and right borders.

- If necessary, drag the placeholder to position it as shown in Figure 6–22.

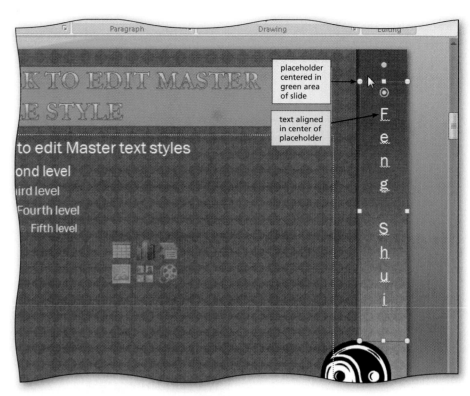

Figure 6–22

- Right-click the text to display the Mini toolbar and shortcut menu, click the Font box arrow on the Mini toolbar, and then scroll down and select Tahoma.

- Click the Decrease Font Size button two times to decrease the font size from 26 to 20 point.

- Click the Font Color box arrow and then change the font color to Orange (column 3 in the Standard Colors area) (Figure 6–23).

Figure 6–23

To Copy a Placeholder to the Slide Master

The new formatted placeholder appears only on the Title and Content layout. If you selected any other layout in your presentation, such as Two Content or Title Only, this placeholder would not display. For consistency, this placeholder should appear on all text slides. You are not given the opportunity to insert a placeholder into the slide master, but you can paste a placeholder that you copied from another slide. The following step copies the new placeholder from the Title and Content layout and pastes it into the slide master.

1

- With the Home tab displayed, click the new placeholder border so that it is displayed as a solid blue line.

- Click the Copy button in the Clipboard group to copy the placeholder to the Clipboard (Figure 6–24).

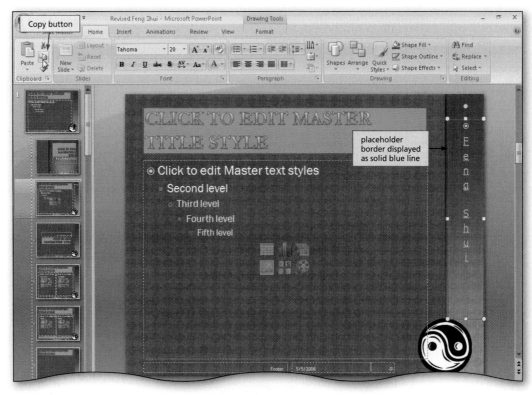

Figure 6–24

2

- Click the Opulent Slide Master thumbnail in the left pane to display the slide master.

- Click the Paste button in the Clipboard group to copy the placeholder from the Clipboard to the slide master (Figure 6–25).

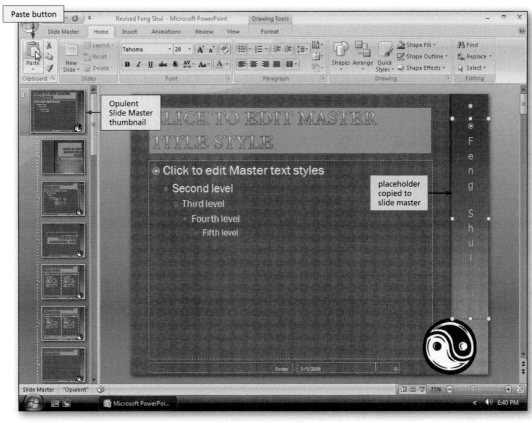

Figure 6–25

To Close Master View

Now that all the changes to the slide master and the Title and Content layout are complete, you can exit Master view and return to Normal view. All slides in the presentation will have the new placeholder, color scheme, fonts, quick style, and yin and yang symbol. The following steps close Master view.

- Click Slide Master on the Ribbon to display the Slide Master tab (Figure 6–26).

Figure 6–26

- Click the Close Master View button in the Close group to exit Master view and return to Normal view (Figure 6–27).

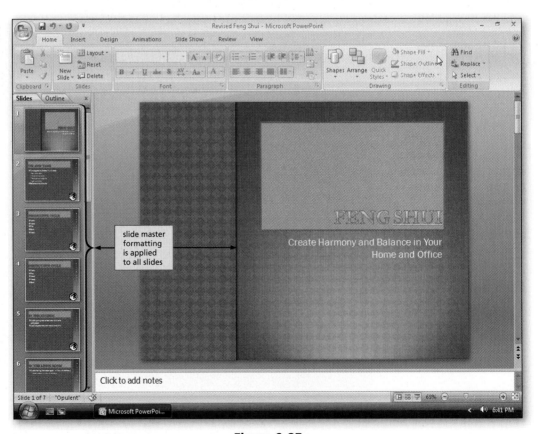

Figure 6–27

Adding and Formatting Numbered Lists

To customize your presentation, you can change the default slide layout bullets to numbers. PowerPoint provides a variety of numbering options, including Arabic and Roman numerals. These numbers can be sized and recolored, and the starting number can be something other than 1 or I. In addition, PowerPoint's numbering options include upper- and lowercase letters.

To Change a First-Level Bullet Character to a Number

PowerPoint allows you to change the default bullets to numbers. The process of changing the bullet characters is similar to the process of changing bullets to symbols. The following steps change the first-level paragraph bullet characters on Slide 2 to numbers.

- Display Slide 2.

- Triple-click the first first-level Slide 2 paragraph, which begins with the words Two opposing forces, to select it.

- Press and hold down the CTRL key and then triple-click the second first-level Slide 2 paragraph, which begins with the word Balance, to select this paragraph (Figure 6–28).

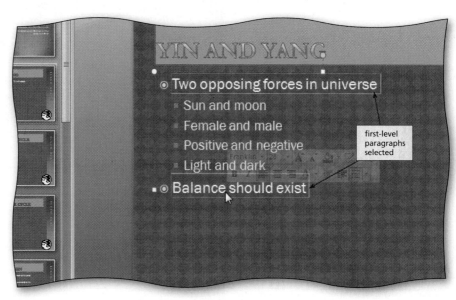

Figure 6–28

- With the Home tab displayed, click the Numbering button arrow to display the Numbering gallery (Figure 6–29).

Experiment

- Point to various numbers in the Numbering gallery and watch the numbers change on Slide 2.

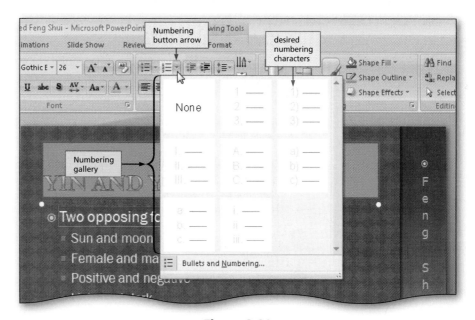

Figure 6–29

❸

- Click the 1) 2) 3) numbering option (row 1, column 3) to insert these numbers as the first-level paragraph characters (Figure 6–30).

Q&A

How do I change the first number in the list?

Click Bullets and Numbering below the Numbering gallery and then click the up or down arrow in the Start at text box to change the number.

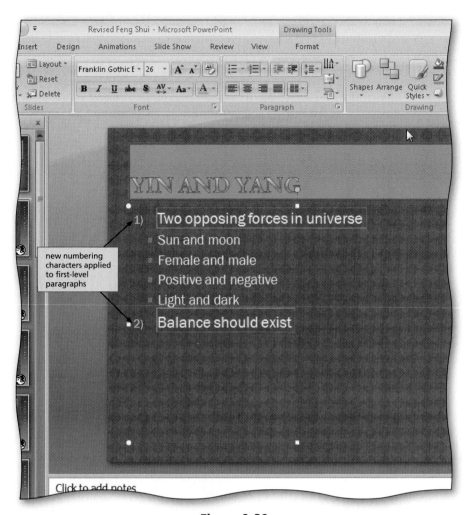

new numbering characters applied to first-level paragraphs

Figure 6–30

Other Ways

1. Right-click paragraph, point to Numbering on shortcut menu, select numbering characters

To Change a Second-Level Bullet Character to a Number

The second-level square bullets can be changed to a sequence different from the first-level numbers. The following steps change the second-level paragraph bullet characters on Slide 2 to lowercase letters.

① Triple-click the first second-level Slide 2 paragraph, which begins with the word Sun, to select it.

② Press and hold down the CTRL key and then triple-click the second second-level Slide 2 paragraph, which begins with the word Female. While holding down the CTRL key, triple-click the third second-level paragraph and the fourth second-level paragraph to select these four paragraphs.

③ With the Home tab displayed, click the Numbering button arrow to display the Numbering gallery.

④ Click the a) b) c) numbering option (row 2, column 3) to insert these letters as the second-level paragraph char acters (Figure 6–31).

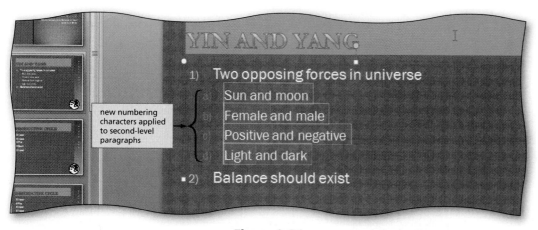

Figure 6–31

To Format a First-Level Numbered List

To add emphasis, you can increase the size of the new numbers and letters inserted in Slide 2. As with bullets, these characters are measured as a percentage of the text size and can range from 25 to 400 percent. The color of these numbers and letters also can change. The original colors are based on the eight colors in the design theme. Additional standard and custom colors are available. The following steps change the size and colors of the first-level numbering characters to 125 percent and Orange, respectively.

- Triple-click the first first-level Slide 2 paragraph, press and hold down the CTRL key, and then triple-click the second first-level Slide 2 paragraph to select these paragraphs.

- With the Home tab displayed, click the Numbering button arrow to display the Numbering gallery (Figure 6–32).

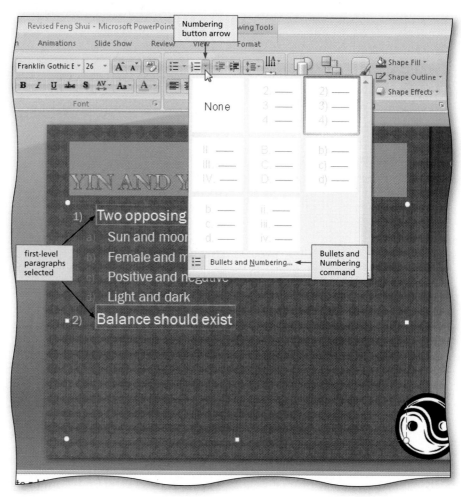

Figure 6–32

- Click Bullets and Numbering to display the Bullets and Numbering dialog box.

- Click the Size box up arrow to change the size to 125%.

Q&A

Can I type a number in the text box instead of clicking the up arrow?

Yes. Double-click the text box and then type the desired percentage.

- Click the Color arrow to display the color palette (Figure 6–33).

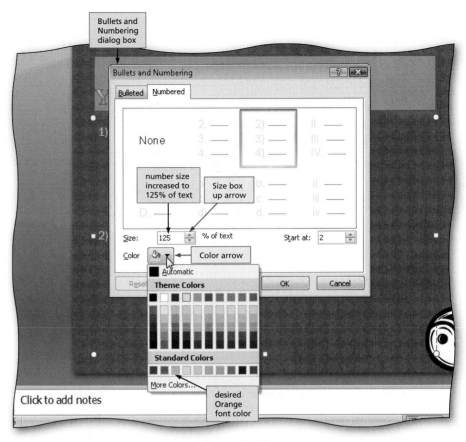

Figure 6–33

- Change the font color to Orange (column 3 in the Standard Colors area) (Figure 6–34).

4

- Click the OK button to change the font size and color.

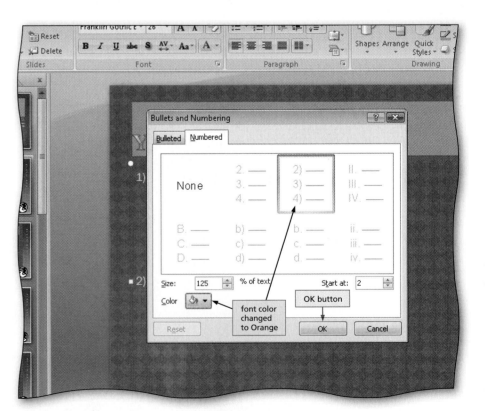

Figure 6–34

To Format a Second-Level Numbered List

For consistency, the letters in the second-level paragraph list on Slide 2 should resemble the numbers in the first-level paragraph list. The font size should be somewhat smaller because the paragraph font size is smaller than the first-level paragraph font size. In addition, the list should be a complementary color. The following steps change the size of the second-level numbered list to 100 percent and the color to Light Green.

1 Select the four second-level paragraphs on Slide 2.

2 Click the Numbering button arrow and then click Bullets and Numbering in the Numbering gallery to display the Bullets and Numbering dialog box.

3 Click the Size box up arrow to change the size to 100%.

4 Click the Color arrow to display the color palette and then click the color Light Green in the Standard Colors area (column 5).

5 Click the OK button to change the font size and letters in the list (Figure 6–35).

Other Ways

1. Right-click paragraph, point to Numbering on shortcut menu, click Bullets and Numbering, click up or down Size arrow until desired size is displayed, click Color button, select color, click OK button

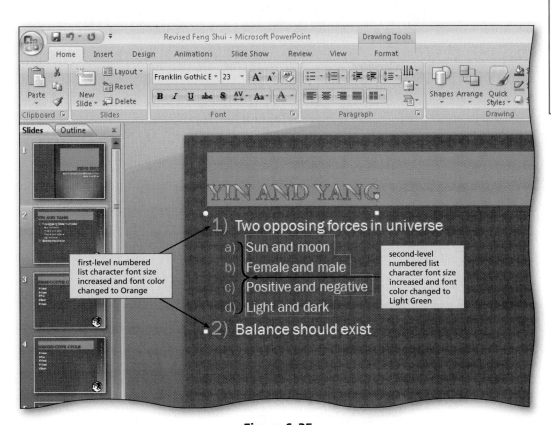

Figure 6–35

To Change the Second-Level Paragraph Line Spacing

The vertical space between paragraphs is called **line spacing**. PowerPoint adjusts the amount of space based on each font size. Default line spacing is 1.0, which is considered single spacing. Other preset options are 1.5, 2.0 (double spacing), 2.5, and 3.0 (triple spacing). You can specify precise line spacing intervals between, before, and after paragraphs in the Indents and Spacing tab of the Paragraph dialog box. The steps on the following page increase the line spacing of the second-level paragraphs from single (1.0) to double (2.0).

- With the Home tab displayed and the four second-level Slide 2 paragraphs selected, click the Line Spacing button in the Paragraph group (Figure 6–36).

- Click 2.0 in the Line Spacing list to double space the second-level paragraphs.

- Click the content placeholder anywhere except the six paragraphs to remove the selection from the second-level paragraphs.

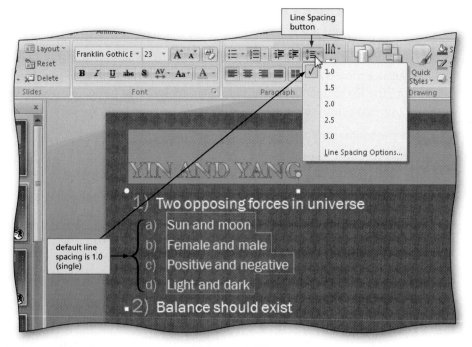

Figure 6–36

Other Ways

1. Right-click paragraphs, click Paragraph on shortcut menu, on Indents and Spacing tab click Line Spacing box arrow, click Double, click OK button

2. Click Paragraph Dialog Box Launcher, on Indents and Spacing tab click Line Spacing box arrow, click Double, click OK button

To Align Text in a Content Placeholder

The four text paragraphs in the content placeholder on Slide 2 are aligned at the top of the text box. This default setting can be changed easily so that the paragraphs are centered or aligned at the bottom of the placeholder. The following steps center the first- and second-level paragraphs in the content placeholder.

- With the Home tab displayed and the content placeholder selected, click the Align Text button in the Paragraph group (Figure 6–37).

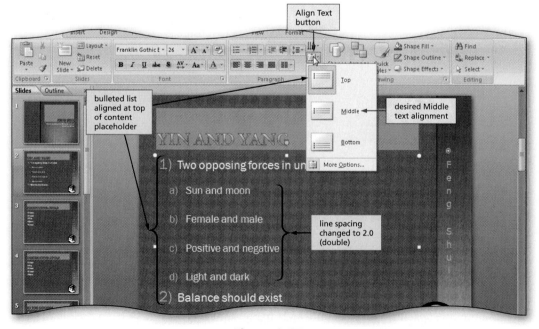

Figure 6–37

2

- Click Middle in the Align Text list to center the paragraphs in the content placeholder (Figure 6–38).

Q&A

What is the difference between centering the paragraphs in the placeholder and centering the text?

Clicking the Align Text button and then clicking Middle moves the paragraphs up or down so that the first and last paragraphs are equal distances from the top and bottom placeholder borders. The Center button, on the other hand, moves the paragraphs left or right so that the first and last words on the longest lines are equal distances from the left and right text box borders.

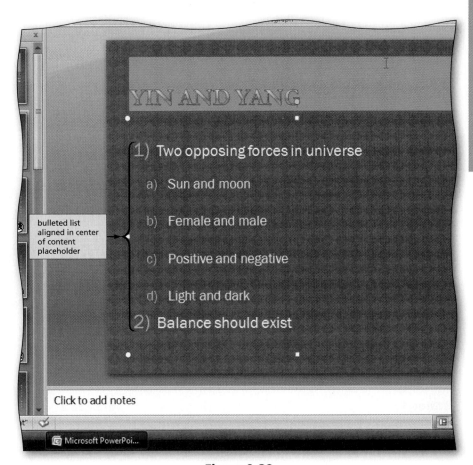

Figure 6–38

Reusing Slides from an Existing Presentation

Occasionally you may want to insert a slide from another presentation into your presentation. PowerPoint offers two methods of obtaining these slides. One way is to open the second presentation and then copy and paste the desired slides. The second method is to use the Reuse Slides task pane to view and then select the desired slides.

SharePoint Servers

In a business environment, PowerPoint presentations may be stored on a centrally located Slide Library that resides on a server running Office SharePoint Server 2007. These slide shows may be shared, reused, and accessed by many individuals who then can copy materials into their individual presentations. The Slide Library functions in much the same manner as your community library, for the SharePoint Server time stamps when an individual has borrowed a particular slide or presentation and then time stamps the slide or presentation when it is returned. If a particular slide in the Library has been updated, anyone who has borrowed that slide is notified that the content has changed. In this manner, people creating PowerPoint presentations can track the changes to presentations, locate the latest versions of slides, and check for slide updates.

BTW

Creating a Document Workspace Site

A SharePoint Server allows coworkers to collaborate efficiently. By creating a Document Workspace site on the server, team members can share and update the same files and keep each other informed about the files' status. Files are stored in a document library, which is a location where team members create, collect, update, and manage files. If a member modifies a file, the team members are notified of the change. The library tracks the file versions so that members can see a history of changes and restore a previous version, if necessary.

To Insert a Slide into a Presentation

The PowerPoint presentation with the file name, Feng Shui Rooms, has room layouts with optimal designs adhering to traditional methods of distributing chi energy. It contains four slides, and you would like to insert three of these slides, shown in Figure 6–39, into your Revised Feng Shui presentation. This Feng Shui Rooms presentation is on your Data Files for Students. See the inside back cover of this book for instructions on downloading the Data Files for Students, or contact your instructor for more information.

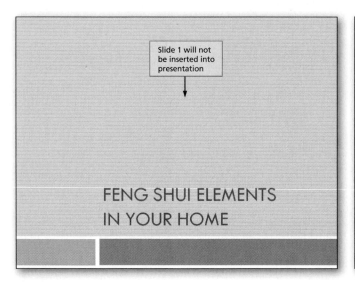

(a) Slide 1

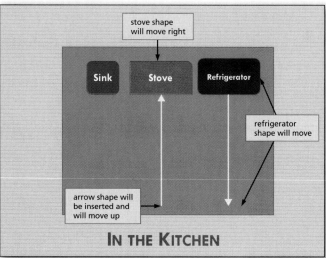

(b) Slide 2

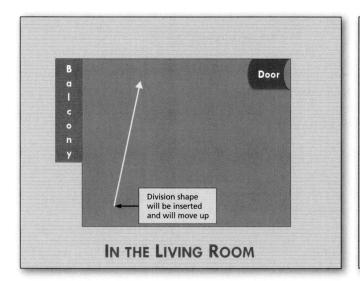

(c) Slide 3

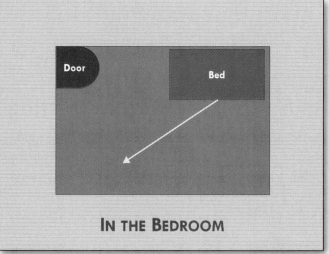

(d) Slide 4

Figure 6–39

The inserted slides will be placed in the presentation directly after Slide 5. They will inherit the styles of the current slide, which is the Feng Shui slide master and layouts, unless the option to keep source formatting is selected. The following steps add these slides to your presentation.

1

- Display Slide 5.

- With the Home tab displayed and your USB flash drive connected to one of the computer's USB ports, click the New Slide button arrow to display the Opulent layout gallery (Figure 6–40).

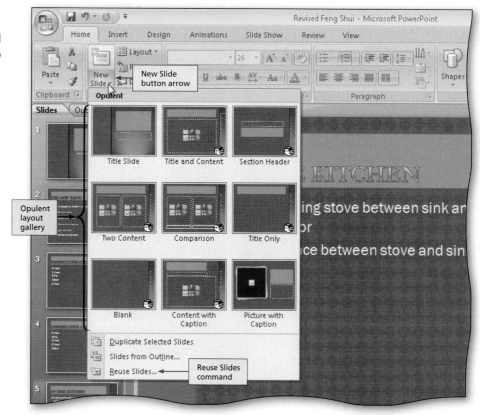

Figure 6–40

2

- Click Reuse Slides in the Opulent layout gallery to display the Reuse Slides task pane.

- Click the Browse button (Figure 6–41).

 What are the two Browse options shown?

If the desired slides are in a Slide Library on an Office SharePoint Server, then you would click Browse Slide Library. The slides you need, however, are on your Data Disk for Students, so you need to click Browse File.

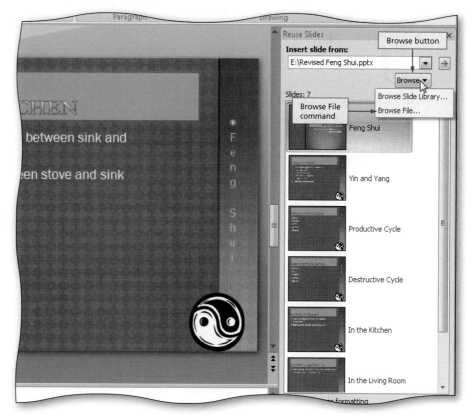

Figure 6–41

- Click Browse File to display the Browse dialog box.

- If necessary, double-click UDISK 2.0 (E:) to select the USB flash drive, Drive E in this case, as the device that contains the Feng Shui Rooms file.

- Click Feng Shui Rooms to select the file (Figure 6–42).

Q&A What if this file is not on a USB flash drive?

Use the same process, but select the device containing the file in the Favorite Links section.

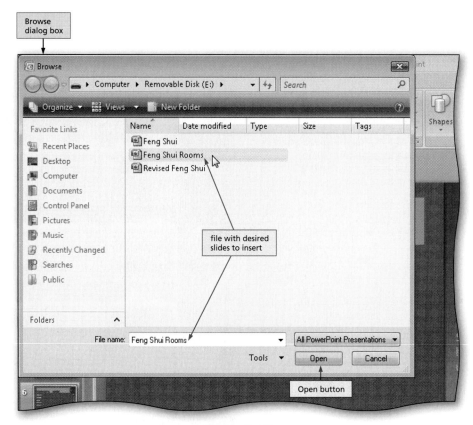

Figure 6–42

- Click the Open button in the dialog box to display thumbnails of the four Feng Shui Rooms slides in the Reuse Slides task pane (Figure 6–43).

Experiment

- Point to each of the thumbnails in the Reuse Slides task pane to see a larger preview of that slide.

Q&A Can I insert all the slides in the presentation in one step instead of selecting each one individually?

Yes. Right-click any thumbnail and then click Insert All Slides.

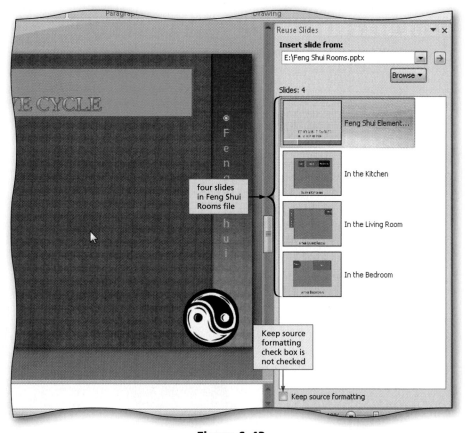

Figure 6–43

5

- Click the 'Keep source formatting' check box at the bottom of the Reuse Slides task pane to preserve the Feng Shui Rooms presentation formatting.

Q&A

What would happen if I did not check this box?

PowerPoint would change the formatting to the characteristics found in the Opulent slide master and layout masters.

- Point to the second slide, In the Kitchen (Figure 6–44).

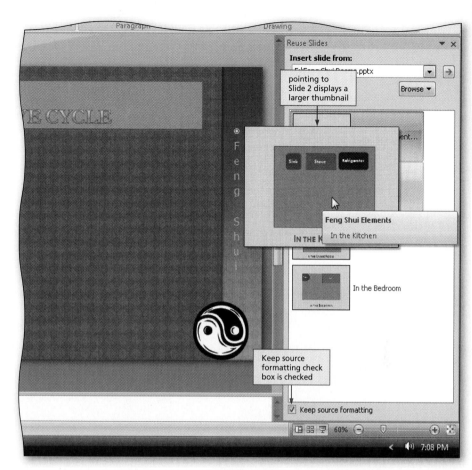

Figure 6–44

6

- Click the In the Kitchen preview to insert this slide into the Revised Feng Shui presentation after Slide 5 (Figure 6–45).

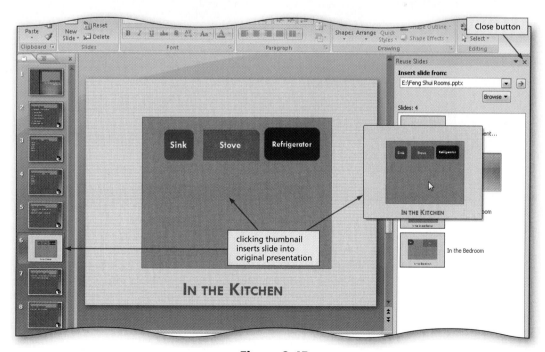

Figure 6–45

To Insert the Remaining Slides into a Presentation

The third and fourth slides in the Feng Shui Rooms presentation can be reused in the Revised Feng Shui presentation. The following steps insert one slide after Slide 7 and another slide as the last slide in the presentation.

1 Display Slide 7 and then point to the third slide in the Reuse Slide task pane, In the Living Room.

2 Click the In the Living Room preview to insert this slide into the Revised Feng Shui presentation after Slide 7.

3 Display Slide 9, point to the fourth slide in the Reuse Slide task pane, In the Bedroom, and then click this preview to insert this slide as the last slide in the Revised Feng Shui presentation.

4 Click the Close button in the Reuse Slides task pane so that it no longer is displayed (Figure 6–46).

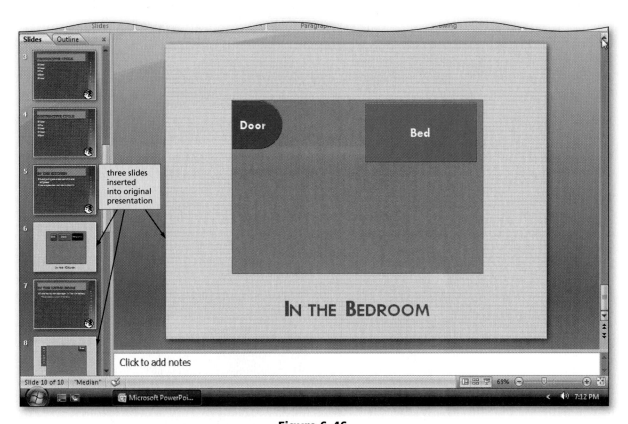

Figure 6–46

Plan Ahead

Use animation sparingly.
Audience members usually take notice the first time an animation is displayed on the screen. When the same animation effect is applied throughout a presentation, the viewers generally become desensitized to the effect unless it is highly unusual or annoying. Resist the urge to use animation effects simply because PowerPoint provides the tools to do so. You have options to decide how text or a slide element enters and exits a slide and how it is displayed once it is present on the slide, but your goal is to use these options wisely. Audiences soon tire of a presentation riddled with abundant animations, which quickly lose their impact.

Using Animations in a Presentation

To add visual interest and clarity to a presentation, you can animate various parts of a presentation, including clips, shapes, text, and other slide elements. **Animation** includes special visual and sound effects applied to text or content. For example, each paragraph on the slide can spin as it is displayed. Individual letters and shapes also can spin or move in a wide variety of motions. You already are familiar with one animation effect: transitions. PowerPoint has a variety of built-in animations that will fade, wipe, or fly-in text and graphics.

Custom Animations

You can create your own **custom animations** to meet your unique needs. Custom animation effects are grouped in categories: entrance, exit, emphasis, and motion paths. **Entrance** effects, as the name implies, determine how the slide element first appears on the slide. **Exit** animations work in the opposite manner as entrance effects: they remove slide elements. **Emphasis** effects modify the text and objects once they are displayed on the screen. For example, letters may darken or increase in font size. The entrance, exit, and emphasis animations are grouped into categories: Basic, Subtle, Moderate, and Exciting. You can set the animation speed to Very Fast, Fast, Medium, Slow, or Very Slow.

If you need to move objects on a slide once they are displayed, you can define a **motion path**. This predefined movement determines where an object will be displayed and then travel. Motion paths are grouped in the Basic, Lines & Curves, and Special categories. You can draw a **custom path** if none of the predefined paths meets your needs.

BTW

Playing Adobe Macromedia Flash Animations
PowerPoint can play an animation created with Adobe Macromedia Flash and saved as a Shockwave file with an .swf extension. The Flash file must be embedded in the presentation, or the ActiveX control named Shockwave Flash Object must be added to the slide and then linked to the Flash file so that it runs using the Adobe Macromedia Flash Player. The Shockwave Flash Object must be registered to your computer. In addition, your computer's security settings must allow ActiveX controls to run.

To Animate a Bulleted List

Used properly, animated text can draw the audience's eyes toward important slide concepts. Slide 2 in this presentation has six paragraphs of text. When you are using PowerPoint to accompany a speech, add animation effects to paragraphs so that you can display only the topic being discussed at a particular time of your speech rather than display the entire slide at once. The following steps insert one entrance effect for these paragraphs.

- Display Slide 2 and then click the text placeholder to select it.

- Click Animations on the Ribbon to display the Animations tab.

- Click the Custom Animation button in the Animations group to display the Custom Animation task pane.

- Click the Add Effect button in the Custom Animation task pane to display the Add Effect menu (Figure 6–47).

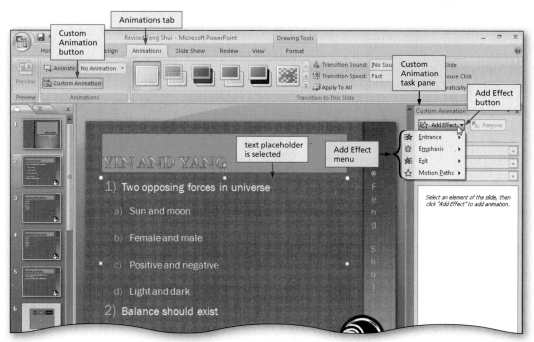

Figure 6–47

2

- Point to Entrance in the Add Effect menu to display the Entrance effects submenu (Figure 6–48).

Q&A Why does my list of effects differ from what is shown in Figure 6–48?

The effects in the list are dynamic, so they change based upon whether you have viewed and applied them previously in a presentation.

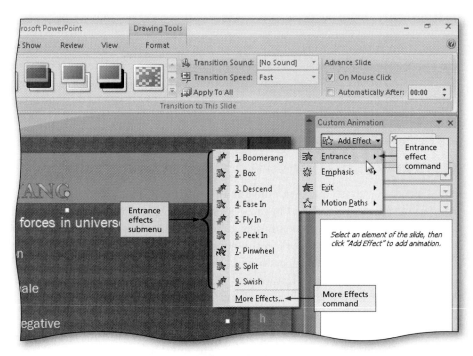

Figure 6–48

3

- Click More Effects on the Entrance effects submenu to display the Add Entrance Effect dialog box (Figure 6–49).

Experiment

- Click some of the entrance effects in the various categories and watch the effect preview on Slide 2.

Q&A Can I move the Add Entrance Effect dialog box so that I can see the entrance effects previews in the paragraph?

Yes. Click the dialog box title bar and drag the box to a location where you can view the first bulleted paragraph.

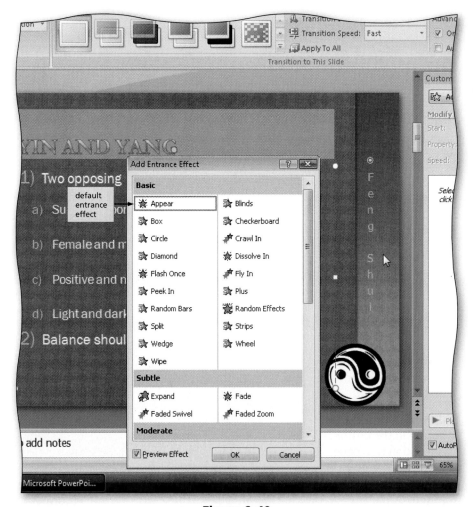

Figure 6–49

- Scroll down and then click Ease In in the Moderate category (Figure 6–50).

Q&A Why do I see a preview of the effects when I click their names?

The Preview Effect box is selected. If you do not want to see previews, click the box to deselect it.

- Click the OK button to apply the Ease In entrance effect to the paragraphs.

Q&A Why do the numbers 1 and 2 display in boxes on the left side of the paragraphs?

The 1 and 2 are sequence numbers. They indicate the first animation is the first first-level paragraph and the four second-level paragraphs and the second animation is the second first-level paragraph.

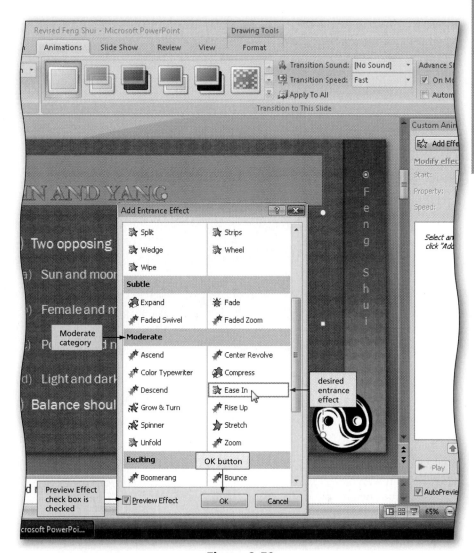

Figure 6–50

To Change Animation Speed and Grouping

Animation can start in one of three ways. The default is On Click, when the slide element is displayed after the user clicks the mouse or presses the SPACEBAR. Another option is With Previous, when the element is displayed simultaneously with whatever item is currently being displayed. The After Previous option specifies that the item will be displayed after a specified interval.

If you want to display a first-level paragraph along with its associated second-level bullets, you would specify that the animation is grouped by first-level paragraphs. If, however, you want the first-level paragraph to display and then pause until you click the mouse or press the SPACEBAR, then you would specify that the animation is grouped by second-level paragraphs. The following steps change the animation speed and group the text by second-level paragraphs.

• Click the Start box
arrow in the Custom
Animation task pane
to display the Start
list (Figure 6–51).

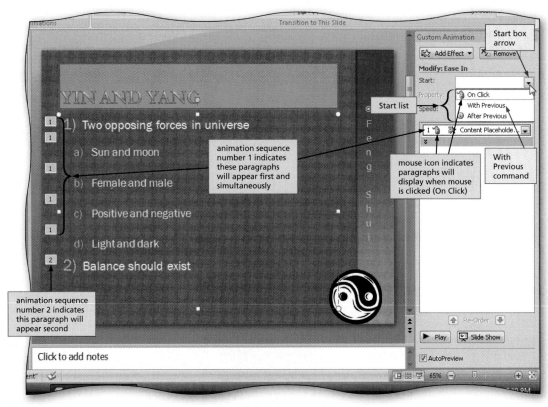

Figure 6–51

2

• Click With Previous
to specify the anima-
tion will start when
the slide is displayed.

Q&A

Why did the
sequence numbers
change to 0?

All animations will
be displayed once
the slide appears on
the screen. You will
not need to click
to show each line
of bulleted text
individually.

• Click the Speed box
arrow in the Custom
Animation task pane
to display the Speed
list (Figure 6–52).

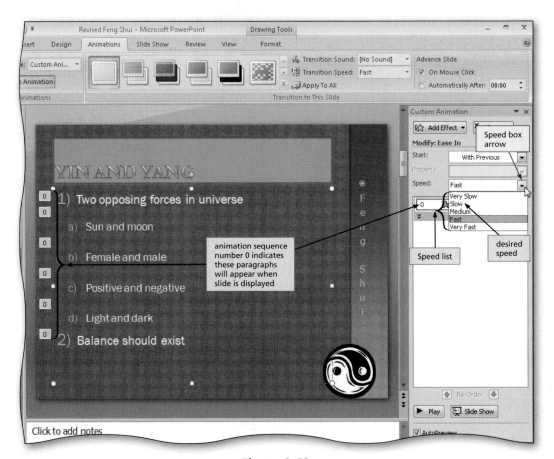

Figure 6–52

3

- Click Slow in the Speed list to change the display speed.
- Click the Animation Order list arrow to display the Animation Order list (Figure 6–53).

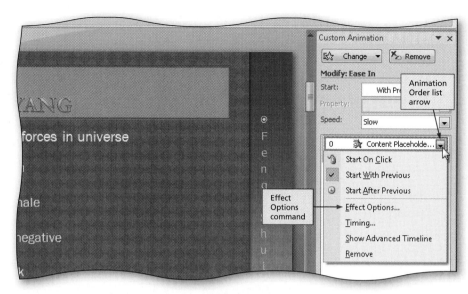

Figure 6–53

4

- Click Effect Options in the Animation Order list to display the Ease In dialog box.
- Click the Text Animation tab and then click the Group text list arrow (Figure 6–54).

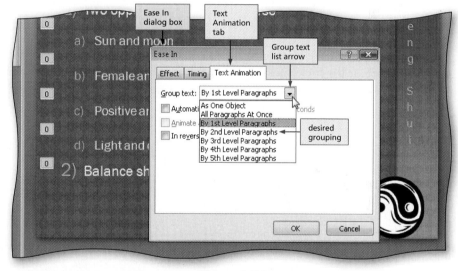

Figure 6–54

5

- Click By 2nd Level Paragraphs to change the entrance animation grouping (Figure 6–55).

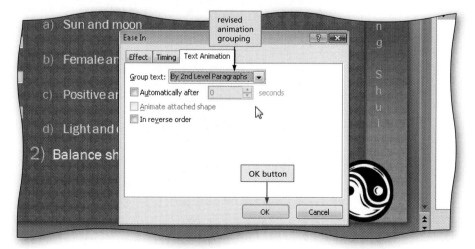

Figure 6–55

• Click the OK button to apply this animation (Figure 6–56).

Q&A How can I change this Ease In effect to another effect?

Click the Change button at the top of the Custom Animation task pane and then select another effect.

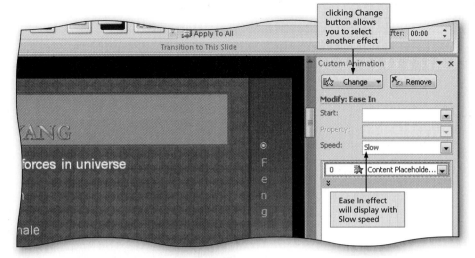

Figure 6–56

To Dim Text after Animation

As each bulleted list item on the slide is displayed, you may desire that the previous paragraph be removed from the screen or the font color be changed. PowerPoint provides several options for you to alter this text by specifying an After Animation effect. The following steps dim each paragraph on Slide 2 by changing the font color to Orange.

• With the Custom Animation task pane displayed, click the Animation Order list arrow and then click Effect Options.

• With the Effect tab displayed in the Ease In dialog box, click the After animation list arrow (Figure 6–57).

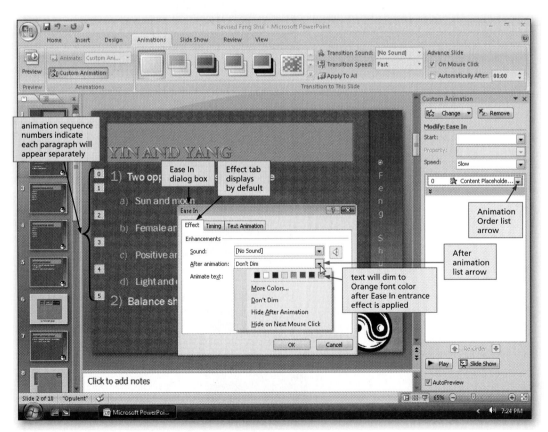

Figure 6–57

2

- Click the color Orange (column 8) in the row of colors to select this color for the dim effect (Figure 6–58).

3

- Click the OK button to apply the dim effect to the Slide 2 bulleted-list paragraphs.

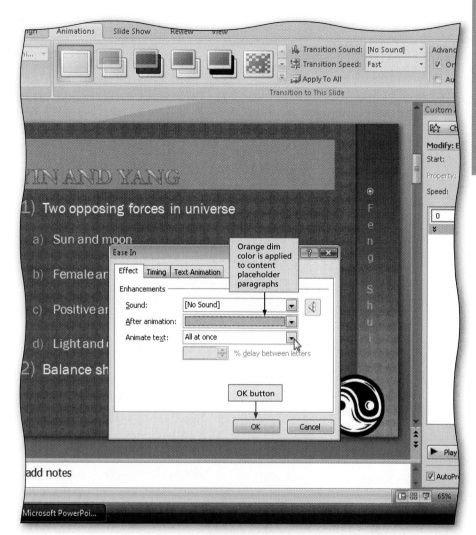

Figure 6–58

To Animate and Dim Text on the Remaining Text Slides

For consistency, you should animate the bulleted-list text on Slides 5, 7, and 9. The following steps apply the Ease In entrance effect and then dim the text on these three slides.

1 With the Custom Animation task pane displayed, display Slide 5 and then click the text placeholder to select it.

2 Click Add Effect, point to Entrance in the Add Effect menu, and then click Ease In in the Entrance effects submenu. Click the OK button to close the Add Entrance Effect dialog box.

3 Click the Start box arrow and then click With Previous. Click the Speed box arrow and then click Slow.

4 Click the Animation Order list arrow, click Effect Options, click the After animation list arrow on the Effect tab in the Ease In dialog box, and then click the color Orange. Click the OK button.

5 Repeat Steps 1 through 4 above for Slides 7 and 9.

6 Click the Close button in the Custom Animation task pane so that it no longer is displayed (Figure 6–59).

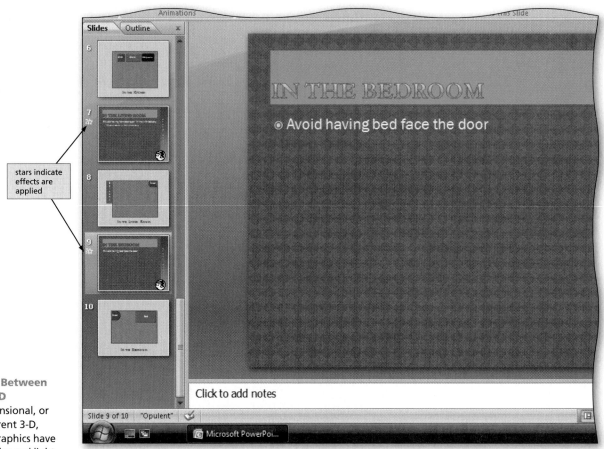

Figure 6–59

Switching Between 2-D and 3-D
Three-dimensional, or scene-coherent 3-D, SmartArt graphics have camera angles and light settings that affect their orientation, shadow, and perspective. Although you can change the text and formatting of each individual shape, you cannot reposition or resize each object. If you want to make these changes, you need to switch to a two-dimensional scene to unlock the graphic and then move and resize the shapes. To switch to two dimensions, click the Edit in 2-D button in the Shapes group on the Format tab. The 3-D SmartArt style remains applied while you modify the objects. When you click the Edit in 2-D button again, the 3-D SmartArt style reappears.

To Convert Text to a SmartArt Graphic, Apply a SmartArt Style, and Change the Color Variation

One basic feng shui concept is that the universe revolves around the five elements listed on Slide 3: water, wood, fire, earth, and metal. The first element, water, is essential for nourishing trees, which produce wood. This wood fuels fire, and the fire's ashes become part of the earth. Metal is one component of earth. When an individual's world is composed of these elements in this order, then this person is happy and successful. This cycle can be presented effectively as a SmartArt graphic. For further emphasis, you can animate each element on this slide. The following steps covert the Slide 3 text to the Basic Cycle graphic, which is part of the Cycle category, apply a SmartArt style, and then change the color variation.

1 Display Slide 3 and then click Insert on the Ribbon to display the Insert tab.

2 Select the five bulleted list items and then right-click the text to display the shortcut menu. Point to Convert to SmartArt in the shortcut menu and then click the Basic Cycle graphic (row 3, column 2) to apply this shape and convert the text.

3 With the SmartArt graphic selected and the Design tab active, click the More button in the SmartArt Styles group to expand the SmartArt Styles gallery. Click the Polished style (row 1, column 1) in the 3-D category to apply this style to the graphic.

4 Click the Change Colors button in the SmartArt Styles group to display the Change Colors gallery. Click Colorful - Accent Colors (column 1) in the Colorful category to apply this color variation to the graphic (Figure 6–60).

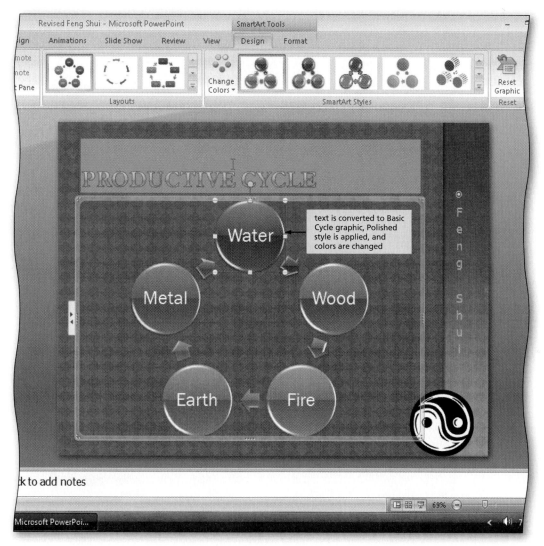

Figure 6–60

Add preset animations to your text and graphics.

To animate all text in a placeholder with the same effect, consider using a preset animation. PowerPoint provides three effects – Fade, Wipe, and Fly In – that give your slide show an interesting element. Previous PowerPoint versions contained many more preset animations with plenty of movement and flashy elements. The three included with PowerPoint 2007 are subtle and appealing. They make great additions to your slide show and are easy to apply. They make terrific animation choices.

Plan
Ahead

To Animate a SmartArt Graphic

The bulleted lists on the text slides are animated, and you can build on this effect by adding animation to the Slide 3 SmartArt graphic. You can add a custom animation to each shape in the cycle, but you also can use one of PowerPoint's built-in animations to simplify the animation procedure. The following steps apply the built-in Fly In animation effect to the cycle diagram.

- With the SmartArt graphic selected, click Animations on the Ribbon to display the Animations tab.

- Click the Animate button arrow in the Animations group on the Animations tab to display the Animate list (Figure 6–61).

Figure 6–61

- Point to One by one in the Fly In category in the Animations list to preview the animation on Slide 3 (Figure 6–62).

Experiment

- Click some of the animations in the various categories and watch the animations preview on Slide 3.

❸

- Click One by one in the Fly In category to apply this animation to the SmartArt graphic.

Figure 6–62

To Delete a Slide

Now that you have been working with the slides to illustrate various feng shui concepts, you decide that the Destructive Cycle material on Slide 4 is not necessary. The following steps delete Slide 4 from the presentation.

1
- Display Slide 4 and then click the Home tab (Figure 6–63).

2
- Click the Delete button in the Slides group to delete Slide 4.

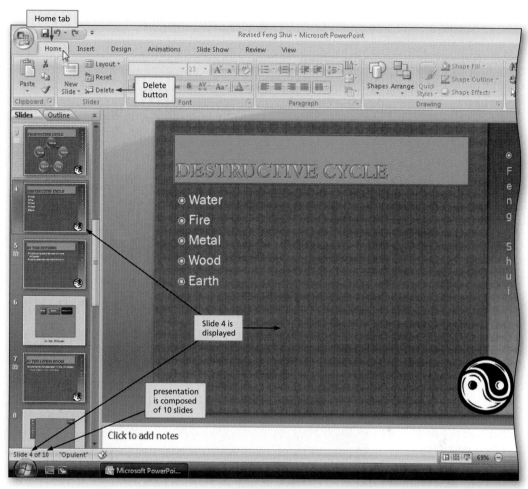

Figure 6–63

Other Ways

1. Right-click Slide 4 thumbnail, click Delete Slide

Deleting Multiple Slides
In this project you deleted only one slide. You may, however, want to delete multiple slides in a presentation. To select multiple sequential slides, click the first slide you want to delete, press and hold down the SHIFT key, and then click the last slide you want to delete. To select multiple slides that are nonsequential, press and hold down the CTRL key while you click each slide that you want to delete. Then click the Delete button.

To Animate a Shape Using a Motion Path

Slides 5, 7, and 9 contain shapes representing basic elements in three rooms of our homes: the kitchen, living room, and bedroom. Some interior decorators use feng shui principles to arrange these elements and thereby direct the flow of chi energy. The slides in your presentation help illustrate these principles, but they can be enhanced with animation to show audience members how to move appliances and furniture or install a screen so that their homes can benefit from enhanced chi movement.

One of the more effective methods of animating shapes is to use a motion path to predetermine the route the shape will follow. In your presentation, the shapes will move from negative locations to optimal locations on the slides along motion paths. The first bulleted list item on Slide 4 states the feng shui guideline that the stove should not be located between the sink and refrigerator. To solve this problem on Slide 5, you first move the refrigerator and then move the stove to the area where the refrigerator initially was located. The following steps apply a motion path to the Slide 5 refrigerator.

- Display Slide 5 and then click the Animations tab. Click the refrigerator shape to select it.

- Click the Custom Animation button in the Animations group to display the Custom Animation task pane.

- Click the Add Effect button and then point to Motion Paths in the Add Effect menu to display the Motion Paths menu (Figure 6–64).

Q&A

Why does my list of motion paths differ from what is shown in Figure 6–64?

As with the entrance effects, the effects in the motion paths list are dynamic; they change based upon whether you have viewed and applied them previously in a presentation.

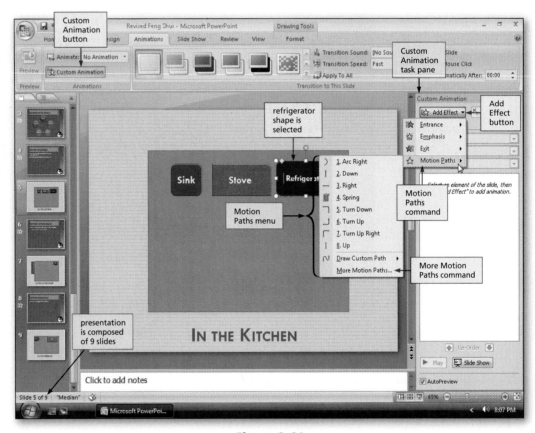

Figure 6–64

• Click More Motion Paths in the Motion Paths menu and then click Turn Down in the Lines & Curves category (Figure 6–65).

Experiment

• Click some of the motion paths in the various categories and watch the refrigerator move on Slide 5.

Q&A Can I move the Add Motion Path dialog box so that I can see the movement on the slide?

Yes. Click the dialog box title bar and drag the box to a location where you can view the refrigerator.

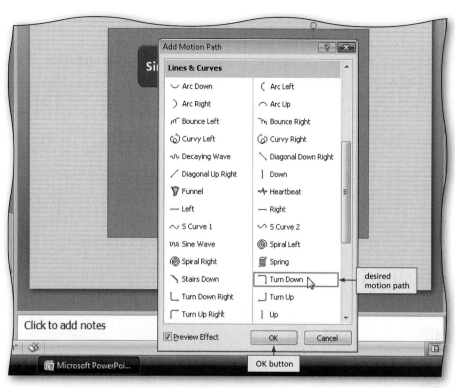

Figure 6–65

• Click the OK button to apply the Turn Down motion path to the refrigerator.

• Click the Start arrow in the Custom Animation task pane to display the Start menu (Figure 6–66).

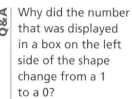

• Click With Previous in the Start menu to change the animation from On Click to With Previous.

Q&A Why did the number that was displayed in a box on the left side of the shape change from a 1 to a 0?

The 0 indicates that the animation will play immediately when the slide is displayed. The presenter will not need to click the mouse or press the SPACEBAR to start the animation.

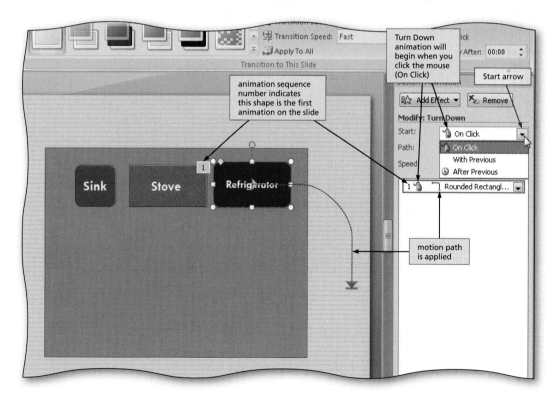

Figure 6–66

To Adjust a Motion Path

The Turn Down motion path moves the refrigerator in the correct direction, but the path is outside the green rectangle representing the kitchen walls. The green triangle in the middle of the refrigerator shape indicates the starting point, and the red triangle along the right side of the slide indicates the stopping point. For the maximum animation effect on the slide, you would like to move the stopping point inside the green rectangle and farther down the slide. The following steps move the stopping point on the Slide 5 refrigerator shape.

1

- With the refrigerator motion path displayed, click the red stopping point triangle to select the motion path.

- With your cursor displayed as a two-headed arrow, drag the stopping point to the location shown in Figure 6–67.

 Q&A My entire motion path moved. How can I move only the red stopping point arrow?

Be certain your cursor is a two-headed arrow and not a four-headed arrow.

2

- Drag the green starting point to the location shown in Figure 6–68.

- Click the Play button in the Custom Animation task pane to view the refrigerator animation (Figure 6–68).

Q&A My animation is not exactly like the path shown in Figure 6–68. Can I change the path?

Yes. Continue adjusting the starting and stopping points and playing the animation until you are satisfied with the effect.

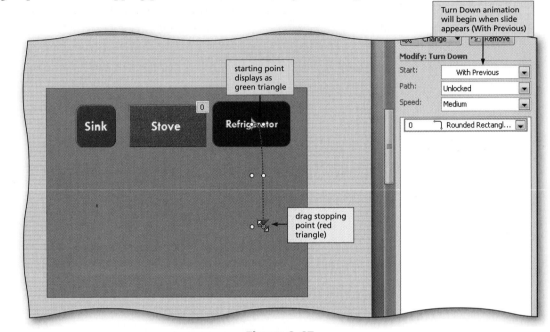

Figure 6–67

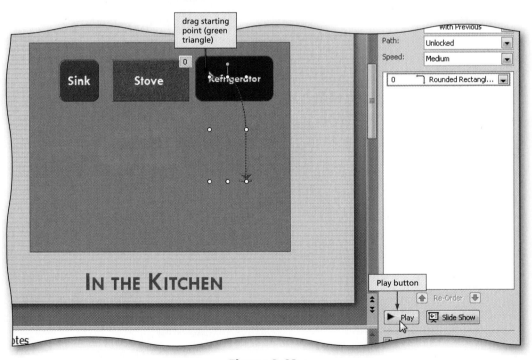

Figure 6–68

To Animate Another Shape

The bulleted text on Slide 4 describes a feng shui principle that sufficient space should exist between the stove and sink. Now that the refrigerator shape is moved on Slide 5, you can animate the stove and move it to the location previously held by the refrigerator. The following steps apply a motion path to the stove to move it to the right.

1 With the Custom Animation task pane displayed, click the stove shape to select it, click the Add Effect button, point to Motion Paths in the Add Effect menu, and then click More Motion Paths in the Motion Paths menu.

2 Click Right in the Lines & Curves category and then click the OK button to apply this motion path to the stove.

3 Click the Start arrow in the Custom Animation task pane to display the Start menu and then click With Previous.

4 Click the Play button in the Custom Animation task pane to view the animations (Figure 6–69).

Figure 6–69

To Insert and Format a Shape and Then Apply a Motion Path

The Turn Down motion path moves the refrigerator in the correct direction and the Right motion path moves the stove to the area previously occupied by the refrigerator. To further emphasize this movement, you can add an arrow in the space where the stove originally was placed. The following steps add an arrow symbol, format this shape, and then apply a motion path.

1. Click Insert on the Ribbon to display the Insert tab. Click the Shapes button in the Illustrations group and then click the Left-Right Arrow shape (row 1, column 5 in the Block Arrows area).

2. Click Slide 5 at the bottom edge of the green rectangle. Drag a corner sizing handle so that the arrow shape is approximately the size shown in Figure 6–70 and then move the arrow to the location shown in this figure.

3. Click the Home tab and then click the Shape Quick Styles button in the Drawing group. Click the Intense Effect – Accent 5 Shape Quick Style (row 6, column 6) to apply this format to the arrow.

4. Click the Add Effect button in the Custom Animation task pane, point to Motion Paths, and then click More Motion Paths. Click Up in the Lines & Curves category and then click the OK button to apply this motion path to the arrow.

5. Click the red stopping point triangle and with your cursor displayed as a two-headed arrow, drag the stopping point to the middle of the stove shape. Drag the green starting point triangle to the middle of the arrow, if necessary.

6. Click the Start box arrow in the Custom Animation task pane to display the Start menu and then click With Previous.

7. Click the Speed box arrow in the Custom Animation task pane to display the Speed menu and then click Very Slow.

8. Click the Play button in the Custom Animation task pane to view the animations (Figure 6–70).

BTW

Creating a Custom Show
A custom show allows you to adapt your presentation to various audiences. For example, you can have one show that fits a 20-minute time constraint and a second show on the same topic that fits an hour schedule. The two types of custom shows are basic and hyperlinked. A basic show is a subset of the original presentation and contains selected slides. A hyperlinked show navigates to one or more separate presentations from your main show. To create a basic custom show, click the Custom Slide Show button in the Start Slide Show group on the Slide Show tab and then click Custom Shows. Create a new show and then select the slides you want to include. To create a hyperlinked custom show, follow the steps above to create a basic show and then click the Hyperlink button in the Links group on the Insert tab. Click Place in This Document under Link to and then select either the custom show or a particular slide that you want to view.

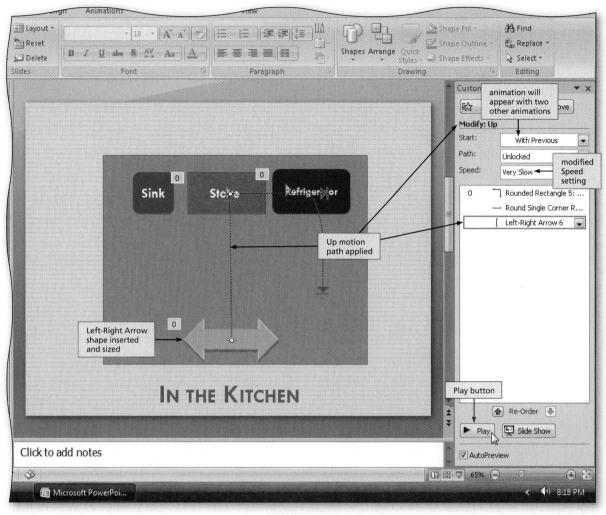

Figure 6–70

To Insert and Format a Second Shape and Then Apply Effects

The feng shui principle on Slide 6 states that a door and a balcony should not directly oppose each other. If they do, the chi energy is likely to enter one side of a room and then quickly exit on the opposite side without having a chance to flow throughout the space. A screen divider placed between the door and balcony will divert the chi. You can represent this concept by adding a rectangle to the room depicted on Slide 7 and then animating this shape. Both of these animations will play automatically in the sequence you specify. The following steps add a rectangle symbol, which is the division sign, format this shape, and then apply both an entrance effect and a motion path.

1 Display Slide 7. Display the Insert tab, click the Shapes button in the Illustrations group, and then click the Division shape (column 4 in the Equation Shapes area).

2 Click Slide 7 at the lower-left corner of the green rectangle. Drag the green rotation handle to the right so that the rectangle displays vertically. Drag a top or bottom sizing handle so that the Division shape is approximately the size shown in Figure 6–71 and then move the shape to the location shown in this figure.

3 Display the Home tab and then click the Shape Quick Styles button in the Drawing group. Click the Light 1 Outline, Colored Fill – Dark 1 Quick Style (row 3, column 1) to apply this format to the shape.

BTW

Translating Text
Bilingual dictionaries can translate words and phrases into different languages. To use this feature, select the text and then click the Translate button on the Review tab. In the Research task pane, click the From list arrow and select the original language and then click the To list arrow and select the translation language. Users are cautioned to have humans check the translation when important or sensitive information is translated because the software translation may not preserve the text's full meaning and tone.

4 Click the Add Effect button in the Custom Animation task pane, point to Entrance, click More Effects, and then click Dissolve In in the Basic category. Click the OK button, click the Start arrow in the Custom Animation task pane to display the Start menu, and then click With Previous.

5 Click the Add Effect button, point to Motion Paths, and then click More Motion Paths. Click Turn Up in the Lines & Curves category and then click the OK button to apply this motion path to the Division shape.

6 Click the red stopping point triangle and then drag the stopping point to the top edge of the green background between the door and the balcony, as shown in Figure 6–71. Drag the green starting point triangle to the middle of the Division shape, if necessary.

7 Click the Start box arrow in the Custom Animation task pane to display the Start menu and then click With Previous. Click the Speed box arrow and change the speed to Slow.

8 Click the Play button in the Custom Animation task pane to view the animations (Figure 6–71).

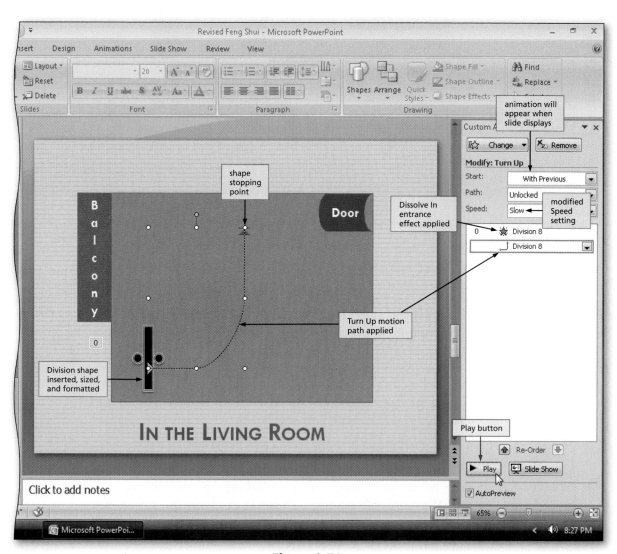

Figure 6–71

To Draw a Custom Motion Path

While PowerPoint supplies a wide variety of motion paths, at times they may not fit the precise animations your presentation requires. In that situation, you can draw a custom path that specifies the unique movement your slide element should make. Slide 8 presents the feng shui concept that the foot of a bed should not face a doorway. To illustrate this principle, you want to move the bed in Slide 9 to a location at the bottom of the slide. No preset motion path presents the exact motion you want to display, so you will draw your own custom path.

Drawing a custom path requires some practice and patience. You click the mouse to begin drawing the line. If you want the line to change direction, such as to curve, you click again. When you have completed drawing the path, you double-click to end the line. The following steps draw a custom motion path.

- With the Custom Animation task pane displayed, display Slide 9. Click the bed shape to select it.

- Click the Add Effect button, point to Motion Paths in the Add Effect menu, and then point to Draw Custom Path in the Motion Paths menu to display the Custom Path menu (Figure 6–72).

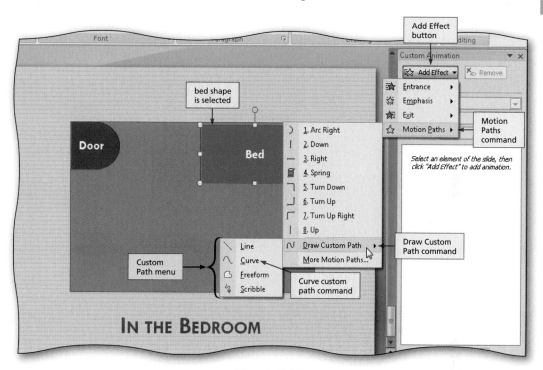

Figure 6–72

2

- Click Curve in the Custom Path menu.

- Click the bed shape and then move the mouse toward the door shape.

- Click the mouse on the right side of the door shape to indicate where the curve will start (Figure 6–73).

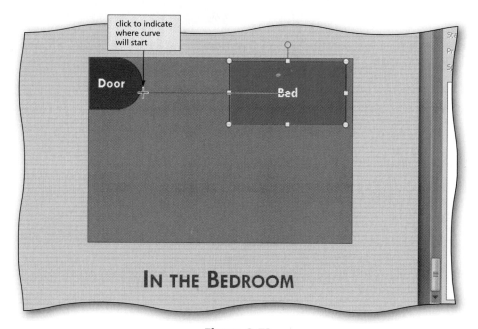

Figure 6–73

- Move the mouse pointer to the location shown in Figure 6–74, which is the ending point of the curve (Figure 6–74).

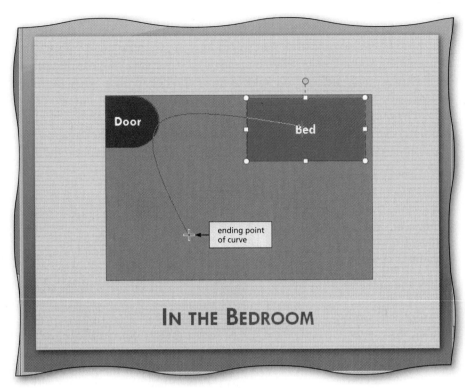

Figure 6–74

- Double-click to indicate the end of the curve.

- Click the Start arrow in the Custom Animation task pane and then click With Previous (Figure 6–75).

Q&A

If my curve is not correct, can I delete it?

Yes. Click the Remove button in the Custom Animation task pane and repeat the steps above.

- Click the Close button in the Custom Animation task pane so that it no longer is displayed.

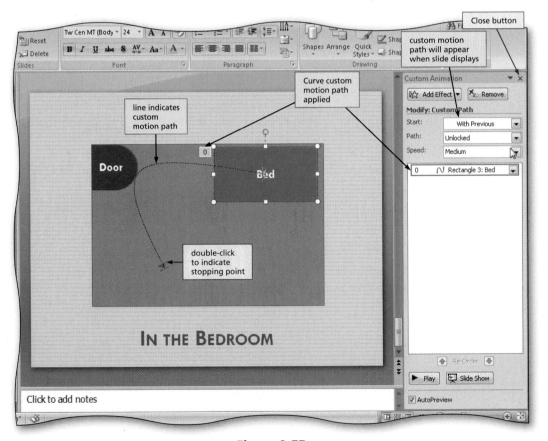

Figure 6–75

To Create a Self-Running Presentation

The feng shui presentation can accompany a speech, but it also can run unattended at furniture stores and home improvement seminars. When the last slide in the presentation is displayed, the slide show **loops**, or restarts, at Slide 1. PowerPoint has the option of running continuously until the user presses the ESC key. The following steps set the slide show to run in this manner.

1
- Click Slide Show on the Ribbon to display the Slide Show tab. Click the Set Up Show button in the Set Up group to display the Set Up Show dialog box (Figure 6–76).

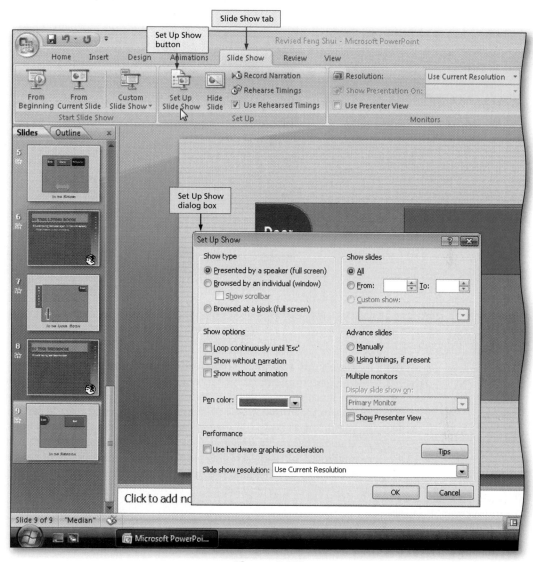

Figure 6–76

BTW

Creating a New Default Document Theme
The Office Theme document theme is applied by default. If you want to set another theme as the default, click the More button in the Themes gallery to expand the gallery, right-click the desired theme to set as the default, and then click Set as Default Theme. Every new presentation will use this new theme. You can reset the Office Theme or select another theme to use as the default.

2

- Click 'Browsed at a kiosk (full screen)' in the Show type area (Figure 6–77).

3

- Click the OK button to apply this show type.

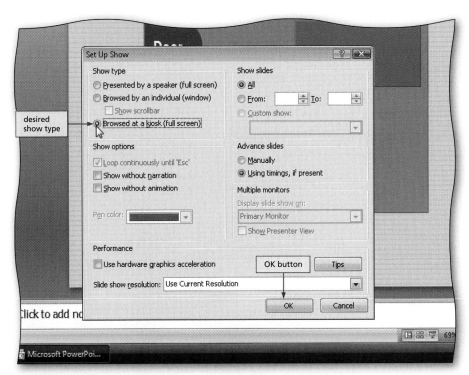

Figure 6–77

Plan Ahead

Give your audience sufficient time to view a slide.
The presentation in this chapter is designed to run at a kiosk continuously without a speaker's physical presence. Your audience, therefore, must read or view each slide and absorb the information without your help as a narrator. Be certain to give them time to read the slide and grasp the concept you are presenting. They will become frustrated if the slide changes before they have finished viewing and assimilating the material. As you set the slide timings, read each slide aloud and note the amount of time that elapses. Add a few seconds to this time and use this amount for the total time the slide is displayed.

BTW

Participating in the Customer Experience Improvement Program
Microsoft encourages Office users to participate in its Customer Experience Improvement Program in an effort to enhance the software's performance, reliability, and quality. Participants sign up for the program in the Trust Center and agree to allow Microsoft to collect information automatically and anonymously about their computers generally once daily. This information includes error messages, type of hardware, performance, and difficulties running Microsoft software. Users can stop participating at any time.

To Add Slide Timings

You need to determine the length of time each slide should be displayed. Audience members need sufficient time to read the text and watch the animations. Table 6–1 specifies the length of time each slide should be displayed.

Table 6–1 Slide Timings	
Slide Number	**Display Time**
1	00:10
2	00:20
3	00:15
4	00:10
5	00:15
6	00:10

Table 6–1 Slide Timings *(continued)*	
Slide Number	**Display Time**
7	00:15
8	00:10
9	00:15

The following steps add slide timings to the presentation.

1 Display the Animations tab, and then display Slide 1.

2 Use the Automatically After up arrow in the Transition to This Slide group to change the time to 00:10.

3 Repeat Steps 1 and 2 above to set the timing for the remaining slides according to Table 6–1.

4 Click the Slide Sorter view button to review the slide timings (Figure 6–78).

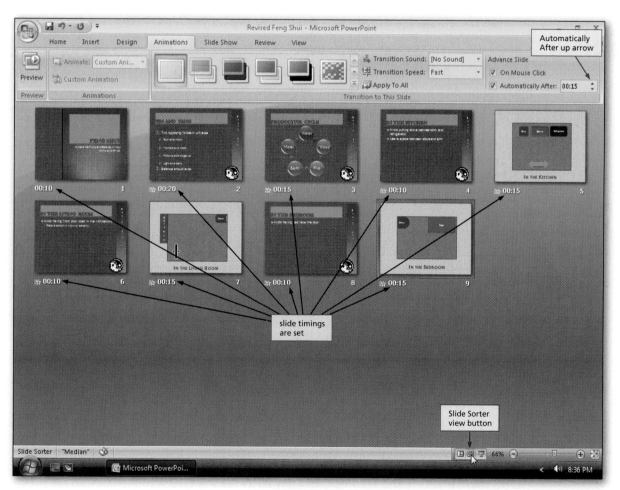

Figure 6–78

Add a Transition between Slides

A final enhancement you will make in this presentation is to apply the Uncover Right transition in the Wipes category to all slides and change the transition speed to Slow. The following steps apply this transition to the presentation.

1 With the Animations tab displayed, click the Normal view button and then expand the Transitions gallery.

2 Click the Uncover Right transition (row 2, column 2) in the Wipes category in the Transitions gallery.

3 Change the Transition Speed to Slow.

4 Apply the transition to all slides in the presentation.

To Run an Animated Slide Show

All changes are complete. You now can view the Revised Feng Shui presentation. The following steps run the presentation.

1 Click Slide 1 in the Slides pane to display the title slide and then click the Slide Show button to display the title slide.

2 As each slide is displayed automatically, review the information.

3 When Slide 1 is displayed again, press the ESC key to stop the presentation.

To Preview and Print Handouts

All changes are complete. You now can create handouts to accompany the slide show. The following steps preview and then print the presentation.

1 Click the Office button, point to Print, and then click Print Preview on the Print submenu.

2 Click the Print What arrow in the Page Setup group and then click Handouts (6 Slides Per Page) in the Print What list.

3 Click the Print button in the Print group.

4 Click the OK button in the Print dialog box to print the handouts (Figure 6–79).

5 Click the Close Print Preview button in the Preview group on the Print Preview tab to return to Normal view.

To Change Document Properties and Save the Presentation

Before saving the presentation again, you want to add your name, class name, and some keywords as document properties. The following steps use the Document Information Panel to change document properties and then save the project.

1 Click the Office Button, point to Prepare, and then click Properties on the 'Prepare the document for distribution' submenu.

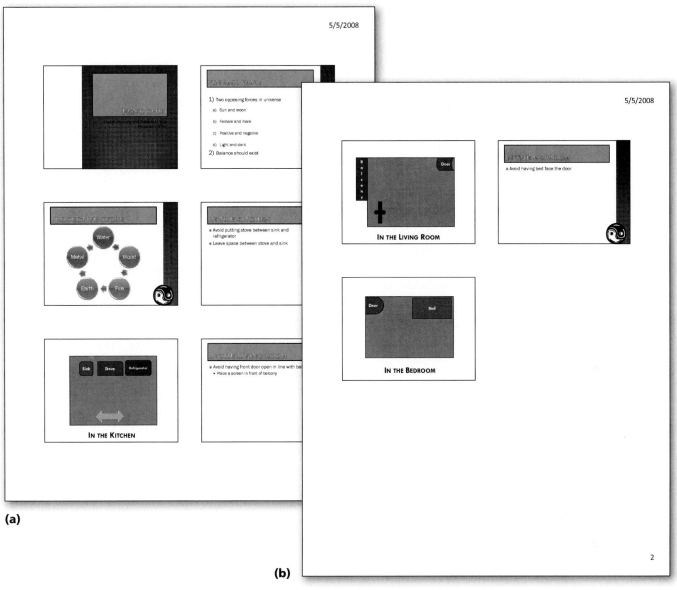

Figure 6–79

② Type your name as the Author property and your course and section as the Subject properties.

③ Type feng shui, chi, Productive Cycle as the Keywords property.

④ Close the Document Information Panel.

⑤ Click the Save button to overwrite the previous Revised Feng Shui file on the USB flash drive.

To Quit PowerPoint

This project is complete. The following steps quit PowerPoint.

1 Click the Close button on the right side of the title bar to quit PowerPoint; or if you have multiple PowerPoint documents open, click the Office Button and then click the Exit PowerPoint button on the Office Button menu to close all open documents and quit PowerPoint.

2 If necessary, click the No button in the Microsoft Office PowerPoint dialog box so that any changes you have made are not saved.

Chapter Summary

In this chapter you have learned how to format a slide master with a font theme, background, Quick Style, background graphic, and new placeholder. You also changed bullet characters to a numbered list, inserted slides from another presentation, animated a SmartArt graphic, added entrance effects, and created motion paths. The items listed below include all the new PowerPoint skills you have learned in this chapter.

1. Display the Slide Master (PPT 382)
2. Apply Slide and Font Themes to a Slide Master (PPT 383)
3. Format a Slide Master Background and Apply a Quick Style (PPT 387)
4. Add a Background Graphic to a Slide Master (PPT 389)
5. Insert a Placeholder into Slide Layouts (PPT 391)
6. Add and Format Placeholder Text (PPT 392)
7. Copy a Placeholder to the Slide Master (PPT 394)
8. Close Master View (PPT 396)
9. Change a First-Level Bullet Character to a Number (PPT 397)
10. Change a Second-Level Bullet Character to a Number (PPT 398)
11. Format a First-Level Numbered List (PPT 399)
12. Format a Second-Level Numbered List (PPT 401)
13. Change the Second-Level Paragraph Line Spacing (PPT 401)
14. Align Text in a Content Placeholder (PPT 402)
15. Insert a Slide into a Presentation (PPT 404)
16. Insert the Remaining Slides into an Original Presentation (PPT 408)
17. Animate a Bulleted List (PPT 409)
18. Change Animation Speed and Grouping (PPT 411)
19. Dim Text after Animation (PPT 414)
20. Animate and Dim Text on the Remaining Text Slides (PPT 415)
21. Animate a SmartArt Graphic (PPT 418)
22. Delete a Slide (PPT 419)
23. Animate a Shape Using a Motion Path (PPT 420)
24. Adjust a Motion Path (PPT 422)
25. Draw a Custom Motion Path (PPT 427)
26. Create a Self-Running Presentation (PPT 429)

 If you have a SAM user profile, you may have access to hands-on instruction, practice, and assessment. Log in to your SAM account (http://sam2007.course.com) to launch any assigned training activities or exams that relate to the skills covered in this chapter.

Learn It Online

Test your knowledge of chapter content and key terms.

Instructions: To complete the Learn It Online exercises, start your browser, click the Address bar, and then enter the Web address `scsite.com/ppt2007/learn`. When the Office 2007 Learn It Online page is displayed, click the link for the exercise you want to complete and then read the instructions.

Chapter Reinforcement TF, MC, and SA
A series of true/false, multiple choice, and short answer questions that test your knowledge of the chapter content.

Flash Cards
An interactive learning environment where you identify chapter key terms associated with displayed definitions.

Practice Test
A series of multiple choice questions that test your knowledge of chapter content and key terms.

Who Wants To Be a Computer Genius?
An interactive game that challenges your knowledge of chapter content in the style of a television quiz show.

Wheel of Terms
An interactive game that challenges your knowledge of chapter key terms in the style of the television show *Wheel of Fortune*.

Crossword Puzzle Challenge
A crossword puzzle that challenges your knowledge of key terms presented in the chapter.

Apply Your Knowledge

Reinforce the skills and apply the concepts you learned in this chapter.

Formatting a Slide Master and Applying Entrance and Emphasis Effects
Instructions: Start PowerPoint. Open the presentation, Apply 6-1 Everglades, from the Data Files for Students. See the inside back cover of this book for instructions on downloading the Data Files for Students, or contact your instructor for more information about accessing required files.

The four slides in the presentation present information about endangered wildlife found in the Everglades. The document you open is an unformatted presentation. You are to display the slide master and then apply slide and font themes, format a background, and apply a Quick Style, so the slides look like Figure 6–80.

Perform the following tasks:
1. Display the Slide Master tab and then display the Two Content Layout slide master. Click the Insert Placeholder button in the Master Layout group and insert a text placeholder above the date, footer, and page number placeholders at the bottom of the slide.

2. Type `Everglades National Park` in this new placeholder, change the font to Baskerville Old Face (or a similar font), change the font size to 24, and then change the font color to Green. Click the Bullets button arrow and then click None to remove the bullet. Align the text in the middle of the placeholder and then center the text.

3. Add the Technic document theme and then change the presentation theme colors to Paper and the theme font to Equity. Exit Master view.

4. Apply the Ease In Entrance effect to the title text on each slide. Change the Start animation from On Click to After Previous and the Speed to Slow. On Slide 1, add the Contrasting Color emphasis effect, change the Start animation to After Previous, and change the Speed to Very Slow.

Continued >

Apply Your Knowledge *continued*

5. Apply the Split Entrance effect to the bulleted lists on Slides 2, 3, and 4. Change the Start animation from On Click to After Previous and the Speed to Slow. Dim the text after animation.

6. Add the Shape Diamond wipe transition (row 5, column 6) to all slides and change the transition speed to Slow.

7. Set the slide timings to 10 seconds for Slide 1 and 15 seconds for the other three slides. Create a self-running presentation to browse at a kiosk. Run the show to check the timings, effects, and transitions.

8. Change the document properties, as specified by your instructor. Save the presentation using the file name, Apply 6-1 Formatted Everglades. Submit the revised document in the format specified by your instructor.

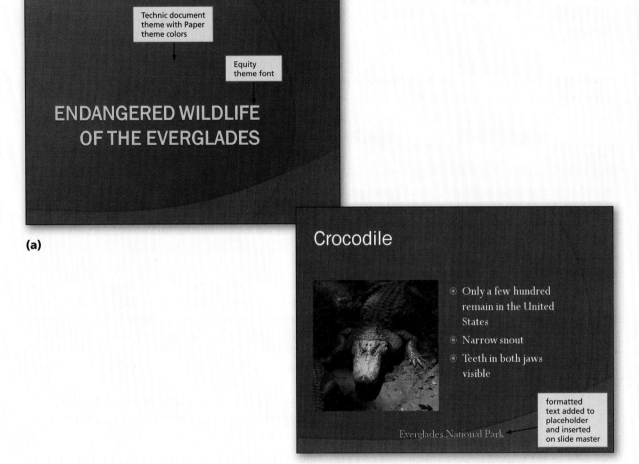

(a)

(b)

Figure 6–80

(c)

(d)

Figure 6–80 (continued)

Extend Your Knowledge

Extend the skills you learned in this chapter and experiment with new skills. You may need to use Help to complete the assignment.

Inserting a Placeholder and Aligning Text

Instructions: Start PowerPoint. Open the presentation, Extend 6-1 Census, from the Data Files for Students. See the inside back cover of this book for instructions on downloading the Data Files for Students, or contact your instructor for more information about accessing required files.

You will insert a placeholder on the left side of the slide and then add text, change the alignment and orientation of the text boxes on the chart bars, and change the animation effect and speed (Figure 6–81).

Perform the following tasks:

1. Display the Slide Master tab and then click the Insert Placeholder button in the Master Layout group. Insert a text placeholder beside the title and text placeholder on the left side of the slide.

2. Select the new placeholder, delete all the default text in this placeholder, type U.S. Census, and then drag the bottom sizing handle down to align with the bottom of the text placeholder. Display the Home tab, click the Text Direction button, and then change the text direction to Stacked. Change the font, the font size, and the font color. Change the text alignment.

Continued >

Extend Your Knowledge *continued*

3. Exit Master view. Change the text direction for each percent label in the 1970, 1980, 1990, and 2000 bars to Stacked and then reduce the font size.

4. Change the Entrance effect for each of the bars from Blinds to another appropriate effect and change the Start animation to After Previous. Select a speed other than Very Fast.

5. Add a background style. Insert your name in a footer along with the date and time updated automatically.

6. Change the document properties, as specified by your instructor. Save the presentation using the file name, Extend 6-1 Revised Census.

7. Submit the revised document in the format specified by your instructor.

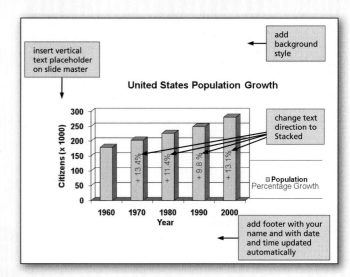

Figure 6–81

Make It Right

Analyze a presentation and correct all errors and/or improve the design.

Formatting a Slide Master Background

Instructions: Start PowerPoint. Open the presentation, Make It Right 6-1 Tents, from the Data Files for Students. See the inside back cover of this book for instructions on downloading the Data Files for Students, or contact your instructor for more information about accessing required files.

The presentation has unsuitable entrance effects applied, small clips, and inconsistent numbering. Correct the formatting problems and errors in the presentation while keeping in mind the guidelines presented in this chapter.

Perform the following tasks:

1. Display the Trek Slide Master. Insert the Tent picture from your Data Files for Students into the slide master, size it, and then position it in the upper-right corner. Insert your name in a footer on all slides.

2. Use the same numbering format on Slides 2, 3, and 4 for the first- and second-level numbered lists.

3. Change the font theme to a theme other than Trek, shown in Figure 6–82.

4. Increase the size of the clips on Slides 2, 3, and 4 so they display prominently on the slides. Insert the Tent picture on Slide 1 and increase its size. Change the entrance effects on the clips on Slides 2, 3, and 4 to one effect in the Moderate category and decrease the speed from Fast.

5. On Slide 2, change the line spacing from 1.0 to another spacing that fits the content placeholder. Also, dim the bulleted list paragraphs after each one is displayed.

6. Change the slide transitions to a fade or dissolve.

7. Set the timings for Slide 1 to 10 seconds and for Slides 2, 3, and 4 to 5 seconds. Create a self-running presentation to browse at a kiosk. Run the show to check the timings, effects, and transitions.

8. Use the spell checker to help correct the misspellings.

9. Change the document properties, as specified by your instructor. Save the presentation using the file name, Make It Right 6-1 Revised Tents.

10. Submit the revised document in the format specified by your instructor.

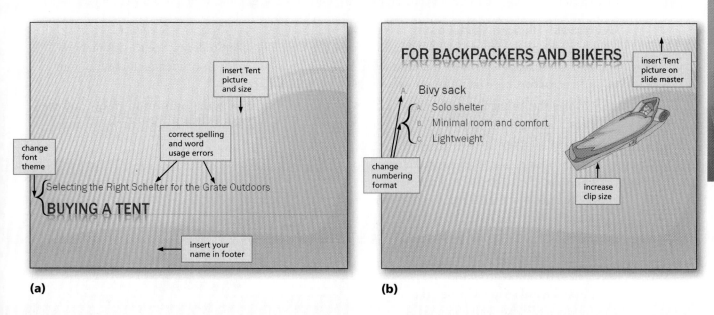

(a)   (b)

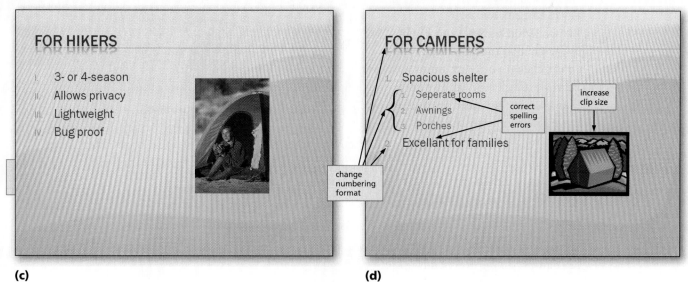

(c)   (d)

Figure 6–82

In the Lab

Design and/or create a presentation using the guidelines, concepts, and skills presented in this chapter. Labs 1, 2, and 3 are listed in order of increasing difficulty.

Lab 1: Removing, Changing, and Adding Animations

Problem: Abraham Maslow attempted to explain the factors that dictate human behavior. You are studying Maslow's Hierarcy of Needs in your Psychology 101 class and want to develop an animated graphic showing this concept. You create a presentation, which is on your Data Files for Students, and then decide to remove, change, and add animations present in the graphic, which is shown in Figure 6–83.

Instructions: Perform the following tasks:

1. Open the presentation, Lab 6-1 Maslow, from the Data Files for Students. See the inside back cover of this book for instructions on downloading the Data Files for Students, or contact your instructor for more information about accessing required files.

2. Display the Animations tab, click the Custom Animation button in the Animation group, and then click Rectangle 4: Maslow's Hierarchy of Needs in the Animation Order list. Click the Change button to display the Change menu.

3. Point to Emphasis, click More Effects to display the Change Emphasis Effect dialog box, and then select Color Wave in the Subtle category. Change the Start animation from On Click to After Previous and the Speed to Fast.

4. Delete the effect from the Physiological shape. Change the entrance effects for the Safety, Love, Esteem, and Self-Actualization shapes from Fly In to Descend in the Moderate category, change the Start animation from On Click to With Previous, and then change the Speed to Medium for these four hierarchy shapes.

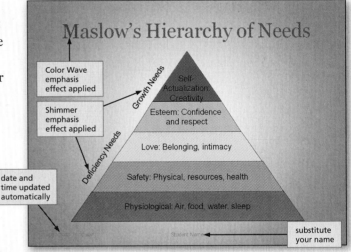

Figure 6–83

5. Add the Shimmer Emphasis Effect in the Moderate category to the two text boxes: Deficiency Needs and Growth Needs. Change the Start animation for both text boxes from On Click to With Previous, and then change the Speed to Slow.

6. Add the Style 9 background style.

7. Insert your name in a footer along with the date and time updated automatically.

8. Change the document properties, as specified by your instructor. Save the presentation using the file name, Lab 6-1 Revised Maslow.

9. Submit the revised document in the format specified by your instructor.

In the Lab

Lab 2: Formatting a Slide Master, Inserting a Slide, Formatting a Numbered List, and Changing SmartArt Animation

Problem: The sources of today's stressors likely come from external factors in our lives and internal reactions while under duress. If we do not release the tension, our bodies react with troubled sleep, back and neck pain, and other health-related problems. You have decided to create the PowerPoint presentation shown in Figures 6-84a through 6-84d to show in your Health 101 class, where you are studying how stress affects our lives.

Instructions: Perform the following tasks:

1. Open the presentation, Lab 6-2 Stress Awareness, from the Data Files for Students. See the inside back cover of this book for instructions on downloading the Data Files for Students, or contact your instructor for more information about accessing required files.

2. Apply the Metro document theme. Display the Slide Master tab and then insert the Stress Photo from the Data Files for Students. Size the photo so that the height is 2" and the width is 1.39". Drag the photo to the upper-right corner of the Metro Slide Master. Copy the resized Stress Photo to the upper-right corner of the Comparison and the Title and Content layouts.

3. Change the presentation theme colors to Solstice. Create a new Theme Font named Stress using Century Gothic for the heading font and Verdana for the body font. Add your name as the Footer text. Close Master view.

4. On Slide 2, change the three bullet characters in each placeholder to the 1. 2. 3. numbering format. Change the numbering color to Red and the size to 100% of text. Change the line spacing to 2.0. Apply the Fade Entrance animation and have the text display All At Once. Dim the text after animation. Move the two pictures to the locations shown in Figure 6–84b.

5. On Slide 3, convert the bulleted list to the Basic Matrix SmartArt style (column 1 in the Matrix category) and apply the Colorful Range – Accent Colors 4 to 5 (column 4 in the Colorful category). Apply the Fade Entrance animation and have the squares display One by one.

6. Delete Slide 4. Insert the one slide in the Stress Graphic file from the Data Files for Students. Do not keep the source formatting. Change the colors to the Colorful Range – Accent Colors 4 to 5.

7. On Slide 1, add the Arc Right motion path to the picture. Change the animation to With Previous and the speed to Slow. Adjust the motion path so that the stopping point is in the area between the title text and the bottom of the slide.

8. On Slide 2, add the Box Entrance effect to both pictures. Change the animation to With Previous, the direction to Out, and the speed to Medium.

9. Apply the Box Out transition (row 3, column 3 in the Wipes category) to all slides. Change the speed to Medium. Check the spelling and correct any errors.

10. Change the document properties, as specified by your instructor. Save the presentation using the file name, Lab 6-2 Revised Stress.

11. Submit the revised document in the format specified by your instructor.

Continued >

In the Lab *continued*

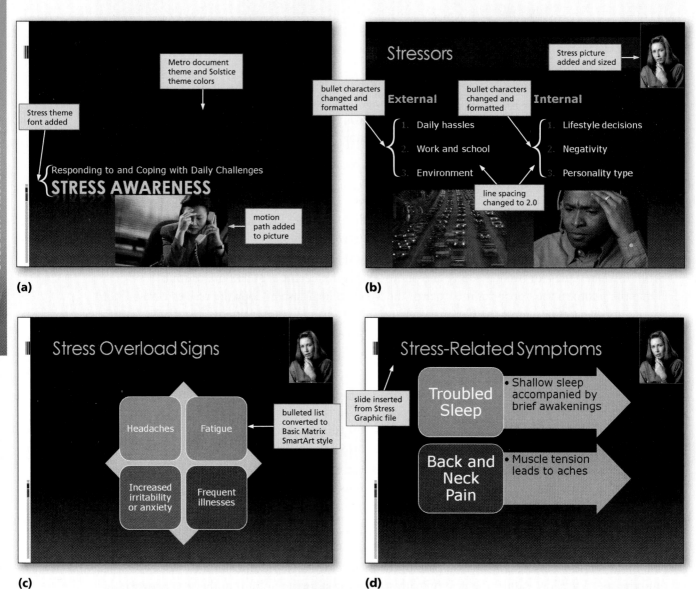

Figure 6–84

In the Lab

Lab 3: Creating a Presentation with Animation

Problem: Credit card debt has more than doubled among college students. More than 83 percent own at least one credit card, and their average balance is approximately $2,300. You survey the students in your Economics 101 class to gather information about their credit card use and then create the presentation in Figure 6–85. Slide 1 contains a resized photograph with a motion path, and Slides 2 and 3 contain SmartArt graphics with animations.

Instructions: Perform the following tasks:

1. Create a new presentation using the Module document theme. Change the presentation theme colors to Foundry and the theme font to Solstice. Insert the Canvas texture (row 1, column 2 in the Texture gallery) to format the background on all slides. Using Figure 6–85, type the Slide 1 title and subtitle text and the Slides 2 and 3 title text. Apply the Title and Content layout to Slides 2 and 3.

2. On Slide 1, insert the Credit Hands picture from your Data Files for Students and size the picture to 60%. Recolor the picture by applying the Sepia variation (column 2 in the Color Modes area). Add a 10 Point Soft Edges picture effect and then position the picture as shown in Figure 6–85a.

3. On Slide 2, insert the Linear Venn SmartArt graphic (row 8, column 1 in the Relationship gallery). Using Figure 6–85b, type the four lines of text in the graphic. Apply the Inset SmartArt Style (row 1, column 2 in the 3-D category) and then change the color to Colorful – Accent Colors (column 1 in the Colorful category).

4. On Slide 3, insert the Vertical Box List SmartArt graphic (row 1, column 4 in the List gallery). Using Figure 6–85c, type the three lines of text in the graphic. Apply the Metallic Scene SmartArt Style (row 2, column 2 in the 3-D category) and then change the color to Colorful – Accent Colors (column 1 in the Colorful category).

5. On Slide 1, animate the Credit Hands picture by drawing a custom motion path. To draw the path, select the picture, display the Custom Path menu, and then click Scribble. Draw the motion path shown in Figure 6–85a so that the picture moves diagonally downward to the bottom-middle edge of the slide and then diagonally upward to the top-left corner of the slide. Change the Start animation to With Previous and the Speed to Slow.

6. On Slide 2, apply the Fade 'One by one' Entrance animation to the SmartArt graphic. Change the Start animation to With Previous and the speed to Very Slow. Add a Spin Emphasis animation, change the Start animation to After Previous, the Amount to Counterclockwise, and the Speed to Very Slow.

7. On Slide 3, add the Peek In Entrance effect to the SmartArt graphic. Change the Start animation to With Previous, the Direction to From Right, and the speed to Medium. Click the Content Placeholder 5 arrow in the Custom Animation list, click Effect Options, and then click the SmartArt Animation tab in the Peek In dialog box. Click the Group graphic arrow and then click 'One by one'.

8. Set the timings for Slide 1 to 5 seconds and for Slides 2 and 3 to 10 seconds. Create a self-running presentation to browse at a kiosk. Run the show to check the timings, effects, and transitions.

9. Insert the slide number and your name in Slides 2 and 3. Apply the Split Vertical Out transition (row 4, column 6 in the Wipes category) to all slides. Change the speed to Slow. Check the spelling and correct any errors.

10. Click the Slide Sorter view button, view the slides for consistency, and then click the Normal view button. Run the slide show.

11. Change the document properties, as specified by your instructor. Save the presentation using the file name, Lab 6-3 Student Credit.

12. Submit the revised document in the format specified by your instructor.

Continued >

In the Lab *continued*

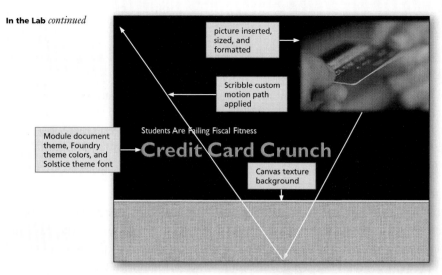

Figure 6–85 (a)

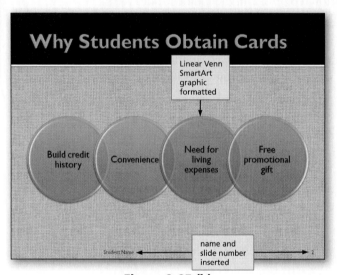

Figure 6–85 (b)

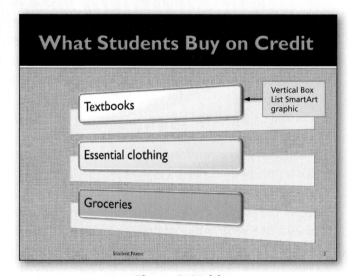

Figure 6–85 (c)

Cases and Places

Apply your creative thinking and problem solving skills to design and implement a solution.

● EASIER   ●● MORE DIFFICULT

Note: Remember to use the 7 × 7 rule as you design the presentations: a maximum of seven words on a line and a maximum of seven lines on one slide.

● 1: Design and Create a Health and Wellness Institute Presentation

Your local fitness center is upgrading its services and programs. In turn, it is changing its name from "health club" to "health and wellness institute." New services are listed in Table 6–2.

New programs are listed in Table 6–3.

Create a self-running presentation announcing the name change. Include slides with SmartArt graphics listing the services and programs. Animate the text and the graphics. Apply at least three objectives found at the beginning of this chapter to develop the presentation. Apply slide transitions and a footer with your name and the page number on all slides. Be sure to check spelling.

Table 6–2 Health and Wellness Institute Services
Steam room and saunas
Massage therapy
Aquatic therapy
Café
Pro shop
Playroom
Conference / Meeting rooms

Table 6–3 Health and Wellness Institute Fitness Programs
Sports specific training
Personal training
Walking / running club
Children's activities
Aquatics
Yoga and Pilates
Self defense

• 2: Design and Create a Telemarketing Scams Presentation

Criminals steal money in a variety of ways, and one of the more profitable is through telemarketing schemes. Law enforcement professionals are reporting an increase in complaints about illegal telephone money solicitations. Con artists claiming to represent charities and law enforcement agencies prey upon unsuspecting citizens by stealing credit card numbers from unsuspecting citizens. Common scams are listed in Table 6–4.

People hearing one of the phrases in Table 6–5 should hang up immediately.

The Better Business Bureau Web site (http://bbb.org) and the Federal Trade Commission Web site (http://ftc.gov) include details about identifying and reporting these scams. Visit these sites and review the facts presented. Create a presentation using this information. Begin by displaying the slide master and applying slide and font themes. Format the slide master background and apply a Quick Style. Include one text slide with a bulleted list and two slides with SmartArt graphics listing the scams and pressure phrases. Animate the text and the graphics. Apply at least three objectives found at the beginning of this chapter to develop the presentation. Apply slide transitions and a footer with your name and the page number on all slides. Be sure to check spelling.

Table 6–4 Telemarketing Scams
Prizes / Sweepstakes
Free or discounted travel
Investments with high returns
Telephone slamming
Telephone cramming
Fake charities

Table 6–5 Pressure Phrases
"You have just won…"
"Congratulations! You have won the grand prize…"
"You have been specially selected…"
"You will receive a bonus if you sign up today…."

•• 3: Design and Create a Carbon Monoxide Presentation

Several thousand people suffer accidental carbon monoxide (CO) poisoning each year, and at least 200 of these people die from inhaling this gas. This colorless, odorless, and tasteless gas is called the "silent killer." Furnaces, ovens, clothes dryers, water heaters, and other fuel-burning appliances produce it, and so do fireplaces, barbeque grills, and wood-burning stoves. When the CO is not ventilated properly, home occupants can suffer flu-related symptoms (dizziness, severe headache, nausea, fatigue, and disorientation). CO detectors can help prevent many of these poisonings. Your local fire department chief has asked you to prepare a presentation about CO poisoning. He would like you to include an animated graphic with a safety checklist to help residents protect their homes. Review information about carbon monoxide on the Consumer Product Safety Commission Web site (http://cpsc.gov) and then develop the presentation for the fire chief. Included animated numbered lists with text aligned in the content placeholders. Apply at least three objectives found at the beginning of this chapter to develop the presentation.

Continued >

Cases and Places *continued*

•• 4: Design and Create a U.S. Senate Presentation

Make It Personal

The U.S. Senate Web site (www.senate.gov) has a wealth of information about Senators' biographies, legislation, and the Constitution. Also included is a chart showing the Senate organization. Review the information and then create a presentation about this governmental body. Include an animated chart displaying aspects of this latest Senate organization chart. Also include two slides featuring the two Senators from the state in which you reside; these two slides should have animated numbered lists with text aligned in the content placeholders and also hyperlinks to your Senators' Web sites. Apply slide transitions and a footer with your name and the slide number on all slides. Be sure to check spelling.

•• 5: Design and Create a Digital Camera Presentation

Working Together

Digital cameras offer convenience and fun for amateur and professional photographers alike. Buying this type of camera can be difficult, however, for people who are unfamiliar with the product. Have each member of your team call or visit a local electronics or camera store or conduct online research and gather information about digital single-lens reflex (SLR), slim, and long zoom cameras. Find details about megapixels, optical and digital zoom, scene modes, image stabilization, and storage media. After coordinating the data, create a self-running presentation with animated bulleted lists and pictures. Include an animated SmartArt graphic that can be used as a buying guide. Apply slide and font themes to the slide master, add a background graphic, and copy a placeholder. As a group, critique each slide. Submit your assignment in the format specified by your instructor.

Online Feature

Importing Files from the Microsoft Office Online Web Site

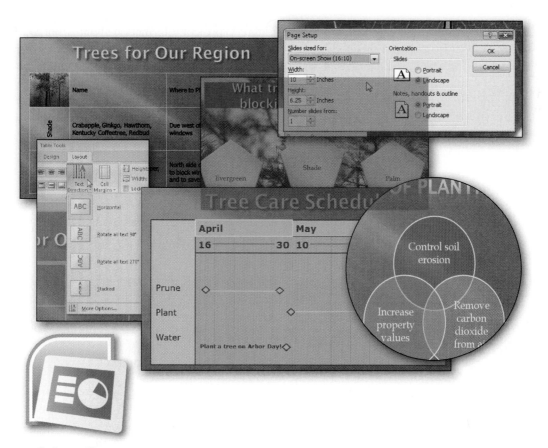

Objectives

You will have mastered the material in this feature when you can:

- Locate and download templates from the Microsoft Office Online Web site
- Save slides as images
- Add images to tables
- Select presentation resolution
- Change presentation orientation
- Write VBA code to create a unique presentation

Online Feature Introduction

The document themes included in Microsoft Office PowerPoint 2007 are visually appealing and present a wide variety of styles and appearances. To give your presentation a unique look, you can search the Microsoft Office Online Web site for additional themes and then download these files. This Web site also includes individual slides that fit a particular purpose, such as a monthly calendar, party invitations, and schedules.

You can customize and extend the capabilities of PowerPoint by using **Visual Basic for Applications** (**VBA**). This powerful programming language allows you to simplify tasks that you repeat frequently, such as updating a PowerPoint presentation with a daily calendar of campus events or featuring the athlete of the week.

Project — Presentation with Imported Templates and VBA

The five slides in the presentation (Figure 1) present information about Arbor Day. J. Sterling Morton started this holiday in 1872 as a day to plant a tree in support of the environment and as a way to emphasize the natural benefits of trees. The presentation has three slides that were imported as templates from the Microsoft Office Online Web site: relationship, hierarchy, and workflow. These templates are modified and then merged with a presentation with a title slide and table. The entire presentation resolution is changed to display favorably on wide-screen monitors, and two slides are saved as images so they easily can be reused in other programs and distributed as a handout.

Another aspect of this chapter is to add VBA code to the presentation so that viewers can be tested on their retention of material presented in the slide show. The inclusion of this programming introduces Visual Basic principles and demonstrates PowerPoint's versatility. One slide displays a question and prompts a user to select one of three answers. A message box displays feedback on whether this choice is correct.

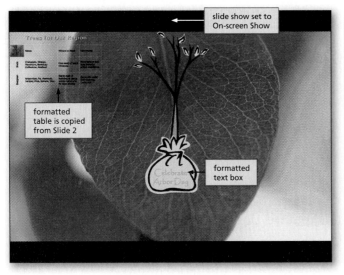

(a)

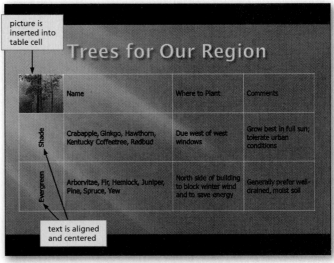

(b)

Figure 1 *(continued)*

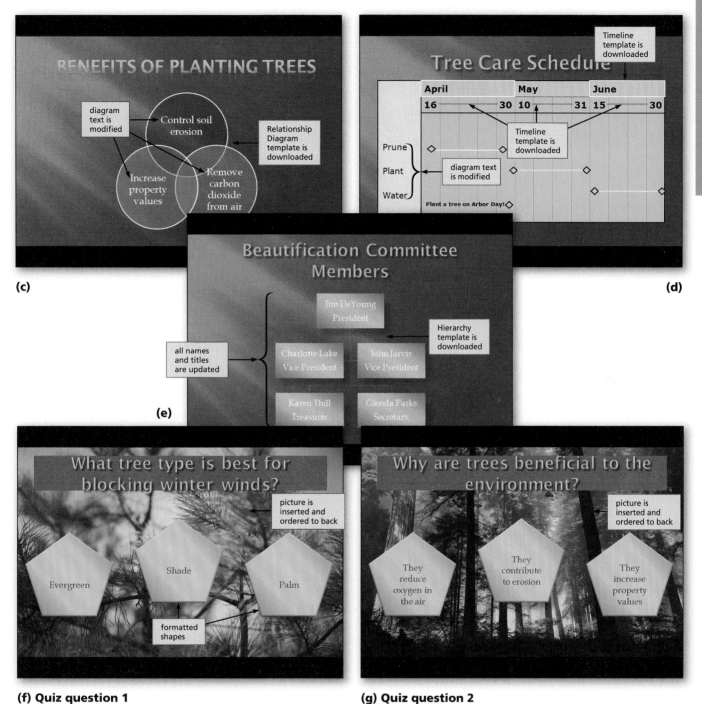

(c)

(d)

(e)

(f) **Quiz question 1**

(g) **Quiz question 2**

Figure 1

Overview

As you read through this feature, you will learn how to create the presentation shown in Figure 1 by performing these general tasks:

- Download SmartArt templates.
- Insert and modify shapes and text boxes.
- Order illustrations and other content.
- Modify tables.
- Write a VBA application.

Plan
Ahead

General Project Guidelines

When creating a PowerPoint presentation, the actions you perform and decisions you make will affect the appearance and characteristics of the finished document. As you create a presentation with templates, such as the project shown in Figure 1, you should follow these general guidelines:

1. **Use a hierarchy chart to depict relationships.** A hierarchy chart is a good tool to help visualize how one concept relates to another. This graphic often is used to show corporate reporting lines and a family's genealogy.

2. **Determine the screen show ratio.** Consider where the presentation will be shown and the type of hardware that will be available. Wide-screen displays are gaining acceptance in the home office and corporate world, but their dimensions present design challenges for the PowerPoint developer.

3. **Desk check the application code before entering it into the Visual Basic Editor.** You can maximize your work time by stepping through your lines of code before you type these instructions on your computer. Viewing the program's structure and working through the instructions helps find errors before they arise during the program execution.

When necessary, more specific details concerning the above guidelines are presented at appropriate points in the feature. The feature also will identify the actions you perform and decisions you make regarding these guidelines during the creation of the presentation shown in Figure 1.

To Start PowerPoint, Open a Presentation, and Rename the Presentation

If you are using a computer to step through the project in this feature and you want your screens to match the figures in this book, you should change your computer's resolution to 1024 × 768. For information about how to change a computer's resolution, read Appendix E. The following steps start PowerPoint and open a presentation.

1 Start PowerPoint and then open the presentation, Arbor Day, from the Data Files for Students.

2 Maximize the PowerPoint window, if necessary.

3 Save the presentation as Arbor Day Revised.

4 Save the document on your USB flash drive.

BTW

Requesting Templates
Microsoft changes the templates based on requests from PowerPoint users and how frequently the templates are downloaded.

Downloading Templates from the Microsoft Office Online Web Site

Designers at Microsoft and other companies have created a wide variety of templates for PowerPoint that are stored on the Microsoft Office Online Web site. They are grouped in useful categories, including Award certificates, Calendars, Diagrams, Invitations, and Schedules. Some of these categories are subdivided into organized groupings. For example, the Presentations category is subdivided into Academic, Business, Design, Healthcare, and other groups. If you cannot locate the templates used in this feature, your instructor can provide the files needed to complete this presentation.

To Locate and Download a Relationship Diagram Template

One template you will use in your presentation is a Relationship diagram, which is a SmartArt graphic. You will locate this template, preview the design, and then **download**, or copy, it to your USB flash drive. Later you will insert it into your Arbor Day Revised presentation. To locate templates, you can type a keyword in the search text box or select a category in the left pane of the New Presentation dialog box. The following steps locate and download the Relationship diagram.

1

• Click the Office Button and then click New to display the New Presentation dialog box.

Q&A Why do I see slides displaying in the Recently Used Templates area of my screen?

Figure 2 does not show any templates, but some may display on your screen if someone previously downloaded templates. They remain in this area until you choose to delete them.

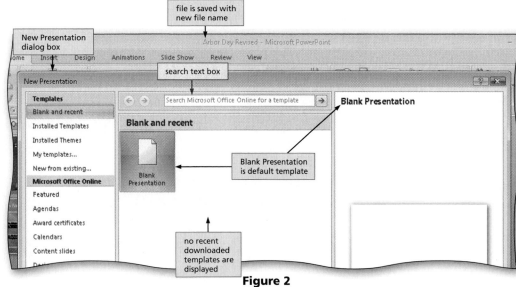

Figure 2

2

• Type relationship in the search text box and then click the Start searching button to search for and display all templates having the keyword, relationship.

Q&A Can I enter more than one search term in the text box?

Yes. Entering more than one word helps narrow the search results.

• If necessary, click the Relationship diagram thumbnail to display a preview of and information about this diagram (Figure 3).

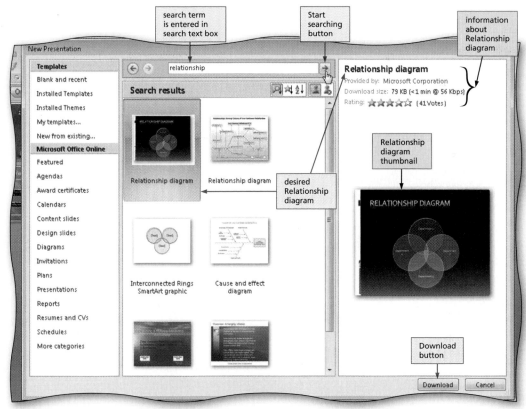

Figure 3

Experiment

• Click various thumbnails in the Search results area to view a larger thumbnail and information about the template.

3

- With the Relationship diagram pictured in Figure 3 selected, click the Download button to download this template.

- If the Microsoft Office Genuine Advantage dialog box is displayed, click the Continue button to download the template.

- Save the Relationship diagram on your USB flash drive with the file name, Tree Relationship (Figure 4).

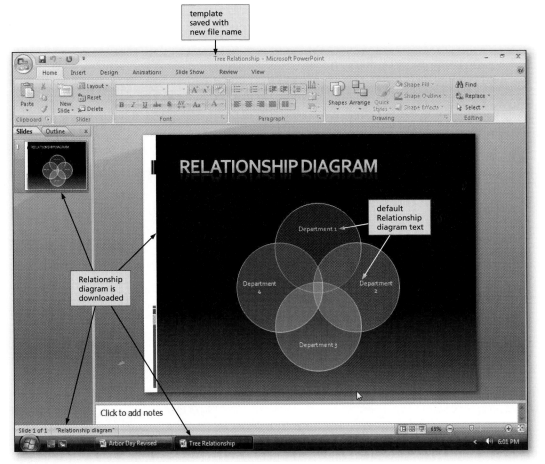

Figure 4

To Locate and Download a Timeline Template

You can increase your audience's understanding of when to prepare for and plant trees by using a timeline. The Microsoft Office Online Web site provides a variety of timelines, many of which are categorized in the Schedules group. The following steps locate and download the Three-month timeline template.

1 Click the Office Button, click New, and then type `timeline` in the search text box in the New Presentation dialog box.

2 Click the Start searching button to search for and display all templates having the keyword, timeline.

3 Click the Three-month timeline thumbnail shown in Figure 5 to select this template (Figure 5).

4 Click the Download button to download this template. If the Microsoft Office Genuine Advantage dialog box is displayed, click the Continue button to download the template.

5 Save the Three-month timeline diagram on your USB flash drive with the file name, Planting Timeline.

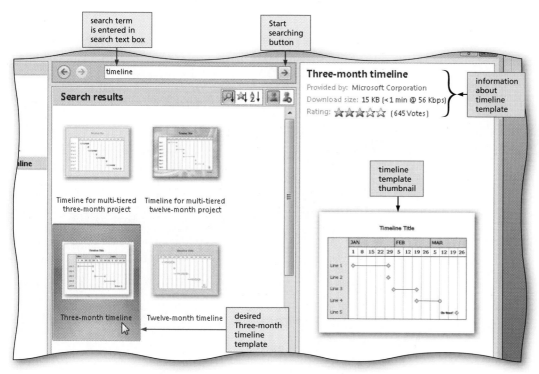

Figure 5

Use a hierarchy chart to depict relationships.

One method of visually showing the structure of people or departments within a organization is to use a **hierarchy chart**. This type of chart, also called an organization chart, depicts various functions or responsibilities as they relate to a company or organization. Hierarchy charts are used in a variety of ways to depict relationships. For example, a company uses a hierarchy chart to describe the relationships between the company's teams. In the engineering and information sciences fields, organization charts often are used to show a process.

Plan
Ahead

To Locate and Download a Hierarchy Template

Your community has a Beautification Committee. One method of displaying the Committee structure is to use a hierarchy chart. The following steps locate and download the Hierarchy diagram template.

1 Display the New Presentation dialog box, type `hierarchy` in the search text box, and then click the Start searching button to search for and display all templates having the keyword, hierarchy.

2 If necessary, click the Hierarchy diagram thumbnail shown in Figure 6 to select this template (Figure 6 on the following page).

3 Click the Download button to download this template. If the Microsoft Office Genuine Advantage dialog box is displayed, click the Continue button to download the template.

4 Save the Hierarchy diagram on your USB flash drive with the file name, Beautification Committee.

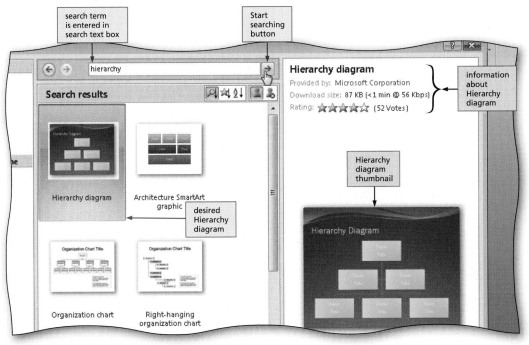

Figure 6

BTW

Deleting Downloaded Templates
If you decide you do not want to use a template you downloaded, you can delete it easily. Right-click a template in the Recently Used Templates area of the New Presentation dialog box and then click Remove template on the shortcut menu. If you want to delete all the templates you downloaded, click 'Remove all recent templates' on the shortcut menu.

Inserting Templates into a Presentation and Modifying Slides

The three downloaded templates are saved on your USB flash drive. You can add them to the Arbor Day Revised presentation and then modify the slide content. To ensure the slides have a consistent look, do not check the Keep source formatting box in the Reuse Slides task pane; the Apex design theme applied to the Arbor Day Revised presentation will then be applied to the newly inserted slides.

To Insert Templates into a Presentation

The three templates you downloaded can be added to the Arbor Day Revised presentation. The following steps insert the templates after Slide 2.

1. Click the Arbor Day Revised button on the Windows Vista taskbar to display this presentation.

2. Display Slide 2. With the Home tab displayed and your USB flash drive connected to one of the computer's USB ports, click the New Slide button arrow and then click Reuse Slides to display the Reuse Slides task pane.

3. Click the Browse button and then click Browse File to display the Browse dialog box. If necessary, double-click UDISK 2.0 (E:) to select the USB flash drive, Drive E in this case, as the device that contains the three templates.

4. Click Tree Relationship in the Browse dialog box to select the file and then click the Open button to display the template in the Reuse Slides dialog box.

5. Click the Tree Relationship preview to insert this slide into the Arbor Day Revised presentation.

6 Repeat Steps 3 through 5 to insert the Planting Timeline and the Beautification Committee templates in the Arbor Day Revised presentation.

7 Click the Close button in the Reuse Slides task pane so that it no longer is displayed (Figure 7).

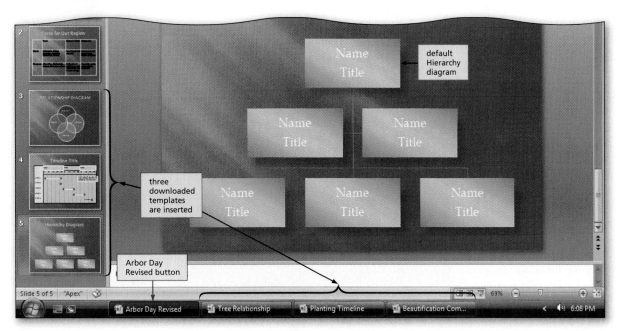

Figure 7

To Set Text Box Margins

The Slide 1 text box appears disconnected from the tree clip. You could reinforce the concept of planting a tree on Arbor Day if you change the margins of this text box and then move the text box on the tan material holding the tree's roots. The following steps set the text box margins.

1

• Display Slide 1, click the text box, and then right-click the text box to display the shortcut menu and the Mini toolbar (Figure 8).

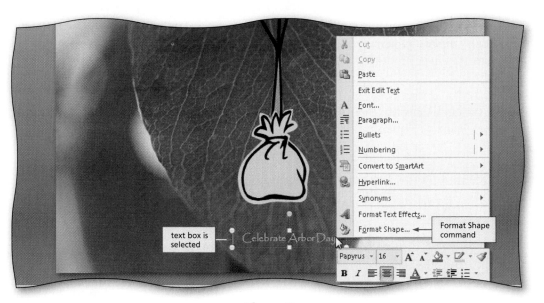

Figure 8

- Click Format Shape on the shortcut menu to display the Format Shape dialog box.

- Click Text Box in the left pane and then click the Left up arrow in the Internal margin area repeatedly until 0.5" is displayed (Figure 9).

Q&A

What are the three Autofit options in the Format Shape dialog box?

By default, PowerPoint changes a shape's size to accommodate text. The three AutoFit options allow you to decide how to use this feature. If you click the Do not Autofit button, automatic resizing is turned off. If you click the 'Shrink text on overflow' button, the font size is reduced to fit within the shape. The 'Reshape shape to fit text' button, which is the default option, increases the size of the shape vertically so that the text fits inside of it.

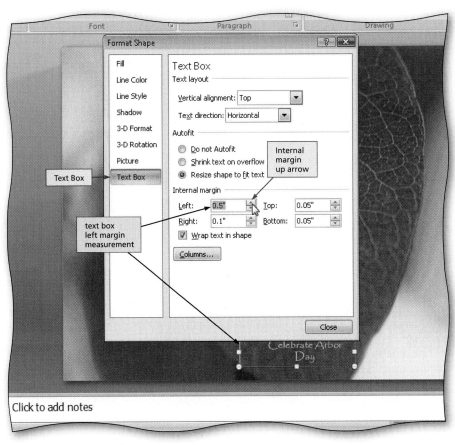

Figure 9

- Click the Right up arrow in the Internal margin area repeatedly until 0.5" is displayed.

- Click the Top down arrow to display a measurement of 0".

- Click the Bottom down arrow to display a measurement of 0" (Figure 10).

- Click the Close button in the Format Shape dialog box.

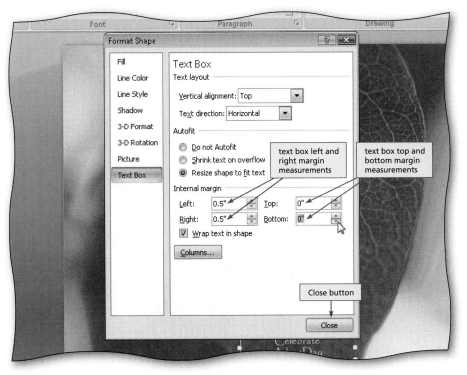

Figure 10

To Order a Text Box on a Slide

The Slide 1 text box now is the proper size to appear with the tree clip. When you drag the text box over the clip, however, it will be positioned behind this clip. You need to change the order of the slide elements so the text box will appear in front of the tree clip. The following steps move the text box and change its order.

 1

- Drag the text box to the center of the tan root ball sack in the tree clip.

- Right-click the root ball to display the shortcut menu and then point to Send to Back to display the Send to Back submenu (Figure 11).

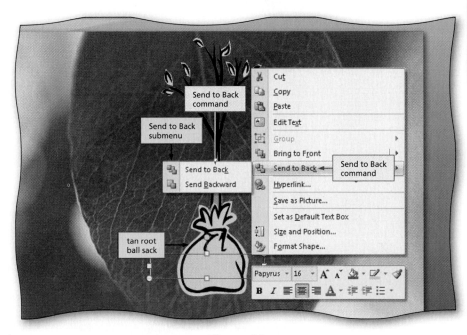

Figure 11

 2

- Click Send to Back in the submenu to display the text box on top of the tan area of the tree clip.

- With the Home tab displayed, select the text box and then click the Shape Outline button in the Drawing group to display the Shape Outline gallery (Figure 12).

3

- Click No Outline to remove the border from the text box.

- If necessary, drag the text box to position it in the center of the tan area.

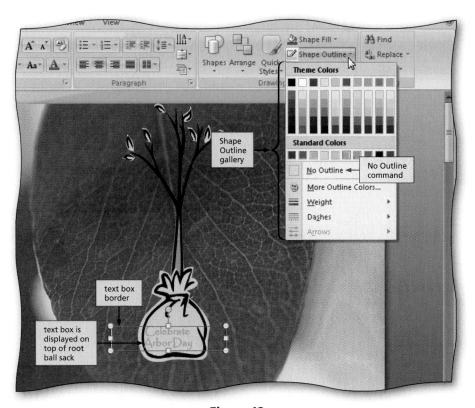

Figure 12

To Change Table Text Alignment

To add visual interest to the table on Slide 2, you change the alignment of each cell. You align table text in a similar manner as centering text in a placeholder. The following steps center the text in each table cell.

1

- Display Slide 2, click a table cell, and then display the Layout tab.

- Click the Select button in the Table group to display the Select menu (Figure 13).

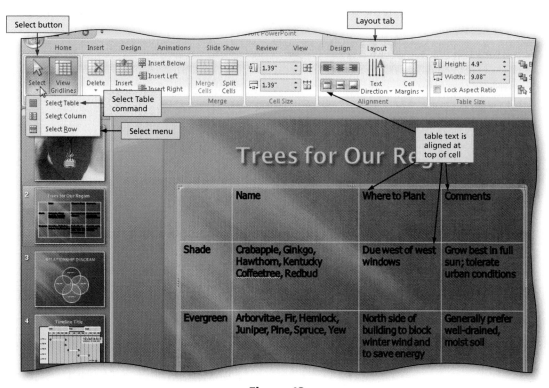

Figure 13

2

- Click Select Table in the Select menu to select the entire table.

- Click the Center Vertically button in the Alignment group to center the text in the middle of each cell in the table (Figure 14).

Q&A Must I center all the table cells, or can I center only specific cells?

You can center as many cells as you deem necessary at one time by selecting one or more cells.

Other Ways

1. Right-click selected cells, click Format Shape on shortcut menu, click Text Box, click Vertical alignment arrow

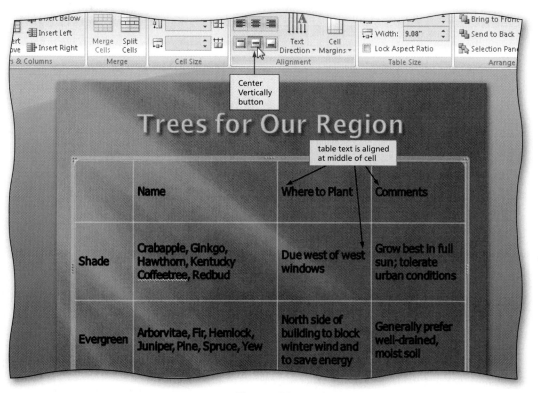

Figure 14

To Change Table Text Orientation

The default orientation of table cells is horizontal. You can change this direction to vertical or stacked, or you can rotate the direction in 90-degree increments. The steps used to align the direction of text in a placeholder are similar to the steps used to align the text in a cell. The following steps rotate the text in two table cells.

1

- With the Layout tab displayed, click the Shade cell and then drag down to select both the Shade and Evergreen table cells.

- Click the Text Direction button in the Alignment group to display the Text Direction gallery (Figure 15).

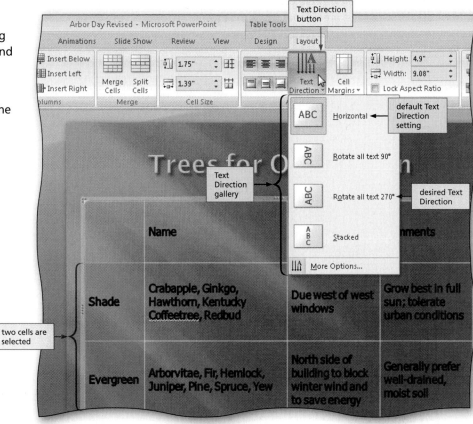

Figure 15

2

- Click 'Rotate all text 270°' to rotate the text in the two cells.

- Click the Center button in the Alignment group to center the Evergreen and Shade text (Figure 16).

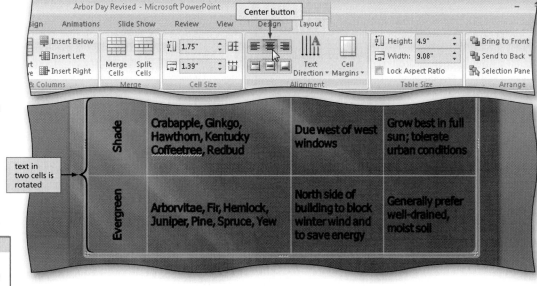

Other Ways

1. Right-click selected cells, click Format Shape on shortcut menu, click Text Box, click Text direction arrow

Figure 16

To Add an Image to a Table

Another table enhancement you can make is to add a picture or clip to a table cell. The following steps add a tree picture to the upper-left table cell.

- Right-click the upper-left table cell to display the shortcut menu and Mini toolbar (Figure 17).

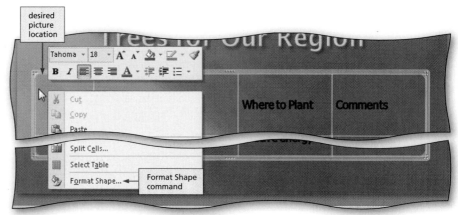

Figure 17

- Click Format Shape to display the Format Shape dialog box and then click Picture or texture fill (Figure 18).

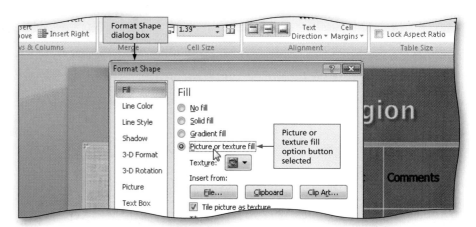

Figure 18

- Click the Insert from File button to display the Insert Picture dialog box.

- Select the Foliage picture on the Data Files for Students and then click the Insert button in the Insert Picture dialog box to insert the picture into the table cell (Figure 19).

- Click the Close button in the Format Shape dialog box.

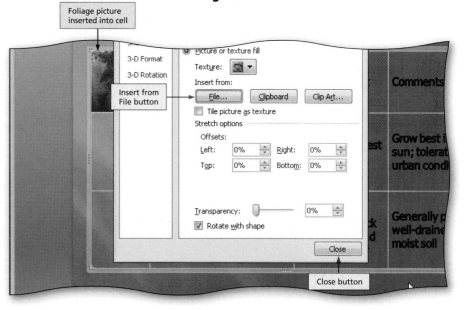

Figure 19

To Enter Text in a Relationship Diagram

The Relationship diagram you downloaded and saved is a SmartArt graphic with default text entered in each of the four circles. You want to change this text to reflect three environmental and social benefits gained by planting trees. If no text is displayed after a bullet in the Text pane, the corresponding shape will not be displayed. The following steps replace the default text in three circles of the Relationship diagram on Slide 3.

1 Display Slide 3 and then click the Relationship diagram to select it and display the Text pane, if necessary, by clicking the Text pane control on the left side of the diagram.

2 Select the Department 1 text in the Text pane and then type `Control soil erosion` in the first bullet line.

3 Select the Department 2 text and then type `Remove carbon dioxide from air` in the second bullet line.

4 Select the Department 3 text and then type `Increase property values` in the third bullet line.

5 Select the Department 4 text and then press the DELETE key to eliminate this shape from the diagram.

6 Select the Relationship Diagram slide title and then type `Benefits of Planting Trees` as the new title text (Figure 20).

BTW

Adjusting AutoRecover Features
PowerPoint creates a recovery file every 10 minutes by default. This feature helps preserve a presentation if a power outage occurs, another program makes your system unstable, or an error occurs in the PowerPoint program. If you want to increase or decrease this length of time, click the Microsoft Office Button and then click the PowerPoint Options button to display the PowerPoint Options dialog box. Click Save in the left pane and then adjust the time in the 'Save AutoRecover information' text box in the Save presentations area.

PowerPoint Online Feature

Other Ways

1. Select text in one shape, type new text

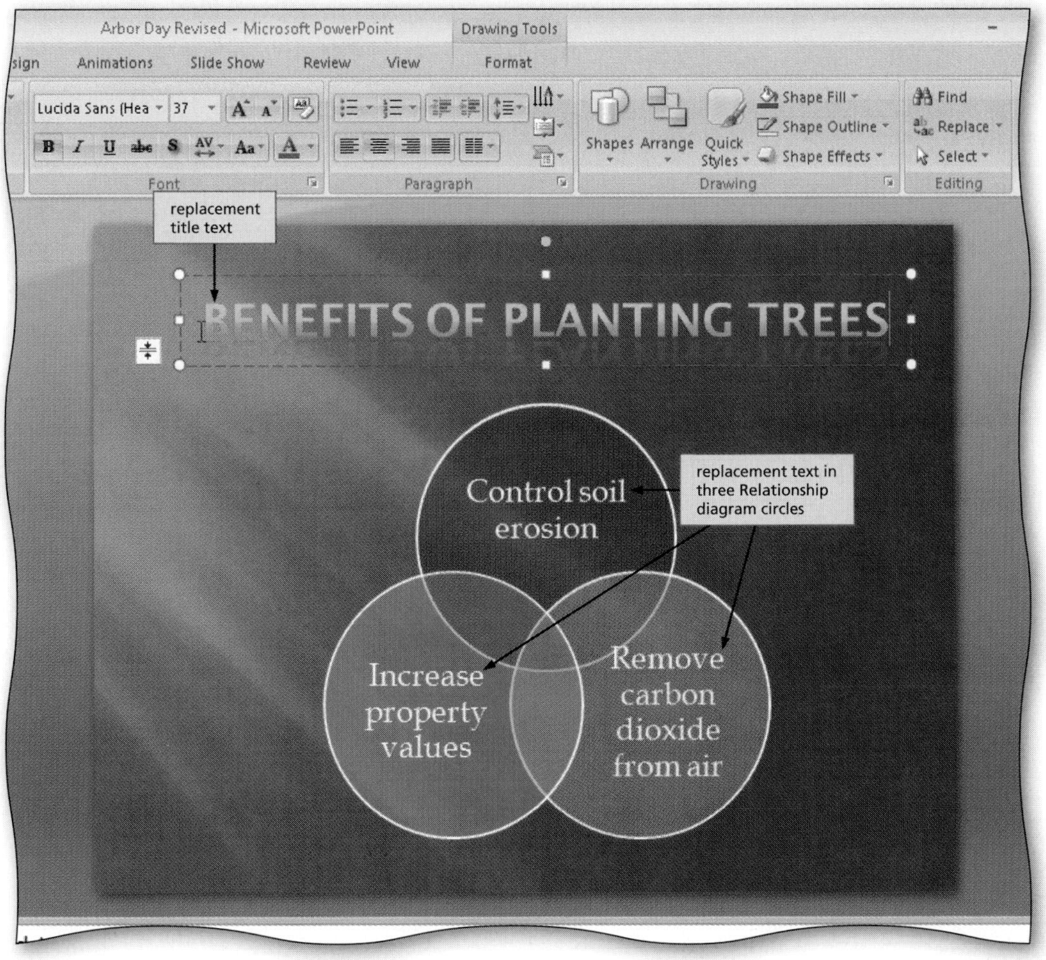

Figure 20

To Zoom a Slide

Slide 5 contains a chart that will display the Beautification Committee members' names and titles. You can decrease or increase the slide size by changing the zoom. When you zoom out, you can view the entire slide and judge its content. When you zoom in, conversely, you can view a small part of the slide and modify the text. The following steps zoom Slide 5.

- Display Slide 5.

 Experiment

- Repeatedly click the Zoom In and Zoom Out button on the status bar and watch the slide size change.

2

- Click the Zoom In button as many times as necessary until the Zoom level button displays 110% on its face (Figure 21).

Q&A Does changing the zoom affect how the slide prints on a handout?

No. The zoom setting changes only how the slide is displayed on the screen.

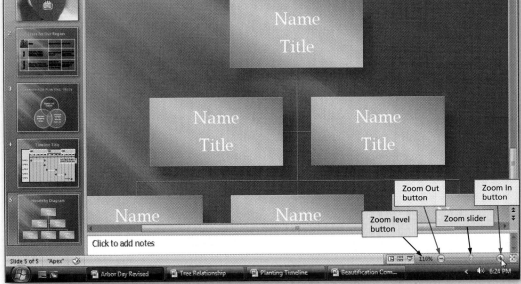

Figure 21

Other Ways

1. Drag Zoom slider on status bar
2. Click Zoom level button on status bar, select desired zoom percent, click OK button
3. Click Zoom button on View tab, select desired zoom percent, click OK button

To Enter Text in a Hierarchy Diagram

The Hierarchy diagram template you downloaded and saved also is a SmartArt graphic. The words Name and Title are the default text entered in each rectangle, and you want to change this text to the Beautification Committee's names and titles, as shown in Figure 22.

As with the Relationship diagram, if no text is displayed after a bullet in the Text pane, the corresponding shape will not be displayed. The following steps replace the default text in the Hierarchy diagram on Slide 5.

1 Click the Hierarchy diagram to select it and display the Text pane.

2 Type Jim DeYoung as the first bulleted Name text and type President as the new Title text.

3 Continue replacing the default text in the Text pane with the names and titles shown in Figure 22.

4 Type Beautification Committee Members as the new Hierarchy Diagram title text (Figure 23).

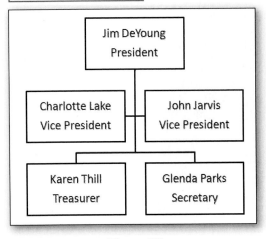

Figure 22

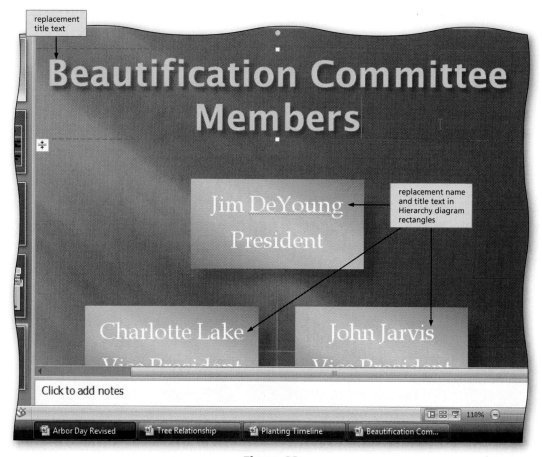

Figure 23

To Modify Timeline Diagram Text

The Timeline diagram template you downloaded and saved is not a SmartArt graphic, so edits will be made directly on this diagram. The modified timeline will show activities that should be performed during the months of April, May, and June. The following steps replace the default text in the Timeline diagram on Slide 4.

- Display Slide 4. Click the Zoom Out button as many times as necessary until the Zoom level button displays 80% on its face.

- Select the Timeline Title slide title and then type Tree Care Schedule as the new title text.

- Select the first column heading, JAN, and then type April as the new column title text (Figure 24).

Figure 24

2

- Type May as the new second column title and June as the new third column title.

- Select the first row title, Line 1, and then type Prune as the new text (Figure 25).

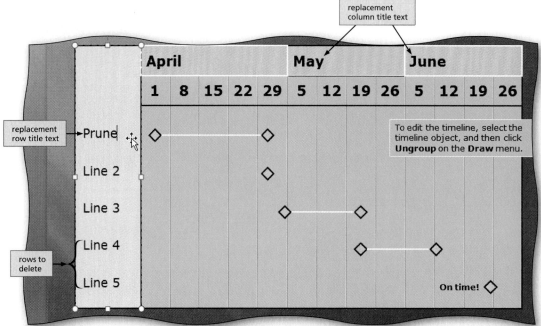

Figure 25

3

- Type Plant as the new second row title and Water as the new third row title.

- Select the Line 4 and Line 5 row titles and then press the DELETE key to delete this text (Figure 26).

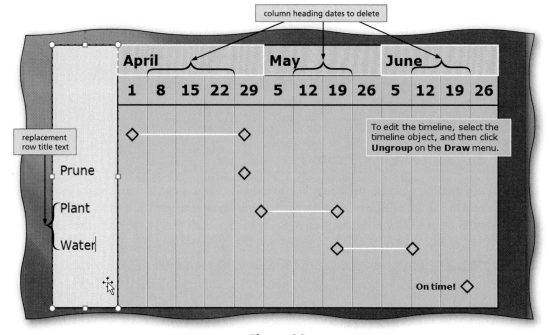

Figure 26

4

- Select the numbers 8, 15, and 22 under the April heading and then press the DELETE key to delete this text.

- Delete the numbers 12 and 19 under the May and June headings (Figure 27).

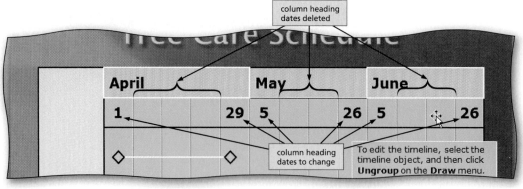

Figure 27

- Change the first April date, 1, to 16 and the second April date, 29, to 30.

- Change the first May date, 5, to 10 and the second May date, 26, to 31.

- Change the first June date, 5, to 15 and the second June date, 26, to 30 (Figure 28).

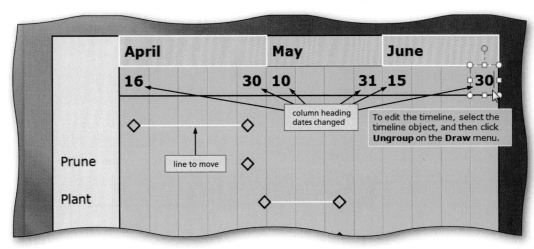

Figure 28

To Modify Timeline Graphics

All the column and row headings and dates are correct. When you deleted the Line 4 and Line 5 row titles, the three remaining row titles were no longer aligned with the timeline graphics. The following steps move the April timeline and the On time! graphic and also delete the edit instruction text box.

- Select the line between the two diamonds under the April heading and drag it down to align with the diamond in the Prune row (Figure 29).

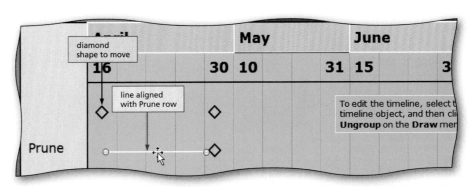

Figure 29

- Select the diamond shape in the April 16 column and drag it down to align with the Prune line, as shown in Figure 30.

- Select the top diamond shape in the April 30 column (Figure 30).

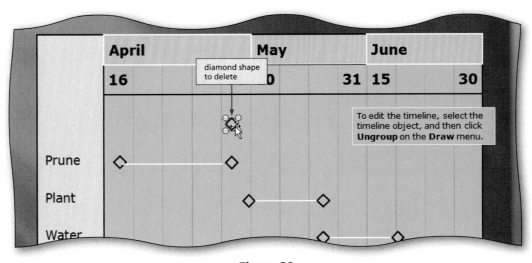

Figure 30

3

- Press the DELETE key to delete this diamond.

- Click the Edit text box border under the June heading to select this object (Figure 31).

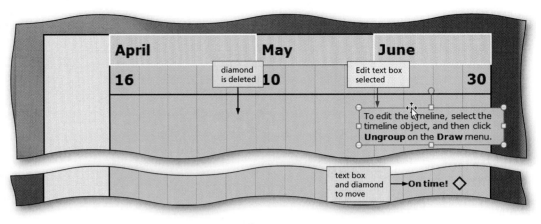

Figure 31

4

- Press the DELETE key to delete the text box.

- Select the On time! text in the bottom-right corner of the diagram and then type Plant a tree on Arbor Day! as the new text box text.

- Drag this text box and the diamond shape to the left so that they are positioned under the April column heading (Figure 32).

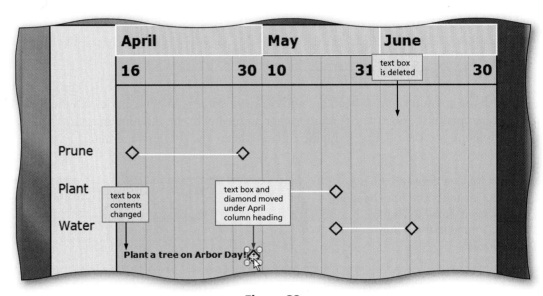

Figure 32

5

- Click the Plant right diamond shape and then drag it under the May 31 heading.

- Click the Water right diamond shape and then drag it under the June 30 heading.

- Click the Water left diamond shape and then drag it under the June 15 heading (Figure 33).

 The line connecting the diamonds is not straight. Can I move it?

Yes. Select the shape again and drag it to a new location.

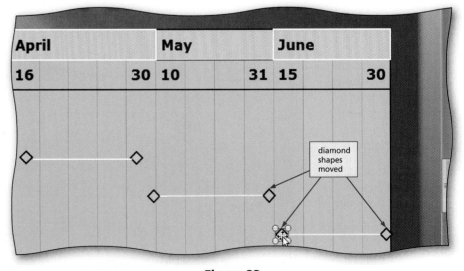

Figure 33

To Add Line Shapes to a Timeline

The three timeline chart elements now are aligned properly under the column headings. The following steps add lines to the column headings.

- Display the Format tab and then click the Line shape in the Insert Shapes gallery (Figure 34).

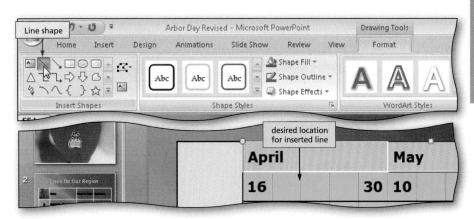

Figure 34

- Position the mouse pointer to the right of the number 16 under the April heading. Click and then drag the line to the left of the number 30 (Figure 35).

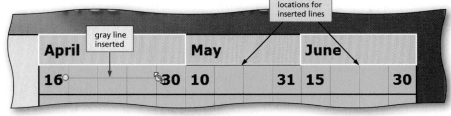

- Repeat Steps 1 and 2 to insert a line between the May 10 and 31 headings and the June 15 and 30 headings.

Figure 35

To Change a Line Shape Color

The default line shape color is gray. To draw attention to the time span between the heading dates, you can change the shape color. The following steps change the line shape color from dark gray to red.

- With the Format tab displayed and June line selected, click the Shape Outline button in the Shape Styles group to display the Shape Outline color palette (Figure 36).

Experiment

- Point to various colors in the Shape Outline gallery and watch the line color change.

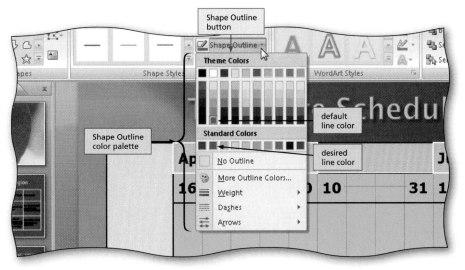

Figure 36

- Click Red (column 2) in the Standard Colors area to apply this color to the line.

- Select the May line and then click the Shape Outline button to apply the Red color to the line.

- Apply the Red color to the April line (Figure 37).

Q&A

Can I change the color of these three lines simultaneously?

Yes. If you select all three lines and then click the Shape Outline button, you can select one color for these lines.

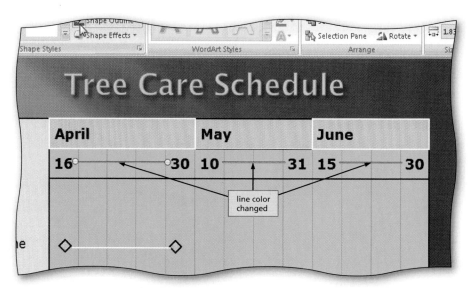

Figure 37

Paste Special

One method of copying a slide object is to copy it to the Clipboard and then use the Paste Special command to insert it on the slide. The **Paste Special** command groups all the individual object elements and then inserts the object as one picture. You specify the type of picture format PowerPoint should use.

To Copy a Formatted Table to the Title Slide

The red leaf picture on Slide 1 is attractive and helps introduce the Arbor Day theme to the audience. You can pique their interest even more by displaying the formatted table and the three templates on this slide. While the text on these objects will be too small to read, its visual nature will give a preview of the concepts that will be explored later in the presentation. The following steps use the Paste Special command to duplicate the table on the title slide.

- Display Slide 2. With the Home tab displayed, click a gray area of the slide other than the table or the title text placeholder and then click the Select button in the Editing group to display the Select menu (Figure 38).

Figure 38

2

- Click Select All in the Select menu and then click the Copy button in the Clipboard group (Figure 39).

 Can I delete the borders between the table cells?

Yes. When you delete the border, you combine the cell contents. To perform this action, display the Design tab under Table Tools and then click the Eraser button in the Draw Borders group. Click a cell border that you want to delete.

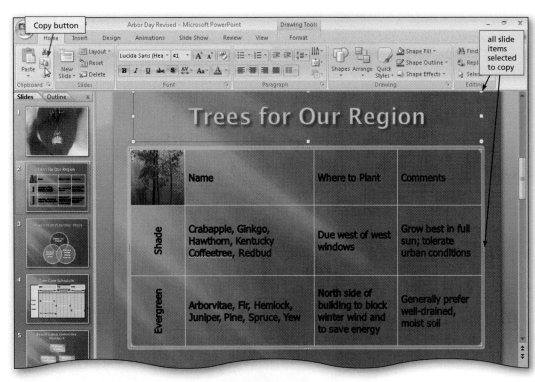

Figure 39

3

- Display Slide 1 and then click the Paste button arrow in the Clipboard group to display the Paste menu (Figure 40).

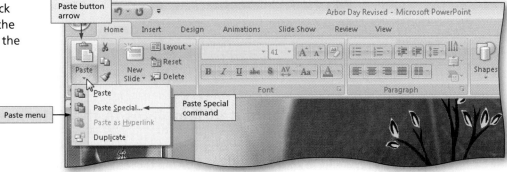

Figure 40

4

- Click Paste Special and then click Picture (PNG) in the Paste Special dialog box to select this picture type (Figure 41).

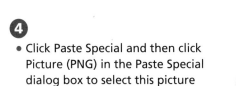 **Can I simply paste the table instead of using the Paste Special command?**

Yes, and the table would look identical to the one displayed on your screen now. The table would be composed of individual pieces, however, which could be a problem if you inadvertently moved or deleted one of these components.

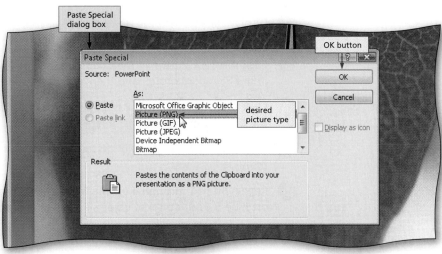

Figure 41

5

- Click the OK button to paste the table in the title slide.

- Display the Format tab and then click the Shape Height down arrow in the Size group to reduce the table height to 2.0".

- Drag the table to the upper-left corner of the slide, as shown in Figure 42.

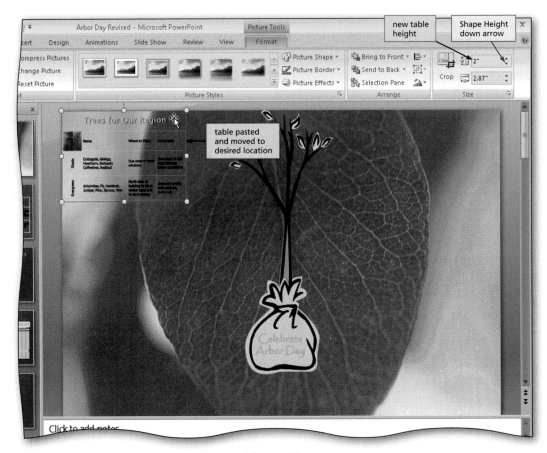

Figure 42

To Copy Formatted Templates to the Title Slide

The tree region table is pasted on Slide 1, and you can copy the three formatted templates to the title slide following the same procedure using the Paste Special command. The following steps copy the formatted Relationship, Hierarchy, and Timelines templates to Slide 1.

1 Display Slide 3. With the Home tab displayed, click a gray area of the slide, click the Select button in the Editing group to display the Select menu, and then click Select All.

2 Click the Copy button in the Clipboard group, display Slide 1, click the Paste button arrow in the Clipboard group, and then click Paste Special in the Paste menu.

3 Click Picture (PNG) in the Paste Special dialog box to select this picture type and then click the OK button to paste the Relationship diagram in the title slide.

4 Size the diagram so its height is 2.0". Drag the diagram to the upper-right corner of the slide.

5 Repeat Steps 1 through 4 for the Hierarchy diagram on Slide 4 and the Timelines diagram on Slide 5. Position these objects as shown in Figure 43.

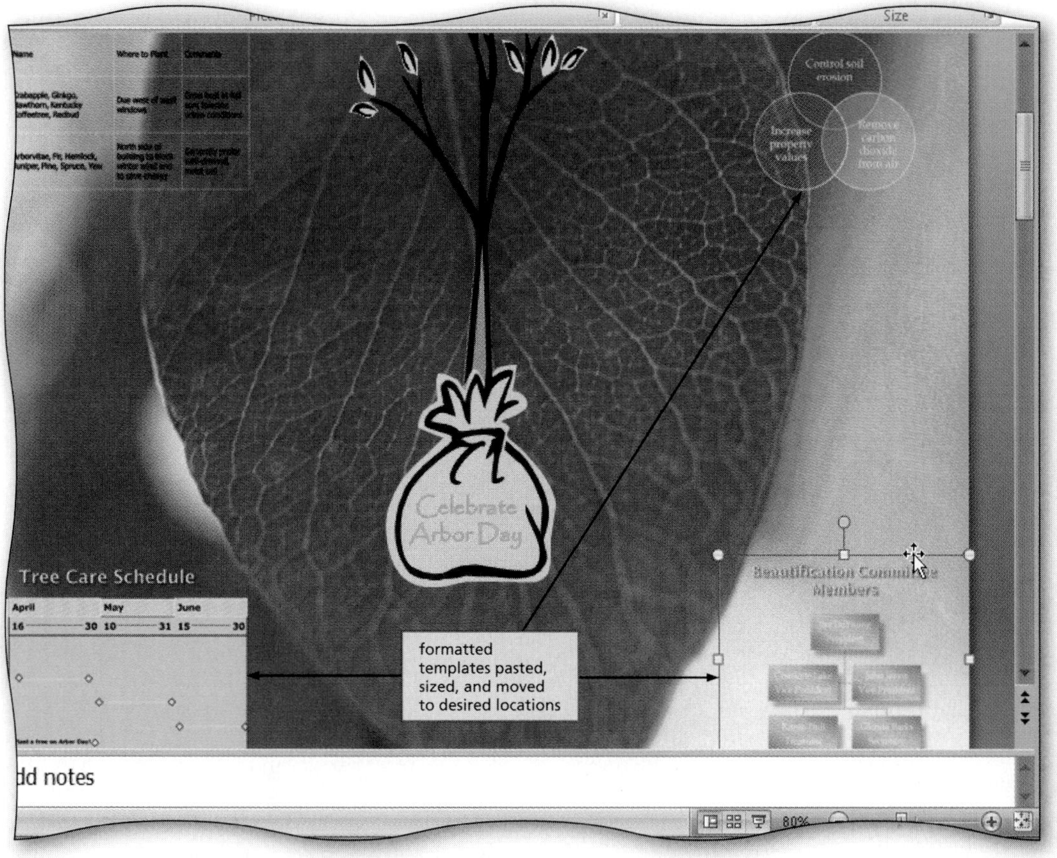

Figure 43

To Animate the Slide 1 Objects

Slide 1 contains many visual elements. Your viewer would be more apt to focus on one aspect of the slide if the objects were displayed one at a time. The following steps apply the Dissolve In entrance effect and a Box exit effect for the objects on the title slide.

1. Click the Zoom Out button as many times as necessary until the Zoom level button displays 70% on its face. Display the Animations tab and then click the Custom Animation button in the Animations group to display the Custom Animation task pane. Select the Trees table object, click the Add Effect button, point to Entrance in the Add Effect menu, and then click More Effects.

2. Click Dissolve In in the Basic category and then click the OK button to close the Add Entrance Effect dialog box.

3. Click the Start box arrow and then click After Previous. Click the Speed box arrow and then click Slow.

4. Click the Add Effect button, point to Exit in the Add Effect menu, and then click More Effects.

5. Click Box in the Basic category and then click the OK button to close the Add Exit Effect dialog box. Change the Speed to Slow.

6. Repeat Steps 1 through 5 above for the Tree Relationship, the Planting Timeline, and the Beautification Committee objects (Figure 44 on the following page).

7. Click the Close button in the Custom Animation task pane so that it no longer is displayed.

BTW

Using the Document Recovery Task Pane
The Document Recover feature can be helpful if PowerPoint or another Microsoft Office program closes abnormally. This feature recovers as many changes as possible that you made after the last time you saved this file. When you restart PowerPoint after it closes unexpectedly, the program may be able to display this file if it can recover all the changes you made. Another possibility may be that PowerPoint displays the Document Recovery task pane and shows a maximum of three versions of your file. In this situation, you can identify which version of the file you want to keep. The most current version is at the top of the list. If you are uncertain which file is the one you want to keep, save all three files using different names and then review each one.

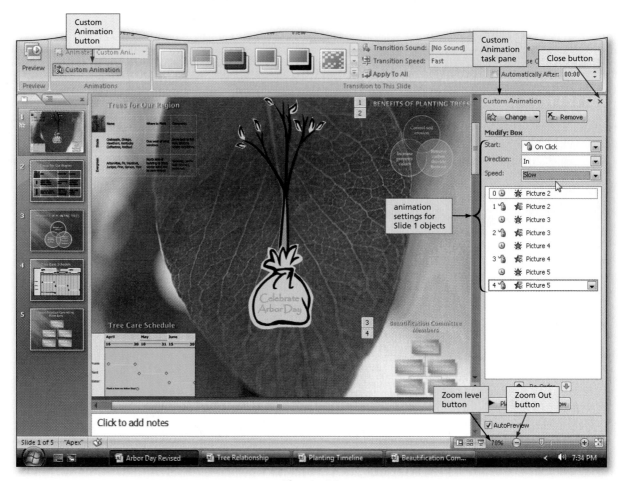

Figure 44

Plan
Ahead

Determine the screen show ratio.

Your presentation can be viewed on one of three different screen sizes. A standard monitor has a ratio of 4:3. Many new wide-screen notebook computers have a 16:10 ratio, and high-definition televisions have displays with a 16:9 ratio. These numbers describe the dimensions of the screen. For example, a display with a 4:3 ratio would be four feet wide if it were 3 feet high. Similarly, a notebook computer screen would be 16 inches wide if it were 10 inches high. While these exact measurements do not fit all displays and screens, the hardware height and width dimensions remain in the same proportion using these ratios.

Changing the default ratio offers many advantages. Audience members perceive a presentation in the wide-screen format as being trendy and new. In addition, the wider screen allows more layout area to display photographs and clips. In rooms with low ceilings, the wide-screen displays mirror the room dimensions and blend with the environment.

Slides created in the 4:3 format and then converted to 16:9 or 16:10 may look distorted, especially if images of people or animals are inserted. You consequently may need to adjust these stretched graphics if they look unnatural. If you present your slide show frequently on computers and screens with varying formats, you may want to save the slide show several times using the different ratios and then open the presentation that best fits the environment where it is being shown.

While the wide screen presents the opportunity to place more text on a slide, resist the urge to add words. Continue to use the 7 × 7 guideline (a maximum of seven lines on a slide and a maximum of seven words on a line).

Setting Slide Size and Slide Show Options and Saving Individual Slides

Today's technology presents several options you should consider when developing your presentation. The on-screen show ratio determines the height and width proportions. The screen resolution affects the slides' clarity. In addition, you may want to save an individual slide as an image so it can be imported into another file or easily printed by itself.

BTW

Changing the Starting Slide Number
The first slide number is 1 by default. To change this number, click the 'Number slides from' up button in the Page Setup dialog box.

To Set Slide Size

By default, PowerPoint sets a slide in a 4:3 ratio, which is the proportion found on a standard monitor. If you know your presentation will be viewed on a wide-screen high-definition television (HDTV) or you are using a wide-screen notebook computer, you can change the slide size to optimize the proportions. The following steps change the default resolution to 16:10, which is the proportion of a notebook computer.

- Display the Design tab and then click the Page Setup button in the Page Setup group to display the Page Setup dialog box.

- Click the 'Slides sized for' arrow to display the size list (Figure 45).

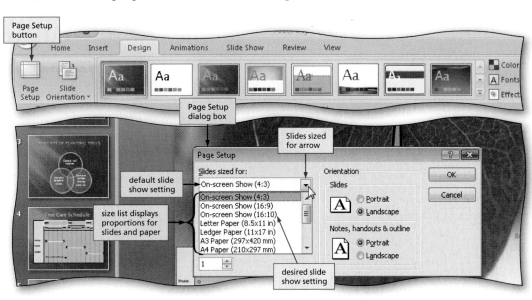

Figure 45

- Click 'On-screen Show (16:10)' to change the slide size setting (Figure 46).

Q&A

Can I also change the default slide orientation from Landscape to Portrait?

Yes, but all slides in the presentation will change to this orientation. You cannot mix Portrait and Landscape orientations in one presentation. If you need to use both orientations during a speech, you can use a hyperlink to seamlessly jump from one slide show in Landscape orientation to another in Portrait orientation.

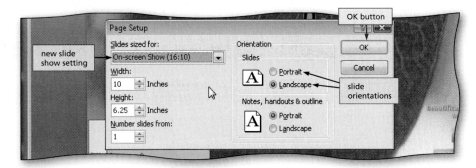

Figure 46

❸
- Click the OK button to change the slide size in the presentation.

To Select Presentation Resolution

As discussed in Appendix E, screen, or presentation, resolution affects the number of pixels that are displayed on your screen. When screen resolution is increased, more information is displayed, but it is decreased in size. Conversely, when screen resolution is decreased, less information is displayed, but that information is increased in size. Throughout this book, the screen resolution has been set to 1024 × 768. The following steps change the presentation resolution to 800 × 600.

- Display the Slide Show tab and then click the Set Up Slide Show button in the Set Up group to display the Set Up Show dialog box.

- Click the 'Slide show resolution' arrow in the Performance area to display the resolution list (Figure 47).

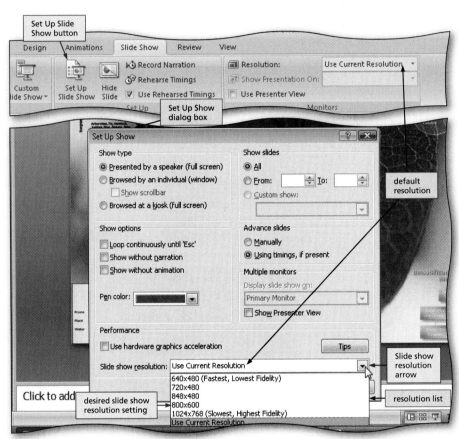

Figure 47

- Click 800 × 600 to change the slide show resolution setting (Figure 48).

- Click the OK button to change the presentation resolution.

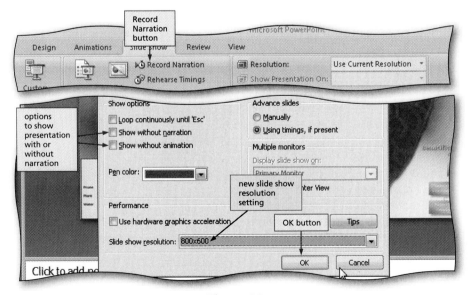

Figure 48

To Record Narration

In special occasions you may want your viewers to hear recorded narration that accompanies slides. If your topic is poetry written by local poets, you may want to hear their voices interpret the poetry that is displayed on slides. You can record narration separately and then add this file to the slide. You also can record narration while the slide show is running. To record this narration, you would perform the following steps.

1. Display the Slide Show tab and then click the Record Narration button in the Set Up group.

2. Click the Set Microphone Level button in the Record Narration dialog box, determine the microphone level, and then click the OK button in the Microphone Check dialog box.

3. Click the Change Quality button in the Record Narration dialog box, click the Name arrow, select the desired recording quality, and then click the OK button in the Sound Selection dialog box.

4. If your narration is lengthy, click the 'Link narrations in' check box to link the narration file to your presentation.

5. If your presentation consists of more than one slide, click Current Slide or First Slide to match the narration with a particular part of the presentation.

6. In Slide Show view, begin speaking into the microphone. When finished, click the black Exit screen.

7. Click the Save button if you want to save the slide timings along with your narration.

To Show a Presentation with or without Narration

If you have recorded narration to accompany your slides, you can choose whether to include this narration when you run your slide show. You would perform the following steps to run the slide show either with or without narration.

1. On the Slide Show tab, click the Set Up Slide Show button in the Set Up group.

2. If you do not want the narration to play, click 'Show without narration' in the Show options area of the Set Up Show dialog box and then click the OK button.

3. If you have chosen to show the presentation without narration and then desire to let audience members hear this recording, click 'Show without narration' to deselect this option in the Set Up Show dialog box and then click the OK button.

To Save a Slide as an Image

Throughout this book you have inserted images into your presentation. The need may arise for you to insert a PowerPoint slide into another file. For example, you may want to insert the information on one slide into a Microsoft Word document. The following steps save Slide 2 as a .jpg image.

- Display Slide 2, click the Office Button, and then point to Save As to display the Save As submenu (Figure 49).

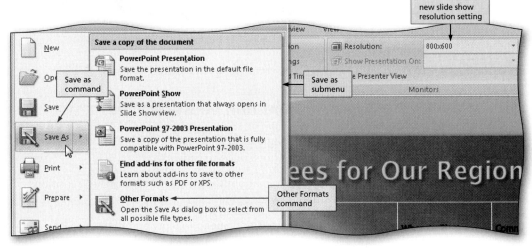

Figure 49

- Click Other Formats on the Save As submenu to display the Save As dialog box.

- Type `Regional Trees` in the File name text box and then click the 'Save as type' arrow to display the Save as type list (Figure 50).

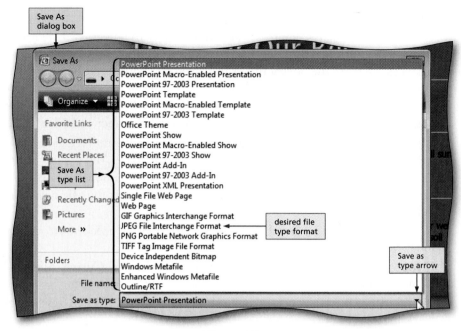

Figure 50

- Click JPEG File Interchange Format in the Save as type list to change the file type (Figure 51).

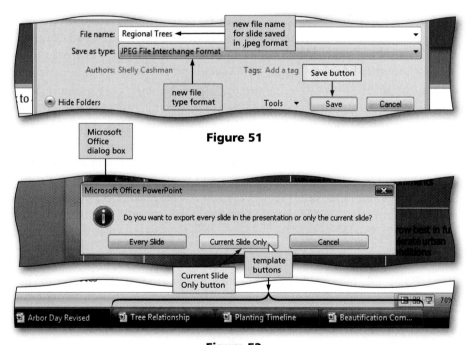

Figure 51

Figure 52

To Add a Transition between Slides

The following steps apply the Uncover Up transition to the presentation and change the transition speed to Slow.

1 Display the Animations tab and then display the Transitions gallery. Click the Uncover Up transition (row 2, column 3) in the Wipes category.

2 Change the Transition Speed to Slow and then apply this transition and speed to all slides.

To Change Document Properties and Save the Presentation

Before saving the presentation again, you want to add your name, class name, and some keywords as document properties. The following steps use the Document Information Panel to change document properties and then save the project.

1 Display the Document Information Panel and then type your name as the Author property.

2 Type your course and section as the Subject property.

3 Type `Arbor Day, regional trees, Beautification Committee` as the Keywords property.

4 Close the Document Information Panel and then save the presentation on the USB flash drive.

To Close the Downloaded Template Files

The five main slides in your presentation are complete. The three templates you downloaded from the Microsoft Office Online Web site are open, but you will not need to reference them to complete this project. You therefore should close these files. The following steps close the three downloaded templates.

1 Right-click the Tree Relationship button on the Windows Vista taskbar and then click Close.

2 Repeat Step 1 for the Planting Timeline and the Beautification Committee files.

> **Other Ways**
> 1. Click Close button on right side of title bar
> 2. Press ALT+F4

Using Visual Basic for Applications to Create a Quiz

Visual Basic for Applications (VBA) programs can add unique features to your presentation. The fundamentals of VBA will be presented later in this feature when you create an interactive quiz with questions for audience members to answer. Before you learn to write the VBA instructions, however, you first need to create the two slides that will display questions pertaining to the Arbor Day presentation and three possible answers for each question.

To Insert a Slide and then Add and Format a Shape

Three possible answers will display on the slide. To add interest, you can display the text of each answer in a shape. One method for creating these answers is to create one shape, copy it, and then position the shapes on the slide. The following steps insert and format a shape.

1 Insert a new slide at the end of the Arbor Day Revised presentation and apply the Title Only slide layout.

2 With the Home tab displayed, click the Shapes button in the Drawing group and then click the Regular Pentagon shape (row 1, column 8 in the Basic Shapes area).

3 Click Slide 6 anywhere below the title text placeholder to insert the shape and then size the Regular Pentagon shape to a height of 2.5" and a width of 2.7".

4 Apply the Intense Effect – Accent 1 Shape Style (row 6, column 2) to the shape (Figure 53).

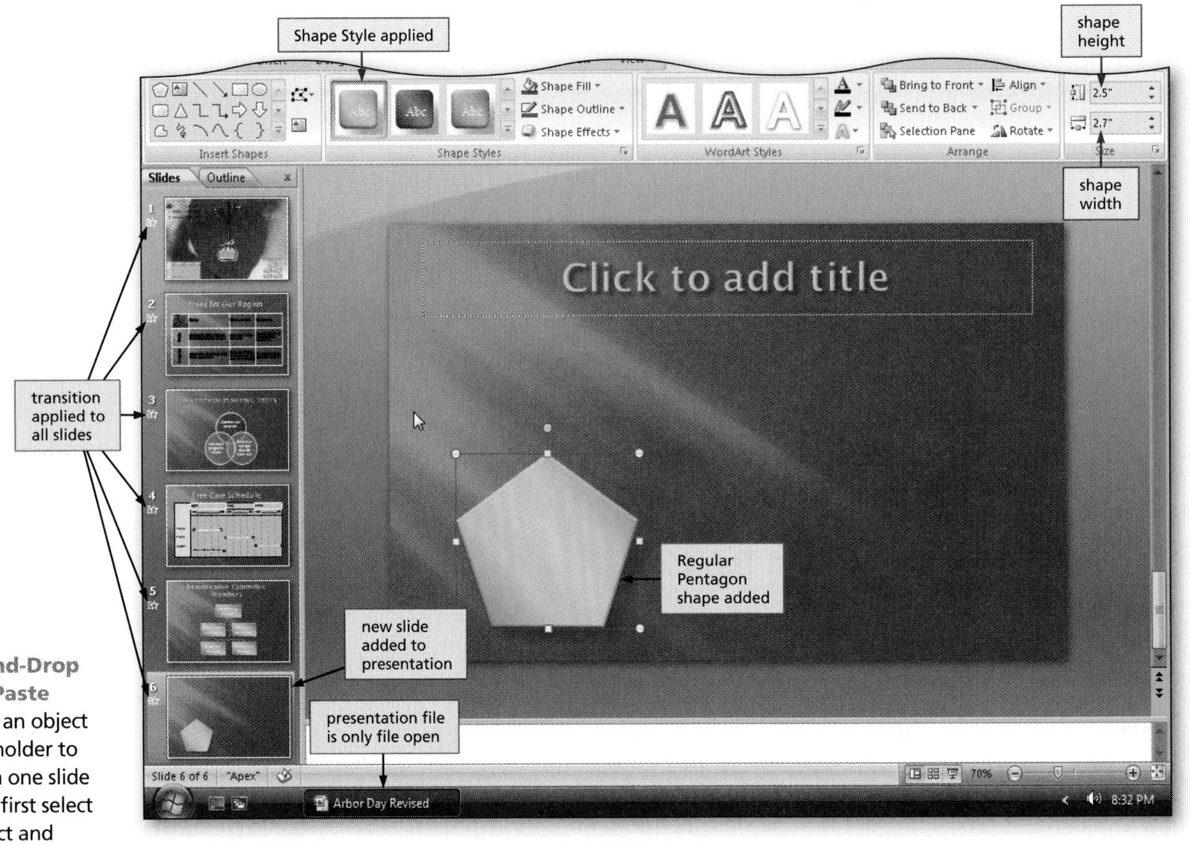

Figure 53

BTW

Using Drag-and-Drop and Cut-and-Paste
To move text or an object from one placeholder to another or from one slide to another, you first select the text or object and then use drag-and-drop editing or the cut-and-paste technique to move these characters or items. With **drag-and-drop editing**, you drag the selected item to a new location on the slide or a different slide and then insert, or drop, it there. **Cutting** involves removing the selected item from the document and then placing it on the Clipboard. **Pasting** is the process of copying an item from the Clipboard into the slide at the location of the insertion point.

Copying and Pasting

With one shape inserted and formatted on the slide, the next step is to create two identical objects for the quiz answers. One way to create these shapes is to repeat Steps 2 through 4 on the previous page. Another way is to copy the original shape to the Clipboard and then paste this shape from the Clipboard into the same slide or another slide at the location of the insertion point. The Clipboard holds text or objects temporarily until you copy another object or character. The same procedure of copying and pasting objects works for copying and pasting text from one text box or placeholder to another.

When moving characters or an object from one slide to another, use the Clipboard to cut and paste; when moving these items a short distance, use the drag-and-drop technique for efficiency. The following steps demonstrate copying and pasting.

To Copy a Shape

Now that the shape is formatted, you can copy it twice on the slide. The following steps copy the Regular Pentagon shape.

1. Display the Home tab and then click the Copy button in the Clipboard group.

2. Click the Paste button in the Clipboard group twice to insert two Regular Pentagon shapes on Slide 6 (Figure 54).

BTW

Cutting Techniques
After selecting the text or object, you can cut your selection using one of three methods: click the Cut button on the Home tab, click the Cut command on the shortcut menu, or press the CTRL+X keys simultaneously.

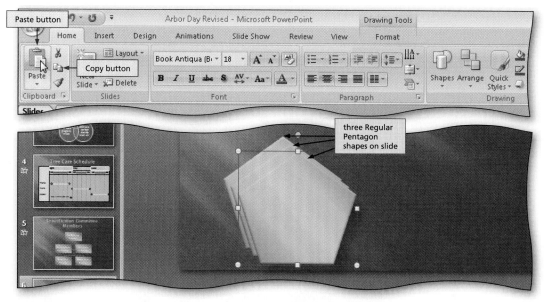

Figure 54

To Display the Gridlines and Align the Shapes

The **grid** is a set of intersecting lines used to align objects on the slide. By default, the **Snap objects to grid** option is active so that objects move to the nearest grid intersection automatically when the object's borders are near the grid lines. The following steps display the gridlines and then move the three shapes to the desired location.

1
• Right-click Slide 6 anywhere except the title text and shapes to display the short-cut menu (Figure 55).

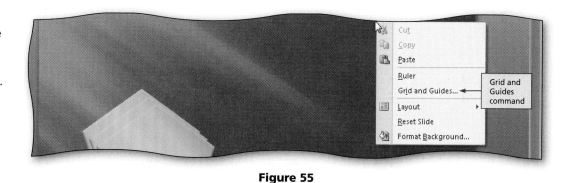

Figure 55

2
• Click Grid and Guides on the shortcut menu to display the Grid and Guides dialog box and then click the 'Display grid on screen' check box in the Grid settings area (Figure 56).

Q&A Can I change the spacing of the grid lines?

Yes. Click the Spacing arrow in the Grid and Guides dialog box and then select the desired measurement.

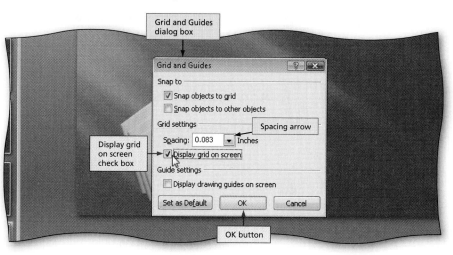

Figure 56

- Click the OK button to display the grids.

- Drag each shape to the locations shown in Figure 57.

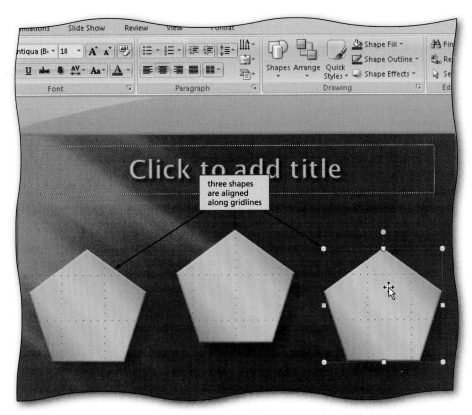

Figure 57

Other Ways

1. Click Gridlines on View tab
2. Press SHIFT+F9

To Duplicate a Slide

Your quiz will have questions on two slides. Now that one slide is formatted, you can duplicate it and then add the questions and answers to both slides. The following steps duplicate Slide 6.

1 With Slide 6 and the Home tab displayed, click the New Slide button arrow to display the Apex layout gallery.

2 Click Duplicate Selected Slides to insert a new Slide 7, which is identical to Slide 6.

To Add Text to Shapes and the Title Text Placeholders

With both quiz slides added to the presentation, you now can type the quiz questions and answers. The following steps add the questions to the title text placeholders and the answers to the Regular Pentagon shapes on Slides 6 and 7.

1 Display Slide 6 and then type `What tree type is best for blocking winter winds?` in the title text placeholder.

2 If necessary, select the title text placeholder, click the Shape Fill button arrow in the Drawing group, and then click Red (column 2 in the Standard Colors area) to add a fill color to the title text placeholder.

3 Select the left Regular Pentagon shape and then type `Evergreen` in the shape.

4 Select the middle shape and then type `Shade` in the shape. Select the right shape and then type `Palm` in the shape.

5 Change the font color of these three answers to Red and the font size to 20 point.

6 Display Slide 7 and then type `Why are trees beneficial to the environment?` in the title text placeholder.

7 Select the title text placeholder, if necessary, and then click the Shape Fill button to add a Red fill color to the title text placeholder.

8 Type `They reduce oxygen in the air` in the left shape, type `They contribute to erosion` in the center shape, and then type `They increase property values` in the right shape.

9 Change the font color of these three answers to Red and the font size to 20 point (Figure 58).

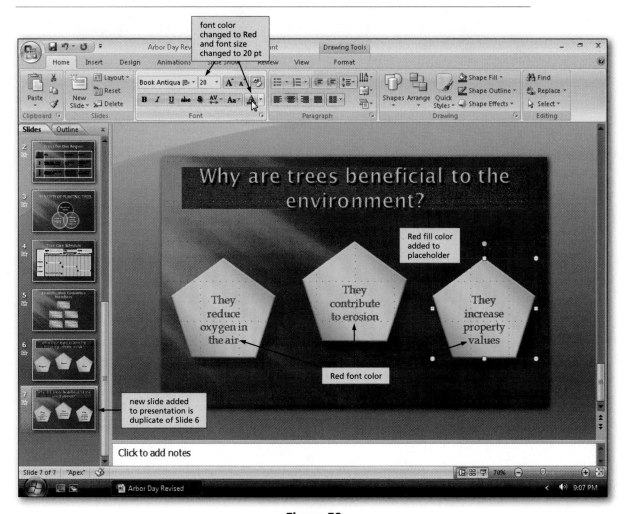

Figure 58

To Insert and Order a Picture on a Slide

Adding pictures of trees on the quiz slides will help add interest. If you insert these pictures now, they will cover the shapes and text you just added. To move these pictures underneath the slide objects, you order the pictures to the back of the slide. The following steps insert photographs and then send them to the back of Slides 6 and 7.

- Display Slide 6, display the Insert tab, and then click the Picture button to display the Insert Picture dialog box.

- Select the Evergreens picture on the Data Files for Students and then click the Insert button in the Insert Picture dialog box to insert the picture on Slide 6.

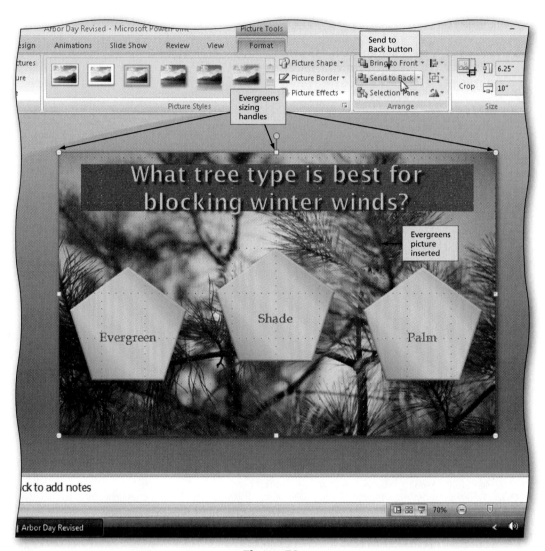

Figure 59

- Drag the Evergreens sizing handles so the picture covers the entire slide.

Q&A Is it acceptable to use the side sizing handles to change the picture dimensions?

In previous chapters you have used the corner sizing handles to change the picture sizes so the picture stays in proportion. This guideline is important for some picture images, such as people or animals. This Evergreen picture, however, does not look distorted when you drag the side sizing handles outward, so enlarging the photograph in this manner is fine.

- Click the Send to Back button in the Arrange group to move the Evergreens picture under the Slide 6 content (Figure 59).

- Display Slide 7, display the Insert tab, and then insert the Forest picture on the Data Files for Students.

- Drag the Forest sizing handles so the picture covers the entire slide.

- Click the Send to Back button in the Arrange group to move the Forest picture under the Slide 7 content (Figure 60).

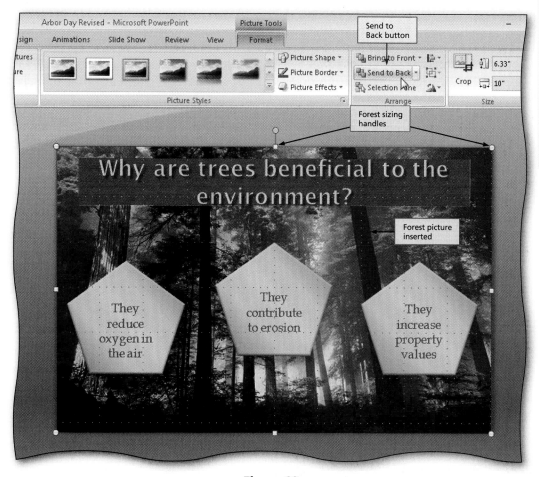

Figure 60

To Hide Gridlines

The shapes and text are entered on the two quiz slides and are located in the desired locations. The grid no longer is needed. The following step hides the gridlines.

 Display the View tab and then click Gridlines.

Visual Basic Code Elements

The lines of instruction, called code, customize and extend PowerPoint's capabilities. The step-by-step set of instructions is called an **application**. Thus, Microsoft created the name Visual Basic for Applications for its programming language used to customize PowerPoint and other Microsoft Office 2007 programs. PowerPoint and other Office programs use the **Visual Basic Editor** to enter, modify, and view VBA code.

Table 1 shows the VBA code you will use to create a quiz. The lines of code, taken as a whole, are called a **macro**, which is a set of instructions that automates multi-step tasks. This quiz macro contains three procedures, each beginning with a **Sub statement** and ending with an **End Sub statement**. The Sub statement begins with the name of

BTW

Indenting Lines
The indents are only for clarity; in this project they help you recognize the three subroutines. Indent these lines three spaces.

the procedure. In Table 1, lines 10, 13, and 16 give the names of the three procedures: WrongAnswer, CorrectAnswer, and LastCorrect. The parentheses following the procedure names allow the passing of data variables, or arguments, from one procedure to another. Passing arguments is beyond the scope of this project, but the parentheses still are required. Every procedure must end with an End Sub statement; the End Sub statements in lines 12, 15, and 18 signify the end of the three procedures.

Line	VBA Code
Table 1 Create Quiz Procedures	
1	' Create Quiz Procedure Author: Shelly Cashman
2	' Date Created: 5/7/08
3	' Function: When the slide is displayed, this procedure accepts data indicating
4	' whether a user has selected a correct or incorrect quiz answer. If the
5	' answer is correct, a message box is displayed indicating the user
6	' entered a correct response. If the answer is incorrect, a message box
7	' is displayed indicating an incorrect answer was chosen. When the
8	' correct answer is selected on the last slide, the procedure ends.
9	'
10	Sub WrongAnswer()
11	MsgBox ("Please select a different answer.")
12	End Sub
13	Sub CorrectAnswer()
14	MsgBox ("You are correct.")
15	End Sub
16	Sub LastCorrect()
17	MsgBox ("You are correct.")
18	End Sub

BTW

Using Comments
Comments contain overall documentation about the procedure and may be placed anywhere in the procedure. Most programmers place comments before the Sub statement. Comments have no effect on the execution of a procedure; they simply provide information about the procedure, such as name, creation date, and function.

The first executable statement in Table 1 is line 10. Adding comments before a procedure will help you remember its purpose at a later date. In Table 1, the first nine lines are comments. **Comments** begin with the word Rem or an apostrophe (').

To enter a procedure, use the Visual Basic Editor. This Editor allows you to type the lines of VBA code as if you were using word-processing software. At the end of a line, press the ENTER key to move to the next line. If you make a mistake in a statement, use the ARROW keys and the DELETE or BACKSPACE keys to correct it. You also can move the insertion point to previous lines to make corrections.

Plan Ahead

> **Desk check the application code before entering it into the Visual Basic Editor.**
> PowerPoint steps through the Visual Basic statements one at a time beginning at the top of the procedure. When you a plan a procedure, remember that the order in which you place the statements is important because the order determines the sequence of execution.
>
> Once you know what you want the procedure to do, write the VBA code on paper. Then, before entering the procedure into the computer, test it by putting yourself in the position of PowerPoint and stepping through the instructions one at a time. As you do so, think about how the instructions affect the slide show. Testing a procedure before entering it is called **desk checking**, and it is an important part of the development process.

To Enter the Create Quiz Procedures

Once you have determined the VBA instructions for the quiz, you can enter this code in the Visual Basic Editor. The following steps activate the Editor and create the three quiz procedures.

1

- Click the Office Button and then click the PowerPoint Options button to display the PowerPoint Options dialog box.

- Click the Show Developer tab in the Ribbon check box (Figure 61).

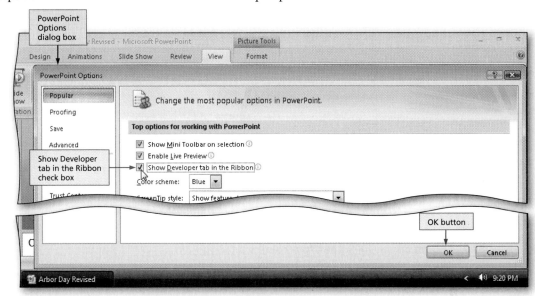

Figure 61

2

- Click the OK button to close the PowerPoint Options dialog box.

- Click Developer to display the Developer tab (Figure 62).

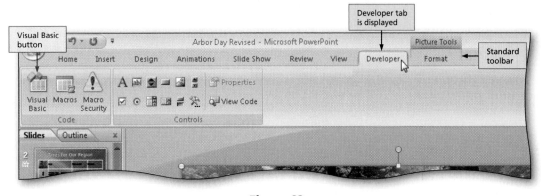

Figure 62

3

- Click the Visual Basic button in the Code group to open the Microsoft Visual Basic Editor.

- Click the Insert UserForm button arrow on the Standard toolbar to display the Insert UserForm list (Figure 63).

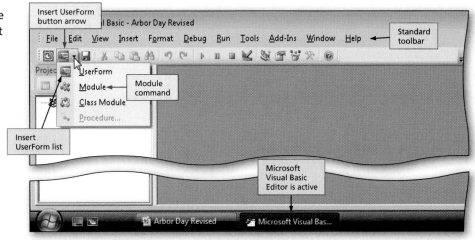

Figure 63

- Click Module in the Insert UserForm list to display the Visual Basic Editor.

- If necessary, click the Maximize button in the Arbor Day Revised – [Module1 (Code)] window to maximize the window.

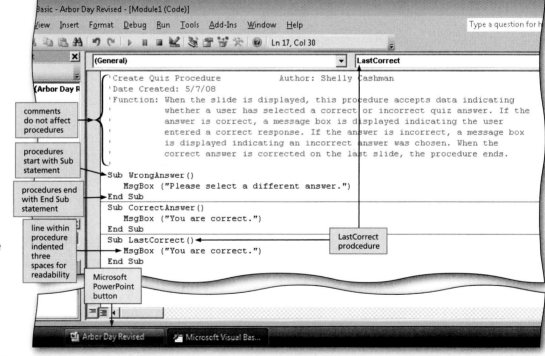

Figure 64

- Type the nine comment statements (lines 1 through 9) shown in Table 1. Be certain to enter an apostrophe at the beginning of each comment line (Figure 64).

 Why do these lines display in a green font color?

The green font color indicates these lines are comments.

- Press the ENTER key to position the insertion point on the next line.

- Enter lines 10 through 18 shown in Table 1 (Figure 65).

Do I need to type the End Sub statements shown in lines 12, 15, and 18?

No. The Visual Basic Editor displays these lines automatically when you type the Sub statements.

6

- Click the Microsoft PowerPoint button on the Standard toolbar to return to Slide 7.

Figure 65

Why did I leave the Visual Basic Editor open?

At this point you are not absolutely certain your VBA code is correct. If you run the presentation and encounter an error, you easily can view the code by clicking the Microsoft Visual Basic – Arbor Day Revised Macro button that is displayed on the Windows Vista taskbar.

To Assign a Macro to the First Quiz Question Shapes

One of the three shapes on Slide 6 displays the correct answer to the question displayed in the title text placeholder. The other two shapes display incorrect answers. You need to assign the CorrectAnswer macro to the corresponding shape and the WrongAnswer macro to the two corresponding shapes. The following steps assign action settings to the three shapes on Slide 6.

1

- Display Slide 6, click the Evergreen shape anywhere but the text, and then display the Insert tab.

Q&A Should the shape border be a dashed or a solid line?

Solid. If your shape has a dashed line, click the shape again. The solid line ensures that the macro will be assigned to the entire shape.

- Click the Action button in the Links group to display the Action Settings dialog box (Figure 66).

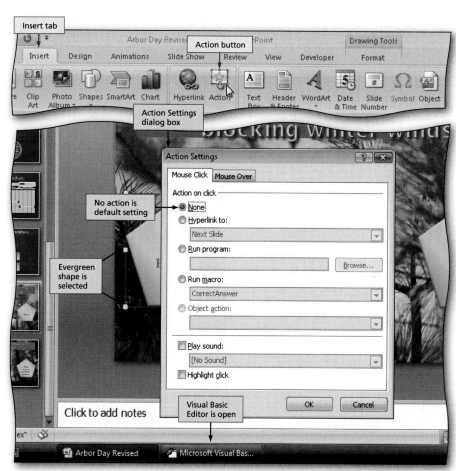

Figure 66

2

- With the Mouse Click tab displayed, click Run macro, and then verify that CorrectAnswer is the macro name displayed in the Run macro box (Figure 67).

Q&A How are the names generated for the macro list?

When you typed the VBA code, you entered the names of three procedures, or macros, followed by parentheses. Those three names are displayed in the macro list.

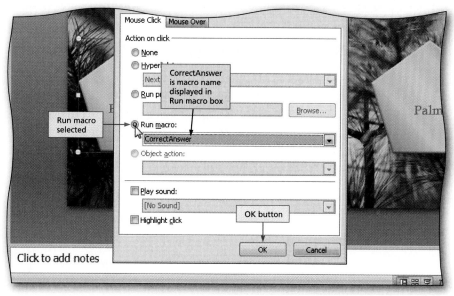

Figure 67

- Click the OK button to apply the CorrectAnswer macro to the Evergreen shape.

- Click the Shade shape anywhere but the text and then, if necessary, display the Insert tab.

- Click the Action button in the Links group, click Run macro in the Action Settings dialog box, click the Run macro arrow, and then click WrongAnswer in the macro list (Figure 68).

- Click the OK button to apply the WrongAnswer macro to the Shade shape.

- Click the Palm shape anywhere but the text, click the Action button in the Links group on the Insert tab, click Run macro, and then select WrongAnswer in the macro list.

- Click the OK button to apply the WrongAnswer macro to the Palm shape.

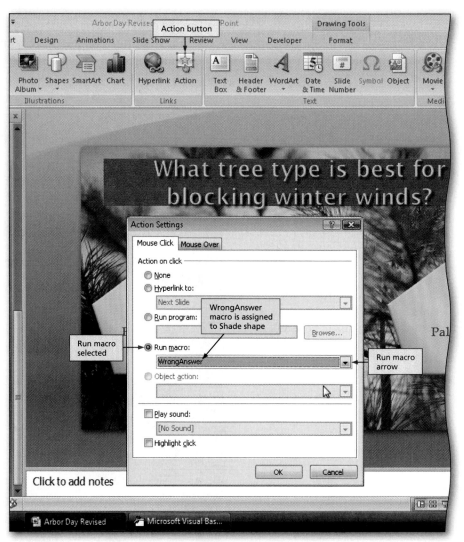

Figure 68

To Assign a Macro to the Final Quiz Question Shapes

The last quiz slide uses a different macro action setting to end the quiz after the user selects the correct answer. The LastCorrect macro will display a message box and then return to the slide show. In this presentation, this last quiz question also is the last slide in the presentation, so the slide show ends when the quiz ends. The following steps assign action settings to the three shapes on Slide 7.

- Display Slide 7. With the Insert tab displayed, click the right shape, which displays the text, They increase property values.

- Display the Action Settings dialog box, click Run macro, and then display the macro list.

- Click LastCorrect to select this macro (Figure 69).

- Click the OK button to apply the LastCorrect macro to the right shape.

- Click the left shape, click the Action button, click Run macro in the Action Settings dialog box, select WrongAnswer in the macro list, and then click the OK button.

- Apply the Wrong Answer macro to the middle shape and then click the OK button.

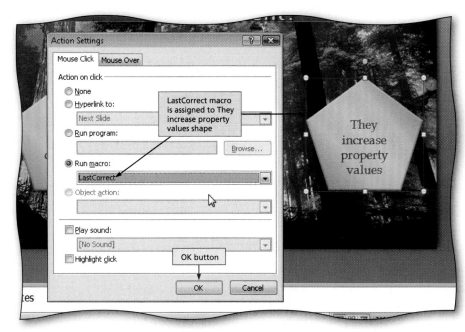

Figure 69

To Save the Presentation with a Macro

By default, PowerPoint will not save this presentation with a macro. You need to save the file as a macro-enabled presentation, which has the .pptm file extension. The following steps save the presentation in this format.

- Display the Save As dialog box, click the Save as type arrow, and then click PowerPoint Macro-Enabled Presentation in the Save as type list.

- Type Arbor Day Revised Macro in the File name text box (Figure 70).

- Click the Save button to save the presentation with a macro.

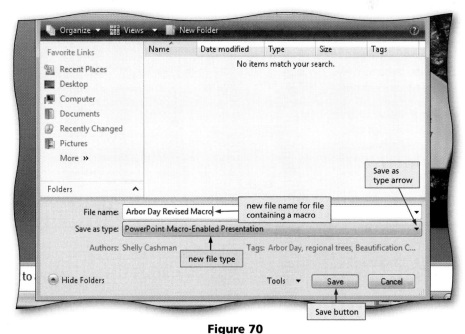

Figure 70

To Test Macro Settings

Unscrupulous people sometimes write macros to damage computer systems or to obtain information illegally. For this reason, Microsoft Office 2007 includes a Trust Center that allows users to determine security levels. In this feature, you should allow all macros to run while you are developing and testing this quiz code. The following steps test the macro level and adjust the setting, if necessary.

• Click the Office Button, click the PowerPoint Options button, and then click the Trust Center link in the left pane (Figure 71).

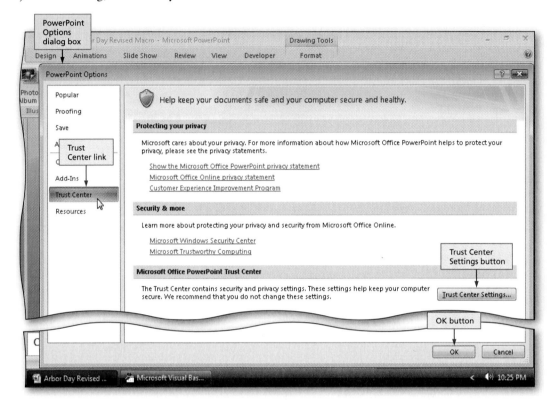

Figure 71

• Click the Trust Center Settings button in the Microsoft Office PowerPoint Trust Center area to view the Macro Settings.

• If is it not already selected, click the 'Enable all macros' option (Figure 72).

• Click the OK button to apply this macro setting and to close the Trust Center dialog box.

• Click the OK button to close the PowerPoint Options dialog box.

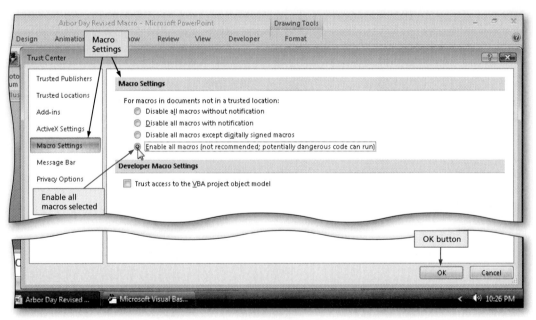

Figure 72

To Run a Slide Show with Macros

Running a slide show that contains a macro is the same as running any other slide show. When a quiz slide is displayed, click one of the shapes to display a message box indicating you have selected a correct or an incorrect answer. The following steps run the Arbor Day Revised Macro presentation.

1 Click Slide 1 on the Slides tab. Click the Slide Show button to run the slide show and display Slide 1. Click to display the template images that are pasted on the slide.

2 Display Slides 2, 3, 4, and 5.

3 Display Slide 6. Click a shape with an incorrect answer and view the message box indicating that your choice was wrong. Click the OK button in this message box to close it. Click the other incorrect answer, view the message box, and then click the OK button in this message box.

4 Click the correct answer and view the message box. Click the OK button to close this message box.

5 Display Slide 7. Repeat Steps 3 and 4 to view the message boxes for the incorrect and correct answers. Click the OK button in the message box.

6 Click Slide 7 so that the black slide appears announcing the end of the slide show.

BTW

Quick Reference
For a table that lists how to complete the tasks covered in this book using the mouse, Ribbon, shortcut menu, and keyboard, see the Quick Reference Summary at the back of this book, or visit the PowerPoint 2007 Quick Reference Web page (scsite.com/ ppt2007/qr).

To Preview and Print Handouts

All changes are complete, and the presentation is saved. You now can create handouts to accompany the slide show. The following steps preview and then print the presentation.

1 Use Print Preview to preview the Arbor Day Revised Macro presentation.

2 Click Handouts (4 Slides Per Page) in the Print What list.

3 Click the Page Orientation button in the Page Setup group and then click Landscape in the Orientation list.

4 Click the Options button in the Print group and then Header and Footer in the Options list.

5 Click Header and then type `Celebrate Arbor Day` in the Header text box. Click the Apply to All button in the Header and Footer dialog box.

6 Print the handouts.

7 Close Print Preview and return to Normal view.

BTW

Certification
The Microsoft Certified Application Specialist (MCAS) program provides an opportunity for you to obtain a valuable industry credential – proof that you have the PowerPoint 2007 skills required by employers. For more information see Appendix G or visit the PowerPoint 2007 Certification Web page (scsite.com/ppt2007/cert).

To Reset Settings and Quit PowerPoint

You should reset the options you changed to their defaults. The following steps reset the resolution and slide size and also disable macros.

1 On the Slide Show tab, click the Resolution arrow in the Monitors group. Click Use Current Resolution or the original setting you changed.

2 On the Design tab, click the Page Setup button. Click the 'Slides sized for' arrow and then scroll up and click On-Screen Show (4:3). Click the OK button to close the dialog box.

3 Display the Office Button menu, click the PowerPoint Options button, click Trust Center in the left pane, click the Trust Center Settings button, and then click 'Disable all macros with notification' or the original setting you changed to run the macro in this project.

4 Click the OK button to close the Trust Center dialog box and then click the OK button to close the PowerPoint Options dialog box.

5 Display the Office Button menu and then click the Exit PowerPoint button to close all open documents and quit PowerPoint.

6 If a Microsoft Office PowerPoint dialog box is displayed, click the Yes button to save the changes.

Online Feature Summary

This Online feature introduced you to downloading templates from the Microsoft Online Web site, adding images to tables and changing the alignment of table text, changing presentation orientation and resolution, using Paste Special to copy objects, and writing VBA code. The items listed below include all the new Office 2007 skills you have learned in this Online feature.

1. Locate and Download a Relationship Diagram Template (PPT 451)
2. Locate and Download a Timeline Template (PPT 452)
3. Locate and Download a Hierarchy Template (PPT 453)
4. Insert Templates into a Presentation (PPT 454)
5. Set Text Box Margins (PPT 455)
6. Order a Text Box on a Slide (PPT 457)
7. Change Table Text Alignment (PPT 458)
8. Change Table Text Orientation (PPT 459)
9. Add an Image to a Table (PPT 460)
10. Enter Text in a Relationship Diagram (PPT 461)
11. Zoom a Slide (PPT 462)
12. Enter Text in a Hierarchy Diagram (PPT 462)
13. Modify Timeline Diagram Text (PPT 463)
14. Modify Timeline Graphics (PPT 465)
15. Add Line Shapes to a Timeline (PPT 467)
16. Change a Line Shape Color (PPT 467)
17. Copy a Formatted Table to the Title Slide (PPT 468)
18. Copy Formatted Templates to the Title Slide (PPT 470)
19. Animate the Slide 1 Objects (PPT 471)
20. Set Slide Size (PPT 473)
21. Select Presentation Resolution (PPT 474)
22. Record Narration (PPT 475)
23. Show a Presentation with or without Narration (PPT 475)
24. Save a Slide as an Image (PPT 475)
25. Close the Downloaded Template Files (PPT 477)
26. Display the Gridlines and Align the Shapes (PPT 479)
27. Insert and Order a Picture on a Slide (PPT 482)
28. Hide Gridlines (PPT 483)
29. Enter the Create Quiz Procedures (PPT 485)
30. Assign a Macro to the First Quiz Question Shapes (PPT 487)
31. Assign a Macro to the Final Quiz Question Shapes (PPT 488)
32. Save a Presentation with a Macro (PPT 489)
33. Test Macro Settings (PPT 490)
34. Run a Slide Show with Macros (PPT 491)
35. Reset Settings and Quit PowerPoint (PPT 492)

In the Lab

Create a presentation using the guidelines, concepts, and skills presented in this feature. Labs 1, 2, and 3 are listed in order of increasing difficulty.

Lab 1: Inserting Photographs in a Table and Adding Narration

Problem: Jim DeYoung, the Beautification Committee president, is planning a series of workshops to teach homeowners how to prune their trees properly. He would like to use a slide during his demonstration that shows an incorrect stem cut and a correct collar cut. He sends you two photographs of these cuts and also records a message describing these cuts. You create the slide shown in Figure 73.

Instructions:

1. Create a new presentation using the Origin document theme and the Title and Table slide layout. Set the slide size to On-screen Show (16:9). Change the slide show resolution to 800 × 600.

2. Type `Pruning Techniques` in the title text placeholder. Insert the OF-1 Pruning narration file from the Data Files for Students and set the narration to start automatically. Drag the speaker icon to the outer lower-right corner of the slide.

3. Insert a table with three columns and one row. Add the OF-1 Incorrect Prune photograph from the Data Files for Students to the left table cell and the OF-1 Correct Prune photograph from the Data Files for Students to the center table cell.

4. Resize the table by pointing to the sizing handle (the cluster of dots) on the bottom edge. When your mouse pointer becomes a double-headed arrow, click and drag the handle down to the location shown in Figure 73.

5. Use the drag-and-drop technique to move the title text, Pruning Techniques, to the right table cell. Rotate the text direction to 90° and then center the text vertically in the cell. Change the font size to 32.

6. Insert a text box in the left table cell and type `Incorrect Stem Cut` in the box. Change the font color to Red. Copy this text from the left cell and paste it into the center cell, and then change the word, Correct, to Incorrect. Change the font color to Green. Apply the Subtle Effect – Accent 3 Quick Style (row 4, column 4) to these two text boxes and add an Orange border (shape outline) with a 3 pt line weight.

7. Set the Left and Right text box margins to 0.1" and the Top and Bottom margins to 0.2". Display the gridlines and align the text boxes with the top-left squares.

8. Type `Keep Your Tree Healthy` as the new title text. Add an Orange (column 3) fill color to the title text placeholder. Insert an Elbow Connector shape (column 4 in the Lines area) to the right of the word, Healthy, and change the color to Green.

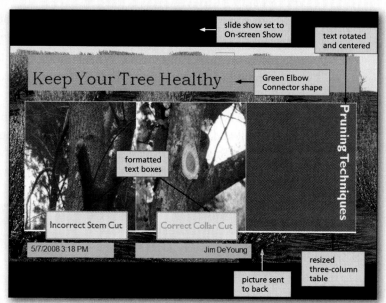

Figure 73

Continued >

In the Lab continued

9. Insert the OF-1 Pear Trees picture and drag the sizing handles to cover the entire slide. Use the Send to Back button to move the picture under the slide content.

10. Display your name and current date and time in the footer. Select each footer placeholder and add a Light Green (column 5) fill color.

11. Change the document properties, as specified by your instructor. Save the presentation using the file name, Lab OF-1 Pruning. Print the slides.

12. Save the slide as a .jpg image with the file name, Lab 0F-1 Pruning Picture.

13. Run the presentation with and without narration.

14. Submit the revised document in the format specified by your instructor. Reset the resolution and slide show settings.

In the Lab

Lab 2: Importing and Modifying a Radical Sports Design Template

Problem: Your local park district is preparing marketing materials for its summer recreational program. You have volunteered to help produce a PowerPoint presentation that will be displayed at the community center. The title slide will be incorporated in the front page of the brochure that will be mailed to all community residents and in print advertisements in the local paper. You create this title slide, which is shown in Figure 74, to show to the Park District marketing director.

Instructions:

1. Start a new presentation. Locate and download the 'Radical sports design template', which is located in the Sports subcategory of the Design slides category on the Microsoft Office Online Web site.

2. Insert the marketing theme, Wheels and Fields, in the title text placeholder and the name of your community along with the words, Parks and Recreation Department, in the subtitle text placeholder. Insert your name in the footer.

3. Insert a two-column table with one row and then insert the OF-2 Skateboard photograph in the left cell and the OF-2 Baseball photograph in the right cell. Both photographs are on your Data Files for Students. Display the Layout tab and then change the table size height to 2.75".

4. Insert a text box with Left and Right margins of 0.5" and Top and Bottom margins of 0.3". Change the Shape Fill color to Red and the Shape Outline color to Yellow. Drag the text box to the right side of the subtitle text placeholder and rotate it to the left, as shown in Figure 74. Then send the text box back so that the subtitle text is displayed on top of this text box.

5. Save the slide as a .jpg image using the file name, Lab OF-2 Summer Brochure. Save the presentation using the file name, Lab OF-2 Radical Sports.

6. Submit the revised document in the format specified by your instructor.

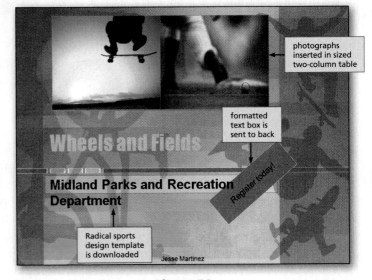

photographs inserted in sized two-column table

formatted text box is sent to back

Wheels and Fields

Midland Parks and Recreation Department

Register today!

Radical sports design template is downloaded

Jesse Martinez

Figure 74

In the Lab

Lab 3: Creating an Interactive Quiz to Reinforce Feng Shui Concepts

Problem: In Chapter 6 you created a presentation illustrating feng shui concepts. You want to see if your message is reaching your audience correctly, so you create a True-False quiz, shown in Figure 75, to test viewers' understanding of this Chinese practice of creating harmony and balance.

Instructions:

1. Open the presentation, Revised Feng Shui, from your USB flash drive. (If you did not complete this presentation, see your instructor for a copy.) Display the slides in Slide Sorter view and then select all slides by clicking Slide 1, pressing and holding down the SHIFT key, and then clicking Slide 9. Click the Advance Slide Automatically After check box in the Transition to This Slide group on the Animations tab to uncheck the box and remove slide timings.

2. Return to Normal view and then add a slide at the end of the presentation. Insert the Isosceles Triangle shape (row 1, column 3 in the Basic Shapes area) in the lower-left side of the slide and size it to a height of 2.5" and a width of 2.9", which is 250% of the original size. Apply the Intense Effect – Accent 1 Shape Style (row 6, column 2) to the shape.

3. Copy the shape to the lower-right side of the slide and apply the Intense Effect – Accent 6 Shape Style (row 6, column 7) to this shape. Change the outline color to Purple. Type True in the left triangle and False in the right triangle. Rotate the True and False text 270° and then change the font color to Dark Blue (column 9) and the font size to 40. Align the text in the left side of the shapes. Rotate the right shape 180° so that it is upside down.

4. Duplicate the slide twice and then type the questions in Table 2 in the title text placeholders.

New Quiz Slide	Question	Answers
1	The two opposing forces active in the environment are called yin and yang.	True
2	The five elements in the Productive Cycle shape daily life.	True
3	This room illustrates the correct placement of kitchen appliances.	False

Table 2 Quiz Questions and Answers

5. Click the AutoFit Options button on the left side of the placeholders and then click Stop Fitting Text to This Placeholder to stop PowerPoint from changing the title text font size. On Slide 1, drag the placeholder's bottom sizing handle down to position the entire placeholder on the slide.

6. Display the gridlines and the ruler. Display the Opulent Slide Master and then copy the Yin and Yang symbol to the first quiz slide. Size this symbol to 150% and then align the upper-left corner with the gridline at 2" left of center and 1" above center.

7. Use the Paste Special command to copy the Productive Cycle from Slide 3 to the second quiz slide. Paste the Productive Cycle as a picture with the .png file format. Size the picture to a height of 5.5" and align the upper-left corner with the gridline at 4" left of center and 2" above center.

8. Use the Paste Special command to copy the kitchen diagram from Slide 5 to the third quiz slide and paste it as a picture with the .png file format. Size the picture to a height of 4.7" and align the upper-left corner with the gridline at 4" left of center and 2" above center.

9. Animate the two triangles and the picture on each quiz slide using the settings in Table 3.

10. Hide the gridlines and the ruler. Delete Slides 1 through 9. Open the Microsoft Visual Basic Editor and then enter the procedure to display a slide, accept a True or False answer, and then display a message box giving feedback. Use the code in Table 1 on page PPT 484 as a guide. The quiz should terminate when the user has selected the correct answer on the final quiz slide.

Continued >

In the Lab *continued*

Table 3 Quiz Objects Animation				
Order	**Object**	**Effect**	**Start Setting**	**Speed**
1	Picture	Entrance Spinner (Moderate category)	After Previous	Medium
2	Left Isosceles Triangle	Entrance Ascend (Moderate category)	After Previous	Slow
3	Right Isosceles Triangle	Entrance Ascend (Moderate category)	With Previous	Slow
4	Picture	Emphasis Blink (Exciting category)	After Previous	Slow
5 (for quiz slides 1 and 2 only)	Picture	Exit Spinner (Moderate category)	After Previous	Medium

11. Assign the macros to the two triangle shapes on each quiz slide.

12. Save the quiz as a macro-enabled presentation using the file name, Lab OF-3 Feng Shui Macro. If necessary, change the Trust Center macro setting to 'Enable all macros'.

13. Submit the revised document in the format specified by your instructor. Reset the macro setting.

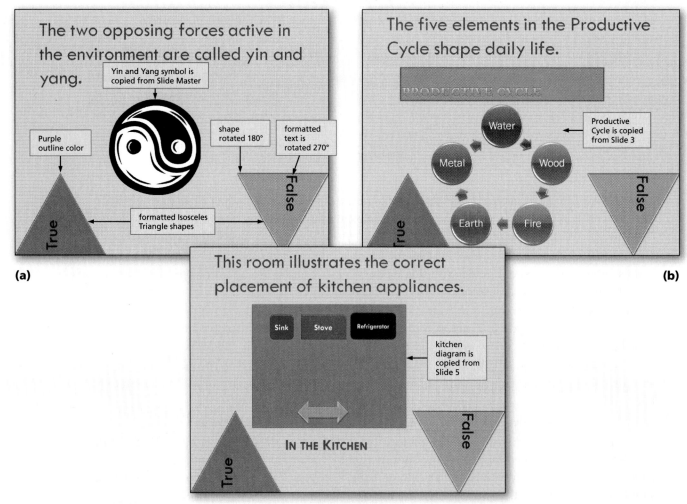

(a)

(b)

Figure 75 (c)

Appendix A
Project Planning Guidelines

Using Project Planning Guidelines

The process of communicating specific information to others is a learned, rational skill. Computers and software, especially Microsoft Office 2007, can help you develop ideas and present detailed information to a particular audience.

Using Microsoft Office 2007, you can create projects such as Word documents, Excel spreadsheets, Access databases, and PowerPoint presentations. Computer hardware and productivity software such as Microsoft Office 2007 minimizes much of the laborious work of drafting and revising projects. Some communicators handwrite ideas in notebooks, others compose directly on the computer, and others have developed unique strategies that work for their own particular thinking and writing styles.

No matter what method you use to plan a project, follow specific guidelines to arrive at a final product that presents information correctly and effectively (Figure A–1). Use some aspects of these guidelines every time you undertake a project, and others as needed in specific instances. For example, in determining content for a project, you may decide that a bar chart communicates trends more effectively than a paragraph of text. If so, you would create this graphical element and insert it in an Excel spreadsheet, a Word document, or a PowerPoint slide.

Determine the Project's Purpose

Begin by clearly defining why you are undertaking this assignment. For example, you may want to track monetary donations collected for your club's fundraising drive. Alternatively, you may be urging students to vote for a particular candidate in the next election. Once you clearly understand the purpose of your task, begin to draft ideas of how best to communicate this information.

Analyze Your Audience

Learn about the people who will read, analyze, or view your work. Where are they employed? What are their educational backgrounds? What are their expectations? What questions do they have?

PROJECT PLANNING GUIDELINES

1. DETERMINE THE PROJECT'S PURPOSE
Why are you undertaking the project?

2. ANALYZE YOUR AUDIENCE
Who are the people who will use your work?

3. GATHER POSSIBLE CONTENT
What information exists, and in what forms?

4. DETERMINE WHAT CONTENT TO PRESENT TO YOUR AUDIENCE
What information will best communicate the project's purpose to your audience?

Figure A–1

Design experts suggest drawing a mental picture of these people or finding photographs of people who fit this profile so that you can develop a project with the audience in mind.

By knowing your audience members, you can tailor a project to meet their interests and needs. You will not present them with information they already possess, and you will not omit the information they need to know.

Example: Your assignment is to raise the profile of your college's nursing program in the community. How much do they know about your college and the nursing curriculum? What are the admission requirements? How many of the applicants admitted complete the program? What percent pass the state Boards?

Gather Possible Content

Rarely are you in a position to develop all the material for a project. Typically, you would begin by gathering existing information that may reside in spreadsheets or databases. Web sites, pamphlets, magazine and newspaper articles, and books could provide insights of how others have approached your topic. Personal interviews often provide perspectives not available by any other means. Consider video and audio clips as potential sources for material that might complement or support the factual data you uncover.

Determine What Content to Present to Your Audience

Experienced designers recommend writing three or four major ideas you want an audience member to remember after reading or viewing your project. It also is helpful to envision your project's endpoint, the key fact you wish to emphasize. All project elements should lead to this ending point.

As you make content decisions, you also need to think about other factors. Presentation of the project content is an important consideration. For example, will your brochure be printed on thick, colored paper or transparencies? Will your PowerPoint presentation be viewed in a classroom with excellent lighting and a bright projector, or will it be viewed on a notebook computer monitor? Determine relevant time factors, such as the length of time to develop the project, how long readers will spend reviewing your project, or the amount of time allocated for your speaking engagement. Your project will need to accommodate all of these constraints.

Decide whether a graph, photograph, or artistic element can express or emphasize a particular concept. The right hemisphere of the brain processes images by attaching an emotion to them, so audience members are more apt to recall these graphics long term rather than just reading text.

As you select content, be mindful of the order in which you plan to present information. Readers and audience members generally remember the first and last pieces of information they see and hear, so you should put the most important information at the top or bottom of the page.

Summary

When creating a project, it is beneficial to follow some basic guidelines from the outset. By taking some time at the beginning of the process to determine the project's purpose, analyze the audience, gather possible content, and determine what content to present to the audience, you can produce a project that is informative, relevant, and effective.

Appendix B
Introduction to Microsoft Office 2007

What Is Microsoft Office 2007?

Microsoft Office 2007 is a collection of the more popular Microsoft application software. It is available in Basic, Home and Student, Standard, Small Business, Professional, Ultimate, Professional Plus, and Enterprise editions. Each edition consists of a group of programs, collectively called a suite. Table B-1 lists the suites and their components. **Microsoft Office Professional Edition 2007** includes these six programs: Microsoft Office Word 2007, Microsoft Office Excel 2007, Microsoft Office Access 2007, Microsoft Office PowerPoint 2007, Microsoft Office Publisher 2007, and Microsoft Office Outlook 2007. The programs in the Office suite allow you to work efficiently, communicate effectively, and improve the appearance of the projects you create.

Table B–1

	Microsoft Office Basic 2007	Microsoft Office Home & Student 2007	Microsoft Office Standard 2007	Microsoft Office Small Business 2007	Microsoft Office Professional 2007	Microsoft Office Ultimate 2007	Microsoft Office Professional Plus 2007	Microsoft Office Enterprise 2007
Microsoft Office Word 2007	✓	✓	✓	✓	✓	✓	✓	✓
Microsoft Office Excel 2007	✓	✓	✓	✓	✓	✓	✓	✓
Microsoft Office Access 2007					✓	✓	✓	✓
Microsoft Office PowerPoint 2007		✓	✓	✓	✓	✓	✓	✓
Microsoft Office Publisher 2007				✓	✓	✓	✓	✓
Microsoft Office Outlook 2007	✓		✓				✓	✓
Microsoft Office OneNote 2007		✓				✓		
Microsoft Office Outlook 2007 with Business Contact Manager				✓	✓	✓		
Microsoft Office InfoPath 2007						✓	✓	✓
Integrated Enterprise Content Management						✓	✓	✓
Electronic Forms						✓	✓	✓
Advanced Information Rights Management and Policy Capabilities						✓	✓	✓
Microsoft Office Communicator 2007							✓	✓
Microsoft Office Groove 2007						✓		✓

Microsoft has bundled additional programs in some versions of Office 2007, in addition to the main group of Office programs. Table B–1 on the previous page lists the components of the various Office suites.

In addition to the Office 2007 programs noted previously, Office 2007 suites can contain other programs. Microsoft Office OneNote 2007 is a digital notebook program that allows you to gather and share various types of media, such as text, graphics, video, audio, and digital handwriting. Microsoft Office InfoPath 2007 is a program that allows you to create and use electronic forms to gather information. Microsoft Office Groove 2007 provides collaborative workspaces in real time. Additional services that are oriented toward the enterprise solution also are available.

Office 2007 and the Internet, World Wide Web, and Intranets

Office 2007 allows you to take advantage of the Internet, the World Wide Web, and intranets. The Microsoft Windows operating system includes a **browser**, which is a program that allows you to locate and view a Web page. The Windows browser is called Internet Explorer.

One method of viewing a Web page is to use the browser to enter the Web address for the Web page. Another method of viewing a Web page is clicking a hyperlink. A **hyperlink** is colored or underlined text or a graphic that, when clicked, connects to another Web page. Hyperlinks placed in Office 2007 documents allow for direct access to a Web site of interest.

An **intranet** is a private network, such as a network used within a company or organization for internal communication. Like the Internet, hyperlinks are used within an intranet to access documents, pages, and other destinations on the intranet. Unlike the Internet, the materials on the network are available only for those who are part of the private network.

Online Collaboration Using Office

Organizations that, in the past, were able to make important information available only to a select few, now can make their information accessible to a wider range of individuals who use programs such as Office 2007 and Internet Explorer. Office 2007 allows colleagues to use the Internet or an intranet as a central location to view documents, manage files, and work together.

Each of the Office 2007 programs makes publishing documents on a Web server as simple as saving a file on a hard disk. Once placed on the Web server, users can view and edit the documents and conduct Web discussions and live online meetings.

Using Microsoft Office 2007

The various Microsoft Office 2007 programs each specialize in a particular task. This section describes the general functions of the more widely used Office 2007 programs, along with how they are used to access the Internet or an intranet.

Microsoft Office Word 2007

Microsoft Office Word 2007 is a full-featured word processing program that allows you to create many types of personal and business documents, including flyers, letters, resumes, business documents, and academic reports.

Word's AutoCorrect, spelling, and grammar features help you proofread documents for errors in spelling and grammar by identifying the errors and offering suggestions for corrections as you type. The live word count feature provides you with a constantly updating word count as you enter and edit text. To assist with creating specific documents, such as a business letter or resume, Word provides templates, which provide a formatted document before you type the text of the document. Quick Styles provide a live preview of styles from the Style gallery, allowing you to preview styles in the document before actually applying them.

Word automates many often-used tasks and provides you with powerful desktop publishing tools to use as you create professional looking brochures, advertisements, and newsletters. SmartArt allows you to insert interpretive graphics based on document content.

Word makes it easier for you to share documents for collaboration. The Send feature opens an e-mail window with the active document attached. The Compare Documents feature allows you easily to identify changes when comparing different document versions.

Word 2007 and the Internet   Word makes it possible to design and publish Web pages on the Internet or an intranet, insert a hyperlink to a Web page in a word processing document, as well as access and search the content of other Web pages.

Microsoft Office Excel 2007

Microsoft Office Excel 2007 is a spreadsheet program that allows you to organize data, complete calculations, graph data, develop professional looking reports, publish organized data to the Web, and access real-time data from Web sites.

In addition to its mathematical functionality, Excel 2007 provides tools for visually comparing data. For instance, when comparing a group of values in cells, you can set cell backgrounds with bars proportional to the value of the data in the cell. You can also set cell backgrounds with full-color backgrounds, or use a color scale to facilitate interpretation of data values.

Excel 2007 provides strong formatting support for tables with the new Style Preview gallery.

Excel 2007 and the Internet   Using Excel 2007, you can create hyperlinks within a worksheet to access other Office documents on the network or on the Internet. Worksheets saved as static, or unchanging Web pages can be viewed using a browser. The person viewing static Web pages cannot change them.

In addition, you can create and run queries that retrieve information from a Web page and insert the information directly into a worksheet.

Microsoft Office Access 2007

Microsoft Office Access 2007 is a comprehensive database management system (DBMS). A **database** is a collection of data organized in a manner that allows access, retrieval, and use of that data. Access 2007 allows you to create a database; add, change, and delete data in the database; sort data in the database; retrieve data from the database; and create forms and reports using the data in the database.

Access 2007 and the Internet   Access 2007 lets you generate reports, which are summaries that show only certain data from the database, based on user requirements.

Microsoft Office PowerPoint 2007

Microsoft Office PowerPoint 2007 is a complete presentation graphics program that allows you to produce professional looking presentations. With PowerPoint 2007, you can create informal presentations using overhead transparencies, electronic presentations using a projection device attached to a personal computer, formal presentations using 35mm slides or a CD, or you can run virtual presentations on the Internet.

PowerPoint 2007 and the Internet   PowerPoint 2007 allows you to publish presentations on the Internet or other networks.

Microsoft Office Publisher 2007

Microsoft Office Publisher 2007 is a desktop publishing program (DTP) that allows you to design and produce professional quality documents (newsletters, flyers, brochures, business cards, Web sites, and so on) that combine text, graphics, and photographs. Desktop publishing software provides a variety of tools, including design templates, graphic manipulation tools, color schemes or libraries, and various page wizards and templates. For large jobs, businesses use desktop publishing software to design publications that are **camera ready**, which means the files are suitable for production by outside commercial printers. Publisher 2007 also allows you to locate commercial printers, service bureaus, and copy shops willing to accept customer files created in Publisher.

Publisher 2007 allows you to design a unique image, or logo, using one of more than 45 master design sets. This, in turn, permits you to use the same design for all your printed documents (letters, business cards, brochures, and advertisements) and Web pages. Publisher includes 70 coordinated color schemes; 30 font schemes; more than 10,000 high-quality clip art images; 1,500 photographs; 1,000 Web-art graphics; 340 animated graphics; and hundreds of unique Design Gallery elements (quotations, sidebars, and so on). If you wish, you also can download additional images from the Microsoft Office Online Web page on the Microsoft Web site.

Publisher 2007 and the Internet   Publisher 2007 allows you easily to create a multipage Web site with custom color schemes, photographic images, animated images, and sounds.

Microsoft Office Outlook 2007

Microsoft Office Outlook 2007 is a powerful communications and scheduling program that helps you communicate with others, keep track of your contacts, and organize your schedule. Outlook 2007 allows you to view a To-Do bar containing tasks and appointments from your Outlook calendar. Outlook 2007 allows you to send and receive electronic mail (e-mail) and permits you to engage in real-time communication with family, friends, or coworkers using instant messaging. Outlook 2007 also provides you with the means to organize your contacts, and you can track e-mail messages, meetings, and notes with a particular contact. Outlook's Calendar, Contacts, Tasks, and Notes components aid in this organization. Contact information is available from the Outlook Calendar, Mail, Contacts, and Task components by accessing the Find a Contact feature. **Personal information management (PIM)** programs such as Outlook provide a way for individuals and workgroups to organize, find, view, and share information easily.

Microsoft Office 2007 Help

At any time while you are using one of the Office programs, you can interact with **Microsoft Office 2007 Help** for that program and display information about any topic associated with the program. Several categories of help are available. In all programs, you can access Help by pressing the F1 key on the keyboard. In Publisher 2007 and Outlook 2007, the Help window can be opened by clicking the Help menu and then selecting Microsoft Office Publisher or Outlook Help command, or by entering search text in the 'Type a question for help' text box in the upper-right corner of the program window. In the other Office programs, clicking the Microsoft Office Help button near the upper-right corner of the program window opens the program Help window.

The Help window in all programs provides several methods for accessing help about a particular topic, and has tools for navigating around Help. Appendix C contains detailed instructions for using Help.

Collaboration and SharePoint

While not part of the Microsoft Office 2007 suites, SharePoint is a Microsoft tool that allows Office 2007 users to share data using collaborative tools that are integrated into the main Office programs. SharePoint consists of Windows SharePoint Services, Office SharePoint Server 2007, and, optionally, Office SharePoint Designer 2007.

Windows SharePoint Services provides the platform for collaboration programs and services. Office SharePoint Server 2007 is built on top of Windows SharePoint Services. The result of these two products is the ability to create SharePoint sites. A SharePoint site is a Web site that provides users with a virtual place for collaborating and communicating with their colleagues while working together on projects, documents, ideas, and information. Each member of a group with access to the SharePoint site has the ability to contribute to the material stored there. The basic building blocks of SharePoint sites are lists and libraries. Lists contain collections of information, such as calendar items, discussion points, contacts, and links. Lists can be edited to add or delete information. Libraries are similar to lists, but include both files and information about files. Types of libraries include document, picture, and forms libraries.

The most basic type of SharePoint site is called a Workspace, which is used primarily for collaboration. Different types of Workspaces can be created using SharePoint to suit different needs. SharePoint provides templates, or outlines of these Workspaces, that can be filled in to create the Workspace. Each of the different types of Workspace templates contain a different collection of lists and libraries, reflecting the purpose of the Workspace. You can create a Document Workspace to facilitate collaboration on documents. A Document Workspace contains a document library for documents and supporting files, a Links list that allows you to maintain relevant resource links for the document, a Tasks list for listing and assigning To-Do items to team members, and other links as needed. Meeting Workspaces allow users to plan and organize a meeting, with components such as Attendees, Agenda, and a Document Library. Social Meeting Workspaces provide a place to plan social events, with lists and libraries such as Attendees, Directions, Image/Logo, Things To Bring, Discussions, and Picture Library. A Decision Meeting Workspace is a Meeting Workspace with a focus on review and decision-making, with lists and libraries such as Objectives, Attendees, Agenda, Document Library, Tasks, and Decisions.

Users also can create a SharePoint site called a WebParts page, which is built from modules called WebParts. WebParts are modular units of information that contain a title bar and content that reflects the type of WebPart. For instance, an image WebPart would contain a title bar and an image. WebParts allow you quickly to create and modify a SharePoint site, and allow for the creation of a unique site that can allow users to access and make changes to information stored on the site.

Large SharePoint sites that include multiple pages can be created using templates as well. Groups needing more refined and targeted sharing options than those available with SharePoint Server 2007 and Windows SharePoint Services can add SharePoint Designer 2007 to create a site that meets their specific needs.

Depending on which components have been selected for inclusion on the site, users can view a team calendar, view links, read announcements, and view and edit group documents and projects. SharePoint sites can be set up so that documents are checked in and out, much like a library, to prevent multiple users from making changes simultaneously. Once a SharePoint site is set up, Office programs are used to perform maintenance of the site. For example, changes in the team calendar are updated using Outlook 2007, and changes that users make in Outlook 2007 are reflected on the SharePoint site. Office 2007 programs include a Publish feature that allows users easily to save file updates to a SharePoint site. Team members can be notified about changes made to material on the site either by e-mail or by a news feed, meaning that users do not have to go to the site to check to see if anything has been updated since they last viewed or worked on it. The search feature in SharePoint allows users quickly to find information on a large site.

Appendix C
Microsoft Office PowerPoint 2007 Help

Using Microsoft Office PowerPoint 2007 Help

This appendix shows how to use Microsoft Office PowerPoint Help. At any time while you are using one of the Microsoft Office 2007 programs, you can use Office Help to display information about all topics associated with the program. This appendix uses Microsoft Office PowerPoint 2007 to illustrate the use of Office Help. Help in other Office 2007 programs responds in a similar fashion.

In Office 2007, Help is presented in a window that has Web browser-style navigation buttons. Each Office 2007 program has its own Help home page, which is the starting Help page that is displayed in the Help window. If your computer is connected to the Internet, the contents of the Help page reflect both the local help files installed on the computer and material from Microsoft's Web site. As shown in Figure C–1, two methods for accessing PowerPoint's Help are available:

1. Microsoft Office PowerPoint Help button near the upper-right corner of the PowerPoint window
2. Function key F1 on the keyboard

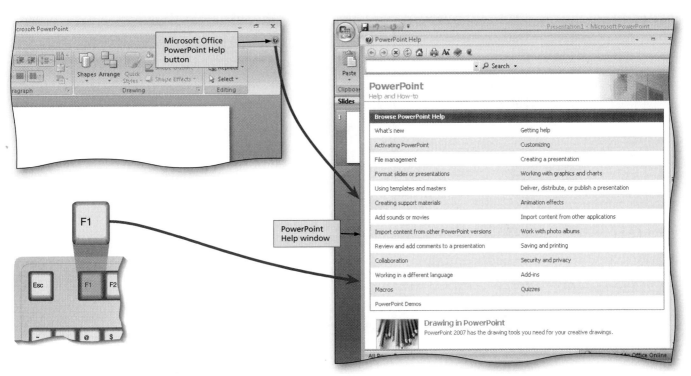

Figure C–1

To Open the PowerPoint Help Window

The following steps open the PowerPoint Help window and maximize the window.

• Start Microsoft PowerPoint, if necessary. Click the Microsoft Office PowerPoint Help button near the upper-right corner of the PowerPoint window to open the PowerPoint Help window (Figure C–2).

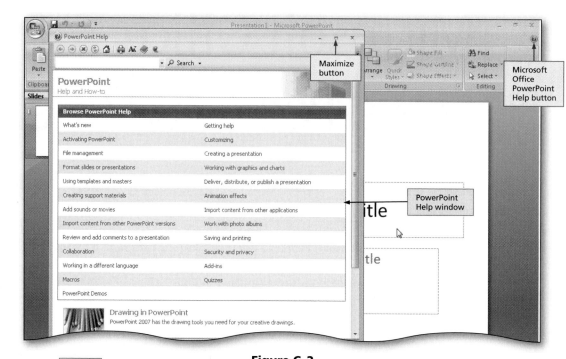

Figure C–2

❷

• Click the Maximize button on the Help title bar to maximize the Help window (Figure C–3).

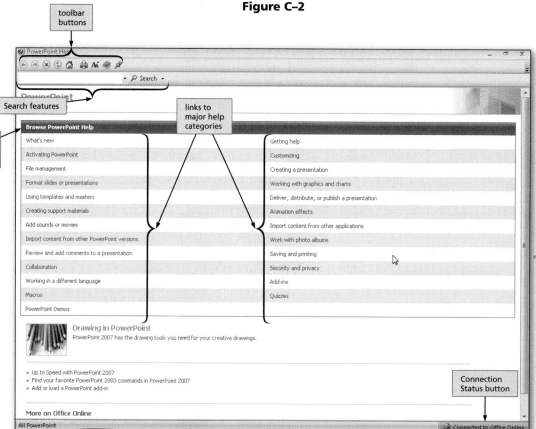

Figure C–3

The PowerPoint Help Window

The PowerPoint Help window provides several methods for accessing help about a particular topic, and also has tools for navigating around Help. Methods for accessing Help include searching the help content installed with PowerPoint, or searching the online Office content maintained by Microsoft.

Figure C–3 shows the main PowerPoint Help window. To navigate Help, the PowerPoint Help window includes search features that allow you to search on a word or phrase about which you want help; the Connection Status button, which allows you to control where PowerPoint Help searches for content; toolbar buttons; and links to major Help categories.

Search Features

You can perform Help searches on words or phrases to find information about any PowerPoint feature using the 'Type words to search for' text box and the Search button (Figure C–4a). Click the 'Type words to search for' text box and then click the Search button or press the ENTER key to initiate a search of PowerPoint Help.

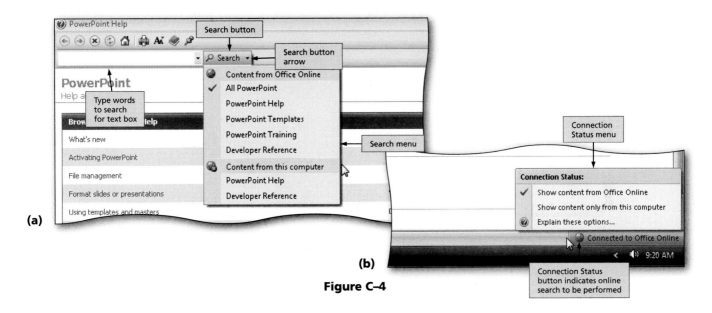

Figure C–4

PowerPoint Help offers the user the option of searching the online Help Web pages maintained by Microsoft or the offline Help files placed on your computer when you install PowerPoint. You can specify whether PowerPoint Help should search online or offline from two places: the Connection Status button on the status bar of the PowerPoint Help window, or the Search button arrow on the toolbar. The Connection Status button indicates whether Help currently is set up to work with online or offline information sources. Clicking the Connection Status button provides a menu with commands for selecting online or offline searches (Figure C–4b). The Connection Status menu allows the user to select whether help searches will return content only from the computer (offline), or content from the computer and from Office Online (online).

Clicking the Search button arrow also provides a menu with commands for an online or offline search (Figure C–4a). These commands determine the source of information that Help searches for during the current Help session only. For example, assume that your preferred search is an offline search because you often do not have Internet access. You would set Connection Status to 'Show content only from this computer'. When you have Internet access, you can select an online search from the Search menu to search Office Online for information for your current search session only. Your search will use the Office Online resources until you quit Help. The next time you start Help, the Connection Status once again will be offline. In addition to setting the source of information that Help searches for during the current Help session, you can use the Search menu to further target the current search to one of four subcategories of online Help: PowerPoint Help, PowerPoint Templates, PowerPoint Training, and Developer Reference. The local search further can target one subcategory, Developer Reference.

In addition to searching for a word or string of text, you can use the links provided on the Browse PowerPoint Help area (Figure C–3 on page App 10) to search for help on a topic. These links direct you to major help categories. From each major category, subcategories are available to further refine your search.

Finally, you can use the Table of Contents for PowerPoint Help to search for a topic the same way you would in a hard copy book. The Table of Contents is accessed via a toolbar button.

Toolbar Buttons

You can use toolbar buttons to navigate through the results of your search. The toolbar buttons are located on the toolbar near the top of the Help window (Figure C–5). The toolbar buttons contain navigation buttons as well as buttons that perform other useful and common tasks in PowerPoint Help, such as printing.

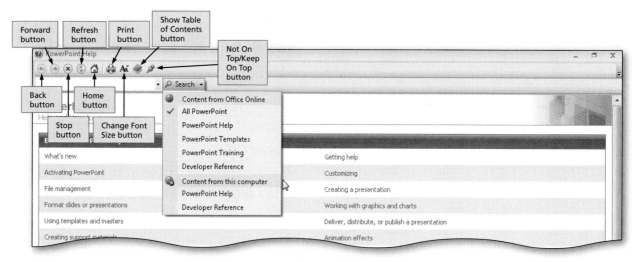

Figure C–5

The PowerPoint Help navigation buttons are the Back, Forward, Stop, Refresh, and Home buttons. These five buttons behave like the navigation buttons in a Web browser window. You can use the Back button to go back one window, the Forward button to go forward one window, the Stop button to stop loading the current page, and the Home button to redisplay the Help home page in the Help window. Use the Refresh button to reload the information requested into the Help window from its original source. When getting Help information online, this button provides the most current information from the Microsoft Help Web site.

The buttons located to the right of the navigation buttons — Print, Change Font Size, Show Table of Contents, and Not on Top — provide you with access to useful and common commands. The Print button prints the contents of the open Help window. The Change Font Size button customizes the Help window by increasing or decreasing the size of its text. The Show Table of Contents button opens a pane on the left side of the Help window that shows the Table of Contents for PowerPoint Help. You can use the Table of Contents for PowerPoint Help to navigate through the contents of PowerPoint Help much as you would use the Table of Contents in a book to search for a topic. The Not On Top button is an example of a toggle button, which is a button that can be switched back and forth between two states. It determines how the PowerPoint Help window behaves relative to other windows. When clicked, the Not On Top button changes to Keep On Top. In this state, it does not allow other windows from PowerPoint or other programs to cover the PowerPoint Help window when those windows are the active windows. When in the Not On Top state, the button allows other windows to be opened or moved on top of the PowerPoint Help window.

You can customize the size and placement of the Help window. Resize the window using the Maximize and Restore buttons, or by dragging the window to a desired size. Relocate the Help window by dragging the title bar to a new location on the screen.

Searching PowerPoint Help

Once the PowerPoint Help window is open, several methods exist for navigating PowerPoint Help. You can search for help by using any of the three following methods from the Help window:

1. Enter search text in the 'Type words to search for' text box
2. Click the links in the Help window
3. Use the Table of Contents

To Obtain Help Using the Type Words to Search for Text Box

Assume for the following example that you want to know more about watermarks. The following steps use the 'Type words to search for' text box to obtain useful information about narration by entering the word, narration, as search text. The steps also navigate in the PowerPoint Help window.

1

- Type narration in the 'Type words to search for' text box at the top of the PowerPoint Help window.

- Click the Search button arrow to display the Search menu.

- If it is not selected already, click All PowerPoint on the Search menu to select the command. If All Word is already selected, click the Search button arrow again to close the Search menu.

Q&A Why select All PowerPoint on the Search menu?

Selecting All PowerPoint on the Search menu ensures that PowerPoint Help will search all possible sources for information on your search term. It will produce the most complete search results.

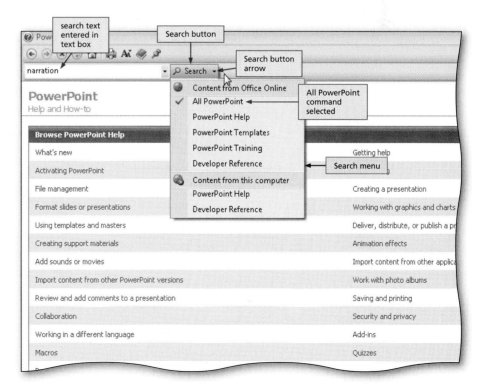

Figure C–6

2

- Click the Search button to display the search results (Figure C–7).

Q&A

Why do my results differ?

If you do not have an Internet connection, your results will reflect only the content of the Help files on your computer. When searching for help online, results also can change as material is added, deleted, and updated on the online Help Web pages maintained by Microsoft.

Q&A

Why were my search results not very helpful?

When initiating a search, keep in mind to check the spelling of the search text; and to keep your search very specific, with fewer than seven words, to return the most accurate results.

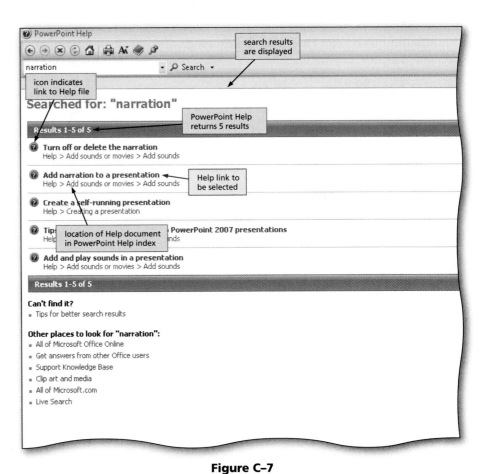

Figure C–7

3

- Click the 'Add narration to a presentation' link to open the Help document associated with the link in the Help window (Figure C–8).

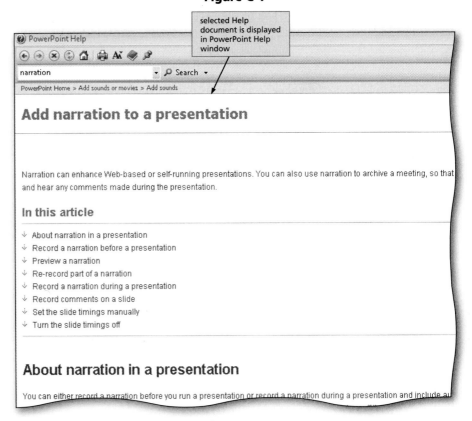

Figure C–8

4

- Click the Home button on the taskbar to clear the search results and redisplay the PowerPoint Help home page (Figure C–9).

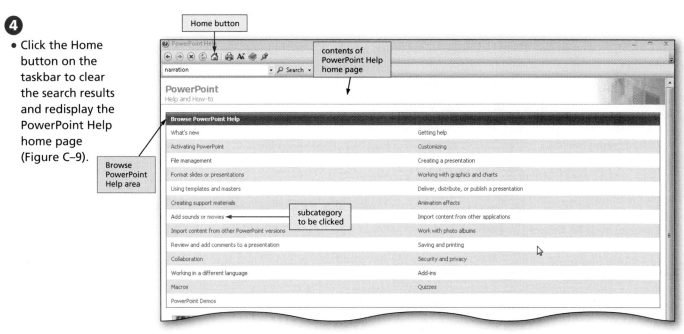

Figure C–9

To Obtain Help Using the Help Links

If your topic of interest is listed in the Browse PowerPoint Help area, you can click the link to begin browsing PowerPoint Help categories instead of entering search text. You browse PowerPoint Help just like you would browse a Web site. If you know in which category to find your Help information, you may wish to use these links. The following steps find the narration Help information using the category links from the PowerPoint Help home page.

1

- Click the 'Add sounds or movies' link, and then click Add sounds in the subcategories of "Add sounds or movies."

- Click the 'Add narration to a presentation' link to open the Help document associated with the link (Figure C–10).

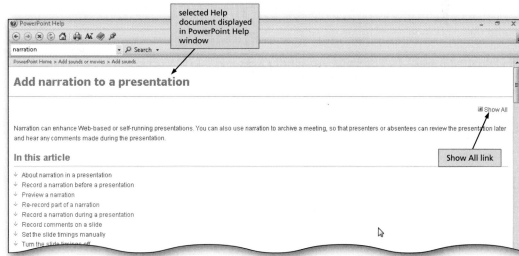

Figure C–10

Q&A

What does the Show All link do?

In many Help documents, additional information about terms and features is available by clicking a link in the document to display additional information in the Help document. Clicking the Show All link opens all the links in the Help document that expand to additional text.

To Obtain Help Using the Help Table of Contents

A third way to find Help in PowerPoint is through the Help Table of Contents. You can browse through the Table of Contents to display information about a particular topic or to familiarize yourself with PowerPoint. The following steps access the narration Help information by browsing through the Table of Contents.

1

- Click the Home button on the toolbar.

- Click the Show Table of Contents button on the toolbar to open the Table of Contents pane on the left side of the Help window. If necessary, click the Maximize button on the Help title bar to maximize the window (Figure C–11).

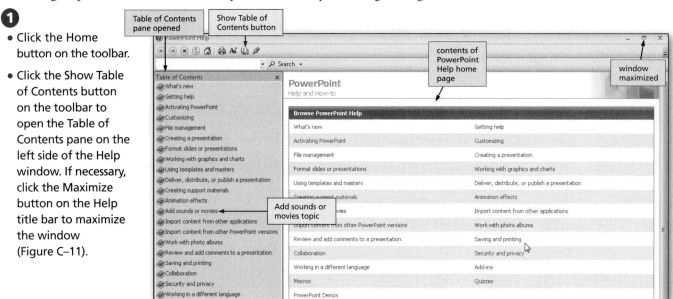

Figure C–11

2

- Click the 'Add sounds or movies' link in the Table of Contents pane to view a list of Help subcategories, and then click Add sounds to view a list of Help subtopics.

- Click the 'Add narration to a presentation' link in the Table of Contents pane to view the selected Help document in the right pane (Figure C–12).

How do I remove the Table of Contents pane when I am finished with it?

The Show Table of Contents button acts as a toggle switch. When the Table of Contents pane is visible, the button changes to Hide Table of Contents. Clicking it hides the Table of Contents pane and changes the button to Show Table of Contents.

Figure C–12

Obtaining Help while Working in PowerPoint

Often you may need help while working on a document without already having the Help window open. For example, you may be unsure about how a particular command works, or you may be presented with a dialog box that you are not sure how to use. Rather than opening the Help window and initiating a search, PowerPoint Help provides you with the ability to search directly for help.

Figure C–13 shows one option for obtaining help while working in PowerPoint. If you want to learn more about a command, point to the command button and wait for the Enhanced ScreenTip to appear. If the Help icon appears in the Enhanced ScreenTip, press the F1 key while pointing to the command to open the Help window associated with that command.

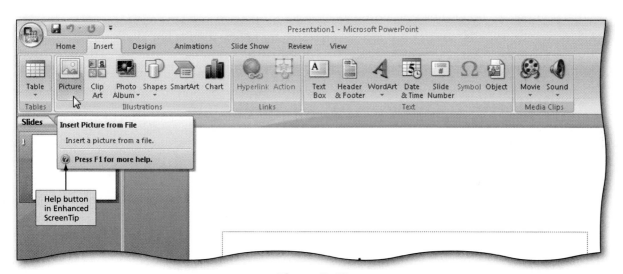

Figure C–13

Figure C–14 shows a dialog box with a Get help button in it. Pressing the F1 key while the dialog box is displayed opens a Help window. The Help window contains help about that dialog box, if available. If no help file is available for that particular dialog box, then the main Help window opens.

Figure C–14

Use Help

1 Obtaining Help Using Search Text

Instructions: Perform the following tasks using PowerPoint Help.

1. Use the 'Type words to search for' text box to obtain help about landscape printing. Use the Connection Status menu to search online help if you have an Internet connection.

2. Click 'Print with landscape orientation' in the list of links in the search results. Double-click the Microsoft Office PowerPoint Help window title bar to maximize it. Read and print the information. At the top of the printout, write down the number of links PowerPoint Help found.

3. Use the Search menu to search for help offline. Repeat the search from Step 1. At the top of the printout, write down the number of links that PowerPoint Help found searching offline. Submit the printouts as specified by your instructor.

4. Use the 'Type words to search for' text box to search for information online about adjusting line style. Click the 'Change the color, style, or weight of a line' link in the search results. If necessary, maximize the Microsoft Office 2007 PowerPoint Help window. Read and print the contents of the window. Close the Microsoft Office PowerPoint Help window. Submit the printouts as specified by your instructor.

5. For each of the following words and phrases, click one link in the search results, click the Show All link, and then print the page: page zoom; date; print preview; Ribbon; word count; and citation. Submit the printouts as specified by your instructor.

2 Expanding on PowerPoint Help Basics

Instructions: Use PowerPoint Help to better understand its features and answer the questions listed below. Answer the questions on your own paper, or submit the printed Help information as specified by your instructor.

1. Use Help to find out how to customize the Help window. Change the font size to the smallest option and then print the contents of the Microsoft Office PowerPoint Help window. Change the font size back to its original setting. Close the window.

2. Press the F1 key. Search for information about tables, restricting the search results to PowerPoint Templates. Print the first page of the Search results.

3. Search for information about tables, restricting the search results to PowerPoint Help files. Print the first page of the Search results.

4. Use PowerPoint Help to find out what happened to the Office Assistant, a feature in the previous version of PowerPoint. Print out the Help document that contains the answer.

Appendix D
Publishing Office 2007 Web Pages to a Web Server

With the Office 2007 programs, you use the Save As command on the Office Button menu to save a Web page to a Web server using one of two techniques: Web folders or File Transfer Protocol. A **Web folder** is an Office shortcut to a Web server. **File Transfer Protocol (FTP)** is an Internet standard that allows computers to exchange files with other computers on the Internet.

You should contact your network system administrator or technical support staff at your Internet access provider to determine if their Web server supports Web folders, FTP, or both, and to obtain necessary permissions to access the Web server. If you decide to publish Web pages using a Web folder, you must have the Office Server Extensions (OSE) installed on your computer.

Using Web Folders to Publish Office 2007 Web Pages

When publishing to a Web folder, someone first must create the Web folder before you can save to it. If you are granted permission to create a Web folder, you must obtain the Web address of the Web server, a user name, and possibly a password that allows you to access the Web server. You also must decide on a name for the Web folder. Table D–1 explains how to create a Web folder.

Office 2007 adds the name of the Web folder to the list of current Web folders. You can save to this folder, open files in the folder, rename the folder, or perform any operations you would to a folder on your hard disk. You can use your Office 2007 program or Windows Explorer to access this folder. Table D–2 explains how to save to a Web folder.

Table D–1 Creating a Web Folder

1. Click the Office Button and then click Save As or Open.

2. When the Save As dialog box (or Open dialog box) appears, click the Tools button arrow, and then click Map Network Drive... When the Map Network Drive dialog box is displayed, click the 'Connect to a Web site that you can use to store your documents and pictures' link.

3. When the Add Network Location Wizard dialog box appears, click the Next button. If necessary, click Choose a custom network location. Click the Next button. Click the View examples link, type the Internet or network address, and then click the Next button. Click 'Log on anonymously' to deselect the check box, type your user name in the User name text box, and then click the Next button. Enter the name you want to call this network place and then click the Next button. Click to deselect the 'Open this network location when I click Finish' check box, and then click the Finish button.

Table D–2 Saving to a Web Folder

1. Click the Office Button, click Save As.

2. When the Save As dialog box is displayed, type the Web page file name in the File name text box. Do not press the ENTER key.

3. Click the Save as type box arrow and then click Web Page to select the Web Page format.

4. Click Computer in the Navigation pane.

5. Double-click the Web folder name in the Network Location list.

6. If the Enter Network Password dialog box appears, type the user name and password in the respective text boxes and then click the OK button.

7. Click the Save button in the Save As dialog box.

Using FTP to Publish Office 2007 Web Pages

When publishing a Web page using FTP, you first must add the FTP location to your computer before you can save to it. An FTP location, also called an **FTP site**, is a collection of files that reside on an FTP server. In this case, the FTP server is the Web server.

To add an FTP location, you must obtain the name of the FTP site, which usually is the address (URL) of the FTP server, and a user name and a password that allows you to access the FTP server. You save and open the Web pages on the FTP server using the name of the FTP site. Table D–3 explains how to add an FTP site.

Office 2007 adds the name of the FTP site to the FTP locations list in the Save As and Open dialog boxes. You can open and save files using this list. Table D–4 explains how to save to an FTP location.

Table D–3 Adding an FTP Location

1. Click the Office Button and then click Save As or Open.

2. When the Save As dialog box (or Open dialog box) appears, click the Tools button arrow, and then click Map Network Drive... When the Map Network Drive dialog box is displayed, click the 'Connect to a Web site that you can use to store your documents and pictures' link.

3. When the Add Network Location Wizard dialog box appears, click the Next button. If necessary, click Choose a custom network location. Click the Next button. Click the View examples link, type the Internet or network address, and then click the Next button. If you have a user name for the site, click to deselect 'Log on anonymously' and type your user name in the User name text box, and then click Next. If the site allows anonymous logon, click Next. Type a name for the location, click Next, click to deselect the 'Open this network location when I click Finish' check box, and click Finish. Click the OK button.

4. Close the Save As or the Open dialog box.

Table D–4 Saving to an FTP Location

1. Click the Office Button and then click Save As.

2. When the Save As dialog box is displayed, type the Web page file name in the File name text box. Do not press the ENTER key.

3. Click the Save as type box arrow and then click Web Page to select the Web Page format.

4. Click Computer in the Navigation pane.

5. Double-click the name of the FTP site in the Network Location list.

6. When the FTP Log On dialog box appears, enter your user name and password and then click the OK button.

7. Click the Save button in the Save As dialog box.

Appendix E

Customizing Microsoft Office PowerPoint 2007

This appendix explains how to change the screen resolution in Windows Vista to the resolution used in this book. It also describes how to customize the PowerPoint window by changing the Ribbon, Quick Access Toolbar, and the color scheme.

Changing Screen Resolution

Screen resolution indicates the number of pixels (dots) that the computer uses to display the letters, numbers, graphics, and background you see on the screen. When you increase the screen resolution, Windows displays more information on the screen, but the information decreases in size. The reverse also is true: as you decrease the screen resolution, Windows displays less information on the screen, but the information increases in size.

The screen resolution usually is stated as the product of two numbers, such as 1024×768 (pronounced "ten twenty-four by seven sixty-eight"). A 1024×768 screen resolution results in a display of 1,024 distinct pixels on each of 768 lines, or about 786,432 pixels. The figures in this book were created using a screen resolution of 1024×768.

The screen resolutions most commonly used today are 800×600 and 1024×768, although some Office specialists set their computers at a much higher screen resolution, such as 2048×1536.

To Change the Screen Resolution

The following steps change the screen resolution from 1280×1024 to 1024×768. Your computer already may be set to 1024×768 or some other resolution.

1

- If necessary, minimize all programs so that the Windows Vista desktop appears.

- Right-click the Windows Vista desktop to display the Windows Vista desktop shortcut menu (Figure E–1).

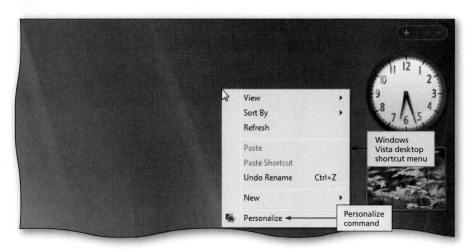

Figure E–1

2

- Click Personalize on the shortcut menu to open the Personalization window.

- Click Display Settings in the Personalization window to display the Display Settings dialog box (Figure E–2).

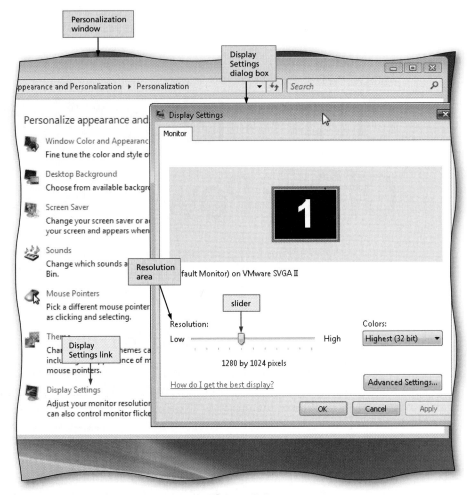

Figure E–2

3

- Drag the slider in the Resolution area so that the screen resolution changes to 1024 × 768 (Figure E–3).

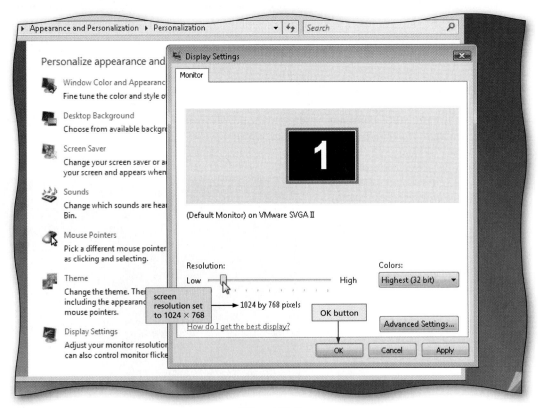

Figure E–3

4

- Click the OK button to change the screen resolution from 1280 × 1024 to 1024 × 768 (Figure E–4).

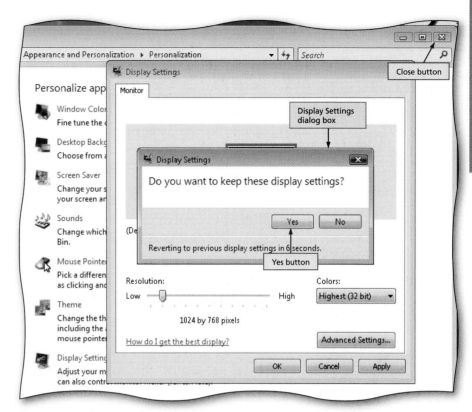

Figure E–4

5

- Click the Yes button in the Display Settings dialog box to accept the new screen resolution (Figure E–5).

Q&A What if I do not want to change the screen resolution after seeing it applied after I click the OK button?

You either can click the No button in the inner Display Settings dialog box, or wait for the timer to run out, at which point Windows Vista will revert to the original screen resolution.

- Click the Close button to close the Personalization Window.

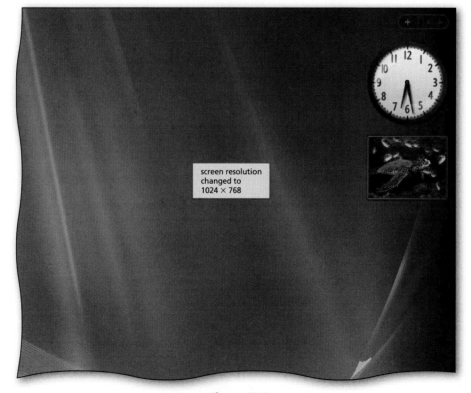

Figure E–5

Screen Resolution and the Appearance of the Ribbon in Office 2007 Programs

Changing the screen resolution affects how the Ribbon appears in Office 2007 programs. Figure E–6 shows the PowerPoint Ribbon at the screen resolutions of 800 × 600, 1024 × 768, and 1280 × 1024. All of the same commands are available regardless of screen resolution. PowerPoint, however, makes changes to the groups and the buttons within the groups to accommodate the various screen resolutions. The result is that certain commands may need to be accessed differently depending on the resolution chosen. A command that is visible on the Ribbon and available by clicking a button at one resolution may not be visible and may need to be accessed using its group button at a different resolution.

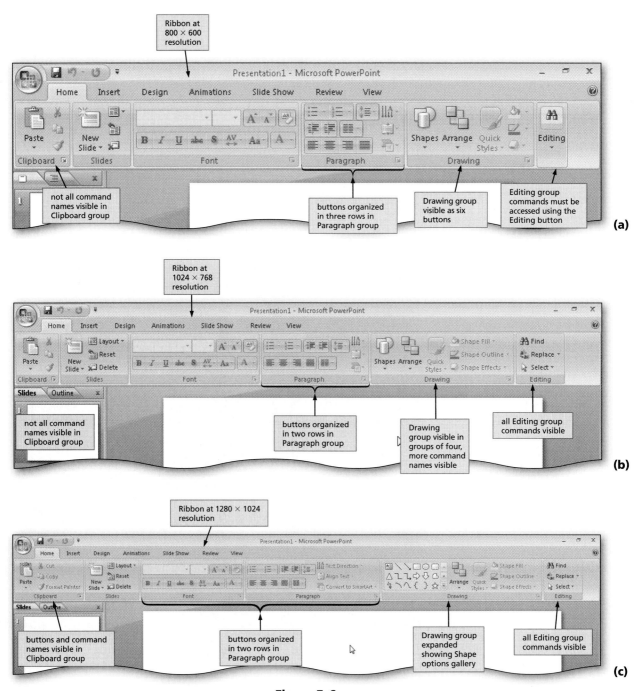

Figure E–6

Comparing the three Ribbons, notice changes in content and layout of the groups and galleries. In some cases, the content of a group is the same in each resolution, but the layout of the group differs. For example, the same buttons appear in the Paragraph group in the three resolutions, but the layouts differ. The buttons are displayed in three rows at the 800×600 resolution, and in two rows in the 1024×768 and 1280×1024 resolutions. In other cases, the content and layout are the same across the resolution, but the level of detail differs with the resolution. In the Clipboard group, when the resolution increases to 1280×1024, the names of all the buttons in the group appear in addition to the buttons themselves. At the lower resolution, only the buttons appear.

Changing resolutions also can result in fewer commands being visible in a group. Comparing the Editing groups, notice that the group at the 800×600 resolution consists of an Editing button, while at the higher resolutions, the group has three buttons visible. The commands that are available on the Ribbon at the higher resolutions must be accessed using the Editing button at the 800×600 resolution.

Changing resolutions results in different amounts of detail being available at one time in the galleries on the Ribbon. The Drawing group in the three resolutions presented show different numbers of buttons. At 800×600 and 1024×768, you need to click a button to display a gallery or menu of options, and at 1280×1024, many of the options within the Shapes gallery are visible.

Customizing the PowerPoint Window

When working in PowerPoint, you may want to make your working area as large as possible. One option is to minimize the Ribbon. You also can modify the characteristics of the Quick Access Toolbar, customizing the toolbar's commands and location to better suit your needs.

To Minimize the Ribbon in PowerPoint

The following steps minimize the Ribbon.

- Start PowerPoint.

- Maximize the PowerPoint window, if necessary.

- Click the Customize Quick Access Toolbar button on the Quick Access Toolbar to display the Customize Quick Access Toolbar menu (Figure E–7).

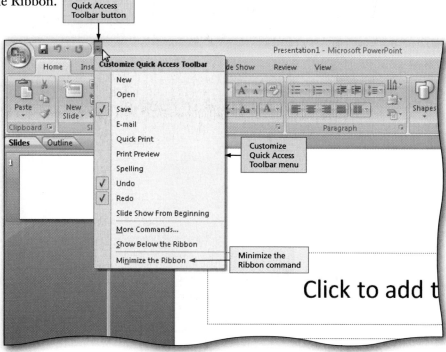

Figure E–7

- Click Minimize the Ribbon on the Quick Access Toolbar menu to reduce the Ribbon display to just the tabs (Figure E–8).

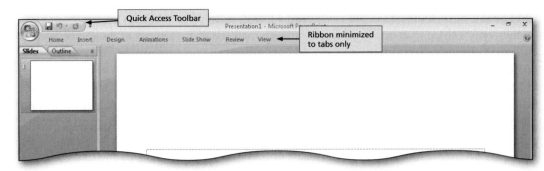

Figure E–8

Other Ways

1. Double-click the active Ribbon tab
2. Press CTRL+F1

Customizing and Resetting the Quick Access Toolbar

The Quick Access Toolbar, located to the right of the Office Button by default, provides easy access to some of the more frequently used commands in PowerPoint (Figure E–7). By default, the Quick Access Toolbar contains buttons for the Save, Undo, and Redo commands. Customize the Quick Access Toolbar by changing its location in the window and by adding additional buttons to reflect which commands you would like to be able to access easily.

To Change the Location of the Quick Access Toolbar

The following steps move the Quick Access Toolbar to below the Ribbon.

- Double-click the Home tab to redisplay the Ribbon.

- Click the Customize Quick Access Toolbar button on the Quick Access Toolbar to display the Customize Quick Access Toolbar menu (Figure E–9).

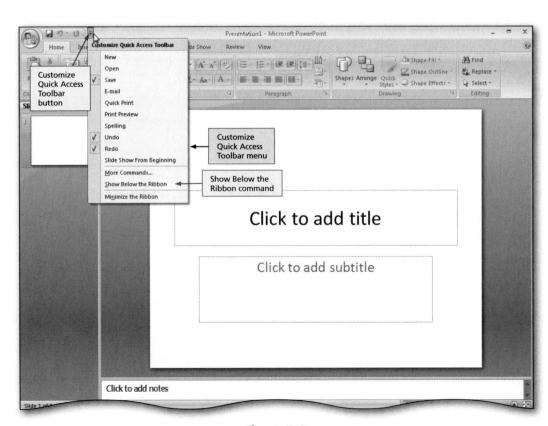

Figure E–9

- Click Show Below the Ribbon on the Quick Access Toolbar menu to move the Quick Access Toolbar below the Ribbon (Figure E–10).

Figure E–10

To Add Commands to the Quick Access Toolbar Using the Customize Quick Access Toolbar Menu

Some of the more commonly added commands are available for selection from the Customize Quick Access Toolbar menu. The following steps add the Quick Print button to the Quick Access Toolbar.

- Click the Customize Quick Access Toolbar button to display the Customize Quick Access Toolbar menu (Figure E–11).

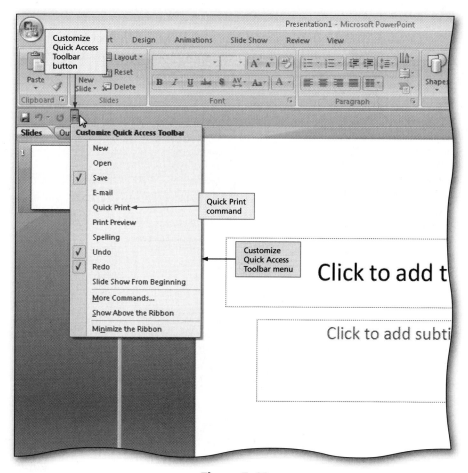

Figure E–11

● Click Quick Print on the Quick Access Toolbar menu to add the Quick Print button to the Quick Access Toolbar (Figure E–12).

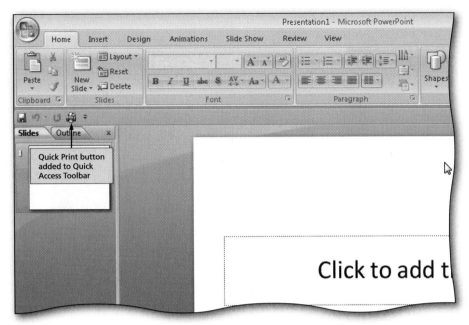

Figure E–12

To Add Commands to the Quick Access Toolbar Using the Shortcut Menu

Commands also can be added to the Quick Access Toolbar from the Ribbon. Adding an existing Ribbon command that you use often to the Quick Access Toolbar makes the command immediately available, regardless of which tab is active.

● Click the Review tab on the Ribbon to make it the active tab.

● Right-click the Spelling & Grammar button on the Review tab to display a shortcut menu (Figure E–13).

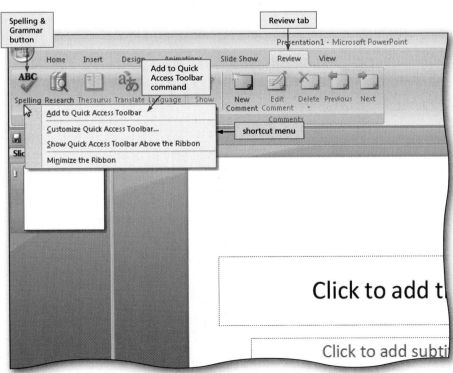

Figure E–13

2

- Click Add to Quick Access Toolbar on the shortcut menu to add the Spelling & Grammar button to the Quick Access Toolbar (Figure E–14).

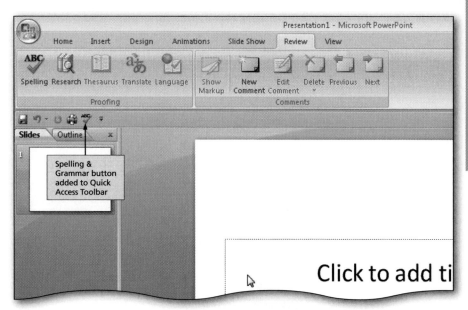

Figure E–14

To Add Commands to the Quick Access Toolbar Using PowerPoint Options

Some commands do not appear on the Ribbon. They can be added to the Quick Access Toolbar using the PowerPoint Options dialog box.

1

- Click Home on the Ribbon to display the Home tab, and then click the Office Button to display the Office Button menu (Figure E–15).

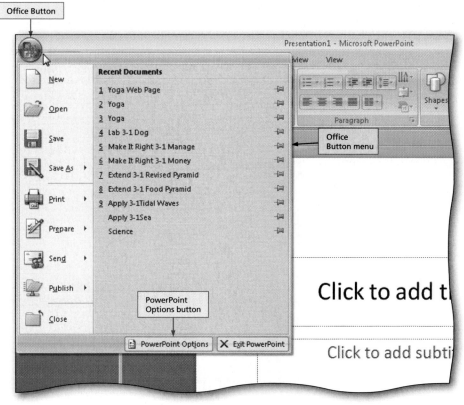

Figure E–15

● Click the PowerPoint
Options button on
the Office Button
menu to display
the PowerPoint
Options dialog box
(Figure E–16).

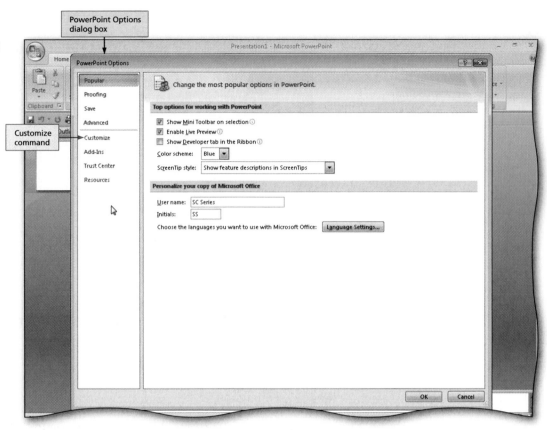

Figure E–16

● Click Customize in
the left pane.

● Click the 'Choose
commands from' box
arrow to display the
'Choose commands
from' list.

● Click Commands Not
in the Ribbon in the
'Choose commands
from' list.

● Scroll to display the
Web Page Preview
command.

● Click Web Page
Preview to select it
(Figure E–17).

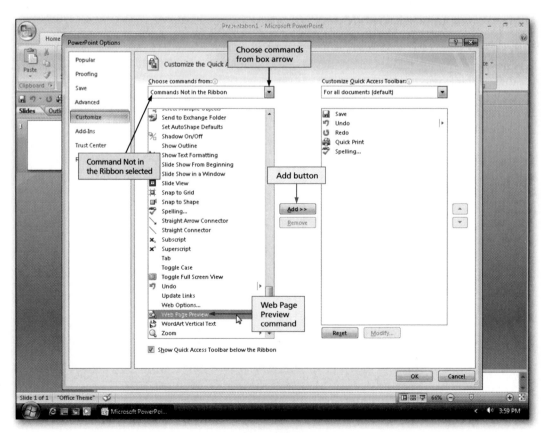

Figure E–17

4

• Click the Add button to add the Web Page Preview button to the list of buttons on the Quick Access Toolbar (Figure E–18).

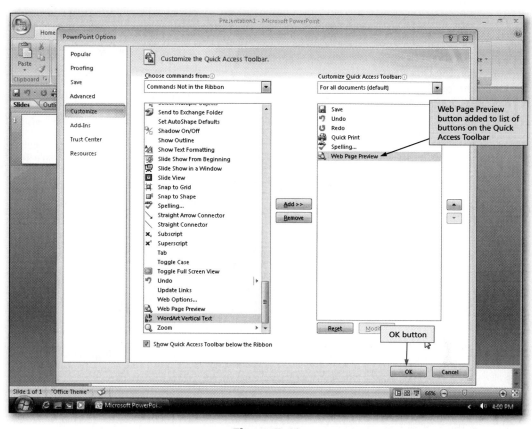

Figure E–18

5

• Click the OK button to add the Web Page Preview button to the Quick Access Toolbar (Figure E–19).

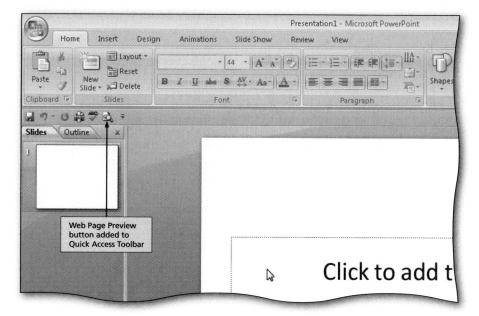

Figure E–19

Other Ways

1. Click Customize Quick Access Toolbar button, click More Commands, select commands to add, click Add button, click OK button

To Remove a Command from the Quick Access Toolbar

- Right-click the Web Page Preview button on the Quick Access Toolbar to display a shortcut menu (Figure E–20).

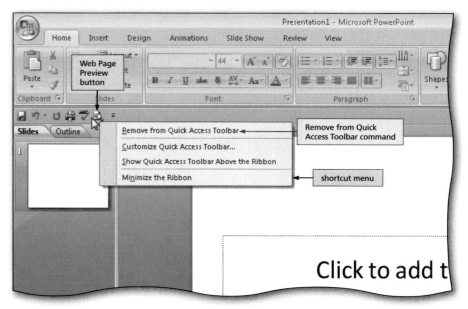

Figure E–20

- Click Remove from Quick Access Toolbar on the shortcut menu to remove the button from the Quick Access Toolbar (Figure E–21).

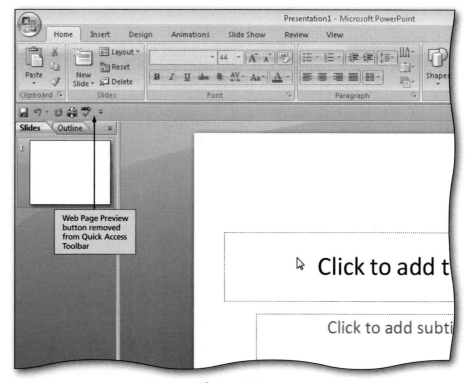

Figure E–21

Other Ways

1. Click the Customize Quick Access Toolbar button, click More Commands, click the command you wish to remove in the Customize Quick Access Toolbar list, click Remove button, click OK button

2. If the command appears on the Customize Quick Access Toolbar menu, click the Customize Quick Access Toolbar button, click the command you wish to remove

To Reset the Quick Access Toolbar

- Click the Customize Quick Access Toolbar button on the Quick Access Toolbar.

- Click More Commands on the Quick Access Toolbar menu to display the PowerPoint Options Dialog box.

- Click the Show Quick Access Toolbar below the Ribbon check box to deselect it (Figure E–22).

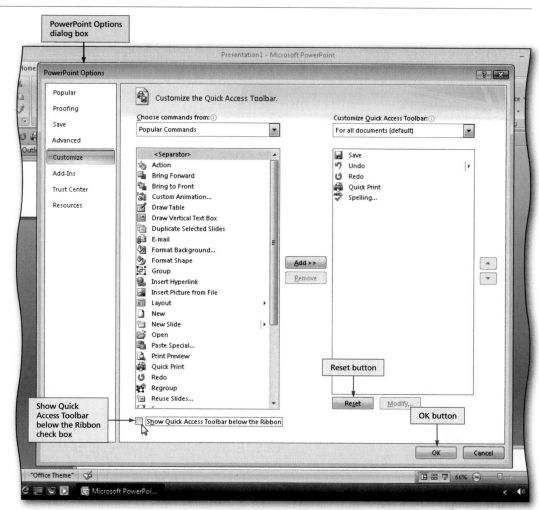

Figure E–22

- Click the Reset button, click the Yes button in the dialog box that appears, and then click the OK button in the PowerPoint Options dialog box, to reset the Quick Access Toolbar to its original position to the right of the Office Button, with the original three buttons (Figure E–23).

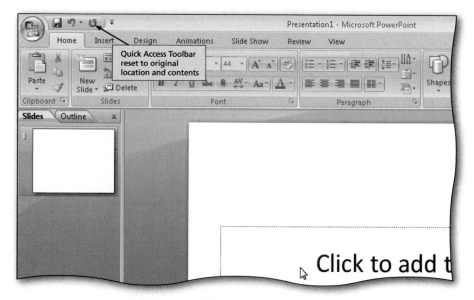

Figure E–23

Changing the PowerPoint Color Scheme

The Microsoft PowerPoint window can be customized by selecting a color scheme other than the default blue one. Three color schemes are available in PowerPoint.

To Change the PowerPoint Color Scheme

The following steps change the color scheme in PowerPoint as well as all other Microsoft Office programs.

1
- Click the Office Button to display the Office Button menu.

- Click the PowerPoint Options button on the Office Button menu to display the PowerPoint Options dialog box.

- If necessary, click Popular in the left pane. Click the Color scheme box arrow to display a list of color schemes (Figure E–24).

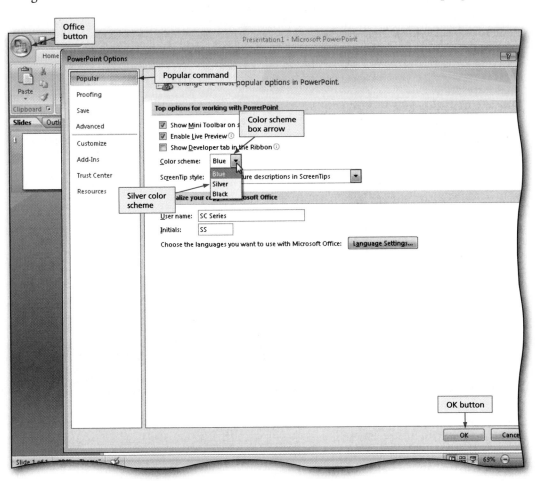

Figure E–24

2
- Click Silver in the list.

- Click the OK button to change the color scheme to silver (Figure E–25).

Q&A How do I switch back to the default color scheme?

Follow the steps for changing the Word color scheme, and select Blue from the list of color schemes.

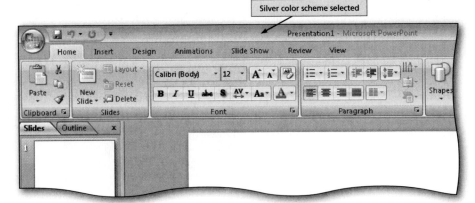

Figure E–25

Appendix F

Steps for the Windows XP User

For the XP User of this Book

For most tasks, no differences exist between using PowerPoint under the Windows Vista operating system and using PowerPoint under the Windows XP operating system. With some tasks, however, you will see some differences, or need to complete the tasks using different steps. This appendix shows how to Start PowerPoint, Save a Presentation, Open a Presentation, Insert a Photograph, and Insert a Media Clip while using Microsoft Office PowerPoint under Windows XP.

To Start PowerPoint

The following steps, which assume Windows is running, start PowerPoint based on a typical installation. You may need to ask your instructor how to start PowerPoint for your computer.

1

- Click the Start button on the Windows taskbar to display the Start menu.

- Point to All Programs on the Start menu to display the All Programs submenu.

- Point to Microsoft Office on the All Programs submenu to display the Microsoft Office submenu (Figure F–1).

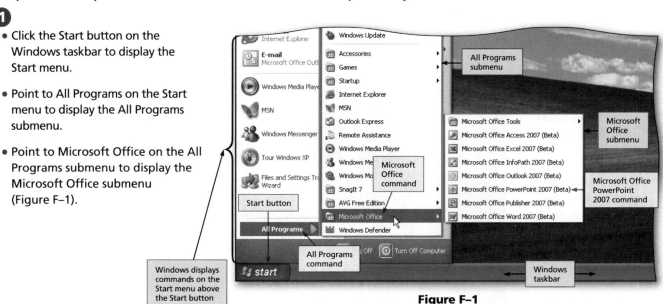

Figure F–1

- Click Microsoft Office PowerPoint 2007 to start PowerPoint and display a new blank document in the PowerPoint window (Figure F–2).

- If the PowerPoint window is not maximized, click the Maximize button next to the Close button on its title bar to maximize the window.

- If the Print Layout button is not selected, click it so that your screen layout matches Figure F–2.

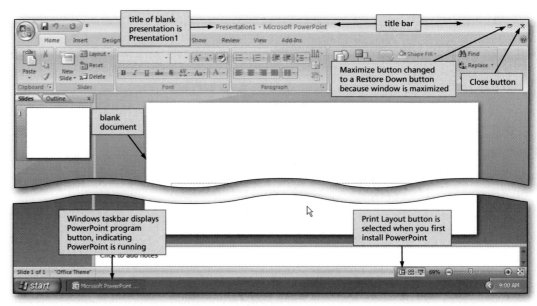

Figure F–2

Other Ways

1. Double-click PowerPoint icon on desktop, if one is present
2. Click Microsoft Office PowerPoint 2007 on Start menu

To Save a Presentation

After editing, you should save the document. The following steps save a presentation on a USB flash drive using the file name, Cabo Package.

- With a USB flash drive connected to one of the computer's USB ports, click the Save button on the Quick Access Toolbar to display the Save As dialog box (Figure F–3).

Q&A

Do I have to save to a USB flash drive?

No. You can save to any device or folder. A **folder** is a specific location on a storage medium. You can save to the default folder or a different folder. You also can create your own folders, which is explained later in this book.

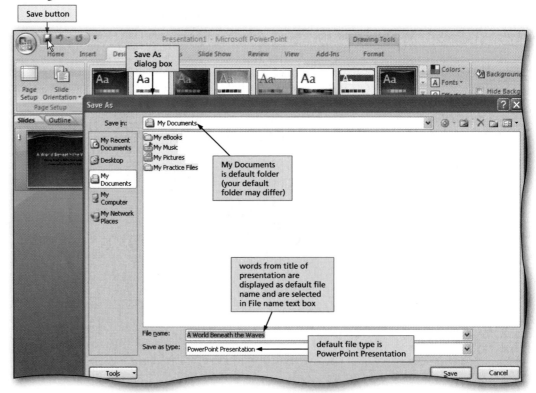

Figure F–3

2

- Type the name of your file (Cabo Package in this example) in the File name text box to change the file name. Do not press the ENTER key after typing the file name (Figure F–4).

Q&A What characters can I use in a file name?

A file name can have a maximum of 255 characters, including spaces. The only invalid characters are the backslash (\), slash (/), colon (:), asterisk (*), question mark (?), quotation mark ("), less than symbol (<), greater than symbol (>), and vertical bar (|).

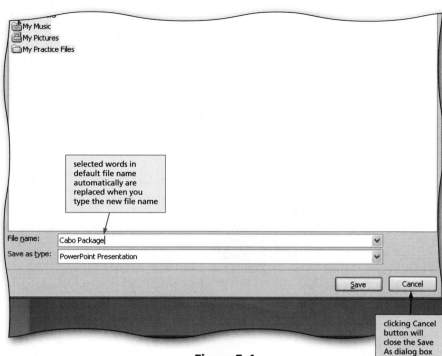

Figure F–4

3

- Click the Save in box arrow to display a list of available drives and folders (Figure F–5).

Q&A Why is my list of files, folders, and drives arranged and named differently from those shown in the figure?

Your computer's configuration determines how the list of files and folders is displayed and how drives are named. You can change the save location by clicking shortcuts on the **My Places bar**.

Q&A How do I save the file if I am not using a USB flash drive?

Use the same process, but be certain to select your device in the Save in list.

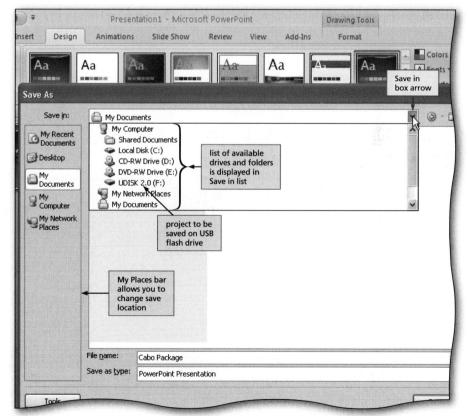

Figure F–5

• Click UDISK 2.0 (E:) in the Save in list to select the USB flash drive, Drive E in this case, as the new save location (Figure F–6).

• Click the Save button to save the presentation.

Q&A What if my USB flash drive has a different name or letter?

It is very likely that your USB flash drive will have a different name and drive letter and be connected to a different port. Verify the device in your Save in list is correct.

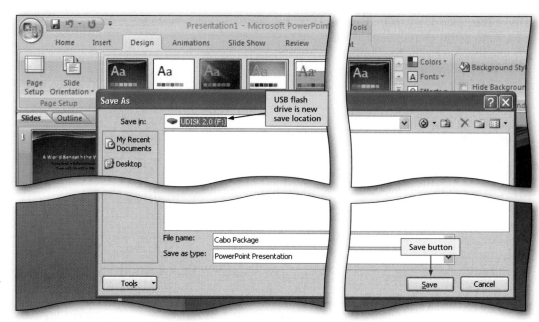

Figure F–6

Other Ways

1. Click Office Button, click Save, type file name, select drive or folder, click Save button

2. Press CTRL+S or press SHIFT+F12, type file name, select drive or folder, click Save button

To Open a Document from PowerPoint

The following steps open the Cabo Package file from the USB flash drive.

1

• With your USB flash drive connected to one of the computer's USB ports, click the Office Button to display the Office Button menu.

• Click Open on the Office Button menu to display the Open dialog box.

• If necessary, click the Look in box arrow and then click UDISK 2.0 (E:) to select the USB flash drive, Drive E in this case, in the Look in list as the new open location.

• Click Cabo Package to select the file name (Figure F–7).

• Click the Open button to open the presentation.

Q&A How do I open the file if I am not using a USB flash drive?

Use the same process, but be certain to select your device in the Look in list.

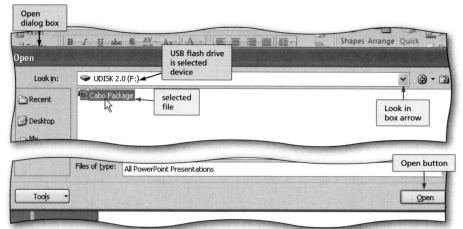

Figure F–7

Other Ways

1. Click Office Button, double-click file name in Recent Documents list

2. Press CTRL+O, select file name, press ENTER

To Insert a Photograph

The following steps insert a photograph, which, in this example, is located on the same USB flash drive that contains the saved presentation.

1 Click the Insert Picture from File icon in the content placeholder to display the Insert Picture dialog box.

2 With your USB flash drive connected to one of the computer's USB ports, if necessary, click the Look in box arrow and then click UDISK 2.0 (E:) to select the USB flash drive, Drive E in this case, in the Look in list as the device that contains the picture.

3 Select the name of the picture file to be inserted.

4 Click the Insert button in the dialog box to insert the picture into the content placeholder.

To Insert a Media Clip into a Slide

The following steps insert a media clip located on the USB flash drive.

1 Click the Insert Media Clip button in the content placeholder (row 2, column 3) to display the Insert Movie dialog box.

2 With your USB flash drive connected to one of the computer's USB ports, if necessary, click the Look in box arrow and then click UDISK 2.0 (E:) to select the USB flash drive, Drive E in this case, in the Look in list as the device that contains the file.

3 Select the file name of the file to be inserted.

4 Click the OK button in the dialog box to insert the file into the content placeholder.

5 Click the Automatically or the When Clicked button.

Appendix G

Microsoft Business Certification Program

What Is the Microsoft Business Certification Program?

The Microsoft Business Certification Program enables candidates to show that they have something exceptional to offer – proved expertise in Microsoft Office 2007 programs. The two certification tracks allow candidates to choose how they want to exhibit their skills, either through validating skills within a specific Microsoft product or taking their knowledge to the next level and combining Microsoft programs to show that they can apply multiple skill sets to complete more complex office tasks. Recognized by businesses and schools around the world, more than 3 million certifications have been obtained in more than 100 different countries. The Microsoft Business Certification Program is the only Microsoft-approved certification program of its kind.

What Is the Microsoft Certified Application Specialist Certification?

The Microsoft Certified Application Specialist certification exams focus on validating specific skill sets within each of the Microsoft Office system programs. Candidates can choose which exam(s) they want to take according to which skills they want to validate. The available Application Specialist exams include:

- Using Windows Vista™
- Using Microsoft® Office Word 2007
- Using Microsoft® Office Excel® 2007
- Using Microsoft® Office PowerPoint® 2007
- Using Microsoft® Office Access™ 2007
- Using Microsoft® Office Outlook® 2007

> For more information and details on how Shelly Cashman Series textbooks map to Microsoft Certified Application Specialist certification, visit scsite.com/off2007/cert.

What Is the Microsoft Certified Application Professional Certification?

The Microsoft Certified Application Professional certification exams focus on a candidate's ability to use the 2007 Microsoft® Office system to accomplish industry-agnostic functions, for example Budget Analysis and Forecasting, or Content Management and Collaboration. The available Application Professional exams currently include:

- Organizational Support
- Creating and Managing Presentations
- Content Management and Collaboration
- Budget Analysis and Forecasting

Index

Quick Reference Summary

In the Microsoft Office PowerPoint 2007 program, you can accomplish a task in a number of ways. The following table provides a quick reference to each task presented in this textbook. The first column identifies the task. The second column indicates the page number on which the task is discussed in the book. The subsequent four columns list the different ways the task in column one can be carried out.

Microsoft PowerPoint 2007 Quick Reference Summary

Task	Page Number	Mouse	Ribbon	Shortcut Menu	Keyboard Shortcut
Action Button, Change Fill Color	PPT 273		Shape Fill button on Format tab	Format Shape | Fill	
Action Button, Edit Hyperlink	PPT 278		Hyperlink button on Insert tab	Edit Hyperlink	
Action Button, Insert	PPT 271		Shapes button on Insert tab		
Add Shapes	PPT 119		Shapes button on Home tab | select shape		
Add Transition	PPT 122		Transition effect on Animations tab or More button in Transition to This Slide group on Animations tab | select transition		ALT+A | T
Animate a Shape Using a Motion Path	PPT 420		Custom Animation on Animations tab | Add Effects button | Motion Paths | More Motion Paths		
Animate Text	PPT 114		Animations tab or Transition button on Animation tab | More button in Transition to this Slide		ALT+D | M
Assign a Macro to a Shape	PPT 487		Action button on Insert tab | Run macro on Mouse Click tab		

Microsoft PowerPoint 2007 Quick Reference Summary *(continued)*

Task	Page Number	Mouse	Ribbon	Shortcut Menu	Keyboard Shortcut
Background, Insert Picture	PPT 171		Background Styles button on Design tab | Format Background | Picture or texture fill | File button | select picture | Insert button	Format Background | Picture or texture fill | File button | select picture | Insert button	
Bullet Character, Animate with Entrance Effect	PPT 409		Custom Animation on Animations tab | Add Effect button | Entrance Effects | More Effects		
Bullet Character, Change to a Number	PPT 397		Numbering button arrow on Home tab	Numbering	
Bullet Character, Change to a Picture	PPT 340		Bullets arrow on Home tab | Bullets and Numbering | Picture button | Picture bullet or Import button | picture file | Add button	Bullets and Numbering | Picture button | Picture bullet or Import button | picture file | Add button	
Bullet Character, Change to a Symbol	PPT 344		Bullets arrow on Home tab | Bullets and Numbering | Customize	Bullets and Numbering | Customize	
Bullet Character, Format Color	PPT 349		Bullets arrow on Home tab | Color arrow	Bullets and Numbering | Color arrow	
Bullet Character, Format Size	PPT 346		Bullets arrow on Home tab | Bullets and Numbering | Size Up or Down arrow	Bullets and Numbering | Size up or down arrow	
Change Animation Grouping	PPT 411		Custom Animation button on Animations tab | Start box arrow | select desired start | Animations Order list arrow | Effect Options | Text Animation tab | Group text list arrow		
Change Animation Speed	PPT 411		Custom Animation button on Animations tab | Speed box arrow		
Change Line Shape Color	PPT 467		Shape Outline button on Format tab		
Change Line Spacing	PPT 401		Line Spacing button on Home tab | *or* Paragraph Dialog Box Launcher | Indents and Spacing tab | Line Spacing box arrow	Paragraph | Indents and Spacing | Line Spacing box arrow	

Microsoft PowerPoint 2007 Quick Reference Summary *(continued)*

Task	Page Number	Mouse	Ribbon	Shortcut Menu	Keyboard Shortcut
Change Size, Clip Art, Photo, or Shape	PPT 101, 103, 117	Drag sizing handles	Dialog Box Launcher in Size group of Format tab | Size tab | enter height and width values or Size group of Format tab | enter height and width values		
Chart, Apply Style	PPT 260		More button in Chart Styles gallery		
Chart, Change Layout	PPT 261		More button in Chart Layouts gallery		
Chart, Insert	PPT 255	Insert Chart button in content placeholder | select chart | OK button	Chart button on Insert tab | select chart | OK button		
Chart Shape, Change Outline Color	PPT 263		Shape Outline button arrow on Format tab		
Chart Shape, Change Outline Weight	PPT 262		Shape Outline button arrow on Format tab | Weight		
Clip Art Border Color, Change	PPT 241		Picture Border button on Format tab		
Clip Art Brightness, Change	PPT 242	Drag Brightness slider or click increase or decrease Brightness arrow in Format Picture dialog box	Brightness button on Format tab		
Clip Art, Insert into Slide with Content Placeholder	PPT 96	ClipArt icon in slide	Clip Art button on Insert tab		
Clip Art, Insert into Slide without Content Placeholder	PPT 234		Clip Art button on Insert tab | type search term | Go button | click clip | Close button		
Clip Art, Regroup	PPT 203		Group button on Drawing Tools Format tab | Regroup	Group | Regroup	
Clip Art, Ungroup	PPT 198		Group button on Format tab | Ungroup | Yes	Group | Ungroup	
Color, Change Object	PPT 199	Shape Fill arrow | select color		Format Shape | Color	
Comment, Delete	PPT 305		Delete Comment button on Review tab		
Comment, Insert	PPT 300		Insert Comment button on Review tab		
Comment, Modify	PPT 303		Edit Comment button on Review tab		
Compatibility Checker, Start	PPT 306	Office Button | Prepare | Run Compatibility Checker			

Microsoft PowerPoint 2007 Quick Reference Summary *(continued)*

Task	Page Number	Mouse	Ribbon	Shortcut Menu	Keyboard Shortcut
Compress Presentation	PPT 312		Compress Pictures button on Format tab		
Copy	PPT 276		Copy button on Home tab	Copy	CTRL+C
Create a Self-Running Presentation	PPT 429		Set Up Show button on Slide Show tab	Browsed at kiosk option		
Cut	PPT 188			Cut	CTRL+X
Date and Time, Add	PPT 173		Date & Time button on Insert tab	Date and time	Update automatically arrow	select date and time format	Apply button or Apply to All button		
Demote a Paragraph	PPT 34	Increase List Level button on Mini toolbar	Increase List Level button on Home tab		TAB or ALT+SHIFT+ RIGHT ARROW
Digital Signature, Create	PPT 313	Office Button	Prepare	Add a Digital Signature			
Dim Text after Animation	PPT 414		Animations tab	Custom Animation button	Animation Order list arrow	Effect Options	Effect tab	After animation list arrow		
Display Gridlines	PPT 479		Gridlines check box on View tab	Grid and Guides	Display grid on screen check box	SHIFT+F9
Display a Presentation in Grayscale	PPT 59		Grayscale button on View tab		ALT+V	C	U
Document Inspector, Start	PPT 307	Office Button	Prepare	Inspect Document	Inspect			
Document Properties	PPT 44	Office Button	Prepare	Properties			
Document Theme, Choose	PPT 16		More button on Design tab	theme		
End Slide Show	PPT 54			End Show	ESC or HYPHEN
Fill, Insert Texture	PPT 168		Background Styles button on Design tab	Format Background	Picture or texture fill	Texture arrow	select background	Apply to All button	Format Background	Picture or texture fill	Texture arrow	select background	Apply to All button	
Final, Mark Presentation as	PPT 316	Office Button	Prepare	Mark as Final	Yes button			
Find and Replace Text	PPT 267		Replace button on Home tab		CTRL+H

Microsoft PowerPoint 2007 Quick Reference Summary *(continued)*

Task	Page Number	Mouse	Ribbon	Shortcut Menu	Keyboard Shortcut
Font, Change	PPT 109	Font button or Font box arrow on Mini toolbar	Font button on Home tab or Font arrow on Home tab | select font or Font Dialog Box Launcher on Home tab | Latin text font arrow on Font tab	Font | Latin text font arrow on Font tab	CTRL+SHIFT+F | Font tab | Latin text font arrow
Font Color	PPT 23, 110	Font Color button or Font Color arrow on Mini toolbar	Font Color button on Home tab or Font Color arrow on Home tab | select color or Font Dialog Box Launcher on Home tab | Font color button on Font tab | select color	Font | Font color button on Font tab | select color	CTRL+SHIFT+F | Font tab | Font color button | select color
Font Size, Decrease	PPT 25	Decrease Font Size button or Font Size arrow on Mini toolbar	Decrease Font Size button on Home tab or Font Size arrow on Home tab | size	Font Size arrow | Size	CTRL+SHIFT+LEFT CARET (<)
Font Size, Increase	PPT 24	Increase Font Size button or Font Size arrow on Mini toolbar	Increase Font Size button on Home tab or Font Size arrow on Home tab | size	Font size arrow | Size	CTRL+SHIFT+RIGHT CARET (>)
Guides, Display	PPT 274			Grid and Guides | Display drawing guides on screen	
Guides, Hide	PPT 279			Grid and Guides | Display drawing guides on screen	
Help	PPT 63 and Appendix A		Office PowerPoint Help button		F1
Hide Slide	PPT 266		Hide Slide button on Slide Show tab	Right-click desired slide thumbnail in Slides tab or in Slide Sorter view | Hide Slide	
Highlight Item	PPT 319	Pointer arrow on Slide Show toolbar | Highlighter		Pointer Options | Highlighter	
Hyperlink, Add	PPT 243		Insert Hyperlink button on Insert tab | type hyperlink text | OK button	Hyperlink | type hyperlink text | OK button	CTRL+K
Ink Color, Change	PPT 320	Pointer arrow on Slide Show toolbar | Ink Color		Pointer Options | Ink Color	
Insert Movie File	PPT 353	Insert Media Clip button | select movie file | OK button | how to start movie	Movie from File button on Insert tab | select movie file | OK button | how to start movie		
Insert Picture under Slide Objects	PPT 482		Picture button on Insert tab | select picture | Open button | size picture to fill entire slide | Send to Back button	Right-click picture | Send to Back	

Microsoft PowerPoint 2007 Quick Reference Summary *(continued)*

Task	Page Number	Mouse	Ribbon	Shortcut Menu	Keyboard Shortcut
Insert Photograph	PPT 98, 99	Insert Picture from File icon on slide	Picture button on Insert tab		
Insert Slide	PPT 404		New Slide button arrow on Home tab | Reuse Slides | Browse button | Browse File | presentation with desired slide | Open button | Keep source formatting check box		
Insert Sound Clip	PPT 355		Sound from File button on Insert tab | sound file | OK button | how to start sound		
Markup, Show	PPT 304		Show Markup button on Review tab		
Next Slide	PPT 47	Next Slide button on vertical scroll bar			PAGE DOWN
Normal View	PPT 91	Normal View button at lower-right PowerPoint window	Normal button on View tab		ALT+V | N
Object, Delete	PPT 202				DELETE
Open Presentation	PPT 54	Office Button | Open | select file			CTRL+O
Open Word Outline as Presentation	PPT 165	Office Button | Open | All Outlines | select file | Open	New Slide button arrow on Home tab | Slides from Outline | select file | Insert		CTRL+O
Package for CD	PPT 321	Office Button | Publish | Package for CD			
Password, Set	PPT 310	Office Button | Save As | Tools | General Options			
Paste	PPT 277		Paste button on Home tab	Paste	CTRL+V
Paste Special	PPT 468		Paste button arrow on Home tab | Paste Special		
Picture, Apply a Shape	PPT 337		Picture Shape button on Format tab		
Picture, Insert into Slide without Content Placeholder	PPT 234		Picture button on Insert tab | select file | Insert button		
Picture Border Color, Change	PPT 237		Picture Border button on Format tab		
Picture Contrast, Change	PPT 238	Drag Contrast slider or click increase or decrease Contrast arrow in Format Picture dialog box	Contrast button on Format tab		
Picture, Recolor	PPT 333		Recolor button on Format tab	Format Picture | Picture in left pane | select color | Close button	

Microsoft PowerPoint 2007 Quick Reference Summary *(continued)*

Task	Page Number	Mouse	Ribbon	Shortcut Menu	Keyboard Shortcut
Picture, Resize	PPT 335	Drag sizing handle in or out	Shape Height or change Shape Width up or down arrow on Format tab	Size and Position | Size tab | change Height or change Width	
Picture, Set Transparent Color	PPT 334		Recolor button on Format tab | Set Transparent Color		
Picture Style, Apply to Clip	PPT 240		More button in Picture Styles gallery on Format tab		
Picture Style, Insert in Picture	PPT 236		More button in Picture Styles gallery on Format tab		
Preview Presentation as Web Page	PPT 151	[Assumes Web Page Preview button has been added to Quick Access toolbar] Web Page Preview button			
Previous Slide	PPT 50, 51	Previous Slide button on vertical scroll bar			PAGE UP
Print a Presentation	PPT 61	Office Button | Print			CTRL+P
Print an Outline	PPT 122	Office Button | point to Print | Print Preview | Print What arrow | Outline View			
Print Speaker Notes	PPT 363	Office Button | Print arrow | Print Preview | Print What arrow | OK button | Close Print Preview button			
Promote a Paragraph	PPT 34	Decrease List Level button on Mini toolbar	Decrease List Level button on Home tab		SHIFT+TAB or ALT+SHIFT+ LEFT ARROW
Quick Access Toolbar, Add Buttons	PPT 148	Customize Quick Access Toolbar button | select from command options			
Quick Access Toolbar, Reset	PPT 154	Customize Quick Access Toolbar button | More Commands | Reset button			
Quit PowerPoint	PPT 53	Double-click Office Button or Close button on title bar or Office Button | Exit PowerPoint		Right-click Microsoft PowerPoint button on taskbar | Close	ALT+F4 or CTRL+Q

Microsoft PowerPoint 2007 Quick Reference Summary *(continued)*

Task	Page Number	Mouse	Ribbon	Shortcut Menu	Keyboard Shortcut
Record Narration	PPT 475		Record Narration button on Slide Show tab | microphone level | OK button | Change Quality button | Name arrow | desired recording quality | OK button | Link narrations in check box for lengthy narrations | Current Slide to match narration to particular part of the presentation | speak into microphone | Save button		
Save a Presentation	PPT 27	Save button on Quick Access toolbar or Office Button | Save			CTRL+S or SHIFT+F12
Save a Presentation with a Macro	PPT 489	Office Button | Save As | PowerPoint Macro-Enabled Presentation in Save as type list | presentation name | Save button			
Save as Web Page	PPT 152	Office Button | Save As | add File name | change Save as type to Single File Web Page | Save button			ALT+F | G or F12
Save in .PPS Format	PPT 317	Office Button | Save As | PowerPoint Presentation | type file name | Save as type arrow | PowerPoint Show | Save			
Set Margins, Text Box	PPT 457			Right-click text box | Format Shape | Text Box in left pane | set margins in Internal margins area	
Set Presentation Resolution	PPT 474		Set Up Slide Show button on Slide Show tab | Slide show resolution arrow		
Show a Presentation with or without Narration	PPT 475		Set Up Slide Show button on Slide Show tab *or* Show without narration		
Slide, Add	PPT 29		New Slide button on Home tab or New Slide arrow on Home tab | choose slide type		CTRL+M
Slide, Arrange	PPT 41	Drag slide in Slides tab to new position or in Slide Sorter View drag slide to new position			

Microsoft PowerPoint 2007 Quick Reference Summary *(continued)*

Task	Page Number	Mouse	Ribbon	Shortcut Menu	Keyboard Shortcut
Slide, Background	PPT 89		Background Styles button on Design tab | select style	Format Background	
Slide, Delete	PPT 419		Delete button on Home tab	Right-click thumbnail in left pane | Delete Slide	
Slide, Duplicate	PPT 40		New Slide arrow on Home tab | Duplicate Selected Slides		
Slide, Save as Image	PPT 475	Office Button | Save As | Other Formats | type desired name | Save as type arrow | select format | Save button | Current Slide Only button			
Slide, Set Size	PPT 473		Page Setup button on Design tab | Slides sized for arrow		
Slide Layout	PPT 92, 94		Layout button on Home tab		
Slide Master, Add a Background Graphic	PPT 389		Insert Picture from File button on Insert tab | graphic file | Insert button		
Slide Master, Add Text to Placeholder	PPT 392	Select text | delete | type new text | drag sizing handles			
Slide Master, Apply a Quick Style	PPT 387		Quick Styles button on Home tab		
Slide Master, Apply Slide Theme Colors	PPT 383		Themes Color button on Slide Master tab		
Slide Master, Apply Slide Themes	PPT 383		Themes button on Slide Master tab | select theme | Theme		
Slide Master, Copy and Paste a Placeholder	PPT 394		Copy button on Home tab | different Slide Master thumbnail in left pane | Paste button		
Slide Master, Close Master View	PPT 396		Close Master View button on Slide Master tab		
Slide Master, Customize Slide Theme Fonts	PPT 383		Theme Fonts button on Slide Master tab | Create New Theme Fonts | heading font | body font | default font name | Save button		
Slide Master, Display	PPT 382		Slide Master button on View tab		

Microsoft PowerPoint 2007 Quick Reference Summary *(continued)*

Task	Page Number	Mouse	Ribbon	Shortcut Menu	Keyboard Shortcut
Slide Master, Format Background	PPT 387		Background Styles button on Slide Master tab		
Slide Master, Format Placeholder Text	PPT 399		Text Direction button on Home tab | select direction | Align Text button		
Slide Master, Insert a Placeholder	PPT 391		Content button arrow on Slide Master tab | select placeholder | click slide		
Slide Numbers, Add	PPT 173		Slide Number button on Insert tab | Slide number | Apply button or Apply to All button		
Slide Show View	PPT 49	Slide Show button at lower-right PowerPoint window	Slide Show button on View tab or From Beginning button on Slide Show tab		F5 or ALT+V | W
Slide Sorter View	PPT 91	Slide Sorter View button at lower-right in PowerPoint window	Slide Sorter button on View tab		ALT+V | D
SmartArt Graphic, Add SmartArt Style	PPT 184		More button in SmartArt Styles group on Design tab		
SmartArt Graphic, Adjust Size	PPT 210	Drag sizing handle to desired location			
SmartArt Graphic, Animate	PPT 418		Animate button arrow on Animations tab		
SmartArt Graphic, Change Color	PPT 186		Change Colors button on Design tab		
SmartArt Graphic, Insert	PPT 205		SmartArt button on Insert tab | select category | select graphic		
SmartArt Graphic, Insert Image	PPT 183	Double-click icon in shape | select picture | Insert button			
Spelling Check	PPT 55		Spelling button on Review tab		F7
Table, Add an Image	PPT 460			Right-click cell | Format Shape | Insert from File | desired image file | Insert button | Close button	
Table, Add Borders	PPT 251		No Border button arrow on Design tab | All Borders		
Table, Add Effect	PPT 252		Effects button on Design Tab		
Table, Apply Style,	PPT 250		More button in Table Styles gallery on Design tab		

Microsoft PowerPoint 2007 Quick Reference Summary *(continued)*

Task	Page Number	Mouse	Ribbon	Shortcut Menu	Keyboard Shortcut
Table, Center Text Alignment	PPT 458		Center Vertically button on Layout tab	Right-click selected cells | Format Shape | Text Box | Vertical Alignment arrow	
Table, Insert	PPT 246	Insert Table button in content placeholder | click Number of columns and Number of rows up or down arrows | OK button	Table button on Insert tab | drag to select columns and rows		
Table, Text Change Orientation	PPT 459		Text Direction button on Layout tab	Right-click desired cells | Format Shape | Text Box | Text direction arrow	
Text, Align	PPT 402		Align Text button on Home tab		
Text, Add Shadow	PPT 110		Text Shadow button on Home tab		
Text, Bold	PPT 25	Bold button on Mini toolbar	Bold button on Home tab		CTRL+B
Text, Change Color	PPT 23	Font Color button or Font Color arrow on Mini toolbar	Font color arrow on Home tab | choose color	Font | Font color button | choose color	
Text, Convert to SmartArt Graphic	PPT 181		SmartArt button on Insert tab	Convert to SmartArt	
Text, Delete	PPT 42		Cut button on Home tab	Cut	DELETE or CTRL+X or BACKSPACE
Text, Formatting with Quick Styles	PPT 119		Quick Styles button on Home tab | select style		
Text, Italicize	PPT 22	Italic button on Mini toolbar	Italic button on Home tab	Font | Font style arrow | Italics	CTRL+I
Text, Select	PPT 21	Drag to select | double-click to select word | triple-click to select paragraph			SHIFT+DOWN ARROW or SHIFT+RIGHT ARROW
Text Box, Adjust Column Spacing	PPT 351		Columns button on Home tab | More Columns		
Text Box, Apply Quick Style	PPT 352		Quick Styles button on Home tab		
Text Box, Create Columns	PPT 350		Columns button on Home tab | number of columns | drag sizing handle up to reduce text box height		
Text Box, Format	PPT 191		Shape Fill button or Shape Outline button or Shape Effects button on Format tab		
Text Box, Insert	PPT 188		Text Box button on Insert tab | click in desired location		
Text Box, Order	PPT 457			Right-click text box | Send to Back | Send to Back	

Microsoft PowerPoint 2007 Quick Reference Summary *(continued)*

Task	Page Number	Mouse	Ribbon	Shortcut Menu	Keyboard Shortcut
Text Box, Remove Border	PPT 457		Shape Outline button on Home tab | No Outline		
Text Box, Rotate	PPT 189	Drag Free Rotate pointer	Rotate button on Format Tab		
Texture Fill, Insert	PPT 168		Background Styles on Design tab | Format Background		
Theme Colors, Change	PPT 233		Theme Colors button on Design tab		
Thesaurus	PPT 269		Thesaurus button on Review tab	Synonyms	SHIFT+F7
Timings, Adjust Manually	PPT 362		Automatically After up or down arrow on Animations tab		
Timings, Rehearse	PPT 360		Rehearse Timings button on Slide Show tab | Next button | repeat for all remaining slides | Yes button		
Transparency, Change	PPT 172	Drag Transparency slider in Transparency text box or click increase or decrease Transparency arrow in Format Background dialog box			
Use Format Painter	PPT 112	Format Painter button on Mini toolbar	Double-click Format Painter button on Home tab | select text with a format you want to copy | select other text to apply previously selected format | press ESC to turn off Format Painter		
WordArt, Apply Style	PPT 175		More button on Format tab		
WordArt Outline Weight, Change	PPT 178		Text Outline arrow on Format tab | Weight		
WordArt Text Effect, Add	PPT 179		Text Effects button on Format tab		
WordArt Text Fill, Format	PPT 176		Text Fill arrow on Format tab		
Zoom for Printing	PPT 128	Drag Zoom slider on status bar or Office Button | point to Print | Print Preview |	Zoom button on View tab | select zoom		
Zoom for Viewing Slides	PPT 127, 462	Drag Zoom slider on status bar	Zoom button on View tab | select zoom		